DOMINIC GOLKER

THE NEW INTERNATIONAL COMMENTARY ON THE OLD TESTAMENT

The Book of
JOB

by

JOHN E. HARTLEY

WILLIAM B. EERDMANS PUBLISHING COMPANY
GRAND RAPIDS, MICHIGAN

255 Jefferson Ave. S.E., Grand Rapids, Michigan 49503

Printed in the United States of America

02 01 00 99 98 97 7 6 5 4

Library of Congress Cataloguing-in-Publication Data

Hartley, John E.
The book of Job.
(The New international commentary on the Old Testament)
Bibliography: p. 56.
Includes indexes.
1. Bible. O.T. Job—Commentaries.
I. Title. II. Series.
BS1415.H37 1988
223′.1077 87-33079

ISBN 0-8028-2528-1

To My Wife
Dorothy
For Her Persevering Help

AUTHOR'S PREFACE

Numbered among the greatest literature of all time, the book of Job addresses the universal problem of suffering with penetrating insight. It is a radical book, for it lets the throes of pain challenge traditional beliefs. Its author has no sacred cows to protect. Although the many advances that have been made in knowledge, especially in the field of medicine, have enhanced the quality of human life, suffering persists. It could be said that suffering has increased among the human race by reason of the global problems that compound human misery. Thus the book of Job is still relevant, because Job stands as an example of faith in God overcoming the severest suffering.

The message of the book of Job plays a vital role in the theology of the canon. It modifies a simplistic, fatalistic understanding of the doctrine of retribution that condemns all who suffer and praises all who prosper regardless of their moral integrity. I believe that Isaiah was so inspired by the account of Job that Job served as one of his models in his portrait of the Suffering Servant. Since Isaiah's Servant Songs play a vital role in the NT's interpretation of Jesus' mission, the tie between those Songs and the book of Job binds this book even more tightly to the NT message of Christ's redemptive work. In that Job's story proves that a righteous person could experience the worst affliction possible and continue to trust in God, it lays the foundation for believing that Jesus truly was a righteous person even though he died a most shameful death, reserved for hardened criminals.

Since this commentary is written for "pastors, scholars, and students," it is designed so that it may be read without a knowledge of Hebrew, yet it is hoped that the comments and the footnotes will be informative for scholarly readers as well. Even though the Hebrew text of Job is unusually difficult, the purpose of this work has been to concentrate on interpreting the book's message rather than to write a linguistic commentary. In an effort to make the MT as intelligible as possible, the insights of Dhorme, Pope, Dahood, Fohrer, Gordis, and others have been drawn on freely.

This leads to a comment about the translation found in the commentary. The Hebrew text of Job requires numerous emendations in order for it to be rendered into readable English. I have made a reading for every line and noted the emendations, of course. As a rule, I have followed the MT as closely as possible, for scholarly study has continued to authenticate its quality, and it offers an objective standard superior to any series of extensive emendations. Also, I have tended to translate literally, in order to give the reader a feel for the way the author expressed his ideas.

I have concentrated on the book's message. My goal has been to interpret each pericope as it relates to that message. To help in this task, at the end of each speech I have added a section entitled "Aim" which discusses its contribution to the work as a whole.

I wish to express my appreciation to Professor R. K. Harrison for inviting me to write this commentary and for his helpful comments and suggestions. I thank the leadership of Azusa Pacific University, especially President Paul Sago, Academic Vice President Don Grant, and Dean of the School of Theology Les Blank, for their encouragement and support. I owe a great debt of gratitude to many who helped in preparing this manuscript, but I shall mention only a few. Special thanks goes to Mrs. Lark Rilling for her editing of the manuscript at various stages of its preparation. I am also grateful to Betty Price, Kathleen Weber, Kelly Martin, and William Yarkin for reading and commenting on the manuscript. Nor can I forget the labor of those who have typed the manuscript. Then, too, I wish to thank Gary Lee, my editor at Eerdmans. Finally, my wife Dorothy has been most helpful.

JOHN E. HARTLEY

CONTENTS

THE BOOK OF JOB

INDEXES

PRINCIPAL ABBREVIATIONS

AB	Anchor Bible
AfO	*Archiv für Orientforschung*
AJSL	*American Journal of Semitic Languages and Literatures*
ALUOS	*Annual of Leeds University Oriental Society*
ANET	J. Pritchard, ed., *Ancient Near Eastern Texts*. 3rd ed. Princeton: Princeton University Press, 1969
AnOr	Analecta Orientalia
Arab.	Arabic
ARW	*Archiv für Religionswissenschaft*
ASTI	*Annual of the Swedish Theological Institute*
ATD	Das Alte Testament Deutsch
AV	Authorized (King James) Version
BAG	W. Bauer, *A Greek-English Lexicon of the New Testament*. Tr. W. F. Arndt and F. W. Gingrich. 2nd ed. rev. by F. W. Gingrich and F. W. Danker. Chicago: University of Chicago Press, 1979
BASOR	*Bulletin of the American Schools of Oriental Research*
BDB	F. Brown, S. Driver, and C. Briggs, *A Hebrew and English Lexicon of the Old Testament*. Repr. Oxford: Clarendon, 1962
BHK	R. Kittel, ed., *Biblia Hebraica*. Stuttgart: Württembergische Bibelanstalt, 1937
BHS	K. Elliger and W. Rudolph, eds., *Biblia Hebraica Stuttgartensia*. Stuttgart: Deutsche Bibelstiftung, 1967–1977
Bib	*Biblica*
BibOr	Biblica et Orientalia
BJRL	*Bulletin of the John Rylands Library*
BK	*Bibel und Kirche*
BKAT	Biblischer Kommentar: Altes Testament
BSO(A)S	*Bulletin of the School of Oriental (and African) Studies*
BWANT	Beiträge zur Wissenschaft vom Alten und Neuen Testament
BZ	*Biblische Zeitschrift*
BZAW	Beihefte zur Zeitschrift für die alttestamentliche Wissenschaft

CBC	Cambridge Bible Commentary
CBQ	*Catholic Biblical Quarterly*
CBQMS	*Catholic Biblical Quarterly* Monograph Series
CJT	*Canadian Journal of Theology*
Diss.	dissertation
DJD	Discoveries in the Judaean Desert
DOTT	D. Winton Thomas, ed., *Documents from Old Testament Times*. Repr. New York: Harper & Row, 1961
ETL	*Ephemerides Theologicae Lovanienses*
ETR	*Études théologiques et religieuses*
EvT	*Evangelische Theologie*
ExpTim	*Expository Times*
Fest.	Festschrift
FF	*Forschungen und Fortschritte*
FOTL	Forms of the Old Testament Literature
GKC	E. Kautzsch and A. Cowley, *Gesenius' Hebrew Grammar*. 2nd ed. Oxford: Clarendon, 1910
HAT	Handbuch zum Alten Testament
Heb.	Hebrew
HKAT	Handkommentar zum Alten Testament
HSM	Harvard Semitic Monographs
HTR	*Harvard Theological Review*
HUCA	*Hebrew Union College Annual*
IB	G. A. Buttrick, et al., eds., *The Interpreter's Bible*. 12 vols. Nashville: Abingdon, 1952–57
ICC	International Critical Commentary
IDB(S)	G. A. Buttrick, et al., eds. *The Interpreter's Dictionary of the Bible*. 4 vols. Nashville: Abingdon, 1962. *Supplementary Volume*. Ed. K. Crim, et al. 1976
Int	*Interpretation*
ISBE	G. Bromiley, et al., eds., *The International Standard Bible Encyclopedia*. 4 vols. Rev. ed. Grand Rapids: Eerdmans, 1979–1988
JAOS	*Journal of the American Oriental Society*
JB	Jerusalem Bible
JBL	*Journal of Biblical Literature*
JJS	*Journal of Jewish Studies*
JNES	*Journal of Near Eastern Studies*
JPOS	*Journal of the Palestine Oriental Society*
JQR	*Jewish Quarterly Review*
JR	*Journal of Religion*
JRAS	*Journal of the Royal Asiatic Society of Great Britain and Ireland*
JSOT	*Journal for the Study of the Old Testament*
JSOTSup	Journal for the Study of the Old Testament Supplement Series

JSS	*Journal of Semitic Studies*
JTS	*Journal of Theological Studies*
KAT	Kommentar zum Alten Testament
KB	L. Köhler, W. Baumgartner, et al., *Hebräisches und Aramäisches Lexicon zum Alten Testament*. 3rd ed. Leiden: Brill, 1967–; 2nd ed. cited where necessary: *Lexicon in Veteris Testamenti Libros*. Leiden: Brill, 1958
KD	*Kerygma und Dogma*
KHC	Kurzer Hand-Commentar zum Alten Testament
LXX	Septuagint
MFO	*Mélanges de la Faculté Orientale de l'Université St. Joseph de Beyrouth*
MGWJ	*Monatsschrift für Geschichte und Wissenschaft des Judentums*
mss.	manuscripts
MT	Masoretic Text
NCBC	New Century Bible Commentary
NEB	New English Bible
NIV	New International Version
OLZ	*Orientalistische Literaturzeitung*
Or	*Orientalia*
OTL	Old Testament Library
OTS	Oudtestamentische Studiën
PEQ	*Palestine Exploration Quarterly*
PRU	*Palais royal d'Ugarit*
RB	*Revue biblique*
REJ	*Revue des études juives*
RevExp	*Review and Expositor*
RevQ	*Revue de Qumran*
RHR	*Revue de l'histoire des religions*
RR	*Review of Religion*
RSP	*Ras Shamra Parallels*. 3 vols. Analecta Orientalia 49, 50, 51. Vols. I–II ed. L. Fisher; vol. III ed. S. Rummel. Rome: Pontifical Biblical Institute, 1972–1981
RSV	Revised Standard Version
SBLDS	Society of Biblical Literature Dissertation Series
SBLMS	Society of Biblical Literature Monograph Series
SBT	Studies in Biblical Theology
SJT	*Scottish Journal of Theology*
ST	*Studia Theologica*
SWJT	*Southwest Journal of Theology*
Syr.	Syriac
Targ.	Targum
T.B.	Babylonian Talmud
TDOT	G. Botterweck and H. Ringgren, eds., *Theological*

	Dictionary of the Old Testament. Vols. I–. Tr. D. Green, et al. Grand Rapids: Eerdmans, 1974–
THAT	E. Jenni and C. Westermann, eds., *Theologisches Handwörterbuch zum Alten Testament.* 2 vols. Munich: Kaiser; Zurich: Theologischer Verlag, 1971–76
TLZ	*Theologische Literaturzeitung*
TRu	*Theologische Rundschau*
TWOT	R. L. Harris, et al., eds., *Theological Wordbook of the Old Testament.* 2 vols. Chicago: Moody, 1980
TZ	*Theologische Zeitschrift*
UF	*Ugarit-Forschungen*
Ugar.	Ugaritic
UT	C. Gordon, *Ugaritic Textbook.* Analecta Orientalia 38. Rome: Pontifical Biblical Institute, 1965
VT	*Vetus Testamentum*
VTSup	*Vetus Testamentum,* Supplements
Vulg.	Vulgate
WMANT	Wissenschaftliche Monographien zum Alten und Neuen Testament
WO	*Die Welt des Orients*
WZKM	*Wiener Zeitschrift für die Kunde des Morgenlandes*
ZAW	*Zeitschrift für die alttestamentliche Wissenschaft*
ZDMG	*Zeitschrift der Deutschen Morgenländischen Gesellschaft*
ZRGG	*Zeitschrift für Religions- und Geistesgeschichte*
ZST	*Zeitschrift für systematische Theologie*
ZTK	*Zeitschrift für Theologie und Kirche*

The Book of
JOB

INTRODUCTION

I. TITLE AND PLACE IN THE CANON

This book, which bears the name of its hero Job, consists of two elements: (1) the account of Job's trial and restoration, and (2) numerous speeches that treat the issue of suffering.

The canonicity of Job has never been seriously questioned, though its location in the various canons has fluctuated. Protestant Bibles follow the order found in the Vulgate, placing it after Esther at the head of the poetical books: Job, Psalms, Proverbs, Ecclesiastes, Canticles. Cyril of Jerusalem and Epiphanius attest this tradition. In the Hebrew Bible Job appears in the third division, known as the Writings. The order in Sephardic manuscripts is Psalms, Job, Proverbs; in Ashkenazic manuscripts it is Psalms, Proverbs, Job. The Syriac Peshitta places Job after Deuteronomy in honor of the tradition that Moses was its author.

II. HEBREW TEXT AND VERSIONS

The many rare words and textual disturbances make the Hebrew text of Job one of the most obscure in the OT. The ancient versions testify to the fact that many passages were unintelligible even to the earliest translators. The versions offer numerous variant readings, but only a few are useful for the restoration of the original reading.

The Greek text (LXX) is essentially a faithful translation of the Hebrew. A few variant readings bear witness to a different Hebrew text; but many of these variants are attempts to cope with an obscure text. Though the translator fluctuated between literal renderings and paraphrases, in an extensive analysis of the LXX Orlinsky has demonstrated that its translator strove to render the Hebrew into Greek as accurately as possible.[1] His work leads

1. See H. Orlinsky, "Studies in the Septuagint of the Book of Job," *HUCA* 28 (1957) 53–74; 29 (1958) 229–71; 30 (1959) 153–67; 32 (1961) 239–68; 33 (1962) 119–51; 35 (1964) 57–78.

him to reject the view that the translator was frequently governed by his theological bias in his translations. Nevertheless, this translator, like any other, was influenced by his theological outlook, e.g., on occasion he slanted the translation toward God's exalted, unassailable perfection.[2] The most remarkable feature of the oldest Greek text is that it is shorter than the MT by some 400 lines.[3] Driver-Gray has listed the number of lines omitted in each section:

prologue	1
chs. 7–14	23–29
chs. 15–21	59
chs. 22–31	124
chs. 32–37	114
chs. 38–42:6	43
epilogue	3

One explanation for these omissions is that the book of Job had been translated into Greek before its development was complete. But because the number of omissions increases significantly in the trite third cycle and in the wordy Elihu speeches, and because many of the lines omitted are recurring lines and thoughts, a more likely explanation is that the Greek translator abridged the speeches intentionally.

The Targum, the Aramaic translation and paraphrase, follows the MT closely but has some of its own idiosyncrasies, e.g., interpreting some verses in the light of Israel's history and adding theological explanations (e.g., 1:6, 15; 20:26–28).

From Qumran Cave XI comes the oldest known Targum of Job (11QtgJob). The paleography of the manuscript leads J. van der Ploeg and A. van der Woude to date it in the 1st century A.D., but Pope and Sokoloff think that the style of the language is closer to the 2nd century B.C.[4] The text is extant from the middle of ch. 17 through 42:11, but it is quite fragmentary. From ch. 32 on more of the text is preserved, including some extensive passages in 37:10–42:11. This Targum ends at 42:11; whether the text stopped here or the remaining verses are missing is unclear. On the whole,

2. Cf. H. Gehman, "The Theological Approach of the Greek Translator of the Book of Job 1–15," *JBL* 68 (1949) 231–40; D. Gard, *The Exegetical Method of the Greek Translator of the Book of Job, JBL* Monograph Series 8 (Philadelphia: Society of Biblical Literature, 1952).

3. In the Hexapla, Origen used Theodotion's Greek translation to restore the lines missing from the LXX; he marked them with an asterisk. A Coptic version of the Greek attests the pre-Origen Greek text.

4. J. van der Ploeg and A. van der Woude, *Le Targum de Job de la Grotte XI de Qumran* (Leiden: Brill, 1971); M. Sokoloff, *The Targum to Job from Qumran Cave XI* (Ramat Gan: Bar-Ilan University, 1974); Pope, pp. XLV–XLVII.

the Qumran Targum supports the MT, including the order of chs. 24–27. The greatest textual variation from the MT is in 42:3, where 11QtgJob reads 40:5 in its place. Also, in 11QtgJob the order of lines is different at 37:16–18: v. 16a, v. 17a, v. 16b, v. 18, with v. 17b omitted. The translator was also puzzled by obscurities in the MT and at times gave a freer translation for clarity. For example, to avoid mythical language he rendered 38:7: "When the morning stars shone [MT sang] together and all the angels [MT sons] of God shouted in unison."

The Syriac Peshitta, which was translated directly from the Hebrew, offers insight into some obscure words and difficult passages.[5] As the textual tradition of the MT becomes more fully understood, the Peshitta's value in textual studies will increase.

After having translated Job into Latin from the Greek at the end of the 4th century A.D., Jerome decided to improve the translation by working directly from the Hebrew text. To help him with this task he engaged a rabbi of Lydda, who opened the rabbinic tradition to him. Therefore, the Vulgate offers some assistance in determining the original Hebrew text of Job.

III. LANGUAGE

The language of the book of Job is notable for its numerous rare words and unique examples of morphology and syntax.[1] Many suggestions have been made to account for its singular nature. Since the story may have an Edomite setting, it has been suggested that the author was an Edomite, a descendant of Esau, Jacob's brother (Gen. 25:23–24).[2] Since Edom was famous for its wisdom (cf. Obadiah), it is possible that Job is an example of that wisdom tradition. The lack of any significant literary documents from that region prevents the testing of this hypothesis.

From the time of Ibn Ezra (12th cent. A.D.) some scholars have thought that Job was translated into Hebrew from another language, perhaps Arabic or Aramaic. For example, Guillaume puts forth the position that the author, a Jew who lived at Tema (the area of present-day Hijaz) sometime between 552 and 542 B.C., wrote the book in Arabic.[3] While scholars

5. See E. Baumann, "Der Verwendbarkeit der Pešita zum Buche Iiob für die Textkritik," *ZAW* 18 (1898) 305–38; 19 (1899) 15–95, 288–309; 20 (1900) 177–201, 264–307; L. Rignell, "Notes on the Peshitta of the Book of Job," *ASTI* 9 (1973) 98–106.

1. See D. Freedman, "Orthographic Peculiarities in the Book of Job," *Eretz-Israel* 9 (1969) 35–44.

2. See R. Pfeiffer, "Edomitic Wisdom," *ZAW* 44 (1926) 13–25.

3. A. Guillaume, "The Arabic Background of the Book of Job," in *Promise and Fulfilment: Essays Presented to Professor S. H. Hooke*, ed. F. F. Bruce (Edinburgh: T. & T. Clark, 1963), pp. 106–27; idem, *Studies in the Book of Job*, ed. J. Macdonald, supplement 2 to *ALUOS* (Leiden: Brill, 1968), pp. 1–14.

frequently resort to Arabic to help explain some of the obscure words, the insights are not frequent enough and consistent enough for the book to have been composed in Arabic. In another effort to account for the peculiarity of the language of this book, Tur-Sinai posits that the MT arose from a partial translation into Hebrew of a lost Aramaic original. In his opinion, the translator left many Aramaic words and phrases untranslated because of their closeness to Hebrew. In addition, the author mistranslated various words. Tur-Sinai identifies the language as the Babylonian Aramaic of the 6th century B.C. Furthermore, he posits that the Masoretes added to the confusion by incorrectly vocalizing many words. Working with these hypotheses, Tur-Sinai makes many new and unique interpretations of the MT of Job. But because he goes so far in his efforts, his ingenious insights are buried amidst many wild speculations.

The Ugaritic texts, which have come to light since A.D. 1939, have greatly enhanced our knowledge of Northwest Semitic languages and of the style of Semitic prosody. Numerous scholars, e.g., Gordon, Dahood, and Cross, have employed the results of Ugaritic studies to improve the interpretation of many OT passages, including many passages in the book of Job.[4] Pope's commentary draws heavily on the present state of knowledge of Ugaritic to enlighten our understanding of the book of Job.

It is clear that the author wrote in a dialect distinct from the Hebrew of Jerusalem, in which much of the OT is composed. His dialect was closer to Aramaic. The author may also have been multilingual, as are many inhabitants of a region in which many related languages are spoken. He drew skillfully on his rich vocabulary and knowledge of the various dialects of Hebrew to probe the depth of his subject.

IV. PARALLEL LITERATURE OF THE ANCIENT NEAR EAST

Israelite Wisdom literature has many parallels to other ancient Near Eastern Wisdom literature. The prime example is the similarity in subject matter and language between Prov. 22:17–24:22 and the Egyptian "Instruction of

4. See, e.g., M. Dahood, "Northwest Semitic Philology and Job," in *The Bible in Current Catholic Thought*, ed. J. McKenzie (New York: Herder & Herder, 1962), pp. 55–74; A. Blommerde, *Northwest Semitic Grammar and Job*, BibOr 22 (Rome: Pontifical Biblical Institute, 1969); W. Michel, "The Ugaritic Texts and the Mythological Expressions in the Book of Job" (Diss., University of Wisconsin, 1970); A. Ceresko, *Job 29–31 in the Light of Northwest Semitic*, BibOr 36 (Rome: Pontifical Biblical Institute, 1980).

Amenemope."[1] In places the verbal identity indicates that one of these texts, more likely the "Instruction of Amenemope," directly influenced the other. The people of the ancient Near East were also quite concerned with disorder and the issue of human suffering. Many texts from this region treat these themes and parallel the book of Job, sometimes in structure and other times in thematic development.[2]

Some Egyptian texts may be compared to the book of Job. "The Protests of the Eloquent Peasant,"[3] a text datable to the 21st century B.C., is similar in format to the book of Job. It consists of nine semi-poetic speeches set between a prose prologue and epilogue. This Egyptian text recounts the story of a peasant who is robbed of his goods on the way to market and then has his complaint denied by local authorities. The peasant appeals for redress to the chief steward of that district. At first he presents his case politely before the steward. But as he has to keep returning day after day to argue his position, his rhetoric becomes more inflammatory. After nine long tirades the chief steward, who has sided with the peasant from the beginning but who has been toying with him to keep him speaking, settles his complaint by awarding him the property of the one who wronged him. The greatest point of contact between these two works is their use of long speeches in the mouth of an offended party to discuss the issue of true justice. In contrast to the peasant, Job becomes more confident as his case drags on. Furthermore, Job's cries of injustice are aimed at God, not at a local official.

The book of Job may also be compared with "The Admonitions of Ipu-wer."[4] The sage Ipu-wer protests the upheaval in society and is distressed at the decline of morality. The desire of this Egyptian sage, though, is more for a stable social order than for moral justice.

Another Egyptian text addressing the issue of despair caused by hard circumstances is "A Dispute over Suicide."[5] This text comes from the second half of the 3rd millennium B.C. Weary and disillusioned with life and considering death to be the escape from the troubles of life, the hero discusses his desire for death with his soul *(ba)*. Fearful that his soul might not accompany him in death if he should take his own life by casting himself in the fire, he pleads with his soul to stay beside him. During his search this

1. *ANET*, pp. 421–24; W. K. Simpson, ed., *The Literature of Ancient Egypt*, rev. ed. (New Haven: Yale University Press, 1973), pp. 241–65.

2. See J. Gray, "The Book of Job in the Context of Near Eastern Literature," *ZAW* 82 (1970) 251–69; H. Preuss, "Jahwes Antwort an Hiob und die sogenannte Hiobliteratur des alten Vorderen Orients," in *Beiträge zur alttestamentlichen Theologie: Festschrift für Walther Zimmerli*, ed. H. Donner, et al. (Göttingen: Vandenhoeck & Ruprecht, 1977), pp. 323–43.

3. *ANET*, pp. 407–10; Simpson, pp. 31–49.

4. *ANET*, pp. 441–44; Simpson, pp. 210–29.

5. *ANET*, pp. 405–407; Simpson, pp. 201–209.

person, like Job, wishes that the gods would come to his defense: "Pleasant would be the defense of a god for the secrets of my body."[6] The soul tries to dissuade him from committing suicide by beckoning him to forget his troubles in the pursuit of pleasure. But he waxes eloquent in rebuttal of his soul's advice. At last the soul agrees to stay with him in life or death. Even though in his darkest hour (ch. 3 and 6:8–13) Job too contemplates death as an escape from his pain, he overcomes that despair, for he never idealizes life in Sheol as sharing with the gods. Job finds greater meaning in life than does his Egyptian counterpart, and his view of God prevents him from contemplating suicide at all. In the Egyptian work the troubled man's speech may be considered a soliloquy, but Job's speeches, for the most part, are addressed to specific parties.

Several pieces of literature from Mesopotamia likewise treat the issue of suffering. A Sumerian poem from the early 2nd millennium B.C. addresses the issue of suffering by looking at the experience of a wise, upright man who is afflicted by a severe illness.[7] The victim laments his plight and longs that members of his family might join him in lamenting. He pleads to his personal god for relief. Then without offering any complaint that he has been treated unjustly he confesses that he has sinned. The god answers his prayer and restores the man's health by driving away the sickness demon. In contrast to Job, the Sumerian sufferer never raises the question of divine justice, for his view is that all people, being sinners, deserve whatever misfortune befalls them.

The most famous parallel to the book of Job is entitled "I Will Praise the Lord of Wisdom" and is known as "The Poem of the Righteous Sufferer" or "The Babylonian Job."[8] A man of high rank is suddenly and unexpectedly reduced to dreadful suffering and laments his malady in gruesome detail. Since he knows of no sin in his life, he searches for some remedy to his plight through the arts of divination, but to no avail. Unlike Job, he does not rebuke or condemn his god. For a year his disease stubbornly resists every effort of the diviners to bring about healing. Meanwhile the sufferer pursues his lament, believing that the gods will show him favor someday. At last he has three dreams in which Marduk, the chief god, sends messengers to perform rites of exorcism to bring about his healing. In

6. Tr. John A. Wilson, *ANET,* p. 405.

7. See S. N. Kramer, "'Man and His God.' A Sumerian variation on the 'Job' Motif," in *Wisdom in Israel and in the Ancient Near East,* Fest. H. H. Rowley, ed. M. Noth and D. Winton Thomas, VTSup 3 (Leiden: Brill, 1969), pp. 170–82; idem, *History Begins at Sumer,* 3rd ed. (Philadelphia: University of Pennsylvania Press, 1981), pp. 114–18.

8. *ANET,* pp. 434–37; W. G. Lambert, *Babylonian Wisdom Literature* (Oxford: Clarendon, 1960), pp. 21–62.

gratefulness he concludes with a long hymn of praise to Marduk. Like Job, the Babylonian hero laments his illness, is troubled by the lack of response from the divine realm, and acknowledges the human limitations, but unlike Job he shies away from the problem of theodicy.

Similarities to Job are also found with an Akkadian work known as "The Babylonian Ecclesiastes" or "A Dialogue about Human Misery" (ca. 1000 B.C.).[9] The work contains twenty-seven strophes arranged acrostically. A sufferer named Shaggil-kinam-ubbib ("May Esagil [Marduk's temple] declare the righteous pure") dialogues with a friend about divine justice and human suffering. In the strophes the hero and the friend exchange ideas. Presenting his tale of woe, the sufferer, an orphan, complains that he has endured trouble from his youth, even though he has sought the help of the gods. The friend answers that people are prone to plan evil, and he accuses the sufferer of intending in his mind to break the ordinances of the god. He also asserts that the wicked certainly get their dues and exhorts his friend to seek God. The sufferer complains that the gods do not restrain the evil demon. Even though he has humbled himself, he still has to obey his own slave and bear the taunt of the prosperous. The friend answers that he is accusing the gods unjustly, for the ways of the gods are remote, beyond human comprehension. He supports his argument by referring to anomalies in nature, e.g., though a cow's first calf is scrawny, its second calf is twice as large. In response the sufferer, like Job, complains that people praise criminals, while they abuse the innocent. The friend concedes that the gods have created humanity with perverse tongues and deceitful ways. In the last preserved strophe the sufferer pleads for understanding from his friend and for mercy from Ninurta, Ishtar, and the king. The ending is abrupt; no doubt it is to be assumed that the gods answer the sufferer's petition by restoring his health. Though the dialogue is only between two parties and their speeches are shorter than those in Job, this text may have influenced the format of the book of Job. But the nature of the hero's suffering and his approach to its solution differ extensively from those found in the book of Job.

An Akkadian text similar to "I Will Praise the Lord of Wisdom" has been found at Ugarit.[10] This sufferer, like Job, can find no answer to his plight from the divine realm. His next of kin console him by imploring him to yield to his fate. They even pour oil over him as though his death were certain. But the afflicted one expects Marduk to restore him. Lying awake at night, tormented by dreams of death, he continues to lament. Amid his lamenting he turns to praising Marduk, the very god who is angry with him. He affirms that the god who has cast him down is the very god who will raise

9. *ANET*, pp. 438–40; Lambert, pp. 63–91.

10. J. Nougayrol, *Ugaritica* V (Paris: Imprimerie Nationale, 1968): 264–73.

him up, because the severity of his affliction testifies to the mercy of his god. Here the text breaks off. This picture is similar to the popular understanding of Job, the righteous sufferer who praised the very God who afflicted him. But this sufferer takes an approach far different from Job's pursuit of litigation with God. That this text was found at Ras Shamra proves that the theme of the just sufferer was known very early in Canannite culture, and such texts may have been available to the author of Job even if he lived all his life in Palestine.

Another similar Akkadian text, dated to the 16th century B.C., is quite fragmentary.[11] It opens with a friend supporting the laments of a sufferer by imploring his god. The sufferer then asserts that he has served his god faithfully despite his suffering. He contrasts his past glory to his present sorrow (cf. Job 29–30), and his friend continues to support him. His god acknowledges the sufferer's lament and declares that his heart is innocent. The god also commends him for bearing his heavy burden, tells him that his future will be bright, and exhorts him not to forget his god. In this text the god declares that the sufferer's heart is innocent (cf. Job 42:7). Unlike Job's friends (e.g., 6:14–24) this sufferer's friend supports him through his lamenting. This Akkadian text is obviously not as complex in theme and literary style as the book of Job, but the points of contact are amazing, particularly the god's acknowledging that the sufferer is innocent. In contrast this sufferer does not complain against his god for acting unjustly in allowing his affliction, at least not in the extant text.

In the search of literature similar to the book of Job, many comparisons have been made with works from more distant lands. In India parallels are found in the story of Hariṣcandra, a wealthy ruler who was tested as the result of a wager between the gods Vasishta and Shiva. Hariscandra suffered all sorts of trials, but endured and was restored to his former estate.[12]

The uniqueness of the book of Job is evident when it is compared to these other works. The author expanded the dialogue from two to four speakers, a major literary breakthrough. More profoundly, according to Roberts, he successfully joined the cultic and the wisdom traditions.[13] He preserved the full pathos of the lament and at the same time kept the intensity of the debate of ideas in the disputation format. His incorporation of lines from the hymnic tradition gives the work a grandeur not visible in the Near

11. J. Nougayrol, "Une Version Ancienne du Juste Souffrant," *RB* 59 (1952) 239–50.

12. Cf. S. Rao and M. Reddy, "Job and His Satan—Parallels in Indian Scripture," *ZAW* 91 (1979) 416–22.

13. J. Roberts, "Job and the Israelite Religious Tradition," *ZAW* 89 (1977) 113.

Eastern parallels.[14] Criticism of the traditional beliefs about reward and punishment is much more severe in the book of Job. This comparison of parallel literature with the book of Job shows that the author may have been influenced by the rich literary tradition of the ancient Near East about suffering, but more in format than in substance.

Throughout the centuries the book of Job has had a great impact on the Western mind, including the great authors.[15] Three examples, Milton's *Samson,* Dostoevsky's *The Brothers Karamazov,* and Kafka's *The Trial,* testify to its impact on thinkers from widely differing perspectives, times, and cultures. Even the psychologist C. J. Jung entered the discussion with his *Answer to Job* (1963). Thus the book of Job continues to speak to the issues of human suffering and theodicy.

V. AFFINITIES WITH OTHER OLD TESTAMENT BOOKS

Many texts in the book of Job are paralleled by phrases and metaphors in other OT books (an equals sign is used where the phraseology is identical):

A. PROVERBS

Job	4:8	Prov.	22:8
	5:17b		3:11a
	12:13		8:14 (cf. Isa. 11:2; Ps. 147:5)
	15:7b	=	8:25b
	18:5a, 6b; 21:7a		13:9b = 24:20b
	18:7a		4:12a
	26:6		15:11a
	26:10b		8:27b
	28:15–19		3:14–15; 8:11, 19

B. PSALMS

Job	5:16b	Ps.	107:42b
	5:17		94:12a
	6:25a		119:103

14. Ibid.

15. See, e.g., M. Friedman, "The Modern Job: On Melville, Dostoievsky, and Kafka," *Judaism* 12 (1963) 436–55; N. A. Francisco, "Job in World Literature," *RevExp* 68 (1971) 521–33.

10:20b + 21a		39:14 (Eng. 13)
12:21a + 24b	=	107:40
18:7–10		140:5–6 (Eng. 4–5)
19:10		52:7 (Eng. 5)
19:13, 14		88:19 (Eng. 18)
22:19a		107:42a
29:12		72:12
33:14		62:12 (Eng. 11)
33:24–25		49:8–10 (Eng. 7–9); cf. Ps. 34:7–8 (Eng. 6–7)
34:14–15		104:29

C. LAMENTATIONS

Job	6:4; 7:20; 16:12		Lam.	3:12
	9:18b	=		3:15a
	12:4			3:14 (similar Jer. 20:7b)
	16:9b + 10a			2:16a + b
	19:7–8			3:7–9
	30:9			3:14; cf. 3:63

D. OTHER BOOKS

Job	1:21		Eccl.	5:14 (Eng. 15)
	19:7		Jer.	20:8
	19:24		Jer.	17:1
	5:18		Hos.	6:1 (cf. Deut. 32:39)
	13:28		Hos.	5:12
	9:8b	=	Amos	4:13d
	9:9a	=	Amos	5:8a
	18:16		Amos	2:9c
	31:15		Mal.	2:10a
	42:2b		Gen.	11:6b
	42:17		Gen.	25:8; 35:29
	4:16c		1 K.	19:12b

E. ISAIAH

Job	9:8a	=	Isa.	44:24c
	12:9b	=		41:20a
	12:24–25			19:14
	14:11	=		19:5
	15:35a	=		59:4d (cf. Ps. 7:15 [Eng. 14])
	16:17a			53:9b
	26:12a			51:15b

These numerous parallels suggest that the author of Job was very familiar with Israel's literature, particularly the hymns and Wisdom literature; without a doubt he knew Pss. 8 and 107. But the direction or nature of the dependency is not always clear. Job may be dependent on other texts, other texts may be dependent on Job, or parallel texts may be mutually dependent on an unknown third source. For example, the interconnection between Job 3:3–10 and Jer. 20:14–18 has been explained both as Job's borrowing from Jeremiah and as Jeremiah's relying on Job. It is also possible that both passages were independently influenced by another source.

F. FURTHER PARALLELS WITH ISAIAH

As the above list shows, Job has affinities with the various divisions of Isaiah. In particular, there is a significant cluster of parallels in phrases, metaphors, themes, and theology between Job and Isa. 40–55.[1]

Both books espouse a high ethical monotheism. Hymnic lines praising God's majesty link the message of each book (e.g., Job 5:9, 16; 9:5–13; 10:8–12; 11:7–11; 12:13–25; Isa. 40:12–14, 25–26; 42:5; 43:15); often God is praised for his marvelous creation. Knowing wisdom fully, he needed no one to instruct him at creation (Job 28:20–27; Isa. 40:14).[2] Verily he has spread out the heaven as the canopy under which he will reveal himself (Job 9:8; Isa. 40:21–23; 44:24). When this God appears, Job fears that he dare not hold him accountable by asking "What are you doing?" (9:12). In Isaiah the people of Israel put this same question to God as a challenge to his wisdom in raising up Cyrus to deliver them (45:9).

This transcendent, holy God, who is mighty of strength (*'ammîṣ kōaḥ,* Job 9:4, 19; Isa. 40:26), reigns supreme over the nations (Job 12:13–25; Isa. 40:15–17) and all cosmic forces, including those symbolized by the sea dragon, Rahab or Leviathan (e.g., Job 9:13; 26:12; 40:25–41:26 [Eng. 41:1–34]; Isa. 51:9). God's sovereignty is also expressed by the metaphor of his having stilled[3] the sea. As supreme Lord he thwarts *(mēp̄ēr)* the omens of diviners (Isa. 44:25) and the devices of the crafty (Job 5:12), and he makes fools of judges (Job 12:17) and skilled magicians (Isa. 44:25). Indeed he calls forth the stars, worshiped by Israel's neighbors as gods, and directs their course (Job 9:7, 9; 38:31–33; Isa. 40:26; 44:24–25; 47:9, 12–13). Enthroned above the vault *(ḥûg̱)* of the earth, he directs the course of events

1. See R. Pfeiffer, "The Dual Origins of Hebrew Monotheism," *JBL* 46 (1927) 202–6; S. Terrien, "Quelques remarques sur les affinités de Job avec le Deutéro-Esaïe," *Volume du Congrès: Genève 1965,* VTSup 15 (Leiden: Brill, 1966), pp. 295–310.

2. A corollary is the statement that God's thoughts are unsearchable (Job 11:7–9; Isa. 40:28).

3. Heb. *rāg̱aʿ* means "still" in Job 26:12 and "stir up" in Isa. 51:15.

on earth (Isa. 40:22). This metaphor is turned around in Job; Job believes that God, enthroned above the vault or zenith *(ḥûg)* of heaven, is so enshrouded with thick clouds that he cannot see things on earth (22:13–14).

The perspectives on humanity's origin and inherent weakness, as well as humanity's great potential, are similar in Job and Isaiah. God has artfully made each person with his own hands (Job 4:19; 10:8; Isa. 45:9, 11), forming him in the womb (Job 31:15; Isa. 44:24). Like a potter he fashions each person out of a lump of clay (*ḥōmer* is used for human beings only in Job 4:19; 10:9; 33:6; and Isa. 45:9; 64:7 [Eng. 6]), and then he breathes into the lump of clay the breath of life (Job 12:10; Isa. 42:5). In addition, *ṣeʾĕṣāʾîm* (lit. "issue, produce") is used for human offspring only in these books (Job 5:25; 21:8; 27:14; Isa. 22:24; 44:3; 48:19; 61:9; 65:23). Truly human life is frail like a flower (Job 14:1–2; Isa. 40:6–7; *ṣîṣ* for human life only in these two passages and in Ps. 103:15). It soon passes away like a wind-driven leaf, or like dry chaff chased by the wind (Job 13:25; Isa. 41:2), or like a moth-eaten garment (Job 13:28; cf. Isa. 50:9; 51:8). Insignificant and weak, a human being is comparable to a maggot and a worm (Job 25:6 and Isa. 41:14).[4] Because life is hard, it is also likened to forced labor or military service (*ṣāḇāʾ*, Job 7:1; 14:14; cf. Isa. 40:2). As for those who fall under divine punishment, they are pictured as drinking deeply from the cup of God's wrath (Job 21:20; Isa. 51:17, 22).

The most significant theme common to both books is that of the righteous sufferer. Job, who suffers the severest pain and humiliation, holds tenaciously to his innocence (19:21). Isa. 40–55 has four portraits of the Suffering Servant, whom God commissioned to redeem Israel (42:1–4; 49:1–7; 50:4–9; 53:1–12). Encountering opposition from every corner, the Servant is beaten, humiliated, and condemned to death (50:5–6; 53:3–4, 7–9). Because the people consider him to be smitten of God (Isa. 53:4; cf. Job 19:21), they despise him (Isa. 53:3; cf. Job 19:18), spit on him (*rōq*, Isa. 50:6; Job 30:10), and then desert him (Isa. 53:3, *ḥdl;* cf. Job 19:14). The Servant's suffering equals or surpasses Job's, even though he too is innocent, never having done violence or spoken deceit (Isa. 53:7, 9; cf. 50:5; Job 6:30; 16:17; 17:4). Both sufferers rest their cases with God (Isa. 49:4; 50:8–9; Job 13:15; 16:19). The Servant suffers vicariously for the sins of all, because he obeys God faithfully (Isa. 53). This idea of vicarious suffering is merely hinted at in the book of Job, e.g., when God instructs Job to pray for his comforters when they offer up burnt offerings (42:7–9; cf. 22:30). In Isaiah God brings the Servant back to life after his cruel death (Isa. 53:10–11) and awards him the spoils of victory (v. 12). While Job ponders the

4. Another point of agreement is that only these two OT books have the Hebrew word for "spider" *(ʿakkāḇîš)* (Job 8:14 and Isa. 59:5).

possibility of escaping his plight by dying for a season and then coming back to life, he finds no possibility that an individual could rise from the grave (14:7–17). Thus in Isaiah the thought of victory over death is developed further than in the book of Job.

The interplay between Isaiah and Job leads to the hypothesis that one of these two authors was well acquainted with the other's work. As Pfeiffer and Terrien point out, it seems most likely that the author of Job wrote before Isaiah, for he only alludes to the vicarious merit of innocent suffering; Isaiah develops this theme fully. If this position is correct, the message of the book of Job prepared the people to understand and receive Isaiah's bold new message that God was going to redeem his people and the world through the innocent suffering of his obedient Servant.

VI. AUTHORSHIP

While the author of the book of Job is anonymous, some insight into his character may be gained from his great work.[1] He may be numbered among the ancient wise men, whose work is attested in Proverbs and Ecclesiastes. Primarily interested in right conduct, the wise men of ancient Israel advocated a disciplined way of life, promising that faithful adherence to their teaching would bring prosperity and a long life (e.g., Prov. 4). Although they paid little attention to cultic ceremony or redemptive history in their writings, they had a deep religious commitment based on a high ethical monotheism. They taught that the fear of Yahweh was the beginning of wisdom (Prov. 1:7; 9:10). Furthermore, in their quest for knowledge they had a keen interest in the literature of other countries, as is attested by the many points of contact among literary texts from the Wisdom circles throughout the Levant. It is not surprising, then, that many of them were conversant in other languages (e.g., 2 K. 18:26, 28).

These wise men served the court as counselors, scribes, and teachers. It can be assumed that they held administrative posts in various cities throughout ancient Israel, including foreign cities under the control of the Israelite or the Judean crown. Possibly some were sent as ambassadors to neighboring countries. Others may have worked for various merchants, being stationed in cities throughout the region. If this was the case, it would help account for their knowledge of the diverse geography, customs, and literature of the surrounding countries.

1. On the author, see A. de Wilde, *Das Buch Hiob,* OTS 22 (Leiden: Brill, 1981), pp. 51–60; M. Crook and S. Elliot, "Tracing Job's Story," *Hibbert Journal* 60 (1961/62) 323–29.

The author of Job fits this characterization well. A wise man, he was skilled in the use of proverbs (e.g., 6:5, 6), rhetorical questions (e.g., 21:29), and enigmatic riddles (e.g., 5:5; 17:5). As Terrien observes, "He was well versed in the art of forensic eloquence (as in 31:1ff.), but he could also restrain his powers of oratory and impose silence upon his volubility (as in 42:6). He ran the whole gamut of tones: he could be coarse (as in 15:2) or vehement (as in 16:18), gruesome (as in 17:14) or humorous (as in 17:16), tender (as in 14:13ff.) or passionate (as in 19:13–19). He used all the shades of irony, from earthly sarcasm (as in 12:2) to heavenly persiflage (as in 38:3ff.)."[2]

This author's knowledge of nature, both plant and animal life, was extensive (cf. 14:7–10). For example, he used five different words for lion in 4:10–11. The series of animal portraits in 38:39–39:30 is a magnificent piece, attesting to his extensive knowledge of the habits of wild animals. He was familiar with precious gems, using thirteen different words for them in 28:15–19, including five words for gold. Quite picturesquely he describes the formation of a human embryo (10:8–11). Furthermore, he was very observant of weather patterns (7:9; 36:27–37:20; 38:34–38) and the constellations (9:9; 38:31–33). Since he so enjoyed contemplating the created order (e.g., 26:5–14; 38:1–15), it is little wonder that he composed the Yahweh speeches around the order, beauty, and marvels of nature. This wise man was also interested in human ingenuity. He was informed about ancient mining practices according to 28:1–11, the most detailed passage about mining preserved in ancient Hebrew. Knowledgeable about hunting and trapping, he employs six different words for traps in 18:8–10.

The author was also well informed about foreign cultures, particularly Egypt: see, e.g., a possible reference to the pyramids (3:14); the speed of swift skiffs made out of papyrus (9:26); the hippopotamus (40:15–24) and Leviathan or the crocodile (40:25–41:26 [Eng. 41:1–34]), two creatures commonly associated with Egypt, though they may have been native to Palestine in an early period. It is possible that the famous Egyptian "Book of the Dead" had some influence on the author's construction of Job's oath of innocence (ch. 31). His knowledge of other cultures is evident in the reference to caravan travel through the Arabian desert (6:18–20). Furthermore, the parallels between the book of Job and literature from Ugarit, noted throughout the commentary, are too specific to be accidental. It is clear from his many allusions to motifs common to them that he was acquainted with many of the Canaanite myths and legends.

This author also had an interest in antiquity. His knowledge of patriarchal history is reflected in his ability to set his work in the patriarchal

2. Terrien, *IB*, III:893.

period. This is particularly seen in the use of archaic names for God and in judging a character by adherence to a patriarchal standard of ethics. Thus the author must have been an avid student of the past.

Although the book makes little reference to the cult, the author had a deep interest in spiritual matters. He recorded Eliphaz's encounter with a spirit (4:12–21), the most detailed account from ancient Israel of a non-prophetic encounter with a numinous being. He alone in the OT alluded to the myth of the primordial man (15:7–8). In accord with the Wisdom tradition in general, he valued the fear of Yahweh as the foundation of true worship and as the basis for upright behavior (1:1, 8; 2:3; 4:6; 28:28; 37:24). Moreover, he struggled earnestly with the discrepancies between his belief that God is just and the actual course of affairs on earth (e.g., 21:7–33; 24:1–17). Rejecting the easy explanations of the various schools of thought, he belonged to those who questioned why the righteous should suffer while the wicked prosper and terrorize the land (e.g., Pss. 10, 12, 13, 49, 73, 88, 109). The speeches in the dialogues may reflect the intensity of his debate with the traditional approaches to the issue of human suffering. His unwillingness to accept standard answers no doubt brought him into conflict with the established priesthood and the scribes. Like Job, he may have suffered much for his apparently unorthodox insights. Fortunately his insights into the issue of suffering have been preserved for us in the book of Job.

Thus the author was a highly educated person and a devout servant of Yahweh; he may be numbered among the great wise men of ancient Israel.

VII. DATE

Scholars vary widely in their dating of the book of Job, from the time of the patriarchs to the postexilic era.[1] Even though there is no obvious indication of its date of composition, two factors are potentially helpful in establishing its date: its language and the points of contact between the book of Job and other OT passages. The use of language to date the book is made very difficult by the author's rich vocabulary and distinct dialect, which differs significantly from the Jerusalem dialect of most of the OT (see section III above). Unfortunately, none of the many Northwest Semitic texts that have been found witnesses to this dialect. The possibility of dating the book by its relationship to other OT passages is complicated by two factors: (1) the uncertainty of the date of those passages (e.g., Pss. 8, 107; Isa. 40–55), and

1. Cf. J. Roberts, "Job and the Israelite Religious Tradition," *ZAW* 89 (1977) 107–14.

(2) the difficulty of establishing which passage is dependent on the other or whether both texts are dependent on a third source.

The dates proposed by contemporary scholars fall into three periods: early 7th century B.C., during Hezekiah's time (e.g., Andersen); mid-6th century B.C., after the fall of Jerusalem (e.g., Terrien, Guillaume); and the 4th–3rd century B.C., the era of the second temple (e.g., Dhorme, Fohrer, Gordis). The evidence cited for the last date includes the following: the order in the list of officials, kings, counselors, and princes in 3:14–15 corresponds to the hierarchy of the Persian empire (cf. Ezra 7:28; 8:25; Esth. 1:3); Job's request that his words be inscribed in stone outlined with lead (19:23–24) may allude to Darius's world-famous Behistun inscription (ca. 520 B.C.); the reference to swift runners in 9:25 may refer to the messenger service instituted by Darius; and caravan trade from Tema and Sheba (6:19) was fostered by the Persians. Three other points that are used to favor the late date are the large number of Aramaisms throughout the book, the emphasis on the individual over the community, and the figure of the Satan in the prologue.

Nevertheless, all these points are debatable. The advance in understanding of the interplay between Aramaic and Hebrew, going back at least to the 9th century B.C., has shown the fallacy in dating documents late because of Aramaisms. The term *the Satan* in the prologue functions as a title, not as a proper name as in the late books of Chronicles and Zechariah. The theme of individual responsibility, which was a strong emphasis at the time of the Exile in the works of Jeremiah (31:29–30) and Ezekiel (chs. 18, 33), is also found in earlier passages (e.g., Exod. 20:22–23:33).

The challenge to the twofold doctrine of retribution and a naive understanding of belief in God has some parallels with Ecclesiastes (cf. 8:14). Unfortunately, these parallels do not assist the dating of Job, for the doctrine of retribution was well entrenched in different ages, as attested by Proverbs, Ezekiel, Kings, and Chronicles; even centuries later Jesus still had to combat this belief (e.g., Luke 13:1–5). The persistence of this doctrine indicates that the book of Job was well aimed but failed to carry popular opinion in any age covered by the OT. Therefore, it is fallacious to assume that Job was written quite late primarily because it challenges the doctrine of retribution.

A sixth-century date has two points in its favor. The Babylonian captivity, a trauma for Judah, certainly could have provided the milieu for this work on suffering. This position is strengthened by the close affinity between Job and Isa. 40–55, which many scholars believe was written ca. 550 B.C. In addition, the few points of contact between Job and Jeremiah, particularly Job 3:3–13 with Jer. 20:14–18, may support a sixth-century date.

While this book, if extant at the time of the Exile, would have been a source of inspiration to those who were suffering under Babylonian lordship, it is highly unlikely that it was composed to address the issue of suffering under foreign captivity, for it looks at the suffering of an innocent person while the Exile is interpreted as the nation's punishment for the gross iniquities of the preceding generation (e.g., 2 K. 22:15–17). Furthermore, a central issue during the Exile for those who suffered was to blame God for making them bear the sins of their forefathers (cf. Jer. 31:29), but nowhere in this book is Job's suffering considered to be the result of his father's sin. Not even the death of his sons is explained as caused by Job's supposed sins; according to Bildad, they died because of their own sins (8:4). Given the impact of the Exile on the national consciousness, one finds it difficult to explain the origin and preservation of a work on suffering from that era that did not at least allude to the Exile. Another point against an exilic date is the unlikelihood of an author's associating either the hero or his closest companions with Edom, because after Babylon destroyed Jerusalem, Edom apparently took over some Judean cities, thereby stirring up in Judah a deep national hatred of Edom (cf. Ezek. 25:12–14; 35:1–15; Ps. 137:7).[2]

An early seventh-century date has more support than these later dates. The many allusions to Canaanite religion and the numerous contacts between the book of Job and the texts found at Ugarit are more easily accounted for in a book written when Israel was flirting with Baalism, i.e., before the Exile. Also, the close ties between the book of Job and portions of Isaiah, especially Isa. 40–55, may indicate the era in which Job was composed. While many scholars divide Isaiah into three books, dating the portions to the late 8th century, the 6th century, and the 4th century, respectively, other scholars, not persuaded by the theory of a Deutero-Isaiah, hold that Isaiah authored chs. 40–55 late in his ministry, during the first half of the 7th century B.C.[3] As for the relationship between the two books, the evidence seems to support the view that Isaiah was influenced by Job, rather than vice versa (see section V.F above). If this is true, then Job was composed before Isaiah, particularly before Isa. 40–55. That would lead to a date for Job no later than the second half of the 8th century.

The numerous points of contact between the book of Job and other OT passages (see section V above) reveal that the author's thought was saturated with his national literature. While the dates of many of the passages that show contact with the book of Job are debated, it is not impossible

2. See B. Oded, in *Israelite and Judaean History*, OTL, ed. J. Hayes and J. Miller (London: SCM; Philadelphia: Westminster, 1977), p. 475.

3. Cf. R. K. Harrison, *Introduction to the Old Testament* (Grand Rapids: Eerdmans, 1969), pp. 764–95; E. Sellin and G. Fohrer, *Introduction to the Old Testament*, tr. D. Green (Nashville: Abingdon, 1968), pp. 363–88.

that a large portion of them could have existed by the 7th century. An analysis of the similarities between Job 3:3–13 and Jer. 20:14–18 indicates that both authors relied on a common prototype.[4] The likelihood that the author was trained in the Wisdom tradition does not eliminate an eighth-century date, for during Hezekiah's reign interest in wisdom revived (715–689 B.C.; cf. Prov. 25:1). Furthermore, the socio-political conditions in the second half of the 8th century would have afforded an appropriate context for the writing of Job: the poor faced great hardship under the oppressive acts of the rich (as witnessed by the prophets Amos and Hosea), and the Assyrians destroyed Northern Israel, taking many captives. Finally, the heavenly council scenes in the prologue are more similar to the ninth-century vision of Micaiah (1 K. 22:19–23) than to the one found in Zech. 3 from the late 6th century B.C.[5]

The evidence for assigning the composition of the book of Job to any of these dates is unfortunately not overwhelming. Nevertheless, the interplay between this book and other OT books, especially Isaiah, can best be accounted for by placing this work in the seventh century B.C.

VIII. LITERARY ISSUES

The literary unity of the book is a major issue. Scholars take three basic approaches to account for the book's complexity and diversity: (1) the book is primarily the product of a single author, who continued to work on his masterpiece over a lifetime (e.g., Snaith, Gordis);[1] (2) the book is a collection of independent pieces from many different authors (e.g., Irwin);[2] (3) the author composed the bulk of the present work and over the centuries others added to it (e.g., Fohrer).[3] This commentary assumes one author for the reasons given below.

The author's style makes the identification of so-called secondary material difficult. A highly literate person, he borrowed materials freely from many sources and incorporated them into his work. If, in some places, the borrowed material was not smoothly integrated according to present-day

4. See the commentary below on 3:3–13.

5. S. Terrien, *IB*, III:888.

1. N. Snaith, *The Book of Job: Its Origin and Purpose*, SBT 2/11 (London: SCM; Naperville: Allenson, 1968), p. 8; R. Gordis, *The Book of God and Man* (Chicago/London: University of Chicago Press, repr. 1978), pp. 100–103, 110–12, 209–15.

2. W. Irwin, "Job," in *Peake's Commentary on the Bible*, rev. ed., ed. M. Black and H. H. Rowley (London: Nelson, 1962), p. 391.

3. G. Fohrer, *Das Buch Hiob*, KAT 16 (Gütersloh: Gerd Mohn, 1963), pp. 29–42.

standards, that does not necessarily signal editorial activity. Apart from manuscript evidence, the criteria for identifying secondary passages are highly subjective. Thus interpreters disagree widely about which portions are secondary.

The major literary problems can be discussed under five headings:

A. The relationship of the prologue-epilogue to the speeches (chs. 1–2; 42:7–17)
B. The unusual brevity of the third cycle of speeches (chs. 24–27)
C. The location of the hymn to wisdom (ch. 28)
D. The authorship of the Elihu speeches (chs. 32–37)
E. The extent and number of the Yahweh speeches (chs. 38:1–42:6)

A. THE PROLOGUE-EPILOGUE

The relationship of the epic account, contained in the prologue and epilogue, to the dialogue has been variously evaluated: (1) the epic account became attached at a later time to the dialogue because of its similar theme; (2) the author kept, primarily unaltered, an old epic account as a framework for the dialogue; (3) the author reworked an old epic account to fit the dialogue; (4) the author composed the epic account. As most contemporary interpreters point out, the epic account is essential to the meaning of the dialogue; thus the first suggestion is highly improbable. The second view falls before the several indications that the epic account has been reworked.[4] The fourth position seems unlikely by reason of the numerous indications of an ancient epic substratum to this prose account.[5] The majority of scholars, therefore, hold some form of the third position.

N. Sarna has demonstrated that an epic substratum underlies the prologue-epilogue.[6] Many details place the prose account in the patriarchal age: wealth is measured in animals and servants (1:3; 42:12); the family head offers up sacrifice (1:5; 42:8); the Sabeans and the Chaldeans are presented as wandering tribes (1:15, 17); the *qᵉśîṭâ* is a unit of currency (42:11; cf.

4. N. Sarna, "Epic Substratum in the Prose of Job," *JBL* 76 (1957) 13–25.

5. In an analysis of the language of the prose, A. Hurvitz ("The Date of the Prose-Tale of Job Linguistically Reconsidered," *HTR* 67 [1974] 17–34) concludes that it was reworked in the postexilic period. The date that the reworking actually took place may not be as late as he suggests, though, for it is hard to assign Hebrew words to a specific period of the Hebrew language as certainly as he assumes with the present knowledge of the growth of the Hebrew language. His work does indicate that the present epic account shows traces that indicate it was edited much later than the patriarchal period. This evidence can be used to favor the view that the author edited an older account to fit his work rather than merely taking it over as he found it.

6. See Sarna, op. cit.

Gen. 33:19 and Josh. 24:32); the description of the glory of Job's long life (42:17).[7] Furthermore, the literary style corresponds to that of an old epic: alliteration and assonance; parallelism; symbolic use of numbers (3, 7, 10, 70, twofold); vivid expressions (e.g., "to swallow," *billaʿ*, for "to wipe out," in 2:3); symmetrical patterns (e.g., the parallel descriptions of the divine council in 1:6–12 and 2:1–7; the characterization of Job in 1:1 par. 1:8 par. 2:3; 1:22 par. 2:10; the alternation between human [1:15, 17] and divine [1:16, 19] causes of the four disasters that befall Job; the naming of Job's daughters in 42:13).[8] These observations lead Sarna to conclude that the prose account comes directly from an ancient Epic of Job.[9]

Furthermore, the characterization of Job in the prologue, especially Yahweh's evaluation of his servant, is essential for a proper understanding of the speeches. Without this prologue the reader would side with the three comforters, thinking Job to be a demented villain, hostile to God and self-deluded about his own moral virtue. The epilogue is more suspect, however, for it seems to reaffirm the doctrine of retribution, which Job has so persuasively refuted. Nevertheless, as the commentary below argues, this work does not reject the doctrine of retribution, but rather corrects misguided applications of that doctrine. The epilogue is a vital part of the message of the book, for it demonstrates that God seeks the ultimate good of his servant despite the tragedies and misfortunes that he has suffered. Without the epilogue the suffering person would appear as the ideal hero and God as a powerful tyrant having no compassion for human beings.

Several scholars have attempted to discover the growth and development of the epic portion.[10] A. Alt argued that ch. 1 and 42:11–17 comprised the original account.[11] His position, though, is too restrictive, for it is hard to understand why portions of ch. 2, which balances the scenes of ch. 1, do not belong to that layer.

G. Fohrer's insightful study offers a reconstruction of the author's

7. Ibid., p. 14. It has also been argued that the style of prose-poetry-prose (a-b-a; prologue-dialogue-epilogue) makes the literary organization of the book of Job comparable to the organization of the Code of Hammurabi and the book of Daniel. It may be more accurate, however, to describe the book of Job as prose with speeches in poetry (see Snaith, *The Book of Job,* pp. 2, 21, 27). This observation takes account of the various prose headings to the speeches, esp. the longer ones to the Elihu speeches (32:1–5) and the Yahweh speeches (38:1), as well as the poetic lines in the prologue (1:21; 2:10).

8. Sarna, op. cit., pp. 15–24.

9. Ibid., p. 25.

10. Cf. J. Lindblom, *La composition du livre de Job* (Lund: Gleerup, 1945); H. Hertzberg, "Der Aufbau des Buches Hiob," in *Festschrift für Alfred Bertholet,* ed. W. Baumgartner, et al. (Tübingen: Mohr/Siebeck, 1950), pp. 233–58; H. Möller, *Sinn und Aufbau des Buches Hiob* (Berlin: Evangelische Verlagsanstalt, 1955).

11. A. Alt, "Zur Vorgeschichte des Buches Hiob," *ZAW* 55 (1937) 265–68.

adaptation of an old epic account as the framework for the dialogue.[12] The key to his approach is 42:11, which records the visit of the friends and relatives to comfort Job after his restoration. That scene appears to be out of place, for one would expect the friends and relatives to come to comfort Job as soon as they had learned of his troubles. Therefore, this incident must have at one time followed Job's wife's tempting words (2:9). Given the doubling of actions and scenes throughout the epic account, one may assume that like his wife, Job's friends and relatives counseled Job to take a course to escape his plight by compromising his integrity. But Job also rejected their counsel. Then Yahweh appeared and addressed his servant in a brief speech whose heading now stands at 38:1. At last Job surrendered himself to Yahweh. Next Yahweh spoke, as in 42:7–9, but to the relatives and friends rather than to Eliphaz and his companions. The old account concluded with a description of Job's restoration (42:10, 12–17). At this point the author of Job modified the ancient epic to incorporate the speeches. He moved the incident about the relatives to the epilogue and put in its place the introduction of the three principal speakers (2:11–13). The similarity of language suggests that the author composed 2:11 after the pattern of 42:11, but he left out the temptation of the relatives and Job's rejection of their faulty counsel. Then in the account of Yahweh's rebuke of Job's counselors he substituted Eliphaz and his companions for the friends and relatives (42:7–9). Also he preserved the introduction to Yahweh's speech (38:1) but replaced Yahweh's brief word with the present Yahweh speeches. Fohrer speculates further that the author recast the indirect style of the speeches in the old epic account into their present poetic form and that he substituted the specific name *Yahweh* for a more general name of God. Thus the author has conformed the old epic account to his composition.

Another supposedly insurmountable obstacle to the literary unity of the prologue and the speeches is that on the surface each portion gives Job a different social setting. The Job of the prose account appears to be a seminomad, the owner of great herds (1:3) grazing over a vast distance (1:14–17), while the Job of the speeches appears as a city dweller (19:15; 29:7; 31:8–11, 38–41). But both settings are more complex than this simple distinction suggests, for the reference to five hundred yoke of oxen plowing fields in 1:3, 14 suggests an agricultural way of life while the reference to living in a tent in 18:6 points to a nomadic way of life. The solution to this problem may be that Job was chief of a tribe, living according to a dimorphic social and political structure, a tribal system that integrated a nomadic and a

12. G. Fohrer, "Zur Vorgeschichte und Komposition des Buches Hiob," *VT* 6 (1956) 249–67; repr. in *Studien zum Buche Hiob* (Gütersloh: Gerd Mohn, 1963), pp. 26–43.

sedentary way of life.[13] The chiefs under this kind of system spent a part of, in some cases the majority of, the year as village residents, or, as Rowton reports, a chief might even have his own village with some four hundred houses along with a fortified residence for himself.[14] Or a tribe might have aligned themselves with a larger urban center in such a way that the tribal elite interacted with the urban upper class.[15] The head of such a city could come from the tribal segment. This picture accords well with the description of Job both as the leader of the town's assembly (ch. 29) and as the owner of vast herds and flocks (1:3).

In conclusion, the author has taken an old epic account and reworked it to serve as the framework for the series of speeches. Thus the marked contradiction between the silent, patient Job of the prose account and the verbose, defiant Job of the dialogue—a contradiction taken by some[16] to be so sharp that they are irreconcilable—is an intended tension, fundamental to the book's message. Thus the epic account is an essential element of the message of the book of Job.

B. THE THIRD CYCLE OF SPEECHES

Given the facts that Bildad's third speech (ch. 25) is very short in proportion to his other speeches, a third speech from Zophar appears to be missing, and Job's last response is unusually long (chs. 26–28), many scholars conclude that the third cycle was disrupted sometime early in the history of the transmission of the text.[17] Moreover, the text of 24:18–24, a part of Job's speech, is almost unintelligible and its argument counters Job's complaint in 24:1–17. No wonder there have been numerous attempts to rearrange the verses found in the third cycle to arrive at a longer speech for Bildad, a more concise speech for Job, and a third speech for Zophar. Here are two examples of reconstructions:

I. Gordis:

Bildad: 25:1–6; 26:5–14

13. M. Rowton, "Dimorphic Structure and the Tribal Elite," *Studia Instituti Anthropos* 28 (1976) 219–57. Cf. also N. Gottwald, *The Tribes of Yahweh* (New York: Orbis, 1979), pp. 437–63.

14. Rowton, op. cit., p. 221.

15. Ibid., pp. 230–37.

16. E.g., H. L. Ginsberg, "Job the patient and Job the impatient," in *Congress Volume: Rome 1968,* VTSup 17 (Leiden: Brill, 1969), pp. 88–111.

17. On the problems of the third cycle, see G. Barton, "The Composition of Job 24–30," *JBL* 30 (1911) 66–77; P. Dhorme, "Les chapitres XXV–XXVIII du livre de Job," *RB* 33 (1924) 343–56; A. Regnier, "La Distribution des chapitres 25–28 du livre de Job," *RB* 33 (1924) 186–200; R. Tournay, "L'ordre Primitif des chapitres XXXIV–XXVIII du livre de Job," *RB* 64 (1957) 321–34; H. Reventlow, "Tradition und Redaktion in Hiob 27 im Rahmen der Hiobreden des Abschnittes Hi 24–27," *ZAW* 94 (1982) 279–93; C. Westermann, *Structure of the Book of Job,* pp. 131–34.

Job: 26:1–4; 27:1–12
Zophar: 27:13–23

II. Hölscher (similarly Duhm):
Bildad: 25:1; 26:2–4; 25:2–6; 26:5–14
Job: 27:1–12 . . .
Zophar: 27:13 . . . 14–23

Each reconstruction is still faced with very rough transitions between sections and lacks the full character of the speeches of the other two cycles. The wide variety of the multiple reconstructions cautions further against major reapportioning of the verses in chs. 24–31 in order to achieve a full third cycle.

Bildad's third speech (25:1–6), lacking both an introduction and a conclusion, seems to have been accidentally cut off. A portion of it may have become relocated in one of the other speeches of this cycle. One section that clearly seems out of place in the mouth of Job is 27:13–23, for it rebutts Job's complaint that evildoers do harm unchecked, for God fails to keep times of judgment (24:1–17). To fill out Bildad's brief speech these verses may be placed after 25:1–6. The lack of transition between these two sections indicates that lines have been lost both before and after 27:13–23. This reconstruction is supported by the content of these two portions. The content of 25:1–6 reveals that Bildad, especially in vv. 4–6, primarily restates Eliphaz's thesis that nothing in heaven or on earth is clean or righteous in God's sight (4:17–19; 15:14–16). As for 27:13–23, they are a restatement of Zophar's teaching that the wicked face certain judgment. From the perspective that the author has Bildad merely reiterate the position of his fellow comforters to intimate that the comforters have nothing more to say, 27:13–23 may be considered the logical sequel to the preserved portion of Bildad's speech.

According to this interpretation Zophar never delivered a third speech. Two observations support this view. First, a survey of the three cycles of the dialogue reveals that the speeches of Eliphaz (98, 68, and 58 lines respectively) and those of Bildad (43 and 41 lines) become progressively shorter while Zophar's second speech is significantly longer than his first (56 lines compared to 40 lines). The author made Zophar's second speech longer as a signal that Zophar would not speak again. The second observation is that since Zophar is the least creative of the three comforters and the most certain that Job is guilty, there would be little loss if he delivered only two speeches. It is concluded, then, that Zophar never made a third speech.

To regain a part of the third cycle and to avoid a highly speculative reconstruction that, if incorrect, would only be further from the original production, only a minor change is made in the commentary. Bildad's third speech is expanded by joining 27:13–23 to 25:1–6 and Job's eighth response is reduced to 26:1–14;[18] 27:2–12. The result is not a full-orbed speech for either person, for the transitions between segments are rough and each speech lacks a conclusion.

C. THE HYMN TO WISDOM

The hymn to wisdom in ch. 28 does not connect smoothly with its immediate context. Its abstract, reflective tone contrasts markedly with the passionately argumentative style of the preceding speeches. Its place in the present text—the last part of Job's last speech of the dialogue—adds to its suspect nature, for its tone seems too tranquil and contemplative for his troubled thoughts, and its meditative nature contrasts markedly with Job's determination in his coming avowal of innocence. Moreover, it is doubtful that the hymn belongs to one of the truncated speeches of the friends, for its insights are fresh, lofty, and speculative in contrast to the friends' sterile rhetoric. On the one hand, nothing in the hymn relates directly to the issue of suffering or contributes to Job's quest for a lawsuit with God; on the other hand, many interpreters judge the hymn secondary because they believe that it anticipates the Yahweh speeches and preempts their impact. Nevertheless, if this hymn comes from a source other than one of the parties of the dialogue, it is well placed, for it bridges the dialogue (chs. 4–27) with the final sets of speeches (29:1–42:6). Since the friends' rhetoric has grown sterile, this hymn judges their efforts as failing to lead Job to wisdom and prepares the way for Yahweh to speak. Therefore, the hymn may be considered to function as an interlude. If the book of Job was presented as a poem, a bard could have intoned the hymn differently; or if the book of Job was presented as a drama, a chorus could have sung it.

Concerning the authorship of this hymn to wisdom, Gordis specu-

18. The majority of modern interpreters reassign the hymnic portion in praise of God's power (26:5–12) from Job to one of the comforters. But there is no serious obstacle to accepting this pericope as Job's. In various speeches Job employs hymnic lines in praise of God's power, e.g., 9:5–13. Since God's majesty occurs in the speeches of Job and the comforters alike, it is only the context that can indicate to which speaker these lines are most appropriate. A comparison of these verses with 9:5–13 is instructive. Both passages praise God as creator (9:8–10; 26:7–10) and describe the remarkable response that God's appearing produces in nature (9:5–7; 26:10–13). Both passages laud God's victory over the cosmic foe Rahab (9:13; 26:12), and they both wonder how any creature, esp. a mortal, can challenge this great God (9:11–12; 26:5–6, 10–11, 14). Moreover, if 27:2–6 comes after 26:5–14, the following pericopes of both passages have remarkable similarities. In 27:2–6 Job resolutely swears that he will hold on to his integrity by maintaining his righteousness, while in 9:14–25 he ponders the absurdity of arguing his case before God. In both sections Job states his resolve to prove his innocence. Thus 27:2–12 is joined to 26:5–14 in order to fill out Job's eighth response.

lates that the author composed it early in his career, and later on a scribe motivated to preserve this fine piece included it in this place, which had already suffered dislocation.[19] While it is possible that this hymn was added to the final edition, the fact that it bridges the two major divisions of the book as well as the ties of v. 28 with other sections of the book (see commentary) indicate that the author skillfully placed the hymn in this location. When the transition from the dialogue to the hymn was lost, along with other portions of the third cycle, resulting in the present text, the hymn appeared to be spoken by Job.

As already stated, many interpreters argue that this hymn destroys the impact of the Yahweh speeches. But this judgment seems to overlook the frequent use of repetition by ancient authors. It was one of their ways of developing a theme more fully and of increasing its impact on the audience. Thus the points of agreement with the words of Yahweh are intended to prepare Job and the audience to hear Yahweh's words by teaching explicitly that Yahweh alone can reveal insight into the true order of the universe, the order Job has challenged. The very fact that numerous interpreters judge the content of the Yahweh speeches to be irrevelant to the issue of Job's suffering supports this view by showing that the author needed to prepare his audience for the approach Yahweh was going to take in answering Job.

Because of the problems mentioned above, some have advocated a different location for this hymn, e.g., just before the Yahweh speeches (Buttenweiser) or after Job's final response to Yahweh (Szczygiel). But these suggestions do not provide the hymn a better setting or improve the book's structure. Their failure serves to point out that this hymn is presently in the best place possible within the book of Job. Since this hymn enhances the work, coincides with the author's style, stands at the place of a major transition in the book, and contributes to the theme of wisdom that reverberates throughout the book, it may be accepted as an integral part of the original work.[20]

19. R. Gordis, *The Book of God and Man,* pp. 102–103.

20. Another issue about the hymn needs mention. The LXX has a shorter text, reading vv. 1–3a, 4b, c, 9b–13, 20–21a, 22b–26a, 27b (see P. Zerafa, *The Wisdom of God in the Book of Job* [Rome: Herder, 1978], pp. 130–36). The translator appears to have reworked this hymn to eliminate the long lists and the sense of redundancy in order to provide a text which would have been more appealing to a Greek audience. The translator made God, not man, the subject of the first stanza and removed the theme of human technical genius. In addition, the translator played down the theme that human beings cannot find wisdom and reordered vv. 22–28 to read that God, who traced out wisdom, makes it available to human beings through the fear of God and the avoidance of evil. These two changes would have made the hymn more palatable to the Greeks, who gave a high place to wisdom and its attainment. If the translator of Job did function as an editor, the LXX does not serve as a witness to a Hebrew *Vorlage* different from that of the MT.

D. THE ELIHU SPEECHES

The authorship of the Elihu speeches has been widely questioned. While a few modern interpreters, e.g., Budde, Snaith, and Gordis,[21] have championed their authenticity, the majority consider them to come from a later hand. Many facts are cited for the latter position. The role of Elihu has not been fully integrated into the final work, for he is not mentioned in either the prologue or the dialogue. Moreover, the style of these speeches differs markedly from those found in the dialogue. One striking difference is that Elihu's speeches lack the rich metaphors that permeate the speeches of the dialogue. Other notable stylistic differences include: Elihu uses the divine name *'ēl* ("God") more frequently than *'ĕlôah* ("God") and *šadday* ("Shaddai"); he prefers the shorter first person singular pronoun *'ᵃnî* to *'ānōkî;* he also prefers the archaic forms of the prepositions *bᵉmô, kᵉmô,* and *minnî* to the shorter, more common *bᵉ, kᵉ,* and *min;* his speeches have a greater number of Aramaisms than the other speeches. Finally, unlike the passionate speeches of the comforters, the Elihu speeches are a reasoned challenge to a position of Job quoted at the opening of the speech. Thus the Elihu speeches differ markedly in structure from the other speeches.[22]

Each of these points may be evaluated from a different perspective. On the one hand, Elihu's absence from the epilogue and the prologue seems inexplicable if one posits an interpolator who inserted the Elihu speeches, for he could have adjusted those places to accommodate his inclusion of Elihu. On the other hand, if one maintains the integrity of the book, the long introduction of Elihu compensates for his absence from the prologue, and his absence from the epilogue corresponds to the author's style—neither the Satan nor Job's wife appears again, even though their absence from the epilogue leaves the modern reader with a sense of incompleteness. If Elihu's role is to prepare Job for the theophany, the author would have had little need to include Elihu in the epilogue, for, having fulfilled his role, he would not stand in need of any judgment like that pronounced against the three comforters. Furthermore, Snaith has carefully compared the alleged differences in vocabulary between the Elihu speeches and the other major sections of the book.[23] He does not find the variations significant. Therefore, he concludes that it is not necessary to posit another author to account for the differences in the Elihu speeches. The differences in the structure of the

21. N. Snaith, *The Book of Job,* SBT 2/11 (London: SCM; Naperville: Allenson, 1968), pp. 72–91; R. Gordis, *The Book of God and Man,* pp. 104–16.

22. On form analysis see C. Westermann, *Structure of the Book of Job,* pp. 139–47; G. Fohrer, "Die Weisheit des Elihu (Hi 32–37)," *AfO* 19 (1959–60) 83–94; repr. in *Studien zum Buche Hiob,* pp. 87–107.

23. N. Snaith, op. cit., p. 77.

Elihu speeches may be explained by Elihu's role being different from that of the comforters.

Elihu is both given prominence and downplayed at the same time. He delivers four unanswered discourses, one more than those of the comforters, and he stands just before the Yahweh speeches. In order to downplay his position before Yahweh's appearance, he is cast as an angry young man, anxious to speak and disturbed by the inability of his elders to answer Job. This characterization offers comic relief to the tension built up by Job's solemn oath.[24] An ancient audience, feeling the full weight of that tension, would be relieved and amused by the bombastic Elihu. Moreover, Elihu's name, which means "he is my God," intimates that he functions as Yahweh's forerunner.[25] That is, he prepares Job to hear what Yahweh will say and to surrender his case against God. This position is strengthened by Freedman's research showing that the Elihu speeches are closely tied to the dialogue and to the Yahweh speeches. The first speech (chs. 32–33) is primarily related to chs. 12–14, especially ch. 13; the second speech (ch. 34) to the third cycle; the third speech (ch. 35) to both the second and third cycles, particularly chs. 21 and 22; but the fourth speech (chs. 36–37), which reiterates some statements from the first speech, is more closely aligned with ch. 38.[26] Freedman's findings mean that the Elihu speeches were composed as a reasoned response to the ideas found in each section of the book. In other words, their author insightfully addressed Job's basic question about the suffering of the innocent and also prepared Job for the answer Yahweh was to give.

Clearly, then, the Elihu speeches are an integral part of the final edition of the work. It is improper to judge them as a clumsy later addition or

24. See J. Whedbee, "The Comedy of Job," in *Studies in the Book of Job*, ed. R. Polzin and D. Robertson, Semeia 7 (Missoula: Scholars Press, 1977), pp. 18–20.

25. See Gordis, op. cit., pp. 115–16.

26. D. Freedman ("The Elihu Speeches in the Book of Job," *HTR* 61 [1968] 51–59) makes some very creative suggestions about the origin and function of the Elihu speeches. He reasons that their author composed three or four speeches—the number depends on whether the third speech is an independent speech or part of another one—in order to insert them at critical places in the dialogue, for he wished to counter the radical ideas found throughout the dialogue. Freedman thinks that the speeches were to be distributed in this fashion: the first speech at the end of the first cycle (ch. 14); the second speech at the conclusion of the third cycle (ch. 27); the third speech, if there is one, possibly at the end of the second cycle (ch. 21); and the fourth after Job's final speech—functioning as a counterbalance to it but more importantly pointing to Yahweh's speech. In Freedman's reconstruction, however, the author failed to complete his project and subsequently abandoned it. Then a later editor, wishing to preserve these speeches, made a place for them between Job's last speech and the theophany. While Freedman's analysis is very interesting, his reconstruction of the speeches' origin and placement in the final edition is more fanciful than credible.

a sanctification of the heretical ideas that Job has entertained.[27] Whether they are the work of the author of Job or of a final redactor is difficult to ascertain. If the author of the book composed them, the variations in style and structure may be accounted for by postulating that he composed them at a later date than the main body of the work, an idea espoused by both Gordis and Snaith. Assuming that the issue of the suffering righteous occupied the author for a lifetime, he may have continued to make changes in this work throughout the years. On this premise Gordis speculates that the author chose Elihu to represent some insights he had gained about human suffering, insights that were too important to put in the mouth of the comforters and yet too limited to be assigned to Yahweh.

Working with Gordis's idea, one might assume that the author of Job often discussed the issue of suffering with others. If he was a teacher, he would have discussed it with his students. Perhaps out of these conversations the Elihu speeches emerged. Or one may theorize that a disciple of this great author composed some of his thoughts about the suffering of the innocent and shared his material with his master; the author reworked and incorporated that material into the final edition as the Elihu speeches. These two proposals are attempts not only to account for the stylistic and structural differences between the Elihu speeches and the dialogue, but also to take seriously the significant contribution that the Elihu speeches make to the final work.

E. THE YAHWEH SPEECHES

A word from God belonged to the oldest stratum of the epic, as the prosaic introduction using the divine name *Yahweh* attests.[28] The author preserved the name *Yahweh* because of its close identification with God's revelation and redemption. Moreover, the Yahweh speeches fit the dramatic action of the book. They are anticipated in Job's repeated demand that God justify him (13:22; 16:18–21; 19:25–27); and his avowal of innocence (chs. 29–31) makes an answer from Yahweh mandatory. Therefore, it is inaccurate to judge these speeches as a secondary addition or a mere appendage.

Nevertheless, the Yahweh speeches present several perplexing problems to the interpreter. On the surface they fail to address the issue of the suffering righteous, and they skirt Job's complaint that God fails to keep times of judgment (e.g., 24:1–17). Amazingly, they seem to ignore Job's avowal of innocence, for Yahweh neither condemns Job nor acquits him.

27. Ibid.
28. Gordis, op. cit., p. 114.

Moreover, modern readers in search of insight into the issue of suffering are often keenly disappointed with the Yahweh speeches.

The major literary issue with the Yahweh speeches is their extent and content.[29] Since large portions of Yahweh's second speech appear verbose and trite in comparison with the first, many contemporary interpreters posit that an original single speech from Yahweh has attracted many additions until a later editor formulated it into two speeches. For example, Fohrer evaluates the portions about Behemoth and Leviathan (40:15–24 and 40:25–41:26 [Eng. 41:1–34]) as secondary additions. He then finds that the remaining material (40:8–14) is too short for a second speech. Furthermore, he judges the rebuking tone of 40:8–14 to be out of place at the head of a speech, so he relocates these verses to the conclusion of the first speech. He also argues for one Yahweh speech on the basis of the literary problems with Job's two answers: Job's first answer appears to be too short (40:3–5), and his second answer is primarily a response to Yahweh's first speech (42:7–17). Therefore, Fohrer reconstructs a single answer from Job, consisting of 40:3–5; 42:2, 3ab, 5, 6, to balance the one Yahweh speech.

Westermann also concludes that originally there was only one Yahweh speech. Using form-critical categories, he reasons that a theophany, unique by its very nature, can consist of only one speech.[30] For Yahweh to deliver two speeches, new ideas would have to be expressed or there would have to have been a new sequence of events. Identifying the genre of the Yahweh speech as a hymn of praise to God that has been transformed into a disputational discourse, Westermann perceives two elements in the speech: praise of God the creator (38:4–30) and praise of the Lord of history (40:6–41:26 [Eng. 41:34]). In this reconstruction the pericope 40:7–14 heads not a new speech but a second division of the one speech. Westermann then evaluates two portions, 40:15–24 and 41:4–26 (Eng. 12–34), as later additions due to their purely descriptive nature, which contrasts with the interrogative style typical of the Yahweh speech.

Nevertheless, a good case can be made for two speeches from Yahweh.[31] The basic structure of the book is composed of sets of twos, threes, and fours.[32] The prologue is cast into sets of twos and fours. The two

29. Cf. G. Fohrer, "Zur Vorgeschichte und Komposition des Buches Hiob," *VT* 6 (1956) 249–67; repr. in *Studien zum Buche Hiob,* pp. 38, 41–42; idem, "Gottes Antwort aus dem Sturmwind, Hi. 38–41," *TZ* 18 (1962) 1–24; repr. in *Studien zum Buche Hiob,* pp. 108–29.

30. Westermann, *Structure of the Book of Job,* pp. 105–23.

31. See V. Kubina, *Die Gottesreden im Buche Hiob* (Freiburg: Herder, 1979). She argues on the basis of form criticism that the literary style of the second speech is continuous with the author's style of the first speech.

32. See section X below.

speeches from Yahweh with Job's two answers make a set of four. This set of four matches the four speeches from Elihu, and corresponds to the twos and fours of the prologue. Furthermore, the integrity of the second speech can be defended. While the portrait of Behemoth (40:15–24) lacks the question format of the portraits found in the first speech (save for v. 24), its use of descriptive sentences is identical to the style found in the portrait of the ostrich (39:13–18).[33] As for the portrait of Leviathan, it is suspect because of its unusual length and the mixture of questions and descriptive sentences. But that portrait is similar in structure to the portraits of the horse (39:19–25) and the birds of prey (39:26–30), which also open with questions and follow with descriptive sentences. This mixture adds variety to the Yahweh speeches. Furthermore, the unusual length of the description of Leviathan is not without parallels; the author elaborates extensively on a theme in a few other passages, e.g., the hymn about God's rule in 12:12–25, the list of injustices in 24:1–17, the list of precious stones in 28:15–19, and the description of ruffians in 30:2–8. Therefore, it is quite possible that the author drew out the description of Leviathan as a rhetorical device; Yahweh kept speaking, as he waited for his words to move Job to change his attitude.

Another reason for two speeches is that they address different issues. The first speech counters Job's accusation that Yahweh fails to administer the world justly, and the second speech challenges Job to surrender his case

33. Cf. G. Fohrer, *Studien,* pp. 108–29. The inclusion of the portrait of the ostrich in 39:13–18 has often been questioned, for it is missing in LXX and lacks the question format found throughout the first speech. Fohrer accepts this passage as original, however, for it balances the two sets of four strophes about animal life with the two sets of four strophes about inanimate life (*Studien,* pp. 115–16; cf. also J. Böhmer, "Was ist der Sinn von Hiob 39,13–18 an seiner gegenwärtigen Stelle?" *ZAW* 53 [1935] 289–91). Nevertheless, Fohrer trims the portrait to four verses, leaving out vv. 15 and 17 as later additions, since they introduce the motif of the ostrich's stupidity, a motif foreign to the original portrait. But a look at the length of the animal portraits is suggestive. While many of them are four verses in length, the first is only three verses (38:39–41). The six verses on the ostrich are followed by the seven-verse portrait of the horse. This sequence of 6-7 is frequent in Semitic poetry (e.g., 5:19). That this sequence is not accidental is suggested by the possible correspondence between the number six, symbolic of that which is incomplete and chaotic, and the description of the ostrich as grotesque and stupid, as well as the correspondence between the number seven, symbolic of that which is complete or perfect, and the description of the horse as a creature of amazing beauty, courage, and strength. The closing portrait of five verses (39:26–30) forms a pattern with the opening portrait of three verses and the usual portrait of four verses (3, 4, 4, 4, 6, 7, 5) to make a total of seven portraits in the first speech. Vv. 15 and 17 set up a marked contrast between the stupidity of the ostrich and the majestic qualities of the horse. Moreover, Keel notes that the ostrich is frequently pictured with other wild animals in ancient Near Eastern glyphs that praise a god as lord of the animals (O. Keel, *Jahwes Entgegnung an Ijob* [Göttingen: Vandenhoeck & Ruprecht, 1978], p. 102). This observation indicates that the portrait of the ostrich properly belongs with the other animal portraits.

before the all-powerful ruler of the cosmos. Both speeches contain the same elements:

Prosaic Introduction	38:1	40:6
Exhortation to Job	38:2–3	40:7
Interrogation of Job	38:4–39:30	40:15–41:26 (Eng. 41:34)
Challenge to Job	40:2	40:8–14

The placing of the challenge to Job at the conclusion of the first speech and at the head of the second speech forms a chiasm designed to heighten the impact of Yahweh's challenge.

In conclusion, the two Yahweh speeches are an integral part of the structure and the message of the book of Job and can be accepted as having been well preserved.

IX. POETRY

An understanding of parallelism, meter, and strophes is an aid to the interpretation of Job. Hebrew poetry is not characterized by rhyme or patterns of alliteration but by parallelism. While a unit may have three, sometimes four, lines, the bicolon is the rule in Hebrew poetry. The second line, which receives greater emphasis, completes the thought begun in the first line. It defines, restricts, or carries forward the idea of the first line. By juxtaposing words and phrases new clarity is given to an otherwise neglected, overlooked, or forgotten concept. Often only parts of the lines are synonymous, while the other parts either expand the thought or set up a contrasting idea. At times the first line expresses an obvious truth and the second line presents an idea not so obvious, but one made more understandable because of the parallel with the accepted idea. In each of these cases the second line does not merely repeat the first, but develops it in some way. Referring to the first line as A and the second line as B, Kugel states "B *must inevitably be understood as A's completion;* A, and what's more, B; not only A, but B; not A, not even B; not A, and certainly not B; just as A, so B; and so forth."[1]

1. J. Kugel, *The Idea of Biblical Poetry: Parallelism and Its History* (New Haven: Yale University Press, 1981), p. 13. Two recent studies on poetry from a syntactical approach are S. Geller, *Parallelism in Early Biblical Poetry,* HSM 20 (Missoula: Scholars Press, 1979); M. O'Connor, *Hebrew Verse Structure* (Winona Lake: Eisenbrauns, 1980). On chiasm, see M. Dahood, "Chiasmus in Job: A Text-Critical and Philological Criterion," in *A Light unto My Path,* Fest. J. M. Myers, ed. H. Bream, et al. (Philadelphia: Temple University Press, 1974), pp. 118–30; and A. Ceresko, "The A:B::B:A Word Pattern in Hebrew and Northwest Semitic with Special Reference to the Book of Job," *UF* 7 (1975) 73–78.

Three examples will serve to illustrate the multiple varieties of parallelism found in the poetry of Job. In the first example, the second line restates the first line, using synonyms:

Can papyrus	thrive	without a marsh?
Can reeds	grow	without water? (8:11; cf. 8:15)

h^{a}yig̱ʾeh-gōmeʾ b^{e}lōʾ ḇiṣṣâ
yiśgeh-ʾāḥû ḇ^{e}lî-māyim

The second line continues the thought of the first line without any synonymous words between the two lines:

If one plans	to enter into litigation	with [God],
he could not answer him	one time	in a thousand. (9:3)

ʾim-yaḥpōṣ lārîḇ ʿimmô
lōʾ-yaʿ^{a}nennû ʾaḥaṯ minnî-ʾālep̱

In the third illustration one element of each line may be parallel while the other elements develop the thought (a:b::a′:c):

If it is regarding strength,	behold,	he is the strong one;
or if it is for litigation,	who	could summon him for me? (9:19)

ʾim-l^{e}ḵōaḥ ʾammîṣ hinnēh
w^{e}ʾim-l^{e}mišpāṭ mî yôʿîḏēnî

The expression "if it is regarding strength" parallels "if it is for litigation," two acceptable ways of settling a dispute. The last phrase, "who could summon him," is a question of doubt that grows out of the contemplation of disputing with God.

Modern studies of Hebrew metrics have produced varying results. A major, still unresolved, difficulty is the length of a foot and the number of feet in a colon. Addressing this problem, F. M. Cross, Jr. and D. N. Freedman have built on the work of W. F. Albright and advocated syllabic meter over stress meter.[2] They count the number of syllables in a colon reconstructed to the supposed original pronunciation. While this method of

2. W. F. Albright, "The Earliest Forms of Hebrew Verse," *JPOS* 2 (1922) 69–86; D. N. Freedman, "Archaic Forms in Early Hebrew Poetry," *ZAW* 72 (1960) 101–107; F. M. Cross, Jr., and D. N. Freedman, *Studies in Ancient Yahwistic Poetry*, SBLDS 21 (Missoula: Scholars Press, 1975); D. Stuart, *Studies in Early Hebrew Meter*, HSM 13 (Missoula: Scholars Press, 1976).

syllabic scansion has not won wide acceptance, it does offer a more objective method for the analysis of cola. Also the reconstruction of difficult texts by this method has yielded some excellent results.[3] Therefore, this approach to prosody is preferred in this commentary.

Almost all the lines in Job are *colum longum,* and the majority of lines fall into the patterns 7/7, 8/7, 8/8, 9/8, 9/9.[4] But some lines appear to be out of balance, e.g., 11/7 (3:7); 8/13 (10:11); 13/9 (12:7). While some of these imbalances may have arisen from textual errors, others may be intentional for variety and emphasis. Here is an example of scansion for 8:2–3:

v. 2	*ʿaḏ-ʾān tᵉmallel-ʾēlleh*	7
	(wᵉ)rûaḥ kabbîr ʾimrê-pîḵā	8(9)
v. 3	*haʾēl yᵉʿawwēṯ mišpāṭ*	7
	(wᵉ)ʾim-šadday yᵉʿawwēṯ-ṣeḏeq	8(9)

Attempts have been made to divide the speeches into strophes (e.g., Kissane and Fohrer).[5] While there are obviously divisions in the speeches according to subject matter, they are not of uniform length, a necessity if there are genuine strophes. Those who arrange the speeches in strophes are often forced to emend the text quite freely and in so doing must omit many verses as secondary. Such wholesale reordering of the text does not seem warranted. Therefore, strophic patterns are not identified in this study; the term *strophe* is used loosely to identify paragraphs of varying lengths.

X. STRUCTURE AND GENRES

A. THE BASIC STRUCTURE OF THE BOOK OF JOB

The book of Job is structured very symmetrically, composed of sets of twos, threes, and fours:

3. For an analysis of ch. 3 using syllabic meter see D. Freedman, "The Structure of Job 3," *Bib* (1968) 503–508.

4. Using stress meter, Fohrer finds that most lines are 3/3 with variations of 3/2, 2/3, 4/4, and very seldom 2/2 and 3/4.

5. Cf. P. Skehan, "Strophic Patterns in the Book of Job," *CBQ* 23 (1961) 125–42; repr. in *Studies in Israelite Poetry and Wisdom,* CBQMS I (Washington: Catholic Biblical Association, 1971), pp. 96–114; E. Webster, "Strophic Patterns in Job 3–28," *JSOT* 26 (1983) 33–60; idem, "Strophic Patterns in Job 29–42," *JSOT* 30 (1984) 95–109.

I. THE PROLOGUE
(chs. 1–2)

A. Introduction of Job
(1:1–5)

B. The First Heavenly Scene
(1:6–12)

C. Job's Misfortune
(1:13–22)

B′. The Second Heavenly Scene
(2:1–7a)

C′. Job's Physical Affliction
(2:7b–10)

A′. Introduction of the Three Friends
(2:11–13)

II. JOB'S CURSE-LAMENT
(ch. 3)

III. THE DIALOGUE
(chs. 4–27)

A. The First Cycle
(chs. 4–14)

1. Eliphaz
(chs. 4–5)
2. Job
(chs. 6–7)
3. Bildad
(ch. 8)
4. Job
(chs. 9–10)
5. Zophar
(ch. 11)
6. Job
(chs. 12–14)

B. The Second Cycle
(chs. 15–21)

1. Eliphaz
(ch. 15)
2. Job
(chs. 16–17)
3. Bildad
(ch. 18)
4. Job
(ch. 19)
5. Zophar
(ch. 20)
6. Job
(ch. 21)

C. The Third Cycle
(chs. 22–27)

1. Eliphaz
(ch. 22)
2. Job
(chs. 23–24)
3. Bildad
(25:1–6; 27:13–23)
4. Job
(26:1–14; 27:1–12)

IV. THE HYMN TO WISDOM
(ch. 28)

V. JOB'S AVOWAL OF INNOCENCE
(chs. 29–31)

A. Job's Remembrance
(ch. 29)

B. A Lament
(ch. 30)

C. An Oath of Innocence
(ch. 31)

VI. THE ELIHU SPEECHES
(chs. 32–37)

VII. THE THEOPHANY
(38:1–42:6)

A. Yahweh's First Speech
(38:1–40:2)

B. Job's Response
(40:3–5)

A′. Yahweh's Second Speech
(40:6–41:26 [Eng. 41:34])

B′. Job's Response
(42:1–6)

VIII. THE EPILOGUE
(42:7–17)

A. Judgment on Friends
(42:7–9)

B. Yahweh's Blessing on Job
(42:10–17)

The prologue is composed of six scenes grouped into three sets of twos. The number three is prominent in the dialogue; three speakers each deliver three speeches in a threefold cycle. In each cycle Job has three responses. Job's avowal of innocence also has three parts. In the next two sets the number four dominates. Elihu delivers four unanswered speeches, and the theophany consists of four units, two long speeches from Yahweh balanced by two short answers from Job. The simplicity and symmetry of this structure contrasts with the profundity of the subject discussed.

B. GENRES

Several form-critical studies have been made of the portions of the book of Job.[1] Two major efforts have attempted to identify the genre of the book. Richter identifies it as a lawsuit.[2] The various sections of the book correspond to different stages of a lawsuit. The first section is the procedure to reach a settlement through a pre-trial hearing (chs. 4–14). Since this attempt fails, a formal trial follows (chs. 15–31). The friends' silence after Job's

1. Cf. G. Fohrer, "Form und Funktion in der Hiobdictung," *ZDMG* 109 (1959) 31–49; repr. in *Studien zum Buche Hiob* (Gütersloh: Gerd Mohn, 1963), pp. 68–86. R. Murphy, *Wisdom Literature: Job, Proverbs, Ruth, Canticles, Ecclesiastes, Esther*, FOTL 13 (Grand Rapids: Eerdmans, 1981), pp. 13–45.

2. H. Richter, *Studien zu Hiob, Der Aufbau des Hiobbuches dargestellt an den Gattungen des Rechtslebens* (Berlin: Evangelische Verlagsanstalt, 1959).

oath of innocence means that they have conceded their case and Job has won. Deeply disturbed by this state of affairs, Elihu enters and appeals the decision (chs. 32–37). Finally, God appears as litigant (chs. 38–41). Under his questioning, the defendant Job withdraws his complaint so that reconciliation between God and himself is achieved (42:1–6).

C. Westermann has presented another major analysis of the structure of this book.[3] He argues that Job is a dramatized lament. Legal language is incorporated into the lament in order to develop Job's complaints and his accusations against God. The friends' speeches are designed as words of consolation, but disputation intrudes into their speeches as they feel compelled to persuade Job of the orthodox position. The Yahweh speeches are also a disputation. Whereas Richter's study is too one-sided, Westermann describes the genres in the book of Job, but "dramatized lament" is a descriptive term, not a literary genre, and it fails to categorize the entire work.[4]

The author, a literary genius, created a masterpiece that is *sui generis*. The book both recounts the story of Job's trial and triumph and debates the issue of human suffering through the medium of speeches. That is, the book is both an epic and a wisdom disputation. In order to probe deeply into the issue of the suffering righteous and its attendant issue of theodicy, the author has drawn on numerous genres in the composition of the speeches. These genres are identified throughout the commentary. At this point an overview of the component parts of the speeches is given to show their interrelatedness and to show how they contribute to the nuance of the message.

The speeches of the friends are essentially disputations, for these men seek to persuade Job to adopt their particular theology. Their speeches consist of multiple genres. The following table lists the broadest categories of genres in their speeches (many of the units are a blend of several genres).

FIRST CYCLE

genre	*Eliphaz*	*Bildad*	*Zophar*
word of consolation	4:2–6		
accusation (in litigation)		8:2–4	11:2–6
wisdom instruction	4:7–11[5]	8:8–10	
fate of wicked	5:1–7	8:11–15	

3. C. Westermann, *Structure of the Book of Job*.
4. See R. Murphy, op. cit., pp. 16–17.
5. The first Eliphaz speech also contains a vision report (4:12–21).

fate of upright	5:17–28	8:16–19, 20–22	
praise of God	5:9–16		11:7–11
			(11:12)
exhortations to seek God	5:8, 27	8:5–7	11:13–20

SECOND CYCLE

accusation	15:2–6	18:2–4	20:2–3
wisdom instruction	15:7–16		
fate of wicked	15:17–35	18:5–21	20:4–29

THIRD CYCLE

accusation	22:2–9	
threat	22:10–11	
praise of God	22:12	25:2–6
disputation	22:13–20	
fate of wicked		27:13–23
call to repentance	22:21–30	

In the first cycle the friends seek to console Job by recounting to him the just and wise ways of God. They juxtapose descriptions of the calamity that befalls the wicked with those of the blessings that attend the righteous. These descriptions function both as a warning of impending doom and as an exhortation for Job to repent. In defense of their instruction the friends quote hymnic lines in praise of God's power and wisdom. They also exhort Job to seek God, promising him prosperity, security, and joy.

In the second cycle the friends, suspecting that Job must have done something seriously wrong to be so afflicted, omit any words of consolation as they deliver harsh accusations against him. Each of them describes the terrible fate that awaits the evildoer as a powerful warning that he must forsake his evil course. Absent from this cycle are hymnic lines in praise of God and calls to repentance; the friends concentrate on trying to convince Job that he is numbered among the wicked.

In the third cycle Eliphaz directly accuses Job of specific sins, and adds a threat about his precarious circumstances. He quotes briefly from a hymn and then proceeds to dispute with Job about the fate of the wicked. He concludes with a vivid, energetic call to repentance. Next, Bildad merely quotes from a hymn in praise of God's majesty and describes the downfall of the wicked. Unfortunately, the end of the third cycle has been disturbed and some lines have been lost (see VIII above).

Job's responses may be divided according to the party addressed—either the friends or God.

Response	*1*	*2*	*3*
First Cycle	Friends (ch. 6)	Friends (ch. 9)	Friends (12:1–13:17)
	God (ch. 7)	God (ch. 10)	God (13:18–14:22)
Second Cycle	Friends (16:1–6)	Friends (ch. 19)	Friends (ch. 21)
	God (16:7–17:16)		
Third Cycle	Friends (chs. 23–24)	Friends (ch. 26; 27:1–12)	

In the first cycle Job's responses are fairly evenly divided: he alternates between the friends and God.[6] The next two cycles are not as balanced. Job's first response of the second cycle is directed primarily to God; in the rest of the dialogue he speaks solely to the friends.

The multiple genres in Job's responses may be listed as follows:

Lament:

- description of suffering: 6:2–4, 11–13; 7:3–6; 9:25–28; 10:1; 16:6–17; 17:1–2, 6–9; 19:13–20; 23:2
- apprehensive fear:
  - of death: 13:28; 14:18–22; 17:11–16
  - of God: 23:15–17
- sorrow at general human suffering: 7:1–2; 14:1–12
- justification of lamenting: 6:5–7
- complaint:
  - against friends: 6:14–27; 12:2–6; 13:1–3; 16:2–5; 17:10; 19:2–6; 21:34; 26:2–4
  - against God: 7:7–10, 11–21; 9:17–18, 21–24; 10:2–7, 13–17; 16:7–14; 19:7–12

Lawsuit:

- with the frends: 13:4–12
- with God: 9:2–4, 14–16, 19–20, (28b), 29–33; 13:13–17 (purposed), 18–27; 23:3–7 (wish)

6. For a further discussion see D. Patrick, "Job's Address of God," *ZAW* 91 (1979) 268–82.

Petition:

to the friends: 6:28–29; 19:21–22

to God:

wish to die: 6:8–10; 7:15

wish for some relief before death: 7:7–10, 16–21; 10:18–22; 14:(5–6), 13–17

request for the easing of his suffering so that he can dispute with God: 9:34–35; 13:20–21

plea for vindication: 16:18; 17:3–4; 19:23–24

plea for deliverance from enemies: 27:7–10

Hymnic lines in praise of God: 9:5–13; 10:8–12; 12:13–25; 23:8–9, 13–14; 26:5–14

Avowal of innocence: 6:28–30; 16:17; 23:10–12; 27:2–6

Affirmation of trust in God: 16:19–22; 19:25–27; 23:6–7

Wisdom instruction: 12:7–12

Warning to friends: 17:5; 19:28–29

Disputation on the success of wicked: 21:2–33; 24:1–17 (followed by a curse on the wicked, 24:18–24, and a challenge to be proven wrong, 24:25)

The skillful blending of genres in Job's speeches yields a splendid result. Through his lamenting Job reveals the depth of his agony. He not only laments his own suffering, but he groans over human suffering in general (7:1–3; 14:1–12). The generalizing tendencies in his laments allow all people to identify with Job. In the hymnic segments Job alludes to the primordial conflict between God and the forces of chaos (e.g., 9:13; 26:12–13). In this way he addresses the cosmic dimensions of his trial and reinforces his belief that God is master over all forces, terrestrial and cosmic. Sorely troubled that his affliction witnesses to some wrongdoing, Job ponders how he can demand that God vindicate him. Thus he draws on the language of a lawsuit to confront God. Thinking of litigation against God, he affirms his own innocence. Also, out of faith he states his trust in God as the one who will prove his innocence.

Two speeches of Job stand outside the dialogue, those in ch. 3 and in chs. 29–31. The first is a curse-lament, a mixture of a curse pronounced against the day of one's birth (3:3–13) and a lament (3:14–26). Job's last formal speech is an avowal of innocence. It is composed by expanding elements of a lament: remembrance of past glory (ch. 29), a detailed description of present suffering (ch. 30), and an oath of innocence (ch. 31). This avowal of innocence is an expression of Job's complete confidence in God's commitment to justice.

As for the Elihu speeches, they are disputations with the intention of teaching Job about God's disciplinary use of suffering and God's just and wise rule. His speeches are very orderly; the elements for the first three are:

	1	*2*	*3*
Introductory apology	32:6–22		
An apology or exhortation to listen	33:1–7	34:2–4	
The presentation of Job's position	33:8–11	34:5–9	35:2–4
A disputation or instruction	33:12–30	34:10–30	35:5–15
An invitation for Job to answer or a judgment	33:31–33	34:34–37	35:16

The fourth speech is composed of two elements—an instruction (36:2–21) and a hymnic description of a theophany (36:22–37:24). Elihu's role is that of Job's instructor and Yahweh's forerunner.

Yahweh's two speeches (38:2–40:2; 40:6–41:26 [Eng. 41:34]) follow the general pattern of a disputation. Yahweh opens by ordering Job to answer his interrogation (38:2–3). The core of the first speech is composed of a hymn praising the Creator and Sustainer of the world. By turning the lines into questions, the author changes the speech into a disputation.[7] The latter part of the speech is made up of animal portraits, an infrequent genre in the OT (38:39–39:30). In his second speech Yahweh comes closer to presenting a direct challenge to the defendant. He challenges Job to prove his superiority (40:6–14) and expands that challenge with the two long portraits of the primordial creatures Behemoth and Leviathan (40:15–41:26 [Eng. 41:34]).

Job's two responses are short. The first one (40:3–5) is simply a statement that he has nothing more to say. His second response (42:1–6) is an acknowledgment of Yahweh's lordship and a recantation.

The identification of the genres that make up the speeches is important to determine more precisely the meaning of the speeches. An understanding of the life setting of each genre clarifies the meaning of its words, phrases, and metaphors. Nevertheless, the author of Job has used these

7. Cf. G. von Rad, "Job XXXVIII and Ancient Egyptian Wisdom," in *The Problem of the Hexateuch and Other Essays,* tr. E. W. Trueman Dicken (Edinburgh/London: Oliver and Boyd; New York: McGraw-Hill, 1966), pp. 281–91; repr. in *Studies in Ancient Israelite Wisdom,* ed. J. Crenshaw (New York: Ktav, 1976), pp. 267–77.

genres freely to his own purpose. Thus the setting in the book is far more important in determining the function of each genre than its setting in life.[8] For example, a description of the fate of the wicked, which usually serves to teach the moral order of the world, functions in 15:20–35 as a warning to Job. Thus for interpreting this work one must give careful attention to the interplay between a genre and its literary setting.

XI. MESSAGE

The message of the book of Job will be presented on two levels: first, on the basis of the book's dramatic framework, and second, in the light of its themes.

A. DRAMATIC FRAMEWORK

A consideration of the dramatic framework of the book of Job offers great insight into the book's message. The author penetrates deeply into the issue of human suffering by setting up many sharp contrasts.[1] The interplay of these contrasts gives dramatic movement to the story.

The basic tension is between one's belief in God and one's personal experience. In the prologue these two dimensions of human existence are in harmony for Job:

Job fears God.	God blesses Job.

Job serves God wholeheartedly, and God's blessing makes Job the noblest, richest chief in the East. God confidently praises Job before the Satan, who questions the integrity of Job's fear of God, claiming that Job does not fear God for nought, but for the great wealth God freely gives him. The Satan then challenges God to let Job's devotion be tested. God accepts the challenge and permits the Satan to afflict Job. Nevertheless, despite his losses and his debilitating illness, Job continues to fear God. Now, however, his daily experience is no longer in harmony with his belief:

Job fears God.	Job is sorely afflicted.

Initially Job mourns his plight in silence, but later he bursts forth in a bitter lament (ch. 3):

Job laments in silence.	Job laments loudly and bitterly.

8. Cf. G. Fohrer, *ZDMG* 109 (1959) 32–33; idem, *Das Buch Hiob,* p. 52.

1. See R. Polzin, *Biblical Structuralism,* Semeia Supplements (Philadelphia: Fortress, 1977), pp. 54–121.

Job's three friends, who have come to comfort him, are sorely troubled by the severity of Job's affliction. At first they try to console him, but in their dialogue with Job they become deeply offended by Job's posture of stubbornly holding onto his innocence and accusing God. Their understanding of retribution leads them to conclude that Job has sinned and has escaped worse punishment only through the mercy of God. Therefore, they earnestly exhort him to repent in order to enjoy God's favor again. Since they place their system of belief above their compassion for their troubled friend, their exhortations to repentance become a temptation by encouraging Job to seek God for reward, not for God himself. The conflict that arises between their purpose and their actions may be charted as follows:

The friends wish to comfort Job.	They accuse him of flagrant sins. Their exhortations tempt him to seek God for material gain.
Job rejects the friends' counsel.	

At the end of the dialogue the hymn to wisdom (ch. 28) teaches that people cannot find wisdom, whose dwelling place is known only to God, save in the fear of God; thus this hymn judges the counsel of the comforters as lacking in wisdom.

The friends are wise men, defenders of accepted beliefs.	The hymn to wisdom denies that humanity knows wisdom.

In the epilogue God will confirm this judgment by saying that the three friends have not spoken about him rightly (42:7–9):

The friends think they honor God in their exhorting and condemning Job.	God condemns them and requires sacrifices for them.

Job's experience of undeserved suffering makes him apprehensive that God may be a ruthless tyrant rather than a merciful Lord. His conviction that he is innocent leads him to call God's justice into question. Therefore, he decides that if he could enter into litigation with God, God would confirm his innocence. But he is apprehensive that God will overpower him. Nevertheless, his conviction that God is just prods him to pursue a lawsuit with God. Job also knows that in court he must have a witness to testify on his behalf, a witness more credible than the condemning testimony of his body. At this point Job's faith in God rises above his experience of suffering, leading him to declare that God is his Witness (16:19), even his Redeemer

(19:25–27), whose testimony will vindicate him. Still, his pain terrorizes him and his dread is compounded by God's silence. Finally, his confidence in his own innocence and God's justice drives him to take a desperate course that will force God to act: he swears an avowal of innocence (chs. 29–31). Now God must answer him; for God to remain silent would be to concede Job's claim to innocence. These conflicting motifs may be charted as follows:

Job believes that he is innocent and God is just.	Job experiences suffering for no apparent reason.
Job pleads for mercy.	God is silent and allows Job's affliction to continue.
Job accuses God of condemning him unjustly.	Job affirms his faith in God as his witness and his redeemer.
	Job swears an avowal of innocence.

Job's belief in God as just and merciful impels him to look to God for a just resolution to his situation.

Job's complaints against God receive two responses, one from Elihu and one from God himself. Elihu teaches that God, who never perverts justice, uses suffering to discipline his servants and that God sends an intermediary to rescue from certain death those who turn to him. Furthermore, he argues that God governs the world in justice and also reveals himself to humanity. Thus Elihu counters Job's complaint by modifying the traditional belief about suffering and by defending the belief that God governs the world justly:

Job suffers	Elihu teaches that God disciplines by suffering
and complains that God is silent.	and that God sends an angel-mediator to rescue those near death.
Job accuses God of injustice.	Elihu argues for God's justice and concludes that Job is wrong in condemning God.

Thus Elihu prepares Job to hear God's speech.

Finally God himself answers Job. God's words sharpen the contrast for Job. Whereas Job is confident of his innocence, God accuses him of darkening counsel. Whereas Job demands that God show cause for his affliction, God questions Job about his knowledge of the world he has created:

Job longs for God's presence.	God appears.
Job claims that he is innocent and that God has wronged him.	God accuses him of darkening counsel.
Job demands a resolution to his case.	God questions him about creation and the government of the world.

Instead of explaining to Job why he has afflicted him, God recounts the marvelous way he has created the world and the wise, judicious way he governs it. If he can both expand Job's understanding of his governance of the world and make him perceive the limits of human understanding of the world order, he can persuade Job that it is possible to believe that he is just and merciful, caring for every creature. Job's initial response to God's questioning is startling—the loquacious Job has virtually nothing to say:

Job states that he is well prepared to argue his case before God.	Job declines to take advantage of the opportunity God gives him to speak.

Next, God challenges Job to don regal garments and rule the world justly, subduing the proud and the wicked. Then God questions him about his ability to master Behemoth and Leviathan. If Job cannot rule more justly than God, he will forfeit his case against God. Persuaded by God's argument, Job relinquishes his complaint and humbles himself before God. This act of contrition stands in stark contrast to his bold claim of innocence:

Job swears that he is innocent.	Job surrenders his complaint and his oath of innocence.

Realizing that to pursue his lawsuit against God, after God has reasoned with him, would be to stand in outright rebellion against God, Job acknowledges God's complete lordship over his life by humbly surrendering himself to God. Thus at the end of the speeches, there is a major resolution to the contrast in the dialogue:

Job asks God to speak to him.	God appears to Job and addresses him.

Job submits to God.

In the epilogue the remaining contrasts are resolved. God accepts Job's act of contrition:

Job submits to God.	God accepts him.

God's earlier accusation against Job gives way to affirmation:

God accuses Job of darkening counsel.	God affirms that Job has spoken rightly.

Whereas Job has darkened counsel in accusing God of ruling unjustly, he has spoken rightly in holding onto his innocence and in asserting that God is his Redeemer. At the same time God holds the friends accountable for their speaking wrongly of him and orders them to make atonement by offering up sacrifices and having Job pray for them. God's instructions both authenticate Job and provide a way for the reconciliation of Job and his friends:

God instructs the friends to offer up sacrifices.	The friends obey God and Job prays for them.

Afterward God manifests his presence in Job's life by blessing him abundantly:

God blesses Job.	Job's estate doubles and Job lives a long, full life.

The epilogue illustrates the basic truth that God is gracious and good, seeking the welfare of his servants. "This realistic this-worldly conclusion of the book shows powerfully that the real decision whether God is truly God falls in *this* life. Here and now faith must prove true."[2]

B. THEMES

The author probes the multiple aspects of human suffering and presents many insights into this issue. Six prominent themes will be noted here: (1) a righteous person may suffer; (2) the dimensions of human suffering; (3) a righteous person's struggle to overcome suffering; (4) qualifications to the doctrine of double retribution; (5) the question of theodicy; (6) an encounter with God.

1. Through Job's experience the author sets forth the tenet that an upright person may suffer terribly, even though he has not sinned. Calamity is not necessarily a hostile witness against a righteous person's integrity.

2. Job, a man of great faith and flawless character, suffers deeply in every dimension of his existence—physical, social, spiritual, and emotional. These dimensions, to be sure, are intertwined in human experience and can be separated only for purposes of discussion. In the physical realm Job loses his vast wealth and all his children in a single day (1:13–14). In these events Job suffers from both the suddenness and the totality of his losses. A little later he is struck down by a dreaded disease (2:8–10). In the social dimension Job, the noblest elder of his community, is alienated from his family and friends as he sits in shame on an ash heap outside the city's walls

2. W. Vischer, "God's Truth and Man's Lie" (tr. D. G. Miller), *Int* 15 (1961) 145.

(2:7–8; 19:13–19). There the crowds, even the lowest rabble, scorn him as they make him the subject of their taunt songs (16:10; 30:1–15). Since even those who have come to console him turn against him, he feels the treachery of disloyal friends (6:14–23). Spiritually God's silence terrifies Job (23:8, 9, 15). God's apparent hostility leads him to imagine that God is a capricious despot, who delights in afflicting his servant (cf. 6:4; 7:17–19; 19:25). Troubled on all sides, Job feels the range of disturbed emotions: troubled thoughts (7:4, 13–14), uncertainty (9:20), rejection and hostility (10:3; 12:4), fear (9:28), dismay (21:6), loneliness (19:13–19), distaste for life (9:2), i.e., the lack of any sense of inner tranquility (3:26). No wonder he often groans that his soul is bitter (7:11; 10:1; 27:2).

3. The center of Job's test is that the anguish caused by God's apparently unreasoned anger threatens to break his moral resolve. Desperately he gropes for some way out of this dark abyss. By vigorously lamenting his bitter feelings, he comes to grips with his anguish and channels his mind to seek some resolution to his predicament. As he probes for a resolution, his thinking is governed by three principles: God is all-powerful and just; he himself is innocent, undeserving of such affliction; and a premature death will be an unbearable disgrace, leaving him unvindicated. His unwavering conviction that he has never departed from God's commandments (23:12) prevents him from becoming trapped in the selfish application of spiritual axioms and wise sayings, a trap set by his friends' counsel. Positively it leads him to swear that he will never speak falsely or act deceitfully by confessing some contrived wrongdoing solely to win God's favor (27:4). By focusing on God as his Witness and his Redeemer, Job makes bold statements of trust in God (16:19; 19:25–27). Finally, with an avowal of innocence he places his destiny in God's hands and demonstrates that a person's moral resolve can grow stronger even amid the worst adversity. Job thus stands as the prime example of how an upright person can maintain his own integrity even when overwhelmed, for no apparent reason, by the most painful suffering.

4. The author challenges directly a simplistic understanding of the doctrine of double retribution—that the righteous are always blessed and that the wicked experience untold hardship, leading to premature death. Job's three comforters articulate the traditional understanding of retribution in its various nuances. Because of their rigid understanding of this doctrine they can only explain Job's suffering as the result of some sin that he has committed. Then the only solution they can offer to him is the way of repentance. Because they encourage Job to repent primarily to escape his suffering and to receive God's blessing, they unsuspectingly tempt him to use God for personal gain, the essence of sin. Therefore, if Job followed their counsel, he would confirm the Satan's proposition that human beings

are totally self-serving in their worship of God. Through the example of these three comfortors the author strongly denounces the practice of using deceptive arguments to defend God (13:7–12).

5. Suffering opens Job's eyes to the discrepancy between the belief that God punishes the wicked and the reality that in numerous cases the wicked are never punished and the innocent are caught by sudden disaster. He wonders whether God is a capricious deity, doing good or ill according to his whims (9:22–24; 21:7–33; 24:1–17). Thus Job raises the issue of theodicy.

Both the Elihu speeches and the Yahweh speeches address the issue of God's being just. Elihu teaches that God uses dreams and suffering as rods of discipline to turn a person from error, even if the error is only potential (33:12–22, 29–30; 36:16–21). Pain is often an instrument of God's mercy. Thus Elihu wishes to direct attention to the purpose of suffering, rather than to try to discover its origin. Furthermore, he acknowledges the great gulf between humanity and God and teaches that God himself directs the deliverance of an afflicted person from death by graciously sending a mediating angel to proclaim that a ransom has been found (33:23–28). If that person will pray, accepting the deliverance God provides, God will deliver his life from death. Moreover, Elihu portrays God as mercifully just in all his dealings (ch. 34), arguing that he has nothing to gain by acting unjustly (ch. 35).[3] Elihu also extols this great God as one who reveals himself in an awesome display of power in order to inspire people to worship him (36:22–37:13).

Addressing Job, God affirms that he has structured the world exactly according to his blueprints (38:4–8). With this metaphor he claims that he has built justice into the structure of the universe. Moreover, God asserts that no corner of the world is outside his authority (38:16–24), thereby refuting any theory that injustice and suffering exist because God is in a struggle with a strong foe. Furthermore, God argues for his wise management of the world by pointing to his ordering of the heavenly elements and his care of the wild animals (38:25–39:30). His argument that he manages the heavenly elements so wisely and provides for the creatures of the desert so caringly implies that he certainly watches over people just as wisely and caringly. Furthermore, in questioning Job so intently about the created order and the creatures Behemoth and Leviathan, symbols of hostile cosmic forces, God brings Job to realize that no human being has a proper perspective to judge the course of matters in the universe, let alone to accuse God of acting unjustly. The foundation of God's argument in his speeches is that power and wisdom (justice) are one in the supreme ruler of the universe. That is, by

3. N. Snaith, *The Book of Job,* SBT 2/11 (London: SCM; Naperville: Allenson, 1968), p. 90.

demonstrating that he exercises his power in wisdom, God proves that he rules the world in justice. Thus the analogies of the created order that God puts before Job offer him the grounds for believing in "the essential rightness of things."[4]

6. Awed by God's majesty and overwhelmed that God in grace reasons with him, Job surrenders his complaint against God, realizing that a person must surrender even his rights to God because God is Lord. In yielding himself to God Job reveals beyond any doubt that he serves God out of love, not for material gain or prestige. Also, in abandoning his avowal of innocence he removes all barriers between himself and God.

In praise of God Job confesses, "I had heard you with my ears, but now my eyes have seen you" (42:5). Clearly the author finds the profoundest personal answer to undeserved suffering to reside in the divine-human encounter. That God both appears to Job and speaks with him means that Job's encounter is more than a mystical experience with a numinous force; it is a meeting with the personal God. God's presence authenticates Job, drawing him out of his self-love to focus his affection on God. Job gladly abandons the complaints against God, conscious of the fact that he can trust God in his grace to accomplish that which is worthwhile from his undeserved suffering. The value of an encounter with God goes beyond the experience itself, as demonstrated by the fact that God continues both to speak with Job after he recants and to work in his life.

God acknowledges Job's faithfulness by giving him the privilege of interceding for his friends as they offer up sacrifices to atone for their having spoken wrongly about God (42:7–9). This divine directive contains many insights. The friends, who have seriously erred by misleading Job in their defense of traditional beliefs, must now seek God's forgiveness. Job now possesses new authority with God by reason of his obedient endurance of undeserved affliction. God's directive also teaches Job that he must not harbor any ill feelings toward his friends for their failure to comfort him.

In conclusion, the book of Job teaches that a person may serve God faithfully, whether his circumstances are bleak or filled with promise, for he has the assurance that God is for him, seeking his ultimate good. A person can triumph over suffering through faith in God.

XII. OUTLINE

I. PROLOGUE (1:1–2:13)

A. JOB'S FAITH AND PROSPERITY (1:1-5)

4. R. Gordis, *The Book of God and Man*, p. 156.

B. THE FIRST SCENE BEFORE YAHWEH (1:6-12)
C. JOB'S TRAGIC MISFORTUNE (1:13-22)
D. THE SECOND SCENE BEFORE YAHWEH (2:1-6)
E. THE AFFLICTION OF JOB'S BODY (2:7-10)
F. THE ARRIVAL OF THE THREE COMFORTERS (2:11-13)

II. JOB'S CURSE-LAMENT (3:1-26)

A. JOB'S CURSE OF THE DAY OF HIS BIRTH (3:1-13)
B. A LAMENT (3:14-26)

III. THE DIALOGUE (4:1–27:23)

A. THE FIRST CYCLE (4:1–14:22)
- 1. Eliphaz's First Speech (4:1–5:27)
  - a. A Word of Consolation (4:1-6)
  - b. The Doctrine of Retribution (4:7-11)
  - c. A Vision Report (4:12-21)
  - d. No Mediator for Mankind (5:1-7)
  - e. An Appeal to Seek God (5:8-16)
  - f. God's Ability to Deliver (5:17-27)
- 2. Job's First Response (6:1–7:21)
  - a. A Rejoinder to the Friends (6:1-30)
    - (1) A Defense of His Lament (6:1-13)
      - (a) The Reality of His Suffering (6:1-7)
      - (b) A Wish for Death as a Release from Suffering (6:8-13)
    - (2) An Accusation against the Friends (6:14-30)
      - (a) Their Treachery (6:14-23)
      - (b) A Request for Their Sympathy (6:24-30)
  - b. A Lament (7:1-21)
    - (1) The Lament Proper (7:1-10)
      - (a) A Description of Great Pain (7:1-6)
      - (b) A Petition (7:7-10)
    - (2) A Complaint against God (7:11-21)
      - (a) The Basic Complaint (7:11-16)
      - (b) A Plea for a Reprieve (7:17-21)
- 3. Bildad's First Speech (8:1-22)
  - a. God's Just Ways (8:1-7)
  - b. Evidence of God's Justice (8:8-19)
    - (1) The Teaching of Tradition (8:8-10)
    - (2) Illustrations from Nature (8:11-19)
  - c. Conclusion and Application (8:20-22)
- 4. Job's Second Response (9:1–10:22)
  - a. Job's Quest (9:1-35)
    - (1) Job's Concerns about Disputing His Case with God (9:1-24)
      - (a) Job's Opening Concerns (9:1-4)

(b) Creation, the Canopy for God's Appearing (9:5-13)
(c) Job's Misgivings about Arguing His Case before God (9:14-24)
(2) Job's Inability to Demonstrate His Innocence (9:25-35)
b. Job's Lament (10:1-22)
(1) A Complaint against God (10:1-7)
(2) Job's Reflection on His Origin (10:8-12)
(3) God's Vigilance (10:13-17)
(4) Job's Preoccupation with Death (10:18-22)
5. Zophar's First Speech (11:1-20)
a. An Accusation against Job (11:1-4)
b. God's Wisdom (11:5-12)
c. A Call to Repentance (11:13-20)
6. Job's Third Response (12:1–14:22)
a. Complaints against the Friends (12:1–13:17)
(1) The First Complaint (12:1-11)
(a) Job's Self-defense (12:1-3)
(b) Job's Disgrace (12:4-6)
(c) Instruction in Wisdom (12:7-11)
(2) Interlude: God's Sovereign Rule (12:12-25)
(3) The Second Complaint (13:1-17)
(a) The Complaint Proper (13:1-12)
(b) Job's Resolve (13:13-17)
b. A Summons to God (13:18–14:22)
(1) Job's Desire for a Legal Resolution to His Complaint (13:18-28)
(a) Job's Statement of Readiness and His Request for Two Pre-Trial Conditions (13:18-22)
(b) An Examination of the Plaintiff (13:23-28)
(2) Human Suffering and Job's Plight (14:1-22)
(a) Human Suffering (14:1-6)
(b) Reflections on the Possibility of Resurrection (14:7-12)
(c) Job's Desire for Relief (14:13-17)
(d) The Terrors of Death (14:18-22)
B. THE SECOND CYCLE (15:1–21:34)
1. Eliphaz's Second Speech (15:1-35)
a. A Disputation Rejecting Job's Claim to Wisdom (15:1-16)
b. An Instruction about the Woes of the Wicked (15:17-35)
2. Job's Fourth Response (16:1–17:16)
a. A Dispute with the Comforters (16:1-6)
b. A Personal Lament with a Complaint against God (16:7-17)
c. The Heavenly Witness (16:18-22)
d. A Personal Lament (17:1-16)

3. Bildad's Second Speech (18:1-21)
   a. A Complaint against Job (18:1-4)
   b. The Terrible Fate of the Wicked (18:5-21)
      (1) The Trapping of the Wicked Person (18:5-10)
      (2) The Death of the Wicked Person (18:11-21)
4. Job's Fifth Response (19:1-29)
   a. A Complaint against the Friends (19:1-6)
   b. A Complaint about God's Enmity (19:7-12)
   c. A Complaint about Complete Alienation (19:13-20)
   d. A Plea for Help and a Statement of Assurance (19:21-27)
   e. A Warning to the Friends (19:28-29)
5. Zophar's Second Speech (20:1-29)
   a. Zophar's Reaction to Job's Speech (20:1-3)
   b. The Sure Fate of Every Evildoer (20:4-29)
6. Job's Sixth Response (21:1-34)
   a. An Appeal for a Sympathetic Hearing (21:1-6)
   b. Tough Questions about the Doctrine of Retribution (21:7-33)
      (1) The Blessings of the Wicked (21:7-16)
      (2) The Infrequency of the Wicked Being Punished (21:17-21)
      (3) The Failure of the Doctrine of Retribution (21:22-26)
      (4) The Rejection of the Friends' Anticipated Rebuttal (21:27-34)

C. THE THIRD CYCLE (22:1–27:23)

1. Eliphaz's Third Speech (22:1-30)
   a. Accusations against Job (22:1-11)
   b. A Disputation concerning God's Activity in Human Affairs (22:12-20)
   c. A Call to Repentance (22:21-30)
2. Job's Seventh Response (23:1–24:25)
   a. A Statement of Confidence (23:1-17)
      (1) Job's Desire to Present His Case before God (23:1-7)
      (2) God's Hiddenness and Job's Confidence (23:8-12)
      (3) Trembling before God (23:13-17)
   b. A Complaint about Unjust Social Conditions (24:1-25)
      (1) The Reign of Evildoers (24:1-17)
         (a) Civil Injustice (24:1-3, 9, 4-8, 10-11)
         (b) Criminal Injustice (24:12-17)
      (2) A Curse on the Wicked (24:18-25)
3. Bildad's Third Speech (25:1-6; 27:13-23)
   a. A Hymn of Praise to God (25:1-6)
   b. The Certain Retribution of the Wicked (27:13-23)

4. Job's Eighth Response (26:1–27:12)
    a. The Rejection of Bildad's Counsel (26:1-4)
    b. The Praise of God's Majestic Power (26:5-14)
    c. Job's Confidence and His Wish (27:1-10)
        (1) An Avowal of Innocence (27:1-6)
        (2) An Imprecation against the Enemies (27:7-10)
    d. Job's Intent to Instruct the Friends (27:11-12)

IV. HYMN TO WISDOM (28:1-28)

A. HUMAN SKILL IN MINING TECHNOLOGY (28:1-11)
B. WISDOM'S VALUE, BEYOND PURCHASE (28:12-19)
C. GOD'S KNOWLEDGE OF WISDOM (28:20-27)
D. WISDOM FOR MANKIND (28:28)

V. JOB'S AVOWAL OF INNOCENCE (29:1–31:40)

A. JOB'S REMEMBRANCE OF HIS FORMER ABUNDANT LIFE (29:1-25)
    1. God's Rich Blessing (29:1-6)
    2. The Respect Job Commanded (29:7-10)
    3. Job's Striving for Justice (29:11-17)
    4. Job's Hope for a Long, Blessed Life (29:18-20)
    5. The Most Respected Elder (29:21-25)
B. A LAMENT (30:1-31)
    1. Job's Present Disgrace (30:1-15)
        a. The Mockers (30:1-8)
        b. The Mockery (30:9-15)
    2. An Accusation against God (30:16-23)
    3. A Self-lament (30:24-31)
C. AN OATH OF INNOCENCE (31:1-40)
    1. The List of Sins Denied (31:1-34, 38-40b)
        a. Lust (31:1-4)
        b. Falsehood and Covetousness (31:5-8)
        c. Adultery (31:9-12)
        d. Mistreatment of Servants (31:13-15)
        e. The Poor and the Weak (31:16-23)
        f. Trust in Wealth and Worship of the Heavenly Bodies (31:24-28)
        g. Satisfaction at a Foe's Misfortune and Failure to Extend Hospitality to a Sojourner (31:29-32)
        h. Concealment of a Sin without Confession (31:33-34)
        i. Abuse of the Land (31:38-40b)
    2. The Sealing of the Oath (31:35-37, 40c)

VI. THE ELIHU SPEECHES (32:1–37:24)

A. INTRODUCTION OF ELIHU (32:1-5)
B. ELIHU'S SPEECHES (32:6–37:24)
    1. Elihu's First Speech (32:6–33:33)
        a. An Apology (32:6-22)

- b. A Disputation about God's Efforts to Redeem (33:1-33)
  - (1) A Further Apology (33:1-7)
  - (2) The Disputation Proper (33:8-30)
    - (a) Presentation of Job's Claim to Be Free from Sin (33:8-11)
    - (b) A Response (33:12-30)
      - (i) The Disciplines of God (33:12-22)
      - (ii) The Angel Mediator (33:23-30)
  - (3) An Invitation for Job to Answer (33:31-33)

2. Elihu's Second Speech (34:1-37)
   - a. A Summons to Listen (34:1-4)
   - b. A Disputation (34:5-33)
     - (1) Presentation of Job's Complaint against God (34:5-9)
     - (2) A Response (34:10-30)
       - (a) The Thesis: God's Just Rule (34:10-15)
       - (b) The Defense of the Thesis (34:16-30)
     - (3) A Call for a Decision (34:31-33)
   - c. A Judgment (34:34-37)
3. Elihu's Third Speech (35:1-16)
   - a. Presentation of Job's Concern about His Own Right (35:1-4)
   - b. A Response: God's Sovereign Justice (35:5-16)
4. Elihu's Fourth Speech (36:1–37:24)
   - a. Introduction (36:1-4)
   - b. God's Disciplinary Ways (36:5-25)
     - (1) The Core Teaching (36:5-15)
     - (2) A Warning to Job (36:16-25)
   - c. God's Greatness (36:26–37:20)
     - (1) God's Glory Visible in the Thunderstorm (36:26–37:13)
     - (2) An Admonition to Job (37:14-20)
   - d. The Divine Splendor (37:21-24)

VII. THE YAHWEH SPEECHES (38:1–42:6)

A. YAHWEH'S FIRST SPEECH (38:1–40:2)

1. Introduction and Opening Challenge to Job (38:1-3)
2. Interrogation about the Created Order (38:4–39:30)
   - a. The Structure of the World (38:4-24)
     - (1) The Fundamental Structure of the World (38:4-15)
     - (2) The Recesses of the World (38:16-24)
   - b. The Maintenance of the World (38:25–39:30)
     - (1) The Inanimate World (38:25-38)
     - (2) The Animate World (38:39–39:30)
       - (a) The Lioness and the Raven (38:39-41)
       - (b) The Mountain Goat and the Hind (39:1-4)
       - (c) The Wild Ass (39:5-8)
       - (d) The Wild Ox (39:9-12)

(e) The Ostrich (39:13-18)
(f) The Horse (39:19-25)
(g) Birds of Prey (39:26-30)
3. An Invitation for Job to Respond (40:1-2)
B. JOB'S ANSWER (40:3-5)
C. YAHWEH'S SECOND SPEECH (40:6–41:26 [ENG. 41:34])
1. Questions concerning Job's Power (40:6-14)
2. Portraits of Two Foreboding Beasts (40:15–41:26 [Eng. 41:34])
a. Behemoth (40:15-24)
b. Leviathan (40:25–41:26 [Eng. 41:1-34])
D. JOB'S ANSWER (42:1-6)
VIII. EPILOGUE (42:7-17)
A. THE CONDEMNATION AND RESTORATION OF THE THREE FRIENDS (42:7-9)
B. GOD'S BLESSING AND RESTORATION OF JOB (42:10-17)
1. Restoration (42:10)
2. The Visit of Job's Kinsmen and Friends (42:11)
3. The Enumeration of Job's Blessings (42:12-15)
4. Job's Epitaph (42:16-17)

XIII. SELECT BIBLIOGRAPHY

Many other works are cited in the commentary. For an extensive bibliography see Lévêque.

A. Alt, "Zur Vorgeschichte des Buches Hiob," *ZAW* 55 (1937) 265–68.

F. I. Andersen, *Job*. Tyndale Old Testament Commentary. Downers Grove: InterVarsity, 1976.

C. Ball, *The Book of Job*. Oxford: Clarendon, 1922.

H. Bardtke, "Prophetische Zuge im Buche Hiob," in *Das Ferne und Nahe Wort*. Fest. L. Rost. Ed. F. Maass. BZAW 105. Berlin: Töpelmann, 1967. Pp. 1–10.

J. Barr, "The Book of Job and Its Modern Interpreters," *BJRL* 54 (1971–72) 28–46.

E. Baumann, "Die Verwendbarkeit der Pešita zum Buche Ijob für die Textkritik," *ZAW* 18 (1898) 305–38; 19 (1899) 15–95, 288–309; 20 (1900) 177–201, 264–307.

F. Baumgärtel, *Der Hiobdialog*. BWANT IV/9. Stuttgart: Kohlhammer, 1933.

M. Bič, "Le juste et l'impie dans le livre de Job," in *Volume du Congrès: Genève 1965*. VTSup 15. Leiden: Brill, 1966. Pp. 33–43.

S. Blank, "'Doest Thou Well To Be Angry?': A Study in Self-Pity," *HUCA* 26 (1955) 29–41.

A. Blommerde, *Northwest Semitic Grammar and Job*. BibOr 22. Rome: Pontifical Biblical Institute, 1969.

E. Bruston, "La littérature sapientiale dans le livre de Job," *ETR* 3 (1928) 297–305.

K. Budde, *Das Buch Hiob*. HKAT. 2nd ed. Göttingen: Vandenhoeck & Ruprecht, 1913.

F. Buhl, "Zur Vorgeschichte des Buches Hiob," in *"Von Alten Testament."* Fest. K. Marti. Ed. K. Budde. BZAW 41. Berlin: Töpelmann, 1925. Pp. 52–61.

M. Buttenwieser, *The Book of Job*. New York: Macmillan, 1922.

A. Caquot, "Un écrit sectaire de Qoumrân: Le 'Targoum de Job,'" *RHR* 185 (1974) 9–27.

_____. "Traits royaux dans le personnage de Job," in *Hommages à Wilhelm Vischer*. Ed. D. Lys. Montepellier: Causse Graille Castleman, 1960. Pp. 32–45.

A. Ceresko, "The A:B::B:A Word Pattern in Hebrew and Northwest Semitic with Special Reference to the Book of Job," *UF* 7 (1975) 73–88.

_____. *Job 29–31 in the Light of Northwest Semitic*. BibOr 36. Rome: Pontifical Biblical Institute, 1980.

D. Clines, "The Arguments of Job's Three Friends," in *Art and Meaning: Rhetoric in Biblical Literature*. Ed. D. Clines, et al. JSOTSup 19. Sheffield: JSOT Press, 1982. Pp. 215–29.

D. Cox, *The Triumph of Impotence: Job and the Tradition of the Absurd*. Analecta Gregoriana 212. Rome: Università Gregoriana, 1978.

J. Curtis, "On Job's Response to Yahweh," *JBL* 98 (1979) 497–511.

M. Dahood, "Some Northwest Semitic Words in Job," *Bib* 38 (1957) 306–20.

_____. "Northwest Semitic Philology and Job," in *The Bible in Current Catholic Thought*. Ed. J. L. McKenzie. New York: Herder & Herder, 1962. Pp. 55–74.

_____. "Some Rare Parallel Word Pairs in Job and in Ugaritic," in *The Word in the World*. Fest. F. L. Moriarty. Ed. R. Clifford and G. MacRae. Cambridge: Weston College Press, 1973. Pp. 19–34.

_____. "Chiasmus in Job: A Text-Critical and Philological Criterion," in *A Light unto My Path*. Fest. J. M. Myers. Ed. H. N. Bream, et al. Philadelphia: Temple University Press, 1974. Pp. 118–30.

A. Davidson, *A Commentary, Grammatical and Exegetical, on the Book of Job*. Edinburgh: Williams and Norgate, 1862.

F. Delitzsch, *Biblical Commentary on the Book of Job*. Tr. F. Bolton. Repr. 2 vols. in 1. Grand Rapids: Eerdmans, 1973.

A. de Wilde, *Das Buch Hiob*. OTS 22. Leiden: Brill, 1981.

E. Dhorme, *A Commentary on the Book of Job*. Tr. H. Knight. Repr. Nashville: Nelson, 1984.

S. R. Driver and G. B. Gray, *A Critical and Exegetical Commentary on the Book of Job*. ICC. Edinburgh: T. & T. Clark, 1921.

B. Duhm, *Das Buch Hiob*. KHC 16. Freiburg/Leipzig/Tübingen: Mohr, 1897.

R. Dunn, "Speech and Silence in Job," in *The Book of Job and Ricoeur's Hermeneutics*. Semeia 19. Ed. J. D. Crossan. Chico: Scholars Press, 1981. Pp. 99–103.

H. Ewald, *Commentary on the Book of Job*. Tr. J. Smith. Edinburgh: Williams and Norgate, 1882.

L. Fisher, ed., *Ras Shamra Parallels*. 2 vols. AnOr 49, 50. Rome: Pontifical Biblical Institute, 1972, 1975.

J. Fitzmyer, "Some Observations on the Targum of Job from Qumran Cave 11," *CBQ* 36 (1974) 503–24.

G. Fohrer, *Das Buch Hiob*. KAT 16. Gütersloh: Gerd Mohn, 1963.

_____. "Zur Vorgeschichte und Komposition des Buches Hiob," *VT* 6 (1956) 249–67. Repr. in *Studien zum Buche Hiob*. Gütersloh: Gerd Mohn, 1963. Pp. 26–43.

_____. "Nun aber hat mein Auge dich geschaut. Der innere Aufbau des Buches Hiob," *TZ* 15 (1959) 1–21.

_____. "Überlieferung und Wandlung der Hioblegende," in *Festschrift Friedrich Baumgärtel*. Ed. L. Rost. Erlangen: Universitätsbund Erlangen, 1959. Pp. 41–62. Repr. in *Studien zum Buche Hiob*. Gütersloh: Gerd Mohn, 1963. Pp. 44–67.

_____. "Form und Funktion in der Hiobdichtung," *ZDMG* 109 (1959) 31–49. Repr. in *Studien zum Buche Hiob*. Gütersloh: Gerd Mohn, 1963. Pp. 68–86.

_____. "Das Hiobproblem und seine Losung," *Wissenschaftliche Zeitschrift der Martin-Luther Universität* 12 (1963) 249–58.

K. Fullerton, "The Original Conclusion to the Book of Job," *ZAW* 42 (1924) 116–35.

D. Gard, *The Exegetical Method of the Greek Translator of the Book of Job*. *JBL* Monograph Series 8. Philadelphia: Society of Biblical Literature, 1952.

_____. "The Concept of Job's Character according to the Greek Translator of the Hebrew Text," *JBL* 72 (1953) 182–86.

_____. "The Concept of the Future Life according to the Greek Translator of the Book of Job," *JBL* 73 (1954) 137–43.

H. Gehman, "The Theological Approach of the Greek Translator of the Book of Job 1–15," *JBL* 68 (1949) 231–40.

E. Gerstenberger and W. Schrage, *Suffering*. Tr. J. Steely. Biblical Encounters Series. Nashville: Abingdon, 1980.

H. Ginsberg, "Job the patient and Job the impatient," in *Congress Volume: Rome 1968*. VTSup 17. Leiden: Brill, 1969. Pp. 88–111.

N. Glatzer, "The Book of Job and its Interpreters," in *Biblical Motifs*. Ed. A. Altmann. Cambridge: Harvard University Press, 1966.

N. Glatzer, ed., *The Dimensions of Job*. New York: Schocken: 1969.

R. Gordis, *The Book of Job*. New York: Jewish Theological Seminary of America, 1978.

_____. *The Book of God and Man: A Study of Job*. Chicago: University of Chicago Press, 1965.

L. Grabbe, *Comparative Philology and the Text of Job: A Study in Methodology*. SBLDS 34. Missoula: Scholars Press, 1977.

J. Gray, "The Massoretic Text of the Book of Job, the Targum and the Septuagint Version in the Light of the Qumran Targum (11QtargJob)," *ZAW* 86 (1974) 331–50.

A. Guillaume, "The Arabic Background of the Book of Job," in *Promise and*

Fulfilment: Essays Presented to Professor S. H Hooke. Ed. F. F. Bruce. Edinburgh: T. & T. Clark, 1963. Pp. 106–27.

_____. *Studies in the Book of Job*. Ed. J. Macdonald. *ALUOS,* supplement 2. Leiden: Brill, 1968.

_____. "The Unity of the Book of Job," *ALUOS* 4 (1962/63) 26–46.

N. Habel, *The Book of Job*. CBC. Cambridge: Cambridge University Press, 1975.

_____. *The Book of Job*. OTL. Philadelphia: Westminster, 1985.

A. Hakam, *Sēper ʾÎyôḇ (Book of Job)*. Jerusalem: Mosad ha-Rab Quq, 1970.

A. Hastoupis, "The Problem of Theodicy in the Book of Job," *Theologia* 22 (1951) 657–68.

H. Heater, Jr., *A Septuagint Translation Technique in the Book of Job*. CBQMS 11. Washington: Catholic Biblical Association, 1982.

J. Hempel, "Das theologische Problem des Hiob," *ZST* 6 (1929) 621–89.

_____. "Was nicht im Buche Hiob steht," in *Wahrheit und Glaube*. Fest. E. Hirsch. Ed. H. Gerdes. Itzehoe: Verlag "Die Spur," 1963. Pp. 133–36.

J. Hertz, "Formgeschichtliche Untersuchungen zum Problem des Hiobbuches," *Wissenschaftliche Zeitschrift der K. Marx Universität* 3 (1953–54) 157–62.

H. Hertzberg, "Der Aufbau des Buches Hiob," in *Festschrift für Alfred Bertholet*. Ed. W. Baumgartner, et al. Tübingen: Mohr/Siebeck, 1950. Pp. 233–58.

Y. Hoffman, "The relation between the prologue and the speech-cycles in Job. A reconsideration," *VT* 31 (1981) 160–70.

G. Hölscher, *Das Buch Hiob*. HAT 17. 2nd ed. Tübingen: Mohr/Siebeck, 1952.

R. Hone, ed. *The Voice out of the Whirlwind: The Book of Job*. Rev. ed. San Francisco: Chandler, 1972.

F. Horst, *Hiob 1–19*. BKAT 16/1. Neukirchen-Vluyn: Neukirchener, 1968.

P. Humbert, "Le modernisme de Job," in *Wisdom in Israel and in the Ancient Near East*. Fest. H. H. Rowley. Ed. M. Noth and D. Winton Thomas. VTSup 3. Leiden: Brill, 1955. Pp. 150–61.

W. Irwin, "An Examination of the Progress of Thought in the Dialogue of Job," *JR* 13 (1933) 150–64.

_____. "Poetic Structure in the Dialogue of Job," *JNES* 5 (1946) 26–39.

R. Jacobson, "Satanic Semiotics, Jobian Jurisprudence," in *The Book of Job and Ricoeur's Hermeneutics*. Semeia 19. Ed. J. D. Crossan. Chico: Scholars Press, 1981. Pp. 63–71.

J. Janzen, *Job*. Interpretation. Atlanta: John Knox, 1985.

M. Jastrow, *A Dictionary of the Targumim, the Talmud Babli and Yerushalmi, and the Midrashic Literature*. New York: Shalom, repr. 1967.

A. Jepsen, *Das Buch Hiob und seine Deutung*. Berlin: 1963.

O. Kaiser, "Leid und Gott: Ein Beitrag zur Theologie des Buches Hiob," in *Sichtbare Kirche*. Fest. H. Laag. Ed. U. Fabricius and R. Volp. Gütersloh: Gerd Mohn, 1973. Pp. 13–21.

B. Kelly, "Truth in Contradiction," *Int* 15 (1961) 147–56.

E. Kissane, *The Book of Job*. Dublin: Browne and Nolan, 1946.

H. Knight, "Job," *SJT* 9 (1956) 63–76.
K. Koch, "Gibt es ein Vergeltungsdogma im Alten Testament?" *ZTK* 52 (1955) 1–42.
W. Koepp, "Vom Hiobthema und der Zeit als Leiden," *TLZ* 74 (1949) 389–96.
L. Krinetzki, "Ich weiss, mein Anwalt lebt. Die Botschaft des Buches Job," *BK* 20 (1965) 8–12.
V. Kubina, *Die Gottesreden im Buche Hiob*. Freiburg: Herder, 1979.
C. Kuhl, "Neuere Literarkritik des Buches Hiob," *TRu* 21 (1953) 163–205, 257–317.
_____. "Vom Hiobbuche und seinen Problemen," *TRu* 22 (1954) 261–316.
E. Kutsch, "Hiob: Leidender Gerechter-leidender Mensch," *KD* 19 (1973) 197–214.
A. Lacocque, "Job or the Impotence of Religion and Philosophy," in *The Book of Job and Ricoeur's Hermeneutics*. Semeia 19. Ed. J. D. Crossan. Chico: Scholars Press, 1981. Pp. 33–52.
B. Lang, "Ein Kranker sieht seinen Gott," in *Der Mensch unter dem Kreuz*. Ed. R. Bärenz. Regensburg: Pustet, 1980. Pp. 35–48.
R. Laurin, "The Theological Structure of Job," *ZAW* 84 (1972) 86–89.
J. Lévêque, *Job et son Dieu*. Etudes bibliques. 2 vols. Paris: Gabalda, 1970.
_____. "Job, ou l'espoir déraciné," *La Vie Spirituelle* 586 (1971) 287–304.
J. Lindblom, *La composition du livre de Job*. Lund: Gleerup, 1945.
V. Maag, *Hiob. Wandlung und Verarbeitung des Problems in Novelle, Dialogdichtung und Spätfassungen*. Göttingen: Vandenhoeck & Ruprecht, 1982.
R. Marcus, "Job and God," *RR* 14 (1949–50) 5–29.
T. Maston, "Ethical Content of Job," *SWJT* 14 (1971) 43–56.
M. Matheney, Jr., "Major Purposes of the Book of Job," *SWJT* 14 (1971) 17–42.
J. Miles, Jr., "Gagging on Job, or the Comedy of Religious Exhaustion," in *Studies in the Book of Job*. Semeia 7. Ed. R. Polzin and D. Robertson. Missoula: Society of Biblical Literature, 1977. Pp. 71–126.
H. Möller, *Sinn und Aufbau des Buches Hiob*. Berlin: Evangelische Verlagsanstalt, 1955.
M. Möller, "Die Gerechtigkeit Gottes des Schöpfers in der Erfahrung seines Knechtes Hiob," in *Theologische Versuche* VI. Ed. J. Rogge and G. Schille. Berlin: Evangelische Verlagsanstalt, 1975. Pp. 25–36.
R. Moore, "The Integrity of Job," *CBQ* 45 (1983) 17–31.
H.-P. Müller, *Hiob und seine Freunde*. Theologische Studien 103. Zurich: EVZ, 1970.
_____. "Altes und Neues zum Buch Hiob," *EvT* 37 (1977) 284–304.
R. Murphy, *Wisdom Literature: Job, Proverbs, Ruth, Canticles, Ecclesiastes, Esther*. FOTL 13. Grand Rapids: Eerdmans, 1981.
A. Néher, "Job: The Biblical Man," *Judaism* 13 (1964) 37–47.
H. Nichols, "The Composition of the Elihu Speeches," *AJSL* 27 (1910–11) 97–186.

H. Orlinsky, "Some Corruptions in the Greek Text of Job," *JQR* 26 (1935–36) 133–45.

_____. "Studies in the Septuagint of the Book of Job," *HUCA* 28 (1957) 53–74; 29 (1958) 229–71; 30 (1959) 153–67; 32 (1961) 239–68; 33 (1962) 119–51; 35 (1964) 57–78; 36 (1965) 37–47.

D. Patrick, "Job's Address of God," *ZAW* 91 (1979) 268–82.

R. Pfeiffer, "Edomitic Wisdom," *ZAW* 44 (1926) 13–25.

R. Polzin, "The Framework of the Book of Job," *Int* 28 (1974) 182–200.

_____. *Biblical Structuralism*. Semeia Supplements. Philadelphia: Fortress; Missoula: Scholars Press, 1977.

M. Pope, *Job*. AB 15. 3rd ed. Garden City, NY: Doubleday, 1979.

G. von Rad, *Wisdom in Israel*. Tr. J. D. Martin. Nashville: Abingdon, 1972.

M. Reddy, "The Book of Job—A Reconstruction," *ZAW* 90 (1978) 54–94.

H. Richter, "Die Naturweisheit des Alten Testaments im Buche Hiob," *ZAW* 70 (1958) 1–20.

_____. "Erwägungen zum Hiobproblem," *EvT* 18 (1958) 202–24.

_____. *Studien zu Hiob: Der Aufbau des Hiobbuches dargestellt an den Gattungen des Rechtslebens*. Theologische Arbeiten 11. Berlin: Evangelische Verlagsanstalt, 1958.

H. Robinson, *The Cross in the Old Testament*. Philadelphia: Westminster, 1955.

J. Roberts, "Job and the Israelite Religious Tradition," *ZAW* 89 (1977) 107–14.

H. H. Rowley, *Job*. NCBC. Rev. ed. Repr. Grand Rapids: Eerdmans, 1980.

_____. "The Book of Job and Its Meaning," *BJRL* 41 (1958) 162–207. Repr. in *From Moses to Qumran*. New York: Association Press, 1963. Pp. 139–83.

E. Ruprecht, "Leiden und Gerechtigkeit bei Hiob," *ZTK* 73 (1976) 424–45.

P. Sanders, ed., *Twentieth Century Interpretations of the Book of Job: A Collection of Critical Essays*. Englewood Cliffs: Prentice-Hall, 1968.

N. Sarna, "Epic Substratum in the Prose of Job," *JBL* 76 (1957) 13–25.

_____. "Some Instances of the Enclitic -m in Job," *JJS* 6 (1955) 108–10.

P. Schmidt, "Sinnfrage und Glaubenskrise: Ansätze zu einer kritischen Theologie der Schöpfung im Buche Hiob," *Geist und Leben* 45 (1972) 348–63.

L. Schökel, "Toward a Dramatic Reading of the Book of Job," in *Studies in the Book of Job*. Semeia 7. Ed. R. Polzin and D. Robertson. Missoula: Society of Biblical Literature, 1977. Pp. 45–61.

S. Scholnick, "The Meaning of *mišpāṭ* in the Book of Job," *JBL* 101 (1982) 521–29.

M. Sekine, "Schöpfung und Erlösung im Buche Hiob," in *Von Ugarit nach Qumran*. Fest. O. Eissfeldt. Ed. J. Hempel and L. Rost. BZAW 77. Berlin: Töpelmann, 1961. Pp. 213–23.

P. Skehan, "Strophic Patterns in the Book of Job," *CBQ* 23 (1961) 125–42. Repr. in *Studies in Israelite Poetry and Wisdom*. CBQMS 1. Washington: Catholic Biblical Association, 1971. Pp. 96–113.

R. P. Smith, *A Compendious Syriac Dictionary*. Ed. J. P. Smith. Oxford: Clarendon, repr. 1976.

N. Snaith, *The Book of Job: Its Origin and Purpose*. SBT 2/11. London: SCM; Naperville: Allenson, 1968.

_____. "The Introduction to the Speeches of Job: Are They in Prose or in Verse?" *Textus* 8 (1973) 133–37.

M. Sokoloff, *The Targum to Job from Qumran Cave XI*. Ramat Gan: Bar-Ilan University, 1974.

J. Stamm, "Gottes Gerechtigkeit, das Zeugnis des Hiobbuches," *Der Grundriss* 5 (1943) 1–13.

M. Stockhammer, "The Righteousness of Job," *Judaism* 7 (1958) 64–71.

_____. "Theorie der Moralprobe," *ZRGG* 22 (1970) 164–67.

E. Sutcliffe, *Providence and Suffering in the Old and New Testaments*. London/New York: Nelson, 1953.

P. Szczygiel, *Das Buch Job*. Bonn: Peter Hanstein, 1931.

S. Terrien, "The Book of Job." *IB* III. Nashville: Abingdon, 1954.

_____. *Job: Poet of Existence*. London: Nelson, 1957.

_____. "The Yahweh Speeches and Job's Response," *RevExp* 68 (1971) 497–509.

D. Winton Thomas, "Types of Wisdom in the Book of Job," *Indian Journal of Theology* 20 (1971) 157–65.

K. Thompson, Jr., "Out of the Whirlwind," *Int* 14 (1960) 51–63.

J. Torrance, "Why Does God Let Men Suffer?" *Int* 15 (1961) 157–63.

M. Tsevat, "The Meaning of the Book of Job," *HUCA* 37 (1966) 73–106.

N. H. Tur-Sinai (Torczyner), *The Book of Job*. Rev. ed. Jerusalem: Kiryat-Sefer, 1967.

_____. "Hiobdichtung und Hiobsage," *MGWJ* 69 (1925) 234–48.

W. Urbrock, "Evidences of Oral-Formulaic Compositions in the Poetry of Job." Diss., Harvard University, 1975.

_____. "Oral Antecedents to Job: A Survey of Formulas and Formulaic Systems," in *Oral Tradition and Old Testament Studies*. Semeia 5. Ed. R. C. Culley. Missoula: Scholars Press, 1976. Pp. 111–37.

_____. "Reconciliation of Opposites in the Dramatic Ordeal of Job," in *Studies in the Book of Job*. Semeia 7. Ed. R. Polzin and D. Robertson. Missoula: Society of Biblical Literature, 1977. Pp. 147–54.

J. van der Ploeg and A. van der Woude, *Le Targum de Job de la Grotte XI de Qumran*. Leiden: Brill, 1971.

W. Vischer, "God's Truth and Man's Lie" (tr. D. G. Miller), *Int* 15 (1961) 131–46.

W. Ward, *Out of the Whirlwind: Answers to the Problem of Suffering from the Book of Job*. Richmond: John Knox, 1958.

A. Weiser, *Das Buch Hiob*. ATD 13. 6th ed. Göttingen: Vandenhoeck & Ruprecht, 1974.

_____. "Das Problem der sittlichen Weltordnung im Buche Hiob," *TBl* 2 (1923) 157–64.

C. Westermann, *The Structure of the Book of Job*. Tr. C. Muenchow. Philadelphia: Fortress, 1981.

J. W. Whedbee, "The Comedy of Job," in *Studies in the Book of Job*. Semeia 7. Ed. R. Polzin and D. Robertson. Missoula: Society of Biblical Literature, 1977. Pp. 1–39.

H. Wildberger, "Das Hiobproblem und seine neueste Deutung," *Reformatio* 3 (1954) 355–63, 439–48.

J. Williams, "'You Have Not Spoken the Truth of Me': Mystery and Irony in Job," *ZAW* 83 (1971) 231–55.

———. "Deciphering the Unspoken: The Theophany of Job," *HUCA* 49 (1978) 59–72.

R. Williams, "Theodicy in the Ancient Near East," *CJT* 2 (1956) 14–26. Repr. in *Theodicy in the Old Testament*. Ed. J. L. Crenshaw. Issues in Religion and Theology 4. London: SPCK; Philadelphia: Fortress, 1983. Pp. 42–56.

E. Würthwein, "Gott und Mensch in Dialog und Gottesreden des Buches Hiob," in *Wort und Existenz*. Göttingen: Vandenhoeck & Ruprecht, 1970. Pp. 217–95.

P. Zerafa, *The Wisdom of God in the Book of Job*. Rome: Herder, 1978.

Text and Commentary

I. PROLOGUE (1:1–2:13)

A short account of Job's trial sets the stage for the long debate between Job and his friends (3:1–42:6). This prose account is divided into two parts, the prologue (1:1–2:13) and the epilogue (42:7–17). It has a very ancient substratum that possibly goes back to the prepatriarchal era.[1] The author of Job took over the ancient form and adapted it as the framework for the dialogue.

The prologue consists of six scenes set up in an a-b-c-b′-c′-d pattern. In the first scene Job is characterized as a great sheikh who worshiped God scrupulously with pure devotion (1:1–5). The next four scenes, which alternate between a meeting of the sons of God (1:6–12; 2:1–7a) and the resulting events that happen to Job (1:13–22; 2:7b–10), recount Job's trial. In the last scene Job's three comforters are introduced (2:11–13).

The epic account is composed in the beautiful, simple, compact style typical of early Hebrew prose. The very short scenes are set with a few bold strokes. Narratives and speeches are uniform; thus a small variance in wording yields maximum effect. The number of characters in each scene is limited, usually to two. Action is swift and definitive. Dialogue between characters is direct and terse. Characterization is developed through speeches and a person's response to an action. Symmetrical patterns contribute to the terse scenes. Numbers are employed to great advantage; the sequence of three, seven, and ten carries great significance.[2] The stark simplicity of the narrative contrasts markedly with the depth of the problem addressed. Consequently the account, though simple, captures the audience's imagination. It has a remarkable fascination that has transcended ages and cultures.

1. Cf. N. Sarna, "Epic Substratum in the Prose of Job," *JBL* 76 (1957) 13–25. For further discussion see section VIII in the Introduction above.

2. E.g., seven sons and three daughters (1:2; 42:13); seven thousand sheep and three thousand camels, five hundred yoke of oxen and five hundred asses (1:3); seven-day feasts (1:14); mourning seven days and seven nights (2:13); and sacrifices of seven bulls and seven rams (42:8).

A. JOB'S FAITH AND PROSPERITY (1:1–5)

1 *In the land of Uz there lived*[1] *a man named Job. This man was blameless and upright, one who feared God and shunned evil.*
2 *Seven sons and three daughters were born to him,*
3 *and he had seven thousand small cattle, three thousand camels, five hundred yoke of oxen, and five hundred asses, and a great many servants. This man was the greatest among all the people of the East.*
4 *His sons used to*[2] *hold feasts, each in his house on his day; and they would send invitations to their three*[3] *sisters to eat and drink with them.*
5 *When a round of feasting had ended, Job would send*[4] *and have them ritually cleansed.*[5] *Diligently making preparations*[6] *in the morning, he would offer burnt offerings for each of them, for Job said,*

"Perhaps my children have sinned
and cursed[7] *God in their hearts."*[8]

Thus Job did regularly.

1 The narrative opens in epic style, *there lived.* Job is simply introduced as a citizen of *Uz.* Unfortunately the exact location of Uz remains unknown. The evidence points in two different directions: a southern location in the

1. This introductory formula, found also in 2 Sam. 12:1 and Esth. 2:5, differs from the more frequent *wayhî 'îš,* "and there was a man." It does not necessarily indicate that the account is late nor does it signal that the account is fictional.

2. Heb. *hālaḵ,* "go, walk," may function as an auxiliary verb and initiate a recurring activity, e.g., Gen. 19:3; Esth. 1:3, 5, 9 (Gordis).

3. The form *šᵉlōšeṯ,* "three," before a feminine noun is irregular, but it is also found in Gen. 7:13; 1 Sam. 10:3. See GKC, § 92c.

4. Heb. *šālaḥ,* "send," may be used to initiate an action expressed in the following finite verb, e.g., Gen. 27:45; 2 K. 11:4 (Gordis).

5. Dhorme points out that the hiphil of *qāḏaš,* "sanctify," means also "convoke to a solemn feast" in ritual contexts such as Exod. 19:10, 14; Joel 1:14; 2:15; Lev. 25:10.

6. Heb. *hiškîm* is generally translated "rise early." The essential idea of the root emphasizes arduous work done eagerly, persistently, and with a sense of urgency. Pope thinks that it may be a denominative of *šᵉḵem,* "shoulder," thus referring to arduous work that requires putting the shoulder to the task. The link with "morning" comes from the frequent use of the phrase "in the morning" after the verb (as here). But "early" is not an essential part of its denotation.

7. The word translated "curse," *bāraḵ* (also in 2:5, 9), which usually means "bless," is used euphemistically. Many consider it a scribal change for an original *qillᵉlû* (which Targ. reads here), but there is no reason why this euphemistic style may not have been original.

8. Heb. *lēḇ, lēḇāḇ,* "heart," represents the thoughts, the will, and the tender emotions. See H. W. Wolff, *Anthropology of the Old Testament,* tr. M. Kohl (London: SCM; Philadelphia: Fortress, 1974), pp. 40–55.

vicinity of Edom and a northern site northeast of Palestine in the Hauran.[9] The evidence slightly favors the latter location. Many explanations have been offered for the name *Job* (Heb. *'îyôḇ* or LXX *Iob*). In 42:18 the LXX identifies Job as Jobab, an Edomite king (Gen. 36:33 = 1 Chr. 1:44; cf. Gen. 10:29), but there appears to be no connection between this Edomite and Job. Some have argued that Job is related to Heb. *'ôyēḇ,* "enemy," the name meaning then "the enemy of God."[10] Another explanation identifies the Hebrew name with the Arabic root *'wb,* "return, repent," i.e., "the penitent one" (cf. Ewald). If this were its meaning, the name would intimate the outcome of the drama, but such a meaning stands in stark contrast to Job's stern conviction that he need not repent. Finally, the appearance of this name in numerous texts from the 2nd millennium B.C. casts doubt on the search for an etymological understanding of Job's name as a literary device. Rather than being a literary invention, Job is the real name of a prepatriarchal hero.[11]

A patriarch is usually introduced in the biblical text with a full genealogy (e.g., Abraham, Gen. 11:26–29); thus it is noteworthy that Job is introduced without genealogy and without reference to his tribe or clan. There is also no specific reference to the time when Job lived. The author

9. On the one hand, many facts connect Uz with Edom. According to Lam. 4:21 the daughter of Edom lives in the land of Uz. In Jer. 25:20–21 Uz is associated with Philistia, Edom, and Moab. Uz was the son of Dishan, a chief of Edom (Gen. 36:28; 1 Chr. 1:42). LXX accepts Edom by reason of its associating, though inaccurately, Job with Jobab, an Edomite king (42:17ff.; Gen. 36:33). On the other hand, there is much evidence for locating Uz in Hauran. Some genealogical evidence points in this direction: Aram had a son named Uz (Gen. 10:23; 1 Chr. 1:17 [one Hebrew ms. and LXX]). Another Uz was the oldest son of Nahor, the Aramean brother of Abraham (Gen. 22:20–21). The reference to the children of the East could mean the area to the east of the Jordan River, if the author lived in Palestine. Josephus (*Ant.* 1.145), along with later Jewish and Arabic traditions, adopted this location of Uz. In addition, there is a monastery close to Damascus named Deir Ayyub in honor of Job. Cf. P. Dhorme, "Le pays de Job," *RB* 20 (1911) 102–107; B. Moritz, "Edomitische Genealogien I," *ZAW* 44 (1926) 92.

10. Job 13:24 (cf. 33:10) has an interesting play on the similarity between Job's name and the Hebrew word for "enemy." There Job accuses God of treating him like his enemy. Support for this view comes from taking the name of Job as developed from the pattern *qaṭṭāl* > *qiṭṭōl;* in this form a person or an object embodies the quality borne by the root (see Fohrer; GKC, § 84[b]e). In a similar direction Gordis interprets the form of the name Job as a passive participle of *'āyaḇ,* meaning "the hated or persecuted one."

11. A Tell el-Amarna letter (no. 256; 14th cent. B.C.) witnesses to a prince of Ashtaroth named *'ayyab.* A Palestinian chief with the name *'ybm* is also attested in the Egyptian Execration Texts (2000 B.C.). The name *'A-ya-bu* occurs in texts from Mari and Alalakh. W. F. Albright (*JAOS* 74 [1954] 223–33) interprets this name as a contracted form of *'Ayya-'abu(m),* meaning "Where is (my) father?" This meaning corresponds well with Job's continual cry for God to reveal himself. In an Ugaritic text (*PRU* II [1957], 35, reverse, line 10) there is a personal name *'yb;* it may have been pronounced *'ay(y)abu* (Pope).

thereby masterfully composes a literary piece in which Job is representative of all who suffer.

Two sets of word pairs characterize Job as a man of untarnished character and devout faith. The first pair, *blameless (tām)* and *upright (yāšār),*[12] indicates that Job was a person of pure motivation. Heb. *tām* frequently designates a sacrificial animal as "spotless, without blemish," but when used with a person it means personal integrity, not sinless perfection (Josh. 24:14; Judg. 9:16, 19).[13] The blameless person is one who walks in close fellowship with God (Gen. 17:1) and who delights in obeying the law (Ps. 119:1). He serves God wholeheartedly. The word *upright*[14] depicts faithful adherence to God's statutes (cf. 1 K. 14:8; 15:5) and an honest, compassionate manner in relating to others. Job treated others, including his servants, fairly and justly (31:13–23). Also he zealously showed mercy to the unfortunate.

The second pair of words describes Job's devout faith. *He feared God and shunned evil.*[15] The *fear of God* is an expression found throughout the OT and frequently in the Wisdom literature. It stands for a solid trust in God. One who fears God loves him devoutly. Therefore he approaches God reverently, filled with awe and deeply conscious of God's contagious love. In daily life he expresses his fear by striving to please God in faithful obedience inspired by love.[16] The Wisdom literature places the highest value on fearing Yahweh, asserting that it is the very foundation for true wisdom (Job 28:28; Prov. 1:7; 9:10). Whoever fears God avoids the very appearance of evil (*raʿ;* cf. Prov. 16:6b). He shuns all enticements to wrongdoing (cf. 31:1–12) and never places his trust in any other god or thing (31:24–28). The combination of these four character traits and his vast wealth bore witness in his culture that Job excelled in wisdom (cf. Prov. 3:9–10).

Job's love for Yahweh and his acts of mercy toward other human beings became legendary. Thus Ezekiel lists him with Noah and Daniel as the most righteous men of all times (Ezek. 14:14, 20).[17]

12. The bond between *tām* and *yāšār* is also attested in Ps. 37:37 and in the phrase *tōm-wāyōšer,* "purity and uprightness" (Ps. 25:21).

13. Throughout the book Heb. *tām* is a pivotal word, for with it the author keeps in focus the fact that Job is "blameless." It appears in 8:20; 9:20–22 (3 times); *tāmîm,* an adjectival form of this root, occurs in 12:4; 36:4; 37:16.

14. Heb. *yāšār,* "upright," is closely associated with the adjectives "righteous" (*ṣaddîq;* Ps. 33:1; 140:14 [Eng. 13]) and "innocent" (*nāqî;* Job 4:7; 17:8).

15. This word pair appears also in Prov. 3:7; 14:16; 16:6.

16. There is a close tie between fear of God and love for God in Deuteronomy (10:12; 13:5 [Eng. 4]). Cf. G. von Rad, *Wisdom in Israel,* tr. J. D. Martin (London: SCM; Nashville and New York: Abingdon, 1972), pp. 65–68; and G. A. Lee, "Fear," *ISBE,* II:289–91.

17. Cf. also Jas. 5:11. The word translated "patience" (AV) is *hypomonḗ,* which

2, 3 God richly blessed his faithful servant. The author uses the numbers three, seven, and ten, all symbolic of completeness, to demonstrate that Job's wealth was staggering. Though he apparently resided in a city, he owned and cultivated land nearby and employed numerous shepherds who tended his flocks at great distances from his home.[18]

God fully displayed his abundant favor on Job by giving Job seven sons and three daughters. This combination symbolized an ideal family.[19] Sons, valued in those days above daughters, are more numerous. In the epilogue the importance of the sons is counterbalanced by the mention of only the daughters' names. God gave Job a rich heritage.[20]

Job had enormous herds. He had *seven thousand small cattle,* i.e., sheep and goats. His holdings included *three thousand camels.*[21] The camel

means "endurance, steadfastness, perseverance" (see BAG, p. 846; cf. Andersen, pp. 100–101). While many think that this reference refers to the Job of the prose account, not to the Job of the dialogue, their position is not necessarily accurate. The context indicates that James is emphasizing that Job endured great tribulation until he saw God. Also the idea common to the OT background and to James is that "Job waited on God," i.e., his attention never deviated from God. Cf. Hauck, *"hypomonḗ," TDNT,* IV:581–88.

18. Numerous commentators have been troubled by the apparently conflicting picture of Job—a city dweller in the prologue and a semi-nomad in the dialogue. Often they have used this discrepancy as evidence that these two parts of the book had distinct and unrelated origins. Recent sociological studies on the Near East have begun to clarify the multiple social structures evidenced there. The cleavage between farmers and shepherds is no longer sharply drawn. As N. K. Gottwald says, "It is abundantly clear, therefore, that agriculture and pastoral nomadism are by no means mutually exclusive but are often combined in the same human community in manifold forms" (*The Tribes of Yahweh* [Maryknoll, NY: Orbis, 1979], p. 439; also cf. pp. 437–63). It is likely that Job was a city dweller who engaged in farming and commerce and employed pastoral nomads to tend his vast herds. M. B. Rowton identifies this social pattern as dimorphic society. Cf. M. B. Rowton, *Al-Bahit, Studia Instituti Anthropos* 28 (1976) 219–57; idem, *Or* 42 (1973) 247–58; idem, *JNES* 32 (1973) 201–15.

19. The ideal of seven children is referred to in 1 Sam. 2:5; Ruth 4:15. But Job is blessed more abundantly, for he has three daughters in addition to his seven sons. Ugaritic mythology has an interesting parallel: Baal had seven sons and three daughters (*UT,* 67:V:8–11), and the daughters, but never the sons, are named.

20. See Ps. 127:3, 5a: "Behold, sons are a heritage from Yahweh, the fruit of the womb a reward. . . . Blessed is the man who has filled his quiver full with them."

21. Dhorme cites Aristotle (*De Historia Animalia* 9.50.5), who mentions that Arabs would at times possess three thousand camels. The camel, the one-humped dromedary, was the means of transportation across the desert. The fact that Job had camels is not anachronistic, as archeological evidence has shown. For instance, excavations at Mari have found camel bones in a house dated to the 24th cent. B.C. Scholars differ, however, as to whether this evidence can support the great size of Job's herd. Cf. W. F. Albright, *From the Stone Age to Christianity,* 2nd ed. (Garden City, NY: Doubleday, 1957), pp. 120, 196, 219; J. P. Free, "Abraham's Camels," *JNES* 3 (1944) 187–93; B. S. J. Isserlin, "On Some Possible Occurrences of the Camel in Palestine," *PEQ* 82 (1950) 50–53; R. Walz, "Zum Problem des Zeitpunkts der Domestikation der altweltlichen Cameliden," *ZDMG* 101 (1951) 29–51; idem, "Neue Untersuchungen zum Domestika-

was a prestigious animal, and such an enormous number symbolizes great status. This large number suggests that Job engaged in caravan trade. To work his farmland he had *five hundred yoke of oxen,* mentioned in pairs because of their use in plowing. By ancient standards this number of oxen could till a considerable acreage. *Five hundred (female) asses,* animals of burden, are listed; their giving milk and bearing offspring made them more valuable than the males. As would be expected, Job had a large staff of male and female slaves[22] for the work of his vast estate. In every way Job's wealth surpassed that of any other sheikh of the East.[23]

4, 5 As a further witness both to Job's affluence and to his piety, a family custom is recounted. This custom is presented in a way that lauds Job's character while setting the stage for the tragic fate that will befall his children.

Each of Job's sons, in turn, held a seven-day feast at his own house.[24] The brothers extended a special invitation to their sisters, who were presumably unmarried and living with their father. While the language may indicate that there were continuous rounds of feasting, it is more probable that each son periodically held a nonreligious feast, possibly a birthday celebration.[25] This detail witnesses to the closeness and the affluence of Job's family, not to the fact that Job's children were given to frivolous living.

Another noble characteristic of Job portrayed in this picture is his fervent spiritual leadership as head of his family. At the conclusion of each round of feasting he offered *burnt offerings,* atoning sacrifices, for all his children, just in case any of them had *cursed God in their hearts.* Before making the sacrifices he sent servants to make sure that his children were *ritually cleansed* for the solemn occasion of offering up sacrifices for expiation. No doubt his children were present the next day when Job, acting as the priest of his family, sacrificed burnt offerings for them. Since the sacrifices were whole burnt offerings, the entire offering was consumed by fire (cf. Lev. 1). Nothing was left for either the children or the offerer to eat. Whole burnt offerings atoned for human sin in general, rather than specific trans-

---

tionsproblem der altweltlichen Cameliden," *ZDMG* 104 (1954) 45–87; A. Parrot, *Syria* 32 (1955) 323.

22. The term *ʿaḇuddâ* is taken as a broken plural for "a household of slaves, male and female" in the pattern of *zāḵûr,* "males," from *zāḵār,* "male," as in Exod. 23:17; 34:23 (cf. Gordis).

23. The term "East" *(qeḏem)* generally stands for the area east of the Euphrates (cf. Gen. 29:1). But for those who lived in Palestine it is the area east of the Jordan (cf. Jer. 49:28; Ezek. 25:4, 10).

24. David's sons also had their own homes (2 Sam. 13:7; 14:28).

25. Heb. *yômô,* "his day," means a birthday, as in 3:1.

gressions, which were expiated with a sin offering (Lev. 4:1–5:6). Job was motivated to present these sacrifices because he was apprehensive that one of his children might have cursed God during the week's festivities. In no way did he want a hasty curse to fester unexpiated in the conscience of one of his children. It is clear that Job took his role as the family's priest very seriously, and this ritual of sacrifice was an expression of the entire family's contrite attitude toward God. As priest of his family he interceded for each member lest any thought disrupt their relationship with God.

At this point it is important to note that the sin of cursing God is pivotal to the prologue. Whereas Job feared that his children might speak lightly about God, the Satan will argue that Job would certainly curse God should he suffer loss (1:11; 2:5). Then Job's wife will urge him to curse God and die (2:9). With this motif the author focuses on the basis of an individual's relationship to God. Does a person worship God out of genuine love or primarily for God's blessing? This is the issue for everyone.

Furthermore, this characterization of Job portrays him as having a pure heart and a dynamic, active faith in God. God confirmed Job's trust by blessing him abundantly. But Job did not grow overconfident. Scrupulously he offered sacrifices continually, seeking to expiate every possible sin—even the incipient thought of denying God—both his own and those of his family. Job lived an exemplary life.

B. THE FIRST SCENE BEFORE YAHWEH (1:6–12)

6 *One day the sons of God came and presented themselves before Yahweh,*[1] *and the Satan also came among them.*

7 *Yahweh said to the Satan, "From where have you come?" The Satan answered Yahweh, "From roaming through the earth and going to and fro in it."*

8 *Then Yahweh said to the Satan, "Have you considered my servant Job? There is no one like him on earth, a blameless and upright man, one who fears God and shuns evil."*

9 *The Satan answered Yahweh, "Does Job fear*[2] *God for nothing?*

1. God is referred to by his personal name Yahweh. This name occurs 7 times in the two scenes of God's conversing with the Satan as compared to only 3 other times in the prologue, all of which are in the adage quoted by Job (1:21). No doubt the name Yahweh appears in these scenes because the author wants to stress Yahweh's sovereignty, specifically his complete superiority to the Satan.

2. MT *yārē'*, "to fear," may be either a perfect form or a participle. As a perfect it means that Job has been fearing God up to the moment when the Satan sees him (Gordis).

10 *Have you[3] not put a hedge[4] about him, his household, and all that he has? You have blessed the work of his hands, and his flocks spread out over the land.*
11 *But stretch out your hand and strike all that he has. Surely, I warrant you,[5] he will curse you to your face."*
12 *Yahweh said to the Satan, "Behold, everything that he has is in your power; only do not stretch out your hand against him." Then the Satan went out from Yahweh's presence.*

6 The setting for this scene shifts to an assembly before God. While the term *one day* is indefinite, the Targum identifies the time of the first meeting with New Year's Day and that of the second session with the Day of Atonement. In the postexilic era it was believed that a preliminary judgment took place on New Year's Day. In that judgment the names of the upright were recorded in the book of life and the names of the wicked removed. Those whose character was marginal received a grace period until the Day of Atonement; at that time their repentance was accepted or rejected and their fate determined.

The sons of God (Heb. *bᵉnê hāʾᵉlōhîm*) are the celestial beings or angels whom God created as his servants. On this day *they came and presented themselves* (Heb. *hiṯyaṣṣēḇ*) as courtiers to give an accounting of their activities to God. One interpretation of the setting of this scene is a session of the council of God.[6] At its sessions the sons of God reported on their activities and received new orders.

On this occasion *the Satan also came among them*. Here the Hebrew word *haśśāṭān* has the article, so it functions as a title rather than as a personal name. The Hebrew root *śṭn* means "to oppose at law." On this basis some scholars conjecture that the Satan may be the prosecuting at-

3. MT *ʾattā* is a defective spelling for *ʾattâ,* which occurs some 5 times in MT (e.g., 1 Sam. 24:19; Ps. 6:4 [Eng. 3]).

4. Heb. *śaḵ,* closely related to the root *skk,* means "hedge or fence in, surround with thorn bushes as with a wall" (cf. Dhorme).

5. Heb. *ʾim-lōʾ* may be taken as an elliptical curse formula in which the consequences of the challenge are affirmed by an oath: "May such and such happen to me if Job does not curse you brazenly and immediately."

6. The setting for this scene closely parallels "the assembly of the gods" that is well attested in ancient Near Eastern literature. Several passages in the OT also seem to assume that God governs the world through a council of the heavenly host (e.g., Ps. 29:1; 82; 89:6–9 [Eng. 5–8]; 1 K. 22:19–23). But in the OT the complete dependence of these sons of God on God himself and their total submission to him is not questioned. In this way Israel altered the ancient Near Eastern understanding of the divine council to conform to its monotheistic belief. Cf. E. T. Mullen, Jr., *The Divine Council in Canaanite and Early Hebrew Literature,* HSM 24 (Chico: Scholars Press, 1980).

torney of the heavenly council.[7] If this view is correct, his task on earth was to discover human sins and failures and to bring his findings before the heavenly assembly. But his role in this scene deviates from this explanation. Instead of uncovering disruptive plans, he acts as a troublemaker, a disturber of the kingdom.[8]

Was the Satan one of the sons of God? The majority of scholars assume that he was.[9] Driver-Gray understand the preposition *among* (Heb. *bᵉṯôḵ*) to indicate that he had a prominent place in this assembly.[10] But some recent scholars understand the text to portray the Satan as an intruder. They come to this position either by taking the term *also* (Heb. *gam*) to mean "other than" or by understanding the preposition *among* to indicate someone who is an outsider.[11] This casting seems to put him as a distinct member of the assembly with a role that stands over against that of the other members. But the main function of this assembly here is to provide an open forum in which Yahweh permits the testing of Job. That is, the plan to test Job was not hatched in a secret meeting between Yahweh and the Satan. Rather it was decided openly before the heavenly assembly. In this setting Yahweh's motivation, based on his complete confidence in Job, was fully known and thus it was above question. This is important, for the author has a doubly

7. Heb. *śṭn* is employed in two ways in the OT. On the one hand, it describes the activity of a political foe bent on overthrowing the king (2 Sam. 19:23 [Eng. 22]; 1 K. 5:18 [Eng. 4]; 11:14, 23, 25). But the personification of the Satan as an evil force hostile to God's reign appears unquestionably only in 2 Chr. 21:1, where the name occurs without the article. On the other hand, it refers to one who, like a prosecuting attorney, brings charges against another in court (Ps. 109:6; Zech. 3:1–2). Many scholars have taken this lead and posited that this figure was patterned after the court life of a large empire. Tur-Sinai looks to the Persian empire. The Persian emperor had secret servants who toured the realm at random to discern the allegiance and behavior of the people and especially of various officials. These agents were called "the eyes and ears of the king" (Herodotus). So in Job the Satan appears as the roving eye of the monarch to report on the loyalty of subjects. In a similar vein A. Brock-Utne ("Der Feind," *Klio* 28 [1935] 219–27) argues that such agents were employed by the Assyrian emperors. His idea is very similar to Tur-Sinai's, but it offers an earlier historical setting for the development of such a role. Also cf. M. J. Gruenthaner, "The Demonology of the OT," *CBQ* 6 (1944) 6–27.

8. While the Satan's role in this test is much simpler than his ominous role as head of all evil powers that the later Judeo-Christian tradition ascribes to him, he reveals numerous characteristics which suggest that he is contiguous with the later Satan, God's primary antagonist. He answered God's questions obtrusively and brusquely, reflecting a contemptuous attitude. He sought to misconstrue a person's actions by imputing impure motives to good deeds. Thus he immediately doubted what God affirmed and sternly resisted persuasion to a different viewpoint. In the second scene before Yahweh the Satan would not even debate the issue of Job's integrity, but rather denied it in an impudent style by challenging God with verbs in the imperative.

9. See, e.g., Driver-Gray, Pope, Fohrer, Gordis.

10. Cf. Gen. 23:6; 42:5.

11. Cf. Andersen, and J. L. Crenshaw, *Old Testament Wisdom* (Atlanta: Knox, 1981), p. 101.

difficult task throughout his work: continually to characterize Job as innocent and not to characterize Yahweh as demonic.

7 This scene focuses on the dialogue between Yahweh and the Satan. Yahweh began by asking the Satan for an accounting of his activities and whereabouts. The Satan responded that he had been *roaming through the earth and going to and fro in it.* The term *roaming* suggests that he moved randomly about the earth, perhaps like an emperor's spy looking for any secret disloyalty to the crown.

8 Yahweh then brought Job to the Satan's attention. Yahweh's purpose was to demonstrate that a human being could live a blameless, upright life. Proudly Yahweh called Job *his servant.*[12] With this title Yahweh was acknowledging that Job was a faithful, obedient follower. Moreover, Yahweh affirmed that Job was truly a righteous man by stating that he was *blameless and upright, one who fears God and shuns evil.* Yahweh hereby authenticated the opening characterization of Job.

9, 10 But the Satan questioned God's praise of Job. He doubted whether any person would fear God *for nothing* or without reason (Heb. *ḥinnām;* cf. 2:3). The Satan's question insinuated that all good deeds spring from selfish motives. To him this would surely be true in Job's case, for Yahweh had both protected Job from all harm and blessed him abundantly. In fact, Yahweh had planted a fence of thorn bushes around all that Job owned so that no plague or misfortune could harm Job's huge herds and productive fields. In addition, Yahweh had so blessed Job that his flocks had multiplied at such a rapid rate that they *spread out* (Heb. *pāraṣ*)[13] over the entire land. Given these facts, how could one believe that Job served God freely out of love?

11 Suspicious of Job's reasons for fearing God, the Satan challenged Yahweh to test Job's fidelity. Using imperatives as though he were ordering Yahweh, he sought to force Yahweh to test Job. He argued that if Yahweh would stretch out his hand and strike all that Job had, Job would surely curse Yahweh to his face. The self-serving basis of Job's loyalty would be revealed. Whereas Job continually feared that one of his children might have cursed God *in his heart,* the Satan projected that Job would become so angry he would curse God *to his face,* i.e., in open defiance (cf. 2:9).

12. The greatest leaders in the OT bear the title *servant,* a title that indicates God himself acknowledges their humble services, which he has commissioned, e.g., Abraham (Ps. 105:6, 42), Jacob or Israel (Isa. 41:8), Moses (Exod. 14:31), Joshua (Josh. 24:29), David (2 Sam. 7:5, 8), Isaiah (Isa. 20:3), and the prophets (2 K. 9:7; Amos 3:7).

13. Heb. *pāraṣ* means "to burst out" beyond limits or expectations; in this case it depicts the phenomenal growth of Job's flocks and wealth (cf. Gen. 28:14; 30:30, 43; Exod. 1:12; 1 Chr. 4:38; Isa. 54:3).

12 Confident of his servant Job, Yahweh accepted the Satan's challenge. He granted the Satan full power over Job's possessions, but not over Job's body. Many scholars speak of this transaction between Yahweh and the Satan as a wager. But this is inaccurate, for no sum was set to be handed over to the winner. The single issue at stake was the motivation for Job's upright behavior and his fear of God. The Satan functions as God's servant, solely an instrument in the testing. The author holds to a pure monotheism wherein God is ultimately responsible for all that happens.

This scene and its counterpart in 2:1–7a are essential for the audience to comprehend the spiritual dimensions of Job's trial. They afford insight into God's evaluation of Job and his confidence that under the severest testing his servant will prove that this evaluation is well-founded. Without knowledge of God's position the dialogue would be meaningless and Job's stubbornness would be thought the height of self-delusion. In order to make a proper assessment of Job's complaint the audience must know God's attitude toward Job and his direction of the events that will befall Job.

C. JOB'S TRAGIC MISFORTUNE (1:13–22)

13 *One day when Job's sons and daughters were eating and drinking wine in their older brother's home,*

14 *a messenger[1] came to Job and said, "The oxen were plowing[2] and the asses were grazing nearby*

15 *when the Sabeans attacked[3] and captured them. They smote the servants with the sword.[4] I alone have escaped to tell you."*

16 *While he was still speaking, another messenger came and said, "The fire of God[5] fell from heaven and burned the flocks and the servants; it consumed them. I alone have escaped to tell you."*

1. The subject *mal'āḵ,* "messenger," stands before the verb to emphasize the sudden interruption of the serene scene.

2. Heb. *ḥōrᵉšôṯ* is a feminine plural participle with the masculine *bāqār* (cf. Gen. 33:13 and GKC, §§ 145b, c). Attempting to deal with the grammar, Guillaume (*Studies in the Book of Job,* ed. J. MacDonald, *ALUOS,* supplement 2 [Leiden: Brill, 1968], p. 77) states that a special characteristic of this Arabian vicinity was the use of cows for ploughing. Unfortunately there is no easy way to document his view. It is more likely, though, that this is a grammatical phenomenon associated with animals; note the masculine plural pronominal suffix, *ʿal yᵉḏêhem,* "by their side," referring to the cattle. The participle is used with *hāyû,* "they were," to describe continuous action in the past (GKC, § 116r).

3. Heb. *tippōl,* "it attacks, falls on," is a feminine form even though people, not the country, is meant by the proper noun *šᵉḇā'* (GKC, § 122i).

4. Lit. "by the mouth of the sword." This phrase pictures the weapon devouring its victims (cf. the arrow drinks blood, Deut. 32:42). Swords have been found with the hilt shaped like a lion's head and the blade protruding from its mouth (T. J. Meek, "Archaeology and a Point in Hebrew Grammar," *BASOR* 122 [1951] 31–33).

5. LXX reads "fire" without the genitive "of God."

17 *While he was still speaking, another messenger came and said, "The Chaldeans formed three bands and swept down on the camels and captured them. They smote the servants with the sword. I alone have escaped to tell you."*

18 *While he was still*[6] *speaking, another messenger came and said, "Your sons and daughters were eating and drinking wine*[7] *in their oldest brother's house,*

19 *when suddenly*[8] *a mighty wind swept across the desert and struck*[9] *the four corners of the house. It collapsed on the young people and they are dead. I alone have escaped to tell you."*

20 *Job arose, tore his robe, and shaved his head. Prostrating himself on the ground, he worshiped,*

21 *saying,*

"Naked[10] *I came from my mother's womb,*
and naked I shall return thither.[11]
Yahweh[12] *gave and Yahweh has taken;*
May the name of Yahweh be blessed."

22 *In all this Job did not sin, and he did not charge God with wrong.*

6. For MT *ʿaḏ,* "until," *ʿôḏ,* "still, yet," should be read as in vv. 16, 17.

7. The word *yayin,* "wine," is absent from LXX and Syr. Perhaps it was added here by the scribal tendency to level the text, making this passage agree with v. 13.

8. The particle *hinnēh,* "suddenly," "behold," introduces a temporal clause, drawing the subject before the verb (Fohrer).

9. Following the feminine *bāʾâ,* "it swept," the masculine *wayyiggaʿ*, "and it struck," is remarkable. Although *rûaḥ,* "wind," may function as a masculine noun (it is usually feminine), there may be a textual error here; or the inflection of the verb following the first predicate may no longer be determined by the subject (GKC, § 145t).

10. Heb. *ʿārōm,* "naked," is an adverb placed before the verb to emphasize a particular state of affairs (GKC, § 118n).

11. The identification of "thither" (Heb. *šāmâ*) is pressed by some. Since one obviously cannot return to one's mother's womb, "there" might mean a return to "mother earth" as the place of humanity's origin. In the words of Eccl. 5:14 (Eng. 15): "As he came from his mother's womb, he will return, naked as he came, and will take nothing for his toil which he may carry away in his hand." The mother's womb, in which a body is knit together, was perceived as an extension of the earth (Ps. 139:13-15). It was common in the ancient Near East to bury a person in a curled position, suggesting a return to the embryonic condition (cf. G. Ricciotti, "Et nu j'y retournerai (Job 1,21)," *ZAW* 67 [1955] 249–51).

Tur-Sinai posits that the fusion of two proverbial expressions here may have resulted in a mixed metaphor: "Naked came I forth from my mother's womb and naked shall I go to my grave"; and "From dust did I come, and thither *[šmh],* to dust, shall I return." This idea is worthy of consideration, for "thither" could be a euphemism for Sheol (cf. 3:17, 19), but the use of the verb "return" is an obstacle to this view (Horst). The emphasis lies on "naked," not on "there."

12. Job uses the divine name Yahweh only here and perhaps in 12:9. God's personal name appears due to the formulaic nature of this expression (cf. Ps. 113:2) and also because of the personal involvement of God in Job's fate.

13 The third scene opens as did the second with the phrase *One day*. Since no one on earth was aware of the agreement between Yahweh and the Satan, all things at Job's household continued as usual. The atmosphere was peaceful. Scrupulous Job would have recently offered whole burnt offerings to atone for any possible sin either in his children's lives or in his life. His sons had joyfully begun a new round of feasting at the home of the eldest. The mention of *wine* is an artistic touch that pictures the children's anticipated joy. That is, the tragedy of the coming events stands out more sharply against the background of the children's excitement at the beginning of a new round of feasting.[13]

14, 15 A serene mood pervaded Job's estate. In the fields his servants were busy plowing with the oxen. Nearby the donkeys that had brought the implements and the supplies to the fields were grazing peacefully. Taking advantage of the unsuspecting atmosphere, a marauding band of Sabeans[14] attacked the workers. They rounded up the animals and drove them off. Mercilessly they killed all the servants with the sword. The only servant who escaped ran to Job with a report.

16 Just as the first servant was finishing his report, a second servant entered and recounted another disaster. Job's flocks were grazing contentedly when *the fire of God,* i.e., a tremendous bolt of lightning,[15] fell from heaven and lapped up everything in the area, including the flocks and

13. Hakam observes that the smiting of Job's possessions occurs in chiastic arrangement to their listing in the first scene:

order of blessing (vv. 2–3)	**order of loss (vv. 13–19)**
sons and daughters	herds and donkeys
flocks and camels	flocks and camels
herds and donkeys	sons and daughters.

14. The Sabeans (Heb. *šeḇāʾ*) are usually identified as a Semitic people living in a fertile district of the southwestern corner of the Arabian peninsula, the area of present-day Yemen. Their capital was located at modern Marib. In the OT Saba or Sheba is associated with Tema (6:19; cf. Isa. 21:13–15; Jer. 25:23) and Dedan (Gen. 10:7; 25:3). The Sabeans are known for trafficking in incense, gold, and precious stones (Isa. 60:6; Jer. 6:20; Ezek. 27:22–23). Since Saba was over a thousand miles from Uz, many have suggested that it was too remote for a band of that tribe to be making a raid on Job's flocks; thus other explanations have been offered. A widely accepted view is that these Sabeans, not yet having settled in southwestern Arabia, were still a roving tribe. Another possibility is that a group of this tribe was roaming widely from their home base in search of plunder. Others suggest that the Sabeans may have had a trading station in northern Arabia from which this raid could have originated. Finally some think there was a North Arabian Sheba in the area of Dedan and Tema on the southern border of Uz. Unfortunately none of these interpretations is compelling.

15. The fire of God usually means lightning; cf. 20:26; Num. 11:1–3; 16:35; 26:10; 1 K. 18:38; 2 K. 1:10–14. Another view takes the phrase "the fire of God" as an example of using the divine name to denote the superlative degree—"a great fire" (D. W. Thomas, "A consideration of some unusual ways of expressing the superlative in Hebrew," *VT* 3 [1953] 209–24).

the shepherds. This calamity has an ironic twist: the Satan used God's fire against God's servant.

17 As that servant was finishing his account, a third servant arrived and told Job that Chaldeans,[16] divided into three bands,[17] had swooped down on his vast herd of camels. So swift and unexpected was their attack that nothing could be rescued. Again only this servant had escaped to bring word back to Job.

18, 19 Immediately a fourth servant entered. The atmosphere was tense; the climax was at hand. This servant recounted the worst tragedy. While Job's sons and daughters were feasting, the east wind[18] struck the house of the eldest. The house collapsed, killing all his children. Only this servant had escaped.

These four plagues revealed to Job that all the forces of heaven and earth had turned hostile toward him. This idea is borne out by the fact that the causes of destruction alternate between earthly and heavenly forces coming from all four points of the compass: the Sabeans from the south, lightning from a storm out of the west, the Chaldeans from the north, and the treacherous sirocco blowing off the desert to the east. The number four also symbolizes full measure, totality.[19]

20 In a moment the richest sheikh had been turned into a pauper. Conscious that the whole world had turned against him, Job was stunned. Grieving deeply, he stood up, ripped his *robe* (Heb. *mᵉʿîl*),[20] an outer garment worn over the tunic, and shaved his head.[21] Then he dropped to the ground and prostrated himself before God. In so doing he acted consciously, according to custom, not impetuously. In this way Job both acknowledged God's lordship over all his possessions and sought consolation from the Almighty.

16. These Chaldeans were probably the forerunners of the famous Neo-Babylonian empire, which reached its height under Nebuchadnezzar in the 6th cent. B.C. At this time they were a semi-nomadic tribe, for their earliest known settlement was in the 9th cent. B.C. to the west of the Euphrates.

17. Heb. *rōʾš,* "head," is used technically to designate a company or party arrayed for combat (Dhorme). The strategy of attacking in three companies is attested several times in the OT, e.g., Judg. 7:16; 9:43; 1 Sam. 11:11; 13:17.

18. The hot desert wind, the sirocco, is legendary, for it sends temperatures soaring and causes unbearably hot, dry weather. Because of its destructive power, it was known as a wind that brought judgment (cf. Jer. 4:11–12; 18:17).

19. In other texts four plagues symbolize the severest tragedy; e.g., in Ezek. 14:12–23 the four woes are hunger, wild animals, sword, and plague; cf. Rev. 9:13–15.

20. This action is also attested in 1 Sam. 18:4; 24:5, 11; Ezek. 26:16; Ezra 9:3, 5.

21. Making the head bald or cutting a bald spot on the head was forbidden by ritual law (Lev. 21:5; Deut. 14:1). This forbidden practice refers to lacerating the skull as a sign of mourning. Job certainly does not gash his body or his head, as was customary in some Near Eastern lands, for shaving the head, not plucking or tearing out the hair, is the clear meaning of *gāzaz* (cf. Jer. 7:29; Mic. 1:16; cf. Jer. 16:6; 41:5; 48:37; Ezek. 7:18).

21 With two aphorisms Job acknowledged God's sovereignty over his entire life, both for good and for ill. His acknowledgment is expressed with the strongest conviction, for he uses God's personal name *Yahweh* three times (Janzen). Job's resignation to the divine will was exemplary. Having entered the world with nothing, he realized he would not take anything with him in death. Just as he came forth from his *mother's womb,* so he would return to the earth, the mother of all the living.[22] More importantly he professed that the God who had given him all this wealth had the right to take it away, even before his death. Job assumed no inherent right to his possessions. In sorrow as well as in blessing he praised God's name.

22 Grieving Job continued to look to God as his source of strength. He did not pursue any course of action to cope with his losses that would blemish his faith in God. He did not charge God with *wrong* (Heb. *tip̱lâ*),[23] i.e., any unseemly or vengeful act. Mourning in silence, he gave his lips no opportunity to utter an angry curse or a cruel vindictive word. Thereby he honored God's trust in him and demonstrated the falsity of the Satan's taunts.

D. THE SECOND SCENE BEFORE YAHWEH (2:1–6)

1 *Another day came when the sons of God came to present themselves before Yahweh, and the Satan also came among them to present himself before Yahweh.*[1]

22. Similar words are found in Sir. 40:1: "Great travail is created for every man, and a heavy yoke is laid on the sons of Adam, from the day that they go out of their mother's womb, until the day that they return to the mother of all the living."

23. The meaning of *tip̱lâ* is obscure. It has been emended variously; e.g., *ʿawlâ,* "wickedness"; *nᵉḇālâ,* "folly" (see *BHK*); it has also been revocalized to *tᵉpillâ,* "prayer," but understood in the sense of "protest" (Ehrlich). Other interpreters relate it to Arab. *tafala,* "be unperfumed, ill-smelling," or to *tifl,* "spittle" (see Driver-Gray). The related Heb. *tāp̱ēl* occurs in 6:6 with the meaning "tasteless," and in Lam. 2:14 it refers to "deceptive" prophecies (here it stands in conjunction with "worthless," *šāwʾ*); *tip̱lâ* appears in Jer. 23:13 in reference to false prophecies. It has the sense of something unsavory or unseemly, an impropriety. Used in regard to Yahweh it means accusing him of an action that is contrary to his holy nature.

1. In the first scene before Yahweh (v. 6) the phrase "to present himself before Yahweh" is not applied to the Satan. It is difficult to know whether this infinitive construct is an intentional addition by the narrator or a scribal dittography. Since LXX omits the phrase, many (e.g., Driver-Gray, Hölscher, Fohrer) prefer to strike it. But it seems best to take it as a part of the narrative designed to emphasize that the Satan, who had acted with such hostility to Job, must still submit to God's authority and questioning. Budde considers that it was a purposeful addition. Gordis interprets it as connoting the insolence and rebelliousness of the Satan; cf. Num. 16:27; Deut. 7:24; Ps. 2:2.

2 *Yahweh said to the Satan, "From where*[2] *have you come?" The Satan answered Yahweh, "From roaming through the earth and going to and fro on it."*

3 *Then Yahweh said to the Satan, "Have you considered my servant Job? There is no one like him on earth, a blameless and upright man, one who fears God and shuns evil. He continues to hold fast to his integrity, and yet you incite*[3] *me against him to ruin him without cause."*

4 *The Satan answered Yahweh, "Skin for skin, a man will give all that he has for his own life.*

5 *But stretch out your hand and touch his bone and his flesh. Surely, I warrant you, he will curse you to your face."*

6 *Yahweh said to the Satan, "Behold, he is in your power; but spare his life."*

1, 2 The fourth scene, like the second, takes place before Yahweh. This account of the assembling of the sons of God and of the dialogue between the Satan and Yahweh is almost identical to the first heavenly scene. Movement and suspense are created by varying the wording at crucial points. It is emphasized that the Satan was present at this assembly to give an accounting of his ways before Yahweh.

3 After the opening formalities Yahweh, as in the first heavenly scene, brought Job to the Satan's attention. Since Yahweh initiated the subject, he obviously was delighted that Job, his servant, had proved that his worship was genuine. To underscore the fact that not a single flaw had been found in Job's character, Yahweh repeated the full fourfold description of Job's moral excellence and added that Job continued to hold tenaciously to *his integrity* (Heb. *tummāṯô*). Job had endured all the losses without compromising his blameless and upright character in any angry outburst against God.

Yahweh then boldly charged the Satan: *yet you incite me against him to ruin him without cause*. The word *incite* (Heb. *sûṯ*) means to allure or stir someone to a course of action that he would not normally take. In this case Yahweh conceded that the Satan had persuaded him to act toward Job

2. The interrogative phrase *ʾê mizzeh,* "from where, whence," varies from the one used in 1:7, *mēʾayin,* "from where." Budde thinks that this phrase indicates that the Satan is further evading God's question. Since both interrogative expressions appear in a compound question in Jon. 1:8, however, it is best not to make too much of the difference.

3. The *waw* consecutive on *wattᵉsîṯēnî* ("and you incited me") does not mean "although" (so Driver-Gray); rather it gives the consequences of the preceding statement (cf. GKC, § 111l). Perhaps Yahweh is anticipating the Satan's response and wishes to express that any future enticement will also prove as futile.

contrary to Job's just desert. With these words Yahweh accepted full responsibility for Job's plight. He would not concede any of his authority to the Satan. This point is crucial, for in the dialogue Job will seek deliverance from Yahweh alone and rightly so, for he has no battle with the Satan. This statement also explains why the Satan does not reappear in the epilogue. Yahweh himself feels obliged to resolve the conflict for Job.

The test against Job had been brutally executed, as attested by the verb *ruin* (Piel of Heb. *bālaʿ*, "swallow"). It also carried a very sharp barb, as connoted by the phrase *without cause* or for no purpose (Heb. *ḥinnām;* cf. 1:9). This wording focuses on the crux of Job's testing. It is difficult enough to endure hardship to achieve a specific goal, but to suffer misfortune for no apparent reason plunges a person into agonizing self-doubt. Coping with the sense of meaninglessness is more difficult than coping with the material losses. The use of *without cause* here sets up a point of tension with the Satan's use of this phrase in the first scene before Yahweh. Whereas the Satan had conjectured that Job's fear of God was not without cause, i.e., Job feared God for selfish reasons, Yahweh in turn rebuked the Satan with the assertion that Job's trial had proved to be without cause, i.e., the Satan's accusations about Job were groundless. Thus the test has proved that the Satan's accusations against Job were "without cause" or had no inherent worth, and that Job feared God "without cause"—Job trusted God with a pure heart filled with love for God, not for the benefits God had bestowed upon him. The Satan's skepticism about Job's character had proved to be completely wrong.

4, 5 Undaunted, the Satan responded without making any concessions to Yahweh's assessment of the reliability of his servant or the absurdity of the testing. Without debating the results of the test, the Satan persisted in his skeptical attitude about the grounds of Job's faith. He posited that Job was acting contritely because he had not really been tested. Yahweh had set up too many restrictions for there to be a true test. Impudently the Satan countered Yahweh's positive evaluation of Job by quoting two short proverbs, asserting that every person is essentially self-serving.

The first proverb is *skin for skin.*[4] Although the exact background of

4. The exact meaning of the proverb "skin for skin" is not clear. It may be similar to the *lex talionis,* "eye for eye, tooth for tooth . . . wound for wound, stripe for stripe" (Exod. 21:24–25). In this instance it means that Job would give up his property and even his children to save his own life. From another viewpoint, Targ. and Rashi take it to mean that one will yield a less important part of the body to protect a more vital member; e.g., one will raise his arm to ward off a blow to the head. Others think of "one skin behind another," i.e., Job has been touched only in the outer skin and there is another layer that could be exposed (Rowley). But there is no evidence that the Semites distinguished the different layers of the skin. Some (e.g., Tur-Sinai) think of skins of animals as used in bartering, but items of the same kind are not usually exchanged in trading.

this proverb is uncertain, it seems to mean that anyone will exchange anything he has for something else of similar or better value. In reference to Job, the Satan means that he has surrendered all of his possessions without complaint in exchange for his own life. The second proverb is clearer: *a man will give all that he has for his own life,* i.e., a person will abandon anything he owns, including his prized possessions and loved ones, to protect his own life. With these proverbs the Satan alleged that Job's losses were ultimately dispensable to Job; in other words, the Satan is still accusing Job of selfishness.

The Satan was seeking to move Yahweh to intensify Job's testing. Insolently he enjoined: *Stretch out your hand and touch his bone and his flesh.* Since *the bones* were considered the seat of illness (e.g., Lam. 1:13), the Satan had in mind a debilitating disease, one that would threaten Job's very life. He believed that if Job's body became sorely afflicted, he would surely curse God to his face. Job would exchange his fear of God for a healthy life.

6 Although Yahweh rejected the Satan's reasoning, he released Job into the Satan's power for further testing. But again he set a boundary to the affliction by prohibiting the Satan from taking Job's life. This concession reveals the full extent of God's confidence in Job, namely, that Job's basic commitment is to God alone. This means that Job, being ignorant of this dialogue, is about to experience the most dire circumstances. The shadow of death will fall over him so heavily that he will think that he is afflicted by a terminal illness with no hope of recovery. In this way God allows Job's faith to be tested to its innermost core.

E. THE AFFLICTION OF JOB'S BODY (2:7–10)

7 *The Satan went out from Yahweh's presence and smote Job with sore boils from the sole of his feet to the top of his head.*
8 *So he took a potsherd to scrape himself as he sat among the ashes.*
9 *His wife said to him, "Do you still hold fast to your integrity? Curse God and die!"*[1]
10 *He answered her, "You are speaking like one of the foolish women. Shall we accept good from God and not misfortune?" In all this Job did not sin with his lips.*

7 Verse 7 may be divided in the middle, the first half placed with the previous heavenly scene and the second half with this earthly scene. The

1. When two imperatives are joined by a *waw,* the second describes an action that follows as a certain consequence of the previous action (GKC, § 110f).

lack of a clear break between the fourth and the fifth scenes conveys the Satan's anxious determination to afflict Job. The Satan went out from Yahweh's presence and smote Job with a grievous illness. In a moment Job's body was covered with *sore boils* (Heb. *šᵉḥîn rāᶜ*) from the sole of his feet to the top of his head.

The exact illness that seized Job is unknown, for *boils* (Heb. *šᵉḥîn*) is a nontechnical term.[2] From Job's speeches some of the symptoms that he suffered included painful pruritus (2:8), disfiguration (2:12), purulent sores that scab over, crack, and ooze (7:5), sores infected with worms (7:5), fever with chills (21:6; 30:30), darkening and shriveling of the skin (30:30), eyes red and swollen from weeping (16:16), diarrhea (30:27), sleeplessness and delirium (7:4, 13–14), choking (7:15), bad breath (19:17), emaciation (19:20), and excruciating pain throughout his body (30:17).

Many have identified this illness as leprosy, a dreaded disease. But the leprosy mentioned in Scripture was a nonfatal disease, very different from modern-day leprosy. Terrien suggests a diesease named *pemphigus folioceus,* for it comes on suddenly and becomes acute at once.[3] This malady strikes virile young men, inflaming the skin, which becomes intolerably itchy. But the multiple symptoms could fit different maladies. As with any major illness Job experienced multiple complications and probably suffered from many ailments. Whether he was struck by a terminal illness is not stated. In the ancient world there probably existed no sharp demarcation between curable and incurable diseases. One patient might survive a dreaded disease while another succumbed to a minor infection. Thus the Satan could have chosen any chronic disease, for ancient people did not assign the death blow to the disease itself but to God. Although God prevented the Satan from taking Job's life, Job, ignorant of this situation, feared that his illness was incurable and that death was inevitable. Since chronic illnesses like boils were often considered a divine curse,[4] Job's contemporaries would quickly conclude that he was being punished for some moral wrong.

2. In personal correspondence Dr. Robert Benninger, with a Diploma in Tropical Medicine and Hygiene from the Ross Institute at the University of London, writes: "To attempt to diagnose the specific disease that afflicted Job on the basis of the symptoms that are given in the Scriptures would appear to be an impossible task. In the seriously afflicted patient the physician may discover not one disease active but several. This could have been the case in Job's situation. A long list of diseases could be included in a listing of a differential diagnosis for Job's affliction. Two that come quickly to mind are *mycosis fungoides* and uncontrolled *diabetes mellitus* with generalized *furunculosis*. It is common to find in seriously ill patients certain mental changes brought on through prolonged suffering. This could have been so in Job's affliction."

3. Terrien, *IB*, III:920.

4. Boils were one of the ten plagues God used to afflict the Egyptians (Exod. 9:8–12). In Deuteronomy they occur in the list of the plagues that punish disobedience to the covenant. As Deut. 28:35 says, "Yahweh will smite you with grievous boils *[šᵉḥîn rāᶜ]* on

8 Humbled, Job went outside the city walls and sat down on the town's ash heap, a collection of the ashes from the city's ovens, broken pots, and other refuse; it was the abode of outcasts. Sprinkling dust on the head, rolling in ashes, and sitting on an ash heap were ancient ways of expressing one's deepest grief.[5] On the ash heap Job sat alone, totally isolated from the community's life, as he mourned his terrible fate in silence. From time to time he picked up a potsherd and *scraped himself.* Was this a form of self-laceration or a desperate effort to relieve incessant itching (cf. Janzen)? The latter is the testimony of those who experience intense itching; they scratch themselves earnestly, mindful that the pain caused by their efforts is worth the slight relief gained from interrupting the itching. That Job was trusting in God and not merely resigned to an impersonal fate becomes clear in the next event.[6]

9 Job's wife enters the picture for the only time.[7] Her role is to show how unusual was Job's silent acceptance of his bodily affliction. Furthermore, her entrance portrays another dimension of Job's trial, namely, the alienation that his affliction caused between him and his wife.

Do you still hold fast to your integrity? Job's wife could not understand why he held so fast to his integrity despite his physical torture. She used the same expression, *hold fast to your integrity* (Heb. *maḥᵃzîq tummâ*), that God had used (2:3). But instead of seeing this quality as her husband's greatest asset, she feared that it inspired a fanaticism in him that refused to face the reality of circumstances. Thus she implored him, *Curse God and die.* The urgency of her appeal is communicated by the fact that both verbs, *curse* and *die,* are imperatives. Whether she believed that Job would die immediately as the consequence of cursing is hard to determine.[8] Certainly she believed that Job should strike out at God, the cause of his troubles, and that such action would hasten his certain death. Possibly she genuinely

---

the knees and on the legs, from which you cannot be healed, from the sole of your foot to the crown of your head." Thus it is evident that Job was smitten by a repulsive disease that not only tormented him but also symbolized that he was encountering the wrath of God.

5. Cf. Isa. 47:1; 58:5; Jer. 6:26; Ezek. 27:30; Jon. 3:6.

6. Cf. Terrien, *IB,* III:921–22.

7. Targ. names Job's wife Dinah, based on the connection that Dinah also acted foolishly (Gen. 34:1–10). In the Testament of Job, Job's wife is named Sitis. LXX assigns to her a much longer speech: "After much time had passed his wife said to him, 'How long will you endure, saying, "Behold, I shall wait a little longer, expecting the hope of my salvation." Behold, your memory is already blotted out from the earth, the sons and daughters, the travail and pangs of my womb, whom I reared with toil in vain. And you sit in decay caused by worms, spending the nights outside, and I am a wanderer and a servant, going from place to place and from house to house, looking for the sun to set, in order that I might rest from my toils and pains which now oppress me. But say some word against the Lord and die.'"

8. See n.5 above.

desired that his cursing God would shorten his misery, for she too was suffering and desperately wanted to end her husband's pain.

His wife's appeal was more trying to Job than the losses themselves, for she spoke out of the strong emotional, marital bond between them. She put into words the essence of her husband's temptation: it is folly to adhere staunchly to one's integrity in the face of such tragedy. According to her view, to compromise one's faith in God in order to ease an intolerable burden is the wisest course to follow. On earth she echoed the Satan's skepticism about human faith in God—"all that a man has will he give for his own life." But if Job followed such a course, it would produce disastrous results. It would undermine the very foundation of his faithful service.

10 With the sternest determination possible Job rebuked his wife. Giving no place to her suggestion, he labeled her counsel as that which comes from *one of the foolish women* (Heb. *ʾaḥaṯ hannᵉḇālôṯ*). Heb. *nāḇāl* is the strongest Hebrew word for "fool." It denotes one who completely renounces God's ways.[9] Thus Job declared her counsel to be utter folly. Thus he turned his back on finding a false way of escape from his suffering and expressed his unwavering allegiance to God.

Then with an aphorism in the form of a question Job puts his wife on the defensive. To rebuff her he asked, *Shall we accept good* [or abundance, Heb. *ṭôḇ*] *from God and not misfortune* [or evil, Heb. *rāʿ*]? Job knows that the faithful must express their trust in God regardless of the circumstances that befall them. The verb *accept* (Heb. *qibbēl*) describes an active, positive participation in what God decrees, not mere passive reception. Job's total submission to God for good or for ill is clear in his response. By his rebuke he renounced his wife's foolish counsel and also sought to prevent his wife from becoming a foolish woman.

The outcome of this state of Job's trial is succinctly stated: *In all this Job did not sin with his lips*. The *lips* express a person's deepest thoughts (cf. Prov. 18:4). Consequently when one strives for moral purity they are the hardest member to bring under control. They are obstinate to discipline. That is why the Wisdom tradition taught that the one who controls his speech has his whole life in focus (Prov. 13:3; 21:23; cf. Jas. 3:2). Therefore to say that Job did not sin with his lips is to state unequivocally that Job did not commit the slightest error. Whereas God had declared prior to this testing that Job was without sin, this statement asserts that Job had come thus far through his trial unscathed by any wrongdoing.

9. As the psalmist says: "The fool says in his heart, 'There is no God'" (Ps. 14:1a).

F. THE ARRIVAL OF THE THREE COMFORTERS (2:11–13)

11 *When Job's three friends, Eliphaz the Temanite, Bildad the Shuhite, and Zophar the Naamathite, heard of all this misfortune that had come*[1] *on him, each set out from his place and they agreed together to go to console and to comfort him.*

12 *When they saw him from a distance, they could not recognize him. They raised their voices and wept; each tore his robe, and they tossed dust into the air and on their heads.*

13 *Then they sat with him on the ground seven days and seven nights. No one spoke a word, because they saw that his suffering was very great.*

This last scene introduces Job's three friends and sets the stage for the dialogue.

11 On learning of Job's affliction, three beloved *friends* (Heb. *rēaʿ*), Eliphaz, Bildad, and Zophar, *agreed together* to travel to Uz in order *to console* Job. The term for *friends* has a wide range of meanings, including an intimate counselor (1 Chr. 27:33), a close friend (Deut. 13:7 [Eng. 6]), a party in a legal dispute (Exod. 22:8 [Eng. 9]).[2] Friends often solemnized their relationship with a covenant, promising to care for each other under all kinds of circumstances. The relationship between Job and his three friends gives every evidence of being based on a covenant (6:14–15, 21–23, 27). Such a relationship was characterized by loyal love (*ḥeseḏ;* e.g., Jonathan and David, 1 Sam. 20:14–15). Motivated by love and their commitment, these men came *to console* and *to comfort* Job. The word *to console* (Heb. *nûḏ*) means literally "to shake the head or to rock the body back and forth" as a sign of shared grief. *To comfort* (Heb. *niḥam*) is to attempt to ease the deepest pain caused by a tragedy or death (e.g., 2 Sam. 12:24; Isa. 66:13). With the noblest intentions, these three earnestly desired to help Job bear his sorrow.

Eliphaz, meaning "God is fine gold," came from *Teman,* "the south land," a principal site in the northern region of Edom (Ezek. 25:13).[3] His identification with Edom fits his role in the speeches as a wise man, for

1. The accent on *habbāʾâ,* "that had come," indicates that it is a perfect verb form with the article functioning as the relative pronoun (GKC, §§ 138i, k).

2. N. Habel, "Only the Jackal Is My Friend," *Int* 31 (1977) 227–36, esp. p. 228.

3. In the patriarchal genealogies Eliphaz was the oldest son of Esau (Gen. 36:4, 10, 12, 15) and Teman was Eliphaz's son (36:11, 15). Cf. Jer. 49:7; Amos 1:11–12; Obad. 9.

Edom was well known for its excellence in wisdom (cf. Jer. 49:7; Obad. 8).[4] *Bildad,*[5] possibly meaning "son of Hadad," lived in *Shuah.*[6] Akkadian documents mention a district Sūḫu, located on the Middle Euphrates River, below the mouth of the Khabur River.[7] Pope thinks that the biblical genealogies place Shuah farther to the south, since it is connected with Dedan and Sheba. *Zophar,* meaning "young bird," came from *Naamah.* Naamah was a female descendant of Cain (Gen. 4:22), and Solomon married an Ammonite princess by this name (1 K. 14:21). A possible identification for Zophar's home is the site ʿAin Ṣopar on the road between Beirut and Damascus.[8]

12, 13 When these friends caught their first glimpse of Job from afar, they were aghast. All of Job's former estate, which once dominated the landscape, had been devastated, and Job himself was scarcely recognizable, his body being so disfigured. Overcome with grief, they wept aloud and rent their mantles. They threw *dust,*[9] symbolic of disease and death, *into the air.* The Hebrew expression is curious; literally, "they threw dust on their heads heavenward."[10] This gesture expressed the depth of their sorrow at such horrifying affliction. Then they sat in silence for seven days and seven nights.[11] This length of time signified the intensity of their sorrow, for such was the period of mourning at the death of a most notable figure (cf. Gen. 50:10; 1 Sam. 31:13).

4. R. H. Pfeiffer, "Edomitic Wisdom," *ZAW* 44 (1926) 13–25.

5. Bildad may be a shortened form of a type of an Amorite name such as *Yabil-Dad(a)* (W. F. Albright, *JBL* 54 [1935] 174n.3; idem, "The Name of Bildad the Shuhite," *AJSL* 44 [1927–28] 31–36; E. A. Speiser, "On the Name Bildad," *JAOS* 49 [1929] 360; idem, "The Name Bildad," *AfO* 6 [1930–31] 23).

6. Shuah may have been a tribal name that became attached to a place. A certain Shuah was born to Abraham by Keturah, a concubine (Gen. 25:2).

7. W. F. Albright (*JBL* 57 [1938] 228).

8. Ibid. Albright mentions another location, a place named Supru on the Middle Euphrates near Mari.

9. Such dry, fine dust was associated with causing the plague of boils that afflicted the Egyptians at the time of the Exodus (Exod. 9:8–10). There may be some symbolic connection between dust and the nature of Job's malady.

10. C. Houtman ("Zu Hiob 2:12," *ZAW* 90 [1978] 269–70) thinks that MT *ʿl-rʾšyhm* means "over their heads," not "upon their heads." While this view removes the tension between the two phrases, it seems more likely that the friends put some dust on themselves to identify with Job. Houtman also suggests that throwing dust toward heaven was an act to entreat God to cover the sources of Job's affliction with dust. Gordis cites B. Elzas for the interpretation that the throwing of dust over one's head was an apotropaic rite to ward off any evil attack. But the context suggests that it was an act of sympathy, not a rite to ward off danger.

11. Ezekiel also sat in silence for seven days, overpowered by his vision of the divine cherub (Ezek. 3:14–15).

2:11–13 The Arrival of the Three Comforters

The seven-day period functions as a turning point in the dramatic action of the account. The atmosphere was tense. Nobody spoke. Job's pain was visibly unbearable. Then like a thunderclap Job's lament broke the silence.

II. JOB'S CURSE-LAMENT (3:1–26)

Aside from the heading (vv. 1–2), ch. 3 is usually divided into three parts: Job's curse on the day of his birth (vv. 3–10); a personal lament (vv. 11–19); a complaint (vv. 20–26). But M. Fishbane's study on the nature of curses has significant implications for understanding the structure of ch. 3.[1] He has shown that the curse itself is contained in vv. 3–13.[2] Therefore the speech has two parts: Job's curse on the day of his birth (vv. 3–13) and a lament (vv. 14–26). Further support for dividing the chapter at v. 13 is the parallel imagery and language in vv. 13 and 26. In both sections Job expresses his ardent longing for inner rest. Also, vv. 11–13 are balanced by vv. 24–26; in

1. M. Fishbane, "Jeremiah iv:23–26 and Job iii:3–13: A recovered use of the creation pattern," *VT* 21 (1971) 151–67. For the structure of the curse see the Excursus below. Cf. also D. Cox, "The Desire of Oblivion in Job 3," *Studii Biblici Franciscani, Liber Annuus* 23 (1973) 37–49; D. N. Freedman, "The Structure of Job 3," *Bib* 49 (1968) 503–508.

2. A close parallel to Job 3:3–13 is Jer. 20:14–18:

v. 3a = Jer. 20:14
v. 3b = Jer. 20:15
vv. 7, 8 similar to Jer. 20:16
v. 10 = Jer. 20:17
v. 11 = Jer. 20:18.

Both men curse the day of their birth. Both suffer from "trouble" (*'āmāl;* Job 3:10; Jer. 20:18) and "sorrow" (*yāgôn;* Jer. 20:18; cf. Job 3:20). Although both bear their burden in obedience to God, they desire to be freed from their painful agony. In contrast to Job, Jeremiah had been forewarned by God that he would experience persecution from his fellow countrymen for preaching a message of doom (Jer. 1:17–19). Both sought relief by cursing the day of their origin. The self-curse in Job is more intricately developed. It is cast in the style of reverse magic. Thus there is no longer the need for the formula "cursed is . . ." (*'ārûr)* as in Jer. 20:14, 15. But in Job's self-curse the author of Job incorporates questions about the cause of his suffering, and such questions are indicative of a lament. The joining of these two elements in both texts suggests that the question *why* may be an integral part of this kind of self-curse.

Since the curse in Job is longer and more complex, one might assume that the author of Job is dependent on the Jeremiah passage. It is more likely, however, that both authors drew on the genre of the self-curse independently. The more complex form may be due not to its lateness but to the author's purpose.

them Job describes his sorrowful state. And vv. 3–10 along with vv. 14–23 have Job searching for death.[3] Finally, these two divisions consist of 26 lines each.[4] The chapter then may be classified as a curse-lament.[5]

Moreover, this curse-lament is not the first speech of the dialogue. The friends are not at all in the purview of Job's thinking. Rather, it is a word that expresses Job's basic wish that God would grant him immediate relief from his suffering. Though set apart, this speech sets the stage for a response from the three friends. The friends may now enter to console and instruct Job.

Overcome by dismay yet observant of tradition, Job's friends offer consolation in sympathetic silence, waiting for Job to speak. Job at last breaks the silence. The words that gush forth from his agitated soul surprise everyone. His words are bold and caustic. Wishing that he had never been born, Job curses the day of his birth.

A. JOB'S CURSE OF THE DAY OF HIS BIRTH (3:1–13)

1 *Afterward Job opened his mouth*
and cursed the day of his birth.
2 *Job said:*

3. One of the great enigmas of the chapter is v. 16. It interrupts two portions dealing with the inhabitants of Sheol. Many commentators either eliminate it as an editorial expansion or place it earlier: Duhm puts it after v. 11, Dhorme after v. 12. But it is hard to imagine that any editor would place v. 16 so far out of context. If it is out of place, it must be a scribal error. The possibility that this verse is in place is accepted by a few: D. N. Freedman ("The Structure of Job 3," *Bib* 49 [1968] 504–505) thinks that v. 16 introduces the conditions among the dead as given in vv. 17–19, just as vv. 11–12 lead to vv. 13–15. While this bicolon seemingly interrupts the flow, it reflects the disturbed state of Job's thoughts and it ties the lament to the curse. It also states that the goal of his lament is to die as soon as possible.

4. Cf. Freedman, op. cit.

5. While this speech has been classified as a self-lament (C. Westermann, *Structure of the Book of Job,* pp. 37–38), the curse structure of vv. 3–13 constitutes an obstacle to this classification. Through a lament a worshiper implores God to deliver him out of his trouble, but he does not request that his existence be annihilated as Job does in the first half of this speech. To overcome this objection Westermann reasons that vv. 3–9 stand for that element of a lament in which the petitioner derides his enemies; in this instance Job's enemy is the day of his birth. This suggestion, though possible, seems somewhat forced. More likely, these verses are a special kind of curse, a counter-cosmic incantation designed to remove a specific day from the calendar, in this case the day of Job's birth. The poet has woven this incantation together with the language of a personal lament and created a new genre, a curse-lament.

3 *"Perish the day when I was born,*
the night[1] which[2] said,[3] 'A male is conceived.'[4]
4 *That day—let it be darkness!*
Let not God above attend to it;
let not a ray of light shine on it.
5 *May darkness and deep dark claim[5] it;*
may a cloud mass[6] settle over it;
may the blackness of day terrify it.
6 *That night—let gloom seize it!*
Let it not be counted[7] among the days of the year;
let it not enter the number of months.
7 *Behold,[8] that night—let it be sterile!*
Let no joyful shout enter it.
8 *Let those who curse the day curse it,*
those prepared to stir up Leviathan.
9 *Let the stars of its twilight[9] be darkened;*
let it hope for light, but have none,
nor see[10] the first rays of dawn,
10 *because it did not shut[11] the doors of my mother's womb,[12]*
or hide trouble from my sight.

1. The article on *hallaylâ,* "the night," may be secondary, having arisen under the influence of the article on *hayyôm,* "the day," in v. 4.

2. The night is personified as speaking. A relative pronoun is assumed before the verb *'āmar,* "he said"; a similar style appears in the first colon, which does not have a relative pronoun before MT *'iwwālēḏ,* "I was born."

3. A. Ehrmann ("A Note on the Verb *'āmar,*" *JQR* 55 [1964] 166–67) takes *'āmar* here to mean "curse."

4. MT *hôrâ,* "is conceived," is most likely an example of a Qal passive perfect (Gordis).

5. Some posit a Hebrew root *g'l* II, "be defiled," related to *gʿl* II, "loathe." But the parallel relationship of *drš,* "seek," and *g'l* I, "claim, redeem," as in Isa. 62:12, favors the root *g'l* I here.

6. *ʿanānâ,* "cloud mass," may have been chosen for assonance with *nehārâ,* "a ray of light" (v. 4).

7. MT *yiḥaḏ* is pointed as though it comes from the root *ḥdh,* "rejoice." But in this context it seems best to revocalize it *yēḥaḏ* from *yḥd,* "be counted," as in Gen. 49:6; see *BHS.* Cf. L. Grabbe, *Comparative Philology and the Text of Job: A Study in Methodology,* SBLDS 34 (Missoula: Scholars Press, 1977), pp. 32–35.

8. Syr. and Vulg. omit MT *hinnēh,* "behold." The line is long, and Horst may be correct in eliminating it.

9. *nešep* may refer either to the twilight at dusk (Job 24:15; Isa. 5:11; Prov. 7:9) or at dawn (Job 7:4; Ps. 119:147).

10. MT *yir'eh,* "see," does not have to be emended to a jussive, *yērē',* for as Dhorme points out, the imperfect is often used for the jussive in *lamed-he* verbs (GKC, § 109a n.2).

11. The subject of *sāgar,* "close," may be indefinite, but in the context it appears to be the night.

12. *biṭnî* (lit. "my womb") is elliptical for "the womb in which I lay."

11 *Why did I not die at birth,*
expire as I came from the womb?
12 *Why did the knees receive me,*
and the breasts that I should suck?
13 *For now I would be lying down and quiet;*
I would be asleep and at rest."

1, 2 This chapter has a special heading (v. 1) before the standard introductory formula of the other speeches (v. 2).[13] The first introduction notes the dramatic shift from Job's silence to his speaking with the sentence, *Job opened his mouth.* Then the nature of Job's speech is defined: he *cursed [qālal] the day of his birth [yômô].*[14] This wording indicates that the curse, rather than the lament, dominates this speech.

Job curses the day of his birth (vv. 3a, 4–5) and the night of his conception (vv. 3b, 6–7) as a single entity. For that reason he entreats the greatest wizards (v. 8) to keep light from giving life to that day (vv. 8–9) and allowing his birth (v. 10). The motivation for his curse lies in the agonizing questions about his being allowed to live in order to experience such pain (vv. 11–12) and not experience the peaceful rest similar to God's on the seventh day of creation (v. 13).

Job wishes that he had never been born, but the only way that such a wish could be realized would be to have the day of his birth removed from the calendar. As long as the day of his birth is recreated every year, his existence continues until his death. But if that day never had been created, he would never have existed. The only way for the day of his birth to be removed from the calendar is to have it removed from the yearly cycle through a counter-cosmic incantation, a spell designed to turn cosmic order, in this case a day ruled by the light of life, into chaos, a gap of time dominated by darkness. A counter-cosmic incantation reverses the stages God took in creating the world. It was believed that God created each day in the same way that he created the world (Gen. 1:1–2:4). Thus every day, being a new creation, bore witness to God's lordship and his creative powers. In contrast, chaos is an unorganized and lifeless mass of water overshadowed by total darkness (cf. Gen. 1:2). But since the day of Job's birth had already been created, the only way that Job might vanish would be to have that day returned to the primordial chaos. If no light had shone on that day, there would have been no life, no birth, particularly Job's. With this spell Job seeks to become totally nonexistent.

13. Verse 2 is unnecessary in the light of v. 1. Either v. 1 was added as a heading to the first speech, or, more likely, v. 2 was a secondary heading added in an effort to level out all the speeches.

14. "His day," *yômô,* means his birthday; cf. Gen. 40:20; Jer. 20:14; Eccl. 7:1.

It should be noted that in his desire for death Job never entertains the option of suicide. Suicide was not acceptable for the person of faith, because it signified that one had lost all hope in God. Having this strong conviction, Job can seek relief from his pain in death only through having the day of his birth removed from time or prompting God to send him to Sheol.

3 Job's curse encompasses both *the day* of birth and *the night* of conception. Those two moments together constitute his origin and are thus inseparable. Ancient thought drew on an analogical approach to life, current today in many parts of the world but foreign to those who adopt a scientific outlook. A magical perspective plus the freedom germane to poetic imagery push the thoughts of these lines beyond the boundary of reality for a modern person. From Job's perspective, though, to eliminate these moments would make it as though he had never been born.

In this verse Job refers to himself as a *male (geḇer).*[15] The several Hebrew words for "man" emphasize various aspects of his being, e.g., *'îš,* his strength, or *'āḏām,* his earthiness and limitedness (cf. *'ᵃḏāmâ,* "earth, ground"), but *geḇer* connotes a powerful man, particularly in contrast to a child or a woman. In the darkest hour of his crisis, Job refers to himself as a full-blooded, stalwart person. Thus his curse is not designed to eliminate from the human race a weakling unworthy of dignity. Rather he views himself as a distinguished person who has been shamed by misfortune.

4 In seeking to remove the day of his birth from existence Job commands, *That day—let it be darkness!* This curse directly counters God's first words in creating the world, "Let there be light" (Gen. 1:3). Any day or block of time that remained in darkness never came into being. That is the reason Job piles up words for darkness in vv. 4–6: *darkness* (*ḥōšeḵ,* vv. 4a, 5a), *deep dark* (*ṣalmāweṯ,* v. 5a),[16] *cloud mass* (*ʿᵃnānâ,* v. 5b), *blackness* (*kamrîr,* v. 5c),[17] *gloom* (*'ōpel,* v. 6a).

15. See H. Kosmala, "The Term *geber* in the Old Testament and in the Scrolls," in *Congress Volume: Rome 1968,* VTSup 17 (Leiden: Brill, 1969), pp. 159–69.

16. *ṣalmāweṯ* used to be taken most often as a compound word, *ṣēl* + *māweṯ,* and translated lit., "shadow of death" (so AV). Others (e.g., Dhorme; KB, p. 964) posited the revocalization *ṣalmûṯ,* i.e., it is the combination of a word for darkness, *ṣelem* (cognate of Akk. *ṣalāmu,* "be dark") plus the abstract ending *-ûṯ.* But D. W. Thomas ("*Ṣalmawet* in the Old Testament," *JSS* 7 [1962] 191–200) argues that *māweṯ,* "death," possesses superlative force; thus he explains that the expression "shadow of death" means "very deep shadow, thick darkness." It is the darkness encountered in a mineshaft (28:3) or in the region of the dead (10:21–22; 38:17). Amos also uses this term to refer to the darkness prior to creation (5:8). In Job 28:3 and 10:22 *'ōpel,* "gloom," accompanies *ṣalmāweṯ.*

17. It seems best to understand MT *kimrîrê* as a noun form from a root *kmr,* "be black," hence "blackness" (cf. Syr.). Grabbe (*Comparative Philology,* pp. 29–31) seriously doubts this position; the cognate evidence is weak and the Syriac root means "be sad, mourn." He also notes that *bmryry ywm,* "bitterness of the day," appears in Sir. 11:4 and *bmrwry ywm* (a slight variant with the same meaning) in the Thanksgiving Hymn,

Job reinforces this injunction by entreating: *Let not God above attend to it; let not a ray of light shine on it*. God's exalted lordship is stressed by the phrase *above* (cf. 31:2, 28; Deut. 4:39). Whatever God *attends to* or seeks *(dāraš)* realizes its fullest potential.[18] Conversely, what God fails to attend to or support perishes. To make sure that day returns to chaos Job says, *Let not a ray of light shine on it*. Where there is no light there is no life. All is stagnant and dormant.

5 Job continues his curse by charging the powers of darkness to *claim* the day of his birth. If they hold it fast, that day would cease to exist. A massive cloud cover *(ʿᵃnānâ)* would *settle over* the world, snuffing out any ray of light. The resulting *blackness (kamrîr)* would *terrify (bāʿaṯ)* that day, i.e., it would keep it imprisoned by fear. The word *terrify* denotes the feeling of dread one experiences in confronting the numinous or the spirit world. It is an uncanny feeling that causes every fiber of one's being to shudder, leaving one powerless. If this incantation is effective, that day would never rise again from the sterile blackness of chaos.

6, 7 Job next addresses the night of his conception. It was a night when life was conceived, life that challenged the disordered lifelessness of darkness. That is, each birth participates in the victory of cosmos over the forces of chaos. In celebration of that victory a *joyful shout (rᵉnānâ)* breaks the stillness of the night, proclaiming that a new life has been conceived and darkness has been defeated (v. 7). But the hopeful expectation of that moment has eventuated in the bitter pain of Job's present suffering. Therefore, Job orders the *gloom (ʾōpel)* of primeval thick darkness to *seize* or abduct that night. If gloom has its way, that night would no longer be counted among the days of the year or enter the number of months. Job also directs a curse to rob the night of his conception of all its fertility. He asks that it *be sterile (galmûḏ)* like rocky soil that fails to yield crops no matter

---

1QH 5:34 (cf. M. Mansoor, "Thanksgiving Hymns and Massoretic Text," *RevQ* 3 [1961–62] 259–66), which for him "leaves no alternative" that the root must be *mrr*, not *kmr*. But the parallelism suggests that *kimrîrê* is the subject of the verb and that it connotes some type of darkness. Dhorme associates it with the mist or fog that hides the sun. Influenced by Rashi and Ibn Ezra, Gordis finds here "the demons of the day." He thinks that *mᵉrîrê* is related to Arab. *mara*, "pass, pass by," and refers to demons in flight. He takes the *kap*, then, as the asseverative *kap*, also known in Ugaritic (R. Gordis, "The Asseverative Kaph in Hebrew and Ugaritic," *JAOS* 63 [1943] 176–78).

18. According to Isa. 62:12, the New Jerusalem will be called, "Sought Out, a City Not Forsaken." God will create the New Jerusalem and establish its environment so that the genuine people of God will worship and live there to the full extent of their created glory. Thus "sought out" in reference to God means that he is present, caring for a place, endowing it with qualities he intended it to have when he created it, i.e., full and complete salvation (e.g., Deut. 11:12; Jer. 30:17); cf. S. Wagner, *"dārash," TDOT*, III:304–305.

how carefully it is tended. If such were the case, no ecstatic shout of joy would *enter* or disrupt that night.

8 To ensure the vitality of his curse Job importunes the most skilled sorcerers in the ancient world to perform the curse against the day of his birth.[19] These sorcerers are known as *those prepared to stir up Leviathan,*[20] the monster that inhabits the sea and that is the personification of all forces that resist God's rule. Leviathan continually seeks to turn beauty into dust and order into confusion. Whoever possessed the magical arts to arouse him could activate the curses of destruction against anything good and noble. That wizard could even curse a specific day and thus annihilate the existence of one who had been born on that day. Job is hereby seeking to invoke the most clandestine powers to accomplish his own annihilation.

9 Job continues his imprecations by cursing *the first rays of dawn* (lit. "eyelids of the dawn") that begin to etch their way across the horizon and *the stars of its twilight,* Venus and Mercury, which shine brightly and announce the end of night. These first signs of light on the horizon foreshadow a new victory of light over darkness. A new day is beginning to be created. Job pronounces this curse to prevent that victory from taking place. If his curse is effective, the night will continue to reign. Light will never shine on that day.

10 Job gives the reason for cursing the day of his birth: *because it* [the forces of nature] *did not shut the doors of my mother's womb, or hide trouble from my sight.* The metaphor of shutting the doors of a womb is used both for preventing conception (Gen. 29:31) and for keeping an embryo from coming forth to life (Job 38:8). If this metaphor goes with the night of conception, the shut womb means that he would not have been conceived

19. The phrase "ones who curse the day" is variously emended. The most popular view is to read "sea" *(yām)* for "day" *(yôm)* (see *BHS*). In Ugaritic myths *Yamm,* or Sea, is the primordial god of chaos that the head of the pantheon must vanquish in order to rule. Yamm thus serves as a fine parallel to Leviathan, the deep-sea monster, for Yamm and Rahab, a creature similar to Leviathan, are parallel in 26:12. But Gordis observes that in the Ugaritic literature those who would curse *yām* are allies of the positive forces trying to defeat chaos. He therefore emends *ʾōrᵉrê,* "those who curse," to *ʿōrᵉrê,* "those who stir up," the same word that comes in the second line. But since this interpretation requires a double emendation, the present text is preferred, taking the second line as a specification of the first. Further, M. Fishbane ("Jeremiah iv:23–26 and Job iii:3–13: A recovered use of the creation pattern," *VT* 21 [1971] 160–61) finds a double entendre in *yôm,* "day," and *yām,* "sea," and he points out that *ʾōrᵉrê,* "those who curse," alludes to *ʿōrēr,* "one who stirs up," and *ʿôr(rî),* "light." This use of assonance and wordplay heightens the magical impact of the curse. Cf. E. Ullendorff, "Job iii:8," *VT* 11 (1961) 350–51. Finally, some interpreters (e.g., Hölscher, Driver-Gray) find here an allusion either to the myth of the Dragon causing eclipses by swallowing the sun or the moon or to the primordial myth in which the ruling god defeats the monsters of chaos.

20. For more on Leviathan see the commentary below on 40:25 (Eng. 41:1).

(1 Sam. 1:5; cf. Gen. 16:2; 20:18). But if it refers to the day of birth, it means that he would have been stillborn. Either way Job would not have experienced the trauma of leaving the warm, comfortable environment of his mother's womb to experience the *trouble (ʿāmāl)*[21] that has befallen him in the world of light.

11, 12 In agony Job asks, *Why did I not die at birth?* If he had been given no breath, he would have expired as he came from the womb. He would simply have been transported from the womb to the grave. Next Job asks, *Why did the knees,* most likely his father's, but possibly his mother's, *receive him?*[22] In holding the newborn the parents bind themselves to the child, signifying their acceptance of the infant and the responsibility of raising the baby. *and the breasts that I should suck?* He wishes that he had been discarded, left to die unattended.

13 *For now I would be lying down and quiet; I would be asleep and at rest.* Job expresses the intent of this curse—he wants to be at rest. This rest recalls the ideal rest that God experienced on the seventh day of the week of creation (Gen. 2:1–3). If Job had such rest, he certainly would not be in such a state of turmoil. Instead he would lie down and drift off into restful sleep.[23] All around him would be quiet; nothing would disturb his slumber. The intensity of his longing for rest is indicated by the use of four different terms: *lie down (šāḵaḇ), quiet (šāqaṭ), sleep (yāšēn),* and *rest (nûaḥ).* Perfect rest is the goal of Job's curse-lament, for v. 13 is reiterated in v. 26.

B. A LAMENT (3:14–26)

14 *"—with kings and counselors of the earth,*
who built ruins for themselves,

21. Job uses *ʿāmāl,* "trouble," as a key word for his plight (4:8; 5:6, 7; 7:3; 11:16; 15:35; 16:2; cf. Habel, OTL). It refers to the agony or the misery caused by severe hardship, such as slavery (Deut. 26:7) or cruel suffering (Isa. 53:11). It also denotes the fatigue that comes from great exertion, as well as the pain and toil that attend one's striving toward goals. Furthermore, Habel (OTL) points out that this word stands for burdensome troubles caused by evil minds (Ps. 94:20; Prov. 24:1–2) or for an evil deed itself (Hab. 1:13). Gordis observes that the friends use it for "doing evil" (4:8; 15:35), while for Job it means "suffering evil or misery."

22. Cf. B. Stade, "Auf Jemandes Knieen gebaren," *ZAW* 6 (1886) 143–56. Although taking a child on the knees may be a father's act to show his acceptance of and concern for his child (Gen. 50:23b; cf. 30:3), it often refers to the motherly custom of gladly taking up the newborn infant to nurse it (cf. Isa. 66:12). She thus recognizes it as her own and commits herself to its nurture and upbringing.

23. The sequence of two verbs in the perfect followed by the imperfect suggests what Job's present state would be if he had had the quiet of a still birth (see GKC, § 106p).

15 *or with princes who had gold,*
who filled their houses with silver.
16 *Or as a discarded miscarriage, I would not be,*
or as infants who never see the light.
17 *There[1] the wicked cease turmoil;*
there the weary have rest;
18 *also prisoners are at ease;*
they hear not the taskmaster's shout.
19 *Small and great alike are there,*
and a servant is free from his master.[2]
20 *Why is light given[3] to the wretched,*
and life to the bitter of soul,
21 *to those who long for death and it comes not,*
and dig[4] for it more than for hidden treasures,
22 *to those who rejoice exceedingly[5]*
and are elated when they find a grave?
23 *To a man whose way is hid,*
whom God has fenced in?

1. The netherworld is referred to in an oblique way by the adverb "there" *(šām)* in vv. 17 and 19.

2. A. C. Blommerde (*Northwest Semitic Grammar and Job,* BibOr 22 [Rome: Pontifical Biblical Institute, 1969], p. 39) finds three different classes in the second line: "slave, freedman, and master." He takes the *mem* on *mēʾᵃḏōnāyw,* "from his master," as an enclitic *mem* and joins it to *ḥopšî,* "free." The parallelism between "small" and "slave," "great" and "lord" is against this possibility.

3. Heb. *yittēn,* "it gives," is indefinite and acts like a passive (Gordis). Driver-Gray indicate that God is the implied subject; thus it is better to follow MT than to emend it to a passive as the versions and Duhm do.

4. The participle in the first line may be continued in the second by an imperfect with a *waw* consecutive (GKC, § 116x).

5. The phrase *ʾĕlê-gîl,* "rejoice exceedingly," is contested. The preposition *ʾĕlê* is a poetic form of *ʾel,* "to," only in Job 5:26; 15:22; 29:19. The phrase *ʾel-gîl* occurs in Hos. 9:1, unfortunately a disputed passage. The parallelism with *qeḇer,* "grave," suggests that *gîl* has something to do with a grave. Duhm and Pope emend MT to Heb. *gal,* "a heap," which appears in Josh. 7:26; 8:29; and 2 Sam. 18:17 in the phrase *gal-ʾᵃḇānîm,* "a heap of stones"; but it is questionable whether *gal* alone can mean grave (cf. A. Guillaume, "The Arabic Background of the Book of Job," in *Promise and Fulfilment: Essays Presented to Professor S. H. Hooke,* ed. F. F. Bruce [Edinburgh: T. & T. Clark, 1963], p. 110, who connects it to Arab. *gâl,* "interior side of a grave"). Grabbe (*Comparative Philology,* pp. 38–41) finds support for "grave" insufficient and prefers MT. In favor of this view is the parallelism of *šmḫ/śmḥ* and *gl* in Ugaritic and Hebrew; cf. Hab. 1:15 and *RSP,* I:354, no. 549g. The question then is which use of parallelism is preferable. Perhaps both parallelisms are operative, with the initial one dominating, for it is possible that there is a wordplay with the primary meaning of *gîl,* "rejoice," going with the first line and the homonym meaning "grave" pointing to the second line (see Guillaume, Gordis).

24 *For my shrieks come as*[6] *my bread;*
my groanings pour out like water.[7]
25 *What I most dreaded has come*[8] *on me,*
and what I feared befalls me.
26 *I have no ease,*[9] *I am not quiet;*
I have no rest, for turmoil comes."

14, 15 Building on v. 13, Job turns from cursing the day of his birth to lamenting his agony. This shift is noted by a dash at the head of v. 14. He begins his lament by longing for the rest that Sheol offers. Job idealizes the existence of those great men who have already passed on. In Sheol he would join *kings and counselors of the earth,* i.e., high state officials, and *princes.*[10] Counselors are closely identified with kings, for such wise men served the king in giving guidance on matters of state (e.g., 2 Sam. 15:30–37; 16:15–17:23).

These great men *built ruins for themselves.* The meaning of *ruins* (*ḥ^{o}rāḇôṯ*) is disputed. Some (e.g., Davidson, Horst, Gordis) take it to refer to cities or other great monuments lying in severe disrepair (cf. Isa. 44:26; 58:12). Frequently a great leader promoted his greatness by rebuilding a famous ruin. By such a deed he extended his authority over that which an enemy had subjugated, even over a place inhabitated by evil spirits. Others think *ruins* refers to the monumental tombs that kings and princes built as their resting place in death. These tombs are called ruins because they were usually left unattended and slowly deteriorated. In support of taking *ruins* as tombs is the parallel term *houses* in v. 15b (cf. 17:13; 30:23; Eccl. 12:5, where "house" stands for Sheol) and the use of this word in association with

6. The preposition *lip̱nê,* "before," is taken to mean "like, as," by reason of its being parallel to *k^e,* "like" (cf. 4:19; 1 Sam. 1:16); so also Dhorme, Horst, and G. R. Driver ("Linguistic and Textual Problems: Jeremiah," *JQR* 28 [1937–38] 122). Another possible meaning is "instead of" (Driver-Gray).

7. "Water" most likely refers to a drink since it is parallel to "bread" or food (cf. Ps. 80:6 [Eng. 5]). Various OT texts associate suffering with bread and water (1 K. 22:27; Ezek. 12:18; Ps. 42:4 [Eng. 3]; 80:6 [Eng. 5]; 102:10 [Eng. 9]; see A. de Wilde, *Das Buch Hiob,* OTS 22 [Leiden: Brill, 1981], p. 101). Other interpreters take "water" to refer to the roaring of a waterfall or a turbulent ocean; then it would refer to the loudness of Job's groanings. Horst takes it to mean that Job's sorrow is as continuous as a flowing stream.

8. Here a common Aramaic word, *ʾ^{a}ṯâ,* "come," is used to parallel a Hebrew synonym, *bôʾ,* "come, befall." This pattern occurs a few other times in the book, e.g., 16:19.

9. The verb *šālawtî,* "I have ease," is written as a *lamed-waw* rather than a *lamed-he* verb, for the *waw* is retained as a strong consonant in some of its forms (GKC, § 75b).

10. The listing together of kings, counselors, and princes also appears in Ezra 7:28 and 8:25 (Horst).

"the pit," the realm of the dead, in Ezek. 26:20. In that case Job is alluding particularly to the motivation that inspired the building of them; i.e., it was believed that the inhabitants of these monuments, regardless of their state of disrepair, had a more peaceful existence in death than the masses who were living. To enhance their existence after death these rich, powerful leaders filled their tombs with valuable objects, including *gold* and *silver.* Along this line many postulate that Job has in mind the great pyramids around which the nobles built smaller pyramid-like tombs to ensure a place in the afterlife for themselves.[11] Lamentingly Job longs for that kind of rest.

16 Job leaves the description of the bliss of Sheol momentarily as he interjects his wish that he might have been *a discarded miscarriage* (*nēpel ṭāmûn;* cf. vv. 11–12). Although this verse appears to be out of place, it may be a reinforcement of his basic desire never to have lived. Job wishes that he would have fallen out of his mother's womb and been cast aside. That lump of organic mass would have been disposed of as though it had no significance. Then he would never have experienced his present distress.

17, 18 Returning to his theme that there is complete rest for the weary in Sheol, Job believes that here all those who are accustomed to stirring up trouble are quiet. Everybody is in the same powerless, limp condition. Although there may be degrees of punishment in the afterlife, the earthly social structure that allows one to lord it over others or a taskmaster to beat his slaves into doing his bidding no longer exists. In Sheol there is no *turmoil (rōg̱ez)* to make one weary, not even for *the wicked (rᵉšāʿîm).* The Hebrew root *rgz* represents strong emotional agitation. It describes the consternation that a terrible ruler causes throughout the earth (Isa. 14:16) and the dreadful panic that a display of God's anger arouses among the populace (Joel 2:11; cf. Isa. 23:11). The wicked are noted for stirring up trouble and creating social havoc as they increase their wealth at the expense of others. In turn their lives are marked by turbulence. Full of apprehension, they explode in anger at any who would challenge them. But in Sheol their turmoil ceases.

also prisoners, i.e., those who have been conscripted into forced labor, either as criminals or as prisoners of war, *are at ease.* On earth they had spent their energies in exhausting labor driven by the *taskmaster's shout (qôl nōg̱ēś),* often accompanied by the stinging blows of his whip. But in Sheol they are released from these heavy burdens and relieved that they no longer hear these terrifying shouts.

11. Working in this direction, some emend *ḥᵒrāḇôṯ* to *hᵃrāmôṯ* on the basis of Arab. *hrm,* "be decayed," a root used by the Arabs to refer to the pyramid ruins (Fohrer and Horst; see *BHK;* cf. Driver-Gray). Fohrer thinks that *ḥᵒrāḇôṯ* is the Hebrew equivalent for the Arabic. Cf. Budde, Duhm, and Dhorme for other explanations.

19 The same restful conditions are for both *small and great.* Andersen points out that these two terms stand in chiastic relationship to the preceding verses: the small *(qāṭōn)* are the wicked of vv. 17–18, and the great *(gāḏôl)* are the kings, counselors, and princes of vv. 14–15. No one lords it over the other; no one is servant to the other. All are free from burdensome responsibilities. The slave is liberated from the demands of his master. The phrase *alike are there (šām hûʾ)* emphasizes that all of them, stripped of any superiority, are in the same predicament, not that they all have the same level of punishment (cf. Driver-Gray; Dhorme).

20–22 In the style of a lament Job asks another disturbing question: *Why is light given to the wretched, and life to the bitter of soul?* These unfortunate creatures are characterized as *wretched* or miserable *(ʿāmēl)* and *bitter of soul* (*mārê nep̄eš;* cf. 7:11; 10:1; 21:25; cf. also 2 Sam. 17:8; Ezek. 27:31). The Heb. *mar* denotes the biting dejection that attends a crushing defeat. Such a fate turns their disposition so sour that they find no joy in living. The light of a beautiful day only makes them more aware of their sorrows and increases their longing for death. Vainly they search for death more eagerly than prospectors who *dig for hidden treasures.* When they finally come to the grave, they *rejoice exceedingly and are elated.* There they find relief from their suffering. Job's question is a strong complaint against God. Since it is God who gives them life and allows them to suffer so, he should recognize their sad state and let them die, if he has any compassion at all.

23 Job applies his general complaint to his own situation. That is, the *why* of v. 20 is implied here: "Why are light and life given . . . *to a man whose way is hid?*" The word *way (dereḵ)* refers to his destiny. That it *is hid* means that in his present plight his life has no purpose. The losses that have befallen him have undercut any sense of meaning he has for life and have left him frustrated and miserable. Light and life, God's greatest gifts to any person, only serve to increase Job's despair beyond measure.

whom God has fenced in. Job imagines that God has surrounded him with a fence so that he cannot find any way of escape from his predicament.[12] His complaint here functions as an ironic twist to the Satan's suspicion (1:10). The Satan argued that God had fenced Job in to keep him safe from any harm and thus Job grew prosperous without any hindrances. But now an anguished Job complains that God has fenced him about to keep any help from reaching him. To Job it appears that God has locked him into turmoil and thrown away the key.

24 *My shrieks come as my bread; my groanings pour out like water*

12. Job also expresses his consternation that God has blocked his access to him in 19:8 (cf. Lam. 3:7; Hos. 2:8 [Eng. 6]).

(cf. Ps. 42:4 [Eng. 3]; 80:6 [Eng. 5]). Daily he must feed on these gruesome morsels. *shrieks (ʾanāḥâ)* is often translated "sighs," but that word is far too gentle in meaning. The Hebrew root refers to the loud moans or wails that arise from those doing oppressive, slave labor or from a people devastated by a tragedy (Exod. 2:23; Lam. 1:4, 8, 11, 21, 22). The shrieks of one afflicted wear out his body and keep him from finding any rest (Ps. 6:7 [Eng. 6]; 102:6 [Eng. 5]).[13] In the OT *groaning* (*šeʾāgâ,* lit. the growling of a lion; Job 4:10; Isa. 5:29) is often used figuratively for mighty sounds: Yahweh's thundering (Jer. 25:30; Amos 1:2), the bellowing of an army as it tears apart a monument (Ps. 74:4), the distressful cries of the afflicted (Ps. 22:2 [Eng. 1]; 32:3; cf. 38:9–10 [Eng. 8–9]).

25 Job laments: *What I most dreaded [paḥaḏ pāḥaḏtî] has come on me.*[14] This statement reveals that before his trial Job had dreaded that some ill might befall his household. His apprehensive nature was evident in his offering sacrifices periodically on behalf of his sons in case they had cursed God in their hearts (1:5). *and what I feared [yāḡar] befalls me.* He had also feared that some tragedy might end his prosperity. Heb. *yāḡar* refers to the apprehension aroused by the wanton hostility of a mighty foe, either earthly (Jer. 22:25) or divine (Deut. 9:19; cf. Job 9:28). Job's qualms about some foreboding calamity have become a terrifying reality.

26 Job concludes his lament with the assertion *I have no ease* (note that v. 26 parallels v. 13). His despondency over his lack of repose is underscored by the negation of three verbs (all in the perfect form) that speak of repose and a fourth verb that states what has happened. The use of the perfect forms suggests that the quality of the action connoted by the verbs is completely absent from Job's present state. Dhorme distinguishes the words as *ease (šālâ)* for mental rest, *quiet (šāqaṭ)* for physical rest, and *rest (nûaḥ)* for rest in general. That delineation may be somewhat artificial, but the rest Job desired encompasses both poise and tranquility. A person with a deep sense of serenity may enjoy life to its fullest. Conversely, one lacking repose is filled with deep agitation, which encompasses physical torment, agony of mind, and social discomfort. Such is Job's case. He exclaims, *turmoil comes!* The word for turmoil (*rōḡez;* cf. v. 17) describes the agitated state that results from complete lack of peace.

13. The words of Baruch, Jeremiah's scribe, are similar to Job's: "Woe is me! Yahweh has added grief to my pains. I am worn out with sighing *[ʾanāḥâ]* and I have no rest" (Jer. 45:3).

14. For a psychological treatment of Job's apprehension expressed in 3:25, see R. L. Katz, "A Psychoanalytic Commentary on Job 3:25," *HUCA* 29 (1958) 377–83.

AIM

These are the harshest words Job utters against himself in the entire book. They startle us. The friends too are shocked. They fear that his faith in God has melted into distrust (e.g., 4:5–6). Why would one who refused to curse God be so hostile toward his own life? The contrast between the Job of the prologue and the Job of the poem could not be sharper. The former Job "did not sin or charge God with wrong" (1:22), but this Job verbalizes his bitterest feelings.

Did Job sin in uttering a curse on his own life? Since life is God's greatest gift to a human being, a curse on it would not only deny that gift but would also speak against God himself. But if Job had sinned in his first speech, there would be no debate. His frequent claims of innocence would be sheer mockeries. Though Job approaches the brink of cursing God, he does not. Instead he vents the venom of his anguish by wishing that he were dead. He survives his darkest hour, since he neither curses God nor takes his fate into his own hands.

EXCURSUS: THE COUNTER-COSMIC INCANTATION

The peoples of the ancient Near East thought that everything, including the gods, emerged from a primordial womb.[1] All beings and forces had their origin in this primordial realm (sometimes called necessity or fate), and they had to obey its decrees. In this system the manipulation of this realm behind the gods made possible the control of someone's destiny or the determination of an outcome. Since this realm was impersonal, it could be addressed only by magic or ritual. This primordial womb was also the basic material out of which the gods created the world; thus, in order to be effective, rituals, incantations, and spells were permeated with the language of birth and creation. Potent spells were believed to tap this mysterious power. Rites for healing unleashed the powers of nature to achieve their purpose. Conversely, spells of doom, made by inverting the language of creation, unraveled the cords binding the universe together and brought death and destruction.

This type of spell served as a model for the structure of Job's curse on the day of his birth. Job pronounces a counter-cosmic incantation designed

1. Y. Kaufmann, *The Religion of Israel,* tr. and ed. M. Greenberg (New York: Schocken, repr. 1972), pp. 21–53.

to reverse the stages of the creation of the day of his birth, which were thought to be essentially the same as the stages of the seven-day creation of the world.[2] To undo the creation of a specific day, each stage of its ordering had to be negated. Furthermore, it needs to be noted that the exactness of the language of the spell guaranteed the result. That is why the counter-cosmic structure of Job 3:3–13 is so closely tied to the language of creation as found in Gen. 1:1–2:4.[3] While the omission of any allusion to the third day of creation in this curse is puzzling, the reason might have to do with the power inherent in numbers. Since seven is the number of order and six the number of disorder, six is crucial to the structure of a curse. In this curse the last day, the day of rest, could not be left out, for rest is the aim of this spell; instead the third day is omitted. The comparison of the two patterns is as follows:

	Job 3:3–13	*Gen. 1:1–2:4*
Day I	let it be darkness (v. 4a)	let there be light (v. 3b)
Day II	let not God above attend to it (v. 4b)	and (God) divided between the waters below the firmament and the waters above the firmament (v. 7b)
Day IV	that night . . . let it not be counted in the days of the year (v. 6b)	let there be light . . . to divide between the day and the night and let them be signs . . . for years (v. 14)
Day V	those prepared to stir up Leviathan (v. 8b)	and God created the great sea monsters (v. 21a)
Day VI	Why did I not die from the womb? (v. 11a)	let us make man (v. 26a)
Day VII	for now I would be lying down and quiet, I would be asleep and at rest (v. 13)	and (God) rested on the seventh day from all his work . . . he sanctified it, because in it he rested (2:2–3)

If this curse were effective, Job would have ceased to exist. It would be as though he had never been born, never existed. Then it would be impossible for him to have been ravaged by such a painful fate. He would never have experienced such agony.

Job takes this approach as the only immediate way out of his misery. Since he has done no wrong, he has no need to repent. There is no sacrifice that he could offer to relieve his sufferings. To take his own life would be inconceivable in view of his faith in God. Therefore, as the last resort he recites this spell. But his curse is illusory, for not even the greatest wizard could accomplish such a feat. Rather, these words reveal the acuteness of Job's misery.

2. M. Fishbane, "Jeremiah iv:23–26 and Job iii:3–13," *VT* 21 (1971) 151–67.

3. Such a reversal of the ordering of the universe is also reflected in Jer. 4:23–26; the prophet foresees the final judgment as the reversal of the stages of creation. Evidently both Jeremiah and the poet are drawing from the same orientation to the power of the curse to negate the ordering of the world.

III. THE DIALOGUE (4:1–27:23)

The dialogue is composed of three cycles. Each cycle has six speeches; each comforter delivers a speech in turn and Job responds to each of them. Job's responses are significantly longer than the speeches of the comforters, though Eliphaz's first speech (98 lines) is about as long as Job's first response (107 lines). The speeches from the other friends are significantly shorter. Bildad's and Zophar's speeches are about the same length, 43 and 40 lines respectively, but less than half as long as Eliphaz's. Conversely, each of Job's responses becomes a little longer: 107, 139, and 157 lines respectively.

In the first cycle the friends clearly state their positions. Eliphaz posits that no human being is righteous before God; Bildad argues that God never perverts justice; Zophar holds that God assuredly punishes every evildoer. All of them exhort Job to seek God that he might again enjoy a prosperous life. Although they wish to console Job, they are so chagrined at the severity of his misfortune that they feel they must reprimand him for some wrong he certainly must have committed. In his responses Job laments his suffering and begins his search for some way to gain reconciliation with God. In this cycle his responses have two basic divisions; in the first division he interacts with his friends, and in the second he addresses God with a lament. As this cycle moves along Job becomes increasingly disappointed in the friends' counsel and searches more earnestly for some way to win an acquittal from God, his Judge.

A. THE FIRST CYCLE (4:1–14:22)

1. ELIPHAZ'S FIRST SPEECH (4:1–5:27)

Being the first to speak, Eliphaz is definitely the most prominent and eloquent statesman of the three comforters. This view of his status is further supported by the fact that in each cycle his speeches are significantly longer than those of the other comforters. He is also the most articulate of the three friends. His rhetoric is filled with a wide variety of forms, e.g., proverbs, parables, analogies, precepts, exhortations, wisdom sayings, hymns, and a vision report.[1] With all these rhetorical devices he argues convincingly for the orthodox understanding of suffering as retribution for wrongdoing and adds greater authority to his teaching (4:8; 5:3, 8, 27).

Eliphaz's central premise is that everyone is guilty of error. From this premise he derives two basic arguments. First, he boldly articulates the law of retribution, i.e., that the righteous prosper and the wicked suffer hardship in this life and face a premature death (4:7–21). Second, he lauds God's greatness and his compassionate care in delivering his own from sorrow (5:9–26). Loss and suffering are not a final tragedy, for God will rescue anyone who is repentant from their grip and he will bestow an abundance of blessings. Therefore, misfortune presents an opportunity for the afflicted to discover hidden errors and to seek God's compassion through contrition.

a. A Word of Consolation (4:1–6)

1 *Eliphaz the Temanite replied:*[1]
2 *"If one ventures*[2] *a word with you will you be irritated?*
But who can keep from[3] *speaking?*[4]
3 *Behold, you have instructed many,*
and you have strengthened feeble hands.
4 *Your words have supported one who was stumbling,*
and you have braced those with shaking knees.

1. See K. Fullerton, "Double Entendre in the First Speech of Eliphaz," *JBL* 49 (1930) 320–74; Y. Hoffman, "The use of equivocal words in the first speech of Eliphaz (Job iv–v)," *VT* 30 (1980) 114–19.

1. Here and in each of the succeeding speeches the author employs the same formula: *wayyaʿan . . . wayyōʾmer,* lit. "and he answered . . . and said."

2. MT *hᵃnissâ* is somewhat problematic. The interrogative particle *hᵃ* may apply to the second line, which is primary here. In this case the first clause functions as a conditional clause with a perfect verb form; the protasis has an imperfect (Driver-Gray; GKC, § 150m; S. R. Driver, *A Treatise on the Use of the Tenses in Hebrew,* 3rd ed. [Oxford: Clarendon, 1892], § 154). The verb *nissâ* is most likely a Piel perfect of *nāsâ,* "try, test." It may also be a variant spelling or an error of audition for the Qal first person plural imperfect of *nāśāʾ*, "take up," i.e., "May we take up a word with you?" (cf. Ps. 4:7 [Eng. 6] for a similar spelling; cf. also Amos 5:1 for the use of *dāḇār,* "a word," with *nāśāʾ*). The former view is preferred, for it not only accepts the text more straightforwardly but also avoids the difficulty of the use of "we" by one of the friends, especially Eliphaz, which the latter proposal requires.

3. This is an example of the omission of the preposition *lᵉ* before an infinitive governed by *yûḵal,* "be able"; cf. 3:8; Exod. 2:3; 18:23 (see Dhorme; GKC, § 114m).

4. Heb. *millâ,* "word," is a favorite term of the poet. Of its 38 OT occurrences, 34 are in Job; of these occurrences in Job the Hebrew plural ending *-îm* is used 10 times and the Aramaic plural ending *-în* 13 times, as here.

5 *But now it has come to you and you are irritated;*
it strikes you and you are aghast.[5]
6 *Should not your piety be your confidence?*
Is not the uprightness of your ways your hope?"[6]

2 Eliphaz's first words reflect his own dilemma. Though he is apprehensive that Job may *be irritated* or wearied *(lā'â)*[7] by a response that challenges the value of his curse-lament, he feels compelled to speak lest Job's bitter words alienate God. With compassion for Job and yet aware that his own speech may add to his friend's burden, he politely asks Job's indulgence before offering a word.

3, 4 Diplomatically Eliphaz affirms Job as a faithful doer of righteous deeds. His judgment is based on the standard of piety found throughout the OT that deeds of mercy to the unfortunate are the sign of true righteousness. Eliphaz enumerates four examples of Job's uprightness: instructing many, strengthening feeble hands, giving an encouraging word to one who is stumbling, and bracing those with shaking knees. In interpreting these acts it is important to observe that the lines of v. 3 are thematically parallel to those of v. 4 (3a par. 4a; 3b par. 4b). Thus the first and third lines will be discussed together, then the second and fourth lines.

you have instructed many (v. 3a). "Instruct" *(yissēr)* means to teach, and refers particularly to moral and religious instruction, both by word and by discipline. That is, to those who were suffering Job gave insight into God's disciplinary use of affliction. His teaching enabled them to overcome their affliction. The parallel statement (v. 4a) is *you have supported* [*hēqîm,* lit. "you have made to rise"] *one who was stumbling.* "Stumbling" describes a person who is about to bow beneath a heavy load (cf. Ps. 31:11 [Eng. 10]). Often iniquity is the cause of stumbling (cf. Hos. 14:2 [Eng. 1]). When Job came across anyone who was about to fall, he directed that person's steps to the path of life with a word of discipline that was at the same time a word of encouragement.

5. The two feminine singular verbs are used for an impersonal subject (GKC, § 144b) and the two second person *waw* consecutives indicate action in the present (GKC, § 111t).

6. "Your hope," *tiqwāṯᵉḵā,* is predicate, for it lacks a *waw;* it comes first to establish chiasm (a:b::b′:a′). Hakam cites many examples where for emphasis a word or phrase stands before the *waw* without attracting the *waw* to itself (e.g., 2 Sam. 15:34); cf. M. Pope, "'Pleonastic' *Waw* before Nouns in Ugaritic and Hebrew," *JAOS* 73 (1953) 95–98.

7. Heb. *lā'â* means "to be weary of" or "to be exhausted from" strenuous effort or "to be weary and fed up" with something that is loathsome, nauseating, or burdensomely repetitious.

According to v. 3b and v. 4b,[8] Job has aided the weak, those with *feeble hands* and *shaking knees*. Drained of all their strength and courage, they must be assisted by someone stronger. Job has performed this service willingly. He has encouraged their rehabilitation by providing emotional support. He does not stand aloof from the needy as though they are parasites wanting to get at his resources. Rather he gladly soils his elegant garments as he reaches out to help them.

5 Eliphaz contrasts vividly Job's past confidence, which led him to perform numerous deeds of mercy, with his present reaction to misfortune. His confidence has melted, leaving him *irritated* (*lā'â;* cf. v. 2) and *aghast* (Niphal of *bhl*). The latter word refers to great inner agitation (cf. Ps. 6:3–4 [Eng. 2–3]) and fear that is close to panic (Ps. 48:6 [Eng. 5]; Jer. 51:32). Such emotion causes trembling and dread (Job 21:6; 23:15) and leads to rash words (Eccl. 5:1 [Eng. 2]). Especially in his curse-lament Job has appeared to counter the advice and encouragement he has extended to others; he fails to live up to the high standards which he has espoused for others. Tragedy has caught him by surprise, and he has attacked the value of his life. The wise trained their students to behave so that they would have a long life (cf. Prov. 3:2, 16); wisdom was even called a tree of life (Prov. 3:18; Sir. 24:13–22). Hence any member of this school would consider Job's challenging the worth of his birth a grave act of impiety. No wonder Eliphaz is shocked by Job's bitter words. Thus he contrasts Job's own response to suffering with the way he has helped the unfortunate in order that he might recognize the error in his lamenting and keep from stumbling over his own agony.

6 Eliphaz continues to upbraid Job with rhetorical questions. He believes that Job's piety should have sustained him in the day of adversity (v. 6). *your piety* (*yir'āṯᵉḵā*) is literally "your fear (of God)," which approximates the modern use of the word "religion." It refers to the inner response of reverence toward God, expressing itself in devotion and in deeds of compassion. *confidence* (*kislâ*)[9] attends genuine faith in God, and one who

8. Isa. 35:3 and Sir. 25:22 have the same parallel expression and use the same words as in v. 3b and v. 4b, except that Isaiah has *kōšᵉlôṯ*, "one stumbling" (as in v. 4a), instead of *kōrᵉʿôṯ*, "one bowing down." These words often refer to an infirmity and may also describe one who has been defeated by a foe (e.g., Ps. 20:9 [Eng. 8]; 27:2).

9. The Hebrew root *ksl* means "be thick" or "fat"; it can refer to the fat on the liver (Lev. 3:4, 10, 15, etc.). Fat is an essential part of the body that sustains life, but too much fat can dull and rob one of agility and power. Thus the major semantic development of this root in Hebrew is toward the meaning "folly" (cf. Job 15:25–27). But a minor development moves in the direction of "confidence"; in 8:14 and 31:24 *kesel* parallels *miḇṭāḥ*, "trust." This meaning may also be connected with the fact that the liver of certain animals, being a vital organ, was used in ancient Near Eastern religion as a form of divination (hepatoscopy), though in biblical thought the human liver is identified as the source of life (H. Wolff, *Anthropology of the Old Testament*, tr. M. Kohl [London: SCM; Philadelphia: Fortress, 1974], p. 64).

has such confidence remembers what God has done for him and is careful to keep God's commandments (Ps. 78:8 [Eng. 7]). Such inner strength guards one from falling into evil (Prov. 3:26). Eliphaz favors this idea, for it appears again in his second and third speeches (15:4; 22:4).

Eliphaz amplifies his concern with a second question: *Is not the uprightness of your ways your hope?* Uprightness should be the foundation of hope. Faith engenders hope, and hope gives buoyancy to life with the result that one joyfully pursues integrity in all areas of one's life. The fear associated with reverence prevents one's self-confidence from giving way to pride. The wholeness of such a faith should provide the one who serves God with the resolution to face every obstacle. This line is not to be taken as a sarcastic statement, but as a mild reproof; Eliphaz earnestly wants Job to avoid speaking so caustically, for he fears that such words will destroy Job's piety.

b. The Doctrine of Retribution (4:7–11)

7 *"Reflect now: who being innocent has ever perished?*
Where have the upright ever been destroyed?
8 *Just as I have seen: those who plow evil*
and sow trouble harvest the same.
9 *At the breath of God they perish,*
and at the blast of his anger they are consumed.
10 *The roar of the lion and the growl of the fierce lion,*
but the young lion's teeth are broken.[1]
11 *The lion perishes for lack of prey,*
and the lioness's cubs are scattered."

7 Eliphaz exhorts Job to *reflect* on the certainty of the doctrine of retribution. For emphasis he adds two rhetorical questions (which expect negative answers) to his exhortation.[2] With these questions he points out that the *innocent (nāqî)* have never *perished, the upright (yāšār)* have never *been destroyed.* With this familiar truth he hopes to rebuild Job's confidence, and so he states the affirmative side of retribution. Eliphaz does not say that the upright will not suffer hardship; rather he is careful to put the emphasis on the final outcome of one's life.

8 The traditional doctrine of retribution is defended by a reference

1. The verb *nittāʿû* is variously understood. It may be related to Ethiopic *natᵉʿa*, "cease" or "vanish" (so Fohrer). It may also be an Aramaism for *nāṭaṣ*, "destroy" (cf. Ps. 58:7 [Eng. 6]). Or it may be a denominative verb from *maltāʿôṯ* ("teeth") with the sense "teeth are removed" (Gordis citing Ibn Janah). The number of Aramaisms in Job favors the second view.

2. Emphasis is further increased by the compound pronoun, "he who" *(mî hûʾ)*.

to a fundamental natural law: "One harvests what he sows" (cf. Gal. 6:7). This law is beyond dispute. Even before the farmer sows, he expends much effort in preparing the soil. So too *those who plow evil (ʾāwen)* purposely and diligently pursue a course of wickedness. They sow *trouble (ʿāmāl)* as they revel in transgressing the moral law. Their sowing determines the kind of harvest they will reap. It is typical of Eliphaz's style that he states that he has personally *seen* this principle at work.

9 The final end of the wicked is administered by God. Although evil produces its own harmful results, God participates in executing judgment so that the sinner will receive a full and proper reward. Here God is angrily present in a gust of wind, a powerful force of destruction.[3] The punishment language of v. 9 parallels that of v. 7. *they perish (ʾāḇaḏ)* is the same as in v. 7a, and *are consumed (kālâ)* is parallel to "be destroyed" *(nikḥaḏ)* in v. 7b. Although Eliphaz is not making a direct allusion to the losses Job suffered when a gust of wind collapsed the house in which his sons were feasting (1:19), it is obvious that he would interpret this tragedy as a direct punishment from God.

10, 11 The doctrine of retribution receives further support from a pictorial proverb regarding the failure of the ferocious lion.[4] Unfortunately these lines are cryptic and obscure; the first line (v. 10a) lacks a verb. The lion here seems to represent the proud evildoer who resists God by pursuing iniquity.[5] Usually the lion roars and growls anxiously for its prey, but this young, vigorous lion is helpless, because its teeth are broken. Its cry is as ferocious as ever, but robbed of its weapons, its growling is hollow and its yearning for prey frustrated. Although this cryptic line does not tell how the teeth became broken, a similar reference in Ps. 58:7 (Eng. 6) suggests that God is responsible for this tragedy. Deprived of quarry, the lion slowly dies

3. For the sake of parallelism the poet splits a phrase which appears whole in 2 Sam. 22:16: *minnišmaṯ rûaḥ ʾappô* (cf. Ps. 18:16 [Eng. 15]), "at the blast of breath from his nostrils" (NIV), using *minnišmaṯ* in v. 9a and *mērûaḥ ʾappô* in v. 9b.

4. The author shows his knowledge of the animal world by using five different words for lion in vv. 10–11. These words probably refer both to varieties in the species and to the stages in their development, though the nuances of the terms are uncertain and hence they are difficult to translate precisely. Heb. *ʾaryēh,* the most frequent word for lion in the OT, is usually identified with the African lion, which in an early period may have also lived in southern Palestine. Heb. *šaḥal,* "young, proud lion," occurs 7 times; Dhorme and others identify it as the panther, but most remain unconvinced of this identification. Heb. *kᵉp̄îr,* "young lion," is one old enough to begin hunting (cf. Ezek. 19:2–6). Heb. *layiš,* which may come from a root meaning "strength" (cf. BDB, p. 539), is used only 3 times in the OT. LXX here translates it *myrmēkoléōn,* "ant lion." Heb. *lāḇîʾ,* "lioness," is possibly the Asiatic lion, which may have inhabited northern Palestine. Cf. G. Botterweck, "*ʾărî,*" *TDOT,* I:374–88.

5. In Scripture the lion serves as a vivid metaphor for the wicked who are brash and fearless in their abuse of God's people (e.g., Ps. 10:9; 17:12; 22:14, 22 [Eng. 13, 21]).

and the lioness's cubs scatter for lack of food. The point is that even a den of majestic lions can be dispersed by an act of God. So too the strongest and the most arrogant evildoer will fall in a short time under God's judgment.

c. A Vision Report (4:12–21)

12 *"Now to me a word came stealthily,*
and my ear caught just a whisper of it.[1]
13 *Amid troubling thoughts*[2] *from night visions,*
when heavy sleep falls on men,
14 *dread seized*[3] *me and trembling,*
and it made all my bones shudder.
15 *A spirit glided past my face;*
a gust[4] *made my skin crawl.*[5]
16 *It stopped,*[6]
but I could not recognize its appearance.
A form was before my eyes;
silence, then I heard a voice:[7]

1. The preposition *menhû* is an older poetic form of *mimmennû;* cf. *minhem* in 11:20.

2. Some relate MT *śeʿippîm* to *seʿippîm* ("branches" or "divided opinions"; cf. 1 K. 18:21), and assign it the meaning "tangled or perplexing thoughts" (Budde, Driver-Gray). But Dhorme relates it to Arab. *šaghifa,* "to be passionately smitten," and thus translates it "what is most deep seated in the heart." BDB (p. 972) and KB (2nd ed., p. 927) relate it to *śarʿappîm,* "disquieting thoughts" (see Ps. 94:19; 139:23).

3. With LXX, Targ., and Syr., the root of *qerāʾanî* is *qrh,* not *qrʾ* (cf. the lexicons, which posit two *qrʾ* roots); *lamed-he* verbs are sometimes confused with *lamed-ʾalep* verbs (GKC, § 75rr).

4. The usual rendering of *śaʿaraṯ* is "hair." It is possible to understand it (a feminine singular) as a collective. Driver-Gray repoint it to read the plural, *śaʿarōṯ,* and they understand the feminine singular verb as being constructed with a plural subject of things (see GKC, § 145k). But M. Dahood ("*śʿrt* 'Storm' in Job 4:15," *Bib* 48 [1967] 544–45), Tur-Sinai, Blommerde (*Northwest Semitic Grammar and Job,* pp. 40–41), and Gordis argue that *śʿrt* means "storm." Their suggestion has the advantage of having "storm" parallel "spirit, wind" (*rûaḥ,* v. 15a; cf. the paralleling of these two words in Isa. 41:16; Ps. 107:25; 148:8; Ezek. 1:4; 13:11, 13). Perhaps *śaʿarâ* is related to *seʿārâ,* which means "gale, heavy windstorm" (e.g., Ps. 107:29; see Tur-Sinai; Blommerde). As for the form here, Gordis suggests that *śaʿaraṯ* is an archaic form of the absolute with the old *-t* ending, while Dahood and Blommerde revocalize it. The meaning then is a "stormy gust" of wind.

5. The Piel *tesammēr,* "crawl," is used transitively, as Gordis argues. Thus it does not need to be emended to a Qal (cf. Driver-Gray).

6. LXX reads the first person form, *ʾaʿamōḏ,* "I stopped"; perhaps it was influenced by the rest of the verbs being in the first person singular. The MT is superior, for it marks a transition from Eliphaz's description of the vision to his reaction to it.

7. This verse is taken to be a quatrastich in the intriguing pattern a::b:c::c:b::c:b. *yaʿamōḏ,* "it stopped," constitutes the first line, which is intentionally abbreviated (note the syllable counts of the lines: 2/7/8/7) to heighten the mystery and the terrifying awe of the experience (cf. Duhm).

17 *'Can a mortal be just before God?*
Or is a man pure before[8] his Maker?
18 *Behold, he places no trust in his servants,*
and he charges his messengers with madness.
19 *Surely, then, those who dwell in houses of clay,[9]*
whose foundations are in dust,
are crushed by a moth.[10]
20 *Between morning and evening they are pulverized;*
unaware[11] they perish forever.
21 *Is not their tent-cord[12] pulled up[13]*
so that they die without wisdom?' "

8. The preposition *min*, "from," on both *'ĕlôah* and *ʿōśēhû* is used not in the sense of comparison but in the sense of "opposite, in front of, before." Emphasis falls on delineating the perspective from which a judgment about the quality is made (cf. Horst).

9. Cf. F. Perles, "Babylonische-biblische Glossen," *OLZ* 2 (1905) 182–83.

10. The third line is very difficult and considered a gloss by some (e.g., Hölscher and Fohrer). The plural verb *yᵉḏakkᵉʾûm* may serve as an impersonal passive (GKC, § 144g; cf. Driver-Gray). The *mem* (attested by LXX) may best be construed either as an enclitic *mem* or as part of *lipnê*, "before." In the OT the moth *(ʿāš)* is viewed as an instrument of destruction. Among other suggestions, Gordis takes *ʿāš* from an Arabic cognate *ʿuš*, "bird's nest," and Tur-Sinai (followed with slight variation by Blommerde, *Northwest Semitic Grammar and Job*, pp. 42–43) reads *ʿōśām*, "their maker." Dhorme takes *lipnê* in the sense of "like" (cf. 3:24): "they are crushed like a moth" (cf. G. R. Driver, "Linguistic and Textual Problems: Jeremiah," *JQR* 28 [1937–38] 121–22). The view taken here is that the moth is the instrument that hastens the destruction of houses composed of mud bricks.

11. The participle *mēśîm* is an ellipsis for the more common *mēśîm lēḇ*, "paying attention" (as in Job 23:6; Isa. 41:20). If v. 20b parallels v. 21b, this view is preferable. Dahood ("Northwest Semitic Philology and Job," pp. 55–56), followed by Pope and Blommerde (*Northwest Semitic Grammar and Job*, p. 43), takes the preformative *mem* on *mēśîm* as an enclitic *mem* and reads *šēm* ("name"), resulting in *mibbᵉlî-m šēm*, "without a name." Rowley favors the view of Dhorme, who follows the LXX reading "to help oneself" and reconstructs *môšîaʿ*, "(for lack of) a savior," for *mēśîm*. But the focus of vv. 19–21 is the vulnerable nature of human beings, not salvation by an intermediary (cf. Habel, OTL).

12. Horst, Gordis, et al. understand Heb. *yeṯer* to mean "tent-cord," while others (see *BHK*) emend it to *yāṯēḏ*, "tent-peg," a more common noun in the OT. The AV "excellency" follows Targ. and Vulg. A few (e.g., Dhorme; cf. Tur-Sinai) find in *yeṯer* a noun meaning "what remains" or "excess," from the common root *ytr*. It means then "excessive wealth" (cf. 22:20). Hence Dhorme translates: "Has not their excess of wealth been snatched from them?" But life, which is symbolized by a tent in Isa. 38:12 and Sir. 9:15, fits the context better than wealth. (Note that Dhorme has to move v. 21a to follow 5:5b.)

13. MT *bām*, the preposition with a pronominal suffix, is used for emphasis at the end of the line; the *bᵉ* may have the sense of "from" (see N. Sarna, *JBL* 78 [1959] 313–14). If it is understood as having an instrumental use, it would emphasize the idea of retribution, the central theme of Eliphaz's argumentation. This word is so difficult to render into English that it has been omitted from the translation.

Within the framework of a vision report Eliphaz states the central tenet of his theology: no human or heavenly creature is just in relationship to God. He recounts his vision to lend irrefutable authority to his position. The report itself consists of two segments: an account of the auditory vision (vv. 12–16) and the message received (vv. 17–21).

The similarity between this account of receiving a word and that of a prophet's receiving a word from God is particularly noticeable when these accounts are contrasted with the way divine messages were received through divination and oneiromancy in neighboring cultures. As with a prophet, the initiative for this vision originated outside of Eliphaz himself. There is no evidence that he followed any incubation rites or induced the vision in any way. Hearing dominates over seeing, as is typical of a vision account in the OT. But the recipient's inability to describe any visual images differs from a prophetic account, for the prophet sometimes sketches briefly, but specifically, what he saw (e.g., Isa. 6). Though Eliphaz's experience was primarily auditory, he did get a glimpse of something resembling a spirit. But no prophet ever mentions hearing a word from "a spirit." More often a prophet speaks as though he stood before Yahweh and there was commissioned to proclaim God's purpose to his people (e.g., Isa. 6, 40). Consequently, the prophet's message was quite specific, being tied to contemporary historical circumstances. In contrast, Eliphaz reports hearing a general truth, the kind of precept valued by the teachers of wisdom. But there is no hint that Eliphaz was an ecstatic, one who frequently enjoyed such encounters. The language suggests that this was a singular experience for him. Since this is the only account of such an auditory vision in the OT, our understanding of it is limited.[14]

12 Eliphaz emphasizes his personal involvement in this vision by beginning with the prepositional phrase *to me*. His use of the terms *a word (dāḇār)* and *came stealthily (y^{e}gunnāḇ)* draws attention to the divine source of the message. This language indicates that the message originated outside himself, i.e., he did not conjure up the idea in his mind. Heb. *gnb* (lit. "steal" in the Qal; here the Pual is used) has a technical meaning in this passage, namely, the reception of a word in an auditory vision.[15] It also connotes the clandestine setting of the experience and the privileged nature of the information received. Its literal meaning "steal" must not be played

14. For a fine discussion of this passage see E. L. Ehrlich, *Der Traum im Alten Testament*, BZAW 73 (Berlin: Töpelmann, 1953), pp. 142–45.

15. R. J. Werblowsky ("Stealing a word," *VT* 6 [1956] 105–106) takes *gunnāḇ* as a technical or semi-technical term for a specific kind of receiving "a word" in a nocturnal revelation. Cf. E. Robertson, "The Role of the Early Hebrew Prophets," *BJRL* 42 (1960) 416–17.

down, for the parallel word *caught* (*lāqaḥ*, lit. "take") sometimes has the extended meaning of stealing (e.g., Judg. 17:2; 18:17, 18, 24; cf. Jer. 23:30). To steal a word Eliphaz had to strain his hearing, for the voice was merely *a whisper (šēmeṣ)*. Perhaps *my ear caught just a whisper of it* means that he received insightful, but only partial, knowledge about God's ways.

13 Eliphaz received his vision in the dark hours of the night.[16] It was the time when *heavy sleep [tardēmâ] falls* on a person, a sleep that may be disturbed by *troubling thoughts [śeʿippîm] from night visions [ḥezyōnôṯ]*. A *vision (ḥizzāyôn)* denotes the reception of a message from the spiritual world, most often at night. While the verb *ḥāzâ* ("see, behold, inspect")[17] may occur in a general, nontechnical sense, the context discounts that interpretation here. Similarly, *tardēmâ,* the word for *heavy sleep,* sometimes describes a deep natural sleep (e.g., Jon. 1:5–6; Prov. 19:15), but more often it signifies a stupor that God causes to fall on a person, blocking out all other perceptions, in order that the person may be completely receptive to the divine word. Such a heavy sleep fell on Abraham at the sacrifice sealing God's covenant with him; in that moment God revealed to him the destiny of his descendants (Gen. 15:12–21; cf. also 2:21). Though the phrase *on men* tones down the visionary meaning of *heavy sleep,* the entire description favors taking this experience as a unique revelatory vision. In fact, the piling up of rare and technical words is designed to heighten the numinous quality of Eliphaz's spiritual encounter.[18]

14–16 *dread seized me and trembling, and it made all my bones shudder*. The uncanny atmosphere of the vision sent chills through Eliphaz. A gust of wind swept across his face, causing his skin to crawl. He knew that *a spirit (rûaḥ)* was present. There is a play here on the Hebrew word *rûaḥ,* which means both "spirit" and "wind." The spirit manifested its presence in a gust of wind. The spirit *glided (ḥālap)*[19] past Eliphaz's face, then halted. In the shadows of the night *a form* (*teмûnâ,* v. 16b) was visible to Eliphaz's eyes, though vaguely; he *could not recognize its appearance*. Heb. *temûnâ*

16. For a similar description of the way God speaks to human beings, see Elihu's description of God's warning a person through visions in 33:15–17.

17. Cf. A. Jepsen, *"chāzāh," TDOT,* IV:283, 290.

18. The extensive use of indeterminate language underlines the mysterious, transcendental nature of Eliphaz's vision: *gunnāḇ,* "came stealthily"; *šēmeṣ,* "a whisper"; *śeʿippîm,* "troubling thoughts"; *ḥezyōnôṯ lāylâ,* "night visions"; *tardēmâ,* "heavy sleep"; *paḥaḏ,* "dread"; *ḥālap,* "glided"; *rûaḥ,* "wind, spirit"; *simmēr,* "crawl"; *mar'eh,* "appearance"; *temûnâ,* "form"; *demāmâ,* "silence." The combined weight of all these words is overwhelming; Eliphaz had a special encounter with a spirit.

19. Heb. *ḥālap* means "to pass by quickly." Its subject may be "a wind" (e.g., Isa. 21:1; Hab. 1:11), though here that would mean *rûaḥ* is masculine in the first line and feminine, as usual, in the second line. Interestingly in 9:11 and 11:10 God is the subject of *ḥālap*.

means "a likeness, a representation, a form," and it is used with the term "idol" (*pesel;* Exod. 20:4; cf. Deut. 4:16, 23, 25) for the form or outer shape represented by the idol. This term is also used for the "form" or semblance of Yahweh (Num. 12:8; Ps. 17:15).

17 Out of the silence Eliphaz *heard a voice.*[20] The soft voice asked him two rhetorical questions: *Can a mortal be just [ṣāḏaq] before God? Or is a man pure [ṭāhar]*[21] *before his Maker?*[22] This dogma is placed in interrogative form for emphasis. Since *the Maker* is far superior to the creature, a human being has no grounds on which he may dispute with God the rightness of his fate. Should he argue that his case is just, he would definitely lose, for God is the absolute standard of justice and moral purity. That is, God, being just and pure by nature, wins every dispute, and each person, no matter how upright on earth, is found guilty by comparison.

While this revealed truth seems so obvious that its being stated is trite, it is central to Eliphaz's thinking. Thus he will repeat it in each of his speeches (15:15–16; 22:2). Whereas the usual basis in the OT for this thought of human unworthiness is humanity's sinful disposition, Eliphaz grounds the doctrine of human insignificance on humanity's inferiority before God. His approach allows him to reject Job's defense of his innocence from the start without directly disputing whether Job is a sinner. From one perspective this revealed word offers Job a little comfort in that he needs to realize that all creatures are flawed. But the primary inference is that no one, not even one who serves God faithfully, is pure in God's sight. By inference no person can gain strength from his own uprightness or place God

20. The phrase *d*ᵉ*māmâ wāqôl,* "silence, then . . . a voice," is similar to the "still small voice" *(qôl d*ᵉ*mānâ daqqâ)* that spoke to Elijah on the mountainside of Sinai (1 K. 19:12–18), but there appears to be more emphasis here on *d*ᵉ*māmâ,* "silence," since that word precedes *qôl,* "voice." Possibly this account is influenced by the report of Elijah's encounter with God at Horeb, yet without claiming that Eliphaz's vision was from God.

21. The root *ṭhr* refers to things that are "pure, free from defect." In cultic texts of the OT it describes persons, objects, or animals that are ritually clean and hence may enter the sacred vicinity of the sanctuary. While Heb. *ṭhr* occurs most often in cultic texts, in a few texts it refers to that which is ethically or morally good (e.g., Job 14:4; 17:9; Prov. 22:11; 30:12; Ps. 12:7 [Eng. 6]; 19:8–11 [Eng. 7–10]; 51:12 [Eng. 10]; Hab. 1:13; cf. Zech. 3:5; H. Ringgren, *"ṭāhar," TDOT,* V:294–95). The parallel with *ṣāḏaq,* "be just," indicates that the moral sense is primary here; cf. J. Lévêque, *Job et son Dieu,* 2 vols. (Paris: Gabalda, 1970), I:202–64.

22. It is difficult to determine if the message given by the divine spirit is contained in v. 17 (18), with a corollary drawn from it by Eliphaz in vv. (18) 19–21, or if it includes all of vv. 17–21. The opening question in v. 17 and the closing one in v. 21, plus the connecting particles *hēn* in v. 18 and *'ap* in v. 19, suggest that vv. 17–21 are to be interpreted as a unit. The repetition of this message in 15:14–15 shows that vv. 17–18 here are to be taken together; also, because of style v. 19 belongs with v. 18. Finally, in 5:1 there is a definite change in style, subject matter, and mood. Therefore, vv. 20–21 are taken as part of the message.

under moral obligation. At this point Eliphaz is denouncing Job's curse-lament, but his argument will become more forceful as Job staunchly defends his innocence, even to the point of accusing God of wrongdoing. In anticipation of Job's claim to innocence Eliphaz is saying that such a claim has no possibility of being true. From his viewpoint no one can make demands on his Creator based on his own worth or moral attainment. With this thesis the author artfully has Eliphaz anticipate the direction Job's argument will take.

18 This dogma about human beings is also true for the heavenly *servants (ʿᵃḇāḏîm)* or *messengers*. The angels or messengers *(malʾāḵîm)* are those who serve *(ʿāḇaḏ)* God (Ps. 104:4). But God does not place unconditional *trust* even in them. In fact, although they are highly exalted creatures, living in a perfect realm close to God, God charges them *with madness* or folly *(tohᵒlâ)*.[23] God is so pure and perfect that by comparison no creature is without fault.

19 The consequences of this dogma for humanity are further developed. This strophe opens with *ʾap̱*, which may mean "how much more" or "how much less." The former meaning is preferred since the argument moves from a given truth to the assured implications, from the heavenly to the earthly. If God does not have complete confidence in the heavenly creatures, who are free from earthly restriction, *surely* he cannot trust human beings, who are greatly handicapped in that they *dwell in houses of clay* (*ḥōmer;* cf. 10:9; 33:6; Isa. 64:7 [Eng. 8]; Sir. 9:15). Such structures are even weaker in that their *foundations are in dust*. Clay and dust symbolize the weaknesses and limitations of the human body. These kinds of houses *are crushed by a moth*. While the *moth (ʿāš)* is famous for devouring garments, none is known to devour houses. Hakam has suggested that there was an insect similar to a moth, also called *ʿāš*, which was known to devastate houses of clay by devouring the straw of the bricks.

20 Eliphaz develops his point. Inhabiting bodies of clay, all people are defenseless, even before a weak opponent. The strongest person may become weakened in a single day, *between morning and evening*. Their destruction is both brutal and total, as shown by the verbs in vv. 19–20:

23. MT *tohᵒlâ* is a hapax legomenon; thus its meaning is uncertain. Blommerde (*Northwest Semitic Grammar and Job*, pp. 41–42) revocalizes it *tᵉhillâ*, "praise" or "glory," and assumes that the negative *lōʾ* of the first line applies to both lines. One common suggestion is that it is related to Ethiopic *tahala*, "error" (Budde). Driver-Gray suggest that it is a miswritten form of *tiplâ*, "folly" (see AV). Following Rashi and Ibn Ezra, Gordis and Dhorme suggest that it is related to the root *hālal*, "be mad" or "make a fool of," forms of which appear in Eccl. 2:2; 7:7, 25; 10:13. The last suggestion is best, for it is built on good philology, has the general support of the versions (LXX, Targ., Vulg.), and does not require any textual change. See Grabbe, *Comparative Philology and the Text of Job*, pp. 41–43.

crushed (Piel of *dk*ʾ, v. 19c), *pulverized* (Hophal of *ktt,* v. 20a), and *perish* (Qal of ʾ*bd,* v. 20b). Caught *unaware* such persons suffer an irreversible fate.

21 Eliphaz continues this theme by using the picture of a tent that collapses before strong gusts of wind. When a tent is pitched, its cords are made taut to keep it erect. But if its cords are pulled up, the tent falls suddenly. No longer stretched out it cannot function as a dwelling place. The thrust of this picture falls on the sudden downfall of the wicked rather than on their physical limitations, which were expressed by the metaphor "houses of clay" in v. 19. When people despise God's ways, *they die without wisdom.* The phrase *without wisdom* means that they have not gained insight into the spiritual values of life or into the reasons for human mortality. Because they have relied on their own reason in their efforts to bring glory to themselves, they die in ignorance of why such a fate has befallen them. Again the author has Eliphaz anticipate the path Job is going to take in seeking an answer from God about his plight. Here Eliphaz is discounting the possibility that anyone who experiences sudden tragedy can understand the reasons for his own ruin.

d. No Mediator for Mankind (5:1–7)

1 *"Call now! Who will answer you?*[1]
To whom among the holy ones will you turn?
2 *Surely*[2] *vexation kills a fool,*
and envy slays the simple.[3]
3 *I have seen a fool taking root,*
and I declared his estate to be suddenly cursed.[4]

1. Heb. ʿ*ônekkā,* "one answering you," is an unusual example of a suffix with a *nun energicum* attached to a participle (GKC, § 61h).

2. Blommerde (*Northwest Semitic Grammar and Job,* p. 43) takes both *kî* and *l*ᵉ as emphatic particles. It seems better to understand the *l*ᵉ as a sign of the direct object, as in Aramaic and often in Job (so Dhorme).

3. In MT both "fool" and "simple" stand first in their respective clauses for emphasis. Here Eliphaz is probably quoting a proverb.

4. The verb *wa*ʾ*eqqôḇ* (lit. "and I cursed") is variously emended, since it is difficult to account for the personal involvement of Eliphaz and for "suddenly" modifying "curse" when it applies to the results of the curse rather than the action of cursing. Fohrer and Hölscher read either *w*ᵉ*rāqaḇ* or *wayyirqaḇ,* "and it rotted," based on LXX (see *BHK*; cf. *BHS*), but as Dhorme points out, LXX nowhere else translates *rāqaḇ* by *bibrṓskō* (lit. "eat, consume"; here a passive), and rotting is not a sudden action. A fine suggestion based on a minor change is *wayyûqaḇ,* "and it was cursed," accepted by Rowley and Pope. Gordis offers a better suggestion that preserves the MT. He takes the verb in a declarative sense: "I declared his dwelling cursed, doomed to sudden destruction." Cf. Syr., which reads a passive verb from a root meaning to perish.

4 *His sons are far from safety,*
and they are crushed[5] *in the gate without a defender.*
5 *His harvest*[6] *a hungry person eats,*
his substance the starving will carry away,[7]
and the famished[8] *long for their*[9] *wealth.*
6 *For hardship does not grow out of the dust,*
nor does trouble sprout from the ground.
7 *But a man engenders*[10] *trouble,*
as[11] *sparks*[12] *fly upward."*[13]

5. MT *w^{e}yiddakk^e'û* is most likely a Hithpael with the *t* assimilated before the *d* (GKC, § 54c).

6. LXX *synḗgagon* suggests the verb *qāṣ^{e}rû,* "they harvested," rather than the noun in MT, *q^{e}ṣîrô,* "his harvest." MT takes the antecedent of the pronoun as the "fool" of v. 3. LXX is in agreement with the plural suffixes in the rest of the verse and goes back to the "sons" of v. 4. MT is followed here, for "the fool," as the center of the description, is the preferred antecedent.

7. Verse 5b is very difficult and many emendations have been suggested. Dhorme takes *'el* after *lāqaḥ* as "to(ward)" and emends *miṣṣinnîm,* "among thorns," to from *ṣāpan* ("hide"): "and carry away to hiding places." Gordis follows Tur-Sinai and keeps the consonants but divides the first two words of the second line differently: *w^e'ulām ṣānîm,* "his substances the starving will carry away." *'ûl,* "strength," is taken to mean "substance, wealth," just as *ḥayil* has both meanings. *ṣānîm,* "starving," is understood as a *qâṭîl* noun from *ṣnm,* "be shriveled up." In the same vein A. Guillaume ("The Arabic Background of the Book of Job," in *Promise and Fulfilment: Essays Presented to Professor S. H. Hooke,* ed. F. F. Bruce [Edinburgh: T. & T. Clark, 1963], pp. 110–11) reads *mōṣnîm,* "the famished," from Arab. *ṣanīm,* "going without food willingly or unwillingly." Tur-Sinai's suggestion seems best, for it enables this line to parallel the first line; the double prepositions, *'el* and *min,* appear to be a scribal error.

8. Many take *ṣammim* as defective writing for *ṣ^{e}mē'îm,* "thirsty," but the verb then should be plural, not singular as in MT. Gordis avoids emendation by seeing *ṣammîm* as a *qaṭṭil* form, parallel to the *qaṭil* pattern, meaning "constricted, famished."

9. The antecedent of the pronoun "their" is both the "fool" of v. 3 and the "sons" of v. 4. Thus v. 5 ties together vv. 3–4. Cf. G. R. Driver, "On Job 5,5," *TZ* 12 (1956) 485–86.

10. Many prefer to revocalize the Pual perfect *yûllaḏ,* "is begotten," to an active verb, either the Piel perfect *yillaḏ* (Horst) or the Hiphil imperfect *yôliḏ* (Duhm, Dhorme, Gordis). The latter reading makes excellent sense and is supported by similar wording in Isa. 59:4b: "They conceive trouble and beget evil." Dhorme and Gordis then explain the *l^e* on *'āmāl,* "trouble," as a sign of the accusative.

11. The second line opens with the *waw* of comparison (GKC, § 161a), though the exact nature of the comparison is difficult to discern; see n. 12 below.

12. The meaning of *b^{e}nê rešep* (lit. "sons of Resheph") is notoriously difficult to determine. It has been taken to mean "members of a flame," i.e., "sparks," since *rešep* means "flame" in some contexts (e.g., Cant. 8:6; cf. "lightning" in Ps. 76:4 [Eng. 3]; 78:48). But LXX, Syr., and Vulg. take it as the name of a bird (cf. Sir. 43:17), which makes sense with the compound verb *yagbîhû 'ûp,* "fly high"; an eagle is also the subject of the verb *yagbîah,* "make high," in 39:27. Since *rešep* is identified with lightning in a few passages and the eagle was associated with thunder and lightning, Dhorme identifies

1 Eliphaz develops the implication of the heavenly message by questioning Job about whom he might turn to for assistance in gaining a hearing with God. The verbs *call (qārā')* and *answer (ʿānâ)* relate to Job's lament and have the sense of presenting a petition or complaint. Eliphaz wonders whether Job thinks that the only way God would hear his complaint would be through the efforts of an intermediary, an angel[14] who would entreat God to hear his request. This is one of the few places in Scripture where an angel is thought to be able to function as an intercessor for a human being (cf. 33:23–28). The belief in heavenly mediators grew during the postexilic period and has been preserved in various branches of Judaism and Christianity. This passage suggests that such an idea was current earlier, in the author's time. Eliphaz resoundingly rejects this idea, however, for he believes that the angels are so tainted (4:18) that they do not have the standing to represent a person before God. Job also needs to realize that he has no grounds to petition God, for his fate is common to every human being.

2 By quoting a proverb Eliphaz alerts Job to the negative consequences that *vexation* (*kaʿaś;* cf. 6:2) and *envy (qin'â)* produce in a person. These words describe the burning, angry emotions that motivate one to erratic behavior and the desire for revenge. Such strong emotion *kills the fool* and *slays the simple*. The words used for *fool* and *simple* encompass the full range of foolish people. The second word, *pōṯeh,* means one who is simple or naive, while the first word, *'ĕwîl,* refers to a hardened fool, an arrogant individual who seeks his own purpose without regard to God. The hardened fool rejects all instruction; instead he quarrels in order to get his own way (Prov. 1:7; 15:5). Such behavior leads to an early death (Prov. 10:8, 10, 14, 21). Through this proverb Eliphaz is warning Job that his present distress, if unchecked, will kill him like a fool.

3 Eliphaz elaborates on his point by recounting the fate of a fool whom he observed beginning to be prosperous. Typically Eliphaz stresses

---

bᵉnê rešep as the eagle. A problem with this view is that *bᵉnê,* "sons of," is plural. Another possibility is to identify the term with the god Resheph, a god of health and well-being as attested in the Karatepe inscriptions. But an Ugaritic text equates him with the Assyrian Nergal, a god of pestilences and the underworld (cf. Pope, and D. Conrad, "Der Gott Reschef," *ZAW* 83 [1971] 157–83). If this view is accepted, the "sons of Resheph" would be "the plagues" that ascend from the lower world to curse human beings (cf. Deut. 32:24; Hab. 3:5).

13. The second verb *ʿûp,* "fly," is related adverbially to the verb *yagbîhû,* "they rise," hence "fly upward."

14. Heb. *qᵉḏōšîm* is generally taken to mean "angels," as in Deut. 33:3; Ps. 89:6–8 (Eng. 5–7); Zech. 14:5; Dan. 4:14 (Eng. 17); 8:13. The angels are holy by reason of their proximity to God, the Holy One, not because of any inherent moral qualities. For a significant new way of interpreting this reference to angels, see D. J. A. Clines, "Job 5,1–8: A New Exegesis," *Bib* 62 (1981) 185–94.

his personal involvement in this incident with *I have seen (rā'îṯî);* the *I* is emphasized by the use of the personal pronoun *'anî.* This fool in his prosperity is comparable to a tree, a frequent symbol for the success and stability of the righteous (e.g., Ps. 1:3). On the surface it appeared that this person was righteous since he was taking root. But Eliphaz, knowing that the man was a fool, became quite aroused (cf. Ps. 37:35–36). Therefore, he *declared his estate to be suddenly cursed.* This does not mean that he actually cursed the estate himself, but that he earnestly bade God to execute the curse entailed in that person's wrongdoing. That is, believing that every wicked deed, even though it may bring initial prosperity, contains its own curse, Eliphaz wished to release the power of the curse contained in that fool's deeds so that the curse would speedily work its ill against that fool's entire *estate (nāweh),* including his family, servants, flocks, and crops.

4 The curse on the fool's estate fell against his sons. Ancient Semitic society considered the family to be a unit; thus all rejoiced or suffered at the success or failure of any of its members. Loss of the family estate, which was both the cornerstone of inheritance and the means for sustaining the clan, was the worst tragedy. Consequently, the fool's children must bear the cruel brunt of the curse against the estate activated by their father's folly. Some of the results of the curse are specified. *far from safety* the sons suffer grave misfortune. The second line indicates that they have been given a harsh sentence for a suspected crime. *they are crushed without a defender in the gate,* i.e., they had no advocate to argue their defense. The city *gate* was the ancient courtroom. The judgment that this court rendered was unusually harsh, as signified by the word *crushed* (*yiddakkᵉ'û;* cf. 4:19; 6:9). Tactlessly Eliphaz makes a pointed allusion to Job's loss of his children, thus aggravating his agony over their death.

5 Furthermore, this family loses all *their wealth,* both the new income from the harvest and their accumulated riches. The desperate poor, referred to here as the *hungry* and *the famished,* await any opportunity to exploit the wealth of the rich. Taking advantage of confusion caused by the curse, these low members of society raid the fields of that rich fool and rob his storehouses.[15] The curse thus reduces this man and his family to vagrancy as visible proof of his folly.

6, 7 Eliphaz continues to argue that punishment is not a part of the natural processes, but is an inevitable outworking of a person's sinful nature. Misfortune is not a capricious act of nature that befalls one at random, for

15. For this picture Eliphaz may be drawing on the theme of the chaotic reversal of the order of society, i.e., the rich are impoverished and the lower classes rule, as evidence of divine judgment on society. Cf. Isa. 3:2–7, 11–12; this theme is very prominent in two Egyptian works describing the First Intermediate Period: "The Admonitions of Ipu-wer" and "The Prophecy of Nefer-rohu" (*ANET,* pp. 441–46).

hardship [ʾāwen] does not grow out of the dust, nor does trouble [*ʿāmāl;* cf. 3:10] *sprout from the ground.* A person harvests what he sows. Suffering and misfortune, then, are direct punishments for wrongdoing. In fact, *man engenders trouble.* During life everyone does things that yield trouble just as surely as *sparks* or flashes of lightning *fly upward.* Perhaps the point of the latter metaphor is that from birth, plagues from the netherworld fly forth to curse a person's life.[16] Caught in the chain of sin-punishment from birth, no person can find release from that chain. To chafe against ill-fate is mere folly. Job, therefore, should not be so distressed—all are sinners destined to experience trouble.

e. An Appeal to Seek God (5:8–16)

8 *"But I would appeal to God,*
and I would commit my cause to God,[1]
9 *who does great deeds beyond searching,*
wonders beyond counting,
10 *who gives*[2] *rain to the land*
and sends water over the countryside
11 *to set*[3] *the lowly on high*
and those who mourn are lifted to safety,
12 *who thwarts the plots of the crafty*
so that their hands do not achieve success,
13 *who takes the wise in their craftiness,*[4]
and the counsel of the clever is hastened to confusion.
14 *In the day they meet*[5] *darkness,*
and at noon they grope as at night.

16. See n. 12 above.

1. The parallelism of *ʾēl,* "God," in the first line with *ʾĕlōhîm,* "God," in the second line occurs elsewhere in Job only in 20:29. This leads some to emend the second, rarer term in Job to the more frequent *šadday* (Pope) or *ʾēlāyw,* "to him" (Horst, who wishes to keep the alliteration). Gordis cautions against such changes, esp. given the alliteration of the lines in MT.

2. The articular participle, *hannōṯēn,* has suggested to Duhm and Fohrer that this verse is an addition, but the participle stands both with and without the article throughout Job. Dhorme thinks it was used because of the syntactical distance of its antecedent, *ʾēl,* "God," and Horst posits that it has demonstrative force.

3. For variation an infinitive construct may parallel a participle (cf. Ps. 113:7–9; 104:21).

4. One would expect *ʿormāṯām* instead of MT *ʿormān,* "their craftiness," since the noun is usually said to be *ʿormâ* (but cf. BDB, p. 791). Dhorme accepts the MT form, which he explains as analogous to *tᵉḇûnām* for *tᵉḇûnāṯām* in Hos. 13:2.

5. Heb. *pāgaš,* "meet," occurs only here in the Piel. Gordis explains that the Piel may have been phonetically induced by the parallel verb *māšaš,* "grope," being in the Polel.

15 *But he delivers from their sharp tongue,*[6]
even from the grip of the strong, the needy.
16 *So the poor have hope,*
and iniquity[7] *shuts its mouth."*

8 Eliphaz jumps to another subject; the shift is marked by the strong adversative conjunction *But (ʾûlām).* True to form Eliphaz emphasizes his own stance in what he is about to say by the emphatic use of the pronoun *I (ʾanî).*[8] Courteously Eliphaz couches his exhortation to Job in a description of what his response would be were he in circumstances similar to Job's. He would *appeal to (dārаš)*[9] God, i.e., he would diligently cry out to God, in a repentant attitude, seeking forgiveness and deliverance. *I would commit my cause to God.* This means he would not have a defiant attitude like Job's. On the surface it appears that Eliphaz is respectfully sensitive to Job, but Job's response will indicate that he detects a condescending tone in Eliphaz's manner.

9, 10 Eliphaz grounds his resolve to seek God earnestly in his view of God, which he recounts by reciting lines from a hymn of praise.[10] The hymn opens by focusing on the marvelous power of God, who performs *great deeds*[11] *[geḏōlôṯ] beyond searching* and *wonders* or miracles *(niplāʾôṯ)*

6. The phrase *mēḥereḇ mippîhem,* lit. "from the sword from their mouth," is difficult. Keil suggests a local use of the preposition *min,* "from the sword which proceeds from their mouth." Davidson understands "from their mouth" to be in apposition to "sword" and to classify which sword, namely, those of their own mouth. Gordis's suggestion makes the best sense of the present text. He takes the two Hebrew words as a hendiadys, meaning "from their sharp tongue" (cf. Ps. 59:8 [Eng. 7]; 64:4 [Eng. 3]). Fohrer arrives at a similar position by reading *pîhem* (attested by Targ., Syr., and Vulg.), "from the sword of their mouth"; the extra *mem* may belong to the preceding word as an enclitic *mem.* Others emend the MT to find a parallel to "needy." Dhorme reads *moḥorāḇ,* "the ruined man," for *mēḥereḇ;* Driver-Gray argue that *yāṯōm,* "orphan," has fallen out and *mēḥereḇ,* "from the sword," was added to fill in the lacuna (cf. RSV); Pope emends *mippîhem* to *peṯāyîm,* "simple ones." But sense may be made of the present text if *ʾeḇyôn,* "needy," is understood as serving both lines.

7. The noun *ʿōlāṯâ,* "iniquity," is a result of the contraction of an original *aw* diphthong in the first syllable and the addition of the *-āṯā* termination, which is used in poetry for the feminine (GKC, § 90g); cf. the Qere *ʿawlāṯâ* (Ketib *ʿōlāṯâ*) in Ps. 92:16 (Eng. 15). The common form of the word is *ʿawlâ.*

8. The first person pronoun is heavily stressed, being repeated in different ways 4 times. This is typical of Eliphaz's style. Nevertheless, God is the focus of the verse, both because God stands at the center of the chiasm (a:b:c::c′:b′:d) and because of the use of the alliteration at this center, *ʾel-ʾēl weʾel-ʾĕlōhîm.*

9. See S. Wagner, *"dārash," TDOT,* III:301.

10. See C. Westermann, *Structure of the Book of Job,* tr. C. A. Muenchow (Philadelphia: Fortress, 1981), pp. 75–76. Job repeats v. 9 in 9:10, with only two minor variations, but from a drastically different perspective.

11. Cf. 9:10; 37:5; Ps. 136:4; 145:3, 6.

so numerous that they are *beyond counting* (cf. Ps. 145:3). In the OT *wonders* may refer to God's deeds in creation[12] or to his deeds of salvation in history, specifically the deliverance of his people from Egypt.[13] The use of participles here indicates God's continuous creative activity. This great God can use the same creative power to overcome the difficulties that his servant is facing.

Eliphaz mentions specific wonders that demonstrate God's great wisdom. He *gives the rain to the land and sends water over the countryside,* i.e., he supplies the great rivers with water from springs and mountain streams.[14] The psalmists often marvel at the wonder of God's creative work and his amazing way of sustaining the creation (e.g., Ps. 104; 107:24–32).

11 This great God also governs human affairs. Specifically he reverses the fortunes of those whom society has wrongly rewarded. He exalts the *lowly* and *those who mourn* in dark apparel with soiled faces expressive of their grief (vv. 11, 15–16).[15] He removes the cause of their distress and sets them in a safe place.

12–14 This same God also condemns those who exercise their power to afflict the weak. God's wisdom is superior to human ingenuity. A bright person relying on his shrewd craftiness plans his own success without acknowledging God. Through his genius he schemes to exert his authority. Early successes give such a person a feeling of security. But God is not deluded by that person's craftiness. At the right time he *thwarts the plots of the crafty [ʿarûmîm]*[16] *so that their hands do not achieve success* [*tûšîyâ;* cf. 6:11–13]. That is, he hastens *the counsel of the clever* (lit. "crooked," *niptālîm*) to *confusion.*[17] He makes these crafty people so anxious about their plans that they lack the patience to carry them out. As they flounder about in confusion their plans fall apart without achieving their purpose. The language paints the picture of one being snared by the very bait he puts out to

12. Cf. Ps. 107:24; 139:14. Fohrer points out that a trait of the wisdom teachers is to reflect on the wonders in creation, esp. with a view to the wisdom and the counsel that are revealed in the created orders (cf. Ps. 104:24; 139:14).

13. Cf. Ps. 78:4; 106:7, 22; 111:4.

14. Tur-Sinai sees here the background picture of a king who sends "emissaries over land and through streets." Winds and rain are God's emissaries.

15. This is a theme that recurs in Job 22:29 and in many Psalms, e.g., 18:29 (Eng. 28); 75:8, 11 (Eng. 7, 10); 113:7–8; 147:6.

16. The word for "crafty," *ʿarûmîm,* refers to incisive perceptions or cunning activity, depending on whether a person exercises this trait in wisdom (1 Sam. 23:22) or folly (Ps. 83:4 [Eng. 3]).

17. It should be noted that this part of v. 13 is the only verse from Job that is indisputably cited in the NT (though Rom. 11:35 is probably quoting Job 41:3 [Eng. 11]). In 1 Cor. 3:19 Paul quotes this line to attest that God's wisdom is far superior to any worldly wisdom.

catch another (cf. 18:7–10; 36:8–10; Prov. 28:10; Ps. 7:16 [Eng. 15]; 35:7–8; 57:7 [Eng. 6]).

The brightest hour for the crafty is turned to *darkness*. Robbing them of their shrewd genius, God turns their wisdom into stupidity. No longer able to make discerning judgments, *at noon they grope* as though it were the blackest hour of *night*.[18] They have lost all of their terrifying power.

15, 16 Having given one line in the poem to God's saving action (v. 11) and three lines to his judging (vv. 12–14), Eliphaz concludes this hymn with two lines that laud the power and mercy of God to help the unfortunate.[19] Though the text has no word for "God," the context makes it clear that it is God who *delivers from their sharp tongue, even from the grip of the strong, the needy*. He rescues the weak from oppression just as surely as he smites the crafty. One might expect that God would be on the side of the strong, but the God of revelation surprises us by always siding with the needy and the poor. He confounds the power of the mighty and aids the abused.

The phrase *from their sharp tongue* is difficult.[20] It seems to refer to the slanderous word uttered to curse the unfortunate, since the wicked often attack their foes with an onslaught of words, seeking to terrify them by shame, intimidation, slander, and curse. The blows of their tongue are as painful as the jabs of a sword. But God delivers the lowly, whether the threat against them be tortuous invectives or a display of force (cf. Ps. 72:12–14). God not only rescues *the poor;* he heals their emotional stress by giving them *hope*, an anticipation of a future in which they will enjoy abundant blessings. When *iniquity shuts its mouth,* the lowly will live in peace, free from threats of violence.

These hymnic lines laud God's governance of his world. In complete control of his world, he shames the haughty and prosperous and exalts the poor and needy. It is hard to determine whether this poem is intended to encourage Job or to condemn him. Is Job an example of a clever, rich man whom God has suddenly and swiftly humbled? Or is he a poor, helpless man whom God will exalt in due time? In the next pericope Eliphaz points toward

18. Cf. Job 12:24–25; Deut. 28:29; Isa. 59:10.

19. As Gordis and others point out, the wording of vv. 16–18 is similar to other OT passages: v. 16b = Ps. 107:42b *(wᵉḵol ʿawlâ);* v. 17a = Ps. 94:12a *(ʾašrê haggeḇer ʾᵃšer tᵉyassᵉrennû yāh);* v. 17b = Prov. 3:11a *(mûsar yhwh bᵉnî ʾal-timʾās);* v. 18a = Hos. 6:1b (similar); v. 18b = Deut. 32:39d. This passage is evidence of how thoroughly the language of the OT tradition permeates the author's thinking. He quotes, adopts, and alludes freely to other texts. That these allusions and quotes come from multiple sources reveals that the author draws widely from the Israelite tradition for the composition of these speeches.

20. See n.6 above.

the latter possibility as his answer for Job by emphasizing God's care for his own, specifically for Job.

f. God's Ability to Deliver (5:17–27)

17 *"Behold, blessed is the man whom God reproves,*
and the discipline of Shaddai[1] *do not reject.*[2]
18 *For he inflicts pain, then he binds up;*
he smites, then his hands heal.[3]
19 *In six sorrows he delivers you,*
and in seven no harm will touch you.
20 *In famine he will ransom*[4] *you from death,*
and in war from the power of the sword.
21 *From*[5] *the scourging of the tongue*[6] *you will be hidden;*
and you will not fear before destruction[7] *when it comes.*

1. This is the first occurrence of the divine name *Shaddai* (Heb. *šadday*) in Job. It occurs 31 times in Job and only 17 times in the rest of the OT. This name is closely associated with the patriarchs (Abraham, Gen. 17:1; Isaac, 28:3; Jacob, 35:11; cf. Exod. 6:3), and no doubt the author of Job uses it to contribute to the patriarchal setting of his work. Translations usually render it "Almighty," on the basis of LXX *pantokrátōr,* "all-powerful." But the precise analysis of *šadday* remains an enigma. The most widely accepted view relates it to Akk. *šadū,* "mountain" (cf. Ugar. *ṯd,* "breast"). Then *šadday* means "the mountain one" (so F. M. Cross, *Canaanite Myth and Hebrew Epic* [Cambridge, Mass.: Harvard University Press, 1973], pp. 52–58; cf. Ps. 121:1–2). Cross goes on to identify *šadday* as a warrior god who is thus ruler and protector of his people (pp. 58–60). Since no explanation is fully satisfactory, the name is simply transliterated in this work. Cf. also W. F. Albright, "The Names Shaddai and Abram," *JBL* 54 (1935) 173–93; F. M. Cross, "Yahweh and the Gods of the Patriarchs," *HTR* 55 (1962) 244–50; V. Hamilton, *TWOT,* II:907; W. Walker, "A New Interpretation of the Divine Name 'Shaddai'," *ZAW* 72 (1960) 64-66; M. Weippert, "Erwägungen zur Etymologie des Gottesnames 'Ēl Šaddaj," *ZDMG* 36 (1961) 42–62; idem, *THAT,* II:873–81; W. Wifall, "El Shaddai or El of the Fields," *ZAW* 92 (1980) 24–32.

2. The length of this verse, the forceful but prosaic "Behold" *(hinnēh),* and its proverbial character cast some suspicion on its authenticity; thus Duhm and Fohrer omit it. But the author quotes freely from the hymnic and Wisdom traditions.

3. Heb. *tirpeynâ,* "heal," is a *lamed-'alep* verb written like a *lamed-he* verb (GKC, § 75qq).

4. The use of the perfect suggests the certainty of God's deliverance from the disasters (cf. GKC, §§ 106m, n).

5. The preposition *bᵉ* is used like the preposition *min,* "from"; thus there is no need to emend it to *min* (as Horst does). Cf. N. Sarna, "The Interchange of the Prepositions *Beth* and *Min* in Biblical Hebrew," *JBL* 78 (1959) 314–15.

6. Many take *šôṭ lāšôn* as "slander" or "backbiting," i.e., "a tongue's lash" which causes slander and strife (cf. Sir. 26:6 [9]; 28:17 [21]; 51:2). Gordis suggests that the phrase is an ellipsis for *šôṭ lᵉšôn 'ēš,* "a tongue of fire" (cf. Isa. 5:24). The advantage of the latter suggestion is that all the plagues remain in a single class of physical phenomena, although with the former view one could think of the results of the tongue's curse rather than of the curse itself.

7. For *šōḏ,* "destruction," some (e.g., Pope; cf. Tur-Sinai) read *šēḏ,* "demon." But this is a conjecture without any textual support.

22 *At devastation from drought*[8] *you will laugh;*
and from the beasts of the land fear not,[9]
23 *because your covenant will be with the stones of the field,*[10]
and the beasts of the field will be at peace with you.
24 *You will know that all is well with your tent,*
and you will inspect your estate and not find anything missing.[11]
25 *You will know that your seed will be many*
and your offspring like the grass of the earth.
26 *You will come to the grave in full vigor,*
as the stacking of grain[12] *in its season.*
27 *Behold, we have searched this out and it is so.*
Attend to it; even you, yourself, come to know it."

17 Eliphaz hopes to alter Job's response to his misfortune by instructing him about the security that the one who trusts in God has during a season of affliction. He opens with a beatitude: *blessed is the man whom God reproves.*[13] God *reproves (hôḵîaḥ)*[14] the one he loves like a faithful father

8. While the distinction between *kāpān* and *rāʿāḇ* (v. 20) unfortunately has not been preserved, Davidson and Gordis understand *kāpān* to mean hunger resulting from failure of crops and *rāʿāḇ* to be a general term for hunger. Gordis's suggestion of taking *lᵉšōḏ ûlᵉḵāpān* as a hendiadys, "the devastation of drought," is excellent.

9. Many eliminate v. 22 as a redundant gloss (e.g., Driver-Gray) that is less forceful than vv. 21 and 23. But it forms a good transition between vv. 21 and 23: v. 22a picks up v. 21b and is explained in v. 23a, while v. 22b is expanded in v. 23b. Thus v. 22 adds weight to these points in the numerical saying.

10. MT *ʾaḇnê haśśāḏeh,* "stones of the field," is problematic, since there are no parallels to making a covenant with inanimate objects, and as Tur-Sinai points out, *ʾaḇnê haśśāḏeh* occurs nowhere else in the OT. Rashi cites an alternate reading, *ʾaḏnê haśśāḏeh,* "lords of the fields" (see Gordis). These lords are understood to be the "spirits" or "demons" of the field that have to be appeased in order for a field to yield produce; cf. K. Köhler, "Seitsame Vorstellungen und Brauche in der biblischen und rabbinischen Literatur," *ARW* 7 (1910) 75–79. G. Beer ("Zu Hiob 5:23," *ZAW* 35 [1915] 63–64) accepts this idea but reads *bᵉnê haśśāḏeh,* "sons of the field"; cf. Pope. Blommerde (*Northwest Semitic Grammar and Job,* p. 45) gains this reading by taking *ʾaḇnê* as *bᵉnê,* "sons of," with a prosthetic ʾ.

11. Dhorme observes that the imperfect *teḥĕṭāʾ*, "it is missing," after a perfect indicates that the latter action is dependent on the former.

12. Heb. *gāḏîš* refers to "a pile of sheaves"; cf. 21:32.

13. The beatitude is at home in the Wisdom tradition. It is a word of promise introduced by *ʾašrê,* "blessed" or "happy" (cf. Prov. 3:13; 8:32, 34; 28:14; 29:18; 26 times in Psalms, e.g., 1:1; 32:1, 2; 94:12; 128:1, 2; and 4 times in prophetic literature) followed by a participle or a subordinate clause. Personal beatitudes are usually addressed to an individual, but sometimes to the whole community (e.g., Ps. 33:12; 144:15). The second line of a beatitude may express a promise, a wish, or even a warning, as here. Cf. Fohrer; H. Cazelles, *"ashrê," TDOT,* I:445–58; and W. Janzen, "*ʾašrê* in the Old Testament," *HTR* 58 (1965) 215–26.

14. In the context *hôḵîaḥ* means "to reprove"; in a legal context it connotes

disciplines his son or like a concerned teacher corrects his student (cf. Prov. 3:11–12; Ps. 118:18; Heb. 12:5–11).[15] Since he who submits to the painful process of discipline will experience blessing, one must *not reject the discipline [mûsār] of Shaddai*. In the end he will come forth a better person, enjoying God's favor in greater measure.

Eliphaz understands discipline or reproof as an intermediate step in the doctrine of retribution. One who needs correcting is reproved in order that he might repent and find forgiveness lest he persist in his error and experience the full punishment his error merits. Misfortune is God's rod of discipline; it reveals his loving care for humanity in that he does not let a person go to the grave without exerting great effort to make that person aware of the consequences of his sinful acts. Consequently, when misfortune befalls a devout follower, it is to be taken as God's attempt to instruct him. Pain is the instrument of discipline long before it becomes the fulfillment of a curse. Thus Eliphaz is encouraging Job to stop chafing against God's discipline with such bitter lamenting.

18 Eliphaz supports the teaching of the beatitude with a hymnic line lauding God's way of acting. God is both the great disciplinarian and the great healer. *He inflicts pain, then he binds up* the wound. Or *he smites, then his hands heal*. These lines are similar to Deut. 32:39: "Then I, I am He! There is no God beside me. I kill and I give life; I wound and I heal" (cf. Isa. 45:7). The same God who inflicts the pain will heal the wound as soon as his instructional purpose is accomplished.

19 God's concern for preserving his own is supported by a numerical saying, a common form in the Wisdom literature.[16] Such a saying was designed to teach certain facts about nature or to elaborate the facets of a particular theme. Here it teaches that a faithful worshiper could experience various misfortunes of discipline, *six*, even *seven* times, yet with God's help he could be delivered from all of them.[17] God's healing power is greater than

---

taking legal action against someone or arguing a case (e.g., Job 13:15). The second person form is probably used here because of the proverbial nature of the statement.

15. The normal method of instruction by the wise made free use of the rod to discipline a student; cf. Prov. 13:24; 19:18; 22:15; 23:13–14; 29:15. Also, the teacher-pupil relationship was often viewed as that of a father and son.

16. Since numbers have no synonyms, in numerical sayings one number is paralleled by that number plus one, hence the sequence x/x + 1. The emphasis falls on the latter number. Proverbs has some numerical sayings, e.g., 6:16–19, 30:15–16, 18–19, 21–23, 24–28, 29–31; cf. Job 40:5. See W. Roth, "The Numerical Sequence X/X + 1 in the Old Testament," *VT* 12 (1962) 300–311. For a thorough study of the whole subject, see W. Roth, *Numerical Sayings in the Old Testament*, VTSup 13 (Leiden: Brill, 1965).

17. It is unclear whether the list contains six or seven plagues, for some seem to be repeated. The plagues that are enumerated depend on which terms are considered to be synonymous (and, for some commentators, which verses are deleted as glosses). The

any punishing plague. The idea is not that God's own people are spared difficulty and misfortune in this life, but that they can endure a sequence of trials confident that God will *deliver* them from each of them. *in seven no harm will touch you* (v. 19b) means that the calamity will not strike the final blow of death. The number *seven* is significant, for it suggests completeness. Thus neither a single calamity nor any sequence of disasters is greater than God's ability to deliver. In 9:20–22, however, Job will directly challenge this thesis.

20 *In famine he will ransom you from death, and in war from the power of the sword.* The first pair that threatens life includes *famine*—a divine act[18]—and *the sword* in *war*—a human act. When one of his people is so threatened, God will pay the ransom *(pāḏâ)* necessary to secure his follower's release *from death.*[19] To the hungry he will give food and to him who is under siege he will give deliverance from the sword.[20]

21 The next set of plagues is *the scourging of the tongue* and *destruction.* Gordis takes the phrase *the scourging of the tongue (šôṭ lāšôn)* as elliptical for "the scourging fire" (*šôṭ lᵉšôn ʾēš;* cf. Isa. 5:24). God protects his own, hiding them from a calamity such as *destruction (šōḏ),* just as he hid Lot in a cave when he rained fire and brimstone on Sodom, or as he hid Noah and his family in an ark when he flooded the earth. During a catastrophe God will provide a way of escape. A follower may lose his possessions, but his life is secure (cf. Jer. 45:5). He need not *fear,* for God is the source of his protection. To endure loss free from remorse and fear is to value God's presence as superior to any loss that might be encountered and to exercise confidence in that position knowing that God is able to bring greater abundance in the season of restoration.

---

plagues are famine and war, v. 20; scourging tongue and destruction, v. 21; devastating hunger and wild beasts, v. 22; stones and beasts, v. 23. V. 22a may contain two plagues, "devastation and drought," but since "devastation" in v. 21b is repeated in v. 22a, the two words in v. 22a may be viewed as a hendiadys for one curse, "devastation from drought" (so Gordis). If the wild beasts mentioned in v. 22b and v. 23b are treated as one plague, the result is a list of seven. According to Gordis they are famine, war, fire, flood, drought, rocks, and wild beasts; he distinguishes *rāʿāḇ,* the famine or starvation caused by, e.g., insects, from that caused by *kāpān,* drought. But if "famine" (*rāʿāḇ,* v. 20a) and "drought" (*kāpān,* v. 22a) are redundant, six plagues are listed, and the seventh item is the opposite, God's abundant blessing (vv. 24–26). Gordis's view fits the context better, since it explains all the elements as "sorrows."

18. Cf. 1 K. 17:1; Ps. 105:16.

19. Cf. Ps. 49:16 (Eng. 15).

20. The combination of "famine" and "sword" is also found in Jer. 18:21. Both of these were military weapons; famine was a potent weapon usually inflicted by cutting off any supplies from entering a city under siege; cf. Jer. 14:13–15. The besieging army knew that in a matter of months the inhabitants would yield without battle, for famine would break their resolve and render them too weak to continue resistance.

22, 23 The last three plagues, *drought, beasts of the land,* and *stones* are woven into two couplets. In contrast to the preceding verses the second couplet is cast as a promise, denying that either stones or beasts will curse their owner. The positive note leads into the rich promises made in vv. 24–26.

In primitive society a village could be threatened with extinction by *devastation from drought* or by *the beasts of the land* or by *the stones of the field*. Drought is a terrible plague that drives people out of their homeland in search of food. In v. 22b *the beasts of the land* and in v. 23b *the beasts of the field* are wild beasts. The raging of a wild beast or a pack of wild animals could cause havoc to an entire village. These animals ravaged the livestock and crops, greatly curtailing an already limited food supply. Afraid for their lives, the villagers would not travel very far from their homes. Also *the stones of the field* could be a real threat, for too many of them rendered a field infertile.[21] An ancient army sometimes punished its foe by strewing stones through the cultivated fields (e.g., 2 K. 3:19, 25).[22] But whoever trusts in God's power is so free from *fear* that when faced by such terrifying catastrophes he *laughs* at them. His relationship with God is actualized in his being in harmony with nature, as guaranteed by a *covenant* with the stones and the beasts of the field. The goal of this covenant is peace between the one who fears God and the various creatures and forces of nature.

24, 25 These two verses articulate the tremendous benefits that result from being at peace with God. *You will know,* i.e., have confidence, *that all is well with your tent*. The *tent* is one's household, whether it be a tent or a house. *all is well* (*šālôm,* lit. "peace") means complete well-being in every aspect of the household. Whenever that person *inspects (pāqaḏ)*[23] his *estate,* either the fields where the crops are growing or more likely the pasture where his flocks are grazing, he will discover that all is prospering. He *will not find anything missing*. After such a tour of his holdings, he returns home filled with relief, gratitude, and confidence in God. At home he hears the joyful shouts of his children, who are as plentiful as *the grass of the earth*. He is content knowing that his heritage is certain. The analogy between children and grass is strengthened by the word *offspring (ṣeʾěṣāʾ)* in

21. Cf. A. S. Peake, "In League with the Stones of the Field," *ExpTim* 34 (1922) 42–43.

22. Ps. 91:11–12 speaks about God charging angels to guard a faithful follower so that he does not stumble over stones and sustain a serious injury (cf. the devil's use of these verses to tempt Jesus, Matt. 4:6 par. Luke 4:10–11). Note also that Ps. 91:13 mentions trampling on lions and snakes, i.e., beasts of the field. These lines indicate that the Hebrews considered both stones and wild beasts as real dangers faced on journeys.

23. The verb *pāqaḏ,* "attend to, muster, visit," is used in the sense of "inspecting" the flocks in Jer. 23:2.

that it can mean both human offspring and the produce from the field (Isa. 34:1; 42:5). Wishing to emphasize the certainty of God's blessing that such a person has, Eliphaz begins both vv. 24 and 25 with *you will know (yāḏaʿtā),* i.e., deep conviction supported by positive experiences.

26 The final promise that Eliphaz gives is that the patriarch himself will live a long life, *in full vigor (kelaḥ).*[24] His life will mature to a ripe old age, similar to *grain* turning golden brown as it ripens for harvest. Death in old age is the fitting conclusion to a life that has run its full course. Thus the three primary goals of an ancient sheikh—security for his flocks, numerous children to continue his name, and a long life—are ensured by God to the person who accepts his discipline. Through these promises Eliphaz is attempting to get Job to cease lamenting his misfortunes and to exercise submissive trust in God. He does not want Job hastening his death by arousing God's anger with more caustic words. But in his coming responses Job will challenge Eliphaz's unilateral application of this teaching of security for the person of faith.

27 Eliphaz concludes his speech with an exhortation. In his personal style he grounds the truth of all that he has spoken in the personal searching of the wise, with whom he identifies himself through the use of the pronoun *we.* The ancient wise men have *searched this out,* i.e., the truth of these hymns, sayings, and teachings, and they have found that they are true. Therefore, he exhorts Job: *Attend to (šāmaʿ)* these principles by putting them into practice. In his opinion, Job will then *come to know (yāḏaʿ)* their truth in his own experience. With this mild but firm exhortation, Eliphaz shows that his counsel is designed to offer Job hope in order that he may come through his suffering to a new, richer life.

AIM

In this first speech Eliphaz earnestly seeks to comfort Job. He desires that Job may find a way out of his suffering and be restored to a richer relationship with God. Acknowledging that Job has lived in the fear of God, he is somewhat shaken by the harsh tones of Job's opening curse-lament. Thus he

24. The understanding of *kelaḥ* as "full vigor," i.e., ripe old age, has a long history, supported by the Targ., "in the plentitude of your years." Driver-Gray find a connection with Arab. *kalaḥa,* "to look hard and stern," and *kulaḥ,* "a hard year (from dearth or famine)," thus implying "firm strength or unimpaired vigor." Ball suggests emending MT to *beleḥakâ,* "in your moisture." But it is not a good principle to eliminate a word primarily because it is unknown, esp. when it appears again in 30:2. Dahood ("Northwest Semitic Philology and Job," p. 56) shrewdly argues that this word results from a blend of *kōaḥ,* "strength," and *lēaḥ,* "freshness," but as Grabbe (*Comparative Philology and the Text of Job,* p. 46) points out, Dahood's idea cannot be proven.

suspects that Job may have inadvertently committed some wrong that has aroused God's anger. Nevertheless, at this time he will not accuse Job of any blatant sin. Rather he grounds the reason for Job's suffering in the limitations and sinfulness of all creatures. No one is without error before God. Consequently, Job's plight is no serious disgrace, but primarily an occasion for him to beseech God's mercy and experience his saving grace. Confession, then, would not be such an act of humiliation that Job would lose status in the community, but an act of obedient response to God as his Lord.

Fearful that Job's attitude will lead him into further conflict with God, Eliphaz emphasizes the doctrine of retribution and exhorts Job to beseech God's mercy so that he may experience God's saving grace. To encourage such a response he lauds God's greatness and in a numerical saying describes the great benefits which attend those whom God delivers from sorrow. By yielding to God Job will find the peace and quiet he desires so earnestly (3:13, 26). God will abundantly bless every aspect of his life; his flocks will richly increase, he will have abundant offspring, and he will die at a ripe old age and be buried in honor. Underlying this instruction is the conviction that God is willing and able to reverse one's plight.

Unfortunately, and obviously without realizing it, Eliphaz sides with the Satan against God in offering this counsel, for he seeks to motivate Job to serve God for the benefits that piety brings. His error is not in his doctrine, but in his inability to counsel Job rightly. Failing to discern that Job is sorely troubled by bearing suffering for no reason at all (cf. 2:3), Eliphaz by his counsel tempts Job to seek God for personal gain, not for God himself. As Andersen observes, "It is not a return to truth to deflect his mind to a promise of health, while he is scratching himself on his ash-heap; to promise him wealth, while the brigands make off with his animals; to give him dreams of numerous descendants, while his children lie crushed by the fallen stones."[1] But should Job follow his advice he would fall into the trap the Satan has set. If Job is to find God, he will have to chart a new course, a route different from the one Eliphaz has laid out.

2. JOB'S FIRST RESPONSE (6:1–7:21)

In his first response to the comforters Job defends his opening curse-lament and continues to lament his grief. In his defense he reasons that his weighty words, being commensurate with his anguish, do not tarnish his piety. He aggressively charges the friends with failing to live up to their responsibilities toward him. Eliphaz has lacked the insight to comfort and to instruct him. His counsel has been too general and indirect, for it is founded

1. Andersen, p. 124.

on the premise that suffering and sin are inexorably bound together, the premise that Job knows he cannot accept in his own case. No wonder Job does not ponder Eliphaz's exhortation to submit to God so that he might be blessed again. Instead he pursues his grievance with God. This time he registers a complaint against God. In deciding to argue with God Job takes the first steps on the path that will lead him to seek a resolution to his misery in an encounter with God himself.

The self-lament form dominates this speech, as attested by several elements: a vivid description of one's suffering (6:2–4; 7:3–6), the expression of distress at the behavior of one's friends (6:14–30), anticipation of death (6:11–13; 7:8–10), and accusations against God (6:4; 7:11–16). The friends take the place that the enemy usually occupies in a psalm of lament, for more agonizing than the taunting of enemies is the dismay caused by the betrayal of friends, a motif found in some psalms of lament (e.g., Ps. 35:13–15; 41:10 [Eng. 9]; 55:13–15 [Eng. 12–14]). Already the distance between the friends and Job is visible. Instead of upholding him they increase his burden by accusing and shaming him. Then in the latter part of this speech Job makes use of legal terms to strengthen his lament. In 7:12 he speaks as a plaintiff arguing his case before the court, and in 7:17–21 he interrogates God, his accuser. Job's use of legal terms is rooted in his conviction that he is innocent.

This speech has two major divisions, distinguished by the party addressed. In the first portion Job speaks to the friends as a group (6:1–30). In the second portion Job complains directly to God, his most formidable opponent (7:1–21).

a. A Rejoinder to the Friends (6:1–30)

(1) A Defense of His Lament (6:1–13)

(a) The Reality of His Suffering (6:1–7)

1 *Job responded:*
2 *"O that[1] my vexation could be weighed,*
and my misfortune[2] put on the scale with it!
3 *For it would outweigh the sand of the seas;*
therefore my words are rash.[3]

1. The particle *lû* here signals an unreal wish (GKC, § 159l).

2. The Qere *wᵉhawwāṯî*, "and my misfortune," is preferred to the Ketib *wᵉhayyāṯî*, "and I was."

3. KB, p. 506, takes *lʿʿ* as cognate to Arab. *laġāʷ*, "chatter"; cf. BDB, p. 534. The only other occurrence of this word is Prov. 20:25, where it expresses the onrush of words in a rash oath.

4 *Because the arrows of Shaddai stick fast in me,*
my spirit drinks their poison;
God's terrors are arrayed against me.
5 *Does the wild ass bray when it has grass,*
or the ox low when it has fodder?
6 *Is bland food eaten without salt,*
or is there taste in the milk of a weed?[4]
7 *My appetite*[5] *refuses*[6] *to touch it;*[7]
it loathes my food like a sickness."[8]

2, 3 Job opens this speech with an outburst of emotion, wishing that there was a dramatic way to demonstrate visibly the enormity of his suffering.[9] He wishes that a huge *scale* could be made available, consisting of two trays balanced from a center pole. On one tray Job would put his vexation and pile on top of it his misfortune. *Vexation* or grief *(kaʿaś)* is the anguish that the

4. The phrase *rîr ḥallāmûṯ* is variously understood. Heb. *rîr* means "saliva" or, with reference to a plant, "juice" or "sap." Hence RSV "the slime of purslane," a plant with mucilage like mallow (Hölscher, Fohrer, Horst). This translation gains support from the later Aram. *ḥallāmûṯ,* "mucilaginous juice of mallow" (M. Jastrow, *A Dictionary of the Targumim, the Talmud Babli and Yerushalmi, and the Midrashic Literature,* 2 vols. [New York: Shalom, 1967], I:471). Duhm, Budde, and Dhorme argue for "white of an egg" (supported by Targ.). Following A. Yahuda (*JQR* 15 [1902–1903] 702–703), Pope thinks the Hebrew is related to Arab. *ḥalūm* or *ḥallūm,* a soft cheese which yields a milky liquid in its raw state. A. Millard ("What Has No Taste?" *UF* 1 [1969] 210) points out that the word may be related to *šamḫilimitu* (occurring in Alalakh Tablets 375 rev. 3, 9; 283b rev. 4), an unknown substance issued in small quantities with grains, thus perhaps some kind of edible plant like purslane. The translation thus uses "milk of a weed" to avoid the unfamiliar "purslane."

5. Heb. *nep̄eš,* "soul," means lit. "throat," and by extension "appetite" (cf. Ps. 107:9; Prov. 6:24; 23:2; 27:7; Isa. 56:11; Jer. 50:19).

6. The perfect form of the verb "refuse" *(mēʾanâ)* indicates that Job continues to hold fast to a position he had already taken (GKC, § 106g).

7. For *lingôaʿ,* "to touch," LXX reads *largîaʿ,* "to rest" (accepted by Duhm and Hölscher).

8. This line is very difficult. The first word *hēmmâ,* "they," has no apparent antecedent (cf. Pope, who thinks that Eliphaz's words are the antecedent); it may have resulted from a scribal error. Thus many scholars suggest reading *zihᵃmâ* (or *zihēm*), "loathes," for *hēmmâ* (e.g., Rowley, Dhorme; see *BHS;* cf. 33:20, which may be an allusion to this verse). Then, if the construct *kiḏwê* (lit. "like a sickness of") is revocalized as an absolute, *kiḏway,* "like a sickness," the line reads as translated here. Other suggestions are to emend *kiḏwê* to *ḥayyāṯî,* "my life" (Ball), or *keḇōḏî,* "my liver/heart" (Dhorme), to gain a parallel to *nap̄šî,* "my self" or "my throat." Pope, however, takes the last word, *laḥmî,* "my food," in the Arabic sense of "meat" and interprets the line as referring to Job's flesh: "They [i.e., Eliphaz's words] are putrid as my flesh."

9. For a discussion of 6:2–3 see E. Sutcliffe, "Further Notes on Job, Textual and Exegetical," *Bib* 31 (1950) 365–78.

trial provoked,[10] while *misfortune (hawwâ)* refers to Job's losses.[11] To find the weight of his agony he would have to put on the other tray all *the sand of the seas*![12] Then all would see that his grief is beyond measure and understand why his *words are rash*. This picture offers a marked contrast to the Egyptian image of weighing a deceased person's heart against the feather of justice. Job chooses the word *vexation (kaʿaś)* as the first word for his agony in order to respond to Eliphaz. Whereas Eliphaz has just said "vexation *[kaʿaś]* kills a fool" (5:2), Job retorts by admitting that he is indeed sorely grieved or vexed, but he denies that he is thus a fool.

4 Using another metaphor, Job claims that God, the superb marksman, has shot a rain of arrows at him. The arrows have hit their mark, unleashing poison in his entrails, thus causing his *spirit (rûaḥ)* to drink deeply of their *poison (ḥēmâ)*.[13] *God's terrors are arrayed against me.* Expanding the metaphor in the third line, Job imagines that God, like a general marshalling a mighty army against a well-fortified city, has arrayed against him an army of terrors.[14] The same horror that the occupants of a besieged city feel floods Job's soul. It is evident that the trial leads Job to struggle with the meaning of his relationship with God. He feels that he is no longer in an I-Thou relationship with God, but in an I-It relationship. God acts toward him as though he were merely a practice target. Since Job has tied his honor so closely to his fear of God, his being reduced to an object crushes him.

5, 6 Using rhetorical questions about that which is absurd, Job supports his lamenting. The first picture (v. 5), composed of two images in synonymous parallelism, observes that as long as animals have food, they do not complain. The *wild ass* is symbolic of lust, roving freedom, and stiff determination (cf. Jer. 2:24). Conversely, *the ox* represents a steady, dependable, mighty work animal. Job is saying that he would not be speaking

10. "Vexation" describes the angry feelings aroused by the hateful actions and disrespectful attitude of an adversary (1 Sam. 1:6, 16; Neh. 3:33 [Eng. 4:1]). Such "vexation" wears down the body (Job 17:7; Ps. 6:8 [Eng. 7]). God too may be vexed by his people. The Israelites provoke God to grief by their sins, esp. by their idolatry (1 K. 14:9; 16:2, 7, 13; Jer. 8:19; 11:17).

11. Heb. *hawwâ* means lit. "gulf, chasm" (see Syr.). Figuratively it refers to a shattering catastrophe that brings ruin or destruction.

12. Sand usually represents an unmeasurable amount, but in this passage it symbolizes a massive weight. Cf. Prov. 27:3; Sir. 22:15.

13. Heb. *ḥēmâ* means lit. "heat"; in this context it refers by extension to the burning sensation caused by poison. Although this is the only mention of poison arrows in the OT, they were common in the ancient world (see Dhorme, Pope). This word is also used in reference to the poison of the adder in Ps. 58:5 (Eng. 4) and Deut. 32:24, 33.

14. Hakam understands the imagery of v. 4c in the light of v. 4b: God has prepared a table for Job and has set before him terrors as the main dish. Then the transition to the food metaphor in vv. 5–6 is smooth.

so rashly if he were not in grave straits, regardless of whether he be compared to a free-spirited man like the wild ass or a hired worker like the ox. The second picture (v. 6), also composed of two images, states that *bland food is not eaten without salt,* being too tasteless. Similarly *the milk of a weed* (specifically purslane) is repulsive for its lack of pleasant taste.

7 Job applies these images to his plight. *My appetite [nepeš] refuses [mēʾ*ª*nâ] to touch it; it loathes my food like a sickness* (cf. 33:20). The *food* could refer either to Job's suffering or to the arguments of his friends. The former seems most likely, for Job focuses on his own sorrow in this pericope. Just as Job's appetite would refuse putrid food, so his inner being recoils before his suffering. No wonder such bitter words pour from his mouth. Lamenting is the natural expression of a person being repulsed by tragic misfortune.

(b) A Wish for Death as a Release from Suffering (6:8–13)

8 *"O that my request were granted,*
that God would grant my hope!
9 *May it please God to crush me,*
may he loose his hands and cut me off.
10 *That would even be my comfort;*
I would leap[1] *in unsparing pain;*[2]
for I have not concealed the words of the Holy One.
11 *What strength do I have to keep on waiting?*
What is my end that I should be patient?
12 *Is my strength the strength of stones?*
Or is my flesh bronze?[3]
13 *Is there*[4] *any help in me,*
since resourcefulness is driven from me?"

1. The root *sld* appears only here in the OT. Many translate it "leap for joy" with the Targ. and LXX (see KB, p. 714). In Mishnaic Hebrew it means "recoil, jump back, shrink," e.g., jerking a hand away from fire (M. Jastrow, *Dictionary of the Targumim,* p. 993). The idea of quick movement is accepted for this root, though no connotation of joy is associated with it.

2. MT *ḥîlâ,* "writhing, pain," is taken as a feminine form of the usually masculine noun. For another view see M. Mers, "A note on Job vi 10," *VT* 32 (1982) 234–36.

3. Most commentators restore Heb. *n*ᵉ*ḥûšâ,* the normal spelling of "bronze" in Job, by attaching the *h* on *haʾim* (v. 13a) to the end of v. 12. Apparently the word was accidentally misdivided at an early stage. See next note.

4. MT *haʾim* is unusual. Dhorme reads *h*ª*lōʾ* with LXX, but the MT form occurs in Num. 17:28 (Eng. 13) and should not be altered too hastily. The best suggestion is to join the letter *h* to the last word of v. 12, thereby preserving the MT consonants. Gordis gains a smooth reading by relating *ʾim* to Arab. *ʾanna,* "indeed."

8–10 In the style of a self-lament Job bemoans his suffering with a wishful request that God would execute the final blow against him. Job continues to lament in a manner that addresses God indirectly. He wishes that God would activate the oath which he has uttered (ch. 3) and would be pleased to crush him. He calls that curse *my request* and *my hope*. At this point the wish for death preoccupies Job's thinking, for he sees it as his only escape from his excruciating pain. And he believes that God could secure his death if he were willing and his hands were unleashed. This wish alludes to the prologue, in which God has tied the Satan's hands. But here Job believes that God's hands are the ones which are bound. Since Job is thinking that God is holding back in afflicting him to the fullest extent possible, he prays that God would crush him by unleashing the full brunt of the attack. *crush (dikkā')* means that one is either brutally beaten or trampled to death (cf. 4:19; 5:4; 22:9; 34:25; Ps. 89:11 [Eng. 10]; Isa. 53:5). The last word in v. 9, *cut off (biṣṣaʿ),* means literally to cut the thread so a fabric can be removed from the loom.[5] In a few OT passages this image depicts death (e.g., Job 27:8; Isa. 38:12).

In describing his curse-lament as *my hope (tiqwâ)* Job is countering the words of Eliphaz. Eliphaz thought Job's hope should be his upright life (4:6) or the assurance that God delivers individuals from troubles (5:15–16). But Job believes that his only hope is death itself. Nevertheless, he resolutely rejects suicide; if death is to come, it must come from God. If he knew his death were near and certain, the present suffering would be a little easier to bear, for the fact that God had answered this prayer would itself be some consolation. He *would leap* up, even though filled with *unsparing pain* (*ḥîlâ,* a word used particularly for labor pains).

Job bases his petition on the fact that he has not *concealed* or denied *(kiḥēḏ)*[6] *the words of the Holy One,* i.e., God.[7] In this way he reaffirms his innocence and uses this affirmation as the basis of his prayer. Job's motivation for this petition is to know that God accepts him as a faithful servant, not to get rid of his pain at any cost. If God hastened his death, it would be a witness to all that God had heard him and granted his prayer.

5. Cf. D. Kellermann, "*bṣʿ*," *TDOT,* II:207.

6. The Piel of Heb. *kḥd* means "hide, conceal (a matter)." It refers to something which is not "made known" (Isa. 3:9) or "spoken" (Ps. 78:4). When one does not hide something, he speaks freely about it and shares his insight and joy with others (Ps. 40:11 [Eng. 10]). Indeed, he who teaches does not conceal (Job 27:11). That Job has not concealed God's words means that he has neither withheld them from others nor failed to obey them.

7. The term "the Holy One" is an epithet for God (cf. Isa. 40:25; 57:15; Hos. 11:9; Hab. 3:3; Sir. 45:6). Although the plural form *qᵉḏōšîm* is sometimes used for "angels" (e.g., Job 5:1; 15:15), the singular strongly favors its identification as a title for God, even though it occurs only here in Job.

Job, therefore, rejects Eliphaz's exhortation completely. He will not repent, for he has never denied God's word. If he did repent, it would in essence be a denial of God rather than a turning to God, as the friends assume. Instead he will address his lament and prayers to God, though such words may seem disrespectful from a human vantage point. Hopeful that God will respond to him, Job is just beginning to formulate the approach that will lead to a demand for God's intervention. Here is the first sign of movement in Job's thinking that will eventually lead him out of deepest despair.

11–13 With a series of rhetorical questions Job deplores his physical weakness and loss of fortitude. His *strength* is not adequate for him to keep waiting for God to answer. Fearful of his end, he has no reason to be patient.[8] *Is my strength the strength of stones? Or is my flesh bronze?* Because the clear answer to these questions is no, Job is unable to go through this trial in silence. Job's experience stands in sharp contrast to Jeremiah's. God promised Jeremiah that he would make him a fortified city, a pillar of iron and walls of bronze against all who would persecute him (Jer. 1:18). But Job has not received any such promise to sustain him during his ordeal. His affliction has sapped his strength. *Is there any help in me, since resourcefulness is driven from me?* Efficient wisdom or *resourcefulness (tûšîyâ),*[9] the quality that has enabled him to gain his riches and lead an upright life, has been driven away.[10] His complaint about the loss of strength adds support to his defense of the intense bitterness of his words. Job's longing is to experience in his life what the psalmist experienced: "My comfort in my suffering is this: your promise renews my life" (Ps. 119:50, NIV).

(2) An Accusation against the Friends (6:14–30)

Job directly charges his friends with dealing treacherously with him. The line of argument here is calmer and more reasoned than the opening utterance. He acknowledges a close relationship with his comforters, calling

8. The expression for "patience" is *heʾĕrîḵ napšô,* lit. "to make one's soul long." This idiom means "to be patient," not "to prolong one's life" (contra Dhorme; cf. Targ. and Syr.). It is the opposite of *qāṣar napšô,* "be short of soul," i.e., "be impatient" (cf. Judg. 10:16; 16:16; Num. 21:4).

9. J. Genung ("Meaning and Usage of the Term *twšyh,*" *JBL* 30 [1911] 114–22) finds the emphasis in *tûšîyâ* on the practical, subjective side of wisdom. Dhorme defines it as "the foresight that plans ahead" (on 5:12). Emphasizing the outcome of competent action, it may be translated "success"; cf. Driver-Gray (on 5:12).

10. The word "drive away, banish" *(nāḏaḥ)* occurs frequently in Deuteronomy; it refers to God's expelling the local inhabitants so that his people may inhabit the promised land. In Jeremiah it becomes a stereotypical phrase for the banishment of the Exile. Perhaps the idea of driving away as a means of punishment may carry over to this statement that God has driven sound wisdom from Job.

them friends and brothers. The word *brothers* (*ʾāḥîm*, v. 15a) and the term *loyal love* or *fidelity* (*ḥeseḏ*, v. 14a) indicate that there probably existed an official bond or covenant between Job and these comforters (cf. 1 Sam. 20:8, 14–15). Their pact certainly included friendship and mutual support. Thus Job accuses his partners of failing to fulfill the obligations of their covenant relationship (6:14–23). Then with a change of tone that indicates he is hopeful of reconciliation, Job seeks to move the friends to soften their rhetoric and teach him his error (6:24–30).

(a) Their Treachery (6:14–23)

14 *"He who refuses[1] loyal kindness to his friend*
also forsakes the fear of Shaddai.
15 *My brothers are unreliable like a wadi,*
like wadi channels they overflow,[2]
16 *when they are murky[3] with[4] ice*
and are swelled[5] by snow;
17 *in the time[6] of their flowing[7] they disappear,*
when it is hot[8] they vanish from their place.

1. The meaning of MT *lammās* is difficult to determine. One possibility is to take it from *māsas*, "melt, despair": "a despairing man should have the devotion of his friends" (NIV). Gordis seeks a cognate in Arab. *lamas* VIII, "to seek, desire something": "he who seeks mercy from his friends." Others relate this word either to *mûš*, "remove" (Hölscher), or *mānaʿ*, "deprive": "he who deprives his friends of kindness" (cf. RSV; Driver-Gray; Targ., Syr., Vulg.). Grabbe (*Comparative Philology and the Text of Job*, pp. 48–51) thinks that *mʾs*, *mʾh*, and *mss* all may be related, with the basic meaning "melt, dissolve, flow." The versions read "refuse"; the parallel word "forsake" *(yaʿᵃzōḇ)* supports their translation. Thus the text may have read *lammāš*, "to the one who refuses" (cf. Fohrer; cf. also *BHS*).

2. The verb *ʿāḇar* can mean "overflow" (Isa. 8:7) or "pass away," i.e., "run dry" (11:6; 30:15); the movement of the passage favors the former meaning. No doubt there is a double image here: both brothers and wadis overflow and then run dry.

3. On the meaning of *qāḏar* see L. Delekat, "Zum Hebräischen Wörterbuch," *VT* 14 (1964) 55–56.

4. The preposition *minnî*, "from," is an old poetic form found 19 times in Job. The line is made very powerful by alliteration: *haqqōḏᵉrîm minnî-qāraḥ ʿālêmô yiṯʿallem-šāleg*. P. Skehan states that the culmination of liquid sounds suggests the "continuous heaping up of snow" ("Second Thoughts on Job 6:16 and 6:25," *CBQ* 31 [1969] 210–12; repr. in *Studies in Israelite Poetry and Wisdom*, CBQMS I [Washington: Catholic Biblical Association, 1971], pp. 83–84).

5. Some (e.g., Dhorme, Tur-Sinai, Gordis) relate *yiṯʿallem*, "it hides itself," to *yiṯʿārem*, "heaped up" (Exod. 15:8). According to Skehan (op. cit.) the scribe intentionally wrote *ʿrm* with a *lamed* for purposes of alliteration. Cf. also Grabbe, *Comparative Philology and the Text of Job*, pp. 51–54.

6. The phrase *bᵉʿēṯ* stands in construct before the independent sentence, forming a temporal clause (GKC, §§ 130d, 155l).

7. The word *zāraḇ* is from an established root in Semitic meaning "flow, rush"

18 *Caravans*[9] *twist their course,*
they go up in the wasteland and perish;
19 *caravans from Tema look for them;*
convoys of Sheba hope for them.
20 *They are ashamed although*[10] *they trusted,*[11]
they come to them[12] *and are confounded.*
21 *Thus*[13] *now you are nothing;*[14]
you see a terror and are afraid.
22 *Have I said, 'Make a gift on my behalf,*
from your wealth[15] *pay a reward for me,*
23 *rescue me from the hand of the adversary,*
or from the hand of the ruthless deliver me?' "[16]

14 Job accuses his friends of falling short in their expression of *loyal kindness (ḥeseḏ)* to him in his time of affliction. They are guilty of failing to fulfill their covenant obligations with him. Job argues that in failing to show

---

(see Grabbe, *Comparative Philology*, pp. 64–65). Thus it is precarious to take it as a Syriac form of *ṣāraḇ*, "burn" (Ezek. 21:3 [Eng. 20:47]); cf. G. R. Driver, "Some Hebrew Medical Expressions," *ZAW* 65 (1953) 261–62.

8. The phrase *beḥummô* is unusual. Perhaps the pronominal suffix has its antecedent in *ʿēṯ*, "time" (Horst), and this phrase corresponds to the more usual expression *keḥōm hayyôm*, "in the heat of the day" (Gen. 18:1; cf. 1 Sam. 11:11). More likely, though, this is a case of the impersonal use of the suffix (GKC, §§ 144b, c; Gordis).

9. Heb. *ʾorḥôṯ*, lit. "paths," is a metonymy for caravans. For this meaning some wish to revocalize it as a participle, *ʾōreḥôṯ* (cf. Gen. 37:25; Isa. 21:13), but that is not necessary. In Assyrian *ḫarrānum* and *aliktum* mean both "road, journey" and "caravan"; the latter is cognate to Heb. *halîḵâ* in v. 19b (W. F. Albright, "Abram the Hebrew: A New Archaeological Interpretation," *BASOR* 163 [1961] 41n.24).

10. Andersen points out that *kî* may carry a concessive meaning.

11. The first line is short. While it is possible to read the singular *bāṭaḥ*, "he trusted" (GKC, § 145u), it is better to emend it to the plural, *bāṭeḥû* (Budde, Duhm, Hölscher, Gordis). The line could be further lengthened with the addition of *bāh*, "in it" (Duhm).

12. The feminine suffix on *ʿāḏêhā*, lit. "to her," refers to the masculine plural *neḥālîm*, "streams," a use of the feminine pronoun for the plural of things (GKC, § 135p).

13. Some (e.g., Fohrer, Pope) prefer *kēn*, "thus," to *kî*, "because," but the latter is fine, for Job is building on his last comparison. See also Blommerde, *Northwest Semitic Grammar and Job*, p. 48.

14. The negative *lōʾ*, "not," in the sense of "nothing," is unusual; but it is possible (see Blommerde, ibid.), and Targ. supports this meaning. Some (e.g., Gordis) read the Qere, *lô*, "it": "you have become it or that." Others (e.g., Dhorme, Fohrer, Pope) follow LXX and Syr. and read *lî*, hence "you have become to me."

15. This is a use of *kōaḥ*, "strength," like *ḥayil*, "strength, arm," in the sense of "wealth, riches" (cf. 5:5; Prov. 5:10; Ezra 2:69).

16. The imperfect is coordinated with the imperative to express a wish or an obligation (GKC, § 107n). Heb. *pāḏâ* here means "to deliver"; the idea of payment has receded into the background (cf. *TWOT*, II:716–17).

him loyalty they *forsake the fear of Shaddai* (cf. 1:1). In this phrase Job specifically uses the divine name *Shaddai* in response to Eliphaz's use of Shaddai in the beatitude (5:17). The phrase "the fear of God" means both reverence toward God and living by a high ethical standard.[17] Therefore, the friends are destroying the basis of their worship of God and the foundation of their wisdom. Whereas Eliphaz is shocked that Job's fear of God does not sustain him during his misfortunes (4:6), Job is distressed that the friends' fear of Shaddai does not move them to support him through his troubles. Both parties are thus attacking the center of the other's worship of God.

15–17 Job points out the seriousness of the friends' offense against him through several picturesque metaphors drawn from the austere environment of the desert.[18] Water is the most crucial item for traversing the desert. Every traveler stakes his life on finding some. The dry streambeds that cut across the desert floor witness to the rainy season when raging torrents of water sweep through these channels. In the spring these wadi channels are filled by melting snow. The rushing water is murky. But as the snow disappears from the mountains, these streams turn to a trickle and gradually dry out. During the hottest days of summer when the traveler desperately needs water, these streams have completely vanished. This analogy claims that the friends overflow with loyal kindness during the good times, but when the heat of trials comes, they dry up; they turn out to be undependable.

18–20 Ancient *caravans* were skilled in crossing the burning desert. In connection with caravan trade Job mentions two famous cities, Tema and Sheba. *Tema* was a center of trade routes in northwestern Arabia, and *Sheba* was a center in southwestern Arabia.[19] Caravans from these cities made regular commercial ventures through this barren land, following a path that had intermittent stations with dependable water sources. But if they came on a dependable well or spring and found it dry, they would be taken by surprise. In desperation a caravan would leave the valley floor and twist its way up through the *wasteland (tōhû)* looking for water, but find no trace of it. The entire caravan would *perish* in the trackless sands. Caught by their folly of relying on that which failed them, they *are ashamed* and *confounded*.

21 Job applies these powerful metaphors directly to his friends. He stands in shame before them just as a thirsty member of a caravan before a dried-up brook. His friends have proved to be *nothing (lōʾ)*. They have no refreshing water to offer him. In looking at Job, *a terror (ḥᵃṯaṯ)*, they *are*

17. See above, p. 67.

18. Cf. S. Perowne, "Notes on I Kings and the Book of Job," *PEQ* 71 (1939) 199–203.

19. In the genealogical tables Tema is a son of Ishmael (Gen. 25:13–15). Geographically Tema is an Arabian locality. On Sheba see 1:15.

afraid. Fear has dissolved their loyalty and preempted their efforts to console him.

22, 23 Job continues by arguing that his ill-fate has not laid a heavy burden on them. A covenant friend was obligated to rescue his partner from any trouble. But Job has not demanded *a gift* from them to pay off some debt nor has he asked them to *pay a reward* (Piel of *šāḥad*)[20] from their wealth to release him from the control of an oppressor. He has not put their wealth in jeopardy. Nor have they had to risk their lives *to rescue* him from *the hand of the adversary* or from *the ruthless (ʿārîṣîm),*[21] i.e., tyrants.

(b) A Request for Their Sympathy (6:24–30)

24 *"Teach me and I shall be silent;*
make me understand[1] *how I have erred.*
25 *How are upright words grievous;*[2]
what does your arguing[3] *prove?*
26 *Do you intend to reprove me with words,*
when the words of a despairing man are counted as wind?
27 *Soon you would cast lots*[4] *over the blameless*[5]
and barter[6] *over your friend.*

20. The Hebrew root *šḥd* means "give a present" or "pay a reward" in order to secure one's desires or to win appeasement (1 K. 15:19; Prov. 6:35; Isa. 45:13). Given the power of a gift, this word often carries the sense of "bribe"; cf. Prov. 17:8, 23; Ps. 15:5; 26:10; Isa. 1:23; 5:23; Exod. 23:8; Deut. 27:25.

21. Heb. *ʿārîṣ* is esp. used of the proud and rich who customarily oppress and extort others, as in Job 27:13; Ps. 54:5 (Eng. 3); 86:14; Jer. 15:21. The word also applies to a ruthless nation that plunders and devastates other peoples; cf. Ezek. 28:7; 30:11; 31:12; 32:12. The idea of rescuing people from such a tyrant is found in Isa. 49:25.

1. The expression *bîn l*[e] means "explain" (Dhorme).

2. Some identify *māraṣ* with Aram. *mrʿ*, "be ill, distressed" (Tur-Sinai, Gordis), or Akk. *marāṣu,* "feel, cause pain" (KB, p. 602); in Ugaritic *mrṣ* means an illness. Others (e.g., Hölscher, Dhorme, Pope) take the root as *mlṣ,* "be sweet," and believe that the spelling has been altered by an exchange of *r* for *l* for purposes of alliteration (cf. also Targ.). The latter view has in its favor the use of *mlṣ* in a similar context in Ps. 119:103. The verse must then be interpreted as ironic or sarcastic, an interpretation that Rowley rejects.

3. The infinitive absolute serves as subject of the verb, which is from the same root, thus emphasizing the verbal idea (GKC, § 113b).

4. The Hiphil of Heb. *nāpal,* "fall," is used often with *gôrāl,* "lot," to mean "cast"; here the complement is suppressed, as in 1 Sam. 14:42. The use of the preposition *ʿal* ("over") favors this interpretation (so Dhorme; cf. Ps. 22:18–19 [Eng. 17–18]; Neh. 10:35 [Eng. 34]). Driver-Gray assign to *nāp̄al* the meaning "fall on," but the action thus depicted seems a little too direct and violent for the context.

5. For MT *ʿal-yāṯôm,* "over an orphan," some commentators (e.g., Duhm) read *ʿly-tm (tōm),* "against the blameless," an allusion to 1:1. This suggestion offers a better parallel with *rēaʿ* and applies directly to Job (Andersen). But cf. Dhorme.

6. The verb *kārâ* is taken from a root *krh* II, "buy, purchase" (KB, pp. 472–73).

28 *But now be pleased to look at me;*
surely I will not lie to your face.
29 *Relent!*[7] *Do not allow false testimony.*
Relent![8] *My cause is just.*[9]
30 *Is there any false testimony on my tongue?*
Does not my palate discern deceptive words?"[10]

24 In a dramatic change of mood Job seeks for sympathetic guidance from his friends. He asks them to *teach* him as wise teachers offering gentle instruction rather than as fierce lawyers arguing his guilt. If they instruct him kindly, he will be silent, attentive to their instruction. Thereby they could ease his pain and help him overcome his alienation from God.

Job wants to learn wherein he has *erred (šāgâ)*. This word refers to unintentional sins. Such sins, though committed unknowingly, must still be atoned for upon becoming known (cf. Lev. 4–5). Throughout the dialogue Job never denies the possibility that he has sinned; rather he denies having sinned as grievously as his suffering would seem to indicate. No wonder he uses such a mild word for any possible sin. But if some specific error can be pointed out, he wants to know what it is so that he can take care of it.

25 Since the friends obviously would think his plea strange and out of place in that Eliphaz has already offered excellent teaching about human nature and how one finds God, Job defends his willingness to receive gentle instruction by pointing out the alienating nature of their arguments. It is true

---

The other context for *kārâ* in 40:30 (Eng. 41:6) suggests the meaning "bargain" (over the price of a fish); cf. Deut. 2:6; Hos. 3:2.

7. Gordis argues that in a few passages *šûḇ,* lit. "turn," being the opposite of "going forward," may mean "stop, halt, stay." Thus he translates the line: "Please stay, there is no wrong in me, stay with me, my integrity is still intact." See further idem, "Some Hitherto Unrecognized Meanings of the Root *Shub,*" *JBL* 52 (1933) 153–62. In this context the verb appears to bear a stronger meaning, however. Cf. Rowley, Pope. For a thorough study of *šûḇ* see W. Holladay, *The Root šûbh in the Old Testament* (Leiden: Brill, 1958).

8. The Qere *šuḇû* is accepted, since Job has been using the plural form throughout this speech, and at certain stages in the evolution of the Hebrew script *y* and *w* were easily mistaken.

9. The reading *bāh* is accepted as the harder reading, though it is untranslated here. The feminine suffix may have a neuter sense, as in Gen. 24:14, "in itself," i.e., "intact" (so Dhorme, Gordis). Others (e.g., Driver-Gray) emend it to *bî,* "in me."

10. The meaning of *hawwôṯ* here is debated. Its usual meaning, "destruction" (KB, p. 232), does not fit the context well. For the translation given here see S. Erlandsson, *"havvāh," TDOT,* III:357. A. Guillaume ("Magical Terms in the OT," *JRAS* [1942] 111–31) takes *hawwâ* to mean "a curse of magical origins"; G. R. Driver ("Witchcraft in the OT *hwh,*" *JRAS* [1943] 6–16) defines it as "windy words"; Pope identifies it with Ugar. *hwt,* "word."

that they have used *upright words,* but these words, being *grievous,* inflict pain on him rather than offer him comfort (cf. Ps. 119:103). The approach they have taken has been argumentative; their intention is to prove him wrong. But his response reveals that their arguing does not accomplish anything.

26 Furthermore, Job wonders why the friends think they can reprove him with words when they count his words to be only wind. Even though he is *despairing (nōʾāš),* his words, and especially the feelings that give rise to them, are worthy of their careful attention, for in them they might discern how to respond to him instructively.

27 Job paints a portrait of the kind of unjust behavior to which their disposition may lead, thereby serving as a warning to the dangers of such an unsympathetic attitude. Those with this attitude use the judicial system to their own advantage to squeeze the most out of someone indebted to them, though that party is an innocent, *blameless (tōm)* person, even *a friend (rēaʿ).* Mercilessly they *cast lots* over their victim or *barter* over him in order to get the most out of him without any regard for his feelings. In ancient society when a party was indebted, the creditor might cast lots over his goods, or even his children, to select that which would be sold against the debt (cf. 2 K. 4:1). Job feels that this is the way his friends have treated him, a blameless man.

This charge against the friends seems harsh in the light of Eliphaz's moderate approach in his first speech. It makes more sense, however, when one recognizes that many of the lines in the first round of speeches need to be understood in the light of the entire dialogue. For instance, here Job has detected in Eliphaz a condescending attitude that will become more evident as the dialogue moves along (cf. 15:4–6; 22:4–7).

28 Seeking to establish a more positive bearing between himself and his comforters, Job requests that they *look* at him. This line suggests that they turned their faces away from him as they spoke. This offensive gesture says that they are rejecting not only his words but also his person. Hurt and disturbed, Job beseeches them to look at him again and not to be so repulsed, neither by the strenuous tone of his lament nor by the horror of his appearance. Although his words may be distasteful to them, they are certainly true. As he speaks he wants to look them in the eye to convince them that he is not lying.

29, 30 Job exhorts them to *relent (šûḇ).* That is, he wants them to change their posture radically. Whereas they now appear to accept *false testimony (ʿawlâ)* against him, they need to recognize that his *cause is just* and so discounts that false testimony.

Job supports his position with a double rhetorical question that denies he has lied in any way. There is no false testimony on his *tongue.*

Since his *palate (ḥēḵ)*[11] can still discern *deceptive words (hawwôṯ),* he is fully conscious of the truth of his words. Heb. *hawwa* refers both to the root of evil in the heart as expressed in wrong desires and to its consequences in falsehood and perversity. It also means "ruin, calamity" as the punishment for such evil desire and falsehood (cf. 6:2; 30:13). No doubt this word was chosen for both nuances. In this context *deceptive words* is the meaning preferred by the many figures for speech, but this term at the same time alludes to Job's misfortune. Job's point is that since he can detect no wrong desire or deception on his part, he believes that the friends need to place some confidence in what he is saying.

b. A Lament (7:1–21)

In the second part of this speech Job leaves off addressing the comforters and speaks directly to God. After lamenting his fate, Job details his own physical agony and bemoans the hard lot of humanity in general. He complains bitterly to God for treating him so harshly, and he reminds God that he will soon die. Then he seeks to motivate God to ease his sufferings for the few days he has left before dying. He reasons that anything that he might have done could not have harmed God and that after his death God will seek him eagerly, but not be able to find him. That Job speaks realistically about his pains here, in contrast to the unrealistic wish never to have been born that he uttered in his curse-lament (ch. 3), means that he is beginning to cope with his real situation. He is reaching beyond his despair to find reconciliation with God. This section is arranged in four subsections alternating between a lament and a petition.

(1) The Lament Proper (7:1–10)

(a) A Description of Great Pain (7:1–6)

1 *"Has not man a term of service on the earth?*
And are not his days like the days of a hired worker?
2 *Like a slave who gasps for the shade,*
and like a hired worker who hopes for his wages,
3 *thus I have inherited months*[1] *of emptiness,*
and nights of misery are allotted[2] *to me.*

11. The palate *(ḥēḵ)* discerns taste (12:11 = 34:3) and functions as an instrument of speech (20:12; 29:10; 31:30).

1. Heb. *yeraḥ,* "month," comes from *yārēaḥ,* "moon," and makes a good parallel with "night" (cf. Tur-Sinai, who translates "moons" here; cf. also Gordis). Rowley points out that "month" stands for the length and "night" for the intensity of Job's suffering.

2. It seems best to take the verb *minnû,* "be allotted," as a third person plural

4 *When I lie down, I wonder, 'When shall I rise?'*
During the length[3] of the evening, I am fed up with tossing until dawn.[4]
5 *My flesh is clothed with worms and crusts;[5]*
my skin forms a scab[6] and oozes.[7]
6 *My days go past faster than a weaver's shuttle;*
they are cut off as the end of a thread."[8]

1, 2 Job laments the hard plight of all human beings, both slave and free.[9] In return for his toil the worker receives only a meager reward, a small wage or a brief time of relaxation. Job considers that his fate is comparable to the hardship borne by one who spends his strength in working for another person.

---

form used for the passive rather than to revocalize it as a Pual (cf. GKC, § 144g); it is also possible that the *u* of the passive has been sharpened to an *i* (Gordis).

3. For *middaḏ* Driver-Gray and Fohrer read *middê*, related to Arab. *madda*, "to extend, stretch out." Gordis argues that *middaḏ* may be a phonetic variant of *muddaḏ:* "the night is extended." The emphasis falls on the end of darkness and not the beginning of light (Fohrer). J. Reider ("*Middaḏ* in Job 7:4," *JBL* 39 [1920] 60–65) gains the same meaning by analyzing the form as *min* ("from") plus *daḏ* ("breast" or "front"): "the front of evening."

4. This verse is long for a distich, but it is difficult to divide it into a tristich. Perhaps the line is intentionally longer to capture Job's emotion. If the *ʾaṯnāḥ* (the principal Masoretic accent that divides a verse) is placed at *ʾāqûm*, "I rise," better parallelism is gained (see *BHS*).

5. The Qere *gûš* (Ketib *gîš*), "lump," is a hapax legomenon in the OT. It may mean "a hard scab"; here it is joined with *ʿāpār*, "dust," which may indicate that dirt has mixed with the various fluids seeping from his sores to form hard crusts. Although *gûš* appears in the Mishna with *ʿāpār*, "a lump of clay," it seems most probable that here *ʿāpār* is a gloss to explain the unusual *gûš* (Budde, Fohrer, *BHS;* but cf. Gordis); in addition, the line is more balanced with its elimination (9/8 syllable count). Thus it is omitted.

6. There are two interpretations for MT *rāgaʿ*. According to Dhorme it means "split"; he cites texts where it parallels *māḥaṣ*, "break, shatter" (26:12; Isa. 51:15; Jer. 31:35). Driver-Gray, Gordis, Fohrer, and KB (2nd ed., p. 874) relate it to Ethiopic *ragaʿa*, "coagulate, congeal," hence meaning "form a scab" (but cf. Dhorme's arguments against this interpretation).

7. It is preferable to take the verb *wayyimmāʾēs* from *māsas* ("flow, melt") and revocalize it *wayyimmās*, "and it oozes," with Driver-Gray. Cf. Dhorme, Tur-Sinai. Perhaps the ʾ entered as a *mater lectionis* (GKC, § 23g).

8. The meaning of Heb. *beʾepes tiqwâ* is ambiguous. Driver-Gray, Pope, Tur-Sinai, and Gordis translate it "without hope," the most common meaning of the terms. Ibn Ezra, Dhorme, Rowley, and Andersen think that the weaving image continues in this part of the verse; hence they translate it "for lack of thread." For *beʾepes* in the sense of "for lack of" see Prov. 26:20; cf. Prov. 14:28; Dan. 8:25; for *tiqwâ*, "thread, cord," see Josh. 2:18, 21. The latter interpretation seems preferable.

9. The comparison of one's sufferings to the general miserable plight of humanity occurs in other psalms of lament, e.g., Ps. 39:5–7, 12 (Eng. 4–6, 11); 62:10 (Eng. 9); 88:5–6 (Eng. 4–5); cf. Fohrer, p. 166.

This analogy emphasizes the weakness and servitude of human beings in general. Three nouns depict the relationship of a laborer to his master. *term of service*. The first noun, *ṣāḇāʾ*, refers to forced service. It was primarily used for military service, but it could also refer to conscripted labor as here. A noteworthy example of forced labor was the corps drafted by Solomon to serve one month out of every three in Phoenicia felling timber (1 K. 5:27-28 [Eng. 13-14]). Corvée labor was hated, for one was forced to work under austere circumstances far from home.

hired worker. The second term, *śāḵîr* (from the verb *śāḵar*, "hire"), could also refer to those hired for military purposes (Jer. 46:21; cf. Isa. 7:20), though it is usually used of domestic workers (e.g., Exod. 12:45; Lev. 25:53). These workers were usually very poor (Lev. 25:40) and often hired themselves out one day at a time for a meager wage that scarcely provided daily food for their families. In the morning they would gather with other laborers at the marketplace and wait patiently to be hired for the day (cf. Matt. 20:1–12). Because of their poverty it was imperative that they be paid at the end of the day so that they could buy food for the evening meal (Lev. 19:13; Deut. 24:14–15; cf. Matt. 20:8).

slave. The third term is *ʿeḇeḏ* (from the common verb *ʿāḇaḏ*, "work, serve"). It has a broad range of reference, including anyone who works for or serves another, from slaves (Deut. 15:15) to ambassadors (2 K. 22:12), from worshipers (all Israel, Lev. 25:55) to the Suffering Servant (Isa. 52:13). Often foreigners were slaves, either captured in war (Josh. 16:10; Neh. 9:36; cf. 1 Sam. 4:9) or sold to pay a debt (Lev. 25:44–46; cf. Deut. 28:68), though Israelites also at times had to sell themselves in service to others for a period of years (limited to seven) in order to pay off debts (Exod. 21:2–11; Lev. 25:39–46; Deut. 15:12–18).[10] The slave was completely bound to his master's will. With these comparisons the author moves beyond the core issue of the suffering of the righteous to the issue of widespread human misery.

The reward of the hired worker differs markedly from that of the slave. The former bears the heat of the day in anticipation of his wages, thinking of the joy he will receive from the morsel he will be able to buy and share with his family. In contrast, the slave endures the burning heat for his master. Beneath the hot sun he *gasps (šāʾaḇ) for the shade*, the coolness of the long shadows of the late afternoon. In the Palestinian hill country the heat of a long summer day is made bearable by the cool, refreshing breeze that one can usually feel in the shade during the afternoon. Since the slave

10. On slavery see R. de Vaux, *Ancient Israel*, tr. J. McHugh (New York: McGraw-Hill, repr. 1965), I:80–90; I. Mendelsohn, *Slavery in the Ancient Near East* (Westwood, CT: Greenwood Press, repr. 1978).

receives no wage, his mind is absorbed with finding moments of relaxation and a little relief like that offered by the shade of a tree.

3 Job mourns that his sorrow is greater than that of these common laborers. Instead of receiving a reward, even a meager one, he has been made to *inherit* [Hophal of *nāḥal*] *months of emptiness [šāwʾ]*. The language of inheritance may allude to his fear that he is made to suffer for the sins of his forefathers. *and nights of misery [ʿāmāl] are allotted to me*. His personal feeling is underscored by the prepositional phrase *to me (lî)*. He can find no relief or joy at all in his allotted position, in contrast to the slave who enjoys the shade or the worker who receives a wage. His lot has brought him lower than the lowest class of men. *allotted* or "measured out" *(minnâ)* indicates his conviction that God has arbitrarily determined his fate.

This verse hints that Job suffered for many months, perhaps stretching into years. While the length of Job's illness is unknown, the Testament of Job (5:9) states that his trial lasted seven years. The dialogue is not concerned with the length of Job's trial, however; it focuses on its inner personal and spiritual dimensions.

4, 5 Job voices some of his specific ailments that fill his nights with misery. At dusk he anticipates a little relief, at least some restful sleep—the laborer's hard work makes him sleep heavily at night. In bed, however, Job becomes so fed up with *tossing* and turning that his mind wonders when it will be time to get up. The night passes so slowly that in its stillness he becomes conscious of every pain in his body. In the morning light Job discovers that *worms* have bred in his sores. Hard scabs have crusted around the sores on his skin, only to break and ooze, leaving his skin painfully raw. This vivid description gives some insight into the multiple physical complications of Job's illness: fever, sleeplessness, delirium, skin ulcers, and running sores infested with worms.

6 Nevertheless, during the slow, agonizing nights, memories of his past make him sadly aware that his days are passing far too swiftly. The speed with which one's life passes is similar to the rapid movement of *a weaver's shuttle* as it flies back and forth across the loom. Soon the cloth is finished and *the thread (tiqwâ)* is cut to separate the cloth from the loom. Like the flying shuttle Job's days are passing so swiftly that it seems God is nearly finished with this piece of cloth and is about to cut it from the loom.[11]

11. Fohrer points out that the poem is full of images relating to the brevity of life, a frequent theme in the OT. Life is compared to a breath (Job 7:7, 16; Ps. 78:39), a fleeting shadow (Job 8:9; 14:2; Ps. 102:12 [Eng. 11]; 109:23; 144:4; 1 Chr. 29:15), a runner (Job 9:25), a blossom (Job 14:2; Ps. 90:5–6; 103:15), and a dream (Job 20:8). The imagery of the fading grass, which appears in Ps. 90:5–6; 102:12 (Eng. 11); 103:15; Isa. 40:6–7, is absent from Job.

Then there will be no cord left to weave into his life. *Cut off* from this earth, he will have no more "hope" *(tiqwâ)* of enjoying life's rich experiences.[12]

(b) A Petition (7:7–10)

7 *"Remember that my life is a mere breath;*[1]
my eyes will not again experience pleasure.[2]
8 *The eye which sees me will look on me no more;*[3]
your eye will be turned my way, but I shall be gone.[4]
9 *As a cloud fades and vanishes,*
so he who descends[5] *to Sheol does not ascend;*
10 *he never again returns home;*
his place never again acknowledges him."

The contrast between this pericope and the first two verses of this chapter is sharp. In vv. 1–2 the wearied laborer had hope for something sweet at the end of his long hours of toil, while in vv. 7–10 Job has no hope for any pleasant moments. His wages, so to speak, would be the taste of life's joys once again. Desire for life is a basic human drive that finds its reward in the enjoyment of pleasant experiences. As it is expressed in Ps. 34:13 (Eng. 12): "Who is the man that delights in life, and loves many days that he may experience pleasure *[rā'â ṭôḇ]*?" Thus Job's request is simple and basic; he longs to experience again the joys of normal life before death robs him of life.

7 *Remember*. This imperative signals that Job is now addressing God directly. Job hopes that God will respond to his present dilemma in conformity with his prior commitments to him.[6] To one who fears God it

12. When the good king Hezekiah was facing death, he too lamented that he would no longer experience the land of the living. In his lament he pictured his death as a shepherd's tent being pulled down and taken away and as a cloth being cut off from the loom (Isa. 38:11–12).

1. Here Heb. *rûaḥ*, "wind, spirit," means "breath" (cf. Eccl. 1:14; Ps. 78:39; Isa. 41:29; Jer. 5:13).

2. *rā'â ṭôḇ*, lit. "see good." See Job 21:13; 36:11; Ps. 4:8 (Eng. 7); 34:13 (Eng. 12); cf. Job 9:25; 21:25, where *ṭôḇâ*, "good," is used.

3. Cf. J. Weingreen, "The construct-genitive relation in Hebrew syntax," *VT* 4 (1954) 56–57. He renders it "no seeing eye shall behold me."

4. Many commentators omit this verse, following LXX. But as Dhorme and Andersen point out, it should be retained.

5. This prayer suggests that Job wishes to experience God's mercy as Israel did in the wilderness (Ps. 78:38–39).

6. "Remember" is a key term in the OT. The worshiping community participates in and realizes the benefits of God's past saving deeds that formed that community. God's remembering means that he is dynamically fulfilling his redemptive purpose in relationship to his promises. When he remember someone in his mercy, he no longer holds that

means that God will act toward him compassionately, will cease being silent, and will become involved in the petitioner's deliverance. *my life is a mere breath,* a vapor that quickly vanishes. That is, Job wishes that God would become mindful of the transient nature of his life and also realize that his servant is close to the limits of what his body can bear.[7] *my eyes will not again experience pleasure.* Job is most fearful that if God does not intervene he will never again experience the pleasant side of life.

8–10 Job grounds his plea for God to remember him in the fact that God will lose out if his servant dies. *your eye will be turned my way, but I shall be gone.* God will look for him, but will not find him. He will have died as quickly and quietly as *a cloud* drifts across the sky and *vanishes.* This image is poignant, because a cloud that moves quickly across the sky soon disappears without a trace,[8] never to return. With this image that captures the transient, insubstantial nature of human life, Job wants God to realize the extreme urgency of his request. His life is now utterly worthless, and it is about to pass with no lasting meaning.

he who descends to Sheol does not ascend. Job knows he is about to die, to descend to *Sheol.* There a person ekes out a ghostly existence, no longer able to do good or to praise God.[9] *he never again returns home.* From an ancient perspective no one returns from Sheol.[10] Never again will Job oversee the management of his house or love his children. His neighborhood, *his place (mᵉqōmô),* will no longer have him frequenting it.

(2) A Complaint against God (7:11–21)

(a) The Basic Complaint (7:11–16)

11 *"Indeed, I shall not restrain my mouth:*
I shall speak in the anguish of my spirit,
I shall complain[1] in the bitterness of my soul.

---

person accountable for his sins. He will not execute the judgment which those sins deserve (Ps. 25:6–7; cf. 79:8). Thus a central theme in psalms of lament is to move God to remember the one afflicted, either an individual or his people. Lam. 5:1 calls for God to remember what has befallen Israel in an effort to activate his saving power in a new way. The summons to remember in a prayer of distress, then, is a fundamental petition for deliverance. Cf. B. Childs, *Memory and Tradition in Israel,* SBT 1/37 (London: SCM; Naperville: Allenson, 1962), pp. 31–44.

8. The images of transience in the OT include smoke that disperses (Ps. 37:20) and clouds and dew that quickly disappear (Hos. 13:3; Isa. 44:22).

9. Cf. Isa. 38:10–20, Hezekiah's prayer for recovery from illness.

10. In Akkadian literature Sheol is called "the land of no return." Cf. "Descent of Ishtar to the Nether World," *ANET,* pp. 106–109, lines 1, 12, 41. For Job's other reflections on the afterlife, see above on 3:14–19 and below on 14:7–12 and 19:25–27.

1. The cohortatives underscore Job's determined resolve.

12 *Am I the sea or the sea serpent*
that you set a guard[2] *over me?*
13 *Whenever*[3] *I think that my bed will comfort me,*
my couch will help bear[4] *my complaint,*
14 *you scare me*[5] *with dreams*
and with visions you terrify me;
therefore my throat chooses[6] *strangling,*
my bones[7] *death.*
16 *I despise it;*[8] *I will not live forever.*
Leave me alone, for my days are a vapor."

11 *Indeed, I shall not restrain my mouth.* Job reaffirms his resolution to lament unrestrainedly his present distress. Because of the reproachful way God is treating him, he feels that it is his right to complain loudly. For one plagued by such excruciating pain, silence is not golden. *I shall speak in the anguish [ṣar]*[9] *of my spirit [rûaḥ], I shall complain in the bitterness [mar] of*

2. M. Dahood ("*Mišmar* 'Muzzle' in Job 7:12," *JBL* 80 [1961] 270–71) assigns to *mišmār* the meaning "muzzle" on the basis of Ps. 68:23b (Eng. 22b), "I muzzled the deep sea" *(ʾšbm mṣlwt ym),* supported by Ps. 39:2b (Eng. 1b); 141:3. Pope accepts Dahood's interpretation of Ps. 68:23 (Eng. 22) but points out that nothing in the present context suggests the same image. In support of the translation "guard" are the references to "the confinement of the sea within bonds" in Jer. 5:22 and Ps. 104:9. For a thorough discussion of Dahood's proposal see Grabbe, *Comparative Philology and the Text of Job,* pp. 55–58.

3. The conjunction *kî* is taken to mean "supposing that, if" (GKC, § 159aa), making v. 13 a subordinate clause to the main clause in v. 14.

4. Davidson understands *nāśāʾ* b^e as "to bear in sharing, to help to bear, to lighten."

5. The *waw* introduces the apodosis (see GKC, § 143d), and the perfect is frequentative (see GKC, § 112hh). This is the only occurrence of *ḥittaṯ* followed by the preposition b^e; standing parallel to *min,* the preposition b^e has instrumental force (cf. N. Sarna, *JBL* 78 [1959] 313; Horst, p. 119).

6. The imperfect consecutive expresses the end result (Budde).

7. The preformative *mem* on *meʿaṣmôṯāy,* "my bones," may be an enclitic *mem* belonging to the preceding word, *māweṯ* (N. Sarna, "Some Instances of Enclitic -m in Job," *JJS* 6 [1955] 108–10; M. Dahood, "Ugaritic Lexicography," in *Mélanges E. Tisserant* [Vatican: Biblioteca apostolica vaticana, 1964], I:93). "Bones" stands as the subject of a suppressed verb implied from the first line, or perhaps the verb has fallen out since the line is short. Many (e.g., Dhorme, Driver-Gray, Rowley) emend "bones" to "pains," *ʿaṣṣ*^{e}*ḇôṯāy*, but this is unnecessary, for "bones" and "soul" may parallel each other; cf. n. 15 below.

8. *māʾastî* is very difficult. Fohrer removes it as a gloss while Pope transfers it to v. 15b. Since the syllable counts of the present line are balanced (9/9), it should not be removed. If *māʾas* bears the usual meaning of "reject," an object such as "life" needs to be supplied (Driver-Gray). Another suggestion is to take this word as *māʾas* II, similar to *māsas* I (cf. v. 5), i.e., "I waste or pine away" (Dhorme; KB, p. 513).

9. Heb. *ṣar* means lit. "narrow, restricted, confined." Tight situations restrict a person's movements and frustrate his desire for freedom, causing distress.

my soul [nepeš].[10] Sorrow from an affliction is suffered in the depths of one's being, and the tongue is the sole avenue for releasing that anguish. He who laments freely has the hope that his words will touch God's compassion, moving God to deliver him.

12 In the style of cross-examining the plaintiff, Job caustically asks God why he has *set a guard* over him. It appears that God must consider him a formidable opponent, comparable to *the sea (yām)* or *the sea serpent (tannîn).*[11] Drawing on the rich mythopoeic imagery of primordial conflict, Job wonders if God is treating him so harshly because he fears that he is a cosmic foe.[12]

13–15 Then in self-defense Job lamentingly recounts his emotional and physical agony (vv. 13–14) and reiterates his longing for death (vv. 15–16). He simply hopes that his bed may offer him some comfort from the guard God has posted over his every action. He thinks that at least *my couch will bear my complaint [śîaḥ].*[13] When he lies down, his load will be eased and he will get some rest. But in the middle of the night Job awakens, sweating and delirious, frightened by *dreams* sent from God.[14] He believes that these *visions* are God's troops ordered to render him impotent before his divine opponent.

At other times in the night he has a hard time catching his breath, coughing so much he feels as though he is about to choke to death. And his bones ache so much he imagines that he is going to die. In a picturesque

10. See Job 10:1; cf. 3:20.

11. Cf. M. Wakeman, *God's Battle with the Monster* (Leiden: Brill, 1973), pp. 55–82; also cf. 26:12; Isa. 51:9–10; Ps. 74:13. Without the article, "sea" represents a cosmic power in the OT; in other Near Eastern cultures the sea was deified.

12. In Mesopotamian mythology the sea and its frightful inhabitant the sea dragon were viewed as the forces of chaos or evil bent on defeating the ruling deity. But Marduk, the god appointed by the council, defeated Tiamat, the primordial salt water, and all her hosts in a furious battle. Later when Marduk set about to create the worlds, he split Tiamat in two; with half of her he formed the heavenly ocean, sealed behind the heavenly vault. A bar was pulled down and guards were posted so that her waters might not escape. Cf. "Enuma Elish," *ANET*, pp. 60–71, esp. pp. 66–68. Ugaritic mythology seems to have two accounts of a cosmic battle, one in which Baal defeated Yamm, and another in which Baal's sister/consort Anat defeated Yamm. In the former, Baal's fate is uncertain; according to some scholars, Baal killed Yamm (see F. M. Cross, *Canaanite Myth and Hebrew Epic* [Cambridge, MA: Harvard University Press, 1973], pp. 113–16; J. C. L. Gibson, *Canaanite Myths and Legends* [Edinburgh: T. & T. Clark, 1978], pp. 44–45; J. Gray in *DOTT*, pp. 129, 132n.16). According to Pope's interpretation, however, Prince Sea was not destroyed as was Tiamat, but was taken captive and placed under guard. So also *ANET*, pp. 131, 132.

13. Heb. *śîaḥ* stands for loud, emotion-filled speech as in a lament or a complaint (cf. 9:27; 10:1; 21:4; 23:2; see also H. P. Müller, *VT* 19 [1969] 364–65).

14. Dreams play an important part in the book of Job; Eliphaz drew much of his authority from a nocturnal confrontation with a spirit (ch. 4), and Elihu will argue that God communicates in dreams (33:15–20).

image, the word *nepeš, throat,* usually translated "soul" or "self," stands with *strangling.*[15] During such a seizure Job's throat would prefer that he choke to death.

16 Job's misery keeps the desire for death constantly before his mind. He despises the cruel truth: *I will not live forever.* He pleads with God to forbear: *Leave me alone, for my days are a vapor [heḇel].* Job often uses "vapor" for the sense of futility that his sorrow causes (9:29; 21:34; 27:12; cf. 35:16). Truly the vanity of life itself should be punishment enough without having undeserved and painful woes added to his lot. If God leaves him alone, his pain might be alleviated and he might enjoy the good for his few remaining days.

Job's affliction defies his every attempt to assign any meaning to his experience. This seemingly meaningless encounter with suffering challenges to the core his view of God, for he knows that God, the source of meaning, is ultimately responsible for his dilemma and must respond to him. Meanwhile, his search for an answer to his fate stretches to the limit his belief in a benevolent God. Because of his faith he earnestly seeks for the answer from God.

(b) A Plea for a Reprieve (7:17–21)

17 *"What is man that you exalt him,*
that you pay attention to him,
18 *that you examine him every morning,*
that you test him every moment?
19 *How long until you look away from me?*
Will you not leave me alone long enough till I swallow my spittle?
20 *If I have sinned,[1] what have I done to you, O Watcher of man?[2]*
Why have you made me your mark so that I have become a burden to you?[3]

15. In this verse internal feelings are related to physical distress. Heb. *nepeš,* "life, person, self," and *ʿeṣem,* "bones," stand for "the self" as a conscious, deciding person. The wordplay on physical terms is strong, for the "throat" is prominent in choking, and one's bones, as a skeleton, suggest death. In Ps. 6:3–4 (Eng. 2–3), where the psalmist desires healing from sickness, *nepeš* and *ʿeṣem* are parallel (cf. also Ps. 35:9–10; Prov. 16:24). This psalm also mentions comfort received by crying on one's bed (v. 7 [Eng. 6]).

1. The perfect may stand in a conditional sentence without a modifier (GKC, §§ 159b, h). See also Dhorme, Gordis.

2. Since the first line is too long, Pope suggests omitting *ḥāṭāʾṯî,* "I have sinned," while Fohrer goes further and removes the whole line as a gloss. Perhaps the vocative phrase *nōṣēr hāʾāḏām,* "Watcher of man," stands outside the scanning.

3. MT *ʿālay,* "to me," is one of the traditional eighteen scribal changes called

21 *Why[4] do you not pardon my rebellion and pass over my iniquity?*
Soon I shall lie down in[5] the dust; then you will seek me eagerly, but I will not be."

17, 18 Job is so frustrated at God's hostility that he parodies two hymnic lines in praise of God's exaltation of humanity. When the psalmist was meditating on human smallness and apparent insignificance in contrast to the vastness of the universe, he marveled that God *exalts* man and *pays attention* to him (Ps. 8:5–6 [Eng. 4–5]; 144:3–4). By giving humanity rulership over the created world, God has endowed humanity with intrinsic value. And God sustains his human creature by *examining him* and *testing him.*[6] Every moment God is at a person's side to encourage and sustain him. The constant divine vigil reveals the supreme value God places on each person. These insights inspired the psalmist to glorify God.

But the psalmist's ardor only deepens Job's despair. Job experiences God's vigilance as unrelenting oppression. So he turns these hymnic lines inside out. Instead of praising God with them Job uses them as a complaint against God's continual effort to find and punish his every flaw. God's testing becomes a burden too heavy for him, a mere mortal, to bear.

19 Using interrogatives to underscore his exasperation, Job implores God: *How long until you look away [šāʿâ] from me?*[7] In a positive sense *šāʿâ* ("gaze") means "to regard someone with interest or approval" (e.g., Gen. 4:4–5; Isa. 17:7–8).[8] Usually the faithful aspire for the eyes of the Lord to shine on their lives, for such observation brings deliverance, security, and blessing (Ps. 33:18–19; 34:16 [Eng. 15]). But Job experiences

---

Tiqqune sopherim. These were changes the scribes made to ease a reading viewed as portraying God in a too human or negative manner. Therefore, it is best to read *ʿāleyḵā,* "to you," with LXX and some mss. As Gordis points out, 2 Sam. 15:33 also supports this change: *wᵉhāyîṯā ʿālay lᵉmaśśāʾ*, "you will be a burden to me." In a different direction Blommerde (*Northwest Semitic Grammar and Job,* pp. 49–50) believes that in several places *ʿly* has not been recognized as *ʿēlî,* "Most High," a title of God (cf. 10:2; 20:4; 36:30; 37:16; 37:22).

4. This word is spelled *meh* rather than the usual *mâ* because of its distance from the principal stress in the verse (GKC, § 37f; Dhorme). It bears the sense of "why."

5. The preposition *lᵉ,* "to," is used for the more usual *ʿal,* "on" (cf. 20:11; 21:26).

6. The psalmists often speak of God's examining and testing both human ways and human motivation for acting (Ps. 7:10 [Eng. 9]; 11:4–5; 17:3; 26:2; 81:8 [Eng. 7]; 139:23). The psalmist believes that God's searching and testing of a person will result in his making the righteous secure and putting an end to the violence of the wicked (Ps. 7:10 [Eng. 9]).

7. Cf. Ps. 39:14 (Eng. 13).

8. Cf. *TWOT,* II:944–45.

God's gaze as sheer pain. Therefore, he pleads, *Will you not leave me alone long enough till I swallow my spittle?*[9] Should God relax his surveillance, Job would win a reprieve, a few moments of rest free from pain, before his certain death.[10] This request reveals how Job's understanding of God has been turned upside down.

20 Job ponders what effect any sin he might have committed could have on God.[11] Assuming that no act that a human being might commit could so affect God that he would be compelled to devastate that person, Job asks rhetorically, *If I have sinned, what have I done to you, O Watcher of man?* Assuredly nothing! The divine title *Watcher of man* has an affirmative meaning expressing the confidence that the afflicted have in divine protection.[12] But Job employs this title with scathing sarcasm, because God's surveillance causes him constant agony.

The three words for sin used in vv. 20–21, *sin (ḥāṭāʾ), rebellion (pešaʿ),* and *iniquity (ʿāwōn),* encompass every kind of transgression (cf. Lev. 16:21). If God wished, he could overlook any sinful deed Job might have done and allow him to live free from such suffering. Job grounds his plea for a reprieve in God's sovereign will, not in his own morality.

In typical lament style Job sets forth a series of questions. He asks God: *Why have you made me your mark,* i.e., that which he strikes *(mip̱gāʿ).*[13] Like a warrior, God has indefatigably continued to inflict severe blows against a single object.[14] Because God has expended such energy in buffeting him, Job states ironically and bitterly: *so that I have become a burden to you?*[15] Job wonders why God is so obsessed with him that God lets his servant become a burden to himself. Such behavior certainly seems to be beneath God's character. Has God himself become a slave, having to bear a heavy burden (cf. vv. 1, 2)?

21 Job persists in asking God: *Why do you not pardon my rebellion and pass over my iniquity?* Then Job could leave him alone. The two words for forgiveness are as strong as the words for sin. *pardon* is *nāśāʾ* (lit. "to

9. Dhorme, Pope, Gordis, and others note a contemporary Arabic expression, "let me swallow my spittle," meaning "wait a minute."

10. A parallel concept is found in Isa. 22:4; here the speaker prayed for God to look away from him while he wept bitterly over the destruction of his own people.

11. Cf. Elihu's discussion of this idea in 35:6–7.

12. Cf. the use of the verb *nāṣar,* "keep, guard," in Deut. 32:10; Ps. 12:8 (Eng. 7); 25:20; 31:24 (Eng. 23); 40:12 (Eng. 11); 61:8 (Eng. 7).

13. The word *mip̱gāʿ*, used only here, means "a mark," something which one strikes (cf. the use of the verb in 1 K. 2:25, 29, 31), rather than "a target" at which one aims (*maṭṭārâ;* cf. 16:12; Rowley).

14. Job returns to the imagery of God's acting against him as an attacking warrior (cf. 6:4). He will use the picture again in 16:12–13.

15. This expression occurs also in 2 Sam. 15:33 and 19:36 (Eng. 35).

bear"). The concept is that the responsibility of a lawless deed is accepted by another who carries it as a burden so that the offender is freed of that responsibility. The glorious revelation of Scripture is that God himself is the one who in his compassionate love bears human sin. The great OT confession proclaims: "Yahweh, Yahweh, the merciful and gracious God, slow to anger, and abounding in loyal love and faithfulness, who keeps loyal love for thousands and bears [or forgives, *nāśā'*] iniquity and transgression and sin, but who will in no way clear the guilty" (Exod. 34:6–7; cf. Num. 14:18; Jon. 4:2; Mic. 7:18; Ps. 99:8). Job wonders why God has not acted as the bearer of his sin. *pass over,* the second word for forgiveness, is *he'ĕḇîr,* "to cause to pass over" or "take away" (cf. 2 Sam. 12:13; 24:10 par. 1 Chr. 21:8). It means that sin is removed so far away that it can no longer produce any evil effects in a person's life. Job wants God to forgive him completely.

Job underscores the urgency of his request for a special pardon by again mentioning the nearness of his death. *Soon I shall lie down in the dust.* "To be in the dust" means "to go to Sheol" (Dhorme), the land of dust. Dust and Sheol are also parallel in 17:16 (cf. Dan. 12:2). There he will no longer be able to render praise to his Creator, and there God will have no opportunity to bestow his mercy on his servant. *then you will seek me eagerly [šiḥar], but I will not be.* Job thinks that too late God will seek him—Job will be dead. Then God will be disappointed. Therefore, it is urgent for God to act right away. As he will usually do in future speeches, Job ends this speech troubled by the immediate threat of his own death (10:21–22; 14:20–22; 17:13–16; 21:32–33).

AIM

In this speech Job laments the treachery of his friends and the agony of his fate. But in comparison with his opening curse-lament, his mood is less caustic. Instead of thinking only about the advantages of dying, he begins to ponder the possibility of relief from his illness in this life. Forcefully, though, he defends his right to lament. While he vividly bemoans his pain, both physical and emotional, the majority of this speech is an attack on his antagonists, both the comforters and God. He denounces his friends for their lack of faithful loyalty in their thinking that he deserves his affliction. And he accuses God, directly and pointedly, of being excessively cruel to him. Although Job has a long way to go before he gains the confidence to challenge God for a resolution of his case, he has taken the first step. By centering his complaint on these specific issues and looking at their impact on his emotional life, Job begins to give focus to his suffering. As he begins to channel some of his hurt into anger toward the friends and God, he is moving away from self-pity. This enables him to muster his few resources to overcome his difficulties by attempting to prove the rightness of his case. Although despairing and wanting to die, he never succumbs to his illness. His desire to be vindicated spurs his will to live. Since he refuses to give up on life, he will never abandon his search for God.

3. BILDAD'S FIRST SPEECH (8:1–22)

Bildad is Job's second friend to speak. He may be younger than Eliphaz, but more likely all the comforters are similar in age, mature and responsible elders with whom a few years makes little difference.[1] The order of speaking is based on their status and their eloquence rather than their age.

Bildad's thesis is that all God's ways are just (v. 3). This conviction rests solidly on the teaching of the fathers (vv. 8–10) and on the ways of nature (vv. 11–19). Bildad expounds and defends this inherited tradition to the questioning Job. In this regard Bildad is a champion of "old-time" religion. He delineates categories sharply. Without any exceptions, the righteous are blessed and the wicked are punished. Any apparent exception is momentary; justice will quickly prevail, reversing these appearances. Nevertheless, Bildad shows some concern for Job in that he desires the restoration of Job's status and wealth.

This speech of Bildad may be divided into three sections, with the central section consisting of two parts: God's just ways (vv. 1–7); evidence for God's justice (vv. 8–19), consisting of the teaching of tradition (vv. 8–10) and illustrations from nature (vv. 11–19); and conclusion and application (vv. 20–22).

a. God's Just Ways (8:1–7)

1 *Bildad the Shuhite answered:*
2 *"How long[1] will you speak such things*
and the words of your mouth be a mighty wind?
3 *Does God pervert justice?*
Or Shaddai[2] pervert the right?
4 *If your sons sinned against him,*
he has released them into the power of their transgression.

1. W. A. Irwin, "The First Speech of Bildad," *ZAW* 51 (1933) 204–16.

1. The particle *'ān,* elsewhere only in 1 Sam. 10:14 and 2 K. 5:25 (Ketib), is the abbreviated form of the more usual *'ānâ* (Job 18:2; 19:2). The abbreviated form may suggest impatience (Davidson).

2. In this bicolon the author splits the name *El Shaddai,* putting one element in each line. This means that these two lines are a single thought (Andersen).

5 *If you will seek God*[3] *eagerly*
and plead with Shaddai for mercy,
6 *if you are pure and upright,*[4]
then he will bestir himself[5] *for you*
and restore[6] *your righteous estate.*
7 *Though your beginning be insignificant,*
your future will flourish greatly."[7]

2 Angered by Job's lament, Bildad opens by reprimanding Job with a sharp rhetorical question, picking up on Job's complaint against his comforters' failure to speak the right words (6:24–25). The interrogative *How long* blames Job for speaking too much, and *such things* refers pejoratively to Job's entire speech (chs. 6–7). Bildad refers caustically to Job's words as *a mighty wind.* Whereas the traditional belief was that words were very potent, potentially as destructive as wind, Bildad contends that Job's speaking so boldly against God vitiates Job's own protests concerning God.

3 Continuing with rhetorical questions Bildad states his major premise: God never *perverts [ʿiwwēṯ] justice* or *the right.*[8] The verb *ʿiwwēṯ* means "twist, bend, make crooked," e.g., to falsify a weight (Amos 8:5) or

3. Some question the preposition in the phrase *ʾel-ʾēl,* "to God." Fohrer strikes it since *šāḥēr,* "seek diligently," takes the accusative, while M. Löhr ("Die drei Bildadreden," *BZAW* 34, Fest. K. Budde, ed. K. Marti [Giessen: Töpelmann, 1920], pp. 107–12) emends it to *ʾeṯ,* the indicator of the direct object. But cf. Driver-Gray, Dhorme, Gordis, Tur-Sinai. Dahood ("Chiasmus in Job," in *A Light unto My Path,* Fest. J. M. Myers, ed. H. N. Bream et al. [Philadelphia: Temple University Press, 1974], pp. 121–22) keeps it as "poetic construction to maintain chiastic parallelism with *ʾēl-šaddai.*"

4. Dhorme and others consider this line a secondary addition, assuming that Bildad would not concede this possibility. But this line adds force to the argument; it drives home to Job his need to follow the course that Bildad offers, even if his claim to innocence is true.

5. J. Reider ("Etymological studies in biblical Hebrew," *VT* 2 [1952] 126) identifies the root of *yāʿîr* with Arab. *ġār,* "to bestow (wealth or provisions)," a meaning that Andersen accepts. H. Ginsberg ("Two North-Canaanite Letters from Ugarit," *BASOR* 72 [Dec. 1938] 18–19) takes it from *nġr,* "watch over," which is joined with *šlm,* "be at peace, preserve," in Ugaritic letters; this connection may account for the parallel here. But the Hebrew cognate of *nġr* is *nāṣar* (cf. H. Richardson, "A Ugaritic Letter of a King to His Mother," *JBL* 66 [1947] 322). The usual definition of *ʿîr,* "stir, act in an aroused manner," is accepted. Cf. Dhorme, Tur-Sinai, and Gordis, who take *ʿîr* to mean "watch over."

6. Since the verb *šillam,* "restore," precedes its feminine subject, it may appear in its simplest form (GKC, § 145o).

7. The verb *yiśgeh,* "it will increase, flourish," is masculine though its subject is feminine and precedes it. According to Dhorme it is masculine to parallel *hāyâ,* "it is," which though itself masculine also has a feminine subject, but properly so since it precedes its subject. This verb is usually written with an ʾ as in Aramaic (cf. 12:23; 36:24), but in 8:7, 11 and Ps. 73:12; 92:13 (Eng. 12) it is written as here with an *h.*

8. Elihu will repeat this position in 34:12.

make a path crooked (Eccl. 1:15; 7:13). *justice (mišpāṭ)* is strict adherence to a standard, and *the right (ṣeḏeq)* is correct behavior. Justice is the basis of God's rule (cf. Ps. 72:1–7; 99:4). An ancient poem says, "The Rock, his work is perfect; for all his ways are justice. A God of faithfulness and without iniquity, righteous and upright is he" (Deut. 32:4). Since justice is the cornerstone of God's relationship with humanity, any accusation that God is perverting justice is tantamont to accusing him of acting demonically. If the charge is true, then God is not God. Such a deity would be a devil, unworthy of a person's devotion. Although Job has not explicitly said that God perverts justice, Bildad hears Job taking this step when he challenges God.

4 Working from the premise that God does not pervert justice, Bildad states that whoever experiences calamity has sinned. *If your sons sinned against him.* Specifically, since Job's children have died in a disaster, they must have sinned against God. *he has released them into the power of their transgression,* i.e., sinful deeds produce their own punishment. Therefore, God is surely just in regard to their death. Bildad proves to be too insensitive to Job's anguish to avoid using his children as an illustration of God's ways.

5 Bildad moves quickly away from forthright condemnation of Job (vv. 2–4) to exhorting him to seek God (vv. 5–7). He seeks to catch Job's attention with the use of the pronoun *you ('attâ).* His rhetoric also contrasts Job's fate with that of his children. Being still alive, Job is experiencing God's mercy and has not sinned as severely as his children had. Therefore, he must take advantage of God's kindness and *seek God eagerly [šiḥar] and plead with Shaddai for mercy [hiṯḥannān].* Such earnest prayer will bring God's blessing.

With the verb *seek eagerly (šiḥar)* Bildad responds specifically to the last line of Job's lament (7:21d), in which Job sought to move God to overlook his sins, for soon God would search diligently *(šiḥar)* for his plagued servant but not find him. Bildad uses this same word to underscore his conviction that Job must change his attitude if he is to regain God's favor. Job should be searching diligently for God rather than imagining that God would some day search eagerly for him. While Job is fearful of death, Bildad thinks that he should be yearning for a prosperous future. Bildad clearly rejects Job's thinking that God would seek for one who has already died, for that person would have encountered the just, final punishment for his sin. Job's position implies that after his death God would admit to having made a mistake, and though he would be eager to correct his error, he would be unable to do so. Such a view of God is too anthropomorphic and limited for Bildad. Therefore, it is Job's view of God that must be corrected.

6 Bildad argues that if Job is truly *pure (zaḵ)* and *upright (yāšār)*

God will answer his petitions for mercy. The use of the word *upright* points back to the prologue (1:1) and reflects the author's incorporation of the prose account into the fabric of his work. Once the upright Job seeks God diligently, God *will bestir himself (ʿûr)*[9] to intervene on Job's behalf. Then he *will restore (šillēm)*[10] Job's *righteous estate*. In a narrow sense this word for *estate (nāweh)* refers to a sheepfold and in a broader sense to a shepherd's holdings. The sheepfold symbolizes a secure resting place, particularly where God as shepherd provides for his flocks.[11] The full phrase *your righteous estate (nᵉwaṯ ṣiḏqeḵā)*[12] means that the extensive holdings of Job bore witness to the righteousness of their sheikh. The image rests on the belief that the condition of the estate bears witness to the character of its owner. God will restore Job's estate to its original glory.

7 Bildad seeks to motivate Job to seek God. He is stating here the positive side of retribution: righteous behavior is rewarded with prosperity. *your beginning (rēʾšîṯ)* refers to the first stage of Job's prosperity, and *your future (ʾaḥᵃrîṯ)* refers to the last and final segment of his life, beginning with his restoration. These two terms together encompass the totality of his life. Even though Job has lost everything, he will receive a restoration that will far surpass his former greatness. Through Bildad's words the author is hinting at Job's restoration as unfolded in the epilogue (42:10–17). In a few places, the author uses the speeches of the friends to allude to the outcome and thus to heighten the contrast between their pious platitudes and the reality of God's treatment of Job, his faithful servant. The friends will be caught by surprise at the fulfillment of their promises without Job's following the conditions they recommend.

b. Evidence of God's Justice (8:8–19)

Bildad develops his thesis that God does not pervert justice by an appeal to the tradition of the elders (vv. 8–10). Then he grounds the validity of this thesis on three illustrations from nature (vv. 11–19): the fate of the papyrus

9. According to Weiser the verb *ʿûr*, "bestir," belongs to the liturgical language of theophany (cf. Ps. 44:24 [Eng. 23]; 59:5–6 [Eng. 4–5]; cf. Isa. 51:9). Similar to this line a psalmist pleads for God to come to his defense, to vindicate him, a troubled servant (Ps. 35:23–24).

10. The root *šlm* in the Piel means "to repair," i.e., "to reestablish" something to its original wholeness (cf. the related noun *šālôm*, "well, whole, peace"). Its meaning is debated. Tur-Sinai and Gordis take it as "be in peace, safeguard," but Dhorme points out that only the Hiphil has that meaning. The Piel, used here, means "restore, complete, reward" (BDB, p. 1022).

11. Cf. *TWOT*, II:561–62.

12. This expression is not unique to the book of Job; it occurs in Jer. 31:23, *nᵉwēh ṣeḏeq* (cf. Jer. 50:7), in reference to the temple mount. In Prov. 3:33 God blesses "the habitation of the righteous," *nᵉwēh ṣaddîqîm*.

(vv. 11–13), the frailty of a spider's web (vv. 14–15), and the ability of a garden plant to grow despite great obstacles (vv. 16–19). The first two pictures show that the godless perish, while the last one demonstrates that the righteous can prosper though confronted by great obstacles.

(1) The Teaching of Tradition (8:8–10)

8 *"Ask now the former generation,*[1]
and reflect on the wisdom of their forefathers[2]*—*
9 *because we are recent and unknowing,*
because our days on earth are a shadow.
10 *Will they not teach you and tell you,*
and from their thinking will they not bring forth words?"

8, 9 Bildad exhorts Job to *ask the former generation* in his search for truth. That is, he is to *reflect on* (lit. "to set his heart on")[3] the *wisdom* or searchings *(ḥēqer)*[4] passed down from their forefathers. Bildad assumes that truth resides with the elderly and beyond that with their fathers all the way back to the patriarchs (cf. Deut. 32:7).[5] The wisdom of the forefathers is prized over an individual's experience, for a single life is too short to afford a personal perspective on the highest wisdom. In comparison to the patriarchs Job's and his friends' lives are *recent* (lit. "of yesterday"). Since their days flee like a shadow,[6] they do not have the time to gain knowledge. With these words Bildad judges Job's challenge of traditional wisdom as invalid and presumptuous.

10 With another rhetorical question Bildad stresses the authority of

1. "Generation" *(dōr)* in the singular refers back to the patriarchs as a whole, not to a single generation.

2. N. Sarna (*JJS* 6 [1955] 108–10) and M. Dahood (*Bib* 46 [1965] 329) find an enclitic *mem* on *'aḇôṯām,* "their fathers" (see also Pope). Others (e.g., Fohrer) emend the form to *'aḇôṯ,* "fathers," for the antecedent is in doubt (cf. LXX, Vulg., RSV). This term appears again in Job 15:18 and also in Sir. 8:9, but in those references the antecedent is clear. For a thorough discussion see Blommerde, *Northwest Semitic Grammar and Job,* pp. 50–51.

3. This assumes that *kônēn,* "prepare oneself," is elliptical for *kônēn lēḇ,* "set one's heart, give heed to" (Dhorme, Gordis). See Driver-Gray for some objections to this interpretation. Driver-Gray and others (e.g., Ball, *BHK*) wish to emend it to *bônēn,* "consider attentively," following Syr. But MT is a valid possibility, for these two roots are parallel in an Ugaritic text (*UT,* 1161:5–6; see *RSP,* I:343, no. 526).

4. Heb. *ḥēqer* stands for the results of an investigative meditation (Dhorme and Pope).

5. Sir. 8:9–12 says about the wisdom of the elderly: "Do not underrate the talk of old men, after all, they themselves learned it from their fathers; from them you will learn how to think, and the art of the timely answer" (JB).

6. Other references to the brevity of human life include Ps. 102:12 (Eng. 11); 109:23; 144:4; Eccl. 6:12; 8:13.

the fathers' wisdom. The question seeks to persuade Job by demanding from him an affirmative answer. He is sure to find instruction from *their thinking* (lit. "their heart") that will guide him in the right way during his affliction. If Job is to find restoration, he must cease challenging honored doctrines on the basis of his own experience and develop a listening attitude to the honored teachings of the fathers.

(2) Illustrations from Nature (8:11–19)

11 *"Can papyrus thrive without a marsh*
or reeds grow without water?
12 *While it is still*[1] *in bloom, uncut,*
it withers more quickly than any grass.
13 *Such is the fate of all who forget God,*
and the hope of the godless will perish,
14 *whose confidence is cut off,*[2]
whose basis of trust is a spider's web.
15 *He leans against the web,*[3] *but it does not stand;*
he grasps it, but it does not hold.
16 *He is a lush plant under the sun;*
its shoots spread over its garden;
17 *its roots become entwined about a stone pile;*[4]
it grasps[5] *a bed of rocks.*[6]

1. As Driver-Gray and Dhorme note, the unusual construction of *ʿōḏennû,* "it is still," plus *lōʾ*, "not," has a parallel in Num. 11:33: *ʿōḏennû* plus *ṭerem,* "not yet." This verse, esp. the second line, influenced Sir. 40:16.

2. MT *ʾᵃšer yāqôṭ* is very difficult. Many, apparently going back to Saadiah, take *yāqôṭ,* a hapax legomenon, to mean "gossamer"; this meaning offers an excellent parallel to "a spider's web." Some commentators offer similar explanations by emending *yāqôṭ* in various ways. One solution is to change it to *qûrîm,* "threads" (Hölscher), or *qiwwim,* "threads" (Gordis), or to read *qûrê qayiṣ,* "threads of summer" (Budde), or *qûrê ʿakkāḇîš,* "spider threads," as in Isa. 59:5, or *qiššûrê qayiṣ,* "bands of summer" (Fohrer). Grabbe (*Comparative Philology and the Text of Job,* pp. 58–60) fails to find any linguistic support for "gossamer" and believes that this translation is solely a desire to find a word parallel to "a spider's web." Dhorme takes a different approach, reading *yālqûṭ* and defining it as "a shepherd's bag or scrip" (cf. 1 Sam. 17:40), the empty bag being a symbol of something unstable. But the versions read a verb, probably from a root *qṭṭ* or *qwṭ,* "cut off," which, being the least speculative, is the best solution.

3. The first line is a little long. Perhaps *ʿal-bêṯô,* "against his house," is a gloss to tie v. 15a more tightly to v. 14, where *bayiṯ* means "web" (cf. Horst).

4. Driver-Gray and Tur-Sinai take *gal* in the first line to mean "spring" (cf. Cant. 4:12) and suggest that *bêṯ ʾᵃḇānîm* in the second line is "the walls of a well-house"; the plant or tree, being planted in a most favorable place in the garden, surpasses all. But *gal* is more usually identified with a heap or monument of stones (e.g., Gen. 31:46–48; Josh. 7:26; 8:29; 2 Sam. 18:17); thus it is best understood here as a stone pile. See n. 6 below; see also 15:28.

5. Many scholars emend *yeḥᵉzeh,* "it sees." Some (e.g., Dhorme, Rowley)

18 *If one snatches it from its place,*
which denies it: 'I have never seen you':
19 *surely it rejoices*[7] *in its way,*
and another will sprout[8] *from the dust."*

11 Bildad supports his teaching by looking at the way papyrus grows. Apparently he has taken an old proverb, possibly from Egyptian wisdom, and presented it as a rhetorical question, a favorite style of his. *papyrus (gōmeʾ)* and *reeds (ʾāḥû)*[9] grow well in damp, swampy areas with a warm climate, such as the Nile offers. An Ugaritic text gives evidence that papyrus grew in the Lake Huleh region in the 2nd millennium B.C.[10] Papyrus was a very valuable plant, being used for swift skiffs (Isa. 18:2), baskets (Exod. 2:3), mats, and parchment. It grows rapidly to a height of eight to ten feet. A tall, straight plant, it appears stately as it waves gently in the breeze. This characteristic is caught in the word used for *thrive (gāʾâ),*[11] or "grow tall," for it also means "be exalted, proud." This picture of the papyrus growing tall speaks of the great pride of the wicked.

---

suggest *yiḥyeh,* "it lives," with the support of LXX (see *BHK*). Others (e.g., Budde, Pope) read *yōḥēz* = *yōʾḥēz,* "it grasps" (cf. Tur-Sinai, *BHK*). This reading offers a fine parallel to *y^{e}subbāḵû,* "they become entwined," and is accepted here. Gordis prefers to see in MT an equivalent of *yeḥ^{e}ṣeh,* "it pierces, divides."

6. The phrase *bêṯ ʾ^{a}ḇānîm,* "a house of stones," may be an expression for a stone wall or a heap of stones (see n.4 above). Some (e.g., Gordis) understand *bêṯ* as "between, among" (Prov. 8:2; Ezek. 1:27; 41:9) or emend it to *bên,* "among" (Fohrer, *BHS*), or understand *bêṯ* as a contraction of *b^{e}ḇêṯ,* the preposition introducing the objective after the verb *ḥāzâ,* "see." But see Dhorme.

7. Many scholars have difficulty with the meaning of MT. Thus for *m^{e}śôś,* "rejoicing," Dhorme prefers a root *sûs,* from which *sās,* "moth," comes; in Akkadian the root is *sāsu* and in Arab. *sūseh,* "to be eaten by worms, to be decayed, rotting" (cf. Sir. 14:18–19). Working with Dhorme's ideas, Horst judges it to be a Qal infinitive construct of *māsas,* "melting, dissolving." Gordis revocalizes MT as *môšēš,* a Polel participle with the *m* elided, from *mûš,* "depart": "thus he departs on his way." But with Driver-Gray and Rowley it seems best to retain MT as the harder reading. See further the commentary below.

8. The verb may be plural because "another" *(ʾaḥēr)* is taken as a collective (so Dhorme). But it seems better either to emend the verb to the singular, *yiṣmāḥ* (LXX, Driver-Gray, Horst, *BHK*), or to consider MT as a survival of an old *yaqṭulu* singular verb form (Blommerde, *Northwest Semitic Grammar and Job,* p. 52).

9. As Pope notes, this word appears in Ugaritic as *aḫ*. Both *gōmeʾ* (KB, pp. 188–89) and *ʾāḥû* (KB, p. 30) may be loanwords from (respectively) Egyptian *qm3,* "reed, papyrus," and *3ḫ3ḫ,* "become green, blossom," or *3ḫy,* "water plant" (see Fohrer; cf. J. Vergote, *Joseph en Égypte* [Louvain: Publications universitaires, 1959], pp. 59–66; T. Lambdin, "Egyptian Loan Words in the Old Testament," *JAOS* 73 [1953] 146, 149).

10. See *UT,* 76:II:9, 12.

11. In reference to nature the feminine noun from this root *gēʾûṯ,* "majesty," depicts a rising cloud of smoke (Isa. 9:17 [Eng. 18]) and the swelling of the sea (Ps. 89:10 [Eng. 9]; cf. Ps. 46:4 [Eng. 3] with *ga ʾ^{a}wâ,* "majesty").

12 Papyrus grows quickly beneath the sun's heat, nourished by abundant water in its swampy bed. But if its water fails while it is in full blossom, it *withers* overnight, before it has been cut for harvest. Shriveled up it loses all value. The stately papyrus is not self-sufficient, and its coming to harvest is not guaranteed.

13 Bildad makes a specific application of this picture. *the fate of all who forget God* is similar to the fate of the papyrus. The wicked are defined as those *who forget God,* paralleled by *the godless* or the profane *(ḥānēp̱).* The forgetting of God is not a mere lapse of memory, but the willful decision to live with no regard either for God or for his precepts. Within Israel it stands for those who strive for their own glory by despising God's laws (Isa. 9:16 [Eng. 17]; Prov. 11:9). Their success vaults them high above the crowds. In their boasting they forget that God is the source of their existence. One day "the water" dries up and they face their *fate (*'*orḥôṯ,* lit. "paths"). In Dhorme's words, "the paths are the tracts of fate, already marked out by God and inevitably followed by man" (cf. Prov. 1:19). Their *hope (tiqwâ),* their anticipation of a long, prosperous future, *will perish.* Indeed, the godless die before they reach a ripe old age.

14, 15 The second illustration, structurally tied to the preceding verse by the relative pronoun *whose,* considers the fragile basis of the godless person's trust. By nature everybody places *confidence* in something. While the faithful rely on God, the Rock (Isa. 26:3–4), the godless place their trust in something they have acquired, e.g., their estate or their wealth. Because their *basis of trust* is like *a spider's web, their confidence [kesel] is cut off* (cf. 4:6). The web represents the frailest of all things. The Koran says, "Verily, frailest of all houses is the house of the spider" (29:40). Anyone who grabs on to a spider web to break his fall finds no support at all. With this illustration Bildad warns Job that no earthly or personal security on which he might rely is any stronger than a spider's web.

16–19 These verses are obscure and have led to many interpretations. Much of the difficulty resides in the apparent discrepancy between v. 18 and v. 19. Does the tearing out of the plant (v. 18) cause it to die, or is it able to withstand this attack and grow into a new beautiful plant (v. 19)? Most interpreters favor the former option, for it continues the comparison with the wicked. Fohrer, for example, visualizes a climbing plant, with long tendrils like a gourd, growing rapidly, since it is exposed to plenty of sunlight in a well-watered garden. The long tendrils of the gourd become so firmly entwined around the rocks that it appears that it cannot be ripped out. But suddenly it is pulled up from its place. Similarly a wicked person prospers, becoming so deeply rooted in his sphere of influence that it appears that no one can uproot him. But God, at will, forcibly removes him, so that his place, i.e., his estate, which supported his prosperity, disowns him.

Thus the fabulous success this wicked person enjoys is illusory and quickly comes to an end. To achieve this reading Fohrer places v. 19 after v. 15 as a concluding statement to vv. 14–15, just as v. 13 is to vv. 11–12 and v. 18 to vv. 16–17.

Another interpretation, offered by Hakam and Gordis, which goes back at least to the medieval interpreter Saadiah, finds in vv. 16–19 a description of the righteous in contrast to the wicked. This solution finds a chiasm between vv. 11–15, 16–19, and the lines of v. 20:

a = vv. 11-15, the wicked	b′ = v. 20a
b = vv. 16-19, the righteous	a′ = v. 20b.

If this literary analysis is correct, the righteous are pictured as a lush plant *(rāṭōḇ)* in vv. 16–19. Heb. *rāṭōḇ* means "moist, juicy"; as a substantive it means a plant that thrives in a damp environment, in this case a flower garden. Well watered, either by the bountiful morning dew or by irrigation from a well, it flourishes beneath the hot sun. It sends out *shoots (yōnaqtô)* that spread out over the garden.[12] In the garden is *a stone pile (gal)*. But when this plant starts to thrive, its life is suddenly threatened. Someone tries to *snatch it* or remove it *from its place* in the garden. At this desperate moment its place also denies the plant, saying, *I have never seen you*. This statement of denial means that the soil refuses to let this plant grow there any longer. The plant begins to wither. All who watch it expect it to die. But, behold, the plant comes back to life: *another will sprout from the dust*. The plant *rejoices*, for it has survived the threat to its life. In a little different direction Gordis reads v. 19b as "from some other dust, it will sprout again." This reading means that God transplants the plant to another place. There it takes hold and begins to root again. In either interpretion of v. 19b the plant endures. Overcoming great obstacles, it is more vigorous and resilient than before.

The identity of this plant is uncertain. Perhaps it is a tree, for the righteous are compared to a stalwart tree in various OT passages, e.g., they are likened to an olive tree (Hos. 14:7 [Eng. 6]) or to a cedar (cf. Ezek. 17).[13] A tree often grows well under adverse conditions. Even if a tree is cut down, a new shoot may sprout from its stump (cf. Job 14:7–9). The tree is thus an

12. The possibility that Bildad is comparing the tenacity of the righteous to a tree is supported by an upcoming reference. When Job speaks of a tree as symbolic of resurrection (14:7–9), he uses several of the words found here: *yōneqeṯ*, "sapling"; *šōreš*, "root"; *ʿāpār*, "soil." Job seems to be responding specifically to Bildad's illustration. He observes that a tree is cut down and appears to die in the dry soil, but at the smell of rain it sends forth a new shoot. This lends some support to interpreting the analogy here as the plant surviving its being snatched from its place.

13. This pattern of contrasting the righteous and the wicked by botanical analogy also appears in Ps. 1 and Jer. 17:5–8.

excellent metaphor for the sturdy character of a righteous person. In any case this picture teaches that the righteous person is able to experience and survive hardship.

Bildad appears to be offering this picture as an illustration of triumph over hardship in order to bolster Job's spirits. If Job is pure and upright (v. 6a), he, like this plant, can expect to overcome his affliction even though his place no longer recognizes him. Bildad desires Job to display a mood of joy and confidence rather than one of mourning and distress. He wants Job to seek God in submission rather than in questioning.

c. Conclusion and Application (8:20–22)

20 *"Surely God does not reject the blameless,*
and he does not strengthen the hand of evildoers.
21 *He will yet fill your mouth with laughter,*
and your lips with shouts of joy.
22 *Those who hate you will be clothed with shame,*
and the tent of the wicked will be no more."

20 The conclusion of the whole matter as taught by the fathers and seen in the ways of nature is that God never reverses the laws of retribution. He never perverts justice. Bildad emphasizes this conclusion through use of litotes, the negation of the contrary: *God does not reject the blameless (tām).* They will never experience enduring punishment. Conversely, God *does not strengthen the hand of*[1] *evildoers (mᵉrēʿîm).* This means that God does not give the wicked special strength to face difficulties. He does not make them prosperous. Should the wicked rise to power, their success is brief and their fall is certain. On the other hand, it is implied that should the righteous experience hardship, God will come to their rescue. Bildad is vigorously objecting to Job's lamenting. He totally rejects Job's fear that God despises the blameless. This may be another instance where the author has a comforter anticipate what Job is going to ponder (cf. 9:20–22).

21 Hopeful of having persuaded Job, Bildad presents Job with two wonderful promises. *God will fill your mouth with laughter, and your lips with shouts of joy,* like those heard at festivals. Bildad has in mind the great joy such as that experienced by one who, having been denied the opportunity of attending the feasts because of hardships, is finally able to attend.[2]

1. To explain the phrase "grasp the hand," *yaḥᵃzîq bᵉyaḏ* (v. 20b), Pope cites the claim of Hattusilis, a Hittite king, to divine election in his Apology: "And my Lady Ishtar took me by the hand; and she guided me" (cf. C. W. Ceram, *The Secret of the Hittites* [New York: Knopf, 1958], p. 188). Also in Isa. 51:18 the word "guide" parallels the phrase "take by the hand"; cf. Isa. 41:13; 42:6; 45:1; Ps. 73:23; Gen. 19:16.

2. Verse 21b is very similar to Ps. 126:2a; that psalm describes the joys of the people on returning from the Babylonian captivity.

22 The second promise speaks of the victory that one has over his enemies. Indeed, *those who hate*[3] Job, namely, those who take pleasure in mocking him during his ill-fate, *will be clothed with shame*. Having disgraced another, they must bear greater public disgrace.[4] Moreover, they will suffer loss of all their possessions. The word *tent (ʾōhel)* may encompass both the place of abode and the family itself. Thus the statement that *the tent of the wicked will be no more* means that everything identified with the wicked will disappear. Neither they nor their offspring will be left to harass Job. Bildad explicitly addresses Job's anxiety of death expressed at the end of his last speech: "I will not be" (7:21c). If Job is righteous, it is the tents of the wicked, not himself, that will be no more.

AIM

After renouncing Job's complaint that God is treating him unjustly, Bildad instructs Job about the cetainty of double retribution. There are no exceptions to retribution. The blameless are always blessed by God and the wicked always punished. Any circumstances to the contrary are either illusory or momentary. This can be proved by the teaching of the fathers and by the patterns of nature. In Bildad's opinion it is unequivocally true that God does not pervert justice. He thus equates justice with double retribution.

A prisoner of tradition, Bildad refuses to allow any experience, particularly Job's, to temper his doctrine. Rather, experience must always be interpreted in the light of known precepts. There can be no exceptions to the precept, for an exception would challenge not only this precept but also the doctrine that God is just, the very cornerstone of orthodox theology. Bildad's error lies in building his entire theology on the premises of the doctrine of retribution, for earthly retribution is not the backbone of divine justice, as the book of Job itself demonstrates.

In his conclusion Bildad offers Job a measure of hope. If Job is truly blameless, he will be vindicated and he will experience festive joy again, and, moreover, his enemies will be shamed. This backdoor support, however, is a long way from the commitment to his personal integrity and the rightness of his case that Job so desperately needs. Upset by Job's lament and aware that suffering is evidence of wrongdoing, Bildad definitely rejects Job's argument, but he has not yet decided whether Job is righteous or

3. This term occurs frequently in the Psalms; in psalms of lament it refers to those who persecute or seek to destroy the righteous (Ps. 9:14 [Eng. 13]; 18:18 [Eng. 17]; 21:9 [Eng. 8]; 35:19).

4. "To be clothed with shame" means to be viewed by everyone as the object of God's judgment (cf. Ps. 35:26; 132:18; similarly 109:29).

wicked. Sadly he fails to stand with his friend during the time of his greatest need.

4. JOB'S SECOND RESPONSE (9:1–10:22)

Job gives vent to the deep agitation of his inner thoughts.[1] In this speech he tends to state a position boldly, then abandon it when he sees its difficulty and jump to another idea, which is also quickly abandoned. Other times he reverts to despair, almost the utter despair of his opening curse-lament (ch. 3). His jumping about reflects his frustration at the lack of any insight into the reasons for his plight.

This speech falls into two sections: Job's quest (9:1–35), and Job's lament (10:1–22). In the first section Job ponders the possibility of resolving his plight by entering into litigation with God (ch. 9). It is not readily discernible to whom he is speaking in this section, but since God is spoken of in the third person, it is assumed that Job is addressing the friends. In contrast to his last speech, in which he chided them much, he has no special words for them in this speech. To the extent that Job is addressing his friends, he may be trying to win their sympathy. But his discourse concentrates on finding a way out of his dilemma. On finding no hope of being acquitted in a trial, he takes up a lament, addressed to God, in the second section (ch. 10).

In this speech Job draws on three fields of language found in the OT: legal (9:3, 14–16, 19–20, 28–30, 32–35; 10:2, 6, 14, 17), psalms of lament (9:22–26; 10:1–22), and hymns of praise (9:5–13; 10:8–12). The language of the court dominates the first part. Here Job ponders the possibility of challenging his plaintiff, God, to enter into debate in order that the causes of God's hostility against him may be faced and removed. Since his case never comes to the docket of the court, he is enduring punishment as though he had already been sentenced. The delay of his trial is thus a grave injustice. But believing in God's commitment to justice, he wishes to enter into litigation and resolve the conflict. His resolve quickly wavers, however, as he meditates on God's majestic power and marvelous wisdom as expressed in the hymnic lines. He realizes that God may do as he wishes; no force can restrain him. In despair, but not giving up, Job takes up a lament in the second part. His uneasiness at God's treatment moves him to fill his lament with accusations against God. Most poignantly he charges God with violating his obligations of kindness toward his creature, the very obligations that are inherent

1. Cf. K. Fullerton, "On Job 9 and 10," *JBL* 53 (1934) 321–49; idem, "Job, Chapters 9 and 10," *AJSL* 55 (1938) 225–69.

in the act of creation. Nevertheless, in his lamenting he recites lines from hymns of praise, thereby keeping alive his longing to have fellowship with God restored. Recitation of these hymnic lines also enables him to cope with his bitterest feelings. That is why he can keep looking to God for help despite God's apparent hostility.

a. Job's Quest (9:1–35)

(1) Job's Concerns about Disputing His Case with God (9:1–24)

(a) Job's Opening Concerns (9:1–4)

1 *Job responded,*
2 *"Surely[1] I know that it is so.*
How can a man be declared innocent by God?
3 *If one plans[2] to enter into litigation[3] with him,*
he could not answer him, not even one out of a thousand.
4 *Wise in thought and mighty in strength[4]—*
who could defy him and win?"

2 Startlingly Job opens with the concession, *I know that it is so.* The immediate antecedent of the pronoun *it* is Bildad's thesis that "God does not pervert justice" (8:3). Then in the second line Job restates Eliphaz's thesis as a question, "How can a man be just before God?" (4:17). Job, though, moves away from the moral dimension of Eliphaz's thesis to the forensic (cf. Habel, OTL). He ponders how a person can be acquitted when it is God who is his accuser. The interrogative indicates that Job does not think there is any likelihood of winning a case against God. Yet his conviction that God does not pervert justice prods him to contemplate the impossible, i.e, of pursuing litigation against God.

3 Job now contemplates the possibility of entering *into litigation* with God in order to prove his innocence. In his mind one may settle such a

1. Heb. *'omnām,* "surely," appears frequently in Job: 12:2; 19:4; 34:12; 36:4; cf. 2 K. 19:17; Isa. 37:18; Ruth 3:12.

2. Heb. *ḥāpēṣ,* "desire, purpose," means to plan a course of action for one's own benefit. It may also mean "delight, pleasure," and in a stronger sense it connotes "will" and "purpose," as here, and "desire, strive after." In the construction *ḥāpēṣ* + *le* + infinitive construct, *ḥāpēṣ* can function as a helping verb, e.g., "to want to do something." Cf. G. J. Botterweck, *"ḥāpēṣ," TDOT,* V:92–107.

3. Heb. *rîḇ* means "to dispute in a court of law, or to enter into litigation." See KB (2nd ed.), pp. 888–89.

4. Heb. *'ammîṣ,* "strong, sturdy," often attracts the noun *kōaḥ,* "power," to connote great strength (so Dhorme; cf. Job 9:19; 36:19; Isa. 40:26).

dispute in two different ways. One way is for both parties to take their case to court. In an ancient court the winner often was the one who argued his position so convincingly and refuted his opponent so persuasively that he reduced him to silence. A second way of deciding a dispute was for the two contestants to engage in a wrestling match.[5] The winner of the match proved the merits of his position and received a settlement to his advantage. While the preponderance of legal language indicates that Job is thinking of a court trial, the references to God's strength and to his cosmic victory over Rahab's cohorts in v. 13 indicate that the latter type of contest is also in his mind.

Job quickly realizes that it would avail him nothing, for *he could not answer (ʿānâ)*[6] God during the cross-examination, *not even one* question *out of a thousand.*[7] Since Job is concerned throughout this speech with getting God into court, it seems preferable to take the human person as the subject in both lines. This interpretation sees that the two parties, a person and God respectively, are in the same position in v. 3 as they are in v. 2b and that the same order occurs in v. 4b. This explanation may account for the use of pronouns instead of proper nouns in v. 3. Another possible interpretation is to translate the second line, "God would not answer him, not one in a thousand times." This rendering is supported by Job's difficulty in believing that God would respond to a summons to hear his case (vv. 16 and 19). In favor of the former translation, however, is Job's fear that he could not find the words to argue with God (vv. 14–15) or that his own mouth would condemn him (v. 20). His apprehension about his own inability to argue his case is stronger than his doubt that God would not answer his case. This interpretation is also favored by the outcome of the book, for in the end when God appears and questions Job, he remains silent, unable to answer God's questions, not even one of them. Therefore, it is best to take a human being as the subject of the verbs in v. 3 and God as their object.

4 The first line, *Wise in thought and mighty in strength,* is a *casus pendens* that may modify either the subject, "who," or the direct object, "God," in the second line. If it modifies the subject, it means that not even the wisest and strongest person could defy God and win. If it modifies the direct object, it is saying that a person could not expect to defy such a wise and strong God successfully. The latter position is preferred, since this epithet prepares the way for the hymnic lines in vv. 5–13. The *who* of the second line then is any human being. Nobody could *defy God and win.* The word *defy (hiqšâ)* is literally "harden, stiffen," used here elliptically for the

5. Cf. C. Gordon, "Belt-Wrestling in the Bible World," *HUCA* 23 (1950–51) 131–36.

6. Heb. *ʿānâ,* "answer," also has a technical legal sense, "respond" to an accusation.

7. This expression occurs also in 33:23; Eccl. 7:28; Sir. 6:5.

usual phrase "harden the neck."[8] It describes the action of a warrior bracing himself for a contest. The word for *win (šālēm)* means literally "be safe, whole, intact." That is, whoever takes on God, no matter how mighty he is, will not escape unharmed.

(b) Creation, the Canopy for God's Appearing (9:5–13)

5 *"He moves the mountains without their knowing it,*
and[1] he overturns them[2] in his anger;
6 *he shakes the earth from its place,*
and its pillars tremble;
7 *he speaks to the sun[3] and it does not shine,[4]*
and he seals the stars.
8 *He stretches out the heavens by himself,*
and treads on the back of the sea.[5]
9 *He made Aldebaran[6] and[7] Orion,*
Pleiades and the Chambers of the South.
10 *He does great deeds beyond searching,*
and wonders beyond counting.

8. The Hiphil *hiqšâ*, "make hard," with *ʿōrep*, "nape of the neck," as its object, means "stiffen the neck," i.e., "to resist someone stubbornly," e.g., Prov. 29:1; Deut. 10:16; Jer. 7:26; 17:23; 19:15. Duhm takes the figure to be that of a warrior making his neck hard for battle.

1. A *waw* before *ʾ^{a}šer* may have fallen out by dittography (Fohrer), or perhaps the *waw* should be removed from *ydʿw* and placed with *ʾ^{a}šer*.

2. MT *h^{a}pāḵām*, "he overturns them," may be a frequentative perfect. But some (e.g., Duhm) would like to revocalize it as a participle, *hōp^{e}ḵām*. Cf. Gordis.

3. A less familiar word for "sun," *ḥeres,* is used here (cf. Judg. 14:18). It appears in place names such as Mount Heres (Judg. 1:35), Ascent of Heres (Judg. 8:13) and Timnath-heres (Judg. 2:9); cf. Isa. 19:18, where MT has *ʿîr haheres,* "city of destruction," as a pun for *ʿîr haḥeres,* "city of the sun," i.e., On or Heliopolis in Egypt (which some mss. and versions read).

4. Heb. *zāraḥ* means primarily "to rise" (so Gordis, Dhorme, Pope), but it may also mean "shine" (so Tur-Sinai, Driver-Gray, Rowley).

5. A few Hebrew mss. read *ʿāḇ,* "cloud," instead of *yām,* "sea." This reading is followed by Fohrer and de Wilde; cf. K.-D. Schunk, *"bāmāh," TDOT,* II:140. Pope, Gordis, and others follow Albright (*JBL* 57 [1938] 227; idem, *Yahweh and the Gods of Canaan* [Garden City, NY: Doubleday, repr. 1969], p. 121n.24) in translating MT *bām^{o}ṯê yām* as "on the back [cf. Ugar. *bmt,* 'back'] of (the) Sea," a reference to Yam, the sea-god in Canaanite mythology. Cf. Deut. 33:29 for a similar expression. This interpretation connects creation (referred to in the first line of this verse) with Yahweh's defeat of the sea-god.

6. This reading assumes that *ʿāš* here and *ʿayiš* in 38:32 are the same. There is alliteration between "he who made" *(ʿōśeh)* and "Aldebaran" *(ʿāš)*.

7. Driver-Gray and others think that there should be a *waw* before *k^{e}sîl,* "Orion"; either it was accidentally omitted or the text order was originally *ʿāš w^{e}kîmâ k^{e}sîl* . . . (cf. Amos 5:8; Job 38:3l; *BHK*) and was altered by an error of metathesis. Cf. *BHS*.

11 *Were he to pass by me, I would not see him;*[8]
were he to glide past, I would not perceive him.
12 *Were he to abduct,*[9] *who could restrain him?*
Who could say to him 'What are you doing?'
13 *God does not restrain his anger;*
under him the helpers[10] *of Rahab lie prostrate."*

These lines in praise of God may be divided into three portions: vv. 5–7, nature's response to God's appearing; vv. 8–10, God's might and wisdom in creating the world; vv. 11–13, God's victory over all foes.[11] These hymnic lines are intricately related to v. 4:

deeds of power	v. 4a′	vv. 5-7
acts of wisdom	v. 4a	vv. 8-10
God's victory over foes	v. 4b	vv. 11-13

All three strophes employ language descriptive of a theophany.[12] When God appears, the earth trembles and the light fails (vv. 5–7). It is under the

8. MT *'er'eh,* "I shall see," may be a defective writing of *'er'ēhû,* "I shall see him" (see *BHK*). Another view suggests that *lô,* "to him," in the second line may do double duty for both lines (Blommerde, *Northwest Semitic Grammar and Job,* pp. 52–53; cf. Gordis). Fohrer thinks that in Hebrew the words "hear" *(šāmaʿ)* and "see" *(rā'â)* do not always need an object. But the English translation demands an object, so one is supplied.

9. According to Dhorme, Heb. *ḥāṯap,* "seize, abduct, despoil," stands for a wicked deed committed by one person against another, like an act of treachery. In Akkadian this root means "to slaughter." The content of v. 13 favors its meaning an act of violence. Dahood ("Some Northwest-Semitic Words in Job," *Bib* 38 [1957] 310–11) and Blommerde (*Northwest Semitic Grammar and Job,* p. 53) divide *yaḥṭōp* into *yaḥaṭ,* "he should snatch away" (from *ḥth),* and the conjunction *pā (pāmî),* which introduces the apodosis. Tur-Sinai takes it as a poetic variant of *ḥtp,* "seize" (cf. Ps. 10:9). Nevertheless, Grabbe (*Comparative Philology and the Text of Job,* pp. 60–63) gives good evidence for a Semitic root *ḥtp,* "match" or "break"; cf. Prov. 23:28; Sir. 15:14; 32:21; 50:4. Cf. Gordis, Rowley. It is best to retain the MT, for there is a play between this word and *yaḥᵃlōp,* "to glide" (v. 11b).

10. H. L. Ginsberg ("A Ugaritic Parallel to 2 S. 1:21," *JBL* 57 [1938] 210) suggests that the Hebrew root *ʿzr* is related to Ugar. *ǵzr,* "be strong," and should be translated "the strong forces of Rahab." But as Rowley points out, the usual meaning, "helpers," makes good sense.

11. The author has borrowed freely from the rich hymnic repertoire of ancient Israel to construct this portion of Job's speech. The composite nature of these lines is visible in three distinct styles: a series of definite participles in vv. 5–7, a series of anarthrous participles in vv. 8–10, and two hypothetical conditions followed by an affirmation in vv. 11–13. While some (e.g., Fohrer) consider vv. 5–10 a secondary addition that interrupts the context, the integral connection between vv. 5–13 and v. 4 points to the integrity of these lines. In addition, Westermann's study (*Structure of the Book of Job,* pp. 71–79) demonstrates that hymnic lines in praise of God are a common feature among the various speakers in the first cycle except Bildad; so this use of hymnic lines is not foreign to a speech by Job.

12. Cf. Jörg Jeremias, *Theophanie* (Neukirchen: Neukirchener, 1965), pp. 23–24, 89, 123–24, 161.

canopy of the heavens, which God has stretched out as his tent, that he rules and does wonders (vv. 8–10). When God draws near, a human being, though unable to see him, is fully conscious of the divine power manifested in the subjection of all hostile forces (vv. 11–13). Job puts himself into the last strophe of this hymn (v. 11) by expressing his agonizing frustration that he would not perceive God even when he passes close by him.[13]

5 When God appears nature acclaims his lordship with a tumultuous uproar. *He moves the mountains,* which are symbolic of antiquity and stability (cf. Gen. 49:26; Deut. 33:15). *he overturns them in his anger.* While this language could describe an earthquake followed by an avalanche, it may also describe a volcanic eruption. Similar descriptions of nature's response to God's coming favor the latter interpretation. When God comes forth from his throne, the mountains melt like wax (Ps. 97:5; Mic. 1:4; Isa. 63:19b–64:1 [Eng. 64:1–2]), or he touches them and they smoke (Ps. 104:32; cf. Deut. 32:22).[14] The explosion happens *without their knowing it,* i.e., unexpectedly.[15]

6 *he shakes the earth from its place.* A mighty earthquake also attends God's appearing.[16] *shakes.* The verb *hirgîz* means "shudder in terror." *and its pillars tremble.* The earth is pictured as a huge house firmly resting on pillars.[17] *tremble.* The verb *hiṯpallaṣ* depicts "being tossed about violently." When God treads on the earth, these supporting pillars quiver beneath the force of his footsteps. Since this line clearly describes an earth-

13. The personal element in v. 11 might indicate that it was not part of the hymnic lines. But vv. 12 and 13 definitely belong to a hymn of praise, for they laud God's victory over all forces. Therefore, v. 11 must also be a part of the hymn. The author has skillfully incorporated this couplet for Job to express his own anticipated response to a theophany without interrupting the flow of the hymn.

14. When God appeared to Israel on Mt. Sinai to give his law (Exod. 19:7, 16, 18), the mount shook, the skies trembled with thunder and lightning, and an eerie darkness hovered over the mount. The prophets employ the same imagery to describe the coming Day of Yahweh (e.g., Joel 3:3–4 [Eng. 2:30–31]).

15. The phrase "without their knowing it" is difficult. Does it mean that God does not know that the mountains quake at his presence because he acts so effortlessly (so Syr., Duhm), that people are too far away to know there has been an earthquake (cf. Tur-Sinai), or that people are caught by surprise when the earth begins to quake (cf. Pope)? Or could it mean that the mountains are caught unaware because their shaking happens so quickly (so Gordis; cf. Dhorme)? If the singular *yāḏaʿ*, "know," is read with Budde and Driver-Gray, it means that God's presence produces these results effortlessly, without special design. But the interpretation that the mountains themselves are caught by surprise, unaware that God is about to shake them, is supported by the texts of Jer. 50:24 and Prov. 5:6 (cf. Isa. 47:11; Ps. 35:8). See Rowley.

16. Palestine has frequently been shaken by severe earthquakes, as is well attested by archeological investigations. This fact is not surprising, for the great Jordan rift runs the length of Palestine.

17. Pillars of the earth are also mentioned in Ps. 75:4 (Eng. 3). Cf. Job 26:11, which mentions the pillars of heaven.

quake, it increases the likelihood that a different natural phenomenon, such as a volcano, is described in v. 5.

7 During such upheavals darkness covers the earth. The great light-giving bodies fail. *he speaks to the sun and it does not shine,* being darkened either by the thick column of smoke from the volcano or hidden by a sandstorm caused by mighty winds that accompany the earthquake. As one puts something in an envelope and seals it, God *seals the stars* so that they cannot come forth and sparkle in their constellations.

8 Next Job reflects on God's great power as manifested in creating the world. The parallelism of *the heavens* and *the back of the sea* is a poetic way to refer to the universe. Each day God *stretches out the heavens* like a great tent (cf. Ps. 104:2; Zech. 12:1; Isa. 44:24; 51:13). This metaphor means that God prepares the heavens as his canopy under which he displays his reign in theophanic splendor.[18] There he manifests his kingly authority: *he treads on the back of the sea.* Since in the OT the sea is symbolic of chaotic powers hostile to God, this expression means that he has subdued the sea and is its master.

9 In particular God has made the constellations and placed them in their respective courses. The stars, by reason of their brilliance and their movement, attracted the wonder and worship of the ancient Semites, above all the Mesopotamians.[19] Believed to be gods and goddesses, the heavenly bodies had a prominent role in the pantheon, e.g., Anu (heavens), Shamash (sun), Sin (moon), and Ishtar (Venus). Those who worshiped the stars absorbed themselves in studying their movements in order to divine their messages and gain insight into the future. While acknowledging the beauty and the power of the stars, Israel acclaimed that God is the Creator and Lord of all the heavenly host. The constellations, being mere creatures, are not worthy of worship.

Either three or four constellations are named here: Aldebaran, Orion, Pleiades, and "the Chambers of the South." The identification of the first star (*ʿāš*) is uncertain.[20] While Ibn Ezra identifies it as "the Great Bear" (Ursa Major), Hölscher considers *ʿāš* as Leo and its encroachment on Cancer.[21] A third possibility, according to Schiaparelli, is Aldebaran, the

18. See N. C. Habel, "He Who Stretches out the Heavens," *CBQ* 34 (1972) 417–30.

19. Isaiah especially accuses the Babylonians of dividing the heavens, possibly referring to the Zodiac, and gazing at the stars in order to divine the future (47:13).

20. Vulg. translates Heb. *ʿāš* as Arcturus, the most brilliant star in the constellation Bootes. But a similar passage, 38:32, has "*ʿayiš* and her children," possibly the Great Bear and the stars of its tail. For a full discussion of various identifications, see Tur-Sinai and Dhorme.

21. This view gains support by taking Arab. *ʿay(y)ût,* "lion," as its cognate.

brightest star in the constellation Hyades and the eye of the bull Taurus.[22] Classical writers group Aldebaran with Pleiades, Hyades, and Orion as heralds of the seasons. Thus it is accepted here as the most likely option.

The second constellation, Heb. *k^e^sîl,* is identified as Orion, a very brilliant constellation. The Hebrew word means literally "fool." It is of interest that Orion, the star which is called "the strong one" in Arabic and translated "the giant" in the Targ. and the Syr., has the name "a fool" in Hebrew. In Greek mythology, Orion, a giant and a great hunter, offended the goddess of the chase and at his death was punished by being placed in the sky and chained.[23]

The third group, Heb. *kûm,* "accumulated, heap up, i.e., a cluster," identifies Pleiades, the most noted cluster of stars. It consists of seven stars.

The phrase *the Chambers of the South (ḥaḏrê tēmān)* may refer either to a constellation or a star or a group of stars in the southern sky, like the Southern Cross or Sirius or Argo.[24] Pope takes this name for the place where the ancient people thought the south wind was stored (37:9). He gets this idea from the fact that the word *tēmān* is related to the south wind (cf. Ps. 78:26; Cant. 4:16). Because the identification of this phrase is so uncertain, it is translated literally here.

10 Beneath the heavenly canopy God performs *great deeds (g^e^ḏōlôṯ)* beyond human comprehension and *wonders [niplā'ôṯ] beyond counting.* That is, God continues to be actively involved within the created order, and all of his wonders bear witness to his wisdom (cf. Isa. 28:29). Whereas Eliphaz employed these same lines to God's judicious governance of the world (Job 5:9), Job's thoughts gravitate toward God's sheer power and cunning, which may be manifested in remarkable, enigmatic upheavals in nature.

11 Moving from the natural phenomena that attend a theophany, Job reflects on how he would respond to God's presence. *Were he to pass by me, I would not see him; were he to glide past, I would not perceive him.*[25]

22. Some identify Syr. *ʿîyûtā',* used here to translate *ʿāš,* with Hyades, whose brightest star is Aldebaran. Cf. G. Schiaparelli, *Astronomy in the Old Testament* (Oxford: Clarendon, 1905), pp. 53–60; W. Brueggemann, "Arcturus," *IDB,* I:216.

23. See W. Brueggemann, "Orion," *IDB,* III:609; and Pope.

24. G. R. Driver ("Two Astronomical Passages in the Old Testament," *JTS* 7 [1956] 8–10) takes *ḥaḏrê* as the Hebraic form of Syr. *ḥdar,* "surround," technically meaning "orbit" or "circuit" of a star and thus referring to the *circulus austrinus* of Martianus Capella. The Babylonians divided the sky into three sections: Enlil, with 33 constellations in the north; Anu, with 23 constellations on both sides of the equator; and Ea, with 13 constellations to the south. The last could equal the "circuit of the South."

25. The verbs in v. 11, *ʿāḇar,* "pass by," and *ḥālap,* "glide past," are technical terms for a theophany. The first one describes God's majestic appearances to Moses and Elijah (Exod. 33:18–23; 34:6; 1 K. 19:11–13), and Eliphaz uses the second term to describe his nocturnal encounter with a divine spirit (Job 4:15).

Job anticipates that he would neither see him nor perceive his presence. Even though nature reacts to God's presence with violent upheavals, God himself is not visible in the natural phenomena (cf. 1 K. 19:11–13). He transcends the elements. As a result, even when God draws near, no human being ever beholds him. All a person perceives are the effects of God's presence. Consequently, one who has a concern with God does not find any opportunity to speak to or argue with him.

12 When God is present, he does whatever he wills. *Were he to abduct, who could restrain him?* He can take a person without anyone stopping him. No victim can call God's actions into question by asking, *What are you doing?*[26] When a bystander puts such a question to a person, he is challenging the rightness of what that person is doing. He is ordering that person to stop and give an account of his actions. But no one can so challenge God.

13 When God is mightily present, he *does not restrain his anger* until all powers, earthly and cosmic, *lie prostrate* before him. Proof of God's incontestable might is his victory over the forces of chaos represented by *the helpers* or cohorts *of Rahab*.[27] Rahab is one of the monsters along with Leviathan (see 3:8; 40:25–41:26 [Eng. 41:1–34]) and Tannin (see 7:12; 30:29; Gen. 1:21; Ps. 74:13; Isa. 27:1) who were thought to inhabit the depths of the sea. By reason of their role in the myths of Israel's neighbors, in the OT these creatures symbolize the forces of chaos in opposition to God. It is always affirmed that God has defeated them as a testimony to the belief that God is master over all cosmic forces, including those that are hostile to his rule.

(c) Job's Misgivings about Arguing His Case before God (9:14–24)

14 *"How then can I answer him*
or choose my words with him?
15 *Whom,[1] though I am in the right, I could not answer;[2]*
to my opponent-at-law[3] I would plead for mercy.

26. A clear parallel is found in Dan. 4:32 (Eng. 35); cf. Eccl. 8:4; Sir. 36:10.

27. The name Rahab *(rahaḇ)* appears in 5 other OT texts (Job 26:12; Ps. 87:4; 89:11 [Eng. 10]; Isa. 30:7; 51:9–10). In Isa. 30:7 and Ps. 87:4 it is a figurative name for Egypt; in the other texts it represents the cosmic dragon.

1. Many omit MT *ʾᵃšer,* "whom." Duhm thinks it entered the passage from v. 17, but Budde argues for its retention. It may have as its antecedent "I" *(ʾānōḵî)* from v. 14, or it may serve as the object of *ʿānâ,* "answer."

2. Dhorme and Fohrer prefer to read MT *ʾʿnh,* "answer," as a Niphal, "I am not answered," with the versions. But Pope, Rowley, and Blommerde (*Northwest Semitic Grammar and Job*, pp. 53–54) point out that this is not necessary. Indeed, that the preceding verbs are active militates against a passive. The direct object of *ʾʿnh* may be *ʾᵃšer,* or the Ketib may be a defective writing of *ʾeʿĕnēhû,* "I shall answer him."

3. MT *limᵉšōpᵉṭî* is best taken as a Polel particle to denote an actor (cf.

16 *If I called and he answered me,*[4]
I do not[5] *believe that he would attend to my voice.*
He bruises me with a tempest[6]
and multiplies my wounds without cause.
18 *He does not permit my spirit to be restored,*
for he satiates me with bitter things.[7]
19 *If it concerns strength, he is the Strong One;*[8]
or if it is for litigation, who could summon him?[9]
20 *Though I am in the right, my mouth*[10] *would condemn me;*
I am blameless, but it would find me perverse.[11]

Dhorme, Gordis). It is similar in form to *mlwšyn,* "the one who slanders," in Ps. 101:5, and to an Arabic form that suggests endeavor and some reciprocity or even enmity: hence "opponent-at-law" (Driver-Gray). Others revocalize it *lᵉmišpāṭî,* "to his justice" (with *-i* meaning "his"; e.g., Blommerde, *Northwest Semitic Grammar and Job,* pp. 53–54), with the interpretation that "justice" is a personified attribute of God.

4. The imperfect consecutive dependent on a perfect represents conditional action (GKC, § 111x).

5. Dahood transfers *lōʾ*, "not," to the end of the first line to translate it as a noun, "nothing" ("Hebrew-Ugaritic Lexicography IV," *Bib* 47 [1961] 408). Andersen also moves in this direction. In his opinion there is a textual problem at this point, for such skepticism is too atypical for Job. He suggests taking *lōʾ* as asseverative, "certainly." But vv. 17–19 seem to demonstrate why Job does not believe God hears him; therefore MT should be retained.

6. For MT *biśʿārâ* Dhorme and Pope read with Targ. and Syr. *bᵉśaʿᵃrâ,* "with a hair," in the sense of "a trifle." This makes a good parallel to *ḥinnām,* "without cause." But *śᵉʿārâ* may be a phonetic error resulting from the writing of a *ś* for a *s*, as in Nah. 1:3, in which case it means "storm" or "tempest." The latter view is preferable, for a storm played a part in Job's losses (1:16). It also establishes a link with Yahweh's address to Job out of a storm (chs. 38–41).

7. MT *mammᵉrōrîm,* a hapax legomenon, may be revocalized to *mimmᵉrōrîm,* "from bitter things" (Driver-Gray), for *śāḇaʿ*, "satiate," occurs with the preposition *min* in Ps. 104:13; Prov. 14:14; 18:20. A close parallel found in Lam. 3:15 uses the preposition *bᵉ* instead of *min,* so some emend MT to *bimrōrîm* (Hölscher, with some mss.). But Gordis accounts for MT by taking this noun as having a preformative *m* and considering the verb *śāḇaʿ* to have a double accusative. It is best to avoid emendation when MT can be explained adequately.

8. To gain a pronoun to complete the first line various proposals have been made: *hinnēhû* (defective script, so Blommerde, *Northwest Semitic Grammar and Job,* p. 56; cf. Gordis, who achieves the same result by assuming an error of haplography), or to remove the *waw* from *ʾim* as an error of word division (Dhorme), or to emend it to *hinnô ʾim* (Duhm).

9. A slight alteration adopted by many commentators is to read *yôʿîḏennû,* "he summons him," instead of MT *yôʿîḏēnî,* "he summons me." Perhaps the present text arose to avoid a bold assertion against God.

10. A slight textual change from MT *pî,* "my mouth," to *pîw,* "his mouth," is supported by some (e.g., Hölscher) but rejected by others (e.g., Duhm, Dhorme, Tur-Sinai). Dahood (*Bib* 38 [1957] 311) makes an interesting suggestion. He takes *pî* as the conjunction *pā: pᵉyaršîʿēnî;* the *pā* then parallels the *waw* in the second line. But the change is without any textual support. Moreover, "his mouth" is not the most natural way

21 *I am blameless!*
I care not for myself.
I loathe my life![12]
22 *It is the same. Therefore I say,*
'He makes an end of the blameless and the wicked.'
23 *Whenever a scourge kills suddenly,*[13]
he mocks at the despair[14] *of the innocent.*
24 *A land*[15] *is given*[16] *into the power of the wicked,*
the faces of her judges he covered.
If it is not he, then who?"

14, 15 Given the fact of God's superior power and wisdom, Job ponders how he could *answer God* in court, especially under cross-examination.[17] There would be no way for him to match words with God. This fear grows out of his recent meditation on God's sovereign power. In these questions Job reiterates his apprehensions of v. 3. Even though he knows himself to *be in the right (ṣāḏaq),* he also knows that he could not defend himself before God. Usually one who is innocent has little to fear from a just judicial process, but Job fears the wise and the mighty God. *to my opponent-at-law I would plead for mercy*. The only action he could take would be to petition

---

to refer to God. Furthermore, Eliphaz makes a similar charge against Job, "Your mouth condemns you" (15:6). And in v. 21 Job finds great limitation within himself (cf. A. Jirku, "Eine Renaissance des Hebräischen," *FF* 32 [1958] 211–12). Therefore, MT is followed.

11. MT *wayyaʿqešēnî,* "he would find me perverse," can be read as a shortened Hiphil or revocalized as a Piel, *wîʿaqqešēnî* (Duhm). Many prefer to read a Hiphil even though this would be the only occurrence of this stem in the Hiphil.

12. Verse 21 is hard to divide. If it is two lines the first line has twice as many syllables as the second (8/4). Pope divides it into three short lines (2:2:2 by stress, but 3/5/4 by syllable count). Whether it is three lines or a long and a short line, it is composed so as to capture the emotional strain Job is under.

13. For MT *piṯʾōm,* "suddenly," F. Zimmermann ("Note on Job 9:23," *JTS* 2 [1951] 165–66) reads *peṯāʾîm,* "simple-minded ones," with the primitive or more basic meaning "innocent, guiltless," as parallel to *neqîyîm,* "pure."

14. A possible interpretation of MT *massaṯ* is "despair" from *māsas,* "flow," which appears in the Hiphil with "heart" to mean "melt" in anguish (Duhm).

15. Heb. *ʾereṣ,* "land, earth," is without the article and probably refers indefinitely to any land, not Israel or Palestine specifically. Duhm and others, however, find a definite historical allusion here to a time when Israel was controlled by a foreign tyrant. But the verse is quoting a general principle rather than referring to a specific historical era.

16. Dahood ("Ugaritic and the Old Testament," *ETL* 44 [1968] 42–43) translates the line, "He puts the earth in the wicked's power." He points MT *ntnh* as *nāṯenāh,* a third person masculine singular, an old *qaṭala* perfect form preserved in poetry. God then is subject of both verbs.

17. In legal contexts the verb "answer" *(ʿānâ)* means "to deliver a defense" under cross-examination.

God for mercy (cf. 8:5). These lines foreshadow the direction the drama will take. Job will press harder and harder for a legal resolution to his unjust suffering. But when God does answer him, he will be silent except to beseech God for mercy. Before God himself he will abandon his legal complaint.

16 Job speculates further about what would happen should he be able to summon God into court.[18] If God should grant him a hearing, he does not believe that God would really listen to his arguments. At best he would be given only an occasion to air his grievances, not a real opportunity to win a court decision.

17 Frustrated, Job complains that God is punishing him brutally. Specifically Job says God is guilty of *multiplying my wounds without cause [ḥinnām]*. The phrase *without cause* means that God is acting capriciously, having no grounds to punish his servant. The author skillfully uses Heb. *ḥinnām,* a pivotal word in the scenes before Yahweh found in the prologue. There the Satan skeptically asked whether Job served God *ḥinnām,* "for nought" (1:9). After Job survived his first test, God retorted to the Satan that the Satan had incited him to afflict Job *ḥinnām,* "without cause." But now Job perceives that God has afflicted him *ḥinnām, without cause*. Whereas the Satan doubted Job's motive for being righteous, the trial leads Job to doubt the justice of God's actions in permitting him to suffer. This dimension of the trial strikes a raw nerve in Job. God allows him to be tested in a way that leads Job to question the very basis of his faith, namely, that God is just and good. No stronger test exists for a faithful servant of God. On the other hand, God has such confidence in his servant that he is not afraid to have his own goodness appear tainted to Job.

At this point the author anticipates the outcome of Job's story with the word *tempest (śᵉʿārâ)*. Job complains here that God *bruises me with a tempest*. Yet it will be from "a tempest" that God will address Job (38:1–42:6).

18 Job intensifies his complaint, declaring that God does not allow him any opportunity for his *spirit to be restored*. The *spirit* means his inner resourcefulness and attitudes. He keeps Job in constant emotional turmoil by continually filling him with *bitter things*. As a result, he is so worn down that he lacks the inner strength to bear himself with dignity. The bitterness that churns deep inside him flavors his speeches.

19 Returning to both his opening thought (vv. 2–4, esp. v. 4a) and a line in the hymn (v. 13), Job reiterates his frustration that there is no way for him to confront God. *If it concerns strength,* the outcome is obvious: God is *the Strong One* (*ʾammîṣ;* cf. 9:4), the sure victor. *If it is for litigation,* no

18. The language of v. 16 has the tone of a legal summons (cf. Isa. 59:4).

one *could summon him* into court on Job's behalf. These terse assertions show that Job cannot conceive of any way to force God into resolving his case.

20 Job bemoans his own inability to defend himself in court. He is convinced that he *is in the right (ṣāḏaq),* because he knows that he is *blameless (tām).* Heb. *tām* appears three times in vv. 20–22, and it was also used in the description of Job's character in the prologue (1:1). Nevertheless, he fears that should he be given a chance to testify before the court, his own *mouth would condemn (yaršîaʿ)* him and find him *perverse* or guilty of wickedness *(yaʿqîš).* Job is apprehensive that his very words in defense of his innocence would prove him guilty.

21 Deeply agitated, Job cries out as though he were standing before the court, *I am blameless! (tām).* Then he desperately exclaims, *I care not for myself! I loathe my life!* Feeling that he has no possible escape from his anguish, he vents his hatred for life. The oblique, literal language, "I do not know myself," may be understood as "I do not care for myself."[19] The conviction of his own moral purity does not ease the deep sense of meaninglessness he feels from his anguish, fed by the lack of any sense of God's presence or any insight into his design.

22–24 Gaining some composure, Job registers a sweeping complaint against God. He complains that when God devastates the world with a plague, he unjustly *makes an end of the blameless [tām] and the wicked [rāšāʿ].* That is, when God *suddenly* sends *a scourge* on the world, like a flood, *he mocks at the despair of the innocent [neqîyîm]. scourge (šôṭ)* means "whip" or "plague" and applies to a devastating judgment that brings widespread death (cf. Isa. 10:26; 28:15–18). *he mocks* means that he gladly lets them vainly cry out for help as a part of their suffering. He lets them struggle hopelessly until they die. This complaint challenges Bildad's conclusion that God carefully distinguishes among people and would never despise the upright (8:20). It also counters Eliphaz's assertion that God offers protection during difficult or troubled times (5:19–22). Eliphaz also used the word *šôṭ* (5:21) and posited that the righteous are able to laugh at destruction (5:22; cf. 22:19–20), rather than being mocked by it. But Job directly challenges his friends' position as well as the mercy and justice of God.

God is guilty of another grave injustice. He gives *a land* or a nation *into the power of the wicked.* Such rulers coerce their subjects and exploit the

19. Cf. Rowley. Dhorme interprets the first line differently: "Am I perfect? I do not know myself!" S. Paul ("An Unrecognized Medical Idiom in Canticles 6, 12 and Job 9, 21," *Bib* 59 [1978] 545–47) argues that "I do not know myself" means that a person is suffering a mental disorder, i.e., he is totally beside himself. But the translation adopted here is supported by the last line of the verse.

land for their own vainglory. In a reign of terror they dominate the law courts by threats and bribes. It appears that God covers *the faces of her judges* so that they allow the mighty to exploit the poor and the weak to build their own wealth. Oppression is rampant, the masses are exploited, and all avenues of redress are shut off. Such rulers relish their cruel exercise of power.

Job ends these charges against God with a poignant question, *If it is not he, then who?* Given the fact that injustices exist throughout the land and that there is only one God, one can only conclude that God himself is the cause of these injustices. Job's questioning leads him to wonder if God is really just. He will have to settle this question himself in order to come to grips with his suffering.

(2) Job's Inability to Demonstrate His Innocence (9:25–35)

25 *"My days pass swifter than a runner;*
they flee without experiencing pleasure.
26 *They skim by like reed[1] skiffs—*
as an eagle swooping down on its prey.
27 *If I say,[2] 'I shall forget my complaint;*
I shall adorn[3] my sad countenance and be cheerful,'
28 *I am appalled by all my pains;*
I know that you will not acquit me.
29 *I am considered wicked;*
why should I toil thus uselessly?
30 *If I were to wash myself[4] with soapwort[5]*
or cleanse my hands with lye,
31 *then you would plunge me into filth[6]*
so that my clothes would abhor me.

1. MT *ʾēḇeh,* "reed," is variously translated by the versions. For example, LXX renders the line "is there any trace left by a ship?" But *ʾēḇeh* may be related to Arab. *ʾabā* and Akk. *abu* and thus mean "reed, papyrus" (KB, pp. 3–4).

2. An infinitive construct after *ʾim* is most unusual. Therefore, it seems best to read the perfect form *ʾāmartî,* "I said" (Duhm; GKC, § 159o).

3. MT *ʿzb* is taken from *ʿzb* II, "fix," used for beautifying the face or changing the mood (M. Dahood, "The Root *ʿzb* II in Job," *JBL* 78 [1959] 303–309; and Pope).

4. Andersen interprets the Hithpael as having iterative force, i.e., the repeated washing of the hands, rather than the reflexive force, as translated here.

5. LXX reads the Ketib *b^{e}mô,* "with," but Targ. and Syr. read the Qere *b^{e}mê,* "with water of." Most modern commentators prefer the Ketib and translate *šeleg* as "soapwort" rather than as "snow." Pope identified soapwort as soap manufactured from the root of the plant *Leontopetalon.* In the Mishna it is written *ʾešlāḡ* and in the Gemara *šalgāʾ* (Pope); it also appears in Akkadian as *ašlāku.*

6. For a detailed discussion of the semantic range of *šḥt* see M. Pope, "The Word *Šḥt* in Job 9:31," *JBL* 83 (1964) 269–78. Budde, Dhorme, Fohrer, and many others read *baššûḥôṯ,* as in Isa. 5:25, from *sûḥâ,* "filth, garbage, manure," a word that is common in Aramaic. But Pope retains *šaḥaṯ,* which stands for the netherworld, the abode of the dead, in 17:14; 33:22, 28. That realm is known for its watery, putrid nature.

32 *For a man like me could not answer him,*
we cannot come together in legal proceedings.
33 *There is no*[7] *arbiter between us,*
that he might lay his hand on us both—
34 *that he might remove his rod from me*
and not let his terror dismay me.
35 *I would speak, not fearing him*
though I[8] *am not right with myself."*

25, 26 Frustrated by the unlikelihood of gaining a hearing before the divine court, Job abruptly drops his last train of thought and begins to lament the hopelessness of his own situation. Since he is not *experiencing pleasure* (*ṭôḇâ,* lit. "good"), his fleeting life seems to be devoid of meaning.[9] On the surface these lines are in conflict with his complaint that his pain-filled moments drag by most slowly (7:3–4). This is the agony of one afflicted by a hopeless illness. Although the moments go by slowly, Job is also aware that his life is flying by with no apparent improvement and will soon be over.

Job compares the rapid passage of his days to that which is noted for being exceedingly swift on land, on sea, and in the air. *A runner* trained as a royal courier could cover long distances quickly.[10] While running, the courier blots out everything around him and endures the pain of the course by focusing on the goal before him (cf. Isa. 52:7; cf. Phil. 4:14). The next figure is the legendary swift *reed skiffs* of the Egyptians. These boats, made out of reeds, had wooden keels, and they were very light (cf. Isa. 18:1–2). They traveled so fast that they seemed to skim over the water. The third image considers the powerful flight of an *eagle* or a falcon *(nešer).* These birds of prey are known for their lightning speed (cf. 1 Sam. 1:23; Jer. 4:13; Hab. 1:8). When the falcon swoops down on its prey, it is estimated that it reaches speeds in excess of 150 mph (Pope). Each of these speedy creatures is spurred on by a desired end. But for Job his days are passing by even more

7. Read MT *lō'* as *lû,* "would that," with Budde and LXX (see *BHS*), for *lō'*, "not," is never used with *yēš* to express "there is not." *lû* introduces a situation contrary to fact.

8. H. Tur-Sinai (Torczyner; "Anmerkungen zum Hebräischen und zur Bible," *ZDMG* 66 [1912] 403) reads *hû'*, "he," for MT *'ānōḵî,* "I": "For he is not honorable with me." This could be another case of a deliberate scribal change *(Tiqqune sopherim).* While this change has much in its favor, MT should be followed, since no textual evidence supports the change.

9. This line resembles 7:6–7.

10. A beautiful picture of the attitude of a king's courier is found in an episode recorded in 2 Sam. 18:19–33. Ahimaaz, a runner, earnestly requests the assignment to carry tidings to the king, but the task is given to a Cushite. Ahimaaz continues to plead for permission to run. Finally gaining permission, he outruns the Cushite (cf. 2 Sam. 2:18).

swiftly, yet without the hope of any reward at the end that would encourage him to blot out the pain of the journey.

27 To overcome this frustration concerning his fleeting life Job ponders the possibility of disciplining his mind: *I shall forget my complaint.* He is considering his friends' advice that he leave off his complaint against God. Resolutely he will *adorn* his *sad countenance* with joy and *be cheerful* (see 10:20; cf. Ps. 39:14 [Eng. 13]). Job's great determination is conveyed by three cohortatives: *forget, adorn,* and *be cheerful.* He is determined to discipline his mind and put on a cheerful attitude.

28 But Job's resolution comes to a sudden end. His effort at positive thinking falters before a surge of pain. The appalling reality of his pain convinces him that God *will not acquit* him. No amount of hopeful thinking can calm his thoughts, which are troubled by God's seemingly capricious power.

29 *I am considered wicked.* Job is deeply disturbed that his illness makes it look like God is punishing him for some wrongdoing. Out of anguish he asks, *why should I toil thus uselessly?* Why should he try to overcome his pain and his guilt by challenging the mighty tyrant God? The word *uselessly (heḇel)* means literally "vapor, mist," that which is fleeting, lacking in substance (cf. Eccl. 1:2). The word *toil (yāgaʿ)* stresses the weariness that comes from hard work. The juxtaposing of *toil* and *uselessly* captures the despair Job feels when he contemplates taking a strenuous course of action to prove his innocence, a course that seems doomed to fail.

30 *If I were to wash myself with soapwort or cleanse my hands with lye.* Job considers a possible way of clearing his character: performing a lustration rite that would prove his innocence to all.[11] In such a ceremony he would use *soapwort* or *lye,* the strongest detergents available.[12] His use of such strong detergents would enhance the outcome of such a rite; then the conclusion that he is morally pure would be incontestable. The most famous

11. The parallel passages in Ps. 26:6 and 73:13 (see n. 12 below) support finding a close connection between Job's longing for innocence (*nāqâ;* v. 28b) and his thinking of a ritual of cleansing his hands (v. 30b). In Ps. 26:6 a psalmist alludes to a person's washing his hands before the sanctuary to show that he is not associated with the wicked. A statute found in Deut. 21:6–9 instructs the elders of a city near where a man has been murdered to wash their hands over a calf to show that they did not spill his blood. A similar rite is alluded to in Jer. 2:22; there Jeremiah preaches that a person cannot cleanse himself from his guilt by washing, no matter how much soap he uses.

12. In this passage the envisioned lustration rite approaches an ordeal; but since the deity is not called on to decide the results of the washing, it is not an ordeal proper (cf. R. Press, "Das Ordal im alten Israel, II," *ZAW* 51 [1933] 245–49). It seems best to take the washing here as a ritual act, one that the community would acknowledge. A psalmist went through a similar experience (Ps. 73). While suffering innocently like Job, he washed his hands in a public rite designed to prove that he was morally pure (v. 13). But that act was in vain, for God continued to plague him (v. 14).

example of the performance of such a public rite is Pilate's washing his hands in front of the crowd before he sentenced Jesus to death, saying, "I am innocent of this man's blood." Pilate wished to demonstrate publicly that he was free from any responsibility for Jesus' death (Matt. 27:24). It is this kind of public rite that Job is contemplating.

31 But Job knows how God would treat him after the completion of such a rite. He is sure that as soon as he finished washing himself as proof of his innocence, God would *plunge him into filth.* He would come forth from that pit so filthy that even his *clothes would abhor* him, i.e., they would refuse to cover his body. Garments are often associated in the OT with a person's moral quality (cf. Job 8:22; Isa. 52:1; 61:10).[13] In a situation similar to Job's, desolate Jerusalem is lamented as a lady clothed in filthy, soiled skirts that bear witness to her sin and loss of regal authority (Lam. 1:8–9). The garments that abhor Job are his garments of nobility, representing his honorable position of authority in the local assembly. Job is certain that if he tried to prove his innocence, God would disgrace him thoroughly.

32 Having pondered these two hypothetical ways of proving his innocence, Job concludes that it is impossible for a man to prove his innocence before God. *For a man like me could not answer him* in a legal proceeding. Therefore, he could not go to court with God, for the distance between God and human beings is too great.

33 Since Job would be at a grave disadvantage if he went to court with God, he looks for some other way to win a favorable settlement with God. He wishes that there were an *arbiter* to mediate his dispute with God. An earthly arbiter may resolve an issue between two parties. He listens to both sides of the controversy and works out a solution that is binding on both of them. Job wishes for such a heavenly umpire, one who could *lay his hand on* both God and himself and effect a reconciliation. In this instance *lay the hand on* means to ensure that both parties abide by the resolution. Of course, there is no official who could require God to act in a set way. Again Job's reasoning comes up against an insurmountable wall. There is no way for him to settle his complaint with God. Nevertheless, the genuineness of his yearning for God shines through this line. Job is grasping after any means to restore his relationship with God. His sense of meaninglessness before inexplicable suffering is deepened by God's absence from his life. That is why his search for vindication is essentially a search for God again to make himself known to him.

13. In the early postexilic period Zechariah had a vision of Joshua, the high priest, standing before an angel in filthy clothes. The angel had him remove them and put on new, rich garments (Zech. 3:3–5). The ritual meant that Joshua's former misdeeds were forgiven and he was thenceforth fully accepted by God to perform the duties of high priest.

34, 35 Job specifically wishes that the arbiter *might remove his* [God's] *rod from me and not let his terror dismay me*. The *rod (šēḇeṭ)* is a staff, like the staff used by a shepherd to protect and guide his sheep. Figuratively God, the Good Shepherd, has a staff. The psalmist finds inner strength by meditating on the comfort that God's staff gives (Ps. 23:4). The same staff, though, may be used as an instrument of punishment (Job 21:9; Lam. 3:1; Isa. 10:5; Prov. 22:8). Thinking about God's staff in this way strikes dismay deep in Job's heart. Job knows that his dismay is so strong that it will prevent him from defending himself with conviction. So if God's rod is removed, he believes that he could speak with clarity and power. His defense of his innocence, free from emotional outbursts and wild accusations, would be persuasive. Perhaps his intense anxiety gives some sense to the puzzling line in v. 35b, *I am not right with myself*. God's hostility so disconcerts Job that he feels at odds with himself (cf. 9:21).

b. Job's Lament (10:1–22)

Job turns from his search for ways to clear himself and laments his affliction. The core of this lament is an accusation against a friend who has proven disloyal.[1] Job's charges against God flow out of conflicting emotions: fear, frustration, anger, and bitter disappointment. He is revealing his distaste at the way God has allowed him to be tested. Unnerved by God's apparent disloyalty, he feels so disgraced that he cannot even lift up his head in public. He concludes that God is either an incompetent judge or a malicious tyrant bent on torturing him without letting him have any rest, not even in Sheol. But God is such a powerful opponent that Job feels there is no way for his misfortune to be changed.

(1) A Complaint against God (10:1–7)

1 *"My soul loathes[1] life;*
I will vent[2] freely my complaint;
I will speak in the bitterness of my soul.
2 *I shall say to God: 'Do not declare me guilty!*
Inform me why you contend with me.'[3]

1. This section ties in with the first sections in carrying through the legal language: "enter into trial" (*rîḇ*, 10:2; 9:3), "be guilty" (*rāšaʿ*; Hiphil in 10:2; 9:20; Qal in 10:7, 15; 9:29), and "be innocent" (*ṣāḏaq*, 10:15; 9:20).

1. MT *nāqeṭâ* is a contracted form of Niphal *nāqôṭâ*, "loathe". This is a case where a middle *waw* root has a form which follows the analogy of an *ʿayin-ʿayin* root (GKC, § 72dd).

2. Cf. M. Dahood, "The Root *ʿzb* II in Job," *JBL* 78 (1959) 303–309.

3. The suffix on the verb *terîḇēnî*, "you contend with me," is an accusative suffix as in Deut. 33:8 (cf. Isa. 27:8; Isa. 49:25), according to Driver-Gray.

3 *Is it advantageous for you to oppress*
and to reject the toil of your hands
while you shine on the counsel of the wicked?[4]
4 *Do you have eyes of flesh?*
Or do you see as man sees?
5 *Are your days as man's days*
or your years as man's days
6 *that you seek my iniquity*
and search for my sin?
7 *Although you know that I am not guilty,*
there is no[5] *one to deliver from your power."*

1 Lamentingly Job vents his pent-up emotions. He despises his ceaseless pain, for it causes him to loathe his own life. The agony churning inside him compels him to speak his thoughts boldly and freely. He is justifying his complaint against God in the fact that God has made his soul so bitter.

2 After his opening comment Job addresses God directly. In a bold move he demands an acquittal by enjoining God with negative imperatives. *Do not declare me guilty [hiršîaʿ]*. The term *declare guilty* (lit. "make one to appear wrong") means that God is treating him as though he had already convicted him of wickedness. Therefore, he bids God: *Inform me why you contend [rîḇ] with me*. Behind this request is the conviction that a plaintiff is obligated to make known to a defendant whom he intends to take to court the charges that he has against him. Job does not question God's right to punish him, but he thinks that God must try him officially before acting with such hostility against one who has been faithful. Ignorant of God's purpose, Job imagines that God is acting capriciously. If Job had knowledge of the proceedings in heaven recorded in the prologue, the trial would be easier for him to bear. In fact, he would most likely have willingly accepted the test in order to vindicate God's trust in him. But for his testing to be as severe as possible Job must be unaware of God's confidence, for trust in God is tested to the ultimate when circumstantial evidence calls into question the integrity of one's devotion to God. God's silence intensifies a person's testing far more than physical and emotional pain.

3 Job probes to discover God's motive for afflicting him by asking three cutting, rhetorical questions (vv. 3–6). First Job asks what is *the advantage* or profit (*ṭôḇ*, lit. "good") that God receives from oppressing

4. Surprised at the mention of the wicked, Duhm, Budde, and Fohrer unnecessarily take the third line as a gloss.

5. The *waw* is taken as *waw apodoseos*, i.e., it introduces the apodosis; therefore v. 7 is a self-contained unit. See Blommerde, *Northwest Semitic Grammar and Job*, pp. 28, 59–60; GKC, § 143d.

Job? Since it is expected that God always acts purposefully and does not profit from human deeds, Job queries as to what God could possibly gain from treating him so harshly. The verb *oppress* (*ʿāšaq*) denotes social injustice that often leads to violence.[6] Only here in the OT does God function as the subject of this negative verb.

and to reject the toil of your hands. Job refers to himself as *the toil of God's hands* (*yᵉgîaʿ kappeyḵā*). Most frequently this epithet is expressed with different Hebrew words, *maʿᵃśēh yāḏeyḵā,* "the work of your hands." This phrase is ordinarily positive, describing a human being as God's creation, the object of his special concern (Ps. 138:8; cf. Job 14:15; 34:19). But Job puts a different Hebrew word for "work" into this phrase, one that expresses "the toil, the painful effort" (*yᵉgîaʿ*) expended to produce something (e.g., Ps. 78:46; 109:11; Jer. 3:24; Ezek. 23:29).[7] While this word is normally used to refer to the toil of human hands (Gen. 31:42), here it speaks of God's strenuous effort to form Job. Moreover, there is usually a tight bond between a worker and his product. The worker takes pride in his creation and gladly accepts the responsibility of caring for it. But by turning this metaphor inside out, Job scathingly charges that God has rejected or renounced (*māʾas;* cf. Job 9:21; 42:6) this bond. He heightens the sarcasm of his question with the words *oppress* and *toil.*

Job charges that not only does God reject his faithful servant, he *shines* [*hôp̱îaʿ*][8] *on the counsel of the wicked.* In reference to God, *shine* means that he blesses someone in a special way (e.g., Ps. 50:2; 80:2 [Eng. 1]). The counsel of the wicked is noted for devising self-serving and hostile plans. Since such counsel leads to destruction (cf. Ps. 1:1, 4–6), it is resolutely avoided by the righteous. Nevertheless, Job accuses God of smiling on the plans of the wicked. Thus God appears to be acting in a way that would deny his very nature and discourage all moral action.

4–6 The second and third questions are absurd questions in the style of a disputation. Job wants to know why God is employing methods that human beings use because of their limitations to gain information on someone they suspect of wrongdoing. He asks God if in making a judgment his eyesight is limited like a human being's. For if he has *eyes of flesh,* he would see only partially, looking only on the externals of a matter, not on the

6. See, e.g., Lev. 5:21, 23 (Eng. 6:2, 4); 19:13; Deut. 24:14; 1 Sam. 12:3, 4; Ezek. 18:18; 22:29; Prov. 14:31; 22:16; cf. J. Lévêque, *Job et son Dieu,* II:413.

7. In Ps. 128:2 "toil" is used positively for the produce of the farmer's labor, since the food sustains his life and gives him great pleasure.

8. Dhorme finds that Heb. *hôpîaʿ* with a personal subject means "to shine on, be radiant, smile." The perfect *hôpaʿtā,* "you shine," may mean that God has already approved the decisions of the wicked and now they will certainly enjoy the benefits of his favor, while the imperfect *timʾas,* "you reject," says that Job is presently rejected and the outcome has not been decided.

inner motivations. But the testimony of the OT is that God is "spirit," not "flesh" (Isa. 31:3), and that in judging people he looks on the heart, not on outward appearances (1 Sam. 16:7). Then why does God so misjudge his innocent servant?

Next Job wonders if God feels limited by a short life span as a human being does in his search to learn if his servant has sinned in any way. Under the pressure of a limited time, God seems to be using cruel tactics to detect any such sin. But since God is eternal, he has no need to press so hard. Job bristles against God's method of investigation. He considers it abusive of justice, because his use of human methods of inquiry makes Job look guilty long before the court has tried his case.

7 Expecting strong negative answers to his questions, Job is sure that God knows that he is not guilty—even though God is acting capriciously and without showing any trust in him. This leaves Job in desperate straits, for *there is no one to deliver* from God's power (cf. Isa. 43:13; Deut. 32:39). A deliverer *(maṣṣîl)* is one who is able to free a person from an oppressor, often by some display of force. Whereas Job had looked for an arbiter to settle his case (9:32–34), now he realizes that he needs a deliverer, rather than an arbiter, to rescue him from God's cruel inquiry. But this insight increases Job's despair, for he knows that there is no such deliverer.[9] This section reveals that Job is so deeply troubled that he is led to doubt that God is true to justice. Such doubt stands at the core of his trial. Thus Job is expressing here the depths of his spiritual struggle brought on by his suffering.

(2) Job's Reflection on His Origin (10:8–12)

8 *"Your hands have fashioned me and made me*
complete:[1] then[2] you consume me.
9 *Remember that you have made me out of[3] clay;*
and you will turn me back to dust.

9. This thought reveals Job's solid commitment to a monotheistic view. In ancient Near Eastern mythology the god of wisdom was often able to outsmart the more powerful gods, and a young god could rise up and defeat the old champion of the gods. But for Job no other power or wisdom could rival God's.

1. MT *yaḥaḏ sāḇîḇ* is difficult. Many emend MT *yaḥaḏ,* "together," to *'aḥar,* "after," on the basis of LXX. MT *sāḇîḇ,* "round about," is variously emended. Duhm takes it as an infinitive absolute, *sāḇôḇ,* "turning around," while Budde and Fohrer read a perfect, *sabbôṯā,* "you have turned" (see *BHS*). Dhorme interprets it as an adverb, "utterly," modifying the verb in the second line. But we take these two words together to mean "complete," and with Gordis connect them to the first line.

2. The *waw* consecutive appears in last position in the line, a style often found in Job.

3. This is a pregnant use of the preposition *kap*—"as it were, by clay" (GKC, § 118w). Fohrer and Horst, however, prefer to read the preposition *bᵉ*, "out of clay."

10 *Did you not pour me out like milk,*
and curdle me like cheese,
11 *clothe me with skin and flesh,*
knit me together with bones and sinews?
12 *You granted me life and loyal love,*[4]
and your providence has guarded my spirit."[5]

8 Job continues his complaint against God by reflecting on the implications of the fact that God's *hands have fashioned (ʿiṣṣēḇ)* him[6] (v. 3a = v. 8a). He states definitely that God, like a potter, has made him,[7] a human vessel, out of clay. These words are similar to lines found in Isaiah: "We are the clay, and thou art our potter; we are all the work of thy hand" (64:8 [Eng. 7]). In this verse from Isaiah the phrase "the work of thy hand" is definitely connected with the image of the potter's making a clay vessel. Job is taking up a theme he mentioned in v. 3b. In v. 3 he emphasized God's effort in making man, while in v. 8 he focuses on the fact that God has artfully designed man (cf. Jer. 18:1–11). But whereas one would expect the potter to display his work proudly and to protect it carefully, God has made his vessel Job *complete,* and is now *consuming* (Piel of *bālaʿ*, lit. "swallowing") him. The same form of *bālaʿ* appears in the prologue in 2:3. There Yahweh charges the Satan, "You have caused me *to consume* him without reason." Job interprets his experience similarly. He attributes the swallowing to God, with no thought about the Satan. From his perspective the divine potter is acting out of character in destroying his own handiwork.

9 Given his distressful situation, Job implores God: *Remember that you have made me out of clay.* The plea for God "to remember" his servant or his people is frequent in the psalms of lament. It is asking God to intervene and rescue them on the basis of his past commitments (e.g., Ps.

4. The juxtaposition of *ḥayyîm,* "life," and *ḥeseḏ,* "loyal love" or kindness, is difficult. Some (e.g., Budde, Davidson, Rowley) understand it as an example of an extreme zeugma: "life blessed with love." Driver-Gray read *ḥēn,* "grace," for *ḥayyîm* to yield a more natural combination of "grace" and "loyal love." But this mass of flesh and bones needs "life," as the parallel in Ezek. 37 shows. Also, the fact that "life" is parallel to "spirit" in the second line supports the MT. On the basis of LXX Duhm suggests emending *ḥeseḏ* to *ḥeleḏ,* "life source." But such changes are unnecessary. As Andersen, Dhorme, and Gordis point out (each in his own way), MT makes sense and should be retained.

5. Hakam offers another interpretation. He takes "spirit" as the subject of the verb, for it is man who is obligated to keep the stipulations of the covenant: "My spirit has kept your charge."

6. "Fashioned" *(ʿiṣṣēḇ)* describes the artistic skill of a craftsman in making an image, as evidenced in the words derived from the same root: *ʿōṣeḇ* or *ʿāṣāḇ* for "idol."

7. Heb. *ʿāśâ,* "he made," is a general term used for the creation of human beings many times in the OT, e.g., Ps. 95:6; 100:3; 119:73.

25:6, 7; 74:2).[8] Here Job is entreating God to treat him in the light of the way he has made him (cf. Job 7:7). Since God has made him out of *clay* (*ḥōmer;* cf. 4:19; 33:6; Ps. 103:14; Isa. 45:9),[9] he is limited and weak by nature. God thus must be mindful of this fact and not expect more from Job than his constitution permits. Also Job wants to make God aware that his rough treatment is about to smash his vessel: *and you will turn me back to dust.*

10–12 Job heightens his complaint by recounting the marvelous way a baby is made. *Did you not pour me out like milk and curdle me like cheese?* Conception is described by analogy to the production of cheese. *milk,* i.e., semen, is poured *(hittîḵ)* into the womb and *curdled* or congealed *(hiqpî')* into a substance like soft *cheese,* i.e., an embryo (cf. Ps. 139:13–16; 2 Macc. 7:22; Wis. 7:2).[10] This soft mass receives form and structure when God *clothes* it *with skin and flesh* and *knits together [sōḵēḵ]*[11] *bones and sinews.* God *grants* this inanimate clump *life (ḥayyîm)* and *loyal love* (*ḥeseḏ;* v. 12). With the breath of life comes God's commitment of loyal love to his new creation. As in Ps. 63:4 (Eng. 3), these two words emphasize both the bestowing of the life principle and the sustaining of that life. After God has breathed the breath of life into each person, he *guards* or protects that life principle or *spirit (rûaḥ)* by his *providence (pᵉquddâ),* which means God's directing the course of events that befall a person.[12] Since Job believes that he has proved faithful to God, he now calls on God to prove true to his commitment by guarding his life from a premature death.

(3) God's Vigilance (10:13–17)

13 *"But these things you hid in your heart;*
I know that this was your intent.
14 *If I had sinned, you would have been watching me,*
and from my iniquity you would not acquit me.[1]

8. See B. S. Childs, *Memory and Tradition in Israel,* SBT 1/37 (London: SCM; Naperville: Allenson, 1962), pp. 34–38.

9. "Clay" is parallel to "dust" also in 4:19; 30:19 (cf. Gen. 3:19).

10. Heb. *qāpā'* (v. 10b) in the Qal means "condense, coagulate," and in the Hiphil, "stiffen, congeal."

11. The Polel *sōḵēḵ* means "entwined" or "knit together." Ezekiel's prophecy (ch. 37) to the valley of dry bones describes the animation of a pile of bones similarly to v. 11. The bones came together, sinews were added, then flesh and skin covered the bones. Finally God breathed into these bodies the breath of life, and they came to life.

12. An example of Heb. *pqd,* "visit, attend to, appoint," having the connotation "help, aid," is attested in a few places. In Jer. 29:10 God "visits" Israel to lead them back from captivity. In Ps. 8:5 (Eng. 4) *pāqaḏ* in the sense "care for" parallels *zāḵar,* "remember" (cf. Job 10:9), and in Ps. 80:15 (Eng. 14) God is asked "to take care of" the vine, i.e., his people, which he has planted.

1. The shift in tenses between the two lines may have a subtle nuance. The perfect verbs in v. 14a, *ḥāṭā'ṯî ûšmartānî,* "if I had sinned, you would have been watching me,"

15 *If I am guilty, woe is me!*
Even if I am innocent, I dare not lift up my head,
being so full of shame and aware[2] of misery.[3]
16 *Proudly[4] you hunt me like a lion;*
you continue[5] to work marvels against me.
17 *You keep sending fresh witnesses[6] against me;*
you multiply your anger against me,
ever sending reinforcements of troops against me."[7]

Job lines his complaint against God for keeping such a vigil against him with legal language: in v. 14 "watch, observe" *(šāmar),* and "clear, acquit" *(niqqâ);* in v. 15 "be guilty" *(rāšaʿ)* and "be innocent" *(ṣāḏaq);* and in v. 17 "witness" *(ʿēḏ).* The complaint emphasizes the prosecutor's hounding the defendant in order to force a confession of guilt from him.

13 Job imagines that God must have been his foe from the start. During the days of Job's prosperity, when he thought that God was showing him love in giving him an abundant life, God had *hid in his heart* the trials that he was going to bring against Job. This interpretation finds the antecedent of *these things* not in what Job has just said but in that which Job is going

---

may indicate that God has already detected some error; and in v. 14b the imperfect verb, *(lōʾ) tᵉnaqqēnî,* "you will (not) acquit," may point to the decision expected at the coming trial.

2. If the root for MT *reʾēh* is *rʾh, reʾēh* is a construct form of *rāʾâ,* "see," functioning as a verbal adjective, "aware of." Many (e.g., Dhorme, Tur-Sinai) emend it to *rᵉwēh,* "watered, saturated," so that the phrase means "steeped in affliction" (cf. Deut. 29:18 [Eng. 19]; Isa. 58:11; Jer. 31:12). But since there is some interrelationship between middle *ʾalep* and middle *waw* roots, Gordis accepts MT as a variant spelling of *rᵉwēh.* Hakam defends MT, for the parallel word *śbʿ*, "full," is also parallel to *rʾh* in Isa. 53:11, and the two occur together in Eccl. 1:8.

3. It appears that the second *y* in *ʿnyy* is a mistake of dittography (Dhorme).

4. The syntax of v. 16a, with a verb in the third person followed by one in the second person, is awkward. Thus the first word, *wᵉyigʾeh,* "and he is proud," has been emended to *wᵉʾegʾeh,* "when I am proud" (Driver-Gray), *wᵉṯigʾeh,* "you are proud," and *wᵉgēʾeh,* "and proud," an adjective modifying the subject (Pope and Gordis). The last suggestion is preferred, for it offers excellent sense with little change.

5. Syntactically Heb. *šûḇ,* "turn," has the sense "begin again, repeat"; cf. 7:7.

6. For MT *ʿēḏeyḵā,* "your witnesses," Dhorme and Pope read *ʿeḏᵉḵā,* "your hostility," as in Aramaic. This reading offers a good parallel to *kaʿaśḵā,* "your anger." In another direction W. Watson ("The Metaphor in Job 10,17," *Bib* 63 [1983] 255–57) has argued that *ʿdyk* in an Ugaritic text means "troops." But Grabbe (*Comparative Philology and the Text of Job,* pp. 63–66) shows that all the versions support MT. Gordis interprets the image by saying, "each blow of fate is a witness testifying against the victim."

7. For MT Driver-Gray suggest reading *wᵉṯaḥᵃlēp ṣᵉḇāʾēḵā ʿimmî,* "And you would renew your hosts against me." But Dhorme and Horst believe that no textual change is necessary, for the MT construction, "reliefs and troops," can be treated as a hendiadys, "relief troops."

to say. As Rowley says, Job thinks that God's kindness was part of his calculated cruelty. Another view interprets Job as saying that God has hidden his care and love deep in his heart so that he can act hostilely in the present toward his servant. Then Job wants God to uncover his love toward him. The former interpretation fits the context better.

14 Job knows that God watches him continuously and would detect his slightest error. If he *had sinned (ḥāṭā'),* God *would have been watching (šāmar)* him to detect his error at once. Heb. *šāmar,* "watch," is used in v. 12b and v. 14a, but with different nuances. The play on this word captures the tension between how Job wishes that God would act toward him and the way God is treating him. According to v. 12b Job expected God to "guard" or protect him, but according to v. 14a he fears that God is "watching" his every move to detect the slightest error so that he might punish him.[8] In his next speech Job will use this same word with a third nuance; he will complain that God "guards" him like a prisoner so that he cannot escape (13:27). The author uses this type of wordplay to portray Job's deep emotional distress. Job is conscious that God *would not acquit* the one who has sinned.

15 Two different ways of interpreting his situation flash through Job's mind. On the one hand, he realizes that *If I am guilty,* he can only exclaim, *woe is me!*[9] On the other hand, *Even if I am innocent* or righteous *(ṣāḏaq), I dare not lift up my head;* i.e., his suffering has filled him *so full of shame* and made him so *aware of misery* that he has no self-esteem left. As a result, he has to "demean (himself) as a criminal" (Davidson). A raised head is a gesture of confident self-worth, while a lowered head expresses shame and humiliation (cf. Judg. 8:28; Zech. 2:4 [Eng. 1:21]; Lam. 2:10). Job feels that his affliction has robbed him of all his dignity even though he is innocent (cf. 11:15).

16 Job explains why he dare not raise his head even though he is innocent. God is stalking Job *like a lion.* He will not let his prey out of sight until he has caught him. Similarly, in a prayer for healing, Hezekiah complains that God like a lion has crushed all his bones (Isa. 38:13). Tur-Sinai and Gordis, however, reason that it is Job who is likened to a lion. They posit that God is hunting him as one hunts a lion. Then God's strategy is similar to a hunting party encircling its quarry and making repeated attacks until it wears down its prey. In this fashion God is wearing Job out. While either interpretation is possible, parallel passages favor the view that God is the one

8. A theme in wisdom circles is that God, the final judge, continually observes the world so that nothing escapes his attention. Qohelet advises not to become too upset over wickedness or perversion of justice because God is high over all and will observe all oppression (Eccl. 5:9 [Eng. 8]).

9. This expression appears elsewhere in the OT only in Mic. 7:1.

being compared to a lion.[10] The adverb *proudly* appropriately fits the metaphor if God is the lion. To weary Job, God continues *to work marvels against* him. The word *hitpallā'*, "to work marvels," refers to deeds that God endows with his creative power (e.g., Isa. 28:29; 29:14). Whereas God had marvelously constructed this child, he now employs his extraordinary power to plague Job in multiple ways.

17 Job laments God's continuous and mighty effort to increase his suffering. He complains that God keeps *sending fresh witnesses* to testify to his guilt. Each new complication in his illness serves as a witness of his guilt. Like a general who keeps ordering fresh troops into the fray against his foe, God gives Job no moments of relief. God *multiplies his anger against* Job by *sending reinforcements of troops against* him. Job feels that his situation is hopeless before such a great general. God's hostility overwhelms him.

(4) Job's Preoccupation with Death (10:18–22)

18 *"Why did you bring me from the womb?*
Would that I had died unseen by an eye.
19 *I should have been as though I had not been.*
I ought to have been brought from the womb to the grave.
20 *Cease, for my days are few,*[1]
leave me alone[2] *that I may smile*
21 *before I go never to return*
to the land of darkness and shadow,
22 *land of gloomy darkness,*
deep shadow and without order,
whose light glows like gloom."

18, 19 In typical lament style Job asks God, *Why did you bring me from the womb?* Only to punish him so? Although he believes that God himself gave

10. A few texts compare God to a lion (Heb. *šaḥal,* as here) about to ravish his people (Hos. 5:14; 13:7); other texts (using other Hebrew words for lion) compare God to a lion who protects his people (Isa. 31:4; Hos. 11:10). Frequently in complaint psalms the lamenter compares his enemies to ferocious lions (e.g., Ps. 7:3 [Eng. 2]; 10:9; 17:12; 35:17; 57:5 [Eng. 4]).

1. For MT *yāmay yaḥᵃdāl,* "my days come to an end" (Ketib), Dhorme reads, with LXX and Syr., *yᵉmê ḥeldî,* "the days of my life." Based on the Qere and Targ., Pope suggests *waḥᵃdāl,* "let me be," to go along with Qere *wᵉšîṯ,* "hold off," in the next line. This suggestion is preferable.

2. The Ketib *yāšîṯ mimmennî* is difficult, for *šîṯ* is a transitive verb. If the Qere *wᵉšîṯ,* an imperative, is followed, one must assume a reflexive pronoun as understood (Dhorme, following Rashi; cf. Rowley). This idea is expressed in 7:16 with *hᵃdal mimmennî.* In a similar mood a psalmist offers the same plea with the words *hāšaʿ mimmennî* (lit. "turn your gaze from me," Ps. 39:14 [Eng. 13]). Accepting the Qere accords with the handling of the parallel *yaḥᵃdāl* (see n. 1 above).

him life at birth (10:12), his experience says that it would have been far better if God had let him die in the womb.[3] Then his fetus would have been taken directly from the womb to the grave. Job is reproaching God for imparting breath to him. Had he been stillborn, no eye would have beheld him at his birth (cf. 3:11). In Job's thinking the fact that another's eye beheld him guaranteed his existence in this world. Job wishes that he had never lived. Then he would feel no pain in the present.

20–22 Given the impossibility of his wish, Job pleads that God grant him some relief in his few remaining days (cf. 7:19). If he is to find such repose, it must come from God, not from within himself. Thus he entreats God, *leave me alone that I may smile (hiḇlîḡ)* before descending to the dark abyss of Sheol. In 9:27 Job considered the possibility of facing his dilemma with new courage and a smile, but he abandoned that idea as futile. Nevertheless, his longing for the repose that will allow him to smile once again continues unabated. If God would leave him alone, he could smile again, for he would have a short time of pleasantness before descending to Sheol. His melancholy words, *I go never to return,* allude to the name for the abode of the dead, "the land of no return" (cf. 7:10). Once a person enters this realm, there is no possibility of returning to earth. Therefore, Job knows that if he is to find any relief, it must be in this life.

The dreary state of Sheol is vividly pictured through the building up of words for darkness.[4] Five different words for darkness are heaped up in seven expressions (cf. 3:4–6): *darkness (ḥōšeḵ), deep shadow* (*ṣalmāweṯ*, 2 times), *(thick) darkness (ʿêpāṯâ), gloom* (*ʾōpel*, 2 times), *without order (lōʾ sᵉḏārîm).*[5] Unfortunately it is hard to capture the nuances of all these words in English. Death is a realm of gloomy darkness. Having no order, it is a land of chaos. Whatever light might shine forth in one of its corners at the brightest time of day is darker than the dead of night on earth.

By reminding God of the dreadful condition awaiting him after his death, Job hopes to move God to answer his petition. Often a lamenter sought to arouse God's compassion with the thought that no praise or love for God is declared in the grave (e.g., Ps. 88:11–13 [Eng. 10–12]; Isa. 38:18). Job is thus desperately seeking to stir God to come to his rescue.

3. The imperfect verbs suggest regret for something which did not happen (Dhorme; cf. GKC, § 107n).

4. The author uses a tristich in v. 22 for emphasis. The third line is balanced with the second by the phrase "like darkness" *(kᵉmô ʾōpel),* and there is similarity in sound with *ʿêpāṯâ*, "darkness," in the first line and *tōpaʿ*, "it shines," in the third line. Thus assonance ties together the first and third lines.

5. N. Tur-Sinai (Torczyner, "A Hebrew Incantation against Night-demons from Biblical Times," *JNES* 6 [1947] 18–29) finds here an allusion to an incantation against night demons; but his evidence is far from conclusive.

AIM

Job is experiencing the full brunt of God's anger. He is certain, however, that God is punishing him wrongly and unjustly. God, the plaintiff, has failed to inform Job, the defendant, of his accusation. If a defendant is not informed in a reasonable amount of time, he has the right to take his accuser to court and demand a resolution. The possibility of exercising his rights as a defendant dominates Job's thinking in this speech. He begins by contemplating the vast power and wisdom of his adversary. This leads him to fear that even if he should have the chance to dispute his case before this mighty God, the One who has mastery over all the forces in the universe, God would easily win. No matter what tactic he might choose, God would be too strong. If it were a contest of strength, God would overpower him. If it were a court case, God would outargue him. Dismayed and despondent, Job accuses God of ruling unjustly and then expresses his hatred of his own life.

Since Job knows no way of proving his innocence, he ponders taking some drastic measure like a public purification ritual to demonstrate to all that he is innocent. But he realizes that God would treat him even more brutally. If he washed himself pure with lye, God would dunk him in a pit of muck and thus make him appear even guiltier. Therefore, in desperation Job wishes that there might be an umpire or arbiter, one who could effect reconciliation between God and himself. Such an arbiter could present his troubled servant to God in a way that God would have to receive him. Job recognizes that it is hard for any person, even a righteous person, to deal with the Holy God. Every person stands in need of an advocate in order to face God. Job's thinking is working with the same inner logic that stands behind the core teaching of the NT, that Jesus Christ, God's Son, has become the Mediator, the Arbiter, between God and man.

Finding no hope in seeking a legal settlement, Job turns to lament his plight. He pleads for God to show him mercy. He reminds God of his obligations as his Creator. God is responsible to sustain each of his creatures. Furthermore, he cannot demand more from a human being than the way he has made him, merely a fragile ceramic vessel. Moving from his thoughts about God's responsibilities as Creator, Job requests that God might ease his suffering in order that he might enjoy his few remaining days before he descends to the realm of total darkness.

For the first time Job speaks as though he wants to come to grips with his situation. A thin ray of hope shines out of his despair as he begins to search in earnest for some way to face God and win a public acquittal. But the way God is treating him causes him to question God's commitment to justice. This struggle in his mind between the God of justice and the afflicting God will dominate his speeches. That is why the legal metaphor will become more prominent in the coming speeches until Job swears his oath of innocence (ch. 31). Job knows that he must win acquittal in order to find renewed fellowship with God and a meaningful life.

5. ZOPHAR'S FIRST SPEECH (11:1–20)

Zophar is the third friend to respond to Job's lament. While many have considered him to be the youngest of Job's companions, little evidence supports this view. All the friends appear to be contemporaries. Nevertheless, Zophar bears the least status, for he delivers only two speeches. His speech is thus far the most poignant, offering Job little comfort except for the elaborate picture of the repentant sinner's peaceful security. Since in Zophar's view people are either contrite worshipers of God or arrogant sinners, he sees little possibility that such a wordy man as Job might be upright, free from wrong. With no apparent sympathy for Job's lament, he coldly reasons that Job's present punishment is only partial, tempered by God's abundant mercy. But he offers Job the promise that if he repents and turns to God with a single mind, he will again enjoy a secure, rich life. His speech consists of three sections: an accusation against Job (vv. 1–4); God's wisdom (vv. 5–12); and a call to repentance (vv. 13–20).

Unlike Eliphaz, Zophar does not appeal to a mystical experience, and unlike Bildad, he does not recall the traditions of the fathers. Instead, his basis is reasoned theology. He reasons deductively from a set of cherished propositions, and he fills his speech with many motifs drawn from the legal, wisdom, and hymnic traditions. He considers it his task to convince Job to leave off his wild statements claiming personal innocence.

a. An Accusation against Job (11:1–4)

1 *Zophar the Naamathite replied:*
2 *"Will a multitude[1] of words go unanswered?*
Or can a verbose man be innocent?
3 *Will your chatter silence[2] men*
that you keep on mocking[3] without anyone to rebuke you?
4 *You say, 'My doctrine is pure,*
and I am clean in your sight.' "[4]

1. Many wish to change MT *rōḇ,* "a multitude," to *rāḇ,* "many." Since *rōḇ dᵉḇārîm* appears in Prov. 10:19 and Eccl. 5:2 (Eng. 3), no change is necessary.

2. Heb. *ḥāraš,* "to silence," is apparently transitive here, although it is usually used intransitively (cf. Job 41:4 [Eng. 12]).

3. The *waw* consecutive is taken to express a consequence of the former idea and describes an action as continuing in the present (GKC, §§ 111r, t).

4. Since Zophar is quoting Job, the change from "in your eyes" *(bᵉʿêneyḵā)* to "in his eyes" *(bᵉʿênāyw)* or "within my eyes" *(bᵉʿênay)* with Duhm and Hölscher is unnecessary.

2 With rhetorical questions Zophar accuses Job of being *a verbose man,* one who is uttering *a multitude of words.*[5] The expression *a verbose man* is literally "a man of lips" *(ʾîš śᵉpāṯayim).*[6] In the OT, idioms that associate speech with the lips, tongue, or mouth stand either for eloquence or for the deceptive nature of human utterance (cf. Isa. 29:13). Zophar cannot believe that such a wordy man could think he *were innocent (ṣāḏaq).* Therefore, he feels compelled to answer Job.

3 *Will your chatter silence men.* The structure of v. 3 could be a declarative sentence, but the context suggests that it is a caustic, rhetorical question. He asks Job if his *chatter (baḏ)* will silence men. Heb. *baḏ* means "empty, idle talk, babbling,"[7] and the word for *men (mᵉṯîm)* means "a weak, powerless group."[8] Job seems to think that he can *keep on mocking (lāʿag)* because there is no one who can rebuke him. *mocking* here describes speaking rashly and impiously. In ancient times the silencing of an opponent in a verbal dispute was tantamount to proving one's own case. Zophar is accusing Job of using such a tactic, i.e., of trying to prove his claim by silencing his opponents. But the very fact that Zophar is addressing Job means that Job has not yet won. Perhaps Zophar views his role as that of one assigned to shame a defendant in a trial (cf. Fohrer). The person in that role countered the defendant's position and ridiculed his arguments.

4 Zophar sets up the theme he wishes to address by quoting Job. This quote is obviously his own construction. *My doctrine is pure (zaḵ)* or unadulterated. The word for *doctrine (leqaḥ)* stands for beliefs received through the tradition of the fathers.[9] Although this supposed quotation approximates Job's position, Zophar is caricaturing Job's view in an attempt to make it look even more absurd. Job never claims that his doctrine is pure. In fact, his thoughts about God and his ways are very disturbed, as his last

5. The wise believed that the voice of a fool is heard in the multitude of his words (Eccl. 5:2 [Eng. 3]). Even stronger is Prov. 10:19: "When words are many, transgression is not lacking."

6. "The lip" as an instrument of speech may parallel "the tongue" (Job 27:4) or "the mouth" (8:21; 15:6; 16:5). It occurs in the phrase "the word of the lips" (2 K. 18:20; Prov. 14:23), which emphasizes mere speech without content. The phrase "a man *[ʾîš]* or an owner *[baʿal]* of a tongue" is used in a negative sense in Ps. 140:12 (Eng. 11); Eccl. 10:11; Sir. 8:3.

7. In Isa. 16:6 and Jer. 48:30 Moab's boasts (Heb. *baḏ*) are declared to be false.

8. Cf. A. Schoors, *I Am God Your Savior,* VTSup 24 (Leiden: Brill, 1973), p. 60.

9. Heb. *leqaḥ* means lit. "what is received" (from the verb *lāqaḥ,* "take, receive"; BDB, p. 544). It is a body of knowledge acquired by instruction (Prov. 1:5; Isa. 29:24). It may also mean a persuasively articulated position (Prov. 16:21, 23). Persuasion to a wrong action, though, is seductive speech. That is why this term represents the argumentation of the adulteress in Prov. 7:21. Perhaps a slight tinge of the negative aspect of this word attends Zophar's composed quote.

speech shows. But Zophar overreacts to Job's challenge of the doctrine of retribution as though Job were putting forth a new teaching.

I am clean [bar] in your sight. Zophar uses the perfect form of the verb "be" *(hāyâ)* to add force to Job's claim. Heb. *bar* refers to that which "shines" (Cant. 6:10) and, by derivation, to that which is "clean, pure, and spotless" (Dhorme). It also describes moral purity, as the phrase "pure in heart" attests (Ps. 24:4; 73:1). Truly Job holds tenaciously to his innocence (e.g., 9:14–21), but he prefers the word *tām,* "blameless" (9:20–21), a word that means personal integrity more than spotless purity.[10] This is important, for Job never says that he has not sinned. His position is that he has not committed any transgression worthy of such punishment. Zophar then has misinterpreted Job in quoting him as asserting his own moral purity.

b. God's Wisdom (11:5–12)

5 *"But would that God[1] might speak[2]*
and open conversation with[3] you
6 *and inform you about the secrets of wisdom,[4]*
because sound wisdom is twofold
(and know that God forgives you some of[5] your iniquity).[6]
7 *Can you fathom the depths of God*
or approach[7] to the limits of Shaddai?

10. References in which Job states that he is innocent include 6:10, 24, 29–30; 7:20-21; 10:5–7.

1. The unusual syntax of having the subject "God," *'ᵉlôah,* before the verb rather than after it may be to strengthen the contrast between Job's words and Zophar's desire for God to speak (Gordis).

2. This construction of *mî-yittēn* with the infinitive *dabbēr,* "speak," instead of the imperfect *yᵉḏabbēr* is unusual; cf. Exod. 14:31; 2 Sam. 19:1 (Eng. 18:33) for a similar construction. Driver-Gray and Horst recommend reading the imperfect *yᵉḏabbēr* as in Job 6:8; 13:5; 14:13, but Fohrer accepts MT (cf. GKC, § 151b).

3. Heb. *ʿim,* "with," is moving in the direction of "against" (so Pope; see also Blommerde, *Northwest Semitic Grammar and Job,* p. 60).

4. Pope takes MT *ḥoḵmâ,* "wisdom," as a gloss to explain *tûšîyâ,* "sound wisdom." But the latter word is hardly "rare and difficult," as Pope contends, for it has already occurred in 5:12; 6:13, and it occurs again in 12:16; 26:3; 30:22 (Qere).

5. The preposition *min* is used as a partitive, i.e., "some of your iniquity."

6. It appears best to take v. 6c as a mutilated distich. Something probably has fallen out, for the line is too long for good poetry. Another possibility is to take this line as a prosaic gloss.

7. Heb. *timṣāʾ,* "find," is used twice. Many (e.g., Budde, Duhm) regard this repetition as prosaic style arising from a scribal error. Two common emendations offered for the second *timṣāʾ* are *tāḇōʾ,* "you come" (Duhm), and (supported by LXX) *tiggaʿ,* "you reach" (Driver-Gray). Nevertheless, the author sometimes repeats words in the same verse, particularly with a shift in nuance. In v. 7a *timṣāʾ* is transitive, but in v. 7b it is intransitive (cf. 8:3).

8 *Higher than the heavens*[8]*—what can you do?*
Deeper than Sheol[9]*—what can you know?*
9 *Its measure*[10] *is longer than the earth*
and broader than the sea.
10 *When he passes by and imprisons*
and summons the assembly, who can restrain him?
11 *Indeed, he knows false men;*
yea, he sees wrongdoing[11] *and he takes close notice of it.*[12]
12 *An empty-headed man may become intelligent*
as[13] *a wild ass can be born a donkey."*

5 Zophar is so upset with Job he wishes that *God might speak* with him. Whereas Job longs to win acquittal from God, Zophar wants God to instruct Job in true wisdom. The phrase *open conversation* is literally "open his lips." The use of "lips" with God is a pun on the taunt found in v. 2a that Job is "a man of lips." God will speak precisely and convincingly in contrast to Job's verbose ramblings.

6 When God speaks, he will make known to Job *the secrets of wisdom*. The *secrets (taʿalumôṯ)* refer to what God knows but human beings do not. God will speak the full scope of *sound wisdom (tûšîyâ).*[14] This wisdom is *twofold (kip̄layim).*[15] Here *twofold* connotes the fullness or totality of a matter (cf. Isa. 40:2). Possibly wisdom is viewed as consisting of two sides, a revealed side manifest in creation and a hidden side which God

8. To bring MT *goḇhê šāmayim* into conformity with the grammatical form of the other three directions, *geḇōhâ miššāmayim*, "higher than the heavens," is read (so LXX; see Dhorme, *BHS*).

9. Dahood ("Northwest Semitic Philology and Job," p. 57) recommends emending the second line to *ʿimqê(h)-m šeʾôl* (cf. Prov. 9:18), with an enclitic *mem*, to make both lines grammatically parallel, but v. 9 shows that the preposition *min* may stand after a word for a dimension.

10. MT *middāh*, "measure," may be read without the *mappiq* in the *h;* it is an adverbial use of the accusative (so Driver-Gray, *BHS*).

11. Horst suggests that *ʾîš*, "man," needs to be supplied before *ʾāwen*, "wrongdoing, evil," hence "a man of evil," offering a good parallel to "false men, men of sin." But since it is doubtful that the ancient mind made a clear distinction between the sin and the sinner, MT is retained.

12. Blommerde (*Northwest Semitic Grammar and Job*, pp. 60–61) takes MT *lōʾ* as another occurrence of its substantive use, meaning "nothing" (cf. Isa. 53:3). Dhorme, however, reads *lô*, "it." This suggestion offers good sense. The *ʾalep* in *lōʾ* could easily be an error of dittography, resulting from the number of ʾs in the line.

13. The *waw* is a *waw* of comparison; see GKC, § 161a.

14. Cf. 5:12; 6:13; 12:16; 26:3; 30:22 (Qere).

15. Some interpret this word as "multiple" (see RSV "manifold"; cf. GKC, § 134r, n.2), while others, e.g., Duhm and Horst, read *kiplāʾîm*, "like miracles." The occurrence of *kip̄layim* in Isa. 40:2 favors the first interpretation here (so Dhorme). Cf. G. von Rad, "*Kip̄layim* in Jes. 40:2—Equivalent?" *ZAW* 79 (1967) 80–82.

keeps with himself (Pope). When God would converse with Job, he would draw on the full scope of wisdom in order to make Job see the errors in his rhetoric.

At the end of this verse Zophar adds a parenthetical note: *and know that God forgives you some of your iniquity*. That is, God is punishing him for only part of his wrongdoing, not for all of it. Zophar believes that God would make this point clear to Job. Therefore, Zophar is the first of the friends to conclude that Job has sinned even beyond the extent of his punishment.

7 Using a series of questions demanding a negative response, Zophar challenges Job's claim that God has misjudged him. Zophar knows that human knowledge is very limited. No one can probe very far into *the depths [ḥēqer] of God* or reach his *limits (taḵlîṯ)*. According to Dhorme, the meaning of Heb. *ḥēqer* goes beyond what is mere research and investigation (5:9; 9:10) to "the object of the inquiry, i.e. what is hidden under appearances, the basis (38:16), the inward essence" (cf. Sir. 42:16; 1 Cor. 2:9–10). Heb. *taḵlîṯ* refers to the furthest boundary, the extent or limit of a matter, and includes the concept of completion or perfection (Ps. 139:22). To gain a full perspective about God's ways a person must have insight into the center of God's being along with knowledge as to the outermost limits of the divine influence. A human being has a difficult time comprehending God's ways, for he observes them only in part. He lacks the full picture that is necessary to understand how a particular occurrence fits within God's comprehensive plan (cf. 1 Sam. 20:12). Therefore, to discuss ultimate questions, as Zophar thinks Job wishes to do, he needs to know the hidden ways of God.

8, 9 Zophar is stressing God's inexhaustible wisdom.[16] God's knowledge extends far beyond every boundary in the created order. The vastness of creation is expressed by the four dimensions[17]—height, depth, length, and breadth—in relationship to four comprehensive geographical terms—heaven and Sheol (which are frequently parallel; cf. Ps. 139:8), and earth and sea[18] (an infrequent pair). God, being higher than the heavens and deeper than the lowest part of the universe, transcends the extraterrestrial

16. Some reject this marvelous piece extolling the greatness and unsearchableness of God's wisdom as redundant to the Yahweh speeches. But, as pointed out elsewhere in this commentary, the author has various themes reverberate through the different speakers in order to show how the same concept has quite different implications. The frequent inclusion of these hymnic lines prepares for the final speeches, enhancing their impact.

17. The four adjectives of dimension may go back to *taḵlîṯ*, "limits," for they are feminine in form.

18. "Breadth" is a dimension used in reference to the sea in Job 37:10 and to the earth in Sir. 1:3.

realm. The created order, though too large for a human being to explore its extremities, is too small to house God.

In relationship to these extremities Job is asked, *what can you do? . . . what can you know?*[19] The meaning of *know (yāḏaʿ)* here goes beyond rational knowledge to include the ability to act on that knowledge. That is why it parallels *do (pāʿal)*. There is nothing Job can do or know that could ever approach, let alone challenge, God's knowing or doing. How then can Job entertain the idea that he could dispute his case with God?

10, 11 While God's presence reaches far beyond the outer limits of the universe, he leaves these distant realms to accomplish his purpose on earth. God *passes by,* detects that somebody is doing wrong, and *imprisons*. Afterward *he summons the assembly* to sit as a court in order to execute a just sentence (cf. Ezek. 16:40; 23:46–47; Prov. 5:14). When God as judge pronounces a sentence, no one *can restrain him* or deter his plan.

Indeed, he knows false men. Here *knows (yāḏaʿ)* means both that God *sees* their *wrongdoing* and that he executes judgment on them. The phrase *false men* is literally "men of nothingness" *(m*ᵉ*ṯê šāwʾ),* those who have no moral scruples.[20] Zophar denounces Job's thought that since God acts capriciously in the way he arrests people, he needs to be stopped and called to give an account of his actions (9:12). Specifically he rejects wholeheartedly this description of God's acting as a possible explanation of Job's plight. Rather he believes that God has passed Job's way and has imprisoned him with illness for some secret sin. Since God knows false men, it is impossible from Zophar's perspective that God could have acted wrongly in afflicting Job.

12 Zophar seeks to prove his point by quoting a proverb. This proverb is a distich full of alliteration and assonance.[21] The point is made by the comparison of the manner or characteristics of two dissimilar objects. The two statements are set in bold relief for maximum impact (cf. 5:7). The truth or falsity of the second line guarantees or denies the point expressed in the first line. Unfortunately, the exact meaning of this ancient saying eludes us.

The interpretation of this verse tends to polarize around two opposing views. Either the proverb teaches that the most stupid, obstinate person can be changed, or it affirms human incorrigibility. The first line is fairly

19. Cf. M. Granoth, "Deeper than Sheol: What Canst Thou Know?" *Beth Miqra* 59 (1973–74) 572–88.

20. "False men" also occurs in Ps. 26:4–5, where it parallels "dissemblers," "evildoers," and "the wicked."

21. The MT reads: *w*ᵉ*ʾîš nāḇûḇ yillāḇēḇ w*ᵉ*ʿayir pereʾ ʾāḏām yiwwālēḏ.*

clear. It considers the likelihood of whether *an empty-headed* [*nāḇûḇ*, lit. "hollow"] *man may become intelligent [lāḇaḇ]*.[22] In postbiblical Hebrew *lāḇaḇ* characterizes a person who is sensible and educated. The second line is very obscure.[23] Thus it is hard to determine whether it affirms or negates the statement of the first line. Its obscurity may have been increased by a textual error or by a word that has been added in transmission. Possibly the word *pereʾ*,[24] "wild ass," has been added as a gloss to explain the less familiar *ʿayir*, "donkey," or, more likely, *ʾāḏām*, "man," has slipped in as a parallel to *ʾîš*, "man."[25] The latter position is favored, for then the point of comparison would be between two types of donkeys, just as in the first line the contrast is between two types of men. The proverb then says that as it is impossible for a donkey to be sired by a wild ass, so it is impossible for a stubborn person to become truly wise by his own efforts. With this proverb Zophar says that there is no natural way for Job to be changed from a stupid man to a wise man. Or referring back to v. 4, it is utterly impossible that Job, a mere man, could be morally pure in God's sight. Therefore, the only way for him to approach God will be the way of repentance, not the way of a legal dispute.

c. A Call to Repentance (11:13–20)

13 *"If you prepare your heart*
and spread out your hands to him,
14 *if wrong is in your hands, remove it,*
and let not injustice dwell in your tents,[1]

22. The Niphal of *lāḇaḇ* is taken as a reflexive, "become intelligent."

23. An example of another reading is to emend MT *yiwwālēḏ*, "he is born," to *yimmālēḏ*, "he is taught": "A male zebra must be trained" (Budde, Fohrer).

24. Some think that especially in the book of Job *pereʾ* means "a zebra," not "a wild ass" (cf. Fohrer). But more likely *ʿayir* refers to the domesticated male donkey and *pereʾ* to the wild ass or onager (Pope). P. Humbert (*ZAW* 62 [1949–50] 201–202) takes *ʿayir* figuratively for "a chief of a herd."

25. The inclusion of *ʾāḏām*, "man," may have been inspired by the phrase *pereʾ ʾāḏām* in Gen. 16:12, referring to Ishmael as a free, roving type of person. Another view, offered by Sutcliffe (*Bib* 30 [1949] 70–71), reads *pereḏ* for *pereʾ ʾāḏām*, i.e., "when a mule is born a stallion," an unreal circumstance since a mule is sterile. He argues that this impossibility led to the corruption of the text and that under influence of Gen. 16:12 it became *pereʾ ʾāḏām*. Also working with *ʾāḏām*, Dahood ("Zacharia 9,1, *ʿên ʾādām*," *CBQ* 25 [1963] 124) postulates that this word can sometimes stand for *ʾaḏāmâ*, "ground," so he renders the phrase "a wild ass of the steppe."

1. Although many wish to emend the plural "your tents" to the singular, that is unnecessary. As in Ugaritic grammar, words for dwellings which appear in the plural may be translated as singular (Blommerde, *Northwest Semitic Grammar and Job*, pp. 12–13; Gordon, *UT*, p. 113, 13.17).

15 *then indeed[2] you will lift up your face free from spot,*
and you will become secure[3] and you will not fear.
16 *For you will forget your trouble,*
you will remember it as water that flowed past.
Life[4] will rise brighter[5] than noon;
darkness[6] will become like morning.
18 *You will be secure because there is hope;*
you will look about[7] and recline in confidence.
19 *You will lie down, with no one to terrify you;*
many will court your favor.
20 *But the eyes of the wicked will fail*
and there will be nowhere for them[8] to flee,
their hope will be turned to despair."

With an elaborate call to repentance Zophar entreats Job to change his ways. He addresses this word directly to Job, as is evidenced by the emphatic position of the pronoun *you* in vv. 13 and 16. The call to repentance consists of a double condition, one affirmative (v. 13) and the other negative (v. 14), followed by a vivid description of the blessed state of the righteous (vv. 15–19) in contrast to the ill-fate of the wicked (v. 20).

13 Zophar exhorts Job, *prepare your heart*. "Preparing the heart" *(hāḵîn lēḇ)* means to make it firm or constant for belief.[9] This expression

2. The protasis (v. 15) to the double apodosis (vv. 13 and 14) is introduced by *kî ʾāz,* which is similar to *kî ʿattâ,* meaning "from then on" or "then indeed."

3. MT *mûṣāq,* "firm," appears to be a Hophal participle of *yāṣaq,* "pour" or "cast." When that which is molten is poured out, it hardens, becoming firmly established. The word is used here to denote security or confidence (cf. Delitzsch's translation: "shalt be firm without fearing").

4. Some emend MT *ḥāleḏ* to *ḥeldêḵā,* "your life" (e.g., Hölscher), based on LXX. But LXX may simply be seeking a good Greek reading, not rendering the Hebrew literally. Heb. *ḥeleḏ* refers to the duration of life and of the world.

5. In comparisons the attributive idea may be omitted in certain pregnant uses of *min* (GKC, § 133e); the quality to be supplied here is brightness.

6. Heb. *tāʿûpâ* may be an emphatic third person verbal form. Being joined with the imperfect *tihyeh,* "it will be," it connotes a contingent condition: "though it be dark" (GKC, § 108e; S. R. Driver, *Hebrew Tenses,* § 152.3). But some (e.g., Duhm, Dhorme, Gordis) prefer to read a noun *t*^{e}*ʿûpâ,* "darkness." Since the latter is only a change in vowel pointing and is more straightforward grammatically, it is preferable.

7. For MT *w*^{e}*ḥāpartā,* "and you will be shamed," Dhorme, Guillaume, and KB (p. 327) read *w*^{e}*udhuppartā,* "you will be protected," cognate with Arab. *ḫafara,* "protect." Another possibility is to treat *ḥpr* as from a more common Hebrew root meaning "search, look for" (Delitzsch).

8. Heb. *minhem,* lit. "from them," is an exceptional form of the preposition plus pronominal suffix (cf. *menhû,* 4:12). It is considered poetic and close to Aramaic.

9. In 1 Sam. 7:3, Samuel, as part of his plea for repentance, exhorts the people to prepare their heart to serve only God and to remove all idols.

stands parallel to "trust" *(bāṭaḥ)* in Ps. 78:8, 37; 112:7. *spread out your hands to him*. His changed inner attitude is to be attested by spreading out his hands *(kap)* to God in earnest supplication.[10]

14 When Job spreads his hands to God (v. 13b), he must make sure there are no stains from his wrongdoing on them (cf. Isa. 1:15–16). Otherwise God will focus on the stains as convicting evidence, not on the pleas of the supplicant. The word for *wrong (ʾāwen),* though encompassing various kinds of sins, specifically depicts covert acts of extortion and oppression. The eighth-century prophets use this word for underhanded violations of the spirit of justice by the rich to enhance their wealth.[11] Zophar may be subtly hinting that Job's wealth came through extortion of the less fortunate. This possibility is strengthened by his injunction, *let not injustice dwell in your tents*. Here *injustice (ʿawlâ)* could refer to anything that was acquired through wrongdoing, committed either by himself, by any member of his family, or by any of his servants.[12] The tribal head, as the moral and spiritual head of the tribe, was responsible for all that was done by those subject to his authority, i.e., those in his *tents*. By removing all the products of wrongdoing from his dwelling, Job will no longer be subject to their influence (cf. Isa. 1:15–16). This call to repentance recognizes both the personal and social nature of sin.

15–19 In order to motivate Job to repent, Zophar next paints an ideal sketch of the blessings that attend God's acceptance of a contrite person.

15 Zophar says to Job: *you will lift up your face free from spot.*[13] His dignity, which has gone so low that he cannot lift up his head (10:15), will return. He *will become secure* or confident *(mûṣāq)* and he *will not fear (yārēʾ).*[14] Zophar addresses Job's agony over the many fears that gnaw at him (e.g., his suffering, 9:28). But Zophar promises that when he meets God all these fears will be gone.

16 Another great blessing will be the forgetting of his troubles. Zophar catches Job's attention by repeating *you (ʾattâ)* in this verse. Job's

10. Heb. *kap,* lit. "palm," picturesquely describes the hands as open, uplifted to God.

11. Cf. K. Bernhardt, "*ʾāwen,*" *TDOT,* I:142–44.

12. An example of removing sin from one's household is Jacob's purging his whole household of foreign gods before moving from Shechem to Bethel so that he could renew his covenant with God without fear of judgment against any member of his household (Gen. 35:2–3).

13. A similar expression appears in Sir. 11:31, which shows that *nāśāʾ*, "lift up," and *mûm,* "blemish," may stand together.

14. 1 John 4:18 contrasts fear and love: "Perfect love casts out fear, for fear has to do with torment." Similarly confidence and fear are contrasted here. If Job gains secure trust in God through repentance, his fear will be removed.

transformation will be extraordinary. He will be so caught up in his new blessing that his *trouble* (*ʿāmāl;* cf. 3:10) will be forgotten. Job uses the word "trouble" frequently to describe his pains and sorrows (e.g., 3:10). To *forget* is to experience release from the obligations and penalties that attend former deeds; it stands in contrast to "remember," which means to act toward someone in the light of past commitments.[15]

This promise is a positive response to Job's despair that he can never forget his lament. Every effort is stifled by a sharp pain that arouses his fears with new force (9:27–28). Fear feeds on apprehension of foreboding situations. But Zophar believes that when Job seeks God with a single mind, the past will cease to haunt him. It will be remembered *as water that flowed past,* an expression similar to "water under the bridge." The image here may be stronger, referring to a threatening torrent of water that is overflowing *(ʿāḇar)*[16] its banks. Such a raging torrent is a frequent picture for a life-threatening danger (Ps. 69:3 [Eng. 2]; 124:4–5; Isa. 8:7–8; Jer. 47:2). But soon the river returns to its normal flow and the danger is gone. So too Job's trials will subside, and the raging torrents will no longer trouble him.

17 Job's life then will be as bright as the sun at high noon. His season of darkness will be turned to joy just as the morning sun dispels the night and inspires hope for a bright new day. This is similar to the words of the psalmist: "[God] shall bring forth your vindication as the light, and your right as the noonday" (Ps. 37:6).[17] Light shining on a person's life brings warmth, buoyancy, and a sense of well-being. The word for *life (ḥeleḏ)* stresses its longevity.[18] Job is being promised a long, enriched life. This picture of brightness contrasts markedly with Job's gloomy description of his fate in death at the end of his last speech (10:20–22).

18, 19 In his new life Job will have inner peace. He will have a strong sense of security because he will have genuine hope. Whereas now Job dreads the future, his hope will inspire him to anticipate the future with joy. Then he may look about with confidence. Like a sheep lying peacefully in a pasture guarded by a shepherd,[19] Job will then be able to *lie down* and

15. Cf. 7:7; and B. Childs, *Memory and Tradition in Israel,* SBT 1/37 (London: SCM; Naperville: Allenson, 1962).

16. The verb "pass by, over" *(ʿāḇar)* may sometimes mean "flood, overflow" (cf. Ps. 124:4–5; Isa. 8:8; Nah. 1:8).

17. Isa. 58:10b offers a similar promise: "Then shall your light rise in the darkness, and your gloom be as the noonday."

18. In contrast, a life of trouble and anxiety is considered a short, vain life (Ps. 39:6 [Eng. 5]; 89:48 [Eng. 47]).

19. Heb. *rāḇaṣ,* "lie down," is frequently used with animals, esp. sheep (cf. Isa. 17:2), but also with a leopard (Isa. 11:6) and a lion (Gen. 49:9). Used figuratively it describes a person in a secure, happy state (Isa. 14:30; Ps. 23:2). In Zeph. 3:13 there is a promise to the remnant of Israel that when they return to the land, they will dwell securely, like a flock grazing freely without any fear.

rest without any fear that someone will terrify him. Zophar is directly countering Job's complaint that God is hunting him like a lion (10:16) with the promise that in the future God will lead and protect him like a shepherd. When he has peace with God, many will court his favor (*ḥillû pānêḵā,* v. 19b). This Hebrew phrase, usually translated "to appease" or "to entreat the favor of," means literally either "to make the face smooth through stroking" or "to sweeten the face."[20] While in the OT a human being may be the object of this action (Prov. 19:6; Ps. 45:13 [Eng. 12]), most often God stands as its object. In passages with God as the object it is associated with words of earnest, contrite petitioning (1 K. 13:6; 2 Chr. 33:12; Zech. 8:21–22). Entreaty is one way an inferior party seeks to win the favor of his superior. This language then means that Job will again stand at the head of his community and be accorded the highest honor.

20 At the end of this call to repentance Zophar presents a terse but vivid description of the fate of the wicked.[21] Their desperate end contrasts markedly with the joys that the penitent have. This portrayal depicts the doom of the wicked in three areas: loss of eyesight, loss of a place of refuge, and loss of hope. When the eyes *fail* (lit. "grow dim"),[22] the joy of living diminishes as one anticipates death (Ps. 69:4 [Eng. 3]; Lam. 4:17; cf. Deut. 28:32). A person needs a place of refuge in a time of trouble. But when the wicked are faced with overpowering danger, they will not be able to escape to a place of refuge (cf. Jer. 25:35; Amos 2:14). Also *their hope,* fed by dreams of great success, *will be turned to despair*. The phrase translated *despair (mappaḥ-nepeš)* means literally breathing out one's breath, i.e., fainting, sighing distressfully (see Sir. 30:12). In Jer. 15:9 it describes a mother's fainting on hearing tragic, humiliating news.[23] This phrase thus means "despair, solemn sadness," not the process of "dying." Zophar is picturing the proud wicked in the prime of life as physically worn out and totally disheartened.

This solemn warning adds a sober note to the glorious promises of blessing that come with repentance. Showing some sensitivity to Job, Zophar casts this line about the wicked in generalities. His style contrasts

20. For the former see KB, p. 304; for the latter see Dhorme. The precise etymology of Heb. *ḥillû* is still uncertain; see K. Seybold, *"chālāh," TDOT,* IV:400, 403, 407–408.

21. In somewhat the same way Bildad closed his description of the blessings that attend the repentant with a verse about the end of the wicked (8:22). But he was more diplomatic than Zophar, for he spoke of the end of Job's enemies.

22. Heb. *kālâ* means "to perish, fail, languish." When used with eyes, it describes eyes wearied with tears (Lam. 2:11) or strained from looking for relief (Job 17:5; Ps. 69:4 [Eng. 3]; Lam. 4:17; see BDB, p. 477).

23. See J. Thompson, *The Book of Jeremiah,* NICOT (Grand Rapids: Eerdmans, 1980), pp. 389–90.

markedly with his use of direct address in reference to the blessings (vv. 15–16, 18–19). Nevertheless, this picture functions as a threat to Job. Should he not repent, such will be his end. Zophar ends with this threat in order to overcome any hesitation to repentance on Job's part.

AIM

Zophar strives to impress Job with the awesomeness of God's wisdom. God's ways are too profound for a mere human being to understand fully. The Creator of the vast universe is aware of all that happens on earth and judges all wrongdoing. Therefore, Job is wrong in thinking that there are wicked who prosper. In fact, in Job's case God is showing mercy by not punishing him even more. It is clear that Zophar has taken the final step in the logic of the doctrine of retribution, concluding that Job is suffering for some hidden sin. For him it means that Job's suffering is justly deserved. Therefore, Job's complaint against God is untenable. Assuredly it is useless for Job to plead that God overlook any wrongs he might have done, for that is God's way with all human beings. There remains only one way for Job to escape his plight—the way of repentance. When he devotes himself fully to God, he will find the peaceful serenity for which his soul longs. But if Job remains obstinate, he will experience the futile end that all the wicked experience.

Zophar unwittingly aligns himself with the Satan's position found in the prologue by encouraging Job to seek God for personal gain. Unfortunately Zophar is blind to the implications of his reasoning. His failure shows that spiritual counsel must be offered in compassionate love, taking into account the peculiarities of a specific situation in order for it to bear the peaceable fruits of righteousness.

6. JOB'S THIRD RESPONSE (12:1–14:22)

Job reacts strongly to the friends' mockery, so strongly that he vigorously asserts his own worth. Boldly he decides that his only hope is to argue his own case before God himself. The decision to take this course leads him to reject his friends' counsel. He makes the most daring statements to date about his confidence in winning an affirmative decision from God himself. His pain, however, moves him to lament his ill-fate in the context of the tragedy of all human suffering. That Job is beginning to come to grips with his situation is evident in the fact that he can contemplate theoretical solutions to his dilemma and reject them rationally, even amid his lamenting. His tenacious determination to find a resolution with God himself holds him firm and allows him, amid his tears, to bring his disturbed thoughts into some focus.

Job's speech consists of two parts distinguished by the party addressed. In the first part Job defends his skill in wisdom as equal to his friends' (12:1–13:17). In the second part he petitions God to try his case before the divine tribunal (13:18–14:22).

a. Complaints against the Friends (12:1–13:17)

Job opens with a stern complaint against his friends. The complaint is found in two places, 12:1–11 and 13:1–12. He feels that his friends have vaunted themselves above him and that in their defense of God they have spoken deceitfully. On the one hand, they need to be better instructed, and, on the other hand, they are placing themselves in danger of a divine rebuke. In the midst of his complaint Job recounts God's sovereign power that can defeat any human dignity and can dispense of any nation at will (12:12–25). Affirmatively Job states his resolve to argue his case directly with God (13:3, 13–17).

(1) The First Complaint (12:1–11)

(a) Job's Self-defense (12:1–3)

1 *And Job answered:*
2 *"Surely you are the gentry,*
and wisdom will die with you.[1]
3 *But I, like you, have a mind;*
I am not inferior to you.[2]
Who does not know such things?"

2 Job reproaches the friends for their pride and insensitivity. Using plural forms, he addresses all of them. He is so upset with the friends that he resorts to scathing sarcasm. Opening with the demeaning *Surely* or "in truth" (*'omnām),* Job captures his bitter ironic murmur by assonance, the piling up of nine *m*s and five gutturals—*'omnām kî 'attem ʿām weʿimmāḵem tāmûṯ ḥoḵmâ* (Gordis). Job judges the friends' superior attitude of belonging to the gentry to say that they think themselves to be the only people with whom

1. J. Davies ("A note on Job xii 2," *VT* 25 [1975] 670–71) takes the second line as a relative clause: "No doubt you are the people with whom wisdom will die."

2. Since v. 3b is identical with 13:2b, it may be a gloss to explain the first line (Duhm, Fohrer). But the author may have repeated the line to tie the two chapters together. The tristich is not a serious difficulty, for there are several tristichs in the speeches. True, this line is missing in LXX, but LXX does not have v. 4a, b, and by itself it cannot be used as a witness for omitting v. 3b (Driver-Gray).

wisdom resides, so much so that when they die the world's storehouse of wisdom will be depleted. In the preexilic period the word for *gentry* (*ʿam*, lit. "people") denoted the upper class, the landed nobility.[3] Job is complaining that the posture of his friends undercuts his own sense of human dignity and adds to his suffering.

3 Job responds to the superior attitude of the friends by defending his own wisdom and dignity. He asserts his self-worth with the words, *I, like you, have a mind* or "am intelligent" *(lēḇāḇ)*. In Hebrew *lēḇāḇ* (lit. "heart") is the center of a person's thinking, tender emotions, and volition. With these words Job forthrightly rejects any personal application of Zophar's proverb, "An empty man may take heart" (11:12). Sensing that Zophar has implied that he is lacking in wisdom, Job counters with the assertion that he is in no way *inferior to (nāp̱āl)*[4] them. Indeed, what they speak is such common knowledge that their wisdom fails to offer him any insight into his sufferings.

(b) Job's Disgrace (12:4–6)

4 *"I have become[1] one who is a laughingstock to his friends,*
one who continually called on God that he might answer him;
a righteous and[2] blameless man is a laughingstock.
5 *A man at ease holds disaster[3] in contempt,*
a blow[4] to those whose feet are slipping.
6 *The tents of marauders are safe;[5]*

3. In preexilic texts "the people of the land" are named along with kings, princes, and priests (cf. Jer. 1:18; 34:19). The word "gentry" is chosen here, because in the kingdom period *ʿam* refers to the educated upper class (cf. Pope).

4. Heb. *nāp̱al,* lit. "fall," has the sense of "be less than" only here.

1. The first person form *ʾehyeh,* "I have become," is problematic, since the other forms in the verse are in the third person. Thus Fohrer reads *yihyeh,* "he has become," while Tur-Sinai suggests revocalizing the consonants *ʾahōyâ,* "(the) woe." But the first person form relates back to v. 3, and it is carried forward by the participles in the rest of the verse.

2. LXX and Targ. read a *waw,* "and," here. Since the third line is short, it is possible that a *waw* may have fallen from *tāmîm,* "a blameless person."

3. Although MT *lappîḏ* usually means "torch," it seems best to divide this word into the preposition *le* plus the definite noun *pîḏ,* "ruin, disaster" (cf. 30:24; 31:29; Prov. 24:22).

4. The meaning of MT *nāḵôn* is unclear. Most take it as a noun from *nāḵâ,* "smite," to mean "a blow or beating" (Dhorme, Fohrer, Gordis). Or it may be a word meaning "it is proper, fitting" (Pope).

5. MT *yišlāyû* is an example of the preservation of an original *yod* in a *lamed-he* verb (GKC, §§ 29t, 75u); cf. Ps. 122:6.

those who provoke God are fully secure[6]—
those who bring God in their hands."[7]

4 Job grieves over the depth of his humiliation. He identifies himself as one *who continually called on God, a righteous [ṣaddîq] and blameless [tāmîm] man.*[8] He echoes here the description of his character found in 1:1, that he was blameless *(tām)* and upright *(yāšār)*. But now he who was accorded the highest honor has become a laughingstock.[9] The use of the imperfect *I have become ('ehyeh)* underscores the change that has taken place in Job's situation. Even his closest friends now mock him. No one likes to be laughed at, but in ancient times to become an object of public scorn was the worst possible disgrace.

5 With a proverb Job reprimands the friends for their contemptuous attitude toward his misfortune.[10] Their ridicule is the direct opposite of the compassion he expects from them. This proverb says that when *a man at ease,* i.e., safe from danger and rich in possessions, has *contempt,* not compassion, for anyone overcome by disaster, his ridicule strikes a mighty blow against him whose feet are slipping.[11] The righteous, particularly the suffering righteous, find it hard to bear the reproach heaped on them by those who are at ease, i.e., those who are self-assured of their own righteousness by reason of their wealth.[12] One psalmist laments: "Too long we have been sated with the scorn of those who are at ease, the contempt of the proud" (Ps. 123:4). By contrast Job will swear in 31:29 that he never assumed a posture of contempt at another's misfortune, not even if that

6. The plural form *baṭṭuḥôṯ,* "fully secure," intensifies the idea of the stem (cf. GKC, § 124e).

7. The third line is very difficult and has received numerous suggestions. The singular forms are problematic in a context of plurals. Most likely the author is quoting a proverbial saying without adapting the forms to the plural.

8. Cf. Gen. 6:9, where Noah is similarly described. The close identification of Job and Noah is also attested in Ezek. 14:14, 20.

9. The theme of becoming a laughingstock or an object of derision is frequent in psalms of lament (Ps. 31:12 [Eng. 11]; 35:15; 41:10 [Eng. 9]; 69:11–13 [Eng. 10–12]; Jer. 20:7; Lam. 1:7; 3:14; cf. Job 19:13–15). Occasionally, however, the righteous mock the wicked during their time of calamity (Ps. 52:7–9 [Eng. 5–7]); perhaps the friends believed that they were doing God a service in taunting Job.

10. According to Hakam, who reads *lappîḏ* as "lamp," the picture in this verse is that when those who are at ease look on one who slips, they act toward him with scorn instead of helping him, i.e., instead of lighting his path with a bright light, they offer him a lamp of contempt.

11. The imagery of an unsteady foot connotes one who is being overcome by the difficulties he faces (4:4; Ps. 18:37 [Eng. 36]; 37:31; Prov. 25:19).

12. Amos rebukes "those who are at ease in Zion," i.e., those who are secure, complacent, and reveling in their wealth (6:1; cf. Isa. 32:4, 11).

person hated him. Since he has been careful not to have such an attitude, he feels that it is not fair that others treat him with such contempt.

6 To counter the teaching of the friends, Job claims that marauding bands, those that inflict sudden terror on unsuspecting settlements, are safe and secure in their tents even though their actions provoke God. They anger God without suffering any ill-consequences. The third line is difficult to interpret. It could be saying that these marauders carry God in their hands, for ancient travelers had pocket-size idols that they would take along with them on a journey. In that case this is a reference to the idolatry of the marauders. A second view, represented by Delitzsch, suggests that the gods in their hands are their swords. Since these bandits are ruthlessly successful, their swords have become their gods. A third alternative understands the line as saying that these marauders believe themselves to be as powerful as God.[13] Therefore, they neither fear God nor see any need for him.

With this description of the wicked, Job refutes the teaching of the friends. Eliphaz tried to encourage him with the teaching that his repentance would bring peace to his tent (5:24), and Bildad reasoned that if he were truly righteous he would have peace (8:6). Similarly Zophar concluded his remarks with a beautiful description of the security and repose of the one who seeks God (11:15–19). Job points out that if they considered the freedom and success of plunderers, forces of terror widely feared in the ancient Near East, they would discover that the secure are not always the righteous. In reality the wicked eniov repose without any hindrance from God.

(c) Instruction in Wisdom (12:7–11)

7 *"But ask now the beasts that they may teach you,*
and the birds of the sky that they may tell you;
8 *or consider[1] the creeping animals[2] that they may instruct[3] you;*
the fish of the sea will also inform you.
9 *Who cannot learn from all of these*
that God's[4] hand has done this?

13. Dhorme and Pope form this interpretation on the basis of the more familiar idiom *yēš le'ēl yāḏî,* lit. "my hand serves me as God," meaning "it is in my power" (Gen. 31:29; cf. Deut. 28:32; Mic. 2:1).

1. Some take MT *śîaḥ* as a word for "bush" (cf. 30:4, 7), but a word for creeping things is expected, since creeping things frequently occur in this kind of a list. It may be best simply to take *śîaḥ* as a verb meaning "consider, meditate on" (cf. Gordis).

2. For the difficult *śîaḥ lā'areṣ,* "consider the earth," Duhm reads *zōḥalê 'ereṣ,* "crawling things of the earth," while Fohrer suggests *ḥayyaṯ hā'āreṣ,* "the game of the earth" (cf. *BHS*). It seems best to accept the MT and understand *lā'āreṣ* as elliptical for "the creeping animals" (Gordis).

3. Plural animal subjects may take a feminine singular verb (GKC, § 145k).

4. MT has *Yhwh,* the special name for God among the Hebrews, which appears only here in the dialogue. Either it was used unconsciously by the author (Gordis) or, more

10 *In his hand is every living creature*
and the spirit of all humanity.
11 *Does not the ear test words*
as the palate tastes its food?"

7–9 The strong adversative conjunction *But (ʾûlām)* indicates that Job is taking up a new subject. Here he exalts God as the creator of all and affirms that wisdom may be found by listening to the creatures God has created. He is probably quoting familiar lines from an instructional poem (cf. chs. 38–39). Poems of this kind belonged to the core of instruction used by the teachers of wisdom. All earthly creatures—*the beasts* of the field, *the birds of the sky, the creeping animals* of the earth, and *the fish of the sea*—are able to instruct man.[5] In contemplating their habits and activities one discovers truths about God and his ways. God has written insight into his ways into every dimension of the world: the earth, the sky, and the sea. The amazing designs throughout creation attest to the skillful work of God's hand (cf. Isa. 66:2; Jer. 14:22). In response to Zophar's quoting from a hymn of praise in 11:7–12, wherein he considers wisdom as inaccessible to humanity, Job counters with the idea that God teaches humanity through that which he has created. Or is Job suggesting that the friends' knowledge does not surpass even that of the beasts of the fields, and that, therefore, they should go back to school?[6]

10 Not only has God made all creatures; he has control over every person's life. The phrase *every living creature* may include the animals, but it specifically refers to people, as the parallel term *humanity (ʾîš)* indicates (cf. 30:23). A human being is similar to an animal in that both are "living creatures" (*nep̱eš ḥay;* cf. Gen. 2:7) and composed of flesh *(bāśār),* but human beings are distinct in that they alone possess spirit *(rûaḥ);* only in one OT passage is spirit associated with beasts (Eccl. 3:21).[7] God sustains human life and directs human destiny. There is nothing that takes place on earth outside of his governance. All is incorporated into his purpose. With these words Job is questioning, without denying God's sovereignty, the proposition that God immediately carries out retribution on all evildoers.

---

likely, it was a scribal error of one who had in mind a familiar phrase using this divine name as he penned this line (cf. Isa. 41:20b). Therefore, *ʾĕlôah* is read with some mss. See *BHS*.

5. See A. de Guglielmo, "Job 12:7–9 and the Knowledge of God," *CBQ* 6 (1944) 476–82.

6. Gordis keenly observes that the singular pronominal suffixes in vv. 7–8 suggest that Job is making an ironic restatement of the friends' inquisition.

7. While the term "spirit" *(rûaḥ)* is associated with animals in that passage, the tone of that passage is hypothetical.

11 Resuming the thought of vv. 7–8, Job asks a rhetorical question implying that God has endowed human beings with the instruments necessary to acquire and test knowledge. Just as the palate tastes food and decides whether it is savory or foul, so the ear tests words to ascertain what is reasonable or irrational, pleasing or discordant, true or false. The ear with its discriminating ability enables one to discern the credibility of words.[8] This role of the ear accounts for the fact that it may sometimes stand parallel to the heart, i.e., the mind (cf. Prov. 2:2; 18:15; 22:17; 23:12). More often, though, "the ear" parallels "the eye," for they are the organs that receive and weigh knowledge.[9] Therefore, when they malfunction, their owner, failing to perceive the truth, follows the way of error.

(2) Interlude: God's Sovereign Rule (12:12–25)

12 *"With the Aged One[1] is wisdom*
and with the Long-lived One is understanding.[2]
13 *With him are wisdom and might;*
he has counsel and understanding.
14 *If[3] he destroys, there is no rebuilding;*
if he imprisons a man, there is no release.
15 *If he holds back the waters, there is drought;*
if he releases them, they overturn the earth.
16 *With him are strength and skill;*
he controls the deceived and the deceiver.
17 *He leads counselors away stripped[4]*
and drives judges mad.

8. In Mesopotamia "the ear" was believed to be the center of intelligence (H. Frankfort, et al., *Before Philosophy: The Intellectual Adventure of Ancient Man* [Baltimore: Penguin, repr. 1973], pp. 145–46).

9. Both these organs, of course, may parallel "the heart" (Deut. 29:3 [Eng. 4]; Isa. 6:10; 32:3, 4; Ezek. 40:4; 44:5).

1. The word for "the aged," *yᵉšîšîm,* appears only in Job in the OT (15:10; 29:8; 32:6; cf. also Sir. 8:6; 25:4–6). In this case it is the plural of excellence (GKC, §§ 124g-k).

2. Verses 11–12 appear to interrupt the flow between v. 10 and v. 13. The singular pronominal suffixes in v. 13 as well as the similarity to the wording in hymns of praise (e.g., Ps. 147:5; Isa. 11:2; and Dan. 2:20) strongly favor taking v. 13 as part of the hymn in praise of God. Blommerde (*Northwest Semitic Grammar and Job,* pp. 62–63) clarifies the obscure relation between v. 12 and v. 13 by understanding the two expressions *yᵉšîšîm,* "the Aged One," and *ʾōreḵ yāmîm,* "the Long-lived One," as two titles for God. Accepting this reading means that v. 12 is the heading of the hymn. This interpretation provides an antecedent for *ʿimmô,* "with him," at the beginning of v. 13. V. 11 then picks up the theme of vv. 7–8 and concludes the pericope.

3. LXX and Syr. appear to have a text reading *mî,* "who," instead of *wᵉlōʾ,* lit. "and not," in both lines. MT is preferred as the more difficult reading (cf. Driver-Gray).

4. Since the basic form of this line is repeated in v. 19a, Duhm (followed by Pope) recasts the colon to read *yôʿᵃṣê ʾereṣ yᵉsakkēl,* "the counselors of the earth deal

18 *He unbuckles the belt*[5] *of kings*
and removes[6] *the waistband from their loins.*
19 *He leads priests away stripped*
and overthrows temple functionaries.
20 *He removes speech from the trusted ones*
and takes away the discernment of the elders.
21 *He pours contempt on nobles*
and loosens the girdles[7] *of the strong.*[8]
22 *He reveals deep things out of darkness*
and brings to light deep darkness.[9]
23 *He makes nations great,*[10] *then destroys them;*
he enlarges[11] *a people,*[12] *then disperses them.*[13]

---

wisely" (see *BHK*). However, all the professional classes in this list appear in the plural absolute, and *'ereṣ,* "earth," does not restrict counselors that significantly. Working from Duhm's reading, Horst suggests the reading *milkê yô'ᵃṣîm yᵉšôlēl,* "He plunders the counsel of advisors." But the author often repeats words and phrases and one should not be too quick to emend the text merely for variety.

5. Since Heb. *mûsār* refers to "moral discipline" (Driver-Gray), many (e.g., Dhorme, Tur-Sinai, Rowley) revocalize it as *môsēr,* "chain, bond," with Targ. and Vulg. Accepting this change, Gordis and Pope understand *môsēr* to mean "belt," a symbol of authority.

6. According to Gordis MT *wayye'sōr* is a plene spelling for *wayyāsar,* "and he removes." Cf. Pope, and Blommerde, *Northwest Semitic Grammar and Job,* p. 63.

7. MT *mᵉzîaḥ* is taken to mean "girdle" and is probably a variant of *mēzaḥ* (Ps. 109:19), which is related to Egyp. *mḏḥ* and Akk. *mēzaḫu* (KB, p. 535).

8. Heb. *'āpîq* usually means "a channel" for a river (Job 6:15) or "a tube" (40:18). But the root can also mean "strong," as is evident in the verb *hiṯ'appēq,* "be strong, restrain oneself." KB (p. 76) relates it to Arab. *'āfiq,* "vigorous" (see also Gordis). Cf. Pope, who follows A. Guillaume (*Studies in the Book of Job,* ed. J. Macdonald [Leiden: Brill, 1968], p. 91) in relating it to Arab. *'ufuq,* "noble qualities," and hence translates it "nobles."

9. Dhorme, Fohrer, Pope, and others think that this line is a disruptive gloss, but poets often juxtaposed lines from various hymns for effect. Perhaps v. 22, which gives the opposite side, is inserted to keep the audience alert and to emphasize both sides of God's sovereignty. The theme of this line appears in Zophar's speech (11:6–10) and reappears in the wisdom hymn (28:11).

10. According to Driver-Gray and Dhorme the preposition *lᵉ* appears before an accusative, as in Aramaic. Blommerde (*Northwest Semitic Grammar and Job,* pp. 64–65) follows Dahood's suggestion that the use of the preposition in both lines means "some . . . others."

11. Hakam takes MT *šōṭēaḥ,* "spread out," in this context to mean "spread a net" in order to capture the nations (cf. Lam. 1:13). Although this view is possible, the parallelism favors the more usual translation.

12. The repetition of *laggôyim,* "to the nations," may be a part of the author's style, or it may be an error from *lᵉ'ummîm,* "to the peoples" (some mss., Targ., Syr.; see *BHK;* cf. *BHS*), or it may have been supplied after the original *'am,* "people," had been misplaced in v. 24. The second possibility is accepted.

13. MT *wayyanḥēm,* "he led them," is antithetical to the first line. One would expect a word similar in meaning to *wayᵉ'abbᵉḏēm,* "he destroys them" (cf. Blommerde,

24 *He deprives the leaders of the people*[14] *of the land of understanding,*
and he makes them wander in a pathless[15] *waste.*
25 *With no light they grope in darkness,*
and he makes them wander[16] *like drunkards."*

These lines laud God as the ultimate source of everything, light and darkness, good and evil, peace and calamity. God is superior to all in wisdom and understanding.[17] As Lord of the universe, he governs the world wisely and mightily. All earthly potentates are subject to him. He gives them power and takes it away according to his pleasure. The very one he exalts he may bring down at his will. God is in control even of the darkness, bringing the hidden things to light. Nothing lies outside his power or beyond his wisdom. In the words of Isaiah: "I am Yahweh and there is no other, who forms light and creates darkness, who makes peace and creates evil; I am Yahweh who does all these things" (45:6b–7; cf. Ps. 107).

In these verses Job focuses on God's devastating power that appears to be used capriciously to curtail the activity of earth's greatest potentates. God overwhelms them with devastating force, seemingly without reason. Thus Job implies that the reason for his troubles resides with God, not with himself. In this way he is countering Zophar's assertion: "When he passes by and imprisons and summons the assembly, who can restrain him?" (11:10). Zophar had argued that those under judgment are the worthless and the stupid. Job reciprocates with a description of God's destructive ability, but he directs the evidence to show that whoever experiences God's destructive power is not necessarily stupid or worthless. People become victims of catastrophes regardless of their social status or moral standing. Therefore, it is with this God that Job must settle his complaint, not with the God of the comforters.

Northwest Semitic Grammar and Job, p. 64). Horst, Ball, and Dhorme suggest *wayyimḥēm,* "and he wipes them out"; others, like Gordis, wish to revocalize MT as *wayyanniḥēm,* "and he leaves them." The latter view is followed, for it is closest to the MT.

14. LXX omits *ʿam,* "people," and Fohrer, Horst, and others consider it a gloss since the line seems long. But the scan with it included is fine: 8/8. Cf. Dhorme, Pope, Rowley.

15. The phrase *lōʾ-ḏārek̠,* lit. "no way," may be a composite noun, "trackless, pathless" (cf. GKC, § 152u; Blommerde, *Northwest Semitic Grammar and Job,* p. 65).

16. For MT *wayyaṯʿēm,* "and he makes them wander," which appears in v. 24b, some read the Niphal *wayyittāʿû,* "and they stagger," with LXX (cf. Isa. 19:14c; so Budde, Duhm, Dhorme, Driver-Gray, Horst). Fohrer and Gordis follow MT.

17. The author is deeply indebted to Israel's hymnic tradition for this long piece. Ps. 107:40 is echoed in v. 21a and v. 24b, and the language is closely identified with Isa. 44:24–28.

12 Building on the accepted idea that wisdom resides with the elders in the community, Job takes two of their epithets and uses them as titles for God, *the Aged One* and *the Long-lived One*. The longer one lives, the wiser one becomes. Since God is the oldest by far, he certainly is the wisest. The hymn will recount God's great wisdom in his sovereign rulership over the world.

13 All aspects of wisdom—connoted by the four terms *wisdom (hoḵmâ), might (gᵉḇûrâ), counsel (ʿēṣâ),* and *understanding (tᵉḇûnâ)*—reside in God (cf. Isa. 11:2). That is, God possesses both the *wisdom* to plan the best course of action and the *might* or power to carry out that course. In ancient Near Eastern myths the qualities of wisdom and power often resided in different gods. The strongest gods, not being the wisest, did things that often had terrible consequences. And since the wisest god was not the strongest, he could be rendered inept before the ferocity of the mighty gods and would have to resort to magic to counter their ill-conceived designs.[18] But in the OT wisdom and strength are one in the true God. The following hymnic lines testify primarily to God's power over all earthly leaders and nations with the inference that all of his mighty deeds are accomplished in wisdom and that no earthly ruler or nation is strong enough or wise enough to resist his purpose.

14 Like a tyrant, God raids a land, destroying property and imprisoning whomever he wills. That which an earthly warrior destroys, however, can be rebuilt, and the one he incarcerates can be set free. God's destructive deeds are more horrendous. His scourge is so total that there will be *no rebuilding* of what *he destroys* and no freeing of him whom *he imprisons*. The language may picture God's imprisoning a tyrant in a pit or cistern and then rolling a stone in front of the entrance to seal the pit (see Delitzsch; cf. Lam. 3:53; cf. Jer. 38:6; Isa. 22:22). No one is strong enough to remove the stone and free the captive.

15 God also manifests his power in his control of *the waters*. When God withholds the rain, the land dries up and the fertile field becomes a desert. Conversely, when God releases the waters (cf. Ps. 104:10), they come with such a sudden rush that *they overturn [hāpaḵ] the earth* (cf. Job 9:5). The destructive thrust pictured by this verb is evident in its use for the overthrow of Sodom and Gomorrah (Gen. 19:21, 25, 29). The mighty waters, before which the gods of mythology flee in terror,[19] are fully subject to God's control.

16 Such a display of God's power is praised in the refrain: *With him*

18. Cf. Y. Kaufmann, *The Religion of Israel*, tr. M. Greenberg (New York: Schocken, 1960), pp. 33–34.

19. E.g., "The Epic of Gilgamesh," XI:113–26 (*ANET*, p. 94).

are strength and skill; he controls the deceived and the deceiver. The structure of this verse parallels v. 13: the first line opens with *ʿimmô* ("With him"), and the second line begins with *lô* ("he has, he controls"; lit. "to him"). God's *strength (ʿōz)* and *skill* or effective counsel (*tûšîyâ;* cf. 5:12) ensure that he is the master of every type of person. Both *the deceived,* i.e., the one who is led astray, and the *deceiver,* i.e., the one who leads another astray, come under his authority. The verbs describe a person's tendency to failure, including moral failings. The greatest among humanity eventually falter and must submit to God's judgment, as the next verses recount. Thus in his wisdom God is the master of all human blunderers.

17 God is able to outwit human wisdom that resides in counselors and judges. The *counselors* are advisors to the court, and the *judges* are those who administered justice (not the charismatic leaders who led Israel in the period of the judges). God has the counselors led away *stripped (šôlāl),* naked and barefoot.[20] With all their insignia of authority removed, their power and prestige have vanished. In the upheaval God *drives* the keenest judges *mad.* Losing their ability of discernment, they are left hopelessly confused.

18 Like a champion wrestler, God *unbuckles the belt of kings.* In some ancient wrestling the victor removed his opponent's belt.[21] *belt* symbolizes a champion's might. In victory he *removes the waistband,* a symbol of their authority (cf. 38:3). Stripped of their power and authority, these rulers are reduced to nothing. Their mastery, which formerly held their subjects in terror, has been broken by the Supreme Ruler of the universe.

19 *Priests,* too, are subject to God's authority. They are not exempt from facing woes, either because of their status in the community or because of their spiritual powers. They too may be stripped and marched off into captivity. The *temple functionaries (ʾēṯānîm)*[22] feel secure in their position, for it was believed that their position was passed from generation to generation under the protection of the deity. But God *overthrows (sallēp̱)* them, removing them from authority.

20 The *trusted ones (neʾĕmānîm)* are those who by reason of their personal integrity and insight were given a special place in government as the monarch's closest advisors. They had trained long and hard to learn

20. For a similar use of *šôlāl,* "stripped, barefoot," see Mic. 1:8 Qere (*šôlāl weʿārôm,* "barefoot and naked"). Also "naked" *(ʿārôm)* is joined with "barefoot" *(yāḥēp)* in Isa. 20:4.

21. See C. H. Gordon, "Belt-Wrestling in the Bible World," *HUCA* 23 (1950–51) 131–36.

22. N. Sarna ("ʾ*ytnym,* Job 12:19," *JBL* 74 [1955] 272–73) demonstrates that ʾ*ēṯānîm* is a special class of temple functionaries, related to Ugar. *ytnm,* but not to Heb. ʾ*êṯān,* "perpetual." This title is similar to, but not identical with, the title *neṯînîm* found in 1 Chronicles, Ezra, and Nehemiah.

wisdom. They were *the elders* who guided a community. Having learned to control their tongues, they were great orators who could hold an audience spellbound and move a governing body to take the wisest course of action. But in judgment God *removes speech* (i.e., their rhetorical skills) and *takes away the discernment (ṭaʿam).* Heb. *ṭaʿam* literally means "taste" and by extension "judgment, discernment." In troubled times, when the city turned to its elders for decisive counsel, God confounded the thoughts of the advisors, leaving the people without good counsel. Their accursed advice would result in a public catastrophe.

21 Next God *pours contempt on nobles (nᵉḏîḇîm),* evidenced perhaps by the people hurling abuse on them. God *loosens the girdles of the strong,* rendering them infirm. The girdle harnesses the strength of the middle of the body, and it serves as a place for the worker to tuck in the skirt of his long robe so that he may labor unhampered. When the worker's girdle is loosed, his ability to work is lost.

22 A hymnic refrain is added at this point to assert that nothing can be hidden from God, not even in the deepest darkness. God *reveals deep things* (*ʿᵃmuqôṯ,* in the plural for intensity), i.e., dark secrets, *and brings to light deep darkness.* The two words for *darkness, ḥōšeḵ,* "darkness," and *ṣalmāweṯ,* "deep darkness," stand for the thick darkness of a cave or the dead of night (cf. 3:5; 10:21). The line implies that the great leaders have been overturned because they have expected to outwit God by devising clever plans in dark places where they thought God could not see them. Nevertheless, God frustrates their mischievous plans by exposing them to the light.

23–25 God rules not only over mighty leaders but also over the great nations. They rise and fall at his command. He allows a people to become great and spread out; i.e., a nation increases its territory through diplomatic intrigue and conquest. But in time God sees to it that that nation falls in defeat and its people are dispersed. He hastens a great nation's demise by removing *understanding (lēḇ)* from *the leaders of the people.* Often as a country prospers the leaders' pride, fed by the increase in their authority, blinds them so that they are unable to cope with the larger problems created by the increased size of their dominion. In the way they administer they appear like a caravan trying to find its way across *a pathless waste* (cf. 6:18–20). They are left to *grope in darkness (ḥōšeḵ)* with *no light* to give any sense of direction, and thus they *wander* aimlessly *like drunkards.*[23] This imagery of drunkenness recalls the metaphor that a rebellious people must drink deeply of the cup of God's wrath (cf. Isa. 51:17–18). That is, their groping in darkness is caused by God's wrath.

23. Cf. Ps. 107:27; Job 5:14.

The picture of God's unchallengeable power is complete. He overthrows every hostile force and reigns supreme. A wise ruler, he exposes all the sinful ways and executes appropriate punishment against human rebellion by turning human-ordered society into chaos. Chaotic upheaval is the ultimate judgment against a community for its corporate sins.[24]

EXCURSUS: REFLECTIONS ON 12:7–25

By juxtaposing these lines about wisdom that the created order teaches (vv. 7–11) and God's sovereign wisdom (vv. 12–25), the author makes a bold statement: the traditions of the fathers, though worthy of great respect, must not be accepted uncritically. In other words, each person has the ability to evaluate accepted beliefs and decide on their validity. In this discussion the tension between corporate morality and individual responsibility is visible. The book of Job reflects on the plight of an individual facing suffering alone while much of the OT operates on the principle of corporate accountability. Although the individual is regarded as a responsible member of the community, his fate tends to be subordinated to the destiny of the nation. The OT emphasizes that God enters into covenant with a people and holds the nation accountable for its response to his demands. So usually the nation as a whole is addressed in the OT. The action of the individual is often evaluated in its corporate impact more than in its personal effects. A shift in this thinking came to the foreground at the time of the Exile. In captivity the individual had a tendency to evade responsibility for his plight by complaining that his fate was caused by the sins of his fathers (cf. Jer. 31:29; Ezek. 18:2). In this way a person avoided acknowledging his own evil ways. In opposition to this attitude both Ezekiel and Jeremiah taught that the individual is responsible to God for both his own righteousness and his own sins, independent of the moral qualities of his fathers or his forefathers (see esp. Ezek. 18; 33). An individual cannot blame his plight solely on the sins of his forefathers. Each one is exhorted, therefore, to repent and to establish a right relationship with God independent of the righteousness or wickedness of his ancestors.

In this book the author separates Job from his community and makes him cope with his losses all alone. Thus the issue of suffering in this work is looked at from the viewpoint of the individual separated from the community. The outcome of Job's struggle will present the position that an individual can reach God through his own perseverance, even when he has no community support.

The book of Job holds that the traditions of the fathers possess high

24. For this idea see Lam. 3:2.

value. Nevertheless, the author finds it necessary to test the ancient precepts in the light of current conditions. The book of Job thus posits that inherited dogma can be corrected through new insights that God leads a person, even one younger than the elders, to discover.

Of course, the great effort to which the author went to accomplish this most significant change in perspective is missed by those in Western society who too readily discount the value of tradition. Instead of abandoning truth from tradition we should listen to it, receptively and critically, in order to hear the hard-won truths. We need to remember that knowledge from the past offers the lens to bring the present age into sharper focus. A holistic perspective does not cast away the old solely for being old. Rather, new insights integrated into the tradition keep the tradition vital and contemporary. At the same time this approach provides perspective for the people, enabling them to understand where they stand in relationship to their heritage without letting that heritage imprison them.

(3) The Second Complaint (13:1–17)

After reflecting on God's power manifest in this world, Job makes a double complaint against his friends: they have not listened to his words and they have defended God's ways falsely (13:1–12). Therefore, he enjoins them to be silent while he argues his case directly with God (13:13–17).

(a) The Complaint Proper (13:1–12)

1 *"Lo, my eye has seen all this;*[1]
my ear has heard and understood it.
2 *What you know, I also know;*
I am not inferior to you.[2]
3 *But*[3] *I would speak to Shaddai,*
and I desire to argue[4] *my case with God.*
4 *You, though, are whitewashers of lies,*
worthless physicians, all of you.
5 *Would that you would be completely silent.*
That would be wisdom for you.

1. Most scholars assume that *zōʾṯ,* "this," or *ʾēlleh,* "these (things)," has fallen out after *kōl,* "all" (cf. Horst, *BHS,* Driver-Gray). The inclusion of the former balances the syllable count, 8/8. But cf. Gordis, who thinks that *ʾēlleh* was understood, though not in the text.

2. This line is identical with 12:3b.

3. The adversative particle *ʾûlām,* "but,"stands outside the metrical pattern by anacrusis (Rowley).

4. The infinitive absolute, functioning as the object of the verb, precedes the verb for emphasis (GKC, § 113d).

6 *Now hear my argument;*
attend to the pleas of my lips.
7 *Is it for God's sake that you speak perversity?*
For him you speak deceit?
8 *Will you show partiality for him?*
Will you argue the case for God?
9 *Will it be well when he examines you?*
Can you dupe[5] *him as men are duped?*
10 *Will*[6] *he indeed vindicate you*
if you secretly[7] *show partiality?*
11 *Will not his majesty terrify you?*
Will not his dread fall on you?
12 *Your maxims are proverbs of ashes;*
your answers[8] *are indeed*[9] *answers of clay."*

1, 2 Job forthrightly restates his opening position that he is equal to his friends in matters of wisdom (cf. 12:2, 3). Confident that he too uses his eyes and ears, the sources of knowledge, well, Job asserts that he himself has spiritual insight equal to theirs. *all* is not to be restricted to the truths which have been expounded; it is to be taken comprehensively. The *eye* signifies that which a person knows through personal observation (cf. Eccl. 8:9, 16–17), while the *ear* receives truth spoken by the wise (cf. 12:11). Job asserts that he *has heard and understood* the tradition of the fathers.

3 Believing in his equality with his comforters, Job informs them that he wishes to argue his case with God himself. In stating his intent to dispute with God as though the two of them were in court, Job is saying that he will pursue a course far different from the one that the friends have

5. With Gordis, MT *t^{e}hāṯēllû,* "you dupe," is interpreted as a Hiphil form of the root *tll* with the preformative *h* preserved (GKC, § 53q). Tur-Sinai prefers another possibility: that it is a Piel of a secondary root *htl.*

6. The interrogative *h* has probably fallen out by haplography; if so, the question form continues throughout vv. 7–11. See Gordis.

7. Gordis recognizes the problem with *basseṯer,* "in secret, covertly," for there is nothing hidden about the friends' defense of God. He suggests, therefore, that MT is an aberrant spelling of *bassēṭer,* "one side in a controversy." This substitution is possible, but the phrase in MT may be used figuratively.

8. There are two main interpretations of MT *gaḇ.* If taken from a root *gbb,* it means lit. "back" and by extension "boss" of a shield (15:26) and possibly a "raised fortification" (Ezek. 16:24, 31, 39; see Rowley, Driver-Gray). Of course, a shield or a defense structure made out of clay would be worthless before any mighty blow. A second interpretation (favored by Dhorme; Gordis; Guillaume, "Background," p. 112) relates *gaḇ* to an Aramaic/Syriac root, *gwb,* "return," "answer," and Arab. *jāba* or *jawāb,* "answer." This possible meaning for *gaḇ* is favored by the parallelism.

9. The *l* is taken as an emphatic *lamed* with Blommerde (*Northwest Semitic Grammar and Job,* p. 66) and Fohrer.

recommended. Instead of appealing to God's mercy, as they have exhorted, he will reason or argue with God. Since the basis of his troubles lies in his relationship with God and since God is known for acting justly, Job hopes that a direct confrontation with God will yield a resolution to his case. He begins with this approach when he addresses God in the second division of this speech (13:18–28). The lack of support from his companions drives Job to God, even overcoming his apprehension expressed so fully in his last speech.

4 Before taking up his case with God, Job makes blatant charges against his comforters. He calls them *whitewashers of lies,* i.e., they smear (Heb. *ṭāp̱al*) the difficulties of explaining his plight with lies in order to make the tradition appear flawless. Their discourses have glossed over the hard facts of his innocent suffering, for they feel compelled to defend their cherished doctrines at his expense (cf. Ps. 119:69, which uses the same expression). Their pious mortar (cf. Heb. *tāp̱ēl*) has been composed of lies. In defense of God they condemn Job. Their approach, unfortunately, is an ingrained human tendency. When faced with a perplexing problem, one often tries to get around it or to cover it over with some type of ideological explanation instead of honestly admitting the difficulties involved.

Because of their inability to face the hard facts, the friends have proved to be *worthless physicians*[10] *(rōp̱eʾîm).*[11] These charlatans are pictured as vainly daubing a sore with a useless salve. They merely go through the ritual in an effort to comfort the patient. At best they arouse false hope. The harsh tone of these accusations shows that the rift between Job and his friends is widening into an irreparable breach.

5, 6 Wishfully, but sternly, Job requests that these friends *be completely silent.* That would be their wisdom! He is applying to them the wisdom of a well-known proverb such as: "Even a fool who keeps silent is considered wise; when he closes his lips, he is deemed intelligent" (Prov. 17:28). If they would be silent, they would be in a position to attend the pleas of his legal argument. Such a summons to *attend to* what one is saying often precedes a significant message; e.g., some singers began their song in this way (Judg. 5:3; Gen. 4:23), and wisdom teachers introduced a speech in a similar fashion (Prov. 7:24). The summons to hear also stands at the opening of a judicial summary (Prov. 4:1) and a prophetic word of judgment (Isa. 1:2, 10; see Horst).

7–11 With a series of questions typical of a disputation, Job seeks

10. The phrase is similar to "worthless shepherds," which appears in Zech. 11:17.

11. Heb. *rāpāʾ*, "heal," means lit. "repair, restore." The root may have originally meant "sew, patch" (see *THAT,* II:803). See further the commentary below on 26:5.

to convince the friends that they are violating justice by showing favoritism to God. Behind their arguments Job has detected a trace of conceited confidence suggesting that they are convinced that God will honor them for exposing another wicked person. Job counters by warning them of the severe consequences that attend deceptive speech, especially false testimony given before the court.

7 Job begins by asking the friends if they are so fearful that his words might insult or threaten God that they defend God's ways with *perversity (ʿawlâ)*[12] and *deceit (r^emîyâ).*[13] Thereby he accuses them of twisting the truth to make him appear wrong and God right. He assumes that they fail to realize that the use of deceit never advances God's cause.

8 Next Job questions the friends about their showing partiality for God. The Hebrew idiom for *show partiality* is *nāśāʾ pānîm,* literally "lifting up the face." This expression can refer to any special favor extended to a person from improper motivation. Such favor may be purchased with a bribe or won by intimidation. In judicial proceedings the showing of favor thwarts justice. To eliminate this possibility the law firmly states that judges are never to exercise partiality in judgment (Lev. 19:15). In showing partiality for God the comforters have prejudiced themselves against speaking justly on God's behalf.

9, 10 With more searching questions Job leads the friends to ponder the responsibility of both their reasoning falsely and their condescending attitude toward him. They must not assume that they will be rewarded or vindicated for their deceptive words when God hears Job's case. Instead they need to realize that they too will be examined by God, being held accountable for the counsel they have offered Job. So Job asks, "When God questions you, will you be able to dupe him as easily as you have duped men?" Of course not!

11 Job asks the friends how they will act in God's presence. Will they not be terrified by *his majesty (ś^eʾēṯ)?* Will not *the dread (paḥaḏ)* of his presence fall on them? The awesomeness of God's presence inspires wonder in his followers (cf. 31:23) but overcomes his foes with panic and terror. When the dread of God falls on a town or a nation, the population is terror-stricken and refuses to act in hostility against God's people (cf. Exod. 15:16; Ps. 105:38; Isa. 2:10, 19, 21).

Job makes a scathing play on the similar sound between the verb *show partiality (tiśśāʾûn)* in v. 10b and the noun *majesty (ś^eʾēṯ)* in v. 11a. Since the friends have wrongly shown favoritism toward God, they will not

12. Heb. *ʿawlâ* means "injustice" or "perversity," and when used with the tongue it means "falsehood," according to Dhorme.

13. Cf. 6:29–30.

be able to stand before God's majesty. The divine majesty will *terrify (bāʿaṯ)* them.[14] Although Job is experiencing terror from his calamity (3:5; 6:4), the friends stand in danger of being overcome by terror, not from misfortune but more ominously from God's presence.

12 Job ends his complaint against the friends by renouncing their instruction. He states sarcastically that their arguments are buttressed by *proverbs of ashes* and their answers are *answers of clay*. Before the truth their wisdom will crumble like a ceramic pot. Wisdom teachers freely used proverbs, maxims, and aphorisms to support their teachings. The word for *maxims (zikkārôn)*[15] comes from the root *zkr,* "remember," and refers to popular, pithy sayings that are easily remembered. Although aphorisms offer insight into life, their brevity and frozen form prevent them from creatively addressing unique situations. Mere repetition of them for every circumstance is an exercise in futility. The proverbs spoken by the friends, then, are like *ashes*—lifeless and lacking substance. There may be a subtle irony in the use of *ashes:* Job's having to sit on ashes and his friends' reducing the wisdom of the ages to ashes.

(b) Job's Resolve (13:13–17)

13 *"Be silent! Let me speak!*
Then let come on me what may.[1]
14 *Shall I put my flesh between my teeth*
and take my life in my hands?
15 *If he were to slay me, I would have no hope.*[2]
Nevertheless, I will defend my ways to his face.

14. This is a favorite word of the author, e.g., 7:14; 9:34.

15. This word does not have to be restricted to "arguments from history," as Gordis postulates. In its passive usage it has a broad range of meaning, including deeds (Esth. 6:1), records (Ezra 6:2), and remembrance (Eccl. 1:11; 2:16). Cf. B. Childs, *Memory and Tradition in Israel,* SBT 1/37 (London: SCM; Naperville: Allenson, 1962), pp. 66–67.

1. In place of MT *mâ,* the phrase *ʿal-mâ* of v. 14a may be read at the end of v. 13b (Fohrer). This change improves the scan of v. 13 from 10/6 to 10/7 and puts v. 14 into balance, 8/8.

2. The first half of the verse has two textual traditions: the Ketib, "If he were to slay me, I would have no *[lōʾ]* hope"; and the Qere, "Though he slay me, yet will I trust in him *[lô]*." Modern interpreters believe that the context strongly favors the Ketib. R. Jacobson ("Satanic Semiotics, Jobian Jurisprudence," in *The Book of Job and Ricoeur's Hermeneutics,* Semeia 19, ed. J. D. Crossan [Chico: Scholars Press, 1981], pp. 67–68) considers the Qere to arise from a pious annotator who sought to find an easy way out of a difficult text. As Rowley observes, the issue in this section is challenging God, not trusting him.

Gordis offers another interpretation. He suggests that the root *yḥl* may have a special nuance, "be silent," as in 32:11, 16. Thus he translates: "Yes, He may slay me; I shall not be quiet." This translation yields a good sense, and is worthy of careful con-

16 *Surely this may be my salvation,*
for a godless man may not come before him.[3]
17 *Listen attentively to my words;*
let my declaration be in your hearing."

This pericope, which stands at the center of this speech, might easily be construed with the second major division of the speech. For two reasons it is placed with the first division. First, Job addresses his friends with imperatives in vv. 13 and 17, as in 13:1–12. Second, he speaks of God in the third person in vv. 15–16, but in the next pericope he will address God alone, using second person singular forms. Therefore, Job's purpose in this pericope is to inform the friends of the course he is about to take.

13 Job petitions the friends to *be silent* in order that he may continue to speak without any hindrance from them. He speaks with resolution by using a cohortative, *let me speak ('ᵃdabbᵉrâ),* with the first person pronoun *('ānî).* This powerful style reveals his determination to take a course that he knows they will not approve. Job is willing to risk any consequences that may result from demanding a hearing with God. He has nothing to lose and much to gain. By resisting the easy solutions the friends have offered and by pushing for a full resolution to his complaint, Job is affirming his faith in God.

14 Job states both his determination to confront God and the risk involved with a vivid picture. *Shall I put my flesh between my teeth?* This figure of speech occurs only here in the OT and its exact meaning is uncertain. The picture may be that of an animal carrying its prey between its teeth. Suddenly another animal cuts across its path and challenges it for its prey. The animal carrying the prey must defend its own life at the risk of losing its food. Or this figure may refer to the convention that when someone is afflicted with excruciating pain, he bites his own flesh to keep from screaming. With a second figure Job says *and take my life [nepeš] in my hands.*[4] This expression means that a person with fierce determination puts his life in peril as he resists the forces arrayed against him. Job accepts the danger of instant death in challenging God to hear his complaint.

---

sideration. It rests, of course, on proving that *yḥl* has this nuance. Habel (OTL) also appeals to 32:11, 16 for the sense of *yḥl,* but he combines the traditional meaning with Gordis's nuance, hence "wait (silently)."

3. The phrase *lᵉpānāyw,* "before him," is made prominent by its position between the negative *lō'* and the verb; such grammatical order is very unusual (GKC, § 152e).

4. This expression occurs also in Judg. 12:3; 1 Sam. 19:5 (cf. 1 Sam. 28:21; Ps. 119:109). In those passages the hero, at the risk of his own life, dared to engage an enemy mightier than himself.

15 Job's determination to clear himself reaches a high pitch.[5] He admits that if he should dare to present his case before the divine court, God might slay him and that would put an end to his hope of vindication. It was inconceivable that a mortal might presume to enter God's presence, let alone challenge him in court. The Hebrews believed that the awesome splendor of the divine presence would so overpower a human being that he would die.[6] But in the urgency of gaining a hearing with God before this illness takes away his life, Job dares to take this brazen step. Aware of the grave risks, he is confident that he can *defend [hôḵîaḥ] his ways* before God. *his ways* means the way he has conducted his life (e.g., Prov. 2:12; 3:6; 4:18, 19). He knows of no instance of ever having deliberately broken God's laws. Therefore, he will take a chance, no matter the cost, to prove that he is truly a righteous man who fears God.

This interpretation does not cancel out the thought of Job's unflinching faith, which is frequently associated with its familiar, though inaccurate, rendering in the AV: "Though he slay me, yet will I trust him." In fact, this rendering goes against the grain of Hebraic thought that teaches that a person's primary opportunity to praise and serve God is in this life. The traditional rendition also suggests irrational trust. But Job's faith is not only daring, it is also rational. Both of these qualities are necessary for him to challenge God to a legal dispute. Job's faith is bold, not blind. It is searching for the justice behind the display of God's power.

16 Job knows that only if he can dispute his case before God will he find *salvation* or deliverance *(yᵉšûʿâ)*[7] from suffering, ignominy, and God's hostility. Since Job knows that there is no salvation outside God, he must win his deliverance from God. Thus he abandons the friends' counsel to find restoration to prosperity through confession of sins. Job reasons that *a godless man (ḥānēp̱)* would never be permitted to come *before God*. Consequently, if God should give him an audience, that in itself would be proof of his innocence.[8]

5. Gordis offers another possible interpretation of the relationship between vv. 14–15. He takes v. 14 as an example of an indirect quote: "You ask, why do I endanger my life (by speaking)? and I answer, Though he slay me, I must justify my ways to his face."

6. Cf. Exod. 33:20; Judg. 6:22–23; 13:22.

7. This verse is alluded to in Phil. 1:12, according to J. Michael, "Paul and Job: A Neglected Analogy," *ExpTim* 36 (1924–25) 67–70.

8. Weiser thinks that the background for the language of vv. 15–16 is the theophany that stands at the center of the old covenant renewal festival. The theophany was the actualization of the salvation promised in the covenant. The participants in this solemn ceremony had to be examined before they entered the sacred precinct (cf. Ps. 15; 24:3–6). Only those who had kept the laws of the covenant were permitted to celebrate; whoever entered unprepared would be consumed by the divine presence. Thus if God would let Job attend such a theophany, that permission itself would be his vindication.

17 Before leaving off addressing his friends directly, Job beseeches them once more: *Listen attentively to my words*. He wants them to hear his declaration without missing a single word. He knows that partial attention leads to misunderstanding and wrong conclusions. He hopes that by paying close attention to each part of the argument he is about to make in his addresses to God, they will come to support him in taking up his case with God.

b. A Summons to God (13:18–14:22)

Since the comforters have feared to side with Job, their lack of moral courage has turned their consolations into ashes.[1] Rightly Job realizes that if he should follow their counsel, he would compromise his own integrity. Unwilling to tarnish his honor, he pleads with God to hear his case (13:18–28). Job has taken a giant step on the way that will lead him to formalize his complaint against God (chs. 29–31). After expressing his resolve, he laments his pain in the context of human sorrow in general, sorrow made acute by the finality of death (14:1–22). With this lament Job identifies his suffering with all human sorrow.

(1) Job's Desire for a Legal Resolution to His Complaint (13:18–28)

(a) Job's Statement of Readiness and His Request for Two Pre-Trial Conditions (13:18–22)

18 *"Behold, I have prepared my case;*
I know that I will be acquitted.
19 *Who is he who can dispute with me?*
Then I should be silent and expire.
20 *Spare me only two things;*
then I need not hide from you:
21 *withdraw your hand far from me;*
let not the terror of you frighten me.
22 *Then call and I shall answer,*
or let me speak and you respond."[1]

1. Cf. Westermann, *Structure of the Book of Job*, pp. 53–55.

1. Driver-Gray say that *dāḇār*, "word," is usually the object of *hēšîḇ*, "return," in such a setting and that it may have been elliptically omitted here; i.e., it is not necessary to restore it for the proper sense, as some recommend. Gordis responds that *hēšîḇ* itself in Mishnaic Hebrew means "refute, respond," and such usage may have been earlier.

18 In anticipation of an opportunity to present his case before the divine court,[2] Job affirms *I have prepared [ʿārak̲]*[3] *my case.* If he is granted an opportunity to present his position, he is confident that he *will be acquitted* or declared innocent *(ṣād̲aq).* With the use of the verb *I know* along with the personal pronoun Job emphasizes his personal conviction about his own innocence, as he did earlier (9:15).

19 Sure of the outcome of the trial, Job asks rhetorically, *Who is he who can dispute with me?* "No one, not even God!" is the implied response. Job is so sure of winning that he taunts his opponent. He believes that no one can ever win a dispute against a righteous or innocent man. Paradoxically he concedes that if someone, i.e., God, should counter his defense, he would *be silent and expire.* He is aware of the consequences should he fail to persuade the court. His boldness is lined with fear and trembling. This contest with God is a life-and-death struggle.

Gordis interprets the verse a little differently. He takes the first line as spoken by God and the second line as Job's response: "But if God says, 'Who dares to argue with Me?' then I must perish in silence." If God refuses to hear the case, then Job can only die in silence. The first interpretation is favored by the fact that v. 19a is a logical consequence of the preparation and personal conviction stated in v. 18 (cf. Isa. 50:8).

20 To ensure a proper trial Job petitions God to grant two pre-trial conditions. Job anticipates that if he is permitted into God's presence, he will have to hide himself from the splendor of God's glory unless God makes it possible for him to stand in his presence. Therefore, he requests that God will permit him to present his complaint. In these requests Job shows that he is very conscious of God's sovereignty and holiness even in his most adventurous statements.

21 Job's first petition to God is *withdraw your hand far from me.* Specifically he is asking God to end his physical suffering. Here the phrase "God's hand" *(kap̱)* means that God is intentionally afflicting Job.[4] Whenever God lifts his hand, Job's illness will be stayed. Then Job will have the fortitude to pursue his case energetically. Job's second plea is that *the terror* attending God's presence may not *frighten* him (cf. 9:34). Anticipation of

2. That Job is seeking to take God to court is evident from the abundance of legal language: "arrange a case" (*ʿārak̲ mišpāṭ,* v. 18a), "be innocent, vindicated" (*ṣād̲aq,* v. 18b), "take up a lawsuit" (*rîḇ,* v. 19a), and a reference to the examination of the participants (v. 22).

3. Heb. *ʿārak̲* means "to arrange in order" so as to achieve a useful purpose; e.g., wood is piled up for a sacrificial fire (Gen. 22:6; 1 K. 18:33), a table is set for a meal (Isa. 21:5; Prov. 9:2), troops are summoned into battle array (Judg. 20:22, 30), and the arguments of a legal case are arranged in a persuasive order (Ps. 50:21).

4. Cf. Ps. 32:4; 38:3 (Eng. 2); Exod. 9:3, using *yād̲* for "hand."

facing the divine terror in court unnerves Job. Therefore, he petitions God to present himself in such a way that the divine glory will not disconcert him.

22 If God grants these two conditions, the setting will be right for the legal proceedings to start. Therefore, Job politely offers God the choice of being either the appellant or the respondent. A discussion over the format for the legal proceedings need not hinder getting the trial underway. Either way Job will have an opportunity to present his side. Job shows his desire that the reconciliation between God and himself be hastened.

(b) An Examination of the Plaintiff (13:23–28)

23 *"How many are my iniquities and sins?*
Show me my rebellion and my sin.
24 *Why are you hiding your face*
and considering me your enemy?
25 *Will you intimidate a wind-blown leaf?*
Will you chase dry chaff?[1]
26 *For you write down bitter things against me*
and make me inherit the iniquities of my youth.
27 *You put*[2] *my feet in stocks,*
and you keep close watch on all my paths,[3]
and you put marks on the soles of my feet.
28 *So I am he who wastes away like a rotten thing,*[4]
like a garment eaten by moths."[5]

23 Job turns to question God. Wanting to learn the specific reasons for his punishment, he asks God either to enumerate his sins (hence the plurals

1. Possibly *wᵉʾim* should be read instead of MT *wᵉʾeṯ* to introduce the second member of a double question (Duhm, Driver-Gray, Tur-Sinai). But GKC, § 150h, gives examples in which a simple *waw* may introduce the second member of a double question. So it is best to leave the text as it stands.

2. MT *wᵉṯāśēm,* "and you put," may be either a defective writing of the imperfect (Fohrer) or a poetic use of the jussive (Dhorme).

3. Some commentators (e.g., Hölscher, Fohrer) take the second line as a gloss from 33:11b; though that is possible, it seems more likely that 33:11 was taken from this reference (so Dhorme, Tur-Sinai; cf. Horst).

4. Tur-Sinai and Fohrer revocalize MT *kᵉrāqāḇ* as *kᵉrōqeḇ,* "a leather skin (wineskin)" from Aram. *rûqbāʾ*, supported by Syr. and LXX. Since the verb *bālâ,* "become old, worn out," may be used with garments (Deut. 8:4; Isa. 50:9; Ps. 102:27 [Eng. 26]) or wineskins (Josh. 9:4, adj. *bāleh*), it supports this view, and this reading affords a good parallel with "a garment" *(beged).* Nevertheless, MT *rāqāḇ,* "decay, dry rot," describes rotting wood in Isa. 40:20 and decaying bones in Prov. 12:4; 14:30. Then the parallel idea may be between "a rotten thing" or dry rot *(rāqāḇ)* and "moths" *(ʿāš),* as in Hos. 5:12.

5. Many consider this verse to be out of context and relocate it. Some (e.g., Rowley) put it after 14:2 as another line which describes human infirmity. Conversely, Fohrer thinks that this verse is a fitting conclusion to the accusation speech in that it gives the grounds for Job's concerns.

iniquities [ʿ^a^wōnôṯ] and *sins [ḥaṭṭāʾôṯ]*), or to make known the specific cause of the breach between them (as denoted by the singulars *my rebellion [pišʿî]* and *my sin [ḥaṭṭāʾṯî]*). The combination of these words for sin encompasses all the possible ways of breaking God's law. This combination of terms also occurs in the high priest's confession of Israel's sins over the scapegoat on the Day of Atonement (Lev. 16:21). Throughout the dialogue Job never denies that he may have sinned, but he is sure that he has done no wrong that deserves such severe punishment. Therefore, God must reveal to him any wrongs he has committed or else be guilty of inflicting punishment unjustly. Job's first question gets to the heart of the matter.

24 Next Job asks God, *Why are you hiding your face and considering me your enemy?*[6] A person's countenance reveals his basic attitude toward another person. The refusal to look at another is a gesture of contempt. In reference to God, those on whom his face shines experience his mercy, but those from whom he hides his face feel the heat of his anger (cf. Ps. 13:2 [Eng. 1]; 44:25 [Eng. 24]). When God hides his face, he no longer hears a person's prayers or acknowledges that person in any way.[7] Since God has turned his face from him, Job *(ʾîyôḇ)* fears that God counts him as *an enemy (ʾôyēḇ)*.

Passages such as this reveal that the loss of God's companionship is the sharpest pain Job must bear. A note of deep sorrow underlies his question. It is clear that Job addresses God in a way that enables him to bring to God's attention the full weight of the pain God's hostile attitude is causing his servant.

25 Pursuing the concern of his last question, Job probes after God's motive for treating him, a frail object, so savagely. A mere man, he feels like *a leaf* driven by a strong wind[8] or like *dry chaff* chased about by a stiff breeze.[9] The leaf and dry chaff represent a human being as a weak, frail creature with no power to withstand a mighty tempest like God. God's power *intimidates (ʿāraṣ)* Job (cf. 31:34). This word represents the fright caused by the anticipation of cruel punishment or the dread aroused by a vision of God's awesome holiness (cf. Ps. 89:8 [Eng. 7]; Isa. 29:23). With the absurd nature of this question Job wishes to make it apparent that God has gone far beyond the standards of justice in treating him, a mere human

6. This theme has been expressed earlier in 7:12 and 10:16.

7. For the expression "God hides his face," see Deut. 31:17–18; 32:20; Ps. 27:9; 69:17–18 (Eng. 16–17); 88:15 (Eng. 14); 104:29; Isa. 54:8. See S. E. Balentine, *The Hidden God: The Hiding of the Face of God in the OT,* Oxford Theological Monographs (Oxford/New York: Oxford University Press, 1983).

8. Cf. Isa. 1:30; 34:4; 64:5 (Eng. 6); Jer. 8:13; Lev. 26:36.

9. Cf. Job 41:20, 21 (Eng. 28, 29); Jer. 13:24; Ps. 83:14 (Eng. 13); Isa. 40:24; 41:2.

being, so harshly. He thereby registers a cutting accusation against his opponent.

26 Dropping his questioning, Job pictures the nature of the affliction he is presently bearing. He likens his situation to a contract that God has filled with bitter stipulations. Perhaps one may think of a written covenant which contains blessings and curses. When one party fails to fulfill his side of the contract, the curses are activated against that party. Job presents this scenario of his suffering so as to win the sympathy of the court. The charges written against him are *bitter things (m^e^rōrâ).*[10] Tur-Sinai takes the phrase *write against* to mean "the assignment of property to an heir."[11] This interpretation makes good sense and is supported by the parallel verb *make to inherit (hôrîš).* The picture then comes from civil, not criminal, law. Job surmises that God is causing him to inherit the iniquities of his youth. Since he has done nothing worthy of his present bitter sufferings (cf. 13:23) and since God has afflicted him, the only possible explanation is that God has decided to make him bear his youthful wrongdoings. The term for *youth (n^e^ʿûrîm)* encompasses a range from the age of an infant to that of a teenager, and in a few cases it may extend to include someone older; but the word refers primarily to one's childhood before initiation into society as an adult. Job assumes that when a person becomes an adult, God no longer holds him accountable for the errors of his youth (cf. Ps. 25:7). So if God is punishing him for sins of his youth, it would indicate rancor on God's part (Dhorme).

27 Still accusing God, Job describes his present predicament as that of a prisoner closely confined and constantly watched. His feet are put in *stocks,* either a block of wood fastened about a prisoner's ankles to restrict his movements or bars that kept him from moving at all.[12] The former situation is more likely, for the second line suggests that Job can move about while God keeps close watch on his paths. In this verse *path* means a way of escape, rather than one's life-style, as it often means in the Wisdom literature. The prisoner's feet were marked or banded in order that he might be easily tracked.[13] The phrase *the soles of my feet* is literally "the roots of my feet." Dhorme argues that the word "root" refers both to the soles and to the

10. Heb. *m^e^rōrâ* means "bitter thing, gall, poison." In the plural it may mean "bitter things," or it may be a plural of intensification: "extreme bitterness" (GKC, § 124c).

11. He appeals to the Babylonian Talmud, *Baba Qamma* 88a.

12. Fohrer has an interesting interpretation of this verse. He reads *bassîḏ,* "in lime," for MT *bassaḏ,* "in stocks." God marks the prisoner's feet so that he can track his prints wherever he goes.

14. Interpreting the verse differently, Fohrer takes the verb *śîm,* "put, place," in the first line from a secondary root *śmm* = *smm,* "smear, stain." This would mean that the soles of the feet were smeared with chalk or something similar so that the prisoner could be easily tracked.

traces they leave on the ground. Two other interpretations are that God draws a ring around Job as a barrier that he cannot step across (cf. Prov. 8:27; Rowley) and that a rope is tied tightly around Job's ankle to keep him from straying (Budde). Although the exact figure escapes us, it is clear that Job is complaining about his lack of freedom to move about in order to prepare his defense. The incomprehensible contradiction in Job's experience is clearly verbalized. On the one hand, God refuses to recognize him by speaking to him; on the other hand, Job cannot get beyond the divine vigilance even for a moment. Practically this means that Job has no reprieve from his suffering, not for a day or even for an hour, nor does he have any insight into its purpose.

28 Deploring his situation, Job portrays his condition as that of rotting wood that is wasting away or like a garment which is being devoured by moths. God is the dry rot or the moth. Although these forces of destruction work slowly, they are persistent and pervasive. In this line Job laments the dreadful results of God's persistent pursuit. Daily he feels weaker. He will soon expire unless relief comes quickly. In the rest of his speech Job seeks to move God to hear his case.

(2) Human Suffering and Job's Plight (14:1–22)

(a) Human Suffering (14:1–6)

1 *"Man, born of woman,*
is short-lived and sated with turmoil.
2 *Like a flower he comes forth,*[1] *then withers;*[2]
like a shadow he flees and does not stay.
3 *Indeed, on such a one do you fix your eyes?*
Will you bring him[3] *into judgment with yourself?*

1. Possibly the MT perfect form *yāṣā'*, "go out," should be revocalized as an imperfect, *yēṣē'* (Budde and Driver-Gray), for the imperfect would better convey a general truth, as in v. 10. Either reading, though, is possible.

2. MT *wayyimmāl* is most likely a Qal of *mālal* (cf. Gordis), a secondary root of *'āmal,* "be weak, languish"—a word that the author favors (cf. 18:16; 24:24; see Horst). In Ps. 37:2 it parallels *yibbōlûn,* "wither, fade," a verb that has *ṣîṣ,* "flower," as its subject in Isa. 28:1 and 40:7–8. It is difficult to tell whether LXX "fall off" came from a *Vorlage* different from MT *wayyibbōl* or whether it translated MT by sense or was influenced by the Isaiah passages. Another possibility is to take the verb as a Niphal of *mālal,* related to *mûl,* "cut off," i.e., "circumcise" (see Fohrer).

3. For MT *'ōṯî,* "me," it is better to read *'ōṯô,* "him," with the versions (see *BHS*); the writing of a *y* for a *w* is a frequent scribal error. Hakam and Gordis resist this change, for Job vacillates between describing his tragic fate and that of humanity in general, but Job does not apply these general truths to himself until vv. 13–15. The lead position of the accusative is for emphasis.

4 *Who can make the unclean clean?*
No one![4]
5 *Indeed,*[5] *his days are determined,*
the number of his months is with you;
you have set limits which he cannot pass.
6 *Look away from him and desist*[6]
until he enjoys his day like a hired worker."

1, 2 Every person's life is filled with sorrow from birth. The language in these verses is generic. The word for *man* is *'āḏām,* which serves as the name of the first man, Adam. This term connotes that man is "from the ground" *('ᵃḏāmâ)* and is thus limited and weak by nature. Three short phrases further underscore human limitations: *born of woman, short-lived,* and *sated with turmoil.* Since a person is *born of woman,* he is conditioned by his origin (cf. 15:14; 25:4; Sir. 10:18; Matt. 11:11; Luke 7:28). Some interpret this phrase as emphasizing frailty (e.g., Rowley), while others find a reference to the ritual impurity that attends birth (e.g., Tur-Sinai). The latter view is anchored in the cultic laws that regulate the uncleanness of the mother after she gives birth, seven days for a male child and fourteen days for a female child (Lev. 12:2–5). Since bodily discharges were categorically treated as unclean, the discharges that attend the birth process led to the declaration of the new mother as ritually unclean. Whether any theological reasons lie behind these rules is difficult to ascertain. Certainly the ritual made the parents

4. Thinking that the second line is too short, Duhm supplies *mēḥaṭṭā'ōṯ,* "(not one is) without sin." In the opposite direction Hölscher eliminates the line, considering it to be poor poetry (cf. 4:17). Blommerde (*Northwest Semitic Grammar and Job,* pp. 69–70) revocalizes the consonants of MT to *mᵉṭummā',* a Pual participle meaning "impure," for MT *miṭṭāmē',* "from an unclean thing," and in the second line he reads *lē',* "the mighty one," instead of *lō',* "not": "Who can make the impure clean? The Mighty One alone." This translation offers fine sense, but it does not seem to fit the context, which is discussing human limitations rather than God's ability to create change. Gordis translates: "Who can distinguish the pure from the impure? No one!" He sees this as an oblique response to Eliphaz's unanswerable argument that no one is pure (4:17–19), meaning that God should have no trouble telling the pure from the impure, for he knows each person's nature.

5. It is better to take *'im* as "indeed" (Gordis) rather than "if"; it governs the whole verse (Driver-Gray).

6. Many read an imperative *waḥᵃḏal,* "leave alone," instead of MT *wᵉyeḥdāl,* "and let him cease." The sequence of *y*s and *w*s makes dittography quite possible. MT is the harder reading. The verb is a jussive used in a final clause after an imperative (Horst). P. Calderone ("*ḤDL II* in Poetic Texts," *CBQ* 23 [1961] 451–60) suggests a root *ḥdl* II, "to be fat, to fill oneself with food, to be prosperous," and reads the next word *'aḏ* as "food" to gain a reading "that he may be filled with food." Blommerde (*Northwest Semitic Grammar and Job,* pp. 70–71) works from this suggestion. For MT *'aḏ,* "until," he reads *'ōḏî,* "his lifetime": "That he may enjoy his lifetime." This reading, though, moves further from the original.

aware that both the mother and the child had to prepare themselves to enter God's presence. The context favors the interpretation that *born of woman* means that the child is frail and subject to all human weaknesses.

At best a person's life is *short-lived.* This phrase is an intentional reversal of the standard language denoting a happy life as "full of days" or "satisfied by days" (e.g., Gen. 25:8; 1 Chr. 29:28). During the person's brief stay on earth his days will be *sated with turmoil* (*rōgez;* cf. 3:26). That is, he will have to bear the emotional anguish that results from many ailments and difficult circumstances.

The analogies of *a flower* and *a shadow* illustrate well a person's short life span. In Palestine after the spring rains, flowers bloom in abundance and the fields glow from their splendor. But they last for only a moment. They soon fade from the hot desert winds (cf. Isa. 40:6–8; Ps. 103:15; 90:5–6). Not only is life brief; even worse, it passes so gradually into nothingness that a human being is hardly aware of the process. It is like a shadow, which grows longer as the daylight wanes, only to disappear at sunset leaving no trace of its existence (cf. 8:9; Ps. 102:12 [Eng. 11]; 144:4; Eccl. 6:12). The swift passage of time compounds the sorrows of a hard life. Amazingly, contemporary human beings have an even harder time than the patriarchs had in coping with the aging process. Through fashion, ointments, and exercise, we seek to retard the decline of strength, but aging inevitably wins the battle.

3 If humanity is so powerless, Job asks God caustically why he must keep everyone under continual scrutiny. *your eyes* means that God constantly surveys every person's ways. Lamentingly Job asks God, *Will you bring him into judgment with yourself?* The thrust of this question is that God is so mighty that no human being can survive a trial in which God is his plaintiff. Job is so distraught by God's hard line that he turns inside out another traditional concept. The belief that God's eyes see all things was a source of comfort to those afflicted, encouraging them to pray for God's help, for they were confident that God knew the truth of their petitions and the desperateness of their situation and would come to their rescue (cf. Isa. 37:17). But Job's thought is similar to the psalmist's: "Do not bring your servant into judgment, because no living person is righteous before you" (Ps. 143:2). With these probing questions Job challenges Bildad's proposition that God cuts off only the wicked in the prime of life (8:12–13). From Job's viewpoint, no one, not even a righteous person, is exempt from suffering. And if a righteous person should suffer unjustly, he cannot stand before the divine judge to win redress.

4 The interpretation of this verse is a puzzle.[7] It expresses an unreal

7. See J. K. Zink, "Uncleanness and sin: a study of Job xiv,4 and Psalm li,7," *VT* 17 (1967) 354–61.

possibility, as signaled by *Who can (mî yittēn)* in the first line and the answer *No one* in the second line. A straightforward reading of this verse seems to have Job saying that something is impossible even for God. To avoid that interpretation the Targum translates the verse: "None, but God, can make man clean who is naturally unclean" (see Kissane). But is that the issue? "Clean" and "unclean" may be used both in a physical sense, e.g., "pure gold" (28:19), and in a moral sense, e.g., "clean hands," i.e., hands that have done no wrong (17:9). These terms may relate to the birth process mentioned in v. 1. In giving birth a mother becomes ritually unclean. While it is not explicitly stated in any OT passage that this ritual impurity relates to inherited sin, a connection seems to be implied. That is, the ritual impurity attending birth foreshadows the certainty that the newborn child will become morally impure by transgressing the law. Not even God can prevent this from happening. He cannot make pure that which is impure by nature. Since this is true, Job is asking God why he holds a person accountable for every wrong he has done. Surely God cannot expect a human being to be flawless.

5 God has placed a limit to the number of days of each human life. Mention of such a restriction goes back to the time when God expelled the man and the woman from the Garden of Eden so that they would not have access to the tree of life (Gen. 3). Later, before the flood, God set a limit of 120 years to human life (Gen. 6:3). Whether that number referred to a period of grace between the announcement and the flood or to the limit for the length of any human life after the flood is not so much the issue as the fact that God set a limit as to the number of years that a person may live. Of course, God allows for great variance among individuals and the race as a whole. Yet long life is exceptional. In the OT seventy years became the ideal length of life (cf. Ps. 90:10). Anyone who surpassed that mark believed that he had received a rich blessing from God. The concept here is that the length of a human life is firmly fixed, for *determined (ḥārûṣ)* refers to a strict decree (cf. 1 K. 20:40; Isa. 10:22), and *limits (ḥōq)* means a prescribed amount.[8] In this tristich the reference to time moves from days to months to a lifetime.

6 Feeling the constraints of a limited life span, Job petitions God to turn his gaze from humanity in general. If God would spare humanity his constant surveillance, everybody would be able to experience some joy during his days (cf. Job 7:19; 9:34; 13:21). Their joy would be like that experienced by a hired worker (cf. 7:1–2). Satisfied and tired from a hard day's work, he rests well at night. His pleasure,[9] though it is limited, is rich.

8. Originally *ḥōq* meant "a statute," a law literally inscribed in stone. Then its meaning was extended to something "prescribed" as "an allowance" of food (Driver-Gray).

9. Another way to render Heb. *rāṣâ* is "pay or requite a debt" (Lev. 26:34, 41, 43). But the emphasis in this context moves in the direction of delight.

Job feels that God should grant each person at least that much relief from his painful burden.

(b) Reflections on the Possibility of Resurrection (14:7–12)

7 *"However, there is hope for a tree;*
if it is cut down, it will sprout again,
and its new shoots[1] will not fail.
8 *Though its roots grow old in the earth*
and its stump dies in the soil,
9 *at the scent of water it will sprout*
and put forth[2] shoots like a sapling.
10 *But a virile man dies and is helpless,*
a man expires and where is he?
11 *As[3] water disappears from the sea,*
or a river becomes parched and dry,
12 *so man lies down and will not rise;*
until the heavens are no more,[4] they will not awake,
and they will not rouse[5] from their sleep."[6]

7–9 Job speculates as to whether a person might live again after he dies. He observes that when a tree is cut down, sometimes a new shoot sprouts from the old stump. If that happens, a new tree eventually stands in place of the old. Even though a stump may be dormant for a long time, a good soaking rain often spurs new growth. Such a marvel suggests that the new

1. Heb. *yôneqeṯ* is "a twig or branch" (BDB, p. 413), but it can also mean "a tender, juicy sucker" (Delitzsch).

2. MT *weʿāśâ* is a perfect consecutive to carry on the idea of process (GKC, § 112m). Heb. *ʿāśâ* usually means "do, make"; here it has the sense of "yield, produce" (cf. Gen. 1:11, 12; Ezek. 17:6, 8, 23).

3. Duhm and others have questioned the authenticity of v. 11 because of its similarity to Isa. 19:5 (see n.7 below). But it is possible to take the introductory *waw* of v. 12 as the *waw adaequationis,* making v. 11 an analogy to v. 12 (see GKC, § 161a; Delitzsch; Gordis). Cf. Dhorme, who favors viewing v. 11 as presenting a pure impossibility.

4. For MT *biltî,* "not," many (e.g., Dhorme and Pope) prefer to read an infinitive construct *belōṯ,* "wasting away, disappearing," supported by the versions plus Ps. 102:27 (Eng. 26) and Isa. 51:6. But MT is possible, as Ps. 72:7; Isa. 14:6; and Mal. 3:10 demonstrate (Gordis).

5. The plural verb forms in the second and third lines may indicate that individuals as a group serve as the subject. But Blommerde (*Northwest Semitic Grammar and Job,* p. 71) suggests that the verbs preserve old indicative endings. Horst thinks that these lines were added as a quote from another context and consciously kept in the plural. If they were a secondary addition, v. 14a may have been parallel to v. 12a.

6. Cf. H. M. Orlinsky, "The Hebrew and Greek Texts of Job 14:12," *JQR* 28 (1937–38) 57–68.

growth has shot up at the scent of water. The stump has been waiting, so to speak, for a chance to send forth new life. A farmer takes advantage of this natural characteristic in trees. When a tree in his orchard begins to grow old and its branches split beneath the weight of its fruit, he cuts it down and grafts a new shoot into the stump. That shoot will grow into a tree that will bear fruit sooner than a newly planted sapling would. This custom was practiced in the Near East for vines, figs, pomegranates, and walnuts (Driver-Gray).

10 While a tree possesses great vitality, a human being, by comparison, is found wanting. He has no root system that will infuse new life into his decaying body. Nor is there a fountain of youth from which he may drink. A virile man is certain of death! As he falls, so he lies. A dead man remains dead forever. The first word, *a virile man* (*geḇer;* cf. 3:3) emphasizes a human being's strength and virility in contrast to his earthiness and limitedness connoted by the second word for *man* (*'āḏām;* cf. 14:1). When he dies, the breath that gave him life escapes his body and he is gone. He is nowhere to be found. The question—*where is he?*—hauntingly affirms the finality of his death. In the present world order no evidence exists that a person may return to life.

As a sage comparing a person's future to the way of a tree, Job stands in the center of OT tradition, for often the righteous are compared very favorably to a tree planted by a stream (e.g., Ps. 1). A tree has great resilience to stand before mighty storms. And if it should be blown down, a new, beautiful tree may grow from its stump. But Job finds that the tree is an inadequate analogy for insight into the question of whether a person may live again after death. Hakam thinks that with this analogy Job is rejecting Bildad's illustration of the righteous as a luxurious plant (Job 8:16–19). In that passage Bildad may have hinted at a second life for a person who is cut off from his prosperity and health just as there would be new growth for a tree torn from its place. If so, Job finds his view faulty, for he realizes that a human being lacks the power of renewal that is inherent in a tree.

11, 12 Job continues his search by comparing death with the way of water. This comparison, being vaguely stated, is variously interpreted. Job seems to refer to an inconceivable occurrence. It is improbable that all the water in *the sea* (*yām,* any large body of water such as a lake) would disappear or that a major river *(nāhār)* like the Jordan or the Nile would run dry.[7]

7. In Ugaritic poetry Prince Sea *(yamm)* parallels Judge River *(nāhār)*. The parallel here is thus ancient and deeply embedded in Northwest Semitic poetic imagery. In the OT this concept emerges in the picture of God's providing a way across the Reed Sea *(yām sûp)* and the River Jordan (*nāhār;* cf. Ps. 114:1–8). There is no allusion to Israel's history in this passage; more likely it draws on the rich mythopoetic imagery of the sea and

It is just as impossible that a human being who lies down in death will ever *awake,* i.e., rise from the dead. "A dead man is . . . like a dried-up *lake*" (Andersen). Since there was no technical word for resurrection when the book of Job was written, the concept was expressed by the piling up of words associated with "awakening from sleep":[8] "arise" *(qûm),* "awake" *(qîṣ),* "stir up, rouse" *(ʿûr).*[9] Job knows that an individual will not rise from the dead *until the heavens are no more.* Ancient people thought the continuance of the world was as certain as the movement of the sun and stars across the heavens (cf. Jer. 31:35–36; Ps. 72:5, 17; 89:30 [Eng. 29], 37–38 [Eng. 36–37]). The heavens would never disappear save in a special, catastrophic divine judgment (Isa. 51:6; cf. Ps. 102:27 [Eng. 26]). Therefore, Job sees no possibility for an individual to be brought back from the dead and given a second life on earth in compensation for having some unjust suffering.[10] That is, no concept of an individual's resurrection will alleviate either his anguish or his feeling that God has been unfair to him.[11]

(c) Job's Desire for Relief (14:13–17)

13 *"Would that you might hide me in Sheol,*
and keep me secluded until your wrath ceases,
and set a mark for me that you might remember me.
14 *If a man dies, will he live again?*[1]
All the days of my service I would hope,
until my renewal would come.

---

its defeat by the powers of order. In Isa. 19:5, an oracle against Egypt, this same image occurs. The second line is identical in both places, but in the first line Isaiah reads *weniššeṯû,* "they will dry up," instead of *ʾāzelû,* "they disappear," and in place of the usual writing of the preposition *mē-,* "from," the author of Job uses the poetic *minnî.* In Isaiah the waters will dry up under God's great judgment on Egypt.

8. Both Isa. 26:19 and Dan. 12:2, clear resurrection passages, use similar expressions for resurrection: *yiḥyû,* "they will live"; *yeqûmûn,* "they will rise"; *hāqîṣû,* "they will wake up."

9. Cf. J. Thomson, "Sleep: an aspect of Jewish anthropology," *VT* 5 (1955) 420–33.

10. Sirach too considered death as final for a human life (38:16–24). Job is correct in affirming that his resurrection would require a radical alteration in the world order. Other texts teach that only at the end of this age will God raise the dead. Since Job is reflecting on his personal predicament separate from any eschatological concerns, he is correct in denying resurrection as a way of escape from his dilemma. Because his aim is purely personal, there is no conflict between his rejection of an individual's return to life and the NT doctrine of resurrection.

11. Cf. N. H. Snaith, *The Book of Job,* SBT 2/11 (London: SCM; Naperville: Allenson, 1968), p. 96.

1. For MT *hayiḥyeh,* "will he live," LXX reads *zēsetai* (i.e., *yiḥyeh*), "he will live." LXX seems to have erred in omitting the interrogative particle; Driver-Gray and Gordis suggest that LXX intentionally made this change to remove the theological heresy.

15 *You would call and I would answer you,*
you would yearn for the work of your hands.
16 *But now you count my steps,*
and surely you notice my sin;
17 *my rebellion is sealed*[2] *in a bag,*
and you coat over my iniquity."

13 Realizing that an individual has no hope for a return to life after death, Job in anguish utters an unrealistic wish. He pleads to God: *hide me in Sheol . . . until your wrath ceases.* This request makes clear that Job attributes the cause of his suffering to God's wrath. He is also conscious of the axiom that when God acts in hot anger, it is only for a moment (Isa. 54:8). Therefore, if he could find a refuge during this time of wrath, he would escape the painful punishment inflicted by that wrath. Since there is no place on earth for Job to hide, his only hope is for a place of refuge in Sheol. Job is not thinking of Sheol as his final resting place, but as a hideout safe from the blasts of the divine anger (cf. Ps. 139:8; Amos 9:2–3). But since Sheol is the land of no return and the place where one is forgotten, in order to be remembered Job requests that God *set a mark,* i.e., erect a stela *(ḥōq),* inscribed with his name so that when his wrath has cooled, God will be reminded of his servant hidden in Sheol and restore him to life. Job believes that if God would grant this petition, he will in time restore and vindicate his servant. The deep-flowing current of Job's genuine trust in God surfaces again. He appeals to God's mercy as the way of escape from God's wrath.

14 The thought of a marker leads Job to ponder again the question "If a man dies, will he live again?" If God hides him in Sheol, there would have to be some way for him to be restored to earthly life. Although he has just discounted the possibility of personal resurrection, Job's wish pulls his mind back to this possibilty. He affirms that he would bear the days of his *service* (*ṣāḇā'*; cf. 7:2),[3] his time of undeserved suffering, in hope until his *renewal (ḥᵃlîpâ)* would come. *renewal* means a new vigorous life in a restored body. The Hebrew root is the same one translated *will sprout again* in reference to a tree in v. 7b. Returned to life, Job would have left his old, diseased body and be given a body full of vitality. Accompanying his renewal would be release from conscripted service. Given this possibility,

2. Gordis would like to revocalize the passive participle *ḥāṯûm,* "sealed," as an infinitive absolute, *ḥāṯōm,* "seal" (cf. 15:3, 35; Esth. 2:3). The consecutive infinitive absolute would function syntactically as an imperfect.

3. Heb. *ṣāḇā'* refers to military service and corvée labor. Here it is possible that the term "my service" in v. 14b refers to the time Job would spend hidden in Sheol (Horst). But since the time in Sheol is viewed as a respite, it seems unlikely that the time spent there would be considered "service." In 7:1–3 Job compares his affliction to a laborer's service. So "service" is taken to mean his term of suffering.

he could endure his present affliction sustained by the vision of the wonderful future that would be his. This possibility, though, is just as hypothetical as his being hidden in Sheol.

The NT teaches that Christ has defeated death, mankind's bitterest foe, and that God will raise the dead to a final judgment. But this doctrine becomes central to biblical faith only after the resurrection of Christ, for it gains its validation in Christ's triumph over death.[4] Without that foreknowledge Job can only conclude death is final for a human being. Furthermore, Job is thinking of an individual's returning back to life for a limited time. His view here is closer to a concept of resuscitation than to resurrection. By contrast the biblical doctrine of resurrection posits that the entire human race will be raised from the dead, some to eternal life and others to eternal damnation.

15 With a renewed life would come a welcomed revitalization of Job's relationship with God. Their communication would be open and reciprocal. God *would call* or summon Job to court, and Job *would answer* him, i.e., defend himself (cf. Habel, OTL). Job would be vindicated. Then he would have fellowship with God, for once again God would yearn for the work of his own hands (*maʿaśēh yāḏêḵā;* cf. 10:3). The word for *yearn* or long for *(kāsap̱)* comes from the same root as the word "silver" *(kesep̱)*. It may mean "to turn pale, i.e., the color of silver, from intense longing or desire" (Pope).[5] It depicts the intensity of God's desire. When God seeks him again, Job will no longer feel that he is the spurned object of God's toilsome labor (10:3). Rather he will again have a life filled with the spontaneous joy that attends God's presence.

16, 17 In the meantime God afflicts Job unceasingly. The reference to God's vigilance may be understood in two different ways. The opening particles *kî ʿattâ* may mean either "for then," a continuation of Job's wishful thinking, or *but now,* signaling that Job returns to lament his real dilemma. The metaphor *count my steps* may connote either scrupulous attention to detect the slightest wrong that the observed party might commit (cf. 10:14) or protection and care (cf. 31:4; 34:21). The ambivalence continues in the statement *my rebellion is sealed in a bag*. The picture could be that of storing valuables like gems or silver coins in a bag. Such valuables were put into a bag, which was fastened, daubed with wax, and pressed with a seal (cf. Gen. 42:35; Prov. 7:20). The bag could not be opened without breaking the seal. Or the picture could be that of an old accounting practice

4. For a discussion of the OT view of "death and beyond" see H. H. Rowley, *The Faith of Israel* (London: SCM; Philadelphia: Westminster, 1956), pp. 150–76.

5. See, e.g., Gen. 31:30; Ps. 17:12 (the lion yearning after its prey); 84:3 (Eng. 2; a person longing for Yahweh's courts); Zeph. 2:1.

in which a stone was placed in a bag to represent one item of a commodity, e.g., a sheep.[6] Whenever a sheep was added or deleted from the flock, a stone was added or removed from the bag. The basic question of interpretation is, does God seal Job's sins in a bag in order to put an end to Job's accountability for them, or does he store them in a bag in order that he might open that bag at the final judgment and execute a full sentence against Job for all his sins? Usually forgiven or passed-over sins are described as forgotten or cast away, while anything classified as sealed is kept in store for the future. For example, Hosea warns Israel that Ephraim's iniquity is bound up and their sin is stored up for God's coming judgment (13:12; cf. Deut. 32:34–35; Rom. 2:5). In the light of the context the imagery of vv. 16–17 is taken to mean that God observes all of Job's ways, notices every failure, and stores up these errors in a bag or possibly keeps count of them by placing a stone in his bag for each sin. Instead of atoning for Job's sins or wiping them out, as some interpret the phrase *coat over my iniquity,* God merely daubs them with whitewash, a coating that the rain of judgment will easily wash away. Thus Job's imaginative hope for a brighter future evaporates before his apprehension that worse affliction is in store for him.

Job's craving for God's love is deeply frustrated by his present experience of God as a relentless tyrant. The juxtaposition of these verses accentuates the deep spiritual agony that stands at the center of Job's testing. Job's faith struggles against the harsh realities of the divine curse on his life. His hopes for relief are dashed by the gloomy manner in which God is treating him. Fortunately, Job does not yield either to depression or to his utopian fantasies, but rather copes with his situation as it is and reaches out to God, seeking a real change in their relationship.

(d) The Terrors of Death (14:18–22)

18 *"But as a mountain surely crumbles,*[1]
and as a boulder is moved from its place,

6. An interesting practice of accounting in ancient Mesopotamia is noted by A. L. Oppenheim ("On an Operational Device in Mesopotamian Bureaucracy," *JNES* 18 [1959] 121–28). An ovoid clay pouch was found with an inscription on the outside listing stones for forty-eight sheep and goats, their kind and condition, and the pouch contained forty-eight stones. Apparently as an animal was used for sacrifice or became lost or was sent for shearing, a pebble was transferred from one pouch to another, marking the specific status of that animal. This separation enabled an accurate and ready accounting of one's inventory. Such a practice may bear on the picture of a sealed bag in this passage. At least it suggests that Job's sins were being accurately accounted for by God's diligent surveillance. This background lends weight, though far from conclusive, to the view that Job's sins are being stored up for judgment.

1. MT *nôpēl yibbôl,* lit. "falling, it withers," is problematic. Heb. *nāḇēl,* "sink, wither and fall, fade," is used of leaves fading or falling (Isa. 1:30; 34:4) and of the earth withering (Isa. 24:4). Its use with mountains appears strange. Driver-Gray suggest the

19 *as water pulverizes stones,*
and as a torrent[2] *sweeps away the earth's soil,*
so you make man's hope to perish.
20 *You attack him powerfully*[3] *and he passes away;*[4]
him whose countenance is changed you send away.[5]
21 *His sons receive honor, but he does not know;*
or they are brought low, but he does not perceive it.
22 *Rather his own flesh pains him,*
and his soul mourns for himself."

18, 19 Job expresses his fearful thoughts by reciting hymnic lines that recount God's awesome power as manifested in natural catastrophes. His mind muses on themes similar to those found in 9:5–10. *Mountains* and *boulders,* symbols of prominence and steadfastness, *crumble* and *move* about in a great avalanche caused by God's appearing. Rushing *water pulverizes stones,* and *a torrent,* swelled by drenching rains and filled with debris, *sweeps away the earth's soil,* cutting deep trenches in the landscape. Such is the way of *man's hope.* It perishes before the overwhelming might of God's actions. Job is saying that his hope, like the landscape, has been scarred by ominous forces of destruction.

---

meaning "crumbles away." If this meaning is possible, MT offers a vivid text with fine assonance. Duhm reconstructs the text with the root *nbl: nāḇôl yibbōl,* "it surely withers." Since it was easy to confuse the letters *b* and *p* both in ancient script and in pronunciation, it is quite possible to understand the path to the present text. Here Duhm's reading is followed, and *nāḇôl* is given the meaning proposed by Driver-Gray. Another reconstructed reading, based on LXX and Syr., is *nāpôl yippôl,* "it surely falls" (see Dhorme, *BHS*).

2. For MT *s*^{e}*pîḥeynâ,* "branch," it seems better to read *s*^{e}*ḥîpâ,* "rainstorm, torrent," cognate to Arab. *saḥīfeh,* "torrential rain" (Dhorme, Tur-Sinai, Gordis). MT is then an error of metathesis.

3. Hakam understands *lāneṣaḥ* as "powerfully" (cf. 15:18). D. W. Thomas takes it as denoting a superlative ("The Use of *nēṣaḥ* as a Superlative in Hebrew," *JSS* 1 [1956] 106–109). Blommerde (*Northwest Semitic Grammar and Job,* p. 72) sees it as modifying *wayyah*^{a}*lōḵ,* "and he passes," in second position by reason of an emphatic *waw.*

4. MT *wayyah*^{a}*lōḵ* is a poetic form for *wayyēlēḵ,* "and he passes."

5. The precise meaning of the phrase *m*^{e}*šanneh pānāyw* is not obvious; it occurs only here in the OT. In addition, the subject of the verb is uncertain—is it God or Job? Taking God as the subject, Budde and others emend the participle to an imperfect *t*^{e}*šanneh.* But the fact that this verse is a chiasm, a:b::b':a', indicates that Job is the subject of the participle. The meaning of this phrase may be clarified by its use in Sir. 12:18; 13:25 (Hebrew text v. 24), where it refers to the change of face caused by one's feelings (Dhorme). Following Ibn Ezra, Fohrer and Gordis take this phrase to describe rigor mortis. But based on the Amarna correspondence, B. Halpern ("Yhwh's summary justice in Job xiv 18," *VT* 28 [1978] 472–74) argues that *m*^{e}*šannen pānāyw* means "he contemplates treachery." While this is an intriguing suggestion, the former translation is kept because death dominates this context.

20 Similarly God overpowers an individual. Having no resources to withstand the divine onslaught, a person *passes away (hālaḵ)*. This verb, which means literally "walk, go," can be used euphemistically for dying (cf. 10:21; Ps. 39:14 [Eng. 13]; Eccl. 3:20). As death steals the soul a person's countenance turns ghostly pale. In this way God sends a person to the netherworld.

21 In Sheol that person is aware of only his own disembodied, shadowy existence. He is oblivious to any other events, including the fate of his beloved children. Whether they *receive honor (kāḇēḏ)* or *are brought low (ṣāʿar)* happens without his knowing it.[6] This perspective counters any view of retribution that argues that a wicked person who is successful is punished through the misfortunes that beset his children, or conversely that an ill-fated upright man will receive his due in the bestowing of honor on his children.

22 Before death the entire person is caught in the throes of pain and is reduced to mourning solely for himself. The totality of a person's preoccupation with himself at this time is conveyed by the parallel terms *flesh* or body *(bāśār)* and *soul* or self *(nepeš)*. The use of *flesh* suggests that such pain is experienced in anticipation of death rather than in Sheol itself, for in OT thought at death the body remains behind in the grave and the person or self descends to Sheol. The idea of continued pain in the netherworld is mentioned only in Isa. 66:24 in the OT. Even though it was developed later in some Jewish beliefs as evidenced in Jdt. 16:17, it is not part of Job's thinking, for above he had entertained the idea of escape from God's wrath in Sheol or the grave (14:13; cf. ch. 3). The fact that the sufferer centers his thoughts on his own predicament is emphasized by the prepositional phrase "on him" *(ʿālāyw)*,[7] standing at the center of both lines.

AIM

In the first cycle the friends seek to comfort Job by instructing him in God's ways and exhorting him to seek God. But Job perceives that his friends have

6. The two verbs "honor" *(kāḇēḏ)* and "be brought low" *(ṣāʿar)* are also juxtaposed in Jer. 30:19b. Their meaning in that context is quantitative, but here the emphasis is qualitative (Gordis).

7. This prepositional phrase is difficult to render smoothly in the translation; cf. Dhorme: "His flesh is grieved only for himself, His soul laments only over himself"; Tur-Sinai: "Only with his flesh on him doth he feel pain, and while his soul is with him doth he mourn"; Driver-Gray: "Only his flesh upon him hath pain, And his soul upon him mourneth"; Gordis, "Indeed, his flesh is pained within him and his spirit is in mourning."

failed to comprehend the uniqueness of his experience. Therefore, he straightforwardly accuses them of false teaching. They have whitewashed the hard facts of his misfortune with easy platitudes. In fact, they have deviated so far from truth and have so failed to show compassion that Job issues a warning: even they may not be able to stand in the divine presence. When God appears, their lies will be exposed and they will cower before the divine splendor. At the conclusion of the first cycle Job is abandoning any hope that his friends will be able to aid him in his effort to achieve reconciliation with God.

Job resolves, therefore, to pursue his complaint directly with God himself. He will prepare his case and argue it before the divine Judge, for that Judge alone can pronounce him innocent.

Job supports his resolve by lamenting his bitter feelings. He complains that God has weighed him down with an intolerable burden. If God would give him a reprieve, he could defend himself before the heavenly court. Job mourns the hardship of human life in general. Very troublesome to one in pain is the brevity of life. Inspired by the way new shoots grow from an old stump, Job wishes that he could die and then return to life. This hope quickly fizzles as he realizes that the human body is not like a tree—it has no inner reserve to give birth to a second life. Death for a human being is final. In desperation Job wonders if it would be possible for God to hide him in Sheol until his wrath subsides. But this wish fades before the reality of God's present treatment of him. Therefore, Job concludes by meditating on the terribleness of death. He realizes that if he is to find vindication, it must be in this life.

Job's words reveal the sense of futility that haunts him. But they also portray the steel nerve deep inside him that will neither let him succumb to his illness nor seek any easy solution that will relieve his pain by compromising his integrity. His struggling faith now and then compels him to make remarkable assertions of confidence in God. These assertions lead Job to persevere on the path of seeking God while he holds on to his integrity.

B. THE SECOND CYCLE (15:1–21:34)

The second cycle contains a full round of speeches. Nevertheless, each of the comforter's speeches is shorter than in the first cycle, save for Zophar's, which is longer (56 lines vs. 40). As in the first cycle Eliphaz's speech (68 lines) is significantly longer than those of the other two friends (47 and 56 lines respectively). Also, Job's speeches continue to be longer than the preceding comforter's speech (79, 58, 67 lines respectively). It is interesting that Zophar's speech is longer than Bildad's, and Job's speech following Zophar's is longer than his speech following Bildad's. This variation in speech length adds to the movement of the dialogue. Furthermore, instead of Job's speeches consisting of two parts as in the first cycle—one part addressed to the friends and a second part addressed to God—Job speaks primarily to one party, either God (chs. 16–17) or the friends (chs. 19, 21).

In this cycle the friends are becoming impatient with Job as they suspect that his affliction means that he must be guilty of some serious sin. Therefore, they focus their rhetoric on the terrible fate that befalls the wicked person, for they wish to convince Job that he will undergo greater hardship if he does not repent. But Job firmly rejects their calls to repentance. Amid his agonizing laments he expresses his faith in God as his heavenly witness (chs. 16–17), even his Kinsman-Redeemer (ch. 19), the one who will vindicate his honor by testifying to his innocence. In his last speech of this cycle Job complains regretfully that in the real world the wicked do prosper (ch. 21). With this complaint he directly challenges the doctrine of retribution that the comforters defended ardently. It is clear that Job has turned away from the traditional theology as expressed by the comforters. Remaining convinced of his innocence, he searches diligently for some way to find reconciliation with God other than the way of repentance.

1. ELIPHAZ'S SECOND SPEECH (15:1–35)

Eliphaz's second speech has two major divisions: a disputation rejecting Job's claim to wisdom (vv. 2–16), and an instruction about the woes of the wicked (vv. 17–35). In the first division Eliphaz delivers a reprimand speech. It comprises a mixture of rhetorical questions (vv. 2–3, 7–9, 11–13, 14) and definitive statements (vv. 4–6, 10, 15–16). Eliphaz adopts this style to ridicule Job's self-defense. Also, taken aback by Job's passionate claim of innocence, he wants to persuade Job that the teaching of the wise, among whom the friends are numbered, far outweighs Job's knowledge. He believes that Job must abandon his claim to innocence, for his own words are proving him guilty, and certainly he must leave off his harsh complaints against God.

In the second division, after requesting Job's attention (vv. 17–19), Eliphaz, like a wisdom teacher, vividly describes the plight of the wicked person (vv. 20–35). That person is characterized as a tyrant who brazenly defies even God. For Eliphaz, the ways of nature guarantee that such a person will not escape his destined ill-fate. By implication he is warning Job of the consequences that will befall him if he does not repent from his stubborn way.

a. A Disputation Rejecting Job's Claim to Wisdom (15:1–16)

1 *Eliphaz the Temanite answered:*
2 *"Does a wise man answer with windy knowledge*
or fill his belly with the east wind
3 *by arguing[1] with useless rhetoric*
or words[2] without value?
4 *Surely you break faith*
and diminish meditation before God,
5 *because your iniquity teaches your mouth,*
and you choose the tongue of the crafty.
6 *Your mouth condemns you—not I;*
your lips answer against you.
7 *Were you the first[3] man born?*
Were you brought forth before the hills?
8 *Did you listen[4] in on the council of God,*
or do you monopolize wisdom?
9 *What do you know that we do not know,*
or understand that we do not?
10 *We have the gray-headed[5] and the aged with us,*
older in days than your father.
11 *Are God's consolations too little for you,*
the words which are spoken gently with you?
12 *Why have you let your heart carry you away?[6]*
And why do your eyes flash[7]

1. The infinitive absolute forms a circumstantial clause that describes the manner of the actions mentioned in v. 2 (GKC, § 113h).

2. LXX reads *en lógois,* "with words," suggesting a text with *bemillîm* instead of *ûmillîm* (or for syllable count possibly *ûḇemillîm*). LXX may not have had a different *Vorlage,* however; perhaps it merely supplied the preposition *be* from the first line.

3. MT *riʾyšôn* is a plene spelling of *rʾšwn,* "first"; cf. *rîšôn* in 8:8.

4. Driver-Gray suggest that the imperfect signifies either a vivid description of the past, referring to a particular council session, or it denotes repeated attendance at the council.

5. The Qal participle *śāḇ,* "the gray-headed," is also found in Sir. 32:3 and in Aramaic, e.g., Ezra 5:5; 9:6, 7, 8, 14.

6. The suffix on *yiqqāḥaḵā,* "it has taken you," stands as a dative (Pope, and Blommerde, *Northwest Semitic Grammar and Job,* p. 73; cf. Hos. 4:11; Cant. 4:9). G. R. Driver ("Misreadings in the OT," *WO* [1947–52] 235) posits that *yiqqaḥ* is related to the Arab. *waqiḥa,* "be bold, shameless," hence "Wherein has thy heart emboldened thee?" (cf. Num. 16:1; Prov. 6:25).

7. The verb *yirzemûn* is usually taken as a by-form of *rāmaz,* "make a sign," or used with the eyes to mean "wink, flash," common in Aramaic. It could be an error of metathesis for *yirmezûn* (see Targ., Syr.; Dhorme; Horst; Grabbe, *Comparative Philology,* pp. 66–67; cf. Tur-Sinai). Another possibility based on LXX is to read *yerûmûn,* "be haughty," as in Prov. 6:17.

13 *that you vent your anger against God*[8]
and pour out words[9] *from your mouth?*
14 *What is man that he could be pure,*
or one born of woman that he could be righteous?
15 *Behold, he puts no trust in his holy ones,*
and the heavens are not pure in his sight.
16 *Surely, then, vile and corrupt*[10] *is man,*
who drinks injustice like water."

2, 3 Opening in the same style as his first speech (4:2), Eliphaz asks Job a rhetorical question expecting a negative answer. The question seeks to make a distinction between a truly wise person and one who exhibits only a show of learning. Since one's use of language betrays his origin and training, those who had received their training under a wise teacher were identified by their discipline in speaking and by their eloquence. Conversely, verbose ramblings like those that pour out of Job identify him as a fool.

The subject of the question, *a wise man (ḥāḵām),* stands first for emphasis. The Hebrew is vague about the identity of the wise man. Does it refer to Eliphaz or Job? If it refers to Eliphaz, the question is, Should he, a wise man, make a response to one whose knowledge is so windy? But if it refers to Job, it asks how can he count himself among the wise and continue to utter so many words? The latter interpretation is favored, for this question seems to be a rebuke of Job's assertion that he is as wise as his comforters (12:3 and 13:2). That is, Job is speaking far too much to be numbered among the wise. In fact, his words have been so irate that one suspects that he must *fill his belly [beṭen] with the east wind.* The *east wind (qāḏîm)* is the strong, hot wind that blows off the desert. It is dreaded in the Near East because its dry burning heat brings days of irritability and listlessness. The *belly* refers to the lower abdomen, the chambers of deepest thoughts and feelings (cf. Prov. 18:8; 20:27, 30; 22:18).[11] But Eliphaz uses "belly" disparagingly. He is ridiculing Job, saying that his words flow from a belly filled with hot air, not from his heart, the center of reason. He thus judges Job's resolve to argue

8. L. Fisher ("An Amarna Age Prodigal," *JSS* 3 [1958] 115) takes *tāšîḇ'el-'ēl* to mean "to turn against God," i.e., "to break a relationship." In an Ugaritic passage (RS 16.129; cf. also 16.157) *za-ki* (cf. Heb. *yizkeh* in v. 14) means "being free" from servitude and obligation to parents; see KB, p. 258.

9. MT *millîn,* "words," is considered too mild by Duhm. He recommends reading *m^erî* (or in pause *merî*), "bitter." But GKC, § 125c considers MT an example of "indeterminateness for the sake of amplification"; this phrase is then translated "reproachful words" (cf. 8:10).

10. The forms *niṯʿāḇ,* "vile," and *neʾĕlāḥ,* "corrupt," are Niphal participles functioning as gerunds (GKC, § 116e).

11. Cf. D. Freedman and J. Lundbom, *TDOT,* II:96–97.

his case directly with God to be merely *useless rhetoric*. His words, being *without value,* will have no power to persuade God.

4 Eliphaz then accuses Job: *Surely you break faith* (*yirʾâ,* lit. "fear," elliptical for "the fear of God," hence "faith" or "devotion"; cf. 4:6). The structure of the accusation with the particle *Surely (ʾap̱)* and the personal pronoun *you (ʾattâ)* underscores the fact that Job, not God, is responsible for breaking faith. In addition, his haughty, heated words *diminish meditation before God.* Being parallel to *faith, meditation (śîḥâ)* means conversation with God or meditative prayer.[12] Is Eliphaz concerned that Job's much speaking harms the faith of those listening to him or his own faith? Since in this pericope Eliphaz is distressed by the heresy he hears in Job's reasoning, he is troubled that Job is destroying his own faith in God.

5 Eliphaz concludes that the reason Job is destroying his own faith lies in the fact that his iniquity teaches his mouth. That is, his wrongdoing moves him to defend himself by complaining against his friends and God. To cover up his error he *chooses [bāḥar] the tongue of the crafty.* The word *bāḥar* describes a deliberate choice. *crafty (ʿᵃrûmîm)* may be used in a positive sense to mean "sensible, prudent," or, as here, in a negative sense to mean "cunning, shrewd." Thus Job is fully responsible for his deceptive, cunning rhetoric.

6 Eliphaz states poignantly, *Your mouth condemns you—not I.* The words that come from his own lips testify against him. Therefore, Eliphaz has no need to prove that Job is guilty and thus deserving of his present affliction. He is agreeing with Job's anxiety that in a dispute with God his own mouth would show him guilty (9:20), while soundly rejecting Job's personal conviction that he is blameless. Because Eliphaz cannot fathom that Job's complaints could possible come from a genuine search for meaning amid suffering, he can only conclude that Job is guilty of speaking too harshly against God.

7, 8 With scathing sarcasm Eliphaz responds to Job's claim that he is not inferior to his friends in wisdom (12:3; 13:1–2). Overinterpreting Job's self-defense, he reacts as though Job implied that his possession of wisdom was superior to everybody else's. Therefore, he puts to Job three sets of rhetorical questions. Caustically he asks Job, *Were you the first man born?* Though he may be referring to Adam, whose name simply means "man" *(ʾāḏām),* he seems to have in mind the myth of the heavenly Adam, the primordial man who served as the model for the earthly Adam.[13] This

12. In Ps. 102:2 (Eng. 1) *śîaḥ* is parallel to "prayer," *tᵉpillâ.*

13. Hakam understands the first line as asking: Are you the first man that was born; hence all those before you are beasts, none of them understand anything! But vv. 7–8 interpreted together refer to a heavenly Adam. They seem to draw from a hymn in praise of man's origin. Unfortunately that hymn has not been preserved. It may have been similar

primordial Adam was the first of God's creative acts. God brought him into existence prior to his creation of the earth, as the phrase *brought forth before the hills* indicates, for the hills were considered the oldest part of the earth. This heavenly man was exceedingly wise, since he sat in the heavenly council (cf. 1:6) and had access to God. That is why Eliphaz asks Job, *Did you listen in on the council of God, or do you monopolize wisdom [tigraʿ ʾēleyḵā ḥoḵmâ]?*[14] i.e., draw wisdom from the heavenly storehouse for yourself? This man would have been present at the creation of the world and learned the key knowledge associated with origins (cf. chs. 38–39). If Job were identified with this man, he would be far wiser than the trusted elders could ever be, even wiser than Eliphaz, who had received a special revelation from God (4:12–21). Of course, Eliphaz's point is that such a claim is absurd.

9, 10 Continuing with rhetorical questions, Eliphaz directly asks Job, *What do you know that we do not know?* The implied answer, of course, is, Nothing. Job has no significant insights that his comforters do not have, for he has no claim to wisdom. Eliphaz proves his position by pointing out that the gray-headed, the oldest, are numbered among the comforters. He even seems to be stating that in their company there is at least one older than even Job's father, rather than merely saying that the comforters are numbered among the most venerated of the aged. But the interpretation that Eliphaz is literally as old as Job's father is doubtful. There is no indication in the narrative that Job's father is still living. Eliphaz then is using hyperbole. Nevertheless, his wording might suggest that Job is younger than some of the three comforters. Eliphaz is arguing that since the three comforters are counted among the aged, their speeches, not Job's, are endowed with wisdom.

11 Eliphaz derides Job for not accepting the comforts of God. *God's consolations (tanḥumôṯ ʾēl)* are *the words spoken gently* by the friends, who represent God to Job and who utter the wisdom of the ages. Thus, in Eliphaz's opinion, to reject their consoling advice is tantamount to rejecting God's consolations. In particular, Eliphaz means that Job has not heeded the message he had received in a vision (4:12–16). Therefore, Eliphaz reiterates that message at the end of this pericope (vv. 14–16).

---

to the poetic account of wisdom's origin found in Prov. 8:22–31, for the language of v. 7a is almost identical to that of Prov. 8:25b. Like wisdom, this heavenly man was the first of God's creative acts (cf. Ezek. 28:11–19 and Sir. 49:16).

14. Hakam thinks that Heb. *gāraʿ* means either "to take a large swallow of a drink," i.e., gulp down wisdom in one swallow, or "to subtract or diminish," i.e., to diminish the supply of wisdom from the heavenly treasure. Ringgren understands it to mean "draw wisdom to himself" (*TDOT*, III:67).

12, 13 Next, Eliphaz asks Job a double question. *Why have you let your heart carry you away? And why do your eyes flash?* In Semitic thought the heart *(lēḇ)* is the center of one's volitional and rational life as well as the tender affections. The eyes are closely associated with the heart, for they both send information to the heart (cf. 31:1, 7) and reflect the heart's disposition. Eliphaz is claiming that the flashing in Job's eyes reveals his anger at God for punishing him. The word translated *anger, rûaḥ* (lit. "wind, spirit"), may stand for a dominant mood, e.g., lust (Hos. 4:12), anger (Judg. 8:3; Prov. 16:32), or extreme displeasure (Eccl. 10:4). Eliphaz uses *rûaḥ,* for he perceives that Job's crafty thinking is controlled by his anger.[15] That is why Job's mouth is pouring out such caustic and reproachful words against God. Whereas Job has stated that his distress arises from being discredited (12:2–6; 13:1–12), Eliphaz says that the cause of his anger is frustrated pride.

14–16 To buttress his condemnation of Job's reasoning, Eliphaz reiterates the message revealed to him in a night vision.[16] He opens with a rhetorical question about human purity (v. 14), and then makes an assertion about heaven (v. 15), in order to draw his weighty conclusion about humanity (v. 16). His thesis is that it is impossible for a person to *be pure* or accounted *righteous,* since *one born of woman* (the very phrase used by Job in 14:1) is morally weak by nature. In contrast to his presentation of the inspired message in 4:17, which speaks of a person never being purer than God, Eliphaz now posits that no person may achieve moral virtue because of the limitations of human nature. The impossibility that there could exist a virtuous human being is established by the fact that God does not even put any *trust in his holy ones,* i.e., the angels (cf. 5:1). Since the angels are mere creatures, they too may err or fail (4:18). Not even their place of abode, *the heavens,* is *pure* or spotless in God's sight. Here the term *the heavens* could refer to the beings who inhabit heaven more than to a place; cf. 38:7, where "the morning stars" parallel "the sons of God," another name for "angels" (cf. 25:2).

15. A similar thought is expressed in Hos. 4:11. Hosea says that harlotry and wine have stolen "the understanding" *(lēḇ)* of God's people so that they cannot find their way back to God (cf. Cant. 4:9). And in Prov. 6:25 the wisdom teacher warns his student not to be taken in by a harlot's beauty, lest her beauty capture his heart so that he can no longer choose to avoid her wiles.

16. The wording is slightly different from that in 4:17–18. The word "be pure" *(zāḵâ)* is used in place of "be clean" *(ṭāhar),* and the verbs are inverted in these lines. Instead of *geḇer,* "a strong man," the phrase "born of a woman" *(yᵉlûḏ ʾiššâ)* is used, and the position of man opposite God is missing here. Also in v. 15 "his holy ones" *(qᵉḏōšîm)* is substituted for "his servants" (*ʿăḇāḏîm;* 4:18), and "heavens" replaces "his messengers."

Eliphaz concludes emphatically that it is impossible for any human being to be pure. He describes humanity as *vile [niṯʿāḇ] and corrupt [neʾᵉlāḥ]*. The first word refers to something that is disgusting and repulsive.[17] The second means "filthy"; in Arabic it is used for the souring of milk.[18] Man by nature *drinks injustice like water*. That is, humanity is prone to do evil. Believing thoroughly in human depravity, it is no wonder that Eliphaz is utterly astounded that Job could think that in himself he is innocent. All his knowledge of theology and logic denies such a possibility. In other words, Eliphaz evaluates Job's claim of innocence to be a strong delusion. In fact, he sees in Job's bearing the very reasons why God is punishing Job and will continue to punish him until his attitude changes.

b. An Instruction about the Woes of the Wicked (15:17–35)

17 *"I shall tell you;[1] listen to me;*
that which[2] I have seen let me recount,[3]
18 *that which the wise have told*
and their fathers have not concealed[4]—
19 *to them alone the land was given,*
and no alien passed among them.
20 *All his days the wicked person is racked with pain,*
even throughout the years[5] stored up for the tyrant.

17. The Hebrew root *tʿb* occurs in Ps. 14:1, "Their [i.e., those who deny good] deeds are corrupt." That psalm emphasizes man's total inability to do good. Cf. P. Humbert, "Le substantif *toʿēbā* et le verbe *tʿb* dans l'Ancien Testament," *ZAW* 72 (1960) 217–37.

18. In Hebrew this root appears in only one other place, and it refers to man's moral corruption (cf. Ps. 14:3 = 53:4 [Eng. 3]). G. R. Driver ("Some Hebrew Words," *JTS* 29 [1927–28] 391–94) traces the root *ʾlḥ* to Akk. *alāḫu*, "luxuriant in abundance." In Hebrew it moved from the meaning "debauched with luxury" to "corrupt."

1. Dhorme, Driver-Gray, Preuss (*TDOT*, IV:248), et al. consider *ḥawwâ*, "tell," an Aramaism; elsewhere in the Hebrew sections of the OT it occurs only in 32:6, 10, 17; 36:2; Ps. 19:3 (Eng. 2); cf. Sir. 16:23; 42:19.

2. The demonstrative pronoun *zeh*, an accusative, comes first to introduce an independent relative clause (GKC, § 138h).

3. The *waw* on *waʾᵃsappērâ* is the *waw apodosis* and is not translated (GKC, § 143d).

4. In the second line N. Sarna treats both *m*s on *mēʾᵃḇôṯām* as enclitic ("Some Instances of the Enclitic -m in Job," *JJS* 6 [1955] 108–10). While the first *m* may be an enclitic particle and should be attached to the verb *kiḥᵃḏûm*, it is better to interpret the second *m* as the plural ending; cf. the same form in 8:8 in a similar context.

5. The meaning of *mispar šānîm* is not "fewness of years" (contra Pope), for that would be *šᵉnôṯ mispār*, but "throughout the years" (Driver-Gray, Dhorme, Rowley, Gordis). Cf. Blommerde, *Northwest Semitic Grammar and Job*, pp. 75–76, who follows Dahood in rendering the phrase "beyond number are the years."

21 *Terrifying sounds are in his ears;*
while he is at peace the marauder[6] *may assail him.*
22 *He has no confidence that he will escape*[7] *from darkness;*
he is marked[8] *for the sword.*
23 *He wanders about for bread, 'Where is it?'*[9]
He knows that ruin[10] *is prepared for him.*
24 *The day of darkness terrifies him;*[11]
distress and anguish overpower him,
like a king prepared for an attack,
25 *because he has stretched out his hand against God,*
and against Shaddai he has vaunted himself.
26 *He charges at him with outstretched neck,*[12]
with his thick-bossed shield,
27 *though he puffed his face with fat*
and bloated his loins with flesh.[13]
28 *He will dwell in devastated cities,*
houses without inhabitant[14]
which are destined to become a rubbish pile.
29 *He will no longer be rich and his wealth will not endure;*
his possessions[15] *will not spread over the earth.*

6. M. Dahood (*Bib* 53 [1972] 403) considers *šôḏēḏ* an epithet for death, "Devastator." While this suggestion has good possibilities, the context describes a series of woes that terrorize a person and slowly rob him of life.

7. The phrase headed by the infinitive construct functions as the object of the verb (GKC, § 114c).

8. According to Gordis the Ketib *weṣāpû* is an older form of the Qal passive participle, "look forward to" or "expect" (see also Dhorme, who translates it "marked" and notes *heʿāśû* in 41:25 [Eng. 33]). Therefore, it is not necessary to read the Qere *ṣāpûy* or to change MT to *ṣāpûn,* "reserved," on the assumption that an *n* has fallen out (contra Driver-Gray; cf. Fohrer).

9. Another possible reading for *ʾayyēh,* "where is it," is *ʾayyâ,* "a vulture"; cf. 28:7; LXX; Dhorme). Then *nōḏēḏ,* "he wanders," is taken from the root *ydd,* "throw": "He is thrown as food for the vulture."

10. It seems best to consider MT *beyāḏô,* "in his hand," as a corruption of *pîḏô,* "ruin, disaster" (12:5; 30:24; 31:29; Dhorme, Pope, Rowley). Cf. Driver-Gray and Gordis, who offer different emendations; Tur-Sinai defends MT.

11. Since v. 23b is quite long and its last two words, *yôm-ḥōšeḵ,* "the day of darkness," are an excellent parallel to *ṣar ûmeṣûqâ,* "distress and anguish," in v. 24a (cf. Zeph. 1:15), it seems best to join this phrase to v. 24, as in LXX (followed by most commentators). As a result, v. 24 becomes a tristich. Cf. Gordis and Tur-Sinai, who defend MT.

12. Tur-Sinai thinks that the phrase "with the neck" refers to "the neck of his armour," i.e., "a hauberk."

13. Heb. *pîmâ,* "flesh," is likely related to Akk. *piāmu,* "robust" (Pope).

14. The preposition *lāmô* functions as an ethical dative, i.e., "for themselves" (Driver-Gray), so lit. "houses which they will not inhabit for themselves."

15. No convincing solution for the strange MT *minlām* has been given. Possibly it is two words, *min lām,* "what is theirs?" (see Tur-Sinai, Gordis). Other suggested

30 *He will not escape darkness;*
his shoots the flame will dry out,
and he will be swept away by the blast of his mouth.[16]
31 *Let not the broken*[17] *trust in vain,*
for his date palm[18] *will be worthless.*
32 *Before its day, it will wither;*[19]
its branches will no longer flourish.
33 *He lets fall his unripened grapes like a vine,*
and he casts[20] *his blossoms like an olive tree.*
34 *For the band of the profane is sterile,*
and fire devours the tents of the briber.
35 *Conceiving mischief and bearing iniquity,*
their womb fashions deceit."

17–19 Eliphaz opens his instruction on the woes of the wicked with an extended introduction. Using his typical style, Eliphaz promises to recount what he has seen and heard, and he exhorts Job to pay careful attention to his teaching. He gives Job the assurance that the insights he is going to offer may be trusted, for he has not only observed them personally but they also come from *the wise*. It is the truth that *their fathers* have passed on (cf. v. 10). With the words *have told (higgîḏ)* and *have not concealed (lōʾ kiḥēḏ;* cf. Isa. 3:9),

---

readings include *šibbᵒlîm* (Gen. 41:5), "ears of corn" (Dillmann), and *mᵉlîlām* or *mᵉlîlô*, "their (or his) ears of corn" (see Budde). Dahood (accepted by Pope) vocalizes the word *mᵉnōlem* (with an enclitic *mem*), "possessions," related to Arab. *manāl*, "give, donate," and he takes *ʾereṣ*, "earth," to mean the "netherworld" ("Northwest Semitic Grammar and Job," pp. 60–61). The context favors a word relating to possessions, and Dahood's suggestion for *minlām* is tentatively followed here; cf. Grabbe, *Comparative Philology*, pp. 67–69; Rowley.

16. Many, like Dhorme, emend *pîw*, "his mouth," to *pirḥô*, "his bud, flower," or *piryô*, "his fruit," based on LXX. For MT *wᵉyāsûr*, "and he will be removed," *wîsōʿar* is read (Duhm): "His fruit (or buds) will be swept away by the wind." This offers a fine line, but how then did MT arise? MT is followed, being the more difficult reading. See Tur-Sinai.

17. MT *niṯʿâ* could be a Niphal participle of *nāṯaʿ*, "break" (cf. 4:10), i.e., "that which is broken."

18. For MT *tᵉmûrāṯô*, "his exchange," LXX reads *zᵉmôrāṯô*, "his (vine) shoots," and takes it as the subject of 15:32a (Dhorme and Fohrer accept this reading). Tur-Sinai reads *timmôrāṯô*, "his date palm." This reading is supported by Dhorme's observation that *kippâ*, v. 32b, is equivalent to Akk. *kippatu*, which specifically refers to a branch of the palm tree.

19. Dhorme suggests reading *timmāl*, "wither," with LXX and Syr., for MT *timmālēʾ*, "it will be filled"; the extra ʾ was accidentally transposed from *šāw (= šāwʾ)* in v. 31b. The subject's antecedent is either *timmôrāṯô*, "his date palm" (v. 31b), or *yōnaqtô*, "his shoots" (v. 30b), but the latter is quite distant.

20. MT *yašlēḵ*, "he casts," is a poetic use of the jussive (Dhorme).

Eliphaz stresses that he is giving the whole counsel, holding nothing back (cf. Ps. 78:5–7).

Eliphaz states that the earth or *the land* was given to the wise as an inheritance. The precise meaning of *the land ('ereṣ)* is uncertain, but its general sense is clear. In the land where the fathers lived, *no alien passed among them.* Since no foreigner lived among them, no foreign influence corrupted their teachings. It was a common belief that one must guard against foreign influence in order to preserve a tradition's purity.[21] What Eliphaz has received from them is thus fully reliable.

20 Eliphaz now turns to his main theme, a detailed description of the wretched fate of the wicked. The *wicked* person *(rāšā')* is *the tyrant* (*'ārîṣ;* cf. 6:23; 27:13), one who arrogantly defies God. Such a person is *racked with pain* all his days. The word used for *pain* literally means the pain of travail *(hiṯḥôlēl).* With this forceful language Eliphaz counters Job's observation made against the doctrine of retribution that "the tents of marauders are safe" (12:6).

21 The wicked person is filled with anxiety. He continually hears *terrifying sounds.* Even when his dwelling place *is at peace,* i.e., free from threat, he imagines that a marauder is waiting in the shadows to assail him, for he knows that the quietest times are the most opportune for an opponent to make a surprise raid. Apprehensive that the worst is about to happen, he is startled by every noise. Never able to relax, he has no inner tranquility (cf. Prov. 28:1).

22 The wicked person has *no confidence,* nothing in which to place his faith so that he may have the assurance that *he will escape from darkness (ḥōšeḵ),* i.e., Sheol, the realm of the dead (as in Job 10:21–22). *darkness* also conveys the trauma of dying. The wicked person has no hope that he will live a long, peaceful life and die in the quiet of his sleep. Rather, he fears a violent death, symbolized by the phrase *marked for the sword.* Having lived lawlessly, he fears that a lawless band, even more ravaging than his own troops, will devastate his house and take his life (cf. Matt. 26:52).

23 Driven by such anxiety, a wicked person is turned into a vagabond, wandering about begging for bread.[22] In this picture the rich, wicked

21. Since this concept parallels the belief that God has given the promised land to Israel alone, some, like Duhm, find in this verse an historical reference either to the captivity of Northern Israel or to the Babylonian captivity when the local population became a mixed race. But no significant political-religious insight is to be gained from this statement, for peoples at all times have been concerned with racial purity. Thus this verse simply expresses a general truth.

22. An altered translation (see n. 9 above and n. 24 below) reads the line to say that his body is cast out as bread for vultures. One of the worst fates ancient man could envision was to die and have his corpse left lying about without proper burial. In such a state the deceased soul would continue to wander, always longing for a moment of rest, never finding repose.

person has lost all his wealth. In this wretched condition he knows with certainty that disaster awaits him.

24, 25 Thoughts about *the day of darkness,* i.e., the day of death, terrify the wicked. *Distress [ṣar] and anguish [mᵉṣûqâ] overpower him.*[23] He feels as though a mighty king were commanding *a swooping attack (kîḏôr)*[24] against him. The reason for his great anguish is that he has defiantly stretched out his hand[25] against God (cf. Isa. 5:25). Thinking that he possessed extraordinary strength, he vaunted himself against Shaddai. But now filled with terror, he faces the full punishment for his ruthless behavior.

26 In his days of prosperity when he felt like an invincible champion, this tyrant welcomed any challenge. Protected by his armor, he felt invincible. His gallant victories have made him self-assured. In his new arrogance he believes that he could defeat even God, should such an opportunity present itself. His haughty presumption has grown out of the fact that he has been able to victimize the morally upright, those whom God is supposed to protect, without suffering any divine reprisals. In full armor and protected by *a thick-bossed shield,*[26] he *charges* at God with *an outstretched neck.*[27]

27 This boastful champion has forgotten that his style of living has robbed him of his great strength. Indulging himself in much feasting, his face has become chubby and fat enlarges his loins. This fat, at first symbolic of health (cf. 2 Sam. 1:22), affluence, and ease, robs him of his agility and prowess.[28] In similar fashion Jeremiah portrays the wicked as becoming

23. "Distress" *(ṣar),* lit. "narrow," suggests that one who is cramped and confined is made anxious. Similarly, Heb. *ṣûq,* the root of *mᵉṣûqâ,* "anguish," means "bring into straits, constrain." The opposite image is that one who occupies a broad place is victorious and blessed.

24. Heb. *kîḏôr* means "to swoop down"; it may be cognate with Arab. *kadara,* "pour out" or "dart down" like a bird of prey (Driver-Gray; cf. Gordis). Cf. also Syr. *kudrāʾ*, "vulture."

25. The phrase "an outstretched hand" is frequently used in the OT to describe a great display of God's power, e.g., when he brought Israel out of Egypt (Deut. 26:8; Ps. 136:12). In some prophetic texts, however, it is used negatively to mean that God is acting mightily against his people (Isa. 5:25; 9:16, 20 [Eng. 17, 21]; 10:4; and Jer. 21:5).

26. For Dhorme "the boss of the buckler" is a technical term for a buckler made in a bulging shape; the thick embossment forms a hump. He translates the phrase "with the mass of his thick-bossed bucklers."

27. Often the strength of a warrior is thought to reside in the neck (cf. Job 41:14 [Eng. 22]; Ps. 75:6 [Eng. 5]).

28. Ancient generals took pride in their prowess, the most noted examples being the pharaohs of the 18th Dynasty, who made great exploits not only on the battlefields but also on hunting expeditions and in sports like archery. Indulging themselves in the luxury of their successes, however, they lost much of their great physical ability. Amenophis III is a noteworthy example. A strong, agile sportsman, he became plump and inactive in his later years. Cf. J. Wilson, *The Culture of Ancient Egypt* (Chicago: University of Chicago Press, 1965), p. 204.

wealthy through deeds of injustice and then growing fat and sleek (Jer. 5:26–28). Even though they have experienced no bounds to the success of their evil schemes, they will not escape God's punishment (Jer. 5:29).[29] With this description of an arrogant warlord attacking God, Eliphaz is criticizing Job for his eagerness to dispute with God himself as the height of presumptuous arrogance.

28 This mighty warlord pays a high price for his foolish arrogance. He is driven from his place of rule and can find lodging only in vacant, crumbling houses in a devastated city.[30] Such a city was thought to be under God's curse; thus they were left a heap of ruins. No one dared even to venture near one, let alone rummage through it (Deut. 13:13–17 [Eng. 12–16]; 1 K. 9:8; Jer. 19:8).

29 This person's *wealth* and authority will vanish quickly.[31] Conceding that a wicked person might become rich for a season, Eliphaz states that his wealth *will not endure* and *his possessions will not spread over the earth*. That is, he will not be able to continue in power indefinitely. One day a mighty blow will knock him down so forcefully that he will never be able to recuperate his losses and rebuild his wealth.

30 This wicked person *will not escape darkness,* i.e., death. Eliphaz defends his teaching by an illustration of a withered tree. In the OT the tree serves as a symbol of an upright, dignified person (e.g., 14:7–10; Ps. 1:3). But Eliphaz observes that a stately tree may wither and die. The tree in this picture faces severe heat and a strong wind.[32] Its tender shoots dry out, scorched by the burning heat. Then a mighty gust of wind blows this tree over. That gust of wind may possibly be seen as coming from God's own mouth.

31, 32 The wicked person who has been broken should not trust in vain, hoping that he will rule again. He is not like a broken tree which may again grow stalwart and yield fruit (cf. 14:7–9). This is not his fortune, for his stately date palm will be worthless. Before its day, i.e., the harvest, it

29. This imagery of self-satisfaction is also applied to Israel; in waxing fat, Israel forsook her God (Deut. 32:15; cf. Ps. 73:7; 119:70).

30. Another interpretation maintains that the evildoer is so confident in his own strength that he fearlessly visits such ruined sites out of curiosity and in search of valuable finds (cf. Fohrer) or that he has even defied a divine curse by reconstructing such a ruined city (cf. Josh. 6:26; 1 K. 16:34).

31. In vv. 28–30 Hakam identifies three curses that befall the wicked: in v. 28 he is removed from his place; in v. 29 he loses his possessions; and in v. 30 he is attacked by adversity.

32. Hakam finds in the imagery that the tree must face three successive evils—first, darkness, which is dispelled by the light; second, the bright sun, which is relieved by the wind; and third, mighty gusts of wind, which uproot the palm from its place. Thus the wicked person is worn down by every element. Each sign of relief becomes only a more severe instrument of punishment.

will wither. Its branches will turn brown, and its young fruit will drop off. Renewal is not possible for this tree, because an austere environment squeezes out its energy, its life. With this illustration from nature Eliphaz is discouraging Job's speculation that there might be hope beyond death for a person, a thought prompted by his observation that a felled tree may sprout again (14:7–9; cf. Ps. 55:24 [Eng. 23]; Ps. 102:24 [Eng. 23]).

33 Using two more illustrations from nature, Eliphaz asserts that the early success that the wicked person enjoys is illusory. Like a vine he *lets fall his unripened grapes [bōser].*[33] The unnaturalness of this occurrence is indicated by the verb *lets fall* (*ḥāmas,* lit. "injure, do violence"). As in the case of this vine, something unexpected strikes the evildoer with a devastating blow so that his success is totally wiped out. Or he is like *an olive tree* that casts its blossoms. Every other year the olive tree produces a vast number of blossoms that never set. In those years the early promise of fruit never materializes. So too the undertakings of the wicked person which promise to produce wealth will never again bear fruit.[34]

34, 35 Eliphaz closes with metaphors picturing the certainty of the doctrine of retribution, particularly the tenet that the wicked assuredly suffer a hard fate. He first compares the failure of the wicked to unprofitable farming. *The band of the profane* is like *sterile* soil (*galmûḏ;* cf. 3:7). No matter how many wicked join forces and no matter how hard they strive for their own success, they never reap a harvest, for they are working soil that is hard and sterile. In their pursuit of wealth and power this company is so notorious for offering bribes that their dwellings are labeled *the tents of the briber* (*ʾohᵒlê šōḥaḏ;* cf. Ps. 26:10). With bribes they sought to corrupt the authorities and get their own way. Nevertheless, in due time they are judged: *fire devours* their tents. In Scripture fire is frequently the instrument God uses to punish the profane, whether it be the fire of war or lightning from heaven.[35] Here it probably means that this band will fall prey to a raid in which their possessions will be consumed by fire.

Second, Eliphaz quotes a proverb using birth language. When an animal gives birth, its offspring is similar in looks and disposition to its parents. Likewise in the moral realm, if one conceives *mischief* or trouble (*ʿāmāl;* cf. 4:8; 5:6, 7), he will surely bear *iniquity* (*ʾāwen;* cf. Ps. 7:15 [Eng.

33. Heb. *bōser* refers to unripened or sour grapes in Isa. 18:5; Jer. 31:29–30; Ezek. 18:2.

34. Hakam writes that this picture depicts the children of a wicked man dying at a young age before they become fully established. Thus a portion of the wicked person's punishment falls on his children. While this idea may be incorporated in the imagery, the fuller picture is that the early signs which indicate that a wicked person will be very prosperous never materialize.

35. E.g., Gen. 19:24; Num. 11:1–3; 2 K. 1:10–14; Isa. 66:15–16.

14]; Prov. 22:8). Bernhardt points out that in passages like this one, Heb. *'āwen* has the sense of "self-deception, vanity."[36] That is, the one who mischievously plans to cause another person trouble for his own personal gain produces results that are not simply worthless to him—they even deceive him into thinking he has something when he has nothing. The second line, *their womb fashions deceit (mirmâ),* reinforces this meaning. It is saying that what is conceived in mischief produces that which is unreliable, faulty, and treacherous. The use of *womb (beṭen)* ties the conclusion to the opening verse, where Eliphaz said that Job's belly *(beṭen)* is filled with the east wind. Disparagingly Eliphaz is locating the source of Job's trouble in his belly, charging that it is filled with hot air and deceitful thoughts.

Eliphaz's description of the demise of the wicked person is powerful. Whoever benefits from wrongdoing enjoys greater and greater power, making his thoughts heady. The flame of his arrogance is fueled to the point that he defies even God. When he appears like a stately, enduring palm tree or like an olive tree covered with blossoms promising an abundant crop, God employs natural forces to dry up this proud tree. Over a period of time the arrogant evildoer experiences bad luck and serious reversals. Then one day a catastrophe destroys all his wealth and power. Overnight he is reduced to wandering, inhabiting desolate ruins. Plagued by physical distress and emotional agony, he finds no rest. As a vagabond alone in the world with no sense of belonging, he falls prey to the terrors of death long before reaching a venerable age.

AIM

After harshly reproving Job with sarcastic rhetoric and claiming that his teachings are reliable, Eliphaz tries to impress on Job that the state of the wicked person is desolate and hopeless. His underlying motive is to convince Job that he is suffering the fate of a very wicked person. Job's earlier blessings were ephemeral, a disguise that concealed his profane behavior. At last God has uncovered his wickedness. In order to lead Job back to God, Eliphaz paints a vivid portrait of the turmoil that the wicked face when God punishes them for their evil deeds. He wants to impress on Job that the doctrine of retribution is an inviolable, moral law.

In this speech Eliphaz offers Job no consolation. His primary purpose is to persuade Job to accept the traditional teaching of the wise. However, he is warning Job that if he has any sense at all, he must abandon his desperate hope of disputing directly with God. Otherwise, he will produce a worse fate for himself.

36. K. Bernhardt, *TDOT,* I:142.

2. JOB'S FOURTH RESPONSE (16:1–17:16)

After an opening complaint (16:1–6), Job bewails his miserable lot. He is addressing his words to God (16:17–17:16), words that feature a mixture of lamenting and judicial language. When he thinks of proving his innocence in court, Job's faith reaches a new height as he states that he has a witness in heaven who will defend his honor (16:18–22). These thoughts also lead him to petition God to stand security for him in order that he might be released from his present affliction while awaiting his vindication (17:3). Thus through the legal metaphor Job finds a way to seek a resolution to his complaint. Nevertheless, his deep personal sorrow continues to echo throughout his lamenting. This speech is divided into four sections: a dispute with the comforters (16:1–6); a personal lament with a complaint against God (16:7–17); the heavenly witness (16:18–22); and a personal lament (17:1–16).

a. A Dispute with the Comforters (16:1–6)

1 *Job answered saying,*
2 *"I have heard many such things;*
all of you are miserable comforters.
3 *Is there no end to windy words?*
Or what irritates you that you keep answering?
4 *I too would speak like you,*
if you were in my place;
I would join[1] words with you;
I would shake my head[2] for you.
5 *I would encourage you with my mouth,*
and the trembling[3] of my lips would not be restrained.[4]

1. The verb *heḥbîr* is explained in three different ways: (1) related to Arab. *ḥarbara,* "beautify, adorn" (Horst, Fohrer, KB, p. 276; "I could be brilliant in words against you"); (2) from an original *ḫbr* (cf. Ugar. *ḫbr*), "make noise, harangue" (Pope; J. J. Finkelstein, "Hebrew *ḥbr* and Semitic *ḥbr,*" *JBL* 7 [1956] 328–31; cf. O. Loretz, "*Ḥbr* in Job 16:4," *CBQ* 23 [1961] 293–94); (3) from Heb. *ḥbr,* "unite, join" (Gordis). The third option is preferable since it is derived from a Hebrew word.

2. The preposition *beₘô* is explained by Gordis as the *bₑ* of means, an alternative to the accusative case (cf. Ps. 22:8 [Eng. 7]).

3. Gordis understands *nîḏ* as an ellipsis for *nîḏ rōʾš,* "shake the head, sympathize" (cf. *nûḏ* in 2:11; 42:11). He translates the line: "And sympathy would restrain my lips."

4. Driver-Gray, Dhorme, Rowley, and *BHK* follow LXX and Syr., which seem to have read *lōʾ ʾeḥśōḵ,* "I would not restrain," instead of the third person *yaḥśōḵ*. Possibly the verb is intransitive (Fohrer; G. R. Driver, "Studies in the Vocabulary of the Old Testament, VI," *JTS* 34 [1933] 380).

6 *If I speak, my pain is not eased,*
and if I resist, it does not[5] *leave me."*[6]

2, 3 Job complains that often he has *heard many such things* as the comforters speak. But in his present plight such pious platitudes serve only to increase his sorrow. Therefore, he accuses his friends of being *miserable comforters (m^e^naḥ^a^mê ʿāmāl).*[7] The byword *miserable comforters* is a pungent oxymoron; i.e., the more words they speak to comfort, the more pain they inflict. This interchange boldly marks the difference between Job's perspective and Eliphaz's. Whereas Eliphaz believes that the speeches of the friends are the very consolations of God (15:11), Job considers them to be harbingers of misery. And whereas Eliphaz concludes his speech with the aphorism "conceiving mischief *[ʿāmāl],* bearing iniquity" (15:35a), Job retorts that it is their theologizing that conceives mischief to produce misery in him.

With a biting rhetorical question Job charges Eliphaz with uttering *windy words (diḇrê rûaḥ),* i.e., eloquent speech devoid of content. He is directly countering Eliphaz's reproach that his knowledge is empty wind (15:2) and Bildad's retort that his words are a mighty wind (8:2). Next Job asks Eliphaz *what irritates (himrîṣ)*[8] him so much that he feels compelled to *keep answering.*[9] Job cannot fathom why Eliphaz is so upset with him.

4, 5 Job speculates about how he would act if their places were reversed. Indeed, he would speak with the same eloquence as his friends. Although much of his rhetoric would be the same as theirs, he would show more sympathy. He would *join words* to bring comfort (vv. 4c, 5a) and *shake* his head in sympathy (vv. 4d, 5b).[10] He would not restrain his trembling lips from uttering supportive words. Job is saying that he has expected far more consolation from his friends than he has received.

5. Here we take Heb. *mah* as a negative particle, with Dhorme, Pope, et al. Cf. Gordis and Tur-Sinai, who take *mah* in its usual sense of "what"; cf. also Driver-Gray; Blommerde, *Northwest Semitic Grammar and Job,* p. 77, who translate it "how much."

6. MT *yah^a^lōḵ* is a poetic form of *yēlēḵ,* "he goes."

7. Hakam says that Heb. *ʿāmāl* comprises *heḇel,* "breath, vanity," *ṣaʿar,* "sorrow," and *rešaʿ,* "wickedness."

8. In the Qal *māraṣ* means "be grievously ill" (cf. 6:25). In the Hiphil as here it means a malady or ill-temperament that compels one to act in an undesirable manner.

9. The use of the singular personal pronoun "you" suggests that v. 3 is addressed directly to Eliphaz. This style is unusual for Job, for he generally addresses his comforters collectively with the plural form of "you," as in vv. 2 and 4.

10. The expression of wagging or moving the head may be a gesture of stunned sympathy (2:11; 42:11) or, more frequently, a sign of contempt and scorn (Ps. 22:8 [Eng. 7]; Sir. 12:18; 13:7; cf. Ps. 44:15 [Eng. 14]; Jer. 18:16). The correct nuance depends on the bearing of the person. Verse 5a suggests that Job would seek to help one in distress. Thus the gestures mentioned in vv. 4d and 5b are understood as sympathetic gestures.

6 Job breaks off his thought abruptly with a brief apology for his continued speaking. He uses cohortatives, *I speak* (*ʾaḏabberâ*) and *I resist* (*ʾaḥdelâ*), for emphasis. Since his pain is not eased with his speaking nor does it leave him when he resists speaking, he sees no advantage in keeping silent. So he decides to keep on speaking in the hope of capturing God's attention. He pours out to God a despairing lament, though tempered with a ray of hope.

b. A Personal Lament with a Complaint against God (16:7–17)

7 *"Surely now, he has wearied me;*
you have devastated my whole company.[1]
8 *You have shriveled me up;*[2] *this has become a witness against me.*
My gauntness[3] *rises up against me; it testifies to my face.*[4]
9 *In his anger*[5] *he tears and assails me.*
He gnashes his teeth at me;
my adversary pierces me with his eyes.
10 *Men gape at me with*[6] *their mouth;*
they slap my cheeks in scorn;
they mass together against me.
11 *God has turned me over to the vicious*[7]
and has tossed me[8] *into the hands of the wicked.*

1. The shift between third (v. 7a) and second (v. 7b) person forms is not unusual in ancient Hebrew poetry.

2. The verb *qāmaṭ* is taken as related to the Syr. *qmṭ* (Ethpaal), which means "seize" or "wrinkle" (cf. AV, Driver-Gray, Gordis). This meaning makes fine sense and finds a parallel in *kaḥašî*, "my gauntness," v. 8b.

3. With Gordis, Driver-Gray, and Andersen, MT *kaḥašî* is taken to mean "my gauntness" from the Aram. *keḥaš*, "lean, weak" (cf. Ps. 109:24). See Rowley; cf. Tur-Sinai, Dhorme.

4. A glaring problem with vv. 7 and 8 is the length of v. 8b. The easiest solution is to take *bepānay yaʿaneh*, "it testifies to my face," as a gloss on *wayyāqām bî*, "it rises up against me." The removal of these words restores some, but not complete, symmetry to the line. Duhm offers another possible solution, with few textual changes. In v. 7 he reads *hašimmānî*, "you have made me desolate," with v. 7a; v. 7b then reads *kol rāʿtî* (for MT *ʿaḏāṯî*) *tiqmeṭēnî:* "All my misery grips me." In v. 8 the *ʾaṯnaḥ* (the principal Masoretic accent) is placed on *bî*. But having two perfect verbs following one another in v. 7a is not the best solution. Also, the context suggests that Job is lamenting with intensity. The varied lengths of the lines of the text may capture his misery.

5. It is possible that the preposition *be* is implied before *ʾappô*, "his anger"; Job 18:4 has a preposition *be* before *ʾappô*. But Amos 1:11 supports MT here.

6. According to Gordis the preposition *be* on *bepîhem*, "with their mouth," is another example of the *be* of means, as in v. 4; cf. Isa. 5:14.

7. For MT *ʿawîl*, "small children" (as in Job 19:18; 21:11), it is best to read *ʿawwāl*, "an unrighteous, vicious person." The emendation is favored by the parallel

12 *I was at ease and he crushed me;*
he seized me by the neck and shattered me.
He set me up as his target;
13 *his arrows[9] surround me.*
He pierces my kidneys without pity;
he spills my gall on the ground.
14 *He rends me breach on breach;*
he rushes at me like a warrior.
15 *I have sewn sackcloth over my scabby skin;*
I have buried[10] my brow in the dust.
16 *My face is inflamed[11] with weeping,*
and dark shadows circle my eyes,
17 *although[12] there is no violence in my hands*
and my prayer is pure."

7 Job complains that God[13] *has wearied* him, taking away all his strength, and has left him desolate by devastating his *whole company,* i.e., all his closest relatives and friends. Job's use of the third person form in v. 7a and

---

rᵉšāʿîm, "wicked" (cf. the same parallelism in 27:7). The singular *ʿawwāl* is also parallel to a plural in 31:3. Hakam, though, suggests the existence of a form *ʿᵃwîl,* "wicked," like *gᵉḇîr,* "lord."

8. Most explain MT *yirṭēnî* as an imperfect of *yāraṭ,* cognate of Arab. *waraṭa,* "hurl, fling." The Piel might be expected here. While this view is followed since it provides a good parallel to *hisgîr,* "turn over to," Gordis follows Rashi in preferring to understand it on the basis of a root in Mishnaic Hebrew, *rṭh,* which means "wring out" and is used to interpret this passage in *Midr. Cant. Rab.* 4:5.

9. The versions have taken *rabbāyw* as "arrows, missiles." But many interpreters (Driver-Gray, Tur-Sinai, Pope, Gordis, Hakam) take the noun as an agent, "archers." The singular verb in vv. 12–14 suggests that a change in subject is not anticipated. Thus "arrows" is preferred. See Dhorme.

10. MT *ʿōlaltî,* "thrust in, bury," is related to Arab. *ǵalla,* "go in"; Aram. *ʿᵃlal,* "enter, thrust"; Syr. *ʿal,* "enter"; Ugar. *ǵll,* "enter, wade in" (KB, p. 789).

11. The Ketib reading of a feminine singular verb, *hᵒmarmᵉrâ,* "be inflamed," after the plural *pānay* is explained as the use of the feminine singular verb after the name of something (Dhorme; GKC, § 145k), or *pānay* may be a feminine form as in Mishnaic Hebrew (Tur-Sinai). Gordis agrees with the latter and understands the verb *hᵒmarmᵉrâ* as an old third feminine plural form which survives in Arab. *qatala.* This position, though, is not widely held (cf. GKC, § 44m). The verb is usually taken either from the Arabic root *ḫamara,* "ferment, be agitated," or from Arab. *ḫamara,* "be red, reddish brown" (Driver-Gray; cf. D. Payne, *ASTI* 5 [1966–67] 64). The latter meaning is best, for the coloring also conveys the idea of being swollen (cf. Lam. 1:20; 2:11).

12. The preposition *ʿal,* "on," appears to govern the clause and is rendered "although"; it may be short for *ʿal-ʾᵃšer* (GKC, §§ 104b, 160c; cf. Isa. 53:9).

13. Although the antecedent for the verb "he has wearied" is not grammatically defined, the context makes it clear that "God" is the subject (so Driver-Gray, Pope, Andersen, Gordis). Perhaps Job is using the pronoun because of the deep disappointment he feels toward God. Cf., e.g., Tur-Sinai and Dhorme, who think MT is corrupt and hence reconstruct the text; Rowley, who follows Vulg. in taking "my pain" from v. 6 as subject.

v. 8b and the second person in vv. 7b–8a reflects his disturbed emotions. Feeling the stab of Eliphaz's point that judgment falls on the entire company of the profane (15:34), Job counters that it is God who is making him look like a godless man by destroying his entire household.

8 Even more disturbing is the trouble brought by his trial, the severity of his physical illness coupled with its condemning testimony. God has *shriveled up (qāmaṭ)* Job. His body has become a painful cage. And the community interprets his skinny body as proof that he has sinned arrogantly: The sores and wrinkles in his body are the convicting evidence that he is guilty. God has split Job in two, so to speak. His body witnesses against his own words. As a result, no one who sees him believes his verbal testimony of innocence.

9 Job fervently laments God's brutal treatment. God's anger is burning so hotly against him that he perceives that God is his adversary *(ṣar).*[14] In accusing God of assailing him Job uses the Hebrew word *śāṭam,* "hate actively" (Driver-Gray), which is similar in sound to, if not directly related to, Heb. *śāṭān,* "prosecutor, satan" (cf. 1:6). Unable to fathom God's role in his affliction, Job fears that God has become his enemy. Here Job comes close to reconstructing the scenes of the heavenly counsel in the prologue, but he turns them inside out. He identifies God as his enemy rather than as his advocate. At this crucial point he is tested to the ultimate. From his perspective he is led to wonder if the God in whom he has trusted is not in reality his satan.

Job portrays God to be like a wild animal voraciously tearing its prey in repeated assaults. When it backs away, it snarls at its prey, its eyes fixed in a glassy stare and its teeth glistening behind quivering lips. Like this wild animal God enjoys terrorizing his victim as he relentlessly wears down any resistance that the victim could muster.[15]

10 Job's sorrow is multiplied as the masses revile him with gestures and insulting blows. Seated on the dung heap outside the city gate, Job has become a spectacle attracting the attention of all. The passersby *gape* at him with wide open mouths, a gesture expressive of their disdain. They slap Job's cheeks contemptuously and reproach him with taunts and insulting gestures.[16] The lower the status of the mockers, the more insulting are their

14. In Lam. 2:4 God is portrayed as an enemy in his devastating attack on Jerusalem. The one who suffers under God's punishment very often views God as his opponent.

15. Cf. Ps. 17:11–12; Lam. 2:16. In psalms of lament the mockers that surround the spectacle of a distressed person are described as animals gloating over their prey (Ps. 22:13–14, 17 [Eng. 12–13, 16]; cf. Lam. 2:16; 3:46).

16. "Striking one's face" is a stinging blow of angry contempt (Lam. 3:30; Mic. 4:14 [Eng. 5:1]; Ps. 3:8 [Eng. 7]; Isa. 50:6). Delitzsch points out that the phrase "with reproach" means that insulting words accompanied their act of contempt (cf. 1 K. 22:24).

jeers against a nobleman. In their gaping mouths (v. 10a) and their slapping of his cheeks (v. 10b) Job sees God's gnashing teeth (v. 9b) and his piercing eyes (v. 9c).[17] This loss of dignity is just as agonizing for Job as the excruciating physical pain, since a person gets much of his identity and personal worth from his society; in rejecting one of its members a community inflicts severe emotional pain.

11 Job states the reason that he has become an object of scorn: *God has turned me over to the vicious.* Instead of his punishing the wicked as the friends have described (8:22b; 11:20; 15:20–34), God has tossed him into the hands of the wicked. Given free rein by God they shame Job wrongfully and make his ill-fate unbearable.

12–14 Job's lament crescendos to an emotional peak in vv. 12–14, as evidenced by the poetic style: two tristichs, the use of assonance,[18] and vivid word pictures. Job contrasts his former blissful state with God's sudden onslaught. The attack was so surprising and so fierce that Job the victim has been left shattered. Like a strong man God seizes him by the nape of the neck (cf. Gen. 49:8) and administers a torturous beating. Or like a marksman God has set Job up as a target (cf. Job 6:4; 7:20; Lam. 3:12). Taking careful aim, he shoots scores of arrows at the target with no relenting. Many hit Job's vital midsection, piercing his kidneys and spilling his gall on the ground (cf. Ps. 38:3 [Eng. 2]; 64:8 [Eng. 7]). Mortally wounded, he is left alone with no hope of physical recovery.

Another picture likens God to a mighty *warrior (gibbôr),*[19] marshalling his troops against a fortified city. Each surge renders breach after breach in the wall.[20] Soon the city is razed. So too Job has been besieged. The disease has destroyed one member of his body after another. Only death awaits him. This picture contrasts sharply with Eliphaz's perception that Job is an armed warrior attacking God (15:26).

15 Grievously wounded, Job mourns in sackcloth sewn over his scabby skin. The term for *scabby skin (gēleḏ)* may refer specifically to the crusty scabs that form over a wound.[21] *sackcloth* was the clothing of those

17. If this is an accurate interpretation, vv. 10–11 do not have to be taken as a later insertion, as some (e.g., Duhm) have argued. See Gordis.

18. The assonance is conveyed by two verbs in the Pilpel, *wayᵉparpᵉrēnî* and *wayᵉpaṣpᵉṣēni,* plus *bᵉʿorpî* (v. 12a, v. 12b).

19. Usually the word *gibbôr* in reference to God represents his mastery over all foes (cf. Jer. 20:11; Isa. 42:13; Zeph. 3:17; Ps. 24:8; 78:65). Like a mighty warrior he secures victory for his own people. By turning the metaphor inside out, Job reveals how treacherous God's ways appear to one who has been faithful.

20. For this imagery of God's pouring out his wrath in terms of breaching a city, cf. 2 Sam. 6:7–8; Ps. 89:41 (Eng. 40). The assonance continues: *yiprᵉṣēnî pereṣ ʿal pᵉnê pāreṣ; yārûṣ ʿālay kᵉg̱ibbôr.* There is obviously a play on the root *prṣ,* "breach," a technical term of siege warfare (Andersen).

21. Cf. A. Cohen, *AJSL* 40 (1923–24) 167.

who were sorrowing before some grave blow or loss. Delitzsch suggests that this garment had to be specially sewn since Job's body was so hideously distorted. And to express his humiliation, Job buries his brow in the dust as a wounded animal in defeat buries its horns in the ground.[22]

16 Job describes the marks left by his protracted weeping.[23] *My face is inflamed,* i.e., raw and chapped. *dark shadows,* portentous of death, encircle his eyes. His woeful countenance moves Job to lash out at God, not out of pride, but out of deep hurt and frustration.

17 Job grounds the intensity of his lament in his innocence. Because he has done *no violence* and his *prayer is pure,* he cries out for vindication. Job chooses language similar to that found in the liturgy of confession that worshipers made before entering the temple precinct (cf. Ps. 24:4). Job is confessing that he has done no wrong. There is no transgression of his which could be the reason for the hostile way God is treating him. He asserts that his *prayer is pure.* His words have been spoken to God honestly and fervently. He has not uttered empty or false words merely to get God to help him. An ancient worshiper believed that God would more likely answer a prayer from pure motives (cf. Ps. 17:1). Job is earnestly seeking to move God to respond to him through his words, even though these words are filled with a biting complaint against God's treatment of him. The daring of Job's approach is only tempered by his uncompromising search for an encounter with God.

c. The Heavenly Witness (16:18–22)

18 *"Earth, cover not my blood!*
my cry, find no resting place![1]
19 *Even now[2] my witness is in heaven;*
my defender[3] is on high.[4]

22. Conversely, "to raise one's horn" is a sign of exalted victory and proud confidence; cf. Ps. 75:5–6 (Eng. 4–5).

23. Powerful emotion is caught by assonance and the use of reduplicated forms: *ḥ^{o}marm^{e}râ,* "inflamed," and *ʿapʿappay,* "my eyes or my eyelids."

1. Heb. *māqôm,* "a place," is a nonspecific term, but the context restricts it to mean a place where the blood of one slain may be covered to keep it from crying out. Dahood ("Northwest Semitic Philology and Job," pp. 61–62) and Pope argue from inscriptional evidence (Panamuwa and Eshmunazar) that *māqôm* may mean "tomb" (cf. Ezek. 39:11). Grabbe (*Comparative Philology and the Text of Job,* pp. 69–72) admits that this word may stand for a tomb, but he concludes that the word is general and does not have that specific meaning in this text. Thus it is best to translate *māqôm* "(resting) place" and consider "tomb" as an implied meaning.

2. The particles *gam ʿattâ,* "even now," and *hinneh,* "behold," are somewhat redundant. Since the first line is a little long, balance (8/8 syllable count) is restored by the deletion of *hinnēh.*

3. Aram. *śāh^{a}ḏî,* "my defender, witness," parallels Heb. *ʿēḏî,* "my witness." A

20 *Behold,[5] my interpreter[6] is my friend;[7]*
to God my eyes drip[8] tears.
21 *And he argues for a man with God,*
as between[9] a man and his fellow,
22 *for a few years will pass,[10]*
and I shall go the way of no return."

18 Like an innocent victim of murder Job petitions the earth, *cover not my blood,* for he does not want his cries for vengeance to cease until they have been answered. The ancient peoples thought that the spilled blood of a slain victim was crying out for revenge.[11] The crying would cease only when the blood was covered or the revenge was accomplished. It was believed that the spirit of one deceased would never rest in the next life until the corpse was buried (see Isa. 26:21; Ezek. 24:7–8). Moreover, it was believed that if the

---

similar paralleling of a Hebrew word with its Aramaic counterpart is also found in 15:3; 37:23; 39:5 (cf. Gordis).

4. Heb. *m^erômîm,* "on high" or "heights," being in the plural suggests a place of spacious expanse (GKC, § 134b; Fohrer); a similar paralleling of "heights" with "heavens" occurs in Ps. 148:1; cf. Isa. 33:16.

5. Verse 20a is unusually short and filled with problems. The length of the lines may be balanced by reading *hinnēh,* "behold," from v. 19a at the beginning of v. 20 (giving a 7/7 syllable count).

6. Some (e.g., Driver-Gray) take MT *m^elîṣay* as a Hiphil participle from *lîṣ,* hence meaning "my scorners," but this would create a single occurrence against the normal Qal participle *lēṣ,* which is used for "scorners." It seems best to take MT as the same word that occurs in 33:23; Isa. 43:27; Gen. 42:23. In these passages its meaning is "interpreter or intercessor" (cf. P. Joüon, "Notes de Lexicographie Hébraïque," *MFO* 5 [1912] 440–43).

7. To agree with the singular subject in v. 19 and the singular verb in v. 21 the plural forms are emended to the singular, which requires only a change in vocalization: *m^elîṣî rē'i.* For MT *rē'ay* many interpretations are possible. A standard interpretation is "my friends." But it could mean "my thoughts," esp. if *'elayw,* "to him," is restored with the LXX, perhaps having fallen out by haplography after *'ĕlôah.* This last suggestion fits the context well and is a good alternative. Thus Pope translates the line: "Interpreter of my thoughts to God" (cf. M. Dahood, *Bib* 53 [1972] 391).

8. There are two interpretations for the verb *dālap:* either "stream, flow," related to a rare Aramaic word, *d^elap,* hence "my eyes drip or weep" (Dhorme); or "be sleepless, exhausted," related to Akk. *dalāpu* (Horst, Fohrer), hence "my eyes are sleepless." The Aramaic, being closer to Hebrew, is followed here.

9. It is possible that *ben,* "son," may be a defective spelling for *bên,* "between," as attested in some mss. (see *BHS*). The construct *ben-'āḏām,* "son of man," does appear in 25:6, but it is not common in Job, while *bên . . . l^e* is fine Hebrew (cf. Gen. 1:6).

10. MT *ye'ĕṯāyw,* "it will pass," is an example of a masculine plural verb after a feminine plural subject (GKC, § 145u).

11. In a similar social setting the blood of Abel cried from the ground, beseeching God himself to punish Cain (Gen. 4:8–15).

next of kin did not answer the cry, God in heaven would vindicate the one slain. Still living but fearful of expiring soon, Job, like one whose life is threatened, cries out, "Murder!" He wants God to avenge him before it is too late.[12] He enjoins his cry not to find any resting place until it is answered. The only answer that will satisfy his cry is an acquittal issued by the divine tribunal.

19 Since there is no earthly party who will come to his defense, Job asserts that his *witness is in heaven,* he will testify to his innocence.[13] This heavenly witness is his *defender.* Who is this heavenly defender? Is it an angel or some other heavenly creature? Considering the various passages in which Job thinks about arguing his case before God, the best candidate for the defender that can be found is God himself. While it is difficult to think that God would serve as witness against himself, as Mowinckel argues, the concept is not impossible. In fact, the whole drama of redemption centers around the antinomy between God's justice that is sometimes expressed in wrath toward sinful man and his love that reaches out to redeem that same sinful man. For love to be genuine, it must be true to justice. In his redeeming work God is motivated by love and acts true to justice. Here Job appeals to God's holy integrity in stating his earnest hope that God will testify to the truth of his claims of innocence, even though such testimony will seem to contradict God's own actions. Such risking is the essence of faith. For a moment Job sees God as his steadfast supporter. In this plea he is expressing the trust God had expressed in him in the prologue because he is pushing through the screen of his troubles to the real God. He is not essentially pitting God against God; rather he is affirming genuine confidence in God regardless of the way it appears that God is treating him. Since Job, in contrast to his friends, will not concede that truth is identical with appearances, he presses on for a true resolution to his complaint from God himself.

20, 21 Job declares confidently that his interpreter is his friend. The *interpreter* is one who advocates a party's case, explaining the situation to the court and defending him against any charges. Who could that party be save God himself in the light of the last verse. That is, as Job's interpreter he will argue the merits of his case with God just *as between a man and his fellow,* i.e., just as human beings do. Since Job's earthly friends have failed

12. An interesting variant interpretation is presented by M. Buttenwieser (*Book of Job* [New York: Macmillan, 1922], pp. 218–22). He takes these lines as Job praying that he might be saved from the grave.

13. Cf. W. Irwin, "Job's Redeemer," *JBL* 81 (1962) 217–24. S. Mowinckel ("Hiobs *gō᾿ēl* und Zeuge im Himmel," in *Vom Alten Testament,* Fest. K. Marti, ed. K. Budde, BZAW 41 [Giessen: Töpelmann, 1925], pp. 207–12) points out that Job is appealing to a heavenly guardian angel who will intercede for him before the divine throne. He compares this verse with other references to such an angel in 5:1 and 33:23. But his interpretation is forced, requiring textual changes.

him, God will take their place by defending his accused friend, even before himself. No wonder these great thoughts cause Job's eyes to flow with tears.

22 Job underlines his plea with a note of urgency. He reminds God that if his petition is not granted, he will perish in dishonor. His end is approaching so fast that he can count the few years left.[14] Soon he will descend to hell on the way that allows *no return* (cf. 7:9). In the realm of the dead he will have no way to defend his reputation. What is decided must be decided on earth. So the closer death approaches, the more urgent his cry for help becomes. Such reasoning, i.e., that the faithful servant will be unable to praise God in the land of the dead, is frequently found in OT prayers, for the distressed petitioner is groping for some way to motivate God to act redemptively (cf. Ps. 30:10–11 [Eng. 9–10]). The appeal is that it is imperative for God to attend to the cry for help for his own sake, attesting his commitment to the upright and to the honor of his name among men.

d. A Personal Lament (17:1–16)

1 *"My spirit is broken;*[1]
my days run out;[2]
the graveyard[3] *awaits me.*[4]
2 *Surely*[5] *there are mockers*[6] *about me;*

14. The phrase "years of number" means "few," for that which can be numbered is considered small and insignificant (e.g., "men of numbers," Deut. 4:27; cf. Ps. 105:12) in contrast to abundance expressed by the phrase "there is no numbering" (Job 5:9; 9:10).

1. BDB (p. 287) and KB (p. 274) accept a root *ḥāḇal* meaning "ruin, destroy," occurring in the Piel. Used with "spirit" it means "break, shatter." The idea in this passage is that Job's inward resources have dissipated; cf. J. Gamberoni, "*chābhal* III," *TDOT,* IV:185–86.

2. MT *nizʿāḵû* is another difficult hapax legomenon. Most take it as a by-form of *dāʿaḵ,* "extinguish," which is read in some mss. (see *BHS*). The new JPS translation reads "run out." Others, like Fohrer, emend it to *neʿezḇû,* "be left to," and join it to the second line to make a bicolon: "The grave is left for me."

3. The plural "graves" *(qᵉḇārîm)* is a plural of extension, "a graveyard, a cemetery" (GKC, § 124c). Duhm points out that Job is thinking of an ordinary grave, not of one for a great noble. For the latter, *bayiṯ,* "house," would have been used.

4. Generally the line is read as a distich, but it is best to keep a tristich of short, crisp lines that communicate strong emotion.

5. Andersen takes the *ʾim-lōʾ* as an oath which binds God to act on Job's behalf. In uttering the curse Job puts himself in jeopardy. The penalty appears in v. 4b, "God must not let them triumph." This interpretation takes seriously the *ʾim-lōʾ*, but it is hard to maintain it as solely an oath, for four lines intervene between the two parts of the oath. It is best to view the *ʾim-lōʾ* as meaning "surely, indeed."

6. The word *hᵃṯulîm,* a by-form from the root *tll,* is taken as an abstract plural meaning "mockery." Gordis suggests that it is a *qāṭūl* participle with middle force, hence "mockers."

my eye dwells[7] on their hostility.[8]

3 *Put up a pledge[9] for me with you;*
who else will permit my hand to be shaken?[10]

4 *Because you have closed their minds to understanding,*
so you will not be exalted.[11]

5 *He who informs against a friend for a reward,*
the eyes of his children will fail.

6 *He has made me a popular byword;[12]*
I am one before whom men spit.[13]

7 *My eye is dimmed from grief;*
all my limbs are like a shadow.

8 *The upright are appalled at this;*
the innocent stirs himself up against the godless.

9 *But the righteous holds to his way,*
and the man with clean hands grows continually stronger.

10 *But, all of you,[14] change, come on;*
I shall not find a wise man among you.

7. The verb *tālan,* from *lûn,* "spend the night, abide," is strange with "my eye" as subject, but it may be taken in the sense of "dwell on." The eye may be a synecdoche for the whole person, for sorrow fills the eye with bitter weeping. Hölscher and Fohrer read *tilʾeynâ ʿênāy,* "my eyes are tired."

8. MT *ûḇᵉhammᵉrôṯām* is difficult. To gain an abstract noun parallel to "mockery," Duhm and Dhorme read *ûḇᵉṯamrûrîm,* "and in bitterness" (with some support from Syr.). Others, like Driver-Gray, take the form as a Hiphil infinitive construct from *mārâ,* "be rebellious," i.e., "on their defiance." The latter solution is best, for it requires no emendation.

9. The parallelism suggests that the noun *ʿerᵉḇōnî,* "pledge for me," should be read for the verb *ʿorḇēnî,* as most interpreters suggest (Gordis).

10. According to Gordis the Niphal *yittāqēaʿ* is an example of the Niphal expressing permission, "allow it to be struck."

11. MT *tᵉrōmēm* is emended to gain an object, as in LXX, either *tᵉrōmᵉmēm* (so *BHS*) or *tᵉrîmēm* (Duhm, Budde, Tur-Sinai). Haplography could easily account for the first possibility. Gordis suggests reading a Polal *tᵉrômām,* "you shall (not) be exalted," for he thinks that the first emendation results in a bland, obvious line. His reading means that God's action of blinding the friends will result in God's not being exalted. This suggestion is followed, for it requires the least textual change. The next-best solution is Dhorme's *tārûm yāḏām,* "their hand is not raised." This wording would explain why no one is in a position to strike Job's hand as a guarantor.

12. MT *limšōl,* "to say or give a proverb," should be vocalized *limšal,* "for a proverb," with LXX (so Budde, Dhorme, Gordis).

13. The noun *tōpeṯ* may be related to Ugar. *wpṯ,* "spit"; cf. M. Dahood, *Bib* 55 (1974) 390.

14. MT *kullām,* "all of them," appears to be an error for *kulleḵem,* "all of you" (with a few mss.; see *BHS*) since the verb is a second person plural. But the MT form makes good use of assonance, and Dhorme points out that the third person plural is used as a vocative in Mic. 1:2; so the MT here would refer unambiguously to Job's friends.

11 *My days*[15] *have passed;*
my plans[16] *are undone,*
the desires of[17] *my heart.*[18]
12 *They turn night to day, saying,*
in the face of darkness, 'Light is near.'
13 *If*[19] *I mark out*[20] *my house in Sheol,*
if I spread my couch in darkness,
14 *if I say to the pit, 'You are my father,'*
or to the worm, 'My mother and my sister,'
15 *where then is my hope?*
My hope[21]*—who can see it?*
16 *Will it go down*[22] *to the chambers*[23] *of Sheol?*
Will we descend[24] *together to the dust?"*

1 With great emotion Job expresses the depth of his despair in three short lines. His *spirit (rûaḥ),* the desire for life in him, has been broken. Depression is robbing his inner resources for bearing his shame. His days are about

15. Blommerde ("The Broken Construct Chain. Further Examples," *Bib* 55 [1974] 549–50) vocalizes MT as *y^{e}mê,* a plural construct which is separated from its *nomen rectum* by the verb. This is quite unusual and not a widely adopted possibility.

16. Hölscher suggests reading *b^{e}zimmâ,* "with plan," instead of MT *zimmōṯay,* "my plans," so that it belongs to the first line, making the verse a distich.

17. MT *môrāšê* is best taken as equivalent to *m^{e}'ōrāšê,* "desires of," from the root *'rš* (cf. Dhorme, Gordis).

18. This verse is most likely a tristich like v. 1. Many have worked on forging it into a distich (cf. n.16 above), but none of the solutions is convincing. Cf. B. Liebermann, "Note on Job XVII,11," *ExpTim* 34 (1922–23) 330–31.

19. The particle *'im* is variously understood. Dhorme takes it as interrogative, but Budde thinks that it introduces a condition, with v. 15 as the apodosis. Gordis takes it as an emphatic, "indeed" (related to Arab. *'inna*).

20. MT *'^{a}qawweh* is generally taken from the root *qwh,* hence meaning "I hope," but Gordis sees it as a denominative from *qaw,* "line," hence "I mark out" (cf. Tur-Sinai). This suggestion achieves an excellent parallelism.

21. Many make emendations to eliminate the double *tiqwāṯî*. For the second line many (e.g., Duhm) with LXX suggest *ṭôḇāṯî,* "my good things." But the author likes to repeat the same word in the second line.

22. MT *tēraḏnâ,* "it goes down," appears to be a third feminine plural verb, but Dahood ("Northwest Semitic Philology and Job," pp. 62–63), Pope, and Gordis take it as a third feminine singular with the *-nâ* as a *nun energicum*.

23. MT *baddê* is variously interpreted. Gordis takes it as a noun, "sections, chambers." Duhm and others read *ha'immāḏî,* "is it with me," based on the LXX, but Horst's suggestion of *h^{a}ḇa'^{a}ḏî* is closer to MT. Dahood ("Northwest Semitic Philology and Job," pp. 62–63) suggests that it is a contraction of *ba-yāḏê (biḏê),* "in the hands of," as in Ugar. *bd* for *byd* (cf. Ps. 49:16 [Eng. 15]).

24. Assuming that MT *nāḥaṯ,* "we descend," is a first person plural Qal imperfect, one would expect that it would be vocalized *nēḥaṯ;* many revocalize it thus.

to run out. The *graveyard* awaits him. Completely disgraced, he will be buried in a common grave *(qeḇer)* instead of receiving honorable interment in a noble sepulcher.

2 Job deplores the public dishonor that accompanies his misfortune. Mockers have surrounded him. Their insults devastate his self-esteem. While the crowds jeer him, his eyes focus on the hostility reflected in their faces. Their gestures coupled with the tone of their voices send shivers through him. Perhaps the reference to the *eye* indicates that their hatred moves Job to tears.

3 In the light of the hostility of his mockers, Job pleads for God to put up a pledge with himself for his servant. Earlier Job had said that if the situation required it he would expect his friends to go surety for him (cf. 6:14–23), but they have not. At this time he needs someone to put up bail so that he can be released from his affliction while he waits for the court to hear his case. There is no one to whom Job can turn as his guarantor, one who will seal the agreement to defend him with a handshake, save God himself. Since the security would be made by God to himself, the same tension between the God of wrath and the God of mercy exists here as in 16:19–21.[25] Job's words are similar to the psalmist's: "I have done justice and righteousness; do not surrender me to my oppressors. Be surety for your servant for good; let not the arrogant oppress me" (Ps. 119:121–22).[26] This parallel passage makes it clear that Job is now pleading to God for immediate relief from his suffering while he has to wait for the heavenly court to hear his case. This plea offers evidence that Job's faith in God remains firm and that God is the witness spoken of in 16:19.

4 Job reminds God why he must turn to him as his bondsman. The reason is that his friends are not willing to go bail for him since God himself has closed their minds. Blinded from the real issues in Job's case, they are afraid to help an apparent object of God's wrath. God then must bear the responsibility for both Job's unjust treatment and the friends' blindness, or else he *will not be exalted.* That is, God will not receive any glory if Job's trial continues unresolved. Only the most daring faith would venture such an accusation against God, for if the charge should be in error, the consequences would be onerous. But if true, it is a compelling way to arouse God to intervene on the supplicant's behalf.

5 Speaking to the friends, Job warns them of the danger that their false accusations against him may incur with a proverb about the retribution exacted against the children of him who informs against a friend for personal

25. For a fine discussion see Horst.
26. Cf. Isa. 38:14; *TWOT,* II:693–94.

gain.[27] By using this proverb as a warning Job is employing the same logic and method as the friends in order to penetrate the hardness of their thoughts toward him. A witness who perjures himself to condemn a defendant must bear the penalty of the offense he had charged the innocent person of committing (cf. Deut. 19:16–19). In this proverb *the eyes of the children fail* because their fathers gave "false eyewitness testimony in order to defraud *his* friends' children" (Andersen).

6 Job now mourns how deeply God has humiliated him among men. He has become *a byword* to the whole community. When passersby behold his deteriorated condition, they are filled with such repulsion that they shout reproaches and *spit* in his face, a revolting, insulting gesture. Undeserved mockery is a serious offense, for it darkens people's minds, preventing them from discerning the truth.

7 Job is further distressed by the deterioration of his body. His eye has grown dim from grief and his limbs have faded to a mere shadow.[28] Thin, with poor eyesight, Job feels powerless.

8–10 These three verses are so hard to understand, especially in this context, that some commentators (e.g., Hölscher, Fohrer) eliminate them. Here we will try to explain them in this context.

Job deplores the attitude that his woes produce in his friends. To disclose the inappropriateness of the friends' approach to him, Job describes the response to ill-fate that is expected from a truly *upright (yāšār)* or *innocent (nāqî)* man. An upright person is so appalled at the abuse borne by an innocent victim that he, also an innocent person, stirs himself to oppose this kind of behavior from the godless. He defends the innocent and condemns the guilty. But Job's friends have not followed this standard of conduct. Instead they have sided with the scoffers and added to his suffering.

The principles presented in v. 9 may be applied either to the friends or to Job. It is true that the righteous person holds firmly to his way. In Job's case his righteousness gives him the fortitude to hold to the true way no

27. Verse 5 is very difficult. It appears to be a cryptic proverb, quoted to defend Job's oath. In the proverb a contrast is made between "friends" and "children." A man does something for others in a way that puts his own children at a grave disadvantage. An older interpretation understands the root *ḥlq* as "flattery"; "he that speaketh flattery to his friends" (AV). Gordis (in his commentary and in *HUCA* 22 [1949] 197–98) finds here a folk saying that describes an effort to host a great feast beyond one's means: "He invites friends to a feast, While his own children's eyes fail with longing (for food)." The friends' display of wisdom to Job is pretentious, being at best very limited. This interpretation fits well with v. 4. Another view takes *ḥēleq* as "a share of an inheritance." A man divides his estate to include others who will help take care of it for his children. But the friends take advantage of the situation and exclude the children. The idea is that one does something for others without meeting the needs of his own family.

28. Cf. Ps. 6:8 (Eng. 7); 31:10 (Eng. 9).

matter how powerful the opposition. Nothing separates him from God, neither pain nor abuse nor insults nor death. Also he, a *righteous* man, has *clean hands,* for he has undergone the act of ritual purification as a testimony of his moral purity. Perhaps Job is quoting a general truth to explain his tenacity in holding on to his innocence. Or, applying these principles to the friends, perhaps Job wishes that they as righteous men would help him to endure his great sorrow in order to preserve his own integrity.[29] Or maybe he is taunting them for their failure to help him.

The vague language of the first line of v. 10 is very difficult to interpret, with the jussive "turn" *(šûḇ)* followed by the imperative "come on" *(bôʾ).*[30] According to Gordis it means "try once again to justify your position." Since *šûḇ* means also "repent, change," Job may be asking the friends to take a different, more sympathetic approach toward him (cf. Habel, OTL). But Job quickly states the conclusion to his exhortation. He still will not be able to find a wise man among his comforters. If correctly interpreted, these lines serve as a searing incrimination of the three companions.

11 In the final segment of this personal lament (vv. 11–16), Job muses on the gloom of death. He deplores the swift passing of his days, for suffering preempts them of any meaning. His plans *(zimmâ)*[31] are undone. And *the desires of my heart,* namely, to be respected and accomplish good for others, are turned to ashes. With these thoughts Job's hope sinks to a low ebb.

12 Verse 12 seems to interrupt the flow of the passage. Often it is explained as Job's stating his friends' approach, using a virtual quote in the second line. Seeking to encourage Job, they optimistically see the turning of his night into day, and so they say, "Light is nearer than darkness." They are telling him that his fortune will be turned to good before he dies (cf. 5:17–26; 8:20–22; 11:13–19). But with these promises they seek to lead Job into false repentance. Another explanation, put forth by Gordis, sees this line expressing the desires of Job's heart (v. 11c), namely, that night would be turned to day and light would be nearer than darkness and death. The shifting of subject from first to third person favors the former view.

13–16 Job reflects on the conflict between the certainty of his

29. Prov. 1:23 has similar language: "Return to my reproof; behold, I shall pour out my mood to you, I shall tell you my words." It suggests that one is willing to open up to a wise man in hope of finding insight and guidance.

30. On this unusual grammatical style see GKC, § 120e.

31. Heb. *zimmâ,* "device, wickedness," is always used in a negative sense outside this passage. But it does not need to be emended, for the similar word *mᵉzimmâ* carries both positive and negative meanings: "purpose or device." See S. Steingrimsson, *"zmm," TDOT,* IV:87–90.

death and his hope. Vv. 13–14 are the apodosis of a conditional sentence, while the protasis consists of rhetorical questions (vv. 15–16). Job is expressing his frustration at his dilemma. In order to find relief from his pain he is marking out a *house in Sheol.* There are some indications in the OT that Sheol was believed to be composed of houses, each with a door and windows.[32] In this dismal abode he would spread out his couch. There he would lie down and get some rest. Without any family left on earth that acknowledges him, he adopts *the pit,* or the grave (*šaḥaṯ;* cf. 9:31; 33:18), as his father, and its occupant, *the worm,* as his mother and sister.[33] These would be his only family to mourn his death. These words are uttered in grim despondency.

Concluding these possibilities with a rhetorical question, Job inquires after the location of his *hope,* by which he specifically means his vindication that would eventuate in the restoration of his honor and his health. Is there anyone who can foresee a brighter future for him? No is the answer, for the darkness chokes every ray of hope that one might have, and if any hope was found, would it pass with him to the chambers of Sheol? The answer is no; since hope is synonymous with life it could have no existence in death. Therefore, the dust will be the end for both his hope and himself.

AIM

In this speech Job vents the agony of his ignominy among men and his estrangement from God. As his pains wear him down, his desire for vindication grows stronger. Presently God seems to be an architect of the cruelest suffering, a tyrant inattentive to his pleas. Like a mighty general leading his army against a well-fortified city, God marshals the forces of affliction against Job. By emaciating his body God has made Job a witness against himself. Socially too God has increased his suffering by blinding the friends from discerning matters accurately, and so he has turned them into mockers.

32. J. Reider ("Contributions to the Scriptural Text," *HUCA* [1952–53] 102–103) notes that earthen ossuaries from Hederah in the plain of Sharon are formed in the shape of a house, including a door and three windows. This suggests that the people considered the dead to be living in houses in the other world.

33. Gordis (in his commentary and in "'My Mother and My Sister'—A Note on Job 17:14 and the Name *'aḥ'aḇ,*" *Leshonenu* 36 [1971–72] 71–72) reasons that a person can bear a compound title drawn from family relationships such as "father-brother." The first indicates the person's higher status and the second their equivalent status. The name Ahab means "father-brother," both epithets of God. Thus Gordis interprets this passage: the worm is called "mother," for it has power over the body, and "sister," for both the worm and the body inhabit the dust (cf. 30:23).

They have become inflicters of suffering rather than sharers in his sorrow, easing its sting.

In a step of daring faith, Job declares that he has a witness in heaven, a defender who will someday verify his claim to innocence. He requests that his defender not only settle his case favorably by attesting his innocence, but also that he serve as his guarantor so that he may be freed from his illness in the immediate future. Only a reprieve will grant the time necessary for the resolution of his case in normal procedure. If God should attend to any of his words, the error in the friends' argument would become plain to all. But Job's ray of hope flickers before the lengthening shadows of death. Therefore, it is urgent that this heavenly witness come to his aid before death claims him as its victim. Since his hope cannot outlive him and bring about a change of his reputation after he has gone, Job bitterly laments the fate before him, seeking to move God to act on his behalf before it is too late.

3. BILDAD'S SECOND SPEECH (18:1–21)

Bildad takes up the task of instructing Job for the second time. His speech is developed quite simply in two sections: a complaint against Job (vv. 2–4), and a discourse on the terrible fate of the wicked (vv. 5–21). Obviously provoked by Job's words and his manner, Bildad delivers a passionate oration on the terrors that await the evildoer. Whereas in his former speech he emphasized the possibility that Job might have a bright future, because the righteous are blessed, he now details the horrid fate that befalls the ungodly. He paints a bleak picture without a single bright stroke. He offers Job no hope, for he wants to persuade him that his questioning God is wrong and will have dire consequences.

The pictures in this speech include a sheikh's lamp (vv. 5–6), numerous traps and snares (vv. 8–10), mythopoetic images of Sheol (vv. 11–14), a curse executed against a defeated foe (v. 15), and the death of a stalwart tree (v. 16). While these images are at home in OT Wisdom literature, the author may have been influenced by individual psalms of lament that depict the evil person's way as laden with traps (e.g., Ps. 140:5–6 [Eng. 4–5]) or as under a military attack (e.g., Ps. 7:13 [Eng. 12]).[1] Moreover, Ps. 73 illustrates how these pictures may be expanded into a motif about the end of transgressors in an inquiry into the wisdom of God's ways. On the other hand, this speech lacks any hymnic praise to God and any exhortation to Job. Interchange between the parties is also missing. It appears that Bildad has abandoned dialoguing with Job; here he delivers only a diatribe on the wicked man's demise.

1. Cf. Westermann, *Structure of the Book of Job*, p. 85.

a. A Complaint against Job (18:1–4)

1 *Bildad the Shuhite responded,*
2 *"How long[1] until you[2] make an end[3] of words?*
Be sensible and then we can speak.
3 *Why are we regarded as cattle,*
considered dumb[4] in your sight?
4 *You who tear yourself in anger,*
will the land be forsaken for you
or a boulder moved from its place?"[5]

2 Annoyed and insulted by Job's words, Bildad asks Job how long it will be before he quits speaking. This question is a stiff rebuke, for a wise man was known for controlling his rhetoric and for his ability to address each situation with precise language. Thus Bildad feels that Job's verbosity reveals his guilt. Also, in his opinion Job is complicating his plight by his much speaking. Therefore, he enjoins Job to *be sensible,* i.e., to display some basic wisdom, in order that his friends can speak to him.

3 Bildad reproaches Job specifically for speaking down to the friends. Job's attitude makes Bildad feel that he and his companions are being regarded *as cattle,* very dumb (cf. Ps. 73:22). Thus he rejects Job's assertion that if their places were reversed he could compose speeches as

1. Bildad began his first speech with this same phrase, *ʿaḏ-ʾānâ,* "how long" (8:2). Job too will begin his next speech with this interrogative (19:2).

2. The plural forms in vv. 2–3 are puzzling. Many emend them to singular forms and claim support from LXX, but LXX may reflect concern for a better literary style rather than a different Hebrew text. The plural is hard to discount in the light of the *nun energicum* on *teśîmûn* (v. 2a) and the plural pronominal suffix on *ʿênêḵem* (v. 3b). Guillaume (*Studies in the Book of Job,* p. 99) thinks that the plural is a mark of politeness at the beginning of a speech; Pope reasons that Bildad is classifying Job with the impious. Certainly the plural "you" does not include the other friends, for he identifies them with the first person plural "we." Maybe the plural "we" influenced the plural "you."

3. The unusual construct form *qinṣê,* "an end of," is difficult before a prepositional phrase (cf. GKC, § 130a). Horst suggests that it is an Aramaic plural form of *qēṣ,* "end." Pope interprets it as cognate to Akk. *qinṣu,* "trap." This last suggestion is attractive, for it offers a play on Bildad's accusation that Job's words are setting a trap for himself with the certainty that Yahweh will ensnare him (vv. 8–10). But the parallel suggests that Bildad feels Job is speaking too much.

4. MT *niṭmînû* is variously treated. It may be a Hiphil of *ṭāmēʾ,* "be defiled." But the context suggests that its meaning is stupidity. To obtain this meaning Rashi (followed by Driver-Gray) reads *temûmîm,* "stupid," but Gordis interprets the MT form as a metaplastic form of *ṭmm,* "stop up," i.e., "be considered stupid." LXX, however, seems to have read *niḏmînû,* "we are put to silence"; Dhorme accepts this as the reading of LXX, but he takes it from the root *dmh* with the meaning "we are likened to," and he restores *kabbaʿar,* "like cattle," before the verb.

5. This verse is a tristich with the first line taken as a *casus pendens* (Driver-Gray).

good as those of his friends, but that his words would offer more comfort (Job 16:4–5). And he is unnerved by Job's statement that he cannot find a wise man among the friends (17:10).

4 Bildad denounces Job further with a biting rhetorical question. The first line, a participial clause, is a *casus pendens,* giving an expanded description of the one addressed. Thus Bildad addresses Job as *you who tear yourself in anger*. He judges that much of Job's agony comes from his chafing against God's discipline. Such resistance is futile and only creates greater discomfort for the one afflicted. Bildad is countering Job's complaint that "[God] has torn me in his wrath and hated me" (16:9). The truth is that it is Job, not God, who is the mad, raving animal.

Bildad then asks Job if for his own benefit he actually expects God either to cause the world to be forsaken or to move a boulder from its place. A *forsaken* land is a territory that has been devastated either by enemy troops or by a natural catastrophe. *a boulder moved from its place* suggests an earthquake (14:18). With this question Bildad takes up Job's words in 14:18 about God's power that both changes the landscape and destroys a person's hope (cf. also 9:5–6). For Bildad the moral order is so integrally related to the natural order that asking for a change in the moral law—Job asking God to acquit him without his repenting—is the same as asking for a remarkable event in nature. But it is beyond his imagination that God would so alter the universe to redeem one man. Bildad thus believes that Job's line of reasoning brings him to the brink of arrogant insanity.

b. The Terrible Fate of the Wicked (18:5–21)

Bildad leaves off his personal dispute with Job and delivers his instruction. He depicts the veil of horror through which an ungodly person must pass on his way to the abode of the dead. The sinner is first caught in his sinful deeds (vv. 6–10), and then a disaster consumes his life and destroys every person and possession belonging to him (vv. 11–20). In summary, this is the fate of everyone who does not know God (v. 21). Bildad believes that God has so designed the world that just judgment is executed against every wicked person.

(1) The Trapping of the Wicked Person (18:5–10)

5 *"Indeed, the light of the wicked is extinguished;*
the flame of his fire ceases to shine.
6 *The light in his tent grows dark;*
the lamp above him[1] *is extinguished.*

1. The preposition with a pronominal suffix *ʿālāyw* is difficult with the suffix on lamp *(nērô)*. It could mean "against him" as in Mic. 3:6 (cf. Job 14:22; Hakam) or it could mean "above him," i.e., the lamp hung from the roof of his tent (Rowley; cf. 29:3).

7 *His vigorous stride is shortened,*
and his own plans[2] *trip him.*[3]
8 *For he is caught by his feet*[4] *in a net;*
he steps on a webbing.
9 *A gin holds him by the heel;*[5]
a snare seizes him.
10 *A noose for him lies hidden on the ground,*
a trap for him on the path."

5, 6 Taking issue with Job's questioning of God's just rule, Bildad affirms that retribution against the wicked is operative in the present. He defends this truth by quoting two proverbs. The first one (v. 5) presents a general truth, as indicated by the use of plural forms. It says *the light of the wicked is extinguished.* This proverb is similar to Prov. 13:9: "The light of the righteous rejoices, but the lamp of the wicked will be snuffed out" (cf. Prov. 20:20; 24:20). Even though the wicked may be able to kindle a brilliant flame *(šeḇîḇ ʾēš),*[6] it will not continue to burn before the strong winds of God's judgment.

The second proverb speaks about a sheikh's lamp (v. 6). The light inside the sheikh's *tent,* his most private abode, *grows dark.* When this lamp is lit, it signifies that all is well in the chief's household. But now the very lamp that hangs above his head is extinguished. Darkness totally enshrouds his tent. The doctrine of retribution is often illustrated by the metaphors of light and darkness. Light is symbolic of life (3:20), wealth (22:28), and happiness; conversely, darkness represents loss (15:30), sadness, and death (3:5). This proverb means that the fate that befalls a wicked person darkens every corner of his life. He cannot see any ray of hope penetrating this darkness. Perhaps by shifting from the plural forms in v. 5 to the singular forms in v. 6 Bildad is making an application indirectly, subtly, to Job.

7 Bildad pictures a wicked person's life as a journey that is unexpectedly halted. Each traveler takes strides appropriate to the path he treads

2. G. R. Driver ("Mistranslations," *ExpTim* 57 [1945–46] 192–93) seeks to prove that *ʿaṣāṯô,* "his counsel," is a noun that means "disobedience" (so NEB).

3. MT *weṯaślîḵēhû,* "and he sent him," appears to be an error of metathesis for *weṯaḵšîlēhû,* "and he causes him to fall, trips him," as read by LXX (see *BHS*). This change is supported by the text of Prov. 4:12 and Ps. 64:9 (Eng. 8). Thus most commentators adopt it.

4. The emendation of *beraglāyw* to *raglô,* "his feet," so that it may function as the subject does not commend itself in the light of a similar reading in Judg. 5:15. G. Gerlemann ("*brglyw* as an Idiomatic Phrase," *JSS* 4 [1958] 59) suggests that *beraglāyw* means "on the spot, instantly."

5. Some (e.g., Budde and Driver-Gray) add a third masculine singular pronominal suffix to *beʿāqēḇ,* but that is not necessary since the noun names a part of the body.

6. This phrase appears also in Dan. 3:22; 7:9; Sir. 8:10; 45:19.

(cf. Prov. 4:10–27). The one who starts down the path of evil begins with long, *vigorous* strides. His strides are lengthened by great successes: the greater each success, the longer his strides become. Because his way is easy, the wicked person at first appears to be making swift progress. But soon his vigor wanes, his stride *is shortened (ṣārar).*[7] He trips over his own grandiose plans, stumbles, and falls. This picture teaches that no wicked person can enjoy prosperity for a great length of time. Neither his strength nor his subtle planning will sustain him indefinitely.

8–10 Bildad illustrates the fact that a wicked person is sure to stumble on the path he is taking by enumerating the many traps that are set to ensnare him. He uses six different words for trapping devices. Such a person's path is dotted with many traps, like a present-day minefield. While a wicked person is traveling on his road to success, his head raised proudly, his foot will unsuspectingly trip a hidden snare, and he will be caught. A clever person may escape one or more snares, but his path is so lined with traps that it is inevitable that he will trigger one of them. It is impossible for any wicked person to escape the heavenly trapper.

The trapping devices mentioned are various kinds of nets and traps used to catch birds and animals.[8] A *net, rešeṯ,* is used for birds and small animals (Hos. 7:12) and also for larger animals like a lion (Ezek. 19:8). Spread out over the ground, perhaps over a pit, it entangles the animal's feet. Figuratively, a net is used to describe a person or a people caught in the destructive schemes of others (Lam. 1:13; Ps. 140:6 [Eng. 5]). A *webbing, śᵉḇāḵâ,* is a large mesh of branches spread over a pit. This word is also used for latticework. When an animal, thinking that it is walking on firm ground, steps unsuspectingly on the mesh, it collapses and the animal falls into a pit. A *gin, paḥ,* is a snare possibly made out of wood (Ps. 124:7). When stepped on, it grasps the victim's heel. A *snare, ṣammîm,* a little-known word, probably comes from the root *ṣmm,* "constrict, contract, shrivel up." It may be another type of trap that closes on its prey (cf. Gordis). Another hunting device is a rope tied to form a *noose, ḥeḇel.* Set to spring up at the slightest touch, it grabs the animal tightly and raises it off the ground. A *trap, malkōḏeṯ,* is a general term for a snaring device.

(2) The Death of the Wicked Person (18:11–21)

11 *"All around terrors frighten him*
and dog[1] his every step.

7. Heb. *ṣar,* "narrow, restricted, confined," is a negative word. It represents distress, defeat, and punishment.

8. The author's rich knowledge of a wide range of subjects is evident again in this passage. Nowhere else do we have a list of ancient traps and snares.

1. MT *wehĕpîṣuhû* is problematic. Those who relate it to a Hiphil of *pûṣ* assign

12 *His strength is depleted,*
and calamity is prepared for his fall.[2]
13 *His skin is eaten by disease;*[3]
the firstborn of death eats his limbs.
14 *He is torn from his secure tent*[4]
and marched off[5] *to the king of terrors.*
15 *Nothing of his dwells*[6] *in his tent;*
brimstone is scattered over his estate.
16 *His roots below dry up,*
and above his branch withers.
17 *His memory vanishes from the earth;*
he has no name abroad.
18 *He is driven from light to darkness,*
and he is chased out of the world.

---

the meaning "pursue, chase" (Dhorme and Gordis). Horst takes it as a by-form of *pzz* II, "be hasty, rash." G. R. Driver ("Some Hebrew Medical Expressions," *ZAW* 65 [1953] 259–60) argues that it means "piss" by relating it to Arab. *fāṣa,* which in stem IV means "urinate." This is why the NEB translates the line "and make him piss over his feet." This suggestion has not found acceptance. The other renderings continue the imagery of trapping.

2. MT *leṣalʿô* is variously understood. Dhorme takes it to mean "at his side." Tur-Sinai and others argue that *ṣēlāʿ*, "rib," has the extended meaning of "wife." Duhm considers it as from *ṣelaʿ*, "stumbling, fall." The reading *leṣelaʿ nāḵôn,* "I am prepared to fall," in Ps. 38:18 (Eng. 17) supports MT and Duhm's interpretation.

3. Verse 13 in MT appears to be the result of a textual corruption, for it is unusual for the author to repeat the same two words in parallel lines. Dhorme vocalizes the first *baddê* as *biḏway,* "by a disease" (cf. Ps. 41:4 [Eng. 3]; also Job 6:7) and the verb as a Niphal, *yēʾāḵēl:* "His skin is eaten away by a disease." Horst suggests reading *maḏweh,* which yields "a malignant disease eats his skin." Dhorme is followed here, for he accepts the consonantal text. N. Sarna ("The Mythological Background of Job 18," *JBL* 82 [1963] 317) takes a different approach; he thinks that *bdy* means "with two hands" and *bdyw* is "with his two hands." He gets his clue from an Ugaritic passage, *UT,* 67:I:19–20, in which Mot says: "The firstborn of Mot will devour his skin with two hands, yea with his two hands he will devour (him) *[bklat ydy ilhm hm].*"

4. Gordis takes the words *mēʾohºlô,* "from his tent," and *miḇṭaḥô,* "his security," to be in apposition and a case of hendiadys meaning "his secure tent."

5. MT *weṯaṣʿiḏēhû,* "he marched him," is emended by many to a third masculine singular. But Moran ("**taqtul*—Third Masculine Singular?" *Bib* 45 [1964] 82) suggests that this form should be vocalized as a third masculine plural *(weṯaṣʿîḏûhû)* used with a passive sense. Gordis thinks that the third feminine singular may also function with a passive sense. In that case it becomes unnecessary to change the text.

6. For the unusual *mibbelî-lô* Fohrer suggests *lîlîṯ,* "a night demon" (cf. Isa. 34:14; cf. n.14 below). Gordis reads *mabbûl,* "flood" (Gen. 6; Ps. 29:10), which may also mean "flood of fire." But Dahood (*Bib* 38 [1957] 312–14) suggests the reading *mabbēl* on the basis of Ugar. *nblat,* "flames": "Fire is set in his tent" (Pope). The extra *l* is attached to the next word as an emphatic *lamed* at the head of the second line. These ideas are interesting but, as Horst points out, unnecessary, for *mibbelî-lô* is similar to *lōʾ lô* (Hab. 2:6) and *lelōʾ lāh* (Job 39:16) as a way of saying "nothing of his."

19 *He has no posterity or progeny among his people,*
and there is no survivor where he once lived.
20 *At his fate*[7] *Westerners are appalled,*
and Easterners are seized[8] *with horror.*
21 *Surely such are the dwellings of an evil man,*
and such is the place of him who knew not God."[9]

11 When a wicked person discovers that he is treading a dangerous course laden with traps, he is filled with apprehensions; *terrors [ballāhôṯ] frighten him*. The enemy Death arouses the deepest feelings of dread in him (Ezek. 26:21; 27:36; 28:19). Frightening terrors stalk his heels. His sleep is disturbed by nightmares. No longer can he find any moments of relaxation. This description recalls Job's opening lament in which he concedes that in his days of success he had dreadful thoughts that he would suffer great loss (3:25).

12 Whoever is so terrorized loses *his strength (ʾôn).*[10] Instead of possessing the fortitude which enables him to face great obstacles, he is robbed of his nerve by fear. Now a *calamity* is ready to bring down his weakened body to the grave. Certainly Bildad believes that Job, just like an evildoer, has been caught in one of God's traps. This is the reason for his fears and his loss of strength.

13 An evildoer's *skin is eaten by disease*. His body wastes away to skin and bones, and his flesh is covered with sores. His bodily functions slowly degenerate, as *the firstborn of death,*[11] i.e., plague, consumes his limbs, leaving him an immobile cripple at the brink of death. No doubt this

7. The phrase *yômô,* "his day," is taken in the sense of the final day of his fate (Pope).

8. Dahood ("Northwest Semitic Philology and Job," p. 63) takes MT *ʾḥz,* "to seize," as a Qal passive, *ʾuḥᵃzû*. The parallelism in this verse favors a passive verb and also accounts for its being plural.

9. The entire phrase *lô yāḏaʿ ʾēl,* "he does not know God," is governed by the construct *mᵉqôm,* "place of" (GKC, § 130d).

10. Heb. *ʾōnô* may mean "his force" or "his strength." In some passages it parallels "the firstborn child" (Gen. 49:3; Deut. 21:17; Ps. 78:51; 105:36). Thus Tur-Sinai, Hakam, and Gordis find here a reference to one's offspring or children, which then is parallel to *ṣēlāʿ*, "side," taken as a metaphor for "his wife," so called because of the account that God formed woman out of man's side (Gen. 2:21–23). Thus his whole progeny is overtaken by terror. They have departed from him, leaving him alone to face the calamity in its full force. This interpretation has some merit. But at best it may be a secondary idea underlying the more obvious meaning as presented in n.2 above. Poetic language often conveys more than one meaning.

11. Dhorme points out that among the Arabs diseases are called "the daughters of death." And among the Babylonians and Assyrians the god of plagues, Namtaru, is the vizier of the queen of hell. Thus the firstborn of death can be identified with the demon of plague.

description alludes to Job's illness. For Bildad, Job's emaciated body is the convicting evidence of his wrongdoing.

14 The wicked man *is torn from his secure tent.* His tent had been the center of his security.[12] There he felt safe from any harm. But he is forcefully removed from his dwelling place and marched off to *the king of terrors,* the prince of the dead.[13] Such a monarch was believed to reign over the subterranean region that housed the souls of the dead and the demons of plague and terror.

15 When this wicked man is removed from his tent, the forces of destruction have a free hand to decimate everything on earth associated with him. No person or animal that belonged to him is left to live in his dwelling. And the enemy ruins his fields, spreading *brimstone* over them.[14] Such a curse leaves his land desolate for decades.

16 The wicked person languishes and dies just as the *branch of* a beautiful tree withers after its *roots dry up.* Since the attack strikes at the tree's roots, it takes a while before the fatal blow becomes visible. But eventually the leaves of the stricken tree turn brown and fall off. So too, the plague begins to work against the wicked person long before its effects become visible. Obviously, there is no chance of renewed growth for a tree whose roots have dried out. With this metaphor Bildad categorically rejects Job's search for hope in his reflection: "There is hope for a tree, if it be cut down, that it will sprout again" (14:7). Bildad wants to put an end to Job's speculative thinking as a way to reason around the view that God has unleashed against him the terrors of death.

12. This scene is similar to the picture of causing a tent to collapse by pulling up its supporting cords, a picture of a violent death (Job 4:21; Isa. 33:20; cf. Judg. 16:9; Eccl. 4:12).

13. The language pertaining to the frightful encounter with death in vv. 11–15 appears to draw heavily on the mythopoetic language associated with the realm of the dead in the ancient Near East. N. Sarna ("The Mythological Background of Job 18," *JBL* 82 [1963] 315–19) argues that "terrors," *ballāhôṯ,* is an epithet of Sheol, which is ruled over by "the king of terrors," *meleḵ ballāhôṯ,* or the god Mot, as is evident in Ugaritic mythology. The firstborn of Mot is a demon that brings misfortune and expedites the destruction of people to satisfy the great craving of Sheol. This demon attacks a person's body, making that person deathly ill. The sudden loss of health and vigor reduces one to haunting nightmares that leave him stricken with terror. A further mythical allusion may be found. Some, like Fohrer, think that *mibbᵉlî-lô,* "nothing," in v. 15a should be read as the word *lîlîṯ,* Lilith, the night demon (cf. n. 6 above). Thus the vacated tent of the evildoer is occupied by demons; consequently no one dares to venture near that place. Cf. W. Irwin, "Job's Redeemer," *JBL* 81 (1962) 217–29.

14. The spreading of salt on a conquered city was an act of war designed to deter an enemy's quick recovery and ability to take on a military campaign; cf. Judg. 9:45. Deut. 29:22 (Eng. 23) says that God would strew a land with brimstone and salt so that nothing could grow there. This reference speaks of God's final judgment against his people's perpetual sinning.

17 The *memory* of the wicked person *vanishes from the earth.* The memory of a person perpetuates his existence on earth after death. Therefore, to leave behind a good reputation is a blessing. As Prov. 10:7 says: "The memory of the righteous is a blessing, but the name of the wicked will rot." A blessed memory was the prize of the righteous. It spread abroad even after their death. But the wicked *has no name* in the land after his death. The removal of this person's name means he is completely forgotten, making the judgment against him full.

18 The wicked person *is chased out of the world. He is driven from light,* which gives life, and confined to the realm of *darkness.* In Sheol he has no place that he can identify as his own. Disoriented, his soul wanders about listlessly in the gloomy darkness. This curse as applied to the realm of the dead is similar to the curse Cain had to bear on earth when he was cast abroad in the earth as a fugitive for killing his brother (Gen. 4:12–14). This comparison indicates the severity of this curse from the ancient perspective.

19, 20 The blotting out of the wicked person's name is so complete that *no survivor* of his is left to dwell *where he once lived.* Usually there are survivors of the worst plagues, but the force of the fatal blow that strikes this person is harder than any known calamity. There will be no offspring left to him, not any of his children nor any of their children.[15] *His fate* (lit. "his day of judgment") will be so horrible that people everywhere, both *Easterners* and *Westerners,*[16] will be *appalled (šāmam).* As they hear about his terrible fate, they *are seized with horror (śaʿar),*[17] causing them to shudder in the depths of their beings.

21 Bildad closes with a summary statement, marked off by the particle *ʾak̲,* "surely." *An evil man,* i.e., a person *who knew not God,* will be imprisoned in a dreadful dwelling. "Not to know God" means to have no

15. The two Hebrew words are *nîn* and *nek̲ed̲.* These two words are often joined together to refer to one's progeny (cf. Gen. 21:23; Isa. 14:22; Sir. 41:5). In Sir. 47:22b God affirms to his people that he will show his covenant mercy by not allowing them to be annihilated: "He would not cut off progeny *[nyn wnkd]* to his chosen, and he would not destroy the seed of his beloved."

16. Heb. *ʾaḥarōnîm,* "coming after, behind," and *qad̲mōnîm,* "former," may also mean "those of the West" and "those of the East." These words are used with the word "sea" to indicate direction: "the sea behind" is the Mediterranean and "the sea in front" is the Dead Sea (cf. Joel 2:20 and Zech. 14:8). Pope refers to the Ugaritic myth (*UT,* ʿnt II:78) in which Anat slays all the people of the sunrise and the seashore, the East and the West. Others understand the meaning of these terms be "the earlier" and "the later" generations. Although this interpretation is possible, this way of expressing that idea is strange and unusual.

17. Heb. *śaʿar* means "a grave fright." Probably it originally describes the bristling sensation that runs through the body when a person is suddenly scared. It is associated with *šāmēm,* "be appalled, astounded," in Jer. 2:12; Ezek. 27:35; 32:10. In a similar vein to this passage the context of Jer. 2:12 shows that frightful terror and grave apprehension attend the most serious sin, i.e., forsaking Yahweh for false gods.

fellowship with God, either because a person has willfully broken his relationship with God or because he has refused to enter into covenant with God. In death that person will never again experience God's enriching grace, for his abode will be in a chaotic place devoid of light. Sadly there is no escape from his punishment.

AIM

Bildad vividly portrays for Job the terrible fate of the wicked. The bright light that shines in his dwelling is extinguished, forcing him to live in darkness. Using another metaphor, Bildad enumerates the many kinds of snares that are concealed on the way that the wicked person travels. He wants to inform Job that no evildoer can escape being caught in one of God's traps. The person who is caught is terror-stricken. Usually he discovers that he is trapped when he falls to a dreaded illness. His last days are filled with pain and fear. Then at his death no memorial is erected for him on earth. Neither does God leave him any survivors. Even his name vanishes from the earth. His bitter fate appalls all.

It is evident that Bildad thinks that Job has traveled a long way down this path, for he is tormented by apprehensive fears and all his offspring have died. But he is also warning Job that although his pain is now great, the path on which he is traveling will result in a more horrible fate. Perhaps he wishes to stir in Job strong emotions of repulsion at such a fate in order that Job might forsake his claims to innocence and humbly repent. But Bildad does not explicitly extend to Job an invitation to repentance. Possibly he believes that Job's fate is irreversible. Therefore, he considers it his task solely to instruct Job about the certain, miserable destiny of all who do not know God. The sight of Job's emaciated body has fired Bildad's rhetoric, but at the expense of his showing any compassion that would encourage him to find God.

4. JOB'S FIFTH RESPONSE (19:1–29)

This time Job addresses primarily his comforters. His speech is heavily influenced by the language of personal lament, particularly the part in which a lamenter expresses his anguish at the tireless efforts of his enemy in plaguing him. To add clout to his lamenting Job weaves in legal language. Amidst his struggling, his faith reaches out to express great confidence in God even in spite of his circumstances. Then Job ends by warning his friends of the consequences of the way that they are counseling him.

This speech consists of five pericopes: a complaint against the friends (vv. 1–6); a complaint about God's enmity (vv. 7–12); a complaint about complete alienation (vv. 13–20); a plea for help and a statement of assurance (vv. 21–27); a warning to the friends (vv. 28–29).

a. A Complaint against the Friends (19:1–6)

1 *And Job answered,*
2 *"How long will you grieve[1] me*
and crush me[2] with words?
3 *These ten times[3] you have humiliated me;*
you have not been ashamed to despise me.[4]
4 *If I have truly erred,*
with me[5] my error resides.
5 *If[6] indeed you would exalt yourself over me*
and argue my disgrace against me,
6 *know then that God has wronged me*
and drawn his net around me."

2, 3 Job's use of plural forms indicates that, as usual, he addresses his complaint against all the friends. His opening words, *How long,* indicate, however, that he has Bildad in mind, for they are the same words that Bildad used to open his two speeches.[7] Job is greatly disturbed both by the harsh tone of Bildad's speech and by his classifying him among the wicked. Therefore, he asks Bildad and the friends how long they will continue to make him feel worse about his affliction. He complains that, in fact, their insults ridiculing his perseverance in seeking an encounter with God *crush* him because they make his faith in God look like obstinate rebellion against God. No wonder Job rebuffs them so sharply.

Job uses strong words to reprove his friends for the way they are treating him. *grieve (yāḡâ)* refers to deep personal sorrow (cf. Lam. 1:12; 3:32, 33). *crush (dikkāʾ)* means that they are destroying his fortitude for

1. MT *tôgyûn,* "you grieve," is a singular example of a *lamed-he* verb preserving a final *y* (GKC, § 75gg).

2. In MT *tᵉḏakkᵉʾûnanî,* "you crush me," the suffix is added to the *nun paragogicum* (GKC, § 60e). It may be revocalized *tᵉḏakkʾûnanî* with elision of the ʾ (GKC, § 75oo).

3. Cf. Gen. 31:7; Num. 14:22; 1 Sam. 1:8; Lev. 26:26.

4. When two imperfects follow one another without a conjunction, the complementary verbal idea is subordinate (GKC, § 120c).

5. The indirect object is placed first for emphasis (GKC, § 142f).

6. The ʾ*im* is taken as a conditional particle, with v. 5 the protasis and v. 6 the apodosis (Delitzsch and Gordis). Dhorme, however, takes the ʾ*im* as an interrogative, "Is it not true indeed . . . ?" (also Fohrer).

7. Cf. 8:2 *(ʿaḏ-ʾān);* 18:2 *(ʿaḏ-ʾānâ).*

bearing pain. Psychologically Heb. *dikkā'* represents the feelings of worthlessness and futility one experiences when overwhelmed by misfortune. In legal contexts it depicts a powerful person's blatant abuse of the judicial system to exploit the weak and the poor (Job 5:4; Prov. 22:22; cf. Lam. 3:34). With this word Job may be making the innuendo that his friends are crushing him by condemning him without producing any convincing evidence against him. *humiliated (hiḵlîm)* means "to shame or dishonor" someone, usually by public ridicule (cf. 1 Sam. 20:34; Prov. 25:8). The meaning of the Hebrew word translated *despise (hāḵar)*[8] has not been precisely determined. Job is charging that his friends' counsel has turned into obsessive, shameful reproof.

4 Job sternly denounces his friends' endeavor to find some sin in him.[9] Until the final verdict comes from God, he must bear the responsibility of any error *(m^e^šûgâ)* he may have unintentionally committed *(šāgâ)*. This Hebrew root for doing wrong refers to an inadvertent mistake, the kind of wrongful act that everyone commits by reason of being human (cf. 6:24). Remaining confident that he has never sinned as gravely as his misfortune suggests, Job refuses to concede that he has done anything more serious than some unintentional blunder.

5, 6 Job endeavors to alert his friends to the way they are actually treating him. By prematurely accusing him they *exalt* themselves over *(higdîl ʿal)* him.[10] In their shaming him they are vaunting themselves. The psalmist also resents the attitude of those who exalt themselves over him. "Let them be put to shame and confusion altogether who rejoice at my misfortune! Let them be clothed with shame and ignominy who exalt themselves against me!" (Ps. 35:26). In this psalm "those who exalt themselves against me" is parallel to "those who rejoice at my misfortune." This

8. The term *tahk^e^rû* appears only here. Various attempts have been made to establish its meaning. Delitzsch and KB (p. 235) relate it to Arab. *hakara,* "fill with wonder." Others relate it to Arab. *ḥakara,* "wrong, deal harshly with," and read *taḥk^e^rû* with three mss. This last suggestion has the advantage of explaining the form as a Qal rather than as a Hiphil. While Dhorme accepts this identification, he defends the MT as resulting from a weakening of the *ḥ*. The context suggests a meaning of "insult, despise." Gordis notes that Arab. *ḥaqara* has this meaning.

9. The exact sense of v. 4 is debated. Most take the first line as the protasis of a conditional sentence: "even if I have erred." Gordis believes that the conditional sense is signaled by *'ap,* "also." The use of the two particles, *'ap* and *'omnān,* "verily, truly," conveys emphasis with a note of sarcasm: "Yes, really."

10. Guillaume (*Studies in the Book of Job,* p. 100) and Gordis relate MT *higdîl* to Arab. *jadala* (III, "to quarrel"; IV, "to quarrel with another") instead of to Heb. *gāḏal* in Hiphil, "to make great." The use of this word with "mouth" in Ps. 55:13 (Eng. 12) lends some support to their view. But the Hiphil occurs several times in the OT to mean "boast, set oneself forth as great presumptuously and arrogantly" (e.g., Ps. 35:26; 38:17 [Eng. 16]; Jer. 48:26, 42; Ezek. 35:13; Zeph. 2:10; cf. R. Mosis, *"gādhal," TDOT,* II:405).

parallelism indicates that those who vaunt themselves typically take pleasure in another's hardship. Job accuses the friends of defaming him by arguing from his disgrace or reproach *(ḥerpâ)* that he is guilty of wrongdoing. *Disgrace* may include the infamy attached to a crime (e.g., 2 Sam. 13:13; Dhorme). These comforters reproach him with the very suffering they came to help him face.

Job wants the friends to know that it is *God* who *has wronged* *(ʿiwwēṯ)* him. Heb. *ʿiwwēṯ* means literally "bend, make crooked." Legally it refers to an unjust, prejudicial decision that denies a defendant his rightful due (cf. Ps. 119:78; Lam. 3:36). With the choice of this word Job refutes Bildad's major premise that God does not pervert *(ʿiwwēṯ)* justice (Job 8:3). But Job knows that in his own case God has misjudged him. Indeed, it is God who has *drawn his net [māṣôḏ]*[11] *around* him. With this image Job picks up on Bildad's elaborate description of God lining the path of the wicked with all kinds of trapping devices (18:8–10). He is refuting his friend's interpretation by claiming that he has not fallen prey to his own folly. The truth is that God has been the aggressive hunter who has thrown his net around his prey so that there is no possibility for him to get away.

b. A Complaint about God's Enmity (19:7–12)

7 *"Though I cry, 'Violence!' I am not answered;*
though I shout for help, there is no justice.
8 *He has walled up my way so that I cannot pass;*
he has shrouded my paths in darkness.
9 *He has stripped me of my honor;*
he has removed the crown from my head.
10 *He has broken me down on every side till I perish;*[1]
he has uprooted my hope like a tree.
11 *His anger burns*[2] *against me,*
and he regards me as one of his enemies.[3]

11. MT *meṣûḏô* is taken from the Hebrew noun *māṣôḏ*, meaning "a net" used in hunting (cf. Eccl. 7:26) or fishing (Eccl. 9:12, *meṣôḏâ*). Based on Heb. *hiqqîp*, "surround," Gordis postulates that the imagery in v. 6 is that of military action. Thus he identifies the MT form as from Heb. *meṣûḏâ*, "fortress, stronghold," here "breastworks, siegeworks." True, Job frequently uses military language to describe his plight, but he seems to be using the metaphor of God as a trapper to respond to Bildad's use of this metaphor in 18:8–10.

1. Heb. *hālaḵ*, "go," here has the nuance of "perish" (cf. 14:20; KB, pp. 236–37). The vocalization *ʾēlaḵ* is exceptional (GKC, §§ 69p, x).

2. Heb. *wayyaḥar*, "and he became angry," in the Hiphil occurs only here and in Neh. 3:20 (which has a textual variant). This vocalization may be for assonance, since a *patah* comes before *ḥ* three more times in vv. 11–12 (cf. Gordis). This could also account for an oral error. That is why most prefer to read the Qal *wayyiḥar*.

3. The plural noun *ṣārāyw*, "his enemies," is striking. Most take it as an error for

12 *His troops advance in columns;*
they construct a siege ramp against me,
and they encamp around my tent."

7 Job laments God's treating him like an enemy. He takes this tactic in order to shock his friends into realizing that God himself is the cause of his plight, not some wrong that he has done. Languishing under God's attack, Job cries out, *Violence! (ḥāmās),*[4] the plaint of one in desperate need of help (Deut. 22:23–24). Without sufficient strength to resist his attackers, the victim's only hope is that his cry will be heard in some quarter or by God himself. But no one, not even God, comes to Job's rescue (cf. Lam. 3:8). No matter how loudly he cries, *there is no justice* for him.

8 Job feels that God has built such a high wall across the way that he was taking that there is no way for him to get through. To use another metaphor, God has shrouded Job's paths with darkness so dense that he cannot find his way (cf. Lam. 3:2, 6). This darkness conceals all avenues of escape. There is a strong note of irony in Job's phrasing his complaint this way.[5] In the prologue the Satan argued that Job's faith was not real, for God had protected Job and his holdings by enclosing them with a hedge (1:10). But now that God has removed that hedge to allow the Satan to test Job, Job sees things inside out. He fears that God has built up a wall around him to keep his cries for help from escaping and any assistance from entering. Even though he looks to God for deliverance, God, in turn, appears to treat him with unprovoked enmity. As a result Job receives neither answers to his earnest prayer as to why he is suffering nor any relief from his persistent pain. Job is expressing his deep inner struggle caused by the conflict between his dreadful circumstances and his faith in God.

9 Job details his complaint against God under numerous metaphors. He charges God with dethroning him (v. 9), uprooting him (v. 10), and besieging him (vv. 11–12). When God stripped him of his *honor (kāḇôḏ),* which had adorned him like a garment, and *removed the crown* from

---

ṣārô, "his enemy." But Gordis views the plural to be distributive, "as one of his foes." Hakam thinks that Job perceives himself to be treated by God as though he were many enemies.

4. In similar fashion Jeremiah cried out under duress, "Violence and destruction" (*ḥāmās wāšōḏ,* Jer. 20:8; cf. Hab. 1:2). "Violence" was the cry for help by one threatened by injustice; he hoped to receive the protection of the community, especially of the court (Jer. 20:8; Hab. 1:2), according to G. von Rad, *Old Testament Theology,* I:157n.34; also cf. H. Stoebe, *THAT,* I:583–87.

5. Many of the words in this strophe appear in Lam. 3:7–9: "He has walled *[gāḏar]* me in so that I cannot escape; he has laden me with chains; though I scream *[zāʿaq]* and cry for help *[šiwwēaʿ],* he shuts out my prayer; he has walled up *[gāḏar]* my ways *[dereḵ]* with hewn stones; he has made crooked *[ʿiwwâ]* my paths *[neṯîḇâ]."*

his head,[6] he deposed Job from his high position as elder statesman. No longer able to take his seat in the council, he now sits on the ash heap in shame. His experience is diametrically opposed to the traditional belief that God crowns a man with glory *(kāḇôḏ)* and honor (*hāḏār;* Ps. 8:6 [Eng. 5]).

10 Job charges God with stamping out his life.[7] *He has broken me down on every side,* that is, God has pounded him as though he were a fortified wall (cf. 16:14). And he has ordered his troops to leave no stone standing. Changing metaphors to that of gardening, Job complains that God *has uprooted my hope like a tree*. Earlier Job had observed that "there is hope for a tree; if it is cut down, it will sprout again" (14:7). But God has acted toward him so ferociously that he has not merely cut down the tree, he has uprooted the stump. Thereby he has snuffed out Job's last hope for renewal.

11, 12 Job feels the full brunt of God's hostility. God has let *his anger* burn hotly against him and has poured it on him in great measure as though he regards Job *as one of his enemies*. That is why he has marshalled *his troops* to *advance in columns* against Job. As though besieging a walled city, the army surrounds Job's tent to shut off all its accesses. Then in the most vulnerable spot they build *a siege ramp* in order to breach the wall. By referring to himself as a *tent* rather than a city,[8] Job focuses on the brutality of God's attack. With this hyperbole Job expresses his utter astonishment at God's treating him so roughly.

c. A Complaint about Complete Alienation (19:13–20)

13 *"My brothers are far[1] from me,*
and my friends are utterly estranged[2] from me.
14 *My relatives and my associates have gone away;*
my house guests have forgotten me.[3]

6. Cf. Jer. 13:18; Lam. 5:16.

7. The dual imagery of being "torn down" *(nāṯaṣ)* and "uprooted" (*nāsaʿ*, though a different word is used for "uproot") appears also in Ps. 52:7 (Eng. 5): "Surely God will tear you down *[nāṯaṣ]* for ever; he will snatch you and pull you from your tent; he will uproot *[šērēš]* you from the land of the living."

8. Fohrer thinks that the word "tent" is chosen as an allusion to Bildad's use of "tent" in 18:5–6. If Job lives in his tent in darkness, it is not because his lamp has gone out like a wicked man's, but because God has unleashed cosmic troops against him.

1. MT *hirḥîq*, "remove," being singular, assumes God as its subject. LXX and Syr. read a plural, and the parallelism also favors a plural. It is possible that the conjunctive *waw* on the next word originally was a *mater lectionis* on the verb (i.e., *hirḥîqû*). It is also possible to account for MT as an error of haplography.

2. For MT *ʾaḵ zārû,* "surely they are estranged," LXX seems to read *ʾaḵzārû,* "they are cruel."

3. Verses 14 and 15 as they stand in MT are out of balance. The simplest solution

15 *My maidservants consider[4] me a stranger;*
I have become a foreigner in their sight.
16 *I summon my servant, but he does not answer;*
I entreat him with my mouth.
17 *My breath is repulsive to my wife;*
I stink[5] to my own children.
18 *Even young children repudiate me;*
when I rise,[6] they jeer at me.
19 *All the men of my council detest me,*
and those[7] I love have turned against me.
20 *My bones cleave to my flesh,[8]*
and I have escaped with the skin of my teeth."

13 God's attack has estranged Job from all his relatives, companions, servants, and fellow citizens. He is left to face his fate alienated from his community. Because they all believe that God has smitten him and they are

---

is to place the *'aṯnāḥ* (the principal Masoretic accent, indicating a pause) for v. 14 at *ûmᵉyuddāʿay,* "my associates," and to place *gārê ḇêṯî,* "my house guests," of v. 15a with v. 14b. The *w* on the following *wᵉ'amhōṯay,* "and my maidservants," is best removed as an error of dittography, having risen from the preceding *y*.

4. There are many explanations for MT *taḥšᵉḇunî*. It may be a third masculine plural with the *taw* prefix (C. Gordon, *JBL* 70 [1959] 160). If this is correct, it is because its subject consists of a masculine noun and a feminine noun; cf. the masculine plural suffix on *bᵉʿênêhem,* "in their sight." Another reason could be that the gender distinction became weakened, particularly in rare feminine forms with a pronominal suffix (GKC, § 135o). If the subject is solely *'amḥōṯay,* "my maidservants," the MT form might be a contraction of the third person feminine plural with a pronominal suffix. Possibly the unusual form arose when the division of vv. 14–15 became blurred.

5. MT *ḥannōṯî* is understood as a hapax legomenon meaning "stink, fetid," related to Arab. *ḫanna* in the 10th stem, "stink" (KB, p. 321); there is also a Syriac root *ḥanîn,* "musty, stale, rancid" (R. P. Smith, *A Compendious Syriac Dictionary,* ed. J. P. Smith [Oxford: Clarendon Press, 1903, repr. 1976], p. 149).

6. The cohortative *'āqûmâ,* "let me rise," expresses a contingent intention (GKC, § 108e).

7. The pronoun *zeh,* "this," is used poetically in place of *'ᵃšer* (15:17; GKC, § 138h); cf. Sir. 6:11 and T. Penar, "Job 19,19 in the Light of Ben Sira 6,11," *Bib* 48 (1967) 293–95.

8. The first line appears to be too long, esp. with both *bᵉʿôrî,* "in my skin," and *ûḇiḇśārî,* "and in my flesh." There are many good suggestions to restore a smoother reading, but it is hard to tell which is best. Perhaps *bᵉʿôrî,* which occurs as *bᵉʿôr* in the second line, was accidentally copied twice; then the first occurrence of it should be removed. That means the *waw* conjunction could be removed from *ûḇiḇśārî,* "and in my flesh." The resulting text is similar to Ps. 102:6 (Eng. 5): *daḇᵉqâ ʿaṣmî liḇśārî,* "My bones cleave to my flesh." This reading is followed as the simplest. However, Duhm and Dhorme take another view, based on LXX, reading *bᵉʿôrî bᵉśārî rāqaḇ,* "In my skin my flesh has rotted away."

repulsed at his grotesque appearance and offensive odor, not one of them gives him any support. Such isolation is a frequent complaint of one enduring illness or an austere hardship.[9] As one psalmist moans: "You, O Yahweh, have removed far from me my loved ones and companions; the darkness is my closest friend *[meyuddāʿ]*" (88:19 [Eng. 18]).

Job's *brothers*[10] head the list of those who shun him. In patriarchal society the bond among family members was very strong, with each one being concerned for his brother's welfare. God, however, has driven a wide wedge into this tight bond. Even Job's trusted *friends (yōḏeʿîm)* are estranged from him. No longer acknowledging their ties with him, they do not come and offer him any help in his time of need.

14 So too have Job's *relatives* and *associates*[11] withdrawn. They offer him no consolation (cf. 42:11). Even his *house guests (gārê ḇêṯ-),* possibly resident aliens who found lodging and protection[12] in Job's house, *have forgotten* their kind benefactor (cf. 31:32). "To forget" means refusing to act toward a person in the light of past associations and commitments.

15, 16 Job's *maidservants,* those who did the daily chores about the house, now regard their master as *a stranger,* i.e., a resident alien *(zār)*[13] or *a foreigner (noḵrî).* Also when he calls to his *servant* as in the former days, he now receives no answer. The best servant does his master's wish even before an order is given. Quick to detect the slightest gesture, he responds to the look in his master's eyes (Ps. 123:2). Out of respect and affection for his lord a faithful servant works from dawn to dusk, always putting his lord first even when he himself is tired and hungry (cf. Lk. 17:7–10). The servants' high esteem for Job has turned to contempt.

17 In addition, the offensive odors given off by his diseased body drive people away. His breath is especially foul; the text reads literally, "my breath is strange" *(ruḥî zārâ).*[14] This foul smell makes him *repulsive* to his wife and to his own children (*benê biṭnî,* lit. "sons of my womb"). The precise identification of *my own children* is difficult to establish. A very

9. Cf. Ps. 31:12–14 (Eng. 11–13); 38:12–13 (Eng. 11–12); 41:10 (Eng. 9); 55:13–15 (Eng. 12–14); Jer. 12:6; 20:10.

10. "Brothers" seems to mean blood brothers instead of the members of his clan, for "my relatives" *(qerôḇay)* occurs in v. 14.

11. Heb. *meyuddāʿ* means "a close friend or associate," e.g., 2 K. 10:11, or possibly "a relative," if it is similar to Heb. *môḏaʿ*, "kindred," in Ruth 2:1 (Ketib; Qere is *meyuddāʿ*).

12. Cf. Dhorme; in Exod. 3:22, *gār bêṯ-* means "a tenant."

13. Cf. L. Snijders, "The Meaning of *zr* in the Old Testament," *OTS* 10 (1954) 1–154.

14. Heb. *rûaḥ,* "wind or spirit," may also mean "breath" (Ps. 135:17) or "sighing" (Lam. 3:56). MT *zārâ* may be taken from *zûr* II, "be strange." Many modern

likely identification is Job's children by his wife. This possibility has led some to argue that the original author did not know the prose section (chs. 1–2), but most interpreters, as has been noted already, no longer hold that position. Since there are no other glaring discrepancies between the speeches and the prologue, the interpretation of this line becomes more difficult. Some think the reference is to children by another marriage or by concubines or possibly to grandchildren. Another conjecture is that the children are orphans whom Job raised (cf. 31:18–19). But none of these explanations has any support from the description of Job's family in the prologue. In another direction it has been postulated that "my womb" is elliptical for "the womb of my mother," as in 3:10. These children would then be Job's blood brothers. In that light, the brothers mentioned in v. 13 would have a broader meaning, referring to the members of his clan. More likely, though, Job is using the stereotyped language of lament without making specific adjustments to the particulars of his case.

18, 19 Even the *young children,* who were trained in those days to give deference to elders on all occasions, now repudiate this noble man. When Job struggles to stand up, instead of being silent out of respect for this dignified elder (cf. 29:8, 10), *they jeer at (dibber bᵉ)*[15] him. Not only the children, but even Job's closest peers *detest (māʾas)* him. His intimate friends whom he has loved *have turned against* him in his time of desperate need. These men are the ones with whom he had sat as ruling members of the local *council* and with whom he had discussed important matters in confidence. Job finds no respect or support from any corner.

20 Feeling totally alienated, Job bemoans his wretched physical condition. His body is so wasted away that his *bones cleave to* his *flesh.*[16] And he is so weak he says: *I have escaped with the skin of my teeth.* The explanations for the last metaphor are multiple and unconvincing. Its meaning eludes us. With it Job seems to express his amazement that his body continues to sustain any life at all. Just as his alienation is total, so too his physical suffering is complete.

---

interpreters (e.g., Rowley; KB, p. 256; Blommerde, *Northwest Semitic Grammar and Job,* p. 87), however, find a root *zûr* III, "be evil, abhorrent, stink"; cf. P. Wernberg-Møller, *VT* 4 (1954) 322–25. But caution needs to be exercised in finding new roots. The meaning "be abhorrent" is possibly understood as an extension of the meaning "be strange" (cf. Gordis). This word then could have been chosen to make a play on *zārû,* "be estranged", in v. 13b.

15. Heb. *dibber bᵉ,* meaning "jeer, scoff, scorn," also occurs in Ps. 50:20; 78:19.

16. Cf. Ps. 102:6 (Eng. 5); Lam. 4:8.

d. A Plea for Help and a Statement of Assurance (19:21–27)

21 *"Have mercy on me, have mercy on me, you my friends,*
for the hand of God has struck me.
22 *Why do you pursue me like God?*
Are you not satisfied with my flesh?
23 *Oh, that my words were written,*
that they were inscribed on a monument
24 *with iron stylus and lead,*
engraved on a rock forever.[1]
25 *But I know that my redeemer is living;*
in the end he will stand on the dust.
26 *After my skin has been so*[2] *marred,*[3]
yet from my flesh I shall see God,
27 *whom I myself shall behold;*
my own eyes will see him and no other.
I am consumed with longing deep within me."

21 In desperation Job pleads with his friends, *Have mercy on me!* The urgency of his appeal is evident from the repetition of this imperative *(ḥonnûnî)* and from the emphatic use of the personal pronoun *you (ʾattem).* Job beseeches his friends to share the weight of his suffering made unbearable by his complete estrangement from the community. They must come to realize that it is not some fault in Job that is the cause of his suffering, but *the hand of God* that has struck him.[4] Then they can freely show him mercy. Job is longing for someone to give him some support in bringing his complaint to God.

22 Fearful that they will not heed his plea, Job scathingly accuses the friends of abusing him. He asks rhetorically, *Why do you pursue me like God? Are you not satisfied with my flesh?* So intent are they on finding wrong in him that he feels that they, *like God,* are pursuing or harassing him relentlessly. It is apparent that they will not be satisfied until Job succumbs

1. For MT *lāʿaḏ,* "forever," some wish to read with Theodotion *leʾēḏ,* "as a witness, testimony." Although this variant reading offers excellent sense, there is not enough textual evidence to depart from MT, which would be the harder reading.

2. The feminine demonstrative pronoun *zōʾṯ* is problematic, and no good explanation has been offered. Here we have followed Budde's emendation, reading *kazzōʾṯ,* "like this." Dhorme solves the problem by eliminating the ʾ as a *mater lectionis* and adding the *z* and *t* to the verb, resulting in *nizqaptî,* "I shall stand up," and making this line synonymous with the second line.

3. The third person plural might be taken as an impersonal use for the passive, or possibly a Niphal, *niqqap* (so Budde, Fohrer), should be read.

4. For illness described as caused by the hand of God, cf. Ps. 32:4; 1 Sam. 5:6.

and confesses to wrongdoing. Job likens them to wild beasts voraciously devouring their prey.[5] This metaphor captures the hostility that Job senses lying beneath the friends' words. His comparison of them both to an irate deity and to ravenous animals indicates that his disdain for them has reached a peak.

23, 24 Anticipating that his friends will fail him, Job searches earnestly for some way to defend his integrity. Fearful that he might die before his honor has been restored, he wishes that his words be preserved forever by being inscribed on a stone *monument [sēper]*[6] *with iron stylus and lead*. While the interpretation of *lead* is debated, the best explanation is that the engraved letters are to be lined with lead so that the sun will make them glisten.[7] Stone, because of its durability, was often used for writing in all periods of the ancient Near East. Inscribed stone monuments called stelae were erected as witnesses of various matters, including laws, events, boundary marks, and personal accomplishments. The exact style of the monument Job has in mind is uncertain, but he looks for a stela that would stand forever, a perpetual witness of his claim of innocence. Job is aware that if he does nothing, his claims will be forgotten soon after his death and his fate will serve as a prime example of a hypocrite's tragic end. Therefore, he desires that his testimony might be preserved so that some day when it is proven true he will be vindicated on earth. Then his honor will be restored, even though it happens posthumously. Although he does not specify the content of the inscription, he surely has in mind his lament, his declaration of innocence, his affirmation of trust in God, and his appeal for vindication.

5. This idiom appears in Ps. 27:2. There is a similar idiom in Akkadian, *akālu qarṣē,* "eat morsels of," which occurs also in Aramaic, e.g., Dan. 3:8 and 6:25 (Eng. 24), meaning "slander." Although the literal meaning certainly recedes with the use of an idiom, the skill of the author would indicate he may be employing another double entendre.

6. Heb. *sēper* means "book, scroll, tablet." It may also be used in a more general sense for any type of written record. In the light of v. 24 it is clear that Job thinks of a stone stela inscribed with his words. Dhorme, Pope, et al. relate *sēper* to Akk. *siparru,* "copper." Copper was used for writing, as is attested by the copper scroll from Qumran. But such a scroll could easily have been lost. Job has a more permanent monument in mind. Fohrer and Blommerde (*Northwest Semitic Grammar and Job,* p. 88) follow H. Gehman ("*Sēper:* An Inscription in the Book of Job," *JBL* 63 [1944] 303–307), who pointed out that in Phoenician *spr* can mean inscription. Cf. J. Stamm, "Versuche zur Erklärung von Hiob 19,24," *TZ* 4 (1948) 331–38; idem, "Zu Hiob 19,24," *ZAW* 65 (1953) 302; C. Conner, "Notes on Biblical Antiquities," *PEQ* 37 (1905) 156.

7. For MT *weʿōpāreṯ,* "and lead," there have been many suggestions. Driver-Gray and Pope take it to refer to the material inscribed with an iron stylus, i.e., a lead tablet. Dhorme posits that an alloy of lead and iron was used to outline the letters to be inscribed. Rashi, followed by Duhm, Rowley, and others, thought that lead was poured into the engraved letters. Such a practice has been attested in the Behistun inscription of Darius I (cf. K. Galling, "Die Grabinschrift Hiobs," *WO* 2 [1954–59] 6).

25 Job abruptly breaks off his wishful thinking and proclaims his deepest conviction.[8] With the heading *I know (ʾanî yādaʿtî)* Job affirms that his conviction is firm and decisive. Whereas he has just been speaking hypothetically, he now speaks with assurance as he proclaims: *I know that my redeemer lives; in the end he will stand on the dust.* Job is saying that there is a "kinsman-redeemer" *(gōʾēl)* who will come to his defense. With the term *gōʾēl* Job is referring to an ancient Israelite custom by which the nearest of kin guaranteed the security and rights of his fellow kinsman.[9] The purpose of this custom was to preserve each family's life force. There were specific situations that required the next of kin to act on a brother's behalf. Whenever a member of the clan was murdered, a kinsman had the responsibility to avenge his brother's blood (Num. 35:19; Deut. 19:6–12). If a brother was himself taken captive or sold into bondage to pay off a debt, his nearest relative redeemed him by securing his release, either by payment of a price or by an act of force (cf. Lev. 25:23–24, 39–55). Whenever a member of the clan was forced to lease or sell his property to pay a debt, his kinsman paid off the debt to secure his family's title to that land (cf. Lev. 25:25). If a kinsman died childless, his brother took his widow and raised up children in the name of his deceased brother in order to preserve his heritage (Ruth 2:20; 3:9; 4:1–17). The kinsman-redeemer also had an obligation to initiate a lawsuit to win back or redress the rights of a brother who had been wronged (cf. Ps. 119:154; Jer. 50:34; Lam. 3:58–59; Prov. 23:11). In so doing he would restore his kinsman's honor by removing all doubt as to his integrity.

The term "kinsman-redeemer" *(gōʾēl)* also functions as one of Yahweh's titles. It is rooted in the interpretation of Israel's deliverance from Egyptian bondage (e.g., Exod. 6:6; 15:13; Ps. 74:2; 77:16 [Eng. 15]). The theology of this title is that since Yahweh brought Israel into existence as a nation, he recognizes his obligation to deliver them from all hostile foes.

8. On these verses see: J. Speer, "Zur Exegese von Hiob 19,25–27," *ZAW* 25 (1905) 47–140; C. Bruston, "Pour l'exégèse de Job 19,25–27," *ZAW* 26 (1906) 143–46; A. Hudal, "Die Auslegung von Job 19,25–27 in der katholischen Exegese," *Der Katholik* 95 (1916) 331–45; S. Mowinckel, "Hiobs *gōʾēl* und Zeuge im Himmel," in *Vom Alten Testament,* Fest. K. Marti, ed. K. Budde, BZAW 41 (Giessen: Töpelmann, 1925), pp. 207–12; W. Vischer, "The Witness of Job to Jesus Christ" (tr. A. Ellison), *The Churchman* 6 (1934) 52–53; idem, "God's Truth and Man's Lie" (tr. D. G. Miller), *Int* 11 (1961) 138–39; J. Lindblom, "Ich weiss, dass mein Erlöser lebt. Zum Verständnis der Stelle Hi. 19,25–27," *ST* 2 (Riga, 1940) 65–77; L. Waterman, "Note on Job 19:23–27: Job's Triumph of Faith," *JBL* 69 (1950) 379–80; T. Meek, "Job xix 25–27," *VT* 6 (1956) 100–103; W. Irwin, "Job's Redeemer," *JBL* 81 (1962) 217–29; J. Zink, "Impatient Job," *JBL* 84 (1965) 147–52; L. Krinetzki, "Ich weiss, mein Anwalt lebt," *Bibel und Kirche* 20 (1965) 8–12; M. Barré, "A Note on Job xix,25," *VT* 29 (1979) 107–109.

9. A. Johnson, "The Primary Meaning of *gʾl,*" *VTSup* 1 (1953) 67–77; A. Jepsen, "Die Begriffe des 'Erlösens' im AT," in *Solange es "Heute" heisst. Fest. für R. Hermann* (1957) 153–63; H. Ringgren, *"gāʾal," TDOT,* II:350–55.

Drawing on this extensive tradition, Isaiah frequently uses this title for Yahweh in proclaiming that Yahweh will create a new Exodus by redeeming Israel from Babylonian captivity (e.g., 43:1–7). He also chooses this title to communicate Yahweh's unfathomable love for his distraught people (e.g., 41:14; 44:24; 49:7–9, 26).[10]

Who is Job's kinsman-redeemer? The traditional interpretation has been that Job is identifying God as his Redeemer. But several modern interpreters find intolerable the logic of this interpretation that God will help Job against God. Therefore, they identify the redeemer in this passage as the heavenly witness that Job believed would testify for him (16:19). The redeemer is an arbiter, one other than God, who will arise to defend Job before God.[11] While this view has much in its favor, it is not able to account for all the facts. As pointed out above, the title *redeemer* had a special place in Israel's confessional theology. Therefore, the author's choice of this term for Job is an intentional allusion to the special nuances of deliverance and love that are associated with this title for God. Since there are so many ties throughout the speeches to various parts of Israel's theological tradition, the selection of this term must be viewed as designed. If the author did not want to make this identification, he would have chosen another term that would have clearly meant an intermediary between God and man, for he has already used many: angel or holy one (5:1), umpire or arbiter (9:33–34), witness (16:19), and friend (16:20). Furthermore, since his brothers and kinsmen have forsaken him (19:13–14) and his comforters have failed him (6:14–23), the redeemer he has in mind must be someone other than these parties. It is also unlikely that the redeemer is the arbiter or umpire for whom Job has wished (9:33–34), for in that passage Job was fully aware that he was expressing an unrealistic wish, whereas now he is speaking with conviction.

In addition, the use of the adjective "alive, living" *(ḥay)* with "redeemer" adds great weight to this identification of God as the kinsman-redeemer. This adjective *living* stands in bold relief against Job's fear of dying. Job is saying that his redeemer is alive, able to come to his aid. Even should he die, his redeemer will survive him and be able to restore his honor. He realizes that the living redeemer is a far better witness on his behalf than a cold stone. Moreover, the use of *living* brings to mind the reference to God as "the living God" (e.g., Deut. 5:23 [Eng. 26]; Josh. 3:10; Jer. 10:10; 23:36; cf. Job 27:2).[12] As the Living One, God both sustains life and acts

10. Cf. W. Eichrodt, *Theology of the Old Testament*, OTL, tr. J. Baker (Philadelphia: Westminster, 1961), 1:254–55.

11. Mowinckel, "Hiobs *gō'ēl* und Zeuge im Himmel," p. 208.

12. Cf. W. Eichrodt's discussion of the meaning of the epithet "the living God," *Theology*, 1:213–14.

marvelously for the deliverance of those who serve him. Therefore, the title "living redeemer" applies to none other than God.

Job asserts that his redeemer *will stand [qûm] on the dust*. Heb. *qûm*, "rise, stand up," is here a technical legal term meaning "to stand up" as a witness in court.[13] Job is thus saying that his kinsman will fulfill his responsiblity as redeemer by giving the decisive testimony in Job's defense. Heb. *qûm* is also sometimes a technical cultic term for a theophany.[14] While over-interpretation must be guarded against, it is possible that both nuances are present in this text; the author likes to use double entendre. Though the legal meaning is predominant in this line, the theophanic nuance is supported by the context and by the fact that it subtly points forward to God's appearing out of the storm. The presence of the second meaning is also attested by the fact that "seeing" occurs three times in vv. 26–27.

The phrase *in the end (ʾaḥarôn)*[15] often signals things that will take place at the end of the age. Job, however, is thinking not of that distant future, but of a day when God will vindicate him and bring his case to a close. In this context then "the end" or "the last" connotes that God will restore Job's honor before he dies. The word *dust* emphasizes that God will appear at the ash heap on which Job sits (2:8).[16] Since dust and ashes

13. Cf. Deut. 19:15–16; Ps. 27:12; 35:11.

14. With God as its subject *qûm* may stand for his coming forth from heaven to render justice on earth (Zeph. 3:8; Ps. 76:10 [Eng. 9]; cf. Isa. 2:19, 21). Weiser, however, understands *qûm* as a technical term for a theophany; i.e., God appears at an assembly of the people as a sign that he renews the covenant and guarantees his blessing on the nation in the coming year. This tradition serves as the background for Job's hope, but the concept has been transformed to fit Job's situation as an individual. God himself will appear and grant to his servant an acquittal that will result in his healing. In addition, Weiser finds that Job's reference to an inscribed stone fits this social setting well. Often one who was facing hardship offered up a lament at this festival, confident that God's appearing held the assurance that his personal prayer was answered. As a votive offering he sets up the inscribed stone. With this in mind Job wishes that a stone containing his words would be erected as a perpetual psalm of lament, entreating God's deliverance.

15. Heb. *ʾaḥarôn,* often taken adverbially as "at last," is either an adjective or an accusative of state (GKC, § 118n; Driver-Gray). There have been several recent attempts to find in this word a substantive parallel to *gōʾēl,* "redeemer." Isaiah uses *riʾšôn* and *ʾaḥarôn,* "the First and the Last," as epithets of God, e.g., 41:4; 48:12. In Isaiah these two words are tied so tightly that they form one epithet, and in 44:6 this epithet stands parallel to *gōʾēl.* Kissane agrees with this view and offers the translation "the Eternal." In another direction Pope calls attention to the Mishnaic term *ʾaḥarāʾî,* meaning "guarantor" (so too M. Barré, *VT* 29 [1979] 107–108). All these possibilities face the problem that *ʾaḥarôn* has no pronominal suffix to match the one on *gōʾēl* (cf. Dhorme), as well as the fact that in Isaiah a phrase rather than a single word functions as the epithet. Though intriguing, this interpretation has not been substantiated.

16. Some take the phrase *ʿal ʿāpār,* "on the dust," to mean "on the grave." Certainly *ʿāpār,* lit. "dust," can mean "grave" (7:21; 17:16; 20:11; Ps. 7:6 [Eng. 5]; 22:16, 30 [Eng. 15, 29]; Isa. 26:19; Dan. 12:2). Its meaning thus depends on the context

symbolize the depths of Job's sorrow, "dust" is preferable to the word "earth" (RSV) to convey the idea that God will take his stand in defense of his kinsman's integrity on the very place of his humiliation.

This magnificent verse then means that Job is beseeching the God in whom he has faith to help him against the God who is punishing him. While this view seems irrational, this paradox lies at the core of Job's struggle. These two conflicting views of God are at war in his own mind. Although he believes that God is just, he is overwhelmed by God's punishing power as manifested in his suffering. But he reaches beyond his experience of God's wrath to state his trust in God, who will in time secure his acquittal and who will also accomplish his deliverance from suffering. In this passage Job is expressing genuine faith, for he makes an unconditional affirmation about God's commitment to him against all circumstantial evidence to the contrary. Only by pure faith can a person believe in God's justice amidst suffering, assured within his heart that out of his sorrow God will restore his honor.

26, 27 These verses recount when and how Job will behold God's testifying as his kinsman-redeemer. A critical question is, Will Job see God's witnessing for him before or after his death? If after his death, will Job observe this event from the distant realm of the dead or will he be resurrected so that he can be physically present? Scholars are quite divided in the way they answer these questions, especially since the text of v. 26 is so obscure. Four prominent interpretations may be briefly stated.

(1) God will raise Job from the grave so that he will experience his vindication before his accusers. This view is dominant in the Christian community. It goes back to the early church fathers, including Clement of Rome and Origen, and it has been popularized by the major translations in the West. The Latin translation of Jerome, which even identifies the Redeemer as the Messiah, has contributed significantly to this view becoming the traditional interpretation. Luther's translation has also propagated this interpretation among Protestants.

A few early church fathers failed to find any reference to a doctrine of resurrection in this passage (e.g., Chrysostom), and numerous modern scholars have mustered strong support against it. Throughout the book any hope of escape from death is rejected. Sheol is known as the land of no return (7:9; 10:21). Whoever dies is confined to that world with no hope of a better lot (17:15–16). Earlier Job had reflected on the possible hope of returning to life, but in dismay he concluded that while such revitalization is possible for

---

of the passage. In Job "dust" is its primary meaning. The translation "dust" is preferable, for it conveys the ambiguity of the Hebrew. Cf. N. Ridderbos, "*ʿpr* als Staub des Totenreiches," *OTS* 5 (1948) 174–78.

a tree, it is not possible for a human being (14:10–12). Since Job finds no support for a belief in resurrection, the claim that resurrection is the focal point of this passage seems to be a reading back of the NT into the OT. To go a step further: if indeed Job proclaims here definitively that God will raise him from the grave and pronounce him innocent, this passage would be the climax of the book, bringing the debate to an end. Or if the dialogue continued, surely this theme would reverberate throughout the following speeches, above all those of Elihu and Yahweh. They would underscore the significance of this truth. Since, however, the idea of resurrection is not treated in any coming passages, it is hard to contend that Job sees it as the answer to his plight. So the first view is unacceptable.

(2) From the grave, Job, a bodiless spirit, will witness the occasion when God appears before the local assembly to verify Job's innocence. This view goes back to early Jewish interpreters (cf. Jub. 23:30–31). Nevertheless, it seems unlikely to be the position of the author, for he did not believe that the dead were aware of events on earth or in heaven (cf. 14:21). From the ancient perspective of Job, who has suffered such ignominy both from his family and his friends, merely to witness his acquittal as an invisible, disembodied spirit would be a hollow victory. Something more definitive and dramatic must take place for Job's integrity to be fully vindicated.

(3) Job's thoughts in these verses are conditional: if he should see God, he would behold God's vindication of him. This view is rejected because Job's introductory words, "I know," set these lines off as an affirmation in contrast to his wishful thinking expressed in vv. 23–24.

(4) God will intervene before Job's death and restore him to his former status. This view is adopted here. In vv. 26–27 Job emphatically states, *I shall see God . . . my own eyes will see him.* The first person forms are strengthened in v. 27a by the personal pronoun *I (ʾanî)* plus the reflexive pronoun *myself* (*lî,* taken as an ethical dative). Job speaks of seeing God three times (*ḥāzâ,* "see," v. 26b and v. 27a, and *rāʾâ,* "behold," v. 27b). Also in v. 27b he says that he will see God with *my own eyes and no other.* The phrase *and no other* (*welōʾ zār,* lit. "and not a stranger") has received various interpretations. While many take it to mean that Job expects that he will be the only one to see God, this seems unlikely, for how then would the community know that he had been vindicated? Andersen has a better solution; he takes this phrase to mean either that Job will no longer be a stranger to God or that God will no longer act like a stranger to Job. So v. 27 makes it clear that Job hopes to see God from his own body.

Turning to v. 26, we begin with the second line since the first line is so obscure. The phrase *mibbeśārî* can mean "without my flesh" or "from my flesh." The latter option is chosen, for Job stresses in v. 27 that he will see God with his own eyes. The parallel phrase in v. 26a is *after my skin* (*'aḥar 'ôrî*), but the meaning of this phrase is hard to establish. Dhorme thinks it means "behind my skin . . . as behind a curtain." The term *skin* seems to indicate that Job is focusing on his external body. This interpretation of these two phrases continues to support the position that Job expects to be physically present at his vindication. But whether he believes that this event will take place before or after his death rests on the meaning of the verb *niqqᵉpû* in v. 26a. Unfortunately its meaning has not been established. If it comes from *nqp* I, "strip off," the line reads "after my skin is stripped off" (Kissane; cf. Pope) and means that in a resurrected body Job will see God. But this root may mean that his skin has become shriveled up or marred beyond recognition. If one accepts this last possibility on the above interpretation that Job will be physically present at his acquittal, Job is saying that from his weak, emaciated body he will see God's appearing to vindicate him. With this affirmation Job's faith reaches beyond his pressing fear that he is about to die, and he places his confidence in God, that somehow he will restore Job's honor before it is too late. The silent God will have the last word. To express it another way, Job believes that his present experience with God's anger is transitory and ephemeral. In the end he will encounter God in justice and mercy, the God who will fulfill his kinship commitment to his servant by vindicating him before the people.

Job's great adventure of faith, however, drains the little strength left in his body. No wonder he exclaims, *I am consumed with longing deep within me*. The line translated literally is "my kidneys fail (or are consumed) in my bosom." In Hebraic thought deep passions are located in the kidneys. Suddenly Job feels emotionally drained. He will have to wait to see whether his insight of faith will prove true.

Although Job's confession as interpreted does not explicitly support the doctrine of resurrection, it is built on the same logic that will lead to that doctrine becoming the cornerstone of NT faith. Job is working with the same logic of redemption that stands as the premise of the NT doctrine of resurrection. Both hold to the dogma that God is just even though he permits unrequited injustices and the suffering of the innocent. God, himself, identified with Job's sufferings in the sufferings of his Son, Jesus Christ, who suffered unto death even though he was innocent. Jesus overcame his ignominious death by rising from the grave. In his victory he, as God's Son and mankind's kinsman-redeemer, secured redemption for all who believe on him. While his followers may suffer in this life, he is their Redeemer, their Advocate before the Father. In this way Job's confidence in God as his Redeemer amidst excruciating suffering stands as a model for all Christians.

e. A Warning to the Friends (19:28–29)

28 *"Because you say, 'How do we pursue him?*
The root of the matter is in him,'[1]
29 *fear the sword, yourselves,*
for these[2] *are iniquities worthy of the sword*
that you may know there is a judgment."[3]

28, 29 With his thoughts on the event at which God will vindicate him, Job delivers a solemn warning to the friends. He admonishes them so that they might realize the responsibility that goes along with their instruction. Anticipating their blindness to the way they are pursuing or troubling him by arguing tenaciously that the cause of his trouble resides in himself, Job quotes their position in order to penetrate their blindness. Since they never listen to his words and wrongly locate the cause of his affliction in him, he warns them that they are committing *iniquities worthy of* punishment by *the sword*. The *sword* symbolizes God's inflicting fatal, decisive blows against his enemies (cf. Deut. 32:41–42; Isa. 66:16; Ezek. 32:10). Therefore, they need to *fear the sword*. After God strikes them down, they will have to stand before *a judgment*. There they will be held accountable for the ways they have counseled Job and the compassion that they have shown him during his trial.

AIM

In this speech Job laments the grief and shame his friends are causing him. He also complains about how brutally God is treating him. This leads him to deplore his alienation from all his relatives and friends that his suffering has

1. Instead of MT *bî,* "in me," some Hebrew mss. and versions read *bô,* "in him." The parallelism favors this variant. The MT no doubt arose because the ancients did not always clearly distinguish between direct and indirect quotes.

2. This line is impossible in its present construction. Emending MT *ḥēmâ* ("wrath") to *hemmâ* ("they") with Budde and Gordis secures a possible reading. Dhorme reconstructs out of MT *ʿawônôṯ ḥāreḇ* the phrase *baʿawônôṯ tiḥar,* "(when wrath) is kindled against wrongs." This suggestion provides an excellent reading, but it needs more textual support. The former is followed as a simpler solution.

3. The meaning of the Qere *šaddûn* is not clear. Most exegetes work from the Ketib *šdyn,* reading either *šeddayyān,* "that there is a judge," followed by Vulg. and Syr., or *šeddîn,* "that there is (a) judgment" (Gordis). Budde and Fohrer gain the first meaning by reading *yēš dayyān.* The Targ. is an expanded translation containing both ideas. The context favors the second reading. Furthermore, L. Fisher ("*ŠDYN* in Job XIX 29," *VT* 11 [1961] 342–43) believes that in the light of Ugaritic phonology the Ketib *šaddîn* is another way of spelling *šadday,* but his view has not been widely accepted.

caused him. Depressed by the loneliness that his isolation causes, Job exercises genuine faith by boldly confessing that he has a kinsman-redeemer who will stand up to testify on his behalf. Although he is unsure when God will act as his redeemer, he is sure that it will be a public occasion at which he himself will be present. He is convinced that his experience of God as an enemy is not illusory; he is more certain that God, acting as his next-of-kin, will secure his redemption, in his case a full acquittal with honor. In the words of Vischer, "For the sake of God Job holds fast to his God, of whom he can trace nothing save the fact that he rejects him. He has not allowed his friends to 'convert' him, he has not let himself be turned away from uncaused freedom and fidelity to the 'God' whose reward or punishment one can calculate and merit."[1]

It is clear that Job has charted a specific course to win his acquittal. While continuing to lament his agony he will seek to move God to fulfill his legal responsibilities to him, specifically to verify his confession of innocence. This assurance energizes Job's spiritual search and buttresses him against succumbing in depression to his pain. As his body weakens, his faith rises to keep him from wallowing in self-remorse or seeking an easy avenue of escape from suffering, such as repenting in order to receive blessing. His faith, however, will not be authenticated until God breaks through and reciprocates Job's trust.

5. ZOPHAR'S SECOND SPEECH (20:1–29)

Zophar is deeply disturbed by Job's accusations that the friends are increasing his torment and that God is the source of his present affliction. But unfortunately he does not know how to comfort Job. Neither does he know how to address the issues Job has raised. After a brief rebuke of Job he delivers a long discourse on a single topic—the certain evil fate of every evildoer. He is indirectly rejecting Job's assertion that God will appear as his Redeemer to vindicate him. He counters Job's statement of confidence by saying that the heavens and the earth will stand as witnesses against the evildoer, even against Job. In his view Job's hope is false, and it is deluding him.

This speech is essentially a wisdom disputation, the development of a single thesis. Bildad's rhetoric is powerful, for it is filled with numerous picturesque metaphors. To a modern reader, however, it may seem rambling. This speech has only two sections: Zophar's reaction to Job's speech (vv. 1–3), and the sure fate of every evildoer (vv. 4–29).

1. W. Vischer, "God's Truth and Man's Lie," *Int* 15 (1961) 139.

a. Zophar's Reaction to Job's Speech (20:1–3)

1 *Then Zophar the Naamathite answered:*
2 *"Therefore[1] my troubled thoughts give me an answer,*
because of the pain I feel[2] within me.
3 *I have heard a rebuke which insults me,[3]*
and the spirit of my understanding gives me an answer."

2, 3 Zophar's *troubled thoughts (śeʿippîm)*[4] move him to answer Job. This couplet is a chiasm. Zophar expresses his deep agitation at Job's discrediting him as wise in vv. 2b, 3a (cf. Andersen) and retorts in vv. 2a, 3b that he will give a sagacious response even though his thoughts are troubled. Taking Job's complaint about the way the friends have treated him and Job's solemn warnings as a personal rebuke, Zophar feels grieved and insulted. His irritation is visible in the fiery tone of this speech. Nevertheless, he promises an insightful response with the words *the spirit of my understanding gives me an answer*. This phrase means both that Zophar's spirit is compelling him to respond to Job (cf. 32:18) and that his words come from reasoned insight (cf. Fohrer). This is his way of reassuring Job that his speech will convey wisdom.

b. The Sure Fate of Every Evildoer (20:4–29)

4 *"Do you not[1] know this from of old,*
since man was placed[2] on earth,
5 *that the mirth of the wicked is brief,*
and the joy of the godless is momentary.

1. Dhorme points out that Heb. *lāḵēn* ("therefore") "at the beginning of a speech . . . is an allusion to what follows."

2. For MT *ḥûšî ḇî,* "my haste in me," Beer, followed by many (e.g., Fohrer), reads *rāḥaš libbî,* "my heart is agitated." If this reading is accepted, an object is needed after *baʿaḇûr*, either *baʿaḇûrâ,* "because of it" (the loss of the *h* could easily have resulted from a scribal error) or *baʿabûr zōʾṯ,* "because of this." However, there may be a root *ḥûš* II (see Eccl. 2:25; cf. KB, p. 288). This root is common in Aramaic and is used in Mishnaic and modern Hebrew meaning "to feel (pain), have concern for." The MT form then may be taken as an infinitive construct.

3. The noun *kelimmāṯî,* "my insult," stands in apposition to the genitive *mûsar,* "discipline."

4. Heb. *śeʿippîm,* "troubled thoughts," occurs only here and in 4:13.

1. This rhetorical question expects an affirmative answer; the *lōʾ,* "not," is omitted because the speaker is so completely convinced; cf. R. Gordis, "A Rhetorical Use of Interrogative Sentences in Biblical Hebrew," *AJSL* 49 (1932–33) 212–17.

2. Dahood takes MT *śîm* as a Qal passive perfect ("Northwest Semitic Philology and Job," p. 64), but it may be a Qal infinitive construct after a preposition, which is generally vocalized *śûm*. Some texts, however, support spelling the infinitive construct *śîm* (Isa. 10:6 [Ketib] and 2 Sam. 14:7 [Qere]; see Driver-Gray).

6 *Though his height[3] mounts up to heaven*
and his head touches the clouds,
7 *like his greatness[4] he will perish forever;*
those who saw him will say, 'Where is he?'
8 *He will fly away like a dream, and none can find him;*
he will be chased[5] away like a vision of the night.
9 *The eye that caught sight of him will see him no more,*
and his place will not behold him again.
10 *His sons must redress the poor;*
his hands[6] must give back his wealth.
11 *Youthful vigor[7] that filled his bones*
will lie with him in the dust.
12 *Though evil tastes sweet in his mouth,*
and he hides it under his tongue,
13 *he relishes it, not letting it go,*
holding it under his palate;
14 *his food will turn in his stomach,*
becoming asp's venom[8] inside him.
15 *He swallowed riches and vomits them;[9]*
God disgorges them from his belly.
16 *He sucks the poison of asps;*
a viper's tongue will kill him.
17 *He will never enjoy the streams of oil,*
the rivers flowing[10] with honey and curds.

3. MT *śîʾ* may be taken as a noun from the root *nśʾ*, "lift up, bear," to mean a "lofty, exalted position"; cf. *śōʾ* in Ps. 89:10 (Eng. 9).

4. MT *k*^{e}*gel*^{a}*lô* is taken by many to mean "as his own dung"; cf. 1 K. 14:10 for its use for cow chips mixed with straw and burned for fuel. The suffix creates problems for this interpretation, however, as does the fact that the imagery is foreign to the context. It seems better to read with LXX a word for "greatness," either *kgdlw* or *bgdlw* (Dhorme). Either reading could have developed into the present text.

5. MT *yuddaḏ*, "he will be chased," may be either a Qal passive imperfect of *nāḏaḏ* or a phonetic alternative to a regular Qal *yiddaḏ*, according to Gordis. He points out that sometimes the vowels *i* and *u* are interchanged in Job.

6. The noun *yāḏāyw*, "his hands," is somewhat difficult in that it raises the question why the author returns to the man after mentioning his sons. R. Gordis ("A Note on *Yāḏ*," *JBL* 62 [1943] 341–44) offers the possibility that *yāḏ* means "his offspring." This suggestion fits the parallelism well.

7. MT *ʿ*^{a}*lûmāw*, "youthful vigor," is an abstract noun with a plural pronominal suffix defectively written (Gordis). It is the likely subject of the feminine verb *tiškaḇ*, "it will lie" (GKC, § 145k).

8. Heb. *m*^{e}*rôrâ* means "gall, poison," for the ancients identified gall, sometimes used as a liquid poison, with venom, also a liquid poison; cf. D. Pardee, "*m*^{e}*rôrăt-p*^{e}*tanîm* 'Venom' in Job 20:14," *ZAW* 91 (1979) 401–16.

9. Driver-Gray show that the perfect *bālaʿ*, "he swallowed," describes completed action, and the *waw* consecutive suggests the natural consequence of the action.

10. Three successive words for streams, *p*^{e}*laggôṯ*, *nah*^{a}*rê*, and *naḥ*^{a}*lê*, suggest a

18 *He will restore his gain uneaten,*
and the profit of[11] *his trade he will not enjoy.*
19 *For he has crushed and abandoned*[12] *the poor;*
he has seized houses which he did not build.
20 *Because he does not experience rest*[13] *from his craving,*
from his greed[14] *he will not escape.*[15]
21 *No one has survived*[16] *his devouring;*
therefore his prosperity will not endure.
22 *In fullness of plenty*[17] *he will have distress;*
the force of every sufferer[18] *will befall him.*
23 *When he has filled*[19] *his belly,*

---

textual problem. Many emend the text by supplying in the first line a word such as *yiṣhār* ("fresh oil") or *šemen* ("oil"; cf. Mic. 6:7), thus gaining a parallel to "honey and curds," and by deleting *nahᵃrê* from the second line. It is possible that *nahᵃrê* arose from *yiṣhār* because of a spelling error in a ms. plus the influence of *naḥᵃlê*. Gordis and Blommerde (*Northwest Semitic Grammar and Job,* p. 90), however, suggest that *nhry* comes from *nhr,* "shine," and is another word for "oil," just as *yiṣhār,* "oil," is related to *ṣhl,* "shine." The first emendation is followed, for the second creates a new word.

11. For MT *keḥêl,* "like wealth of," *beḥîl,* "from the profit of," is read with several mss. and Syr. The *be* is taken as having the sense of "from." Gordis creatively reconstructs the second line to form a close parallelism to the first line. He vocalizes *bḥl* as a Qal participle, *bōḥēl,* "loathing," and reconstructs MT *yaʿᵃlōs* as *yilʿōs,* "he chews," an error of metathesis: "He will spew forth his gain and not chew it down." His suggestion is good, but there needs to be more textual evidence before it is adopted.

12. The first line is difficult, for two finite verbs, *riṣṣaṣ,* "he crushed," and *ʿāzaḇ,* "he left," are juxtaposed without any conjunction and because the second verb is anticlimactic to the first. But perhaps the idea is that of a rich man wreaking havoc in the neighborhood of the poor, destroying homes and inflicting injury and then abandoning the inhabitants to their plight, devoid of any resources to cope with their difficulty. For MT *ʿāzaḇ* there have been many suggestions; e.g., to emend it to *zerôaʿ,* "the arm of (the poor)." Dahood ("The Root *ʿzb* II in Job," *JBL* 78 [1959] 306–307) has supported Ehrlich's finding in *ʿzb* a parallel to "house" *(bayiṯ)* by relating it to Mishnaic Heb. *maʿᵃzîḇâ,* "hut." This suggestion offers a good reading and is a good possibility. Cf. N. Bronznick ("*kî riṣṣaṣ ʿāzab dallîm* (Job 20:19)," *Beth Miqra* 27 [1981–82] 220–28), who argued that *ʿāzaḇ* may also mean "reject, despise."

13. MT *šālēw,* "rest," is possibly a substantive use of an adjective, or, as Gordis claims, it may be an alternate noun form, like *gāḏēr* beside *geḏer,* "wall."

14. Dhorme interprets *baḥᵃmûḏô* to mean "from his appetite (or desire)," namely, the object of greed. This reading offers a fine parallel to *beḇiṭnô,* "from his belly (or craving)."

15. It is not necessary to revocalize MT *ymlt,* "he will escape," as Niphal, for *napšô,* "himself," may be understood after the verb, as in Amos 2:15.

16. Elsewhere Heb. *śārîḏ,* "survivor," is always a person, not possessions.

17. Qere *bimlôʾṯ,* "being full," is a *lamed-ʾaleph* verb vocalized like a *lamed-he* (GKC, § 74h).

18. Heb. *ʿāmēl,* "one who is miserable, a sufferer," is personal. Although many follow LXX and Vulg. in reading *ʿāmāl,* "sorrow," MT should be retained, for Zophar prefers to speak of people.

19. The opening jussive may be interpreted as forming a clause subordinate to the following two lines (Dhorme).

God will send on him his burning anger,
and he will rain down his munitions[20] *on him.*[21]
24 *He will flee from an iron weapon;*
a bronze-tipped arrow will pierce[22] *him.*
25 *He draws*[23] *and it comes out his back,*[24]
a glittering point out of his gall;
it sends[25] *terrors over him.*
26 *Total darkness is reserved*[26] *for his treasures;*
an unfanned fire will consume him;[27]
whoever is left in his tent will be devoured.[28]

20. MT *bilḥûmô* is variously understood and emended. Dahood (*Bib* 38 [1957] 314–15) suggests reading *ʿālāyw mabbēl ḥammô:* "He shall rain on him the fire of his wrath." Although this suggestion is creative and offers good poetry, it requires too much shifting of the text and produces a new Hebrew word, *mabbēl,* unknown in the cognates to this time. The Hebrew root *lḥm* carries two ideas: (1) "food—eat," and (2) "war—anger" (Grabbe, *Comparative Philology,* pp. 76–77). With the first meaning MT is understood as "on his flesh." This affords a good parallel with "his belly" in the first line. With the second meaning MT reads "in his wrath"; the parallel is then with "his burning anger." Gordis thinks that the form may be a morphological variant of the segholate *bᵉlaḥmô,* "his heat, anger." But the war aspect of the second meaning offers a good possibility. The noun may be a broken plural used collectively to mean "munitions." This meaning affords a good transition between v. 23b and vv. 24–25, as well as having the support of Syr. and Vulg.

21. This form of the preposition, *ʿālêmô,* "on him," occurs in 22:2; 27:3; and a few other places.

22. KB, p. 308, gives a root *ḥlp* II, "cut up" (also in Judg. 5:26), but S. Tengström (*TDOT,* IV:432–35) thinks that the meaning "hit, strike" is within the field of *ḥlp* I.

23. LXX probably read *šelaḥ,* "missile, dart," for MT *šālap̱,* "draw, unsheath." Based on LXX many (e.g., Pope and Fohrer) read the line *šelaḥ yēṣēʾ miggēwōh,* "the dart comes out of his back." But it is possible that Heb. *šālap* refers to the entire action, from the shooting of an arrow up to its piercing a target. In a similar vein Gordis, understanding *šālap* to specify the flight of the arrow, offers the translation "it is drawn forth."

24. For MT *miggēwâ* read *miggēwōh,* "from his back," with Targ. and Vulg., since there is no other occurrence of this noun as feminine (see Dhorme). The present text could have arisen from a mistaken writing of *gaʾᵃwâ,* "pride."

25. MT *yahᵃlōḵ* may be revocalized *yᵉhallēḵ,* "he sends," to gain a Piel with a causative meaning.

26. Some (e.g., Dhorme) wish to omit MT *ṭāmûn,* "hidden, reserved," and read *lô ṣāpûn,* "treasured, hidden for him," with LXX. MT is retained, for it is the more difficult reading and the syllable count is well balanced (7/8/7).

27. According to Gordis, MT *tᵉʾoḵlēhû,* "it devours him," may be a variant spelling of a Piel *tᵉʾakkᵉlēhû* (like *tᵉroṣṣᵉhû* in Ps. 62:4 [Eng. 3]). Budde, Tur-Sinai, Fohrer, and *BHS* consider it best, however, to read Qal *tōʾḵlēhû* to avoid a unique vocalization.

28. The difficult MT *yēraʿ* is variously emended. It may be vocalized as *yērōaʿ*, a Niphal of *rʿʿ*, "suffer evil, harm." Or it could be another example of *rʿʿ* in the sense of *rṣṣ,* "break, smash," and vocalized *yārōaʿ* (cf. Gordis). The best suggestion (Dhorme, Gordis) is that it comes from the root *rʿh,* "pasture, graze; strip, devastate" (cf. Mic. 5:5; Ps. 80:14 [Eng. 13]). This offers a good parallel with *ʾāḵal,* "eat, devour."

27 *The heavens will reveal his iniquity;*
the earth will take its stand[29] *against him.*
28 *A flood will sweep away his house,*[30]
torrents on the day of his wrath.
29 *This is the wicked man's portion from God,*[31]
even the heritage decreed for him[32] *by God."*

4, 5 Zophar begins his exposition with a rhetorical question. The formulation of the question implies that should Job deny the answer, he would in effect be saying that he denies the oldest, most honored teaching of the wise. The wisdom from them is true because of its great antiquity; it goes back to God's placing man on earth. Zophar meets Job's boldest statement of faith in God to this point with a harsh rebuke. Instead of knowing that his Redeemer is living (19:25), Job should know the ancient wisdom, which teaches that *the mirth of the wicked is brief.* While *the godless* may experience the ringing *joy* of festivity *(rᵉnānâ),* their joy is hollow, being but for a brief moment. Zophar is arguing that the punishment of the wicked is an integral part of the world order. It is thus unthinkable that there may be an exception, even in Job's case, to this moral law.

6, 7 The higher a wicked person climbs the ladder of success, the harder his fall. Having gained power and wealth, this person's *height mounts up to heaven* and *his head* appears to touch *the clouds.*[33] Zophar is drawing on the mythic portrait of the mighty ruler who rises from poverty to dominate the world (e.g., Isa. 14; Ezek. 28). Swelled with pride this monarch thinks

29. One would expect an *ē* or *ᵉ* after the second *m* in *miṯqômāmâ;* the *ā* is anomalous.

30. Verse 28a may be translated "the possessions of his house will be taken into exile." But in the light of the second line it is quite possible to interpret this line as describing the rush of flooding waters. MT *yigel* may be vocalized with LXX and Syr. *yāgōl,* "roll" (from the root which yields *gal,* "waves"), and MT *yᵉḇûl,* usually meaning "produce," may be taken as related to *yāḇāl,* "streams" (see Isa. 30:25; 44:4), thus meaning "flood" (with Dhorme). While some wish to revocalize it *yāḇāl,* a better suggestion from Tur-Sinai is *yibbôl* in the light of Akk. *bubbulu* or *bibbulu.*

31. Verse 29a is too long (10/7 syllable count). Gordis suggests deleting *mē'ĕlōhîm* as a dittography from *mē'ēl* in the second line. But the word *'āḏām,* "man," is more suspect. It could have been added by reason of its formulaic nature (cf. 27:13). Its elimination restores balance, 8/7.

32. The suffix on *'imrô,* "decreed for him," applies to the entire idea of the construct (GKC, § 135n). Cf. also I. Eitan, "Studies in Hebrew Roots," *JQR* 14 (1923–24) 31–34; and J. Reider, "Contributions to the Scripture Text," *HUCA* 24 (1952–53) 103–104.

33. Dhorme understands the image to be that of a tree proudly rearing its head to the sky. A stalwart tree serves as a metaphor for a mighty ruler, e.g., Ezek. 31, and elsewhere in Job it is used for a nobleman (8:16–18; 14:7–9; 18:16). Perhaps this metaphor lies behind the language.

that he is a god. But at the peak of his glory this giant falls, tumbling to the abyss as swiftly as he rose to prominence (cf. Amos 9:2; Obad. 4). *he will perish forever*. This godless person who was applauded by the masses will be reduced to insignificance. The same masses will taunt him by asking, *Where is he?* This question underscores the pleasure that the very ones who applauded him take in his disappearance. There will be no lasting memory of his triumph. It will be as though he had never been.

8 Such a wicked person passes from the scene *like a dream*. No trace of his existence will be left behind. Just as the morning light chases away a night vision, so the community will quickly rid itself of all memory of this evildoer.

9 Neither the people over whom this monarch held authority nor the place from whence he ruled in splendor will recognize him any longer. Formerly people pushed and shoved to catch a glimpse of this hero. But now they express no interest in him. Even the beautiful palace where he once ruled will not accept him. Were he to walk there dressed in his royal robes, nothing would happen, for he no longer has authority.

10 The vast wealth this wicked person has accumulated will not endure, not even as a part of his family's inheritance. The nature of his punishment means that his children will also suffer for his wickedness. *His sons* will have to *redress the poor,* those impoverished by the evil deeds of their father. As just retribution, the evildoer's massive wealth will go back to those from whom he has coerced it (cf. 5:5). Zophar is renouncing the faulty belief that one can amass wealth by unjust practices in order to leave it as an inheritance to his children.

11 The remarkable *youthful vigor* that flows from this energetic ruler will vanish in an instant. Although his ruddy countenance gives the impression that he could live forever, he goes to the grave in the prime of life. His great virility has no advantage against *the dust,* nor does it secure any advantage for him in the afterlife. All his prowess dies with him.

12–14 In these verses Zophar vividly sets forth the axiom that evil deeds contain their own penalty.[34] A wicked person savors his evildoing just as a child holds a sweet morsel under the tongue, refusing to swallow it until he squeezes out every bit of flavor. But no matter how long he keeps the morsel under his tongue, it dissolves eventually. While the wicked person also relishes the sweet taste of evil, he will have to swallow his evildoing in time. Then it *will turn in*[35] *his stomach,* unleashing its curse against him. It is

34. The same idea is found in the proverb: "Bread gained by deceit is sweet to man, but afterward his mouth will be full of gravel" (Prov. 20:17).

35. This point is strengthened by the use of the verb *nehpak̲,* "it is turned," in the perfect form.

like poisonous food; even though it has been sugar-coated for a pleasant taste, it unfailingly releases its poison in the stomach. Soon the victim is doubled over in excruciating pain. His insides burn so hotly that it feels as though they are full of *venom.* Without any antidote for the poison, he will die in agonizing pain.

15 The rich delicacies of his evildoing will inflict him with torturous vomiting.[36] God himself will forcefully administer the emetic, as the verb *disgorges (hôrîš)* indicates. While wicked deeds contain their own punishment, God himself activates that punishment. It is important to observe that in this manner of reasoning no clear distinction is maintained between primary and secondary causes.

16 In passionately longing for riches this envious person is as vile as if he were sucking *the poison of asps.* He revels in illicit gain. Intricate plans to outwit another for wealth obsess him. But he falls to his own cunning. The very snake he loved to play with bites him. The phraseology *a viper's tongue will kill him* comes out of the ancient belief that a serpent's tongue carried the poison.

17 Cursed, this greedy evildoer will not even enjoy the land's basic produce. In Palestine *oil, honey,* and *curds,* along with wheat, were the staples. With oil a person anoints himself, cooks his food, and lights his dwelling. Honey, usually date syrup, enriches his diet, and curds offer him refreshment from the heat of the day. When the land produces these staples in abundance, it is said that there are *streams of oil and rivers flowing with honey and curds.*

18 Zophar again states that this evildoer will have to restore the wealth he has accumulated without ever getting any satisfaction from it. Perhaps the phrase translated *uneaten,* literally "without swallowing" *(lōʾ yiḇlaʿ),* means that whatever he tries to enjoy of his ill-gotten gain convulses him and thus prevents him from using it in any meaningful way. The words for *gain* and *profit* usually refer to the rewards of hard labor: *yāḡāʿ* means the gain from toil and *tᵉmûrâ* is the profit from barter. But wealth acquired by unjust means has no lasting profit for its owner.

19 This wicked person is cursed further because he inflicted great hardship on the poor. This point ties back to v. 10. In pursuit of wealth *he has crushed the poor,* taking all that they have. Greedily *he has seized* their *houses,* including everything in the house and the property. He comes to possess what he did not work for. After defrauding the poor of their houses, he has *abandoned* them mercilessly to their plight.[37] Helpless to resist this tyrant's legal schemes, they are driven to deep despair.

36. Cf. Prov. 23:8, which also appears in the "Instruction of Amenemope."
37. Cf. a description of such fraudulent activity in Mic. 2:1–2.

20 That evil person's successes in crushing the poor have inflamed his passion for things and for power. *His craving* constantly gnaws at him. No matter how much he feeds it, it refuses to subside. He finds no satisfaction in what he has accumulated. Controlled by his drives, he never has a moment of rest.

21 No one is safe from such a person's plots to dominate and to extort. Since no one is beyond his evil influence, nothing of his prosperity will endure. The principle is the greater the evil, the greater the punishment.

22 While the evildoer revels in his plans to enjoy the *fullness of plenty,* his whole empire collapses. Amidst plenty *he will have distress* (lit. "it will be narrow for him"). A mighty blow will strike him, a blow that has behind it the force of every person he has made miserable. Possibly Zophar thinks that the very ones whom the evildoer has wronged will turn against their oppressor in anger.

23 When this evildoer *has filled his belly,* God will fiercely attack him as an enraged warrior. The evildoer will discover the truth in the adage that while God's anger kindles slowly, it burns exceedingly hot. When God's anger burns hotly, he *will rain* on his foe an arsenal of *munitions* from his heavenly storehouse: "[God] let loose on them his fierce anger, wrath, indignation, and distress, a company of destroying angels" (Ps. 78:49). God's weapons are multiple, including fire, hail, and brimstone (e.g., Gen. 19:24; Exod. 15:7; Ps. 11:6). Together these two pictures mean that behind all the curses that plague this sinner stands God the mighty warrior.

24, 25 The picture continues by describing the evildoer caught in hand-to-hand combat with God. But terrified by God's *iron weapon,* i.e., a sword, he flees for his life. But he will not escape, for God will raise his bow and shoot *a bronze-tipped arrow*[38] at his fleeing opponent. The arrow is released with such force that it will pierce through his body and extend out his back. Its *glittering point,* resembling a lightning bolt,[39] will split *his gall,* i.e., his gall bladder, bringing certain death. This double imagery shows that there is no escape from the weapons of divine justice (cf. Isa. 24:18; Amos 5:18–19), for they are able to strike at close and long range.

Conscious that God's arrow has torn his viscera, the wounded person is flooded with *terrors.* With this language Zophar alludes to Job's lament in

38. The phrase means lit. "a bronze bow" *(qešeṯ neḥûšâ).* It is most likely elliptical for a bronze-tipped arrow shot from a very strong bow. L. Fisher (*RSP,* I:333) discovers that "darts" *(nṯq)* and "arrows" *(ḥẓm)* stand in a more antithetical relationship to bows *(qšt)* than has been supposed. He thus translates this text: "Should he flee the iron dart, the bow of bronze would transfix him."

39. Heb. *bārāq,* translated here "a glittering point," usually means "a lightning flash." Several times the OT speaks of God's weapons as bolts of lightning (cf. Deut. 32:41; Hab. 3:11; Ps. 18:15 [Eng. 14]; 144:6).

16:13. There Job accused God of attacking him like a fierce warrior. Zophar's response is that Job has discerned correctly, for God is justly fighting a rebellious man. In his opinion Job is experiencing God's mighty blows against his hidden sins and will soon die.

26 In the end the evildoer's *treasures*[40] will be assigned to *total darkness*. God's *fire*, though *unfanned, will consume* him and anyone *left in his tent*.[41] Such total punishment means that the victim has been incorrigibly hostile toward God.

27, 28 At this point Zophar speaks to Job's wish for a trial before the heavenly court. He asserts that at his trial *the heavens* and *the earth* will rise up as witnesses and testify against the accused. They *will reveal* all *his iniquity*. This metaphor recalls the imagery of the divine lawsuit.[42] In many OT passages God as plaintiff and judge summons Israel to trial for breach of covenant. In such a lawsuit the heavens and the earth serve as the jury, and they may also function as witnesses (cf. Mic. 6:1). The theory is that no one ever does anything in total secrecy. The elements of nature observe his every act and will give the convicting testimony when God holds court.

With this metaphor Zophar is undercutting the basis of Job's hope. Job is convinced that he is innocent. Since all the visible evidence is against him, his only hope to prove his innocence rests with his heavenly witness (16:18–20), namely, God his kinsman-redeemer (19:25). But Zophar attacks Job's bold, venturesome statement as presumptuous. For him Job's daring faith is the apex of audacity. In it is contained the cause for the final blow to Job. When the divine court hears Job's case, the heavens will bear witness to Job's guilt. Since God is already convicting Job, it is impossible to believe that the heavens would give testimony that would counter God's judgment. In thinking otherwise Job is deluded. The court will pronounce the sentence of total destruction against the evildoer. *A flood will sweep away his house*, including everything in it, on *the day of his [God's] wrath*.

29 In conclusion Zophar restates his thesis. God has assigned the exact *portion* that will befall the wicked person. *Portion (ḥēleq)* means a

40. Most take *ṣᵉpûnāyw* to mean "his valuables," as in Ps. 17:14; cf. Deut. 33:19. Another possible meaning is "his treasured ones, his loved ones." As Driver-Gray point out, it seems strange that darkness is the calamity threatening the valuables, for they are generally secured in obscure places. The incident of Korah's punishment, however, supports understanding *ṣᵉpûnāyw* as "his treasures," for both the possessions of Korah and his company were swallowed by the earth (Num. 16:31–35).

41. God's fire was one of the curses that took Job's flocks and their attendants (1:16).

42. Cf. K. Nielsen, *Yahweh as Prosecutor and Judge*, JSOTSup 9 (Sheffield: JSOT Press, 1978).

person's rightful share of something, e.g., a share in the spoil from war or a lot of land or a part of an inheritance.[43] Here the sinner's final punishment is called his portion, *the heritage decreed for him by God.* The language of portions and inheritance is used to indicate that the evildoer's lot is just and determined.

AIM

In his first speech Zophar described the destiny of both the wicked and the righteous. He painted for Job a striking contrast of their differing fates in order that Job might throw off his claim to innocence and adopt the way of the righteous. Job would again experience God's blessings. In this speech Zophar treats only the negative tenet of the doctrine of retribution, the certain punishment of the wicked. No matter how high a sinner may seem to rise, his downfall will come quickly. The deceitful deeds that have led to his success bear in themselves a deadly poison that will destroy their doer. God himself enters the fray as a mighty warrior to bring down this arrogant foe. Then God holds court to pronounce the final sentence against that evildoer. In the end a torment sweeps away that guilty party and all that he has.

While speaking in principle, Zophar definitely has Job in mind. Much of his description of the woes of the evildoer alludes to Job's calamity and to the wording in his laments. It is obvious that he is interpreting Job's suffering as just, deserved punishment for arrogant sins.[1] In his view Job's crime would be oppressing the poor to amass his great wealth. If Job remains unconvinced, the divine court will soon convict him of his sins. Possibly Zophar hopes that his description of the woes of the wicked will move Job to repentance, but he extends no call to repentance. Perhaps then he has abandoned hope for Job and is defining his fate and its significance in order that Job might be aware of the outcome of his affliction. If this is true, Zophar has closed his thinking in reference to Job's guilt. That is why he would have no reason to deliver a third speech. Having made up his mind that Job's fate is sealed, he would have nothing more to say.

43. Cf. M. Tsevat, "*chalaq* II," *TDOT,* IV:447–51.

1. J. Holbert ("'The skies will uncover his iniquity': satire in the second speech of Zophar (Job xx)," *VT* 31 [1981] 171–79) attempts to show that Zophar is answering Job directly with "the satiric technique of indirection." "His 'general' speech on the fate of the wicked is in reality a specific attack on Job as wicked. He achieves his satiric goal by picking up Job's self-descriptions and incorporating them into his own description of 'wicked people'" (p. 178).

6. JOB'S SIXTH RESPONSE (21:1–34)

On this occasion Job addresses his remarks entirely to the friends. In the style of a wisdom disputation he challenges their simplified view of the doctrine of retribution.[1] Motivated by a desire to prove his own uprightness even though the evidence of his affliction testifies against him, he argues the opposite side of that thesis, namely, that a person's prosperity does not necessarily mean that he is righteous. Many who are rich in material things reject God openly and blatantly. If this is true so is the opposite, i.e., those suffering beneath heavy burdens are not necessarily sinners. If in God's providence the wicked can prosper, surely the devout may suffer. The friends, therefore, should give him the benefit of the doubt and reach out to him in comfort rather than with caustic and condemning words.

This speech has three major divisions: an appeal for a sympathetic hearing (vv. 1–6), questions about the doctrine of the speedy retribution of the wicked (vv. 7–33), and a final complaint against the friends (v. 34).

a. An Appeal for a Sympathetic Hearing (21:1–6)

1 *Job responded:*
2 *"Listen attentively to my word;*
let this be the consolation which you give.
3 *Bear with me while I speak,*
and after I have spoken, mock on.
4 *Is my complaint against man?*
Why[1] *should I not be impatient?*
5 *Look at me and be appalled;*[2]
place your hand over your mouth.
6 *When I remember this,*[3] *I am terrified,*
and shuddering seizes my flesh."

2 Job entreats the friends to *listen attentively to* his word, for he wants them to ponder his position. If they would adopt the posture of careful listeners, this would be their *consolation (tanḥûmôṯ)*. Earlier Eliphaz had acclaimed the words the friends were offering Job as "God's consolations"

1. Cf. C. Westermann, *Structure of the Book of Job,* pp. 87–90.

1. The phrase *wᵉʾim* is elliptical for *ʾim kēn,* "if it is so" (Dhorme, Tur-Sinai).

2. MT *hāšammû,* "be appalled," could be a Hiphil that is inwardly transitive (GKC, §§ 53d, e), but as Driver-Gray posit, a Niphal *hiššammû* would avoid an anomalous use of the Hiphil.

3. The object of the verb "remember" is omitted. Here it is taken to be "his own shocking condition." But it could be the content of what he is about to say, for the friends are distressed at his claim that the wicked do prosper. For a description of personal dread, cf. Isa. 21:3–4.

(15:11a), but Job rejected this assertion by calling the friends "miserable comforters" (16:2b). So now he asks them to show him genuine compassion by paying attention to his words.

3 Job requests of the comforters, *Bear with me while I speak.* With the use of the personal pronoun *I (ʾānōḵî)* before the verb *speak* Job emphasizes that instead of categorically accepting the account of the fate of the wicked, he is going to speak his mind. He makes, therefore, a special plea that they be silent so that they may attend to his words. Perhaps during his speeches they have been reacting to various points with hisses and disruptive gestures. But if they will be attentive while he defends his position, in due time they may continue their mocking *(lāʿag).*[4]

4 With rhetorical questions Job passionately states that his *complaint (śîaḥ)* is against God, not man (cf. 13:3). The personal nature of his complaint is stressed by the use of the personal pronoun *I (ʾānōḵî),* which reinforces the possessive pronoun used with *complaint.* The first part of the verse is literally "Am I against man (making) my complaint?" Since God, for some unknown reason, remains unresponsive to his lament, Job points out that it is obvious why he is *impatient.*[5] It is out of frustration and fear that God may never clear him.

5 Job entreats his friends to turn toward him and *look at* him, in the hope that they might perceive his desperate state. If so, they will *be appalled (hāšammû)* and will have to place their hands over their mouths in silent astonishment (cf. 29:9; 40:4; Mic. 7:16).[6]

6 When Job remembers or thinks about his own shocking condition, he becomes so *terrified (niḇhaltî)* that *shuddering (pallāṣûṯ)* seizes his flesh. In his first speech Eliphaz had accused Job of being terrified or dismayed and thus lacking in faith (4:5). In response Job justifies his emotional distress as inevitable because of the acuteness of his ordeal. The horror he feels is heightened by his realization that his emaciated body denies his cherished belief that God honors faithful service.

4. MT *talʿîg,* "mock on," is singular in form. Since Job speaks to the friends as a group using plural forms, many think it is best to emend it to plural, with LXX, Syr., Vulg. If the singular is read, Job is addressing Zophar, the last speaker, or possibly Eliphaz, the next to speak. That Zophar is singled out by Job finds some support in that he uses this same word, *lāʿag,* to describe Job's speaking (11:3). A singular verb in reference to a friend also occurs in 16:3 between plurals in 16:1–4; the singular, definitely being the harder reading, is accepted.

5. The idiom for being impatient is "my spirit is short" *(tiqṣar rûḥî).*

6. Dahood ("Northwest Semitic Philology and Job," p. 64) cites a Near Eastern illustration as evidence that the gesture means astonishment and awe.

b. Tough Questions about the Doctrine of Retribution (21:7–33)

Job develops his thesis that the wicked prosper in four parts: (1) the blessings of the wicked (vv. 7–16); (2) the infrequency of the wicked being punished (vv. 17–21); (3) the failure of the doctrine of retribution (vv. 22–26); and (4) a rejection of the friends' anticipated rebuttal (vv. 27–33).

(1) The Blessings of the Wicked (21:7–16)

7 *"Why do the wicked live,*
grow old, and become mighty in power?
8 *Their children are established before them,*[1]
their offspring before their eyes.
9 *Their homes are safe, free from fear;*
no rod of God is on them.
10 *Their bull sires without fail;*[2]
their cow calves without loss.
11 *They send forth their infants like sheep;*
their children dance about.
12 *They sing to the music of timbrel*[3] *and harp;*
they make merry to the sound of the flute.
13 *They spend*[4] *their days in prosperity,*
and in a moment[5] *they go down*[6] *to Sheol.*

1. The sequence of *lipnêhem* ("before them") *ʿimmām* ("with them") seems redundant, but the syllable count is balanced with both terms present (9/9). LXX omits *nāḵôn* and *ʿimmām* and reads instead *lᵉnapšām,* "for themselves." This variation suggests that LXX had a different *Vorlage*. Many eliminate either *lipnêhem* or *ʿimmām,* with the majority favoring the omission of the latter, since it has less textual support. But, of course, the early translators could have been troubled by the tautology. The Syr. supports both phrases, and in Ps. 89:22 (Eng. 21) the sentence *tikkôn ʿimmô,* "it will sustain him," offers a parallel. This translation accepts *lipnêhem* and leaves *ʿimmām* untranslated.

2. While the Hebrew root *gʿl* in the Qal means "abhor" and in the Hiphil "reject as fully unfit," in a context about breeding it may have a technical meaning, "impregnate without fail" (cf. H. Fuhs, *"gāʿal," TDOT,* III:47).

3. The phrase *kᵉṯōp,* "like a timbrel," is a little difficult with the verb *nāśâ,* "lift, bear." Delitzsch suggests that *qôl,* "voice," is suppressed before *kᵉṯōp.* The versions support the preferred reading of *bᵉṯōp,* "with (to the music of) a timbrel," and may be followed (see *BHS*).

4. The Ketib *yᵉḇallû* means "wear out." In a few passages it is taken to mean "wear out by use, to exhaust something (in joy)" (e.g., Isa. 65:22). In Modern Hebrew it means "spend time, amuse." The Qere *yᵉḵallû,* a more readily acceptable reading, means "they complete" or "finish" their days in good. The Ketib is followed as the more difficult reading; nevertheless, Job 36:11 lends strong support to the Qere.

5. The phrase *bᵉregaʿ* usually means "in a moment" (so Syr.), which seems the most natural meaning here. But some (e.g., Gordis) relate *regaʿ* to Arab. *rajaʿa,* "return to rest," and translate the phrase "in peace" (cf. Isa. 34:14; Jer. 31:2; 50:34) with LXX and

14 *They say to God, 'Get away from us!*
We do not desire the knowledge of your ways.
15 *What is Shaddai that we should serve him?*
What profit is there that we should entreat him?'
16 *But their prosperity is not in their own hands,*
the counsel of the wicked is far from me."[7]

7 Job strikes at the center of the doctrine of retribution with the question, *Why do the wicked live?*[8] The verb *live* refers to a full, prosperous life. The wicked *grow old* (*ʿāṯaq*),[9] and they *become mighty in power* (cf. Ps. 73:12). Although the penalty for sin is death, everywhere there are jovial, prosperous evildoers, secure and unafraid of loss. It stands to reason then that either they have avoided the penalty for their wicked deeds or the punishment due them has not yet been executed. In either case their penalty is not speedily executed as the friends have held.

The clause *[they] become mighty in power (gāḇᵉrû ḥayil)* calls to mind the common phrase *gibbôr ḥayil,* "the landed aristocracy." Heb. *ḥayil* means "strength" and "army" and sometimes "wealth." Heb. *gāḇar* bears the idea of "be strong, gain the upper hand."[10] That is, these men become leaders of the nation by supporting the state with their wealth and their troops. From the people they receive the highest recognition. Acclaimed as noble citizens, their status covers the wicked deeds that brought them to that prominence. In the following verses Job will detail the multiple blessings that attend such wicked leaders. With this account he is refuting the assertions of Eliphaz (5:5; 15:20) and Zophar (20:15–18) that the wealth of these faithless men is so ephemeral that it can never be used to advantage. In contrast, he claims that their wealth and prominence is real and lasting. A single proven example would refute the dogmatic theology of the friends.

Targ. Perhaps, as Gordis suggests, this is a case in which the writer wishes both meanings to be present.

6. MT *yēḥāttû* is best taken from the root *nḥt,* "go down," with the Targ. and Syr., rather than from *ḥtt,* "destroy." There may be a confusion in pointing between a *pe-nun* and an *ʿayin-ʿayin* verb, or the *dagesh* may be a *dagesh forte affectuosum* (GKC, § 20i), or it may be best to revocalize it *yēḥāṯû* (so most commentators, *BHS*).

7. The preposition *mennî* may be viewed as an archaic form of *mimmennî* (Gordis).

8. Cf. Jer. 12:1–3. Job questions Zophar's picture that the wicked die before their time (20:11).

9. Heb. *ʿāṯaq* means "go forward, advance" or "remove." In its latter semantic field it can mean "transcribe" (Prov. 25:1), and in the former one it can mean "grow old" (a common meaning for this root in Aramaic), in the sense "grow weak" (Ps. 6:8 [Eng. 7]), "be venerated," or "become arrogant" (Ps. 75:6 [Eng. 5]).

10. Cf. H. Kosmala, "*gābhar,*" *TDOT,* II:368; and GKC, § 117z.

8–13 Job proceeds to paint a graphic picture of the prosperous life of the wicked. Everything goes well for them and their household. Their wealth enables them to ensure their children's and their grandchildren's happiness.

8 *their offspring (ṣeʾĕṣāʾêhem)* may refer to subsequent generations. The statement that the success of the wicked benefits their offspring counters both the argument that nothing gained by wrongdoing is passed on to the children as well as the escape clause in the doctrine of retribution that if an arrogant person does enjoy life the punishment due him will fall on his children (e.g., 18:19; 20:21).

9 The homes of these wicked men are *safe* [*šālôm,* lit. "peace"], *free from fear [paḥaḏ]* or threat of loss (cf. 5:24; 15:21). This is remarkable, for the fear of sudden disaster is supposed to unsettle the godless (Prov. 3:25). But these families do not live under the cloud of such dread. There is no evidence anywhere that God's punishing *rod (šēḇeṭ),* which has smitten Job (19:21b), has struck them with even a single blow. Instead everything goes well for these evildoers.

10 The evildoers'[11] flocks are very fertile, free from any complications that reduce the number of offspring. Their cattle are fecund. *Their bull* impregnates *their cow without fail,* i.e., without spilling its seed, and the cow bears without miscarriage. The fertility of their cattle is representative of the prosperity in every area of this person's estate.

11, 12 The wealth from numerous flocks guarantees the security of the household. With no fear of being molested *their infants and children* play heartily and with abandon, just *like sheep.*[12] *send forth (šālaḥ)* carries the idea of "releasing or allowing to run freely" (cf. Isa. 32:20). Because the children are so happy, their play may be characterized as *dance.* Also there are great festive occasions when all the family dance to the music of timbrel, harp, and flute. This picture represents idyllic happiness. Job underscores the joy of the children to show that the merrymaking is not a facade, as is often the case at a feast put on by the rich. He also is countering the argument that if a wicked person prospers his children will surely be cursed.

13 The wicked live a comfortable life and die a quick, easy death. All of their days are spent *in prosperity* (lit. "good," *ṭôḇ*) and enjoyment. When their days come to an end, they descend to Sheol quietly and quickly, free from any prolonged, agonizing illness. A serene death means that the joy of the wicked is as full as possible. Suffering has never impressed on their mind the horrors of death.

11. As is often the case in Hebrew poetry, in this verse there is a shift in number, from the prevailing plural forms to singular forms. For the sake of a smooth English translation, it seems best to continue the plural pronouns.

12. See also Ps. 107:41; cf. Ezek. 36:37; Ps. 114:4, 6.

14 To focus on how his understanding of the fate of the wicked differs from that of his friends, Job depicts the disposition of these evil, successful men. They do not want God to be active in their midst. To portray their arrogant hostility against God, he quotes them as ordering God, *Get away from us!* Their flagrant words show that their rejection of God is conscious and willful. They have no desire to be taught God's ways. Their disposition is the opposite of the humble person who prays, "Make me to know thy ways, O Lord; teach me thy paths" (Ps. 25:4; cf. Isa. 58:2).

15 These evildoers go so far as to question the authority of Shaddai, the God of their fathers. Boldly refusing to recognize his lordship, they will not *serve him* or worship him. Neither do they see any *profit* or advantage in making entreaty to *(nipgaʿ bᵉ)*[13] God. Such stalwart sinners could never be persuaded to serve God by the utilitarian arguments of the friends. Confident of being masters of their own world and without any fear of reprisal from a superior divine force, they deny the teaching of retribution without ever experiencing any grave consequences.

16 With a parenthetical comment Job emphatically states his own judgment on the happy life of the wicked.[14] Even though they boast of their prosperity, Job, along with the comforters, believes that their success is ephemeral. In the final analysis they do not have ultimate control over *their prosperity*. In v. 16b Job rejects emphatically his being identified with the counsel of such wicked men. He affirms his own integrity and faith in God even in the midst of his lament over the good that befalls those who reject God. Thus he is arguing against the position of Zophar on two levels: (1) since there are wicked men who prosper and live to an old age, his own suffering does not automatically put him into the category of the wicked; (2) since he wholeheartedly rejects the counsel of the wicked, he cannot be categorically identified with them.

(2) The Infrequency of the Wicked Being Punished (21:17–21)

17 *"How often is the lamp of the wicked snuffed out,*
or does calamity come on them,
or pains which God apportions in his anger?
18 *How often[1] do they become like straw before the wind*
and like chaff that the storm snatches away?

13. Heb. *nipgaʿ bᵉ* means "entreat" or "implore" another; cf. Jer. 7:16; 27:18; 36:25; Ruth 1:16.

14. Similarly, in the midst of his description of the suffering servant Isaiah expresses his own reaction (53:6).

1. This verse continues to depend on the *kammâ* ("how often") of v. 17.

19 *'God stores up misery for his children,' you say.*
Let him repay him that he may know it.[2]
20 *Let his own eyes see his ruin;*[3]
let him drink of the wrath of Shaddai.
21 *For what is his interest in his household after him*
when his allotted months are cut off?"[4]

17, 18 Doubting that the law of retribution is speedily enacted in many cases, Job asks a series of questions concerning the actual experience of the wicked. He directly rebuts Bildad's assertion that "the light of the wicked is extinguished" (18:5) by asking, *How often is the lamp of the wicked snuffed out?* The *lamp (nēr)* symbolizes a healthy life, and *snuffed out (dāʿaḵ)* refers to a premature death by a tragedy brought on by God as punishment for evildoing (cf. Prov. 13:9; 20:20; 24:20). Job continues to ask, *does calamity [ʾêḏ] come on them, or pains [ḥ^{a}ḇālîm]*[5] *which God apportions in his anger?*

Shifting to an agricultural metaphor, Job asks, *How often do they become like straw before the wind and like chaff that the storm snatches away [gānaḇ]?*[6] Lacking weight, straw or chaff is driven wherever the wind wishes during winnowing; so too it was believed that the wicked are tossed about before the stormy blasts of the divine wrath.[7] Each of Job's questions expects the answer "very few times, if any." But any exception to the application of the law of retribution means that it cannot be applied categorically. Consequently, the arguments of the friends will have to be tempered.

2. For MT *w^{e}yēḏāʿ*, "and he may know," D. W. Thomas ("The Root *ydʿ* in Hebrew, II," *JTS* 36 [1935] 412) finds a second root *ydʿ* that means "to become still, quiet" and "to be reduced to submission." J. Reider ("Etymological Studies: *ydʿ* or *yrʿ* and *rʿʿ*," *JBL* 66 [1947] 317) thinks that there is a confusion of a *d* and an *r*, so he reads *w^{e}yērōaʿ*, "so he is crushed." Since MT is intelligible, it is retained.

3. Heb. *kîḏ* occurs only here. Guillaume (*Studies in the Book of Job*, p. 104) thinks it is related to Arab. *kaʾdāʾ*, "calamity, loss." Others see an error of audition and read either *ʾêḏô*, "his calamity," or *pîḏô*, "his ruin," both of which occur elsewhere in Job. Interestingly the Qumran Targ. supports MT. See Grabbe, *Comparative Philology*, pp. 77–79.

4. The plural verb *ḥuṣṣāṣû*, "be cut off," is attracted to the plural *nomen regens*, *ḥ^{o}ḏāšāyw*, "his months."

5. The exact meaning of *ḥ^{a}ḇālîm* is disputed. The root may mean (a) "pain," (b) "lot, portion," or (c) "cord." The idea of "lot, portion" moves in the direction of "a lot, a portion of land," rather than a person's fate. Those who accept "cords" emend the MT *y^{e}ḥallēq*, "he will apportion," to *yaḥ^{a}zîqûm*, "he will seize them" (so Duhm, based on LXX, but as Dhorme notes, LXX may be a paraphrase of MT). "Pain" seems the best alternative. Even though *ḥēḇel* is usually restricted to "birth pangs," like other words primarily restricted to the birth process, the term may describe the most agonizing pains caused by the severest suffering.

6. Cf. Ps. 1:4; 35:5; 83:14 (Eng. 13); Isa. 17:13; 29:5; Jer. 13:24.

7. Earlier Eliphaz had spoken about blasts from God "as anger that consumes the doers of evil" (4:9).

More specifically they will need to reevaluate Job's case and come to realize that the reason for his tragedy must lie outside the law of retribution.

19–21 Job proceeds to challenge the corollary of the doctrine of retribution that says that God punishes a wicked person by storing up misery for his children (see, e.g., Eliphaz in 5:4 and Zophar in 20:10). Even the proponents of the strict application of retribution concede that sometimes the wicked do find pleasure in their wickedness, but they assert that God will bring the punishment due them on their children. Job emphatically disagrees with this precept. He believes that if God is going to penalize wrongdoing justly, the full brunt of the discipline must be felt by the person who has done wrong. Each sinner needs to be exposed to the divine wrath that is kindled by that individual's transgression. The verbs *see* and *drink* (v. 20) underscore his position that the wicked person must feel the pain of his own sin. *His own eyes* should *see* the loss of his possessions, and he himself should *drink* deeply of *the wrath of Shaddai* (cf. 6:4).[8] A grave problem with the theory of delayed retribution is that the misfortune that is to come on a wicked person's children after his death cannot affect the sinner himself. In fact, after he has died, he no longer has any personal interest in the fate of his household. If the theory of retribution works, Job reasons, punishment must be executed against the sinner himself in his own lifetime. Since such is not the case, the friends' presentation on the doctrine of retribution is faulty.

(3) The Failure of the Doctrine of Retribution (21:22–26)

22 *"Can one teach God knowledge,*
the very one who judges the exalted ones?[1]
23 *Such a one dies in full vigor,*
wholly at ease[2] *and contented,*
24 *his testes*[3] *full of milk,*
his bones moist with marrow.

8. A picture for God's wrath is that of its being stored in a cup. Thus those who are experiencing God's wrath are said to have drunk deeply from this cup (e.g., Isa. 51:17; Jer. 25:15; 49:12; Ezek. 23:31–34; Ps. 11:6; 75:9 [Eng. 8]).

1. The meaning of Heb. *rāmîm* is disputed. It may refer either to the heavens (cf. Targ. and Ps. 78:69) or to the inhabitants of the heights, i.e., the angels. Blommerde (*Northwest Semitic Grammar and Job,* p. 94) understands the plural as the majestic plural; so it is an epithet for God, "the All-High" or "the Exalted." M. Dahood (*Bib* 38 [1957] 312–13) sees here another enclitic *mem;* this interpretation would eliminate the plural. But the frequent references to heavenly beings in this work favor taking *rāmîm* as an epithet for the angels (cf. 5:1; Dhorme, Rowley, Pope).

2. MT *šal'ᵃnan* seems to be a variant of *ša'ᵃnan.* In Northwest Semitic there are several examples of the insertion of a liquid letter to lengthen a word (see Pope; Guillaume, *Studies in the Book of Job,* pp. 104–105); cf. Heb. *zalʿāpâ,* which is related to *zʿp.* In this line it adds to the force of alliteration: *kullô šal'ᵃnan wᵉšālêw.*

3. Verse 24a contains the otherwise unknown *ʿᵃṭînāyw.* The context suggests that

25 *Another dies in bitterness of soul,*
never having tasted happiness.[4]
26 *Together they lie in the dust,*
and worms cover them."

22 Since the friends have described a pattern of quick retribution that is easily countered by an observation of affairs in this world, Job scathingly puts to them an absurd question: *Can one teach God knowledge, the very one who judges the exalted ones?* The friends would be the first to admit that no one, including themselves, could teach God. He is also telling them that they do not have to defend God's governance so vehemently. After all, God is the judge of the exalted inhabitants of heaven.[5]

23–26 Continuing to object to their rigid application of the doctrine of retribution, Job sketches two very different styles of living, both of which result in a premature death. One person is a dignified, vigorous man and the other an impoverished, bitter person. The prominent, prosperous person *dies in full vigor [ʿeṣem tummô],*[6] *wholly at ease and contented.* His life, free from tension and bitterness, is replete with pleasure. Virile and energetic, he is able to subdue every opponent and bring his whole world into submission. His body is strong and stout, as conveyed by *his bones moist with marrow [mōaḥ].*[7] This person's days add up to a rich, abundant life. Another person has the opposite experience. At every turn he faces

---

it means a part of the body. In that light the word *ḥālāḇ,* "milk," is revocalized as *ḥēleḇ,* "fat." For *ʿaṭînāyw* the versions read different parts of the body: LXX and Vulg. "intestines," Targ. "breasts," Syr. "sides." The verb *ʿṭn* concerns the laying of olives in a vat or press. Related words have to do with vessels used in securing oil from olives. Thus some (e.g., BDB, p. 742) suggest a vessel, e.g., "pails," for this word; cf. Grabbe, *Comparative Philology,* pp. 79–81. Gordis finds here a euphemism for male genitals, and "milk" then stands for "semen." This suggestion is the most creative. Pope offers another possibility, reading *ʿṭm* and *ḥēleḇ; ʿṭm* is defined as "haunches," similar to Akk. *eṣmu* and Arab. *ʿiṭmāʾ:* "his haunches full and plump." But since this reading requires two emendations with no textual support, it is not followed.

4. The preposition *b* on *baṭṭôḇâ* is used partitively, "some goodness or happiness" (Delitzsch).

5. Verse 22 is difficult to interpret in the light of the context. However, a question similar to the one here appears in Isa. 40:14. Another way of viewing this verse is to treat it as Job's quotation of an accusation made against him by the friends (cf. Eliphaz in 4:17 and 15:8–14; Zophar in 11:5–9; so Gordis). Driver-Gray reject this idea, for Job does not counter that accusation. Gordis answers their objection by saying that vv. 22–26 offer an oblique response, since Job cannot deny God's superiority.

6. Heb. *ʿeṣem,* lit. "bones," may also mean the substance or essence of a matter. Here Heb. *tm* refers to the completeness of physical vigor.

7. Heb. *mōaḥ,* lit. "marrow," poetically represents a body full of vigor and resilient against disease, a body that has not been shriveled by hardship. Health is pictured as moisture in the bones in Prov. 3:8 (Gordis).

obstacles and losses. Disappointed and frustrated, he becomes hardened and bitter. He never has the opportunity to nourish his body with fine food or to enjoy the festivities of great banquets. His body becomes frail, thin, and wrinkled as he fades away to nothing. Thus he *dies in bitterness of soul, never having tasted happiness.*

These two types of people are not classified as good and bad, righteous and wicked, but as fortunate and unfortunate, regardless of their moral character. Even though on earth they are members of widely different classes, in death they are on the same level. *They lie in the dust* side by side and *worms cover* both of *them.* Death makes no distinction based on the nature of their earthly existence. The rewards enjoyed by the healthy person melt into nothingness (cf. Isa. 14:11), and the ill-fate of the other person has no further ill-consequences. Therefore, Job finds that the postulate of the doctrine of retribution—that the evildoer, though prosperous for a while, receives his just reward in death—fails to withstand scrutiny. Moreover, Job is reasoning that tragedy has been his fate regardless of his faithful adherence to God's way. That is, the validity of his moral integrity stands apart from his tragic circumstances. If that is true, his case must be tried on grounds other than the appearance of his afflicted body. Such is the search Job has undertaken.

(4) The Rejection of the Friends' Anticipated Rebuttal (21:27–34)

27 *"Behold, I know your thoughts,*
the schemes by which you plot[1] to harm me,
28 *because you say, 'Where is the house of the nobleman?*
Where are the dwellings[2] of the wicked?'
29 *Have you not asked travelers?*
Have you not denied[3] their evidence[4]

1. MT *taḥmōsû* may be a denominative verb from *ḥāmās* ("violence"), meaning "do or plot violence or wrong." Another possibility is the meaning "think" related to Syr. *hms,* "think," and Arab. *hamasa,* "speak audibly," and supported by translations in Targ. and Syr. (cf. B. Jacob, "Erklärung einer Hiob-Stellen," *ZAW* 32 [1912] 286–87; see also Dhorme); then the *ḥ* is either a strengthening of the root or the text should read *tahmōsû.* But cf. Gordis, and Blommerde, *Northwest Semitic Grammar and Job,* p. 95.

2. Since the noun *'ōhel,* "tent," standing beside *miškᵉnôṯ,* "dwellings," is redundant, it is best to remove it as a gloss. Also in favor of reading *miškᵉnôṯ* is that its inclusion in the plural *nomen rectum* matches the plural *nomen regens;* and the change yields a balanced syllable count.

3. The Piel *nikkar* is taken to mean either (a) "recognize" (Dhorme) or (b) "treat as foreign, deny, mistake" (cf. Driver-Gray). Since the form is Piel, the latter meaning is accepted. Working with that meaning, Pope renders the line: "Do you not find their tales strange?"

4. Heb. *'ôṯ* means "sign, token, memorial, ensign." It also can stand for "testimony, evidence," in a concrete sense (cf. Dhorme).

30 *that the evil man is spared in the day of calamity,*
that he is delivered[5] *from*[6] *the day of wrath?*
31 *Who will declare his way to his face?*
Who will pay him for what he has done?
32 *He is borne to the cemetery;*
one keeps watch over his tomb.
33 *Clods of the wadi are sweet to him;*
all men will follow after him,
as before him a countless number.
34 *How can you console me vainly?*
Your answers remain as treachery."

27 Sensing that his arguments are failing to convince his friends, Job states that he knows what they are thinking to answer him. Having deduced from his misfortune that he is guilty of serious evildoing, they are plotting schemes *(mᵉzimmâ)* to harm *(ḥāmas)* or damage him. Heb. *mᵉzimmâ* can refer either to good thoughts (Prov. 3:21; 5:2) or to mischievous plans (Ps. 21:12 [Eng. 11]), but in either case it connotes involved, well-thought-out schemes. By their *schemes* Job has in mind more intricate arguments designed to discredit his argument further. Job thus charges his friends with using their shrewdest reasoning to harm rather than to help him.

28 Job postulates the comforters' line of argument. Attempting to refute his position, they will ask him about the existence of material wealth, such as a *house,* that proves that there is a noble wicked man who lives in security and prosperity (cf. 15:34; 18:21; 20:28). The *nobleman (nāḏîḇ)* is a high-ranking prince. The parallel word, *the wicked (rᵉšāʿîm),* intimates that this dignitary has risen to his exalted position by extortion and violence. The splendor of his dwelling mirrors his prestige. But where is his magnificent house? Not only is his house—perhaps by innuendo meaning Job's own house—not to be found in their opinion, but in general they will claim that the dwelling places of the wicked are missing. Through this type of questioning the friends will attempt to deny that there are any exceptions to the law of retribution.

29, 30 In turn Job answers their supposed objection with a question, a question that seeks to demonstrate that the friends have not accepted the signs or evidence that *travelers* (lit. "passersby") offer from what they

5. The plural form *yûḇālû,* "are delivered," is not a great problem, for, as Driver-Gray point out, the author alternates in using singular and plural forms for classes of people. Rowley says that to be led forth in a day of wrath is to escape the day. Therefore, *yûḇāl(û),* "he is led," is translated "he is delivered." Though many emend this verse because it seems to contradict Job's view, Gordis keeps it by interpreting it as Job's citation of his friends' position.

6. The preposition *lᵉ* on *yôm,* "days," is taken as having separative force (Habel, OTL).

have seen. These passersby are wayfarers who have the opportunity to observe many situations in various lands (cf. Lam. 1:12; 2:15; Ps. 80:13 [Eng. 12]). As they travel about they relate the unusual things they have seen. Their wide experience offers them a broad perspective on the general state of human affairs. Perhaps Job has a tolerant attitude toward the information given by travelers, as is found in Ben Sira: "A much traveled man knows many things" (Sir. 34:9a, JB). Previously Eliphaz had rejected the idea that strangers could give any information to the truly wise (15:18–19), but Job is renouncing such a position as myopic thinking intended to protect his theology from being challenged by any evidence to the contrary. The testimony from travelers, however, will confirm that affairs are just as Job has described them, particularly regarding the prosperous wicked. These travelers have observed *that the evil man is spared in the day of calamity ['êḏ]*, known also as *the day of wrath (ʿaḇārôṯ)*. Job is saying that travelers have seen the houses of the noble wicked still standing after a natural disaster.

31–33 Continuing with a double rhetorical question, Job claims that when such an evil person vaunts himself or exercises his authority, no one is brave enough to withstand that person to his face. God has not established any authority on earth powerful enough to repay such an evildoer *for what he has done*. As a result, when he dies he is given a dignified burial, even though he has lived his life as wantonly as he pleased. With great pomp *he is borne to the cemetery* and interred in a beautiful sepulcher. An honorable funeral was one of the highest honors a community could pay its most respected citizens. *Over his tomb (gāḏîš)*[7] a servant *keeps watch (šāqaḏ)*, i.e., in the succeeding years that servant tends the yard and protects the sepulcher from damage. He also takes care of the rites honoring the deceased. In many ancient Near Eastern countries the rich made endowments to ensure the proper care of their tombs. This custom was designed to guarantee the continuation of the honor of the deceased. The tomb here is pictured as being in a *wadi*. The caves along the walls of a dry riverbed offer excellent burial sites. There the *clods* that cover the dead person's body are *sweet*, suggesting that their occupant rests in peace. His glorious grave honors him. This picture discounts the rhetoric of Bildad (18:13–21) and Zophar (20:20–29) about the woeful end of the wicked. Everyone in attendance at his funeral will eventually follow him in death, just as he has joined the *countless number* that have preceded him.[8] In Job's view "inequity

7. MT *gāḏîš* is taken as related to Arab. *jadaṯ*, "tomb." Dhorme thinks that it refers to a mound heaped upon the grave or to a sculpture of the deceased set up to commemorate the occupant's status.

8. Others (e.g., Gordis) find in these last two lines a funeral procession, a crowd going before and behind the bier.

obtains even in death" (Habel, OTL). Thus Job rejects the corollary of the doctrine of retribution that death preempts the joys and successes of the wicked.

34 In a final line Job castigates his friends for consoling him *vainly (heḇel),* offering exhortations that are only a fleeting puff of air. Heb. *heḇel* is the word that appears in the famous line "Vanity of vanities, all is vanity" (Eccl. 1:2). Job finds that their *answers remain as treachery (maʿal).* This last word is a very strong term that describes the violation of the sacred (e.g., Lev. 5:15) and acts of faithlessness in marriage (e.g., Num. 5:12, 27) or devotion to God (e.g., Deut. 32:51; see Gordis). Thus if Job were to rely on them, he would become confused and lost, instead of being led to God.

AIM

The second cycle of speeches ends with Job's complete rejection of the doctrine of retribution as presented by the friends. He delivers a discourse to prove that the premise that the wicked receive just rewards in this life by suffering an early death or by having misfortune befall their households does not stand before the evidence of the actual state of affairs on earth. He shows that there are evildoers who are secure, enjoying their prosperity. They live a rich life, full of blessing, even though they deny God. Their experience proves that "there is such a thing as blessedness without blessing, divine favor without God, salvation without a saviour!"[1] In fact, those who do evil blatantly are interred with a pompous funeral given for the noblest members of the community. They die in glory with respect, not in shame. Job finds that these case histories contradict the tenets of the doctrine of retribution. So at the close of the second cycle of speeches Job soundly rejects the teaching of the friends.

C. THE THIRD CYCLE (22:1–27:23)

The third cycle begins in good form. There is a full speech from Eliphaz (38 lines) followed by one from Job (99 lines). Whether the final portion of Job's speech (ch. 24, esp. vv. 18–24) belongs to Job or to another is in doubt. After ch. 24 the problems increase. Bildad's speech is far too short, only 10 lines. Job's following speech is not only too long (chs. 26–28), but it also contains material that seems impossible to have come from him (above all 27:13–23 and ch. 28). In addition, there is no third speech from Zophar. It is

1. C. Westermann, *Structure of the Book of Job,* p. 89.

quite obvious that this cycle has suffered severely early in its transmission. To regain some order for the latter portion of this cycle chs. 25–27 are reconstructed as follows:

Bildad's Third Speech (25:1–6; 27:13–23)
Job's Third Speech (26:1–14; 27:1–12)

In this cycle Eliphaz, after pronouncing Job guilty of specific sins, earnestly entreats him to repent. Bildad, for his part, lauds God's perfection and elaborates on the fate of the wicked. Basically he reiterates the position of Eliphaz in the first section and that of Zophar in the second. He brings the words of the comforters to an end in a way that makes it clear that they have exhausted their counsel. Their comfort for Job has turned to condemnation of him. As for Job, he holds on to his conviction that he is innocent, and he asserts in faith that he will emerge from his trial purified like gold. Nevertheless, he complains even more pointedly that God encourages wickedness on earth by not holding times of judgment. Overall, though, his words in this cycle are more rational and less passionate as he appears to focus on his search to find God so that he can dispute his case directly with him. While this cycle seems trite and dull, it moves the plot along by creating in the listener the demand that the plot take a new direction.

1. ELIPHAZ'S THIRD SPEECH (22:1–30)

In his third speech Eliphaz forthrightly accuses Job of violating the high standards of patriarchal piety. Then he disputes Job's complaint that the wicked prosper and never are punished by instructing him as to how God actually treats the wicked. Eliphaz concludes by delivering a stirring call for Job to repent. Thus this speech is composed of three sections: accusations against Job (vv. 1–11); a disputation concerning God's activity in human affairs (vv. 12–24); and a call to repentance (vv. 21–30).

a. Accusations against Job (22:1–11)

1 *Eliphaz the Temanite responded:*
2 *"Can a man benefit God,*
that a wise man should be in harmony with him?[1]

1. The second line is hard to interpret. Many assume that it is parallel with the first line and render it "Can even a wise man benefit him?" Another interpretation is to identify the object of *ʿālêmô* as the wise men, not God (e.g., Driver-Gray, Fohrer, Hakam). The line then is translated: "No, he that acts wisely is profitable unto himself." This rendering takes account of the *kî*, "that, because, when," at the head of the second line. This particle indicates that this line carries forward the idea in the first line rather than simply repeating it. Gordis suggests that the double use of *yiskōn* is an example of

3 *What asset is it to Shaddai that you are innocent,*
or gain that you claim that your ways are blameless?[2]
4 *Does he arraign you for your piety*
and enter into judgment with you?
5 *Is not your wickedness great?*
Is there no end to your iniquities?
6 *For you have exacted pledges from your brothers*[3] *without grounds*
and stripped the naked of their clothing.
7 *You gave no water to the weary;*
from the hungry you withheld bread.
8 *You think yourself to be a strong man who owns the earth,*
a privileged inhabitant of it.
9 *You sent widows away empty-handed;*
the arms of orphans have been crushed.[4]
10 *Therefore snares surround you,*
and sudden terror makes you panic;
11 *the light has become dark*[5] *so that you cannot see,*
and swelling waters are about to cover you."

2 As in his other two speeches, Eliphaz opens with questions. In fact, this time the first four verses are rhetorical questions. The first two sets of questions about the advantage of righteous deeds (vv. 2–3) set the context for the second couplet of double questions about the specific reasons for Job's plight (vv. 4–5). While the first three sets of questions demand a negative answer, the fourth set expects an affirmative response. Between the first and second couplet the mood shifts dramatically—from pressing questions presented in debate style to incriminating questions.

In disbelief at Job's holding on to his innocence so obstinately and

---

paronomasia. His view finds support in the fact that this root occurs in v. 21a in the Hiphil meaning "yield, make reconciliation." The author also makes a play on words in vv. 24–25. Accepting this understanding of the use of Heb. *skn,* we conclude its first use means "benefit" and its second use means "be in harmony." The antecedent of the pronominal suffix on the preposition then is God.

2. MT *tattēm* is the Hiphil imperfect of *tāmam,* "be blameless," with so-called Aramaic doubling. It has a declarative sense.

3. Whether the text is *'aḥeyḵā,* "your brothers" (LXX, Syr., Vulg., Gordis), or *'aḥîḵā,* "your brother" (Targ., Budde), is difficult to decide. The parallelism favors the plural form, as does the weight of the textual tradition.

4. The MT has the Pual *yᵉḏukkā',* "it was broken," but the versions read the Piel *tᵉḏakkē',* "you broke." The MT is preferred as the more difficult reading.

5. For MT *'ô ḥōšeḵ,* "or darkness," one can read either *'ôr ḥāšaḵ,* "the light has become darkened" (LXX, Dhorme), or *'ôrᵉḵā ḥāšaḵ,* "your light is darkened" (Duhm, Driver-Gray). LXX is preferred, for it offers the best sense and there appears to be no grammatical reason for *'ô,* "or," here. Also, *'ôr ḥāšaḵ* occurs in 18:6.

disturbed at his bold complaints against God, Eliphaz seeks to demonstrate to Job the fallacy in his reasoning. He wishes to refute Job's implication from his disputation that since there are wicked people who enjoy prosperity all their lives there may be righteous people who endure calamity in spite of their righteousness (ch. 21). Eliphaz counters this position with the premise that a person *can* not *benefit God*. For emphasis, in the MT *God* comes first in the question. The words he uses for man refer to his strength (*geḇer;* cf. 3:3) and his skill in wisdom *(maśkîl)*. Heb. *maśkîl* means to have insight (Prov. 1:3), to act prudently (Ps. 14:3; Prov. 19:14), and to succeed (1 Sam. 18:14, 15). It is used here because it characterizes the person as both righteous and successful. Eliphaz is arguing that the strongest among mankind is not able to do anything that puts God under obligation, not even when he acts wisely in reconciling himself with God. This means then that misfortune can have its cause only in human sin, never in God's sovereign purpose acting toward an individual irrespective of his righteousness or wickedness. In other words it is unfathomable to Eliphaz that God would permit a righteous person to endure a season of misery even though he has been faithful in obeying God. He, therefore, cannot perceive that Job could get anywhere by seeking to find reconciliation with God (cf. 9:33–34; 16:19; 19:25). His hope is groundless, for a wise person has no advantage with God to demand that God respond to him in a certain way.

3 Eliphaz makes direct application of this premise to Job by asking him, *What asset* [*ḥēpeṣ;* cf. 21:21] *is it to Shaddai that you are innocent [ṣāḏaq]*, or what *gain [beṣaʿ] that you claim that your ways are blameless?* The answer to these questions is plainly "none." God receives no asset or gain from a person being innocent and conducting himself blamelessly. No human being can live a life holy enough to demand anything from God. Eliphaz is arguing that Job is approaching the height of hubris by demanding vindication from God. Weiser finds in Eliphaz's position a dual stripping of biblical faith: God is depersonalized by a mechanical view of justice, and moral deeds possess only utilitarian value for mankind.

4, 5 More directly Eliphaz asks Job if God would arraign him for his *piety (yirʾâ)*.[6] Of course not! Neither does he *enter into judgment* with an upright person. A life of genuine faith precludes such a possibility. It is obvious to Eliphaz that Job is guilty of great *wickedness* and that there is no end to his *iniquity* since God is treating Job so harshly. No other cause than Job's sin can account for his suffering, according to the tenets of Eliphaz's theology.

A complete turnabout has taken place in Eliphaz's attitude toward Job. In the first speech Eliphaz praised Job for his righteousness and piety

6. Eliphaz uses *yirʾâ* for "piety, faith," as in 4:6; 15:4.

(4:3–4). He supposed that Job was suffering misfortune merely for a brief time while God was seeking to lead Job to repent of some hidden sin. He hoped that with encouragement Job would find restoration to divine favor through repentance. But Job has persisted in his obstinate claim of innocence. Since Job appears to be as recalcitrant as a hardened sinner, Eliphaz has reached the end of his patience. Shamed by his friend's stubbornness before the obvious divine displeasure, he seeks to convince Job that he is guilty of grievous sins. In fact, he concludes that there is no end to Job's iniquities *(ʿᵃwōnôṯ)*.

6 Eliphaz enumerates specific sins that he is convinced Job has committed. Without any empirical evidence that Job has sinned, Eliphaz arrives at this position by deduction, reasoning that since Job is being severely reproved, he must be guilty of breaches of hospitality and kindness to the unfortunate. The sins of which Eliphaz accuses Job are listed in vv. 6, 7, 9. Among these verses is a strong reprimand in v. 8. The sins mentioned include economic abuse of the poor, refusal of help to the afflicted, and lack of compassion for the bereaved.

Through shrewd business dealings the rich often increase their wealth by squeezing out of the poor the little that they possess. Israelite law had strict regulations regarding debts, pledges, and interest in order to limit the power of the wealthy over the poor. A creditor could accept as security any object that the debtor himself selected, except for a tool or object which the debtor needed in providing his livelihood (Deut. 24:6, 10–11). If he accepted a poor person's cloak as a pledge for a loan, it was to be returned before evening, for it was the owner's sole protection against the cool evening breezes (Exod. 22:25–26 [Eng. 26–27]; Deut. 24:12–13). Eliphaz charges that Job has violated standards similar to these by exacting pledges from his brothers *without grounds,* i.e., indiscriminately (lit. "without any basis," *ḥinnām;* cf. 1:9). Perhaps this charge means that he has seized something the debtor needs for his livelihood or that he has foreclosed on the loan early, before the debtor has had any opportunity to work out a means of paying off the debt, in order to make sure that he will get possession of the item pledged. Moreover, Job has forcefully removed the clothing from the poor, possibly debtors to him, leaving those persons naked.[7]

7, 8 Moreover, Job has failed to show basic compassion, expected from every righteous person. He has not offered a drink of *water to the weary* or given a piece of *bread* to *the hungry*. Job has so hardened his heart and tightened his purse that he has refused even modest charity. Thus he has behaved like a strong, eminent ruler who thinks that he owns everything.

7. "Naked" *(ʿārôm)* refers to one who lacks the customary clothing (Job 24:7, 10; Deut. 28:48; Isa. 58:7; Ezek. 18:7; cf. Fohrer).

Since *he thinks himself to be a privileged inhabitant*[8] of the earth, he feels that everyone owes him, but he has no obligation to help anyone. His insatiable desire for wealth has driven him to use his strength and power to despoil the weak and unfortunate. But he never shares his wealth with others, not even to show a little kindness to the poor.[9]

9 Eliphaz charges that Job has not shown compassion to the bereaved (cf. 29:12–13; 31:16–21). Specifically he has turned away widows[10] empty-handed; presumably these widows came seeking help, asking either for alms or for correction of abuses against them. Possibly Eliphaz is accusing Job of a more serious injustice. Fohrer defines his abuse as the act of turning a widow out of her home with nothing of value (cf. Gen. 31:42; Deut. 15:13). He has also treated orphans so harshly that they had no strength even to glean a little grain left in the fields of Job's estate. To *crush* or break one's arms is a figurative expression for destroying their strength.

10 Since Job has acted so hard-heartedly, he must endure dreadful hardship. *Snares (paḥîm)* are set all around him; this picture is similar to Bildad's description of God's lining the path of the evildoer with snares (18:8–10). Blinded by his greed, Job has accidentally stumbled into one of these snares (cf. 19:6). Then *sudden terror (paḥaḏ piṯʾōm)* makes him *panic* (Piel of *bhl*) as he watches everything he has built fall apart in a moment. The Hebrew root *bhl* means both "hasten" and "be afraid." It describes the panic or dreadful fear that unexpected, life-threatening tragedy arouses, particularly when its cause seems to be a sinister power.[11]

11 The light by which Job has lived has turned to darkness so that he can no longer see clearly. The *swelling waters (šipʿaṯ-mayim)* that devastate the landscape are rising over him. About to cover him, they are threatening to sweep him away. Cold, dark, swelling waters frequently symbolize the unrelenting emotional pressure of despair (Jon. 2:6 [Eng. 5]; Ps. 69:2–3 [Eng. 1–2]). Before his death the sinner gets a foretaste of Sheol, noted both for its watery chaos and for the shadowy, meager life that has to be eked out in dreary darkness. Eliphaz is saying that Job is suffering the curses of God's judgment for his sins.

8. The phrase *neśûʾ pānîm,* lit. "lifted face," means to show respect or partiality toward another so that one treats such a person with favor (13:8, 10; Lev. 19:15; Deut. 10:17). In this passage its passive use suggests that a person is considered honored and respected (cf. 2 K. 5:1; Isa. 3:3; 9:14 [Eng. 15]).

9. Some prefer to omit v. 8 as a gloss. Although it interrupts the context, Eliphaz appears to quote an aphorism to emphasize the great arrogance Job has expressed in lacking compassion for the weak; cf. Gordis. It may be an aside to put sting into this accusation.

10. The word "widow" in OT times often meant a woman who had lost all her protective male relatives, i.e., father, husband, and most often brothers; cf. H. Hoffner, "*ʾalmānāh,*" *TDOT,* I:288.

11. Cf. Job 4:5; 21:6; cf. also B. Otzen, "*bhl,*" *TDOT,* II:3–5.

b. A Disputation concerning God's Activity in Human Affairs (22:12–20)

12 *"Is not God in the heights of heaven?*[1]
And consider the top of the stars that they are very high.[2]
13 *So you say, 'What does God know?*
Can he judge through the dark clouds?
14 *Thick clouds hide him so he cannot see*
as he walks about on the zenith of the heavens.'
15 *Do you keep to the hidden*[3] *way,*
the path[4] *evil men*[5] *have trod,*
16 *who were untimely cut off,*
their foundation swept away by the river?[6]
17 *They said to God, 'Let us alone!*
What can Shaddai do to us?'[7]
18 *Yet he filled their houses with good things—*
but the counsel of the wicked is far from me.[8]
19 *The righteous see it and rejoice;*
the innocent mock them:

1. The phrase *gōḇah šāmayim* is either an adverbial accusative (Gordis) or an accusative of place without the preposition *b*^{e}, "in" (Dhorme; cf. GKC, § 118g). Dahood (*Or* 34 [1965] 171), however, sees here a title for God, "the Lofty One of Heaven."

2. The *dagesh* in *rāmmû* is a *dagesh forte affectuosum* used to make emphatic the *a* vowel (GKC, § 20i).

3. Heb. *ʿôlām* here means "hidden, dark," being cognate with Ugar. *ǵlm*, "dark" (cf. Dahood, "Northwest Semitic Philology and Job," pp. 65–66).

4. Blommerde (*Northwest Semitic Grammar and Job,* p. 97) gives an interesting alternative reading for *ʾ*^{a}*šer,* "that," namely, *ʾăšûr,* "path" (cf. 23:11). We follow this suggestion, for it improves the poetry and offers good parallelism.

5. Interestingly, in Ps. 26:4 *m*^{e}*ṯê šawʾ*, "vain men," parallels *naʿ*^{a}*lāmîm,* "those who conceal (their thoughts)," i.e., hypocrites. This supports the parallelism of *ʾōraḥ ʿôlām,* "the hidden path," and *ʾăšûr dār*^{e}*ḵû m*^{e}*ṯê ʾāwen,* "the path which evil men trod" (so Blommerde, *Northwest Semitic Grammar and Job,* p. 97; following Dahood, "Northwest Semitic Philology and Job," pp. 65–66).

6. Verse 16b is variously understood. Is *nāhār* ("river") or *y*^{e}*sôḏām* ("their foundation") the subject of *yûṣaq* ("swept away")? This translation accepts *nāhār* as the logical subject and *y*^{e}*sôḏām* as the grammatical subject. Dhorme offers another view. He vocalizes *yûṣaq* as a Pual, *yuṣṣaq,* to gain the meaning "poured out" as in Lev. 21:10; Ps. 45:3 (Eng. 2). With a Pual "the river" becomes the subject and "their foundation" an accusative of place: "When a river poured itself out over their foundations."

7. With LXX and Syr. the prepositional phrase *lānû,* "to us," is read for MT *lāmô,* "to him."

8. The change of *mennî,* "from me," to *mimmennû,* "from him" (with LXX, Dhorme, Fohrer), yields an easier sense, but it is better to keep the present text as an exact quote of 21:16b on the premise that ancient literature incorporated quotes using a standard different from that of modern usage.

20 *'Surely[9] their substance[10] is cut off,*
and their abundance the fire has devoured.'"

12 Eliphaz turns abruptly from accusing Job to instructing him about God's punishment of the wicked. He begins by quoting a hymnic line in praise of God's exaltedness (v. 12) to counter Job's supposed position that God lacks knowledge about what happens on earth (vv. 13–14). God is most high. Whoever observes the heavens is awed by the vastness of the universe and the great distance of the stars, especially the dense Milky Way.[11] But God is more distant than even the farthest stars. Because he is so transcendent, there can be no doubt that he is the exalted Lord of the universe.

13, 14 Against the background of this sublime truth, Eliphaz quotes Job's position. He understands Job to be saying that God is too distant to know about affairs on earth or to concern himself with an individual's problems (cf. Lam. 3:14). High above the earth *on the zenith* or vault *(ḥûg) of the heavens* God walks about. From the ancient perspective, when God created the universe, he drew a circle to hold back the heavenly waters from covering the earth (Prov. 8:27). His abode is located above this circle. There thick clouds surround him so that the heavenly creatures are not consumed by his glory (cf. Ps. 97:2). But according to Eliphaz, Job misconstrues this affirmation about God. He thinks that this dark cloud serves as a dense barrier which keeps God from seeing and judging affairs on earth (cf. Job 9:22–24). Job's supposed position contrasts with that of the devout person who reasons that God's exalted position affords him a great vantage point from which to view all the activities of mankind (Isa. 40:22–23; Ps. 33:13–15). The devout believe that from his lofty dwelling God immediately can thwart the plans of any leader that threaten his purpose for mankind.

Eliphaz fears that a right view of God's transcendence has led Job to a wrong position regarding God's immanence and his constant influence in events on earth. In Eliphaz's opinion Job's view is heretical, being close to what is classified today as modern deism or practical atheism: God created

9. Hakam understands that the particle *'im* at the head of a line in a song has emphatic force.

10. MT *qîmānû* is difficult. Some translate it as "our adversaries." In the light of the unusualness of that meaning for this root and the parallel word "their surplus" *(yiṯrām)*, either *y^{e}qûmām*, "their possessions" (Gen. 7:4, 23; Deut. 11:6), or a feminine noun with the pronominal suffix like *qîmām*, "their substance," should be read. The latter is preferred, for such a change may be explained as the result of metathesis; also the reading of *m* as *n w* would have been possible in the ancient script.

11. Heb. *rō'š* (lit. "head") means either "the top" of the stars, mentioned for their distance at the height of the heavens, or the great cluster (group) of stars in the Milky Way (cf. Gordis).

the world but has left it to its own course. For Eliphaz this view of God is faulty, being far too inadequate for an orthodox faith.[12] Therefore, without a radical change in his belief in God, Job has little hope of escaping the ultimate punishment of death. But Eliphaz has not correctly heard Job's complaints. If he had listened more carefully, he would have heard that it is not Job's concern that God is not active in affairs on earth, but that it seems from appearances that God judges the wicked erratically and capriciously. Sadly, Eliphaz is charging Job with heretical thoughts by overinterpreting his sincere complaints against God.

15, 16 Eliphaz points out that evil men who believe that God is too distant to observe affairs on earth pursue their evil plans without any fear of divine reprisals (cf. Ezek. 8:12). Fearful that such is Job's attitude, Eliphaz warns him with a rhetorical question about the consequences of keeping to the *hidden* or dark *paths* that the infamous *evil men* of the past *have trod.* In describing the devastating punishment that befell such vicious people, he is alluding to legendary, catastrophic events of divine punishment as illustrations of the general theme that gross sin is always severely punished.[13] In the past some societies became so corrupt and violent that God brought against them a devastating calamity in order to purge the earth of their existence, e.g., the destruction of the world by the flood at the time of Noah (Gen. 6:9–8:22) and the annihilation of Sodom and Gomorrah by fire (Gen. 19:1–29). When God rained widespread judgment on these areas all their inhabitants *were untimely cut off (qāmaṭ).*[14] Even those who had anchored their *foundations* firmly in the ground in search of security against such a terrible disaster were *swept away by the* raging current of the *river.* By inference Eliphaz is saying that if Job had lived during the time of such a disaster, he too would have lost everything, including his own life, for in defying God he follows the same evil course that provoked such catastrophic judgments. By establishing an analogy between Job's punishment and those past catastrophes, he identifies Job as the same kind of reprobate as those whom God abandoned to their evil imaginations (cf. Gen. 6:5–8). Therefore, he finds that Job is more than deserving of his present plight.

17, 18 Eliphaz quotes those reprobates' swearing their bold defiance against God.[15] They ordered God to leave them alone so that they could go about the evil ways without any interference from him. Eliphaz concedes that God *filled their houses with good things.* In his opinion their fortune is

12. Cf. Ps. 73:11; 94:7; Jer. 23:23–24.

13. Some see in this illustration a direct reference to the Noachian flood, e.g., Dhorme. While this language would include the flood, it seems too general to be restricted to that one event.

14. Cf. also 16:8. Aram. *qᵉmaṭ* means "compress, fold, tie together, bundle." The image is the binding together of sheaves.

15. The parallels are 22:17a = 21:14a; 22:18a = 21:16a; 22:18b = 21:16b.

God's doing, but only for a brief time. Their affluence certainly does not mean to him, as it does to Job, that they are getting by with their wicked deeds (cf. 21:7–15). By abruptly breaking off his description (aposiopesis), he is stressing that their end is so gruesome that it is too repugnant for him to describe. Then Eliphaz interjects his personal rejection of the *counsel of the wicked.* Such personal statements are typical of his style (e.g., 5:3, 27).

19, 20 To heighten his argumentation and to prepare for the coming exhortation to repentance Eliphaz describes the enthusiastic reaction of the righteous to the destruction of the wicked. The righteous *see* their ruin and *rejoice.* They even participate in the punishment of the wicked by mocking them.[16] Gleefully pointing to the ashes of their destroyed possession, the innocent will say, *their abundance the fire has devoured.* All that they had accumulated as the proof of their power and as the basis of their prestige will be consumed. Nothing will survive them as a memorial. In addition, the survival of the righteous will stand as proof that these wicked people have brought this harsh fate on themselves.

c. A Call to Repentance (22:21–30)

21 *"Yield[1] and be at peace,*
thereby[2] your gain[3] will be good.
22 *Accept instruction from his mouth,*
and place[4] his words in your heart.
23 *If you turn to Shaddai, you will be reestablished.[5]*
Put iniquity far from your tent,[6]

16. Ps. 2:4 is very similar to v. 19. For this idea cf. Ps. 52:8–9 (Eng. 6–7); 58:11 (Eng. 10); 107:42; Prov. 1:26.

1. In support of the causative *hasken* with the sense of "yield" is Ugar. *šskn* (*UT,* 51:I:21; Pope). W. Bishai ("Notes on *hskn* in Job 22:21," *JNES* 20 [1961] 258–59) takes *hasken* to mean "be quiet, acquiesce," and sees in *šᵉlām* the parallel idea of "submit."

2. The preposition with third person plural pronominal suffix, *bāhem,* refers to the activity of the two verbs, although they may be viewed as one action (cf. Ezek. 18:26; 33:14).

3. MT *tᵉḇô'āṯᵉkā* is usually altered into a noun or a verb: *tᵉḇû'āṯᵉkā,* "your produce" (versions, Dhorme), or *tᵉḇô'ᵃkā,* "it comes to you" (Fohrer). Since both emendations are possible, the better reading is the former because it requires less textual change and has better textual support.

4. M. Dahood ("The Metaphor in Job 22:22," *Bib* 47 [1966] 108–109) argues that *śîm,* "put, place," can mean "write down, inscribe" (cf. Job 38:33; Prov. 8:29; Ps. 56:9 [Eng. 8]).

5. Many (e.g., Budde, Driver-Gray) prefer to emend MT *tbnh* to *tē'āneh,* "you will be answered," with LXX, but one would also need to add *wᵉ* (Duhm) to introduce the apodosis. In support of MT is a passage in Aqht I:119, where Ugar. *bny* connotes restoration or the healing of a broken wing. Also, in Hebrew *bnh* means "to prosper" (Mal. 3:15) and "to be restored" (Jer. 12:16; 24:6; 33:7).

6. It seems best to take v. 23a as a conditional sentence, vv. 23b and 24 as exhortations, and v. 25 as expressing the result.

24 *lay*[7] *your gold*[8] *on the dust,*
even the gold of Ophir among the stones of the wadi.
25 *Then Shaddai will be your gold,*
and silver in huge piles[9] *for you.*
26 *For then you will delight in Shaddai;*
you will lift your face to God.
27 *You will pray to him and he will hear you,*
and you will pay your vows.
28 *When you decree a matter, it will be established for you,*[10]
and light will shine on your ways.
29 *When men are low, you will say, 'Be lifted up!'*[11]
He will save the lowly of eyes.
30 *He will deliver the guilty,*[12]
who will be delivered by the cleanness of your hands."

21 Having condemned Job and refuted his supposed false thinking about God's ways, Eliphaz exhorts Job to repent: *Yield (hasken)* to God and *be at peace (š^{e}lām)* with him. With the use of Heb. *hasken* Eliphaz makes a wordplay with *yiskōn,* "is in harmony with," used twice in v. 2. According to Eliphaz, although a person cannot benefit God, he can yield to God and benefit himself by receiving an abundance of good things. As long as a

7. Dhorme and Driver-Gray prefer the perfect *w^{e}šattā,* "and you lay," to the imperative *w^{e}šîṯ,* but MT may be retained.

8. While Heb. *beṣer* is frequently taken to mean a high quality of gold, its exact meaning is thought to be "nuggets or crumbled particles of ore" (Driver-Gray) or the gold as it leaves the crucible (Dhorme).

9. The best suggestion for translating *tôʿāpôṯ* is "something elevated, heaping piles." Dhorme and Driver-Gray think that it comes from an Arabic root *ypʿ* with metathesis, "be elevated, steep." Cf. Grabbe, *Comparative Philology,* pp. 81–83.

10. The first two verbs are jussives and are used to express a condition (cf. Dhorme; GKC, § 159b).

11. Many take MT *gēwâ* as an apocopated form of *gaʾ^{a}wâ,* "loftiness, pride." Dhorme gains excellent sense for this line by eliminating *wattōʾmer,* "and you will say," as a dittography from v. 28a and reconstructing the MT to read *hišpîl ʾeṯ gēwâ:* "For *He* crushes [ ] pride." But vv. 29 and 30 are chiastically related, v. 29a being similar in thought to v. 30b. Then MT *gēwâ* may be taken as an exclamation, "Be lifted up, rise high!"—an exhortation of encouragement (cf. Gordis).

12. The phrase *ʾî-nāqî* means "not innocent" or "guilty"; *ʾî* as a negative particle appears in 1 Sam. 4:21, *ʾî-ḵāḇôḏ,* "no glory," and also in Phoenician and Mishnaic Hebrew (cf. Grabbe, *Comparative Philology,* pp. 83–86). C. Thexton ("A Note on Job xxii.30," *ExpTim* 78 [1966–67] 342–43) accepts this reading as aimed at Job and thinks that the second line is a rhetorical question. Many suggestions to eliminate this strange form have been offered. Some (e.g., Fohrer) read *ʾîš,* "an (innocent) man," or associate it with an independent pronoun *ʾayyû,* "whoever" (cf. Guillaume, "Arabic Background," p. 115; N. Sarna, "A *Crux Interpretum* in Job 22:30 *ymlṭ ʾy nqy,*" *JNES* 15 [1956] 118–19; G. R. Driver, "Once Again Abbreviations," *Textus* 4 [1964] 81).

person fights against God by refusing to accept his circumstances, his inner life will be characterized by turmoil. But by submitting to God one finds inner harmony and a sense of well-being.

22 When a person has a penitent attitude, he gladly accepts instruction from God, storing up his words in the heart. This means that he listens to God's words with eagerness and internalizes them in order that he may obey God spontaneously. *Instruction* or teaching *(tôrâ)* here means the precepts passed down through the wise patriarchs to whom God had given insight into his ways.[13]

23 Repentance requires one to change his direction in life—from moving away from God to walking with him. To *turn to* God results in being *reestablished* or built up *(bānâ),*[14] both personally and materially. A tangible expression of this change is for the penitent to remove all *iniquity,* i.e., the gain gotten from iniquitous ways, from *his tent* or his dwelling place (cf. 11:14).

24 The penitent must not put any conditions or reservations on his repentance. His need for singleness of mind is vividly illustrated by the exhortation, *lay your gold on the dust, even the* precious *gold of Ophir*[15] *among the stones of the wadi,* i.e., the riverbed, where the gold originated. With such a gesture a person makes a statement that the wealth of this world has no claims on his affections. Eliphaz is subtly suggesting that Job has secured his treasures from unjust practices, such as extortion. Therefore, for Job to remove iniquity from his tent is for him to get rid of his ill-gotten wealth. His violating the divine teaching in securing this wealth means that he has valued material treasures more than genuine trust in God.[16] Now he must renounce his gold by laying it on the ground.

25–27 As a motivation for Job to repent, Eliphaz offers a tantalizing promise. He says that when the sinner puts God first, God himself will become his abundant treasure.[17] All that gold and silver bring a person

13. The concept of law as an established body of belief followed by the religious community does not exist in this book. Here *tôrâ* or "law" is used as in the Wisdom tradition for the body of instruction given by the wise.

14. God's affirmative action in a person's life or in a nation is often conveyed by the image of building and planting; cf. Jer. 1:10; 18:9; 24:6; 31:4, 28; 33:7; 42:10.

15. This line uses assonance and double paronomasia: *beṣer,* "gold," with *b*ᵉ*ṣûr,* "among rocks," and *ʿāp̄ār,* "dust," with *ʾôp̄îr,* "(gold of) Ophir." Since *beṣer* means both "gold" and "fortress," it is possible that both meanings may be communicated (see Gordis). Ophir was famous as a source of fine gold and other treasures (cf. 1 Chr. 29:4; Isa. 13:12). During Solomon's reign, expeditions that took parts of three years were made to Ophir to bring back many rich and exotic treasures. The location of Ophir is debated, with South Arabia or the East African coast being the most probable spots.

16. Job will affirm in his oath of innocence that he never puts gold above God (31:24–25).

17. There is a subtle play on the wording of this line and the meaning of Eliphaz's

in security, prestige, and glory will be supplied by God himself. Job will discover that acceptance by God brings joy into his life. He will be able to enter the presence of God unashamed, with his face held high. This promise counters Job's present feelings of shame and worthlessness before God (cf. 10:16). In this new condition he may offer his prayers fervently, for nothing will hinder his petitions from reaching God. He will be able to pay his *vows,* offering the appropriate sacrifices. These promises mean that Job, now exiled on an ash heap, will again joyfully worship God at the local shrine, where he will be accorded great respect.

28 Reunited with God, Job will have great spiritual power in order that he may bless others. Since he has God's will at heart, God will bring to pass whatever Job decrees.[18] His dreams and ambitions will no longer be in vain, for God will give him insight into how to proceed in difficult matters. Whatever he does will prosper, for God's *light will shine on* his ways. This is a direct promise that counters Job's feeling of being lost in darkness (19:8).

29, 30 From his renewed relationship with God, Job will be able to help those who are facing troubles. To the disheartened he may speak an encouraging word: *Be lifted up!* God will hear his righteous servant's charge and honor it by granting deliverance to the oppressed. Job also will be able to intercede for others, for his prayers will be grounded in his righteous deeds, as symbolized by the phrase *the cleanness of your hands.*[19] Although one's acts of righteousness do not transfer directly to the account of another, the righteous person does have power to stand in the gap for another. His prayers, coming from a pure heart that is obedient to God, have authority. God acknowledges his prayers and *delivers the guilty.* While God alone grants them forgiveness, he allows a human being to participate in the process of rescuing that person. The patriarchs were known for their ability to petition God for mercy in order to avert judgment on the rebellious (cf. Ezek. 14:12–20). When Job makes peace with God, he will have the same spiritual power as these great patriarchs.

AIM

Since Job refuses to bend from his claim of innocence and God continues to punish him, Eliphaz feels compelled to convince Job that he has indeed

---

name, "My God is pure gold." It is certainly no accident that the author has Eliphaz describe God as one's "gold and silver." Eliphaz's statements about God reflect the meaning of his own name.

18. See R. Gordis, "Corporate Personality in the Book of Job," *JNES* 4 (1945) 54–55.

19. The author again has a speaker anticipate the outcome, but there will be a twist that will surprise the speaker; see 42:8–10.

sinned and that he can have his relationship with God restored. Therefore, he blatantly accuses Job of specific deeds of wrongdoing. Since no one has endured such severe loss and pain as Job has, he must have sinned boldly. Eliphaz concludes that he has violated the standards of patriarchal religion by abusing the weak and unfortunate. He is thus deserving of every painful moment of his trial.

At this point Eliphaz makes his greatest mistake. Pressed to defend God's honor, he condemns Job. Fearing that Job's view of God has led him into arrogant sins, Eliphaz accuses Job of practical atheism—the belief that God is so distant that it does not matter to him what human beings do on earth. But a genuine defense of God must not downgrade another human being. Eliphaz fails to realize that in condemning Job he is also casting reproach on God, Job's creator. In defending God Eliphaz stumbles over the stone of futility, the "no reason or purpose" *(ḥinnām)* of the prologue, which has been put in Job's path. Furthermore, he fails to apply his own conclusion—that the righteous can intercede for the guilty—to his relationship with Job. Rather than condemning Job, he needs to plead for Job's restoration.

Having some hope for Job, Eliphaz exhorts him to repent. To motivate Job he lists the privileges that attend repentance: reconciliation, prosperity, wisdom, joyful living, security, power in prayer, authority in intercession. Eliphaz wants Job to focus on God alone as the source of his wealth and joy. From such singleness of heart comes great spiritual power. These words regarding repentance are insightful and may be proclaimed as a part of God's word. There is one major caution: a call to repentance loses its power when it is offered from inaccurate perceptions and wrong motivations. As Delitzsch says, "Even the holiest and truest words lose their value when they are not uttered at the right time, and the most brilliant sermon that exhorts to penitence remains without effect when it is prompted by pharisaic uncharitableness." The truth of this statement may be offset by the strange ways of God's working. Nevertheless, the challenge of this truth needs to be carefully considered by all who extend a message of repentance. It needs to be remembered that God wants his followers to call people to repentance out of love purified by intercessory prayer. Then they will bring comfort to a troubled heart as they lead a person from guilt to forgiveness. In ministering, one's theology must be elastic enough to be applied to a particular situation, since rigid application of a dogma hinders the dynamic, spontaneous expression of God's grace. Correctness of expression too often crowds out the authenticity of experience. But a committed faith, aware of wide variances in individual cases, reaches out to communicate God's love in tolerance. Such a vibrant faith, confident about the absolutes of doctrine, still struggles with the difficulties and the inconsistencies that arise in working out these truths in daily life. Without denying these contradictions, true faith seeks to overcome them in compassionate service to the suffering.

A study of the movement of Eliphaz's rhetoric in his three speeches reveals the tension that exists between what one believes and the course of earthly affairs. Unfortunately Eliphaz is unable to hold this tension in balance. His care for Job hardens into condemnation because he feels he has to protect his cherished beliefs from Job's charges. Concern for his beliefs leads him to reprove Job instead of sharing Job's burden. As a result, his rhetoric dampens the dynamic of Job's faith and increases the pain of Job's struggle with undeserved suffering. Let us hope that the example of Eliphaz will awaken us to practice our faith by acting compassionately toward the weak and the suffering, not by trying to force them into a set, dogmatic mold that would turn them from God rather than to God.

2. JOB'S SEVENTH RESPONSE (23:1–24:25)

In his first speech of the third cycle Job ignores the friends. With great confidence he focuses his attention on arguing the merits of his case to God. Then he delivers a long complaint, claiming that the righteous do not see the times of judgment that God is supposed to set for the wicked. These two sections are a statement of confidence (23:1–17), and a complaint about unjust social conditions (24:1–25).

Job ignores Eliphaz's blatant accusations against him. He also rejects wholeheartedly Eliphaz's summons to repentance even though its promise of being at peace with God pulls at his strongest desire. Job will not compromise his integrity by contriving repentance. He knows intuitively that he cannot have peace with God by seeking God for the blessings he gives rather than for God himself. Compelled to abandon the counsel of his friends, he holds on to his perception that the only way of improving his lot is to argue his case before the heavenly throne. He is now more firmly convinced that God would give an upright person the privilege to present his arguments and that that person could win acquittal. This conviction inspires him to make the strongest statements to date about his innocence and about his assurance that he will survive his trial. Job's daring boldness, however, is tempered by his fear of the holy God. Such tempering prevents him from falling into presumptuous sin.

Job is also grieved at injustice in the world. Therefore, he delivers a detailed complaint against God concerning the gross inequities borne by innocent sufferers (ch. 24). His thesis is that workers must labor long and hard for meager wages while criminals stalk their unfortunate victims, accomplishing their evil designs unhindered. Greatly distressed at this state of affairs, Job conclues by cursing the fate of the wicked to make sure that their punishment will be certain.

a. A Statement of Confidence (23:1–17)

(1) Job's Desire to Present His Case before God (23:1–7)

1 *Job answered:*
2 *"Also today my complaint is bitter;*
my hand[1] is heavy against my groanings.
3 *Would that I knew where to find him,*
that I might come to his throne.
4 *I would present my case before him*
and would fill my mouth with arguments.
5 *I would know the words he would answer me;*
I should understand what he would say to me.
6 *Would he oppose me with great legal power?*
No, he would not[2] press charges against me.[3]
7 *There[4] an upright man could argue with him,*
and I should be acquitted[5] forever[6] by my judge."[7]

1. For MT *yāḏî,* "my hand," LXX and Syr. read *yāḏô,* "his hand." Andersen accepts *yāḏî* as an example of the *î* suffix meaning "his." But A. de Wilde ("Eine alte Crux Interpretum, Hiob xxiii:2," *VT* 22 [1972] 368–74) wishes to read *ʾoznô,* "his ear," for *yāḏî.* A heavy ear would mean that God does not hear a person's complaint. Unfortunately, there is no textual support for this creative suggestion. MT, supported by Targ. and Vulg., is accepted as the harder reading (Budde, Dhorme).

2. J. Reider ("Contributions to the Scriptural Text," *HUCA* 24 [1952–53] 104) considers MT *lōʾ ʾaḵ-hûʾ* to be impossible Hebrew. He takes *ʾk* as an abbreviation for *ʾaḵzār,* hence "He is not cruel that he should attack me." It is an intriguing suggestion, but not very likely.

3. Many (e.g., Duhm) take MT *yāśim bî* as elliptical for *yāśim lēḇ,* "pay attention to," but then one would expect the preposition *ʿal* or *le,* not *bî* (Dhorme). Though the object is suppressed, the parallelism favors assigning it a legal meaning.

4. The adverb *šām,* "there," is a little troubling. It may be taken locally to refer to *teḵûnāṯô,* "his throne" (v. 3). Delitzsch and Gordis, however, take it temporally, meaning "then." M. Dahood (*Bib* 51 [1970] 397) and A. Jirku ("Eine Renaissance des Hebräischen," *FF* 32 [1958] 212) argue that *šām* means "if" on the basis of Ugar. *ṯm.*

5. Heb. *napšî,* "my soul, myself," is implied as a complement to *ʾapalleṭâ,* "I should be delivered," i.e., "I should be acquitted," since it is without an object (cf. Dhorme).

6. G. R. Driver (*ZAW* 50 [1932] 140–41) interprets *lāneṣaḥ,* "forever," to mean "successfully," i.e., "truthfully, so successfully" (cf. Prov. 21:28). Also cf. D. W. Thomas, "The Use of *neṣaḥ* as a Superlative in Hebrew," *JSS* 1 (1956) 106–109.

7. A variant accepted by many for MT *miššōpṭî,* "from my judge," is *mišpāṭî,* "my case" (LXX, Syr., Vulg.). But the parallelism of *ʿimmô,* "with him," favors the former reading.

2 Ignoring Eliphaz's eloquent call to repentance, Job opens this speech by stating that his *complaint is bitter (m^e^rî).* His *groanings* (*ʾ^a^nāḥâ;* cf. 3:24), evoked by his agony, are so severe that he has to control himself with a heavy hand. His pain is pushing hard against the threshold of his self-control. Job wishes his friends to know that his strong words do not arise from slight discomfort.

The time reference *today* is unique to the dialogue. While the impression is that the dialogue takes place over several days, maybe even weeks, there are no indications as to its length. Since this is Job's first speech of the third cycle, it has been suggested that "today" refers to the third day. More likely this expression means "even now" (Delitzsch). Agreeing, Fohrer interprets the expression as a negative response to the last speech.

3 After this brief reference to his suffering, Job focuses his attention on his primary wish, an audience with God. If he only knew where to find God, he would enter the hall leading to God's *throne (t^e^ḵûnâ),*[8] if that were possible. There justice would be fully rendered in his regard. Job builds his conviction on the hymnic theme that righteousness and justice are the foundation of God's throne (e.g., Ps. 89:15 [Eng. 14]; 97:2).

4, 5 Before the heavenly court, Job would persuasively present his case before God. Out of his mouth would pour an array of convincing arguments. After resting his case, he would anxiously await God's response. Whatever the judgment might be, he would accept it, confident that justice had been done. Through Job's words the author again gives a hint as to the outcome of the drama. As soon as God addresses Job directly from heaven, Job abandons his desire to argue his case. While the silence of such a verbal person may appear out of character, this passage prepares the way for such a response by Job, in that it reveals that Job is not so anxious to prove his innocence by powerful rhetoric as he is eager to renew communion with God. Nevertheless, Job will be caught by surprise when God does appear.

6 For a moment Job fears: God might *oppose me with great legal power*[9] in order to win a decision against him more by brute force than by reason (cf. 9:32–34; 13:13–14). But Job emphatically rejects this thought. God *would not press* his charges to the point of coercing the court to render a

8. Heb. *t^e^ḵûnâ,* lit. "a fixed place," is taken to mean "throne" in this context. This word refers to a foundation which secures a building; so the throne may be seen as the foundation of a monarch's rule. Similarly, a word from the same root, *māḵôn* ("fixed or established place, foundation," BDB, p. 467), is sometimes used for the place of God's ruling, either from heaven (cf. 1 K. 8:39, 43, 49; Ps. 33:14) or from his earthly temple (Exod. 15:17).

9. As attested in Mishnaic Hebrew, *kōaḥ* may mean "legal power." Tur-Sinai understands the phrase *habb^e^roḇ-kōaḥ* to mean "one who has the power of attorney to plead in the court for another."

guilty verdict against an innocent person. It is obvious that Job rests his hope for a favorable decision on the Judge's just character.

7 Job states his conviction again that before God's throne *an upright man (yāšār),* which Job is confident that he is, may enter into legal argument with God. Job is certain that God will acquit him forever once he has heard his arguments. In this pericope Job's confidence both in his innocence and in the possibility of finding a resolution to his plight has reached a new height.

(2) God's Hiddenness and Job's Confidence (23:8–12)

8 *"Lo, I go forward and he is not there;*
behind,[1] but I do not perceive him;
9 *left, where he is at work, but I do not behold him;*
he turns to the right,[2] but I do not see him.
10 *But he knows the way that I take;[3]*
when he has tested me, I shall come forth as gold.
11 *My feet have closely followed his steps;*
I have kept his way without turning away.
12 *I have not departed[4] from the commandment of his lips;[5]*
in my breast[6] I have treasured the words of his mouth."

8, 9 Job expresses his frustration at being unable to find God. He has searched for him at all points of the compass, but he is nowhere to be found. The points *forward, behind, left,* and *right* are based on an eastward orienta-

1. Cf. N. Boyd, "Notes on the Secondary Meaning of *'ḥr,*" *JTS* 12 (1961) 54–56.

2. For MT *baʿᵃśōṯô,* "when he is at work," Syr. reads *biqqaštîw,* "I sought him." This reading is accepted by many, but it loses some weight by also requiring a change in *yaʿṭōp,* "he turns," to the first person (so Syr.). Gordis gives an interesting possibility. He thinks that there is a second root *ʿśh* cognate to Arab. *ǵaša,* "cover" (cf. Isa. 32:6; Prov. 12:23; 13:6). If Gordis is right, then *yaʿṭōp* has the meaning "he covers himself," not "he turns." This suggestion has good possibilities in the light of the hymnic image that God is enveloped in clouds and thick darkness (see, e.g., Ps. 97:2). MT is followed because the other suggestions require too many changes.

3. The preposition *ʿimmāḏî,* "with me," is somewhat unusual in this position. Gordis takes the meaning to be "my usual path." But it seems more likely that the infinitive construct of *ʿmd* should be read, i.e., *ʿomdî,* hence "the way on which I stand or take." With support from Ps. 1:1, where the verb *ʿāmaḏ,* "stand," is used with *dereḵ,* "way," this suggestion is accepted, for it requires less emendation. Others (e.g., Dhorme) read with Syr. *darkî weʿomdî,* "my going and my staying."

4. The *waw* on the predicate is for emphasis (cf. GKC, § 143d).

5. The phrase *miṣwaṯ śᵉpāṯāyw,* "the commandment of his lips," is a *casus pendens* which emphasizes obeying God's words.

6. For MT *mēḥuqqî,* "from my statute," it is best to read *bᵉḥēqî,* "in my bosom," with LXX, Vulg., and many other interpreters. The same idea occurs in Ps. 119:11 with

tion. Job goes to the east, then to the west, but he perceives no trace of God. Turning to the north where God might be expected to be *at work,* ruling the divine assembly—a Canaanite concept carried over metaphorically into the OT (cf. 26:7; Ps. 48:3 [Eng. 2])—Job fails to behold him. When he looks to the distant south, he does not catch a glimpse of him.

The ever-present God, from whom the troubled psalmist cannot flee (Ps. 139:7–10), is hidden from Job. He is experiencing God as "the hidden God."[7] The essential issue for him is how he, an afflicted person, can discover God's presence. While God haunts those who try to escape him in order to lead them to an awareness of the truth, he becomes imperceptible to his own in seasons of adversity in order that they may search for him, stretching their faith. God's distancing himself from Job's consciousness reflects his trust in Job. That is, by hiding from Job, he allows Job to assert his innocence as a venture of genuine commitment to God.

10 After lamenting God's absenting himself, Job states with conviction that God *knows the way that I take*. That is, he is sure that God has full knowledge of all his thoughts and actions. Therefore, he believes that when God has finished testing him, he will come forth purified in character, just as *gold* is purified by passing through fire. Here Job's assurance that God is concerned with his well-being rises to its highest point.

Job's use of the analogy of purifying gold for his own testing is another indication that the basic motivation behind his lament is the restoration of his own honor, not the restoration of his wealth. With this metaphor Job is rebutting Eliphaz's exhortation to lay aside gold and to make God his gold (22:24–25). Rather than owning the precious metal, Job longs for a golden character.

11, 12 Job rests his confidence in a redemptive outcome to his trial solidly on his faithful obedience to God. He has directed his *feet* to follow the *steps* God has laid out for him without any deviation. In other words, he has *not departed from* God's *commandment*. The *commandment* is identified as the teaching that comes directly from God's *lips* or *mouth.*[8] In fact, Job states that he has *treasured* or stored up God's words in his *breast*. That is,

---

"in my heart" *(bᵉlibbî);* cf. Job 10:13. By taking the *min* to mean "in" and changing only the vowels (to read *mēḥēqî*), Blommerde also arrives at the translation "in my bosom" (*Northwest Semitic Grammar and Job,* pp. 100–101).

7. See K. Miskotte, *When the Gods Are Silent,* tr. J. H. Doberstein (New York: Harper and Row, 1967); S. Terrien, *The Elusive Presence: Toward a New Biblical Theology* (San Francisco: Harper & Row, 1978); S. E. Balentine, *The Hidden God: The Hiding of the Face of God in the Old Testament,* Oxford Theological Monographs (Oxford: Oxford University Press, 1983).

8. This language does not have to be restricted to the law given at Mt. Sinai. It may refer to any word received from God (cf. Jer. 9:19 [Eng. 20]).

he has ingrained God's teachings deep inside him in order to guide his daily life. God's word hidden in his mind keeps him from sinning (cf. Ps. 119:11). With this affirmation Job rejects as meaningless for him Eliphaz's exhortation: "Receive instruction from his own mouth, and place his words in your heart" (22:22). Since God's word has never departed from his thinking, he has no need to restore it back into his heart. These two verses are to this point Job's boldest assertion of innocence.

(3) Trembling before God (23:13–17)

13 *"He is one;*[1] *who can turn him?*
Whatever he desires he does.
14 *For he will carry out that which is decreed for me,*
and many such things are in his mind.
15 *Therefore, I am terrified before him;*
I think on it and I am in dread of him.
16 *God has made my heart faint;*
Shaddai has terrified me.[2]
17 *Indeed, I am surely destroyed before the darkness;*[3]
before me gloom covers all."

Job's self-confidence is tempered by his meditation on God's sovereignty. When Job contemplates God's justice in relationship to his personal obedience of the divine law, he waxes bold and confident. But when his mind turns to the sovereign freedom and majestic holiness of God, fear overwhelms him. Such deep, conflicting emotions account for the fluctuation in Job between confidence and uncertainty. In attempting to build his trust in God, he must fight hard against the terror roused by his suffering.

13, 14 Job confesses, *He* [God] *is one.*[4] This confession alludes to

1. In MT *be'eḥaḏ* the *be* is understood as *bet essentiae;* cf. Ps. 118:7 and GKC, § 119i.

2. C. Westermann takes v. 16 as an accusation against God followed by a self-lament in v. 17 (*Structure of the Book of Job,* pp. 56–57).

3. Verse 17 is variously interpreted. Dhorme eliminates *kî* as a dittography of the final *nî* in v. 16b, and he takes the Hebrew root *ṣmt,* "put an end to," to mean "be silent," a meaning this root has in Aramaic and in Arabic. Thus he translates the line: "I have not been silent because of darkness." While this meaning agrees with Job's resolve to keep on speaking, it creates another *hapax legomenon* in Hebrew. In the opposite direction, Gordis takes *kî* to mean "indeed" and *lō'* to have emphatic force: "Indeed, I am destroyed by darkness." For *lō'* Pope reads the precative *lû',* "O would that." While Gordis's exegesis is followed, this verse remains obscure at present.

4. C. Gordon ("His Name is 'One,'" *JNES* 29 [1970] 198–99) points out that "one" refers to the name of God. Job may be drawing on an earlier confession cast in the same mold as the Shema (Deut. 6:4). Dahood ("Northwest Semitic Philology and Job," p. 67) explains *'eḥāḏ* as "only ruler" in the light of *UT,* 51:VII:49–50: *aḥdy dymlk ʿl'lm,* "I alone will rule over the gods."

the great confession of God in ancient Israel: "Hear, O Israel: Yahweh, our God, Yahweh is One." But this does mean that Job is making that particular confession. His confession means that there is no other God; God is both the source and the sustainer of all that exists. Job asks lamentingly, *Who can turn* or influence this great God? No one! God acts freely—*whatever he desires he does.* Job is not, however, charging God with acting capriciously. Rather his distress is that since God is not bound to a mechanistic application of his own laws, he does not have to execute exact retribution immediately. Job fears then that God may carry out that which he has decreed against him. Therefore, he cries out in apprehensive agony that God may let him die before his honor is restored. In any case, Job realizes that his fate is not in his own hands. Job's struggle for faith reaches its severest test when his confidence in God collides with his fear of God.

15, 16 In pondering God's greatness and sovereignty, Job is *terrified* (*bāhal;* cf. 4:5) and *in dread* (*pāḥaḏ;* cf. 3:25; 4:14). With God's anger reflected in his suffering, Job is bewildered by God's terrible power. *God has made my heart faint* or thin *(hēraḵ).* A thin heart, weakened by fear and worry, lacks courage, rendering its owner enervated.[5] After his great statement of faith, Job feels that all his energy is drained from him (cf. 19:27b).

17 The *darkness (ḥōšeḵ)* cuts Job off from beholding God, and *gloom(ʾōp̱el),* settling over him, obscures God's presence. That is, he cannot detect God's grace anywhere. Since darkness and gloom are closely associated with Sheol (cf. 3:4–7; 10:21–22; 38:17), this strong language indicates that Job feels the breath of death on his face.

b. A Complaint about Unjust Social Conditions (24:1–25)

Feeling the terrors of darkness, Job thinks on the widespread suffering in the world that arises from numberless unrequited evil deeds.[1] The wicked are successful in afflicting others and reaping the benefits, but the upright are poor and suffer great hardship. In this complaint Job addresses the more general question of widespread suffering in a world governed by a just God. Although he sits on the ash heap, alienated from the community, he suffers with all mankind. Job's complaint focuses on three oppressive situations: abuse of the weak (vv. 2–4, 9), onerous working conditions for laborers (vv. 5–8, 10–12), and unrequited criminal acts (vv. 13–17).

Job presents detailed patterns of unrequited wrongdoings in the world in order, on the one hand, to refute the easy, categorical answers of his

5. Cf. Deut. 20:3, 8; Isa. 7:4.

1. On ch. 24 cf. O. Loretz, "Philologische und textologische Probleme in Hi 24,1–25," *UF* 12 (1980) 261–66.

friends, and, on the other hand, to move God to respond to his pitiful condition. He believes that God must act not only to prove false the friends' accusations against him, but also to set right affairs in the world. Job's concern about unjust social conditions then is a part of his overall argument. In his concern with injustice in general Job evidences his own moral integrity and sensitivity.

In the second part of this complaint Job expresses his conviction that there must be a time when God will judge all, including the wicked who are honored in this life (vv. 18–24). Employing a series of curses, he wishes to hasten the execution of the penalty on these wicked. In conclusion Job affirms that his argument is true (24:25).

(1) The Reign of Evildoers (24:1–17)

Job takes up the theme of his most recent speech (ch. 21) and expands on it. In that speech he looked at the glorious success and wanton behavior of the wicked. Now he puts forth multiple examples of civil injustice (24:1–3, 9, 4–8, 10–11) and criminal injustice (24:12–17). God's apparent indifference to human activity compounds the evil that human beings do. These injustices threaten to turn society into chaos.[1]

(a) Civil Injustice (24:1–3, 9, 4–8, 10–11)

1 *"Since times are not hidden from Shaddai,*[1]
why do those who know him never see his days?
2 *Men*[2] *move*[3] *boundary stones;*
they steal flocks and pasture[4] *them.*

1. This section appears to be heavily influenced by the genre of the tirade against upheavals in society, a genre well attested in ancient Near Eastern literature, above all in Egyptian literature: e.g., "The Protests of the Eloquent Peasant" (*ANET*, pp. 407–10); "The Admonitions of Ipu-wer" (*ANET*, pp. 441–44); "The Prophecy of Nefer-rohu" (*ANET*, pp. 444–46).

1. Gordis finds here a special grammatical construction: the interrogative *maddûaʿ*, "why," governs the second line with the first line being a subordinate conditional clause: "Why, since the times of judgment are not hidden from Shaddai, do His Friends not see His day (of judgment)?" Another view takes *ṣāpan* to mean "store up," and takes the preposition *min* as introducing the logical subject (Fohrer; cf. Hölscher). Gordis's exegesis is preferred as the less complex.

2. The subject of the first line appears to be missing. Budde supplies the pronoun *hemmâ*, "they," while Duhm adds *rešāʿîm*, "the wicked," with LXX, but the LXX translators may also have been supplying a subject rather than having a different Hebrew text. The line as it stands has a 6/7 syllable count and may be accepted.

3. MT *yaśśîgû*, "move," is a variant spelling of *yassîgû*, as in 2 Sam. 1:22, and the doubling of the first radical is similar to the form of an *ʿayin-ʿayin* verb (GKC, § 72cc).

4. For MT *wayyirʿû*, "and they pasture," LXX reads *werōʿô*, "and its shepherd." Since the flock and shepherd were often considered as one (cf. Jer. 6:3; 51:23), many follow LXX. When both readings offer excellent sense, it is better to follow MT.

3 *They drive away the orphan's donkey;*
they take the widow's ox for a pledge.
9 *They snatch the fatherless child from the breast;*[5]
they seize the infant[6] *of the poor for a pledge.*[7]
4 *They thrust the needy from the way;*
the poor[8] *of the land are forced together into hiding.*
5 *Like*[9] *wild asses in the wilderness*
they go out to their labor,
searching for food[10] *in the desert,*[11]
even[12] *bread for their children.*[13]
6 *They gather*[14] *fodder*[15] *in the field;*
they glean the vineyard of the wicked.[16]

5. MT *šōḏ,* "devastation," is taken as a rare phonetic variant for *šaḏ,* "breast" (see Targ., LXX; Budde, Driver-Gray).

6. With most commentators, the preposition *ʿal,* "on," is revocalized *ʿul,* "infant," to gain a good parallel (see *BHS*).

7. This verse is a well-composed line, but it fits the context of vv. 2–4 better than its present location in MT. Thus Dhorme, Driver-Gray, and Pope place it after v. 3. This possibility seems much better than striking it from the text as a gloss to v. 3.

8. Some mss. have a Ketib-Qere problem here. The Qere *ʿᵃnîyê,* "poor," is close in meaning to the Ketib, *ʿanwê,* "humble"; cf. similar alternate readings in Amos 8:4 and Ps. 9:13 (Eng. 12). Since the Qere occurs in 36:6 in contrast to *rāšāʿ*, "the wicked," Dhorme favors it here.

9. Gordis takes MT *hēn,* "behold," as the masculine plural pronoun, written this way due to Aramaic influence. Dhorme, however, suggests reading *hêḵ,* equal to *ʾêḵ,* "like," with LXX, Syr., and Vulg. Since Gordis must supply "as" in his translation, whereas Dhorme's slight change yields better sense and has versional support, Dhorme is followed.

10. The syntax of *mᵉšaḥᵃrê laṭṭārep,* "searching for food," is problematic. But it is possible to have the *nomen regens* before a prepositional phrase, esp. since it is a participle (GKC, § 130a).

11. Heb. *ʿᵃrāḇâ,* "desert," is taken as an accusative of place.

12. The prepositional phrase *lô,* "for him," may be revocalized *lû* with asseverative force (Guillaume, "Arabic Background," p. 116).

13. The verse is a tetrastich. Apparently a few minor errors in transmission have occurred in the second half of the verse. It is best to place the *ʾaṯnāḥ* at *ʿᵃrāḇâ,* "desert," making it parallel to *bammiḏbār,* "in the wilderness" (cf. Gordis).

14. The Qere *yiqṣôrû* (Qal) is preferred to the Ketib *yaqṣîrû* (Hiphil) since the verb "harvest" appears elsewhere only in the Qal.

15. For MT *bᵉlîlô,* "its fodder," Dhorme and Fohrer wish to read *bᵉlaylâ,* "at night." Gordis divides this word into two words, forming an idiom *bᵉlî lô,* "not his"; the suffix is singular because the form is frozen (cf. Tur-Sinai). If emendation is necessary, Pope's suggestion of *blyʿl (bᵉlîyaʿal),* "worthless person," forms a good parallel with *rāšāʿ*, "wicked." It is safer to stick close to MT, but the suffix is left untranslated.

16. Many (e.g., Duhm, Driver-Gray, Fohrer) think MT *rāšāʿ*, "wicked," should be emended to *ʿāšîr,* "rich," since the question is not an ethical one but one of social position. But the change is unnecessary, for the rich and the wicked are quite synonymous in OT thought, and this landowner is violating the standards of justice due the poor.

7 *Naked, they sleep without clothing,*
without covering in the cold.
8 *They are drenched by mountain rains;*
for lack of shelter they huddle against the rocks.
10 *Lacking clothes, they go about naked;*
hungry,[17] *they carry sheaves.*
11 *Between the rows*[18] *they crush olives;*
thirsty, they tread the winepresses."

1 Job opens his bold speech against the simplistic teaching about retribution offered by the friends with a caustic question about God's failure to requite flagrant violations of the law.[19] Although *times (ʿittîm),* i.e., set times for assaying earthly events, *are not hidden from Shaddai, those who know him (yōḏʿāw),* i.e., those who serve him faithfully, *never see his days,* i.e., the days of accountability when God judges a person's deeds. This question has a double prick. On the one hand, the wicked take advantage of the lack of times of judgment to pursue their evil designs unhindered. On the other hand, the righteous endure hardship, hopeful of God's rectifying justice, but without ever being rewarded by God for their faithful perseverance. Consequently, God's administration of justice seems sporadic, partial, and inconsistent.

2, 3, 9, 4 Since the day of judgment never comes, the statutes designed to protect the weak members of the community are flagrantly violated. Greed inspires the arrogant rich to exploit the poor, the weak, and the unfortunate, i.e., the *orphan (yᵉṯômîm), the widow (ʾalmānâ;* cf. 22:9), and *the needy (ʾeḇyônîm).* To secure property, the wicked craftily *move boundary stones,* the markers duly erected to delineate and protect a family's property. In Mesopotamia some boundary markers were inscribed with specifications about the property and with reliefs of sacred objects to put the

17. The form *rᵉʿēḇîm,* "hungry ones," is the accusative of state (Driver-Gray).

18. MT *bên šûrōṯām* is variously understood. The easiest solution is to take the final *m* as an enclitic *mem.* Dahood ("Northwest Semitic Philology and Job," p. 68) and Blommerde (*Northwest Semitic Grammar and Job,* p. 102) find a feminine dual: *šûrōṯēm,* "two rows." Dhorme offers a most adventuresome suggestion, postulating for *šûrâ* the meaning "millstone," related to *šûr,* "wall," and similar in meaning to *tûr* and *dûr,* "turn, go around." He takes the ending as a dual, hence "between two millstones." This creative suggestion, however, is quite speculative. Another interesting suggestion from E. Sutcliffe ("A Note on Job 24:10, 11," *JTS* 50 [1949] 174–76) reads *bᵉʾên šîrōṯām,* "without their songs." While farm crews often sing while working, the situation of these workers has become so oppressive that all singing has ceased. This suggestion needs more textual support for acceptance.

19. Westermann views ch. 24 as a counterargument against the friends similar to ch. 21. The opening "why" points to argumentation, not to a complaint against God (*Structure of the Book of Job,* p. 58).

property under divine sanction.[20] In ancient Israel, these stones were considered a sacred trust and were also never to be tampered with (cf. Deut. 19:14; Prov. 23:10). If such an inscribed stone was disturbed, the victim could lose a major portion of his property or possibly all of it.[21] Whoever moved such a marker came under a divine curse (Deut. 27:17).

Furthermore, evildoers *steal flocks* and *pasture* the sheep openly. Driving off an entire flock, of course, wipes out a family's or a clan's means of support. Perhaps the evildoers are so blatant that they dare to pasture the stolen herd on the land gained by moving the boundary stones. Interestingly a variant reading has them stealing both the flock and its shepherd.[22]

3 Wealthy lords collect what is owed them from a lowly *orphan*, perhaps a debt incurred by the deceased father, by entering the field where that young debtor is working unannounced and driving off his donkey.[23] That animal is the orphan's primary asset to keep from starving. But that is no concern to these greedy lords in their drive to amass wealth by every means. In a similar manner they take ownership of *a widow's ox* put up as security *for a pledge*. The severity of this action is attested in the Code of Hammurabi (§ 241): the lord who takes an ox in security was fined one-third mina of silver, a heavy penalty.[24] Such procedures also broke the statutes in the Pentateuch that guaranteed the means of support to the unfortunate (e.g., Deut. 24:6). The grievance in such a case is double. The wicked both insult the weak and impair the possibility of their earning a meager livelihood. Job's concern that such injustices cease indicates that Eliphaz's recent charge that he had been guilty of such evil dealings is false (22:6, 9).

9 A poor family could be deprived of its own children. A powerful lord might take *a child* in payment *or a pledge*, being so brazen as to rip this fatherless child from its mother's breast. This picture is figurative for any coercive method designed to gain custody of small children. In ancient times children were valuable assets. From early childhood they shared in the family's work, being trained to carry out various chores. Hence the more children the mighty controlled, the greater the productivity they could get from the land or from a household industry with minimal labor costs.

4 When the weak live during an era of oppression, they have to guard their every movement, ever conscious of protecting themselves from

20. See A. Oppenheim, *Ancient Mesopotamia* (Chicago: University of Chicago Press, 1964), pp. 123, 159.

21. Cf. P. Craigie, *The Book of Deuteronomy*, NICOT (Grand Rapids: Eerdmans, 1976), pp. 332–33.

22. See n. 4 above.

23. The parallelism suggests that the orphan's donkey is taken to secure or to pay off a pledge against a debt.

24. See *ANET*, p. 176.

harm. Afraid to travel by the worn paths lest they be robbed and beaten, *the poor are forced together into hiding.*[25] While the poor must move about stealthily in fear for their own safety, the rich revel in luxury at the expense of those they oppress. Although the laws and the teachings from God were formulated to prevent such social oppression, God has not called these evildoers to account for breaking his laws so contemptuously.

5 Job complains next about the peasants' austere working conditions. Their lot is comparable to that of *wild asses* that wander about the rugged, arid steppe eagerly searching for a little *food (ṭerep).*[26] Like these wild asses they must search hard and long, while afflicted by hunger and thirst, only to find a little *bread [leḥem] for their children.*

6 The burden of their effort is compounded by the lord's niggardly practices. They are forced to gather grain from fields already harvested. They have to *glean (liqqēš)*[27] in this miser's *vineyard.* The owner is labeled *wicked (rāšāʿ),* because after the initial harvest he is supposed to allow the poor to glean freely in his fields (Lev. 19:10; Deut. 24:21). Under these austere conditions there is little possibility of these poor gathering much food for their own families.

7, 8 The poor suffer even more from lack of clothing. Reduced to the shabbiest clothing, they have no garments heavy enough to keep them warm during the cool nights in the hill country of Palestine and Transjordan. Since this lord fails to offer them shelter or even a warm cloak they must sleep *naked (ʿārôm).* During the rainy season they seek shelter from the driving, chilly rain under a boulder. In desperation they crouch by boulders for a little shelter. But during a heavy rain they *are drenched by mountain rains,* torrents of water sweeping down the hillside. Dire poverty takes away their every means of coping with the elements.

10, 11 Job shifts (though the exact place of the shift is hard to pinpoint) from the miserable conditions of the poor to the harsh working practices afforded day laborers. They are so poor they have to work without protective clothing. In v. 7 the emphasis is on the lack of clothing for warmth; in v. 10 the issue is that the laborers do not have the proper clothing to protect them from the hazards of their work.[28]

25. Cf. Judg. 5:6; Amos 5:11–13.

26. Heb. *ṭerep* most often refers to "prey" or "carrion." In a few passages it means "food." Perhaps here it refers to the meager food the poor find by scavenging.

27. The word for gleaning the vineyards is *liqqēš.* In Aramaic it means "do (anything) late." Forms of this root are associated with harvest: *leqeš,* "after growth" (Amos 7:1) and *malqôš,* "late spring rains." In the Gezer Calendar *lqš,* "harvest," stands in contrast to *zrʿ,* "sowing." Thus the verb may mean "gather the last fruit" (Driver-Gray), which is sparse and the poorest.

28. Perhaps v. 10 has been leveled to v. 7, esp. the phrase *bᵉlî lᵉḇûš,* "without

The conditions under which they must work compound their misery. They are forced to work with the very essentials that their bodies cry out for. Famished by hard work, some have to carry *sheaves* all day long and yet are forbidden to eat any of the grain. Others, like beasts of burden, have to pull the heavy millstones that press out the olive oil. Others must tread the grapes in the winepresses which empty the juice into the vat *(yeqeḇ)*.[29] These laborers are parched with thirst while producing liquids, but they are unable to have any of the liquid to quench their thirst. Sapping a worker's strength without giving him any nourishment or allowing him a share in the joy of his toil is the height of inhumane labor practices (cf. Jas. 5:1–6). According to the highest standards, landlords were supposed to let their workers share in the results of their labor. Note that these two verses mention the three staples, grain, wine, and oil, which represent the products of the soil which God gives to sustain human life (e.g., Hos. 2:11, 24 [Eng. 9, 22]).

(b) Criminal Injustice (24:12–17)

12 *"From the city the dying[1] groan;*
wounded men cry out;
but God does not impute error.[2]
13 *They[3] are rebels against the light*
who do not know its ways
nor stay[4] in its paths.
14 *At twilight[5] the murderer rises,*
that he may kill the poor and the needy.

---

clothing." The context suggests that it would describe the nature of the oppressors' work. Tur-Sinai suggests that *hill^{e}ḵû,* "they go," is an error for *'zlw,* "they *spun* [wove cloth] naked without clothing." Although there is little support for this emendation, Tur-Sinai has caught the thrust of the verse.

29. Hakam points out that the author includes the whole process of making wine by referring to the final stage.

1. MT *m^{e}ṯîm,* "men," is read in Syr. as *mēṯîm,* "dying," while LXX reads *bottîm,* "houses." "Dying" offers the best parallel with *ḥ^{a}lālîm,* "wounded," and gives a reason why they would be "groaning" *(nā'aq)*. In Ezek. 30:24 *nā'aq* appears with *ḥālāl,* "the slain," as subject. Also the Syr. reading is supported by the parallel *mt/npš* attested in Ugaritic literature and Job 33:22 (*RSP,* I:272).

2. For MT *tiplâ,* "error," "unseemly act," there is an alternate reading *t^{e}pillâ,* "prayer," in two mss. and Syr. This is an attractive alternative, but *yišma',* "he hears," would then be the verb expected instead of MT *yāśîm,* "he places" (Hölscher). In addition, *tiplâ* occurs in 1:22 and cannot be easily discarded.

3. This is an unusual use of the personal pronoun. Usually the pronoun has an antecedent, but in this instance it appears to be used generally for a class of people the author has in mind. Gordis observes that this style belongs to this author; cf. 8:16; 13:28; 22:13; 41:1.

4. Some read *yāšûḇû,* "they return to," with LXX, Syr., Vulg., but MT *yaš^{e}ḇû,* "they dwell in, remain," is fine.

5. The opening word *lā'ôr* is taken to mean "at the light," i.e., the first twilight,

14c *At night a thief walks about;*[6]
16a *he breaks into houses in the dark.*[7]
15 *The eye of the adulterer watches for dusk;*
thinking, 'No eye will recognize me,'
he places a veil on his face.
16b *They shut themselves in by day;*
they do not want to know the light.
17 *For all of them their morning is deep darkness,*
a time when one recognizes[8] *the terrors of deep darkness."*

12 While injustice abounds in the countryside, suffering and abuse are rampant in the city. In the streets men lie *dying,* slain in an act of violence. The victims *groan (nāʾaq),* and *cry out (šiwwēaʿ)* for help and for vengeance against their attackers. The blood of *wounded men,* emphasized here by the use of the word *nepeš,* "soul"[9]—based on the ancient belief that the soul is borne by the blood (Lev. 17:11)—refuses to return to the ground in rest until the murderer has been punished. But God does not respond to these woeful cries. He *does not impute error.* Since there seems to be no justice, criminals are emboldened to act violently again.

13 Job describes the stealthy activity of those who are *rebels against the light:* the murderer, the thief, and the adulterer.[10] Such criminals work at night under the protection that darkness affords their evil deeds. They *do not know,* i.e., willingly follow, *the light,* the source of life and

---

with Dhorme. While Fohrer reads *lōʾ ʾôr,* "no light," Gordis relates *lāʾôr* to Aram. *ʾûrtāʾ,* "evening," and translates it "at nightfall."

6. The jussive *yehî kaggannāḇ,* "let him become like a thief," is peculiar. Duhm and many others read *yehallēḵ gannāḇ,* "the thief strolls about." Gordis, however, offers a better solution. He keeps MT and takes the *k* as the asseverative *k* used to emphasize the predicate nominative. Cf. GKC, § 118x.

7. While vv. 14c–18a are missing in LXX, Dhorme restructures vv. 14–16 to enhance their meaning: v. 14a, b; 15a, b, c; 14c; 16a, b; 13a, b, c; 16c. Another possible reconstruction is to make a distich out of v. 14c and v. 16a, giving a more likely subject for v. 16a. Also favoring separation of v. 16a from v. 16b, c is the shift from the singular in v. 16a to the plural in the rest of the verse. Moreover, v. 16a treats the second class of criminal, the thief, while v. 16b–c forms a distich offering a generalization about all the classes. A list of evildoers found in Hos. 4:2 gives a clue on the order of these verses (cf. n. 10 below). The text may be reordered thus: 14a, b; 14c, 16a; 15a, b, c; 16b, c. Then in vv. 12–17 there are three tristichs: vv. 12, 13, and 15. This mixture of tristichs with distichs is not unusual for the author.

8. Gordis interprets MT *kî-yakkîr* as an idiom meaning "daybreak," the time when people begin to recognize one another (cf. Ruth 3:14).

9. Gordis takes *nepeš,* "soul," in its physical meaning of "throat"; i.e., the deep cries come from the throat of the slain.

10. The same three classes of crimes occur in Hos. 4:2: murder *(rāṣōaḥ),* theft *(gānōḇ),* and adultery *(nāʾōp).* This order reflects a long tradition of listing these crimes together.

truth. If they ever were to discover the right way, they would not have the inner strength to stay faithfully on that rugged path.

14a, b *The murderer* prefers the quiet darkness of the early morning to do his ill deeds. At the first light of day he stalks a lonely person in the streets, and at the opportune moment he strikes to kill. His victims are *the poor and the needy,* innocent citizens who are unable to muster any resistance. Since they are of the lowest class, no one in the city really cares about their tragic death. The murderer has no worry of being caught and punished.

14c, 16a The *thief walks about* at night, looking for a dwelling to rob. After picking out a suitable target, he digs through the mud-brick wall to gain an undetected entrance.[11] Such a tactic for gaining entrance to a house is mentioned in Exod. 22:1 (Eng. 2): "If a thief is found breaking in and is struck so that he dies, there shall be no bloodguilt" (cf. Jer. 2:34). Such clandestine activity is an expression of rebellion against the light.

15 *The adulterer watches for dusk* so that he can go looking for a likely victim.[12] Conscious of watching others, he is very careful not to be observed. Fear of recognition leads him to disguise his appearance by donning some type of *veil* or mask. His rebellion against the light is total.

16b, c, 17 All these criminals *shut* [Piel of *ḥāṯam*] *themselves in by day*. The Hebrew word *ḥāṯam* means literally "seal." In their dwelling places they feel as secure as a sealed document. Never taking any risk of discovery, *they do not want to know the light*. Because they live by an opposite standard, their attitude to the times of the day is reversed. Morning, which fills most people with joy and expectation, is for them *deep darkness (ṣalmāweṯ)*. Since light fills them with fear of discovery, they lay low during the day, taking their rest. But at night when *the terrors of deep darkness* reign, they feel at ease. Thus the wicked reject light and accept darkness as their protector and assistant.

(2) A Curse on the Wicked (24:18–25)

18 *"He is swift on the face of water;*
let their portion be accursed in the land;
let him not turn to the way of the vineyards.
19 *Let drought and[1] heat*

11. Fohrer relates that the reason that a thief goes through the wall of a house has its basis in the belief that the demons of the house protected the portal. A thief would certainly be sensitive to superstition and magical beliefs.

12. The first line begins with "eye" *(ʿên),* and the second line ends with "eye" *(ʿayin).* This style places emphasis on the role of the eye in the adulterer's lust. See Job 31:1; Matt. 5:27–29.

1. Heb. *gām,* "also," is interpreted as a conjunction in this context (Dhorme).

steal the snow waters,
Sheol those who have sinned.[2]

20 *Let the womb forget him;*
let the worm[3] *suck on him;*[4]
let him no longer be remembered;
so may injustice be broken like a tree.

21 *Let not the barren lady*[5] *bear,*
and leave the widow without good.[6]

22 *May he*[7] *allure the mighty*[8] *by his power;*
let him rise but never be sure[9] *of his life.*

23 *May he give him security that he may be supported,*
with his eyes on their ways.

2. Dhorme reconstructs the last five words as *mêmê šeleg yigzōl ûšeʾôl ḥôṭēʾ* to arrive at an excellent reading: "The drought and the heat carry away the snow waters, Thus does Sheol *snatch away the sinner*." Similarly, Pope suggests eliminating a redundant word—"drought" and "waters"—from each line to gain a balanced distich: "Heat consumes the snow, Sheol those who have sinned." But instead of adopting one of these emendations, I translate the verse with freer use of syntax.

3. For MT *rimmâ,* "worm," many (e.g., Driver-Gray, RSV) read *šemōh,* "his name," but it is difficult to explain how *rimmâ* could have arisen from *šemōh*.

4. For MT *reḥem meṯāqô* many (e.g., Duhm, Budde, Rowley) read *reḥōḇ meqōmô:* "the square of his place." For *meqōmô* Dhorme emends to the verb *peṯāqô,* "he formed him." He identifies this verb as cognate to Akk. *patāqu,* "make, form": "The womb which has formed him." But MT is kept as superior to the changes proposed, and the verse is divided into a tetrastich.

5. The participle *rōʿeh* is variously understood. It may be taken from the root *rʿh,* "graze," used metaphorically to mean "strip." But this meaning is unlikely with its object being a barren woman. Many follow LXX and Targ. to read *hēraʿ,* either "be treated ill" or "break." This reading makes a fine parallel to "does not do good" *(lōʾ yeyēṭîḇ).* Fohrer accepts a root *rʿh* II, "associates with," and Andersen takes this root to mean "a female companion," as in Ps. 45:15 (Eng. 14). This last idea makes the best sense of the participle, which should be revocalized *rōʿâ*.

6. For MT *yeyēṭîḇ,* "it is good," the more usual vocalization would be *yêṭîḇ*. GKC, § 70c, suggests that "the syllable was broken up" to restore the preformative that had merged with the first radical.

7. God is generally understood to be the subject here (so, e.g., Dhorme, Rowley, RSV).

8. Gordis takes the *m* on *ʾabbîrîm,* "the mighty," as an enclitic *mem* or a case of dittography with the following preposition *be,* making it singular, "the mighty man." But if vv. 22 and 23 are taken together, the author moves from the plural in v. 22a to the singular in vv. 22b and 23a then back to the plural in v. 23b. Thus the MT is preferred.

9. The *lōʾ* before *yaʾamîn,* "he believes," may be an asseverative *lûʾ* (cf. Pope). But a similar phrase occurs in Deut. 28:66, *welōʾ taʾamîn beḥayyêḵā,* "you will not believe in life," i.e., "you will never be sure of your life." This expression describes the effects which a divine curse has on a person's desire to live. LXX, Targ., and Vulg., along with Deut. 28:66, support reading *beḥayyāyw,* "in his life," for the Aramaic form *baḥayyîn,* "in life."

24 *They are exalted*[10] *for only a moment and are no more;*[11]
they are laid low[12] *and shrivel up*[13] *like grass;*[14]
like heads of grain they wither.
25 *If not, who can prove that I lied*[15]
or show that[16] *my words are nothing?"*[17]

The interpretation of this section is extremely difficult. The text is obscure, and there are many variant readings; thus numerous emendations have been proposed. Also, the section is understood to describe the certain downfall of the wicked, and hence it contradicts the above complaint. It supports the doctrine of retribution rather than challenging it. Because it agrees with the teaching of the friends, many contemporary interpreters relocate this passage, making it a portion of either Bildad's or Zophar's third speech. If they are correct, its present location may have resulted from the breaking up of the third cycle. But the style of these verses accords more with ch. 24 than either Bildad's speech in 25:1–6 or a reconstructed speech of Zophar from 27:14–23. It is not correct to assume that because Job questions God's method of governing, he puts aside all belief in retributive punishment. While seriously considering the exceptions to the rule, he does not throw out everything he has believed about justice. Since Job wants God to execute his justice against these wicked as proof that he will act justly in his own favor, he utters a series of curses against the lawless, as the imprecatory style of

10. MT *rômmû* is virtually anomalous (cf. GKC, § 67m, and *rōbbû* in Gen. 49:23). It may be from the root *rmm,* "be exalted," or a special Qal form of *rûm,* "be high, exalted, rise." Otherwise, it may be revocalized *rāmû,* with Driver-Gray, but leveling of forms should be the last resort.

11. If the plural form *rômmû* is kept, *'ênām,* "they are not," is preferred over MT *'ênennû,* "he is not."

12. MT *hummᵉḵû,* "they are laid low," appears to be an Aramaized form of the Hophal (GKC, § 67y). LXX, however, reads the singular.

13. A long-standing emendation of MT *yiqqāpᵉṣûn,* "they draw themselves together," is *yiqqāṭᵉpûn,* "they will be plucked, gathered" (as in 30:4). But the root *qpṣ,* which describes the "shutting" tightly of the hand (Deut. 15:7), in reference to grass may describe its shriveling. In Syriac *qᵉpas,* "contract, close, restrain," may mean "droop" in reference to flowers (see R. P. Smith, *A Compendious Syriac Dictionary,* p. 514).

14. MT *kakkōl* appears to be a miswriting of a word for grass. LXX reads *kᵉmallûaḥ,* "as mallow," and the Qumran Targ. reads *kybl',* "grass" *(cynodon dactylum).* The view that the original was *kîḇûl* and MT *kkl* arose from a confusion of *b* and *k* is accepted. Gordis offers the creative suggestion that *kōl* is a cognate of Arab. *ka'l,* "herbage," and thus means "grass." But the reading of the Qumran Targ. makes this proposal unnecessary.

15. The Hiphil of *kāzaḇ,* "lie, be false," has a factitive sense.

16. Although the *mater lectionis* was not written in *wᵉyāśēm,* it seems best to revocalize it *wᵉyāśîm* with a few mss. (so Driver-Gray).

17. MT *'al* is taken as a substantive meaning "nothing, worthlessness" (with Dhorme, Gordis).

v. 18 suggests (Andersen). Cautiously accepting this interpretation, one can retain these verses as part of Job's speech. As Andersen says in defending their place here, "His position is more balanced, but more baffled."

18 Verse 18a is obscure.[18] Since a curse is pronounced against the wicked in the second and third lines, the first line may be a *casus pendens* describing the precarious station of the wicked person. He is swiftly floating down a river with a strong current. Job pronounces a curse against this kind of a person. He prays that their fertile *portion* of land, possibly acquired by squeezing it from the weak, *be accursed.* He also curses that person so that he is afraid to go out into his vineyards to try and protect them from being destroyed by the curse. While his wealth is disappearing before his own eyes, there is nothing he can do to reverse his ill-fate, for it is divinely initiated.

19 Verse 19 is very problematic. Taking it as a tristich overcomes some of its problems, but the brevity of each line is highly unusual. In a curse Job wishes that just as the dryness and heat of the desert *steal the* cold *snow waters* from the stream beds (cf. 6:16–17), so too Sheol will rob insolent sinners of their life.

20 The curse brings a tragic end on the sinner. The very womb that bore him should forget him, i.e., not care for him. This curse is designed so that his surest source of compassion might fail him in his most desperate hour of need. In the grave that person is left to the mercy of worms that thrive on his body. On earth he is no longer to *be remembered.* No beautiful monument is to mark his grave, and no caretaker is to tend his memorial (cf. 21:32–33). With the removal of his remembrance, the *injustice* he pursued is completely *broken,* like a tree trunk split in two by a powerful wind. Then the injustice that his wicked deeds produced will be terminated, never again to oppress people on earth.

21 This verse is also problematic. Perhaps it is based on the theme of retaliation in kind. The curse is that the evildoer's lady companion might not *bear.* This curse is designed to leave this wicked man without heir. The second part of the curse is that his *widow* might not be left with any *good.* She is not to prosper from his evil deeds.

22 God is assumed to be the subject of this verse. The curse is that God might initially fulfill the desires of the wicked, but never let them enjoy their success. *May God allure [māšaḵ]*[19] *the mighty [ʾabbîrîm],* who are as

18. Although something appears to be missing or miswritten in v. 18a, there is a note of genuineness about this verse, as evidenced in the subtle play of assonance between *qal,* "swift," and *tᵉqullal,* "it is cursed."

19. Cf. *TWOT,* I:532; another view interprets *māšaḵ* to mean "prolong one's lifespan" (see RSV; cf. Fohrer).

strong as a bull,[20] to carry out his evil plans. Endowed by God with unusual strength, he (the mighty) accomplishes great feats for his own glory, and he establishes his control where he will. Lured on by his early successes, he lives for all the pleasure he can get. But once he has attained wealth and power, he becomes disillusioned. Nothing satisfies him. He has no meaning. He loses interest in everything; that is his punishment. God robs him of his zest for life.

23, 24 Verses 23–24 continue this theme. Job prays that God *may give* the wicked *security* on which to lean for support, while he continually keeps *his eyes on their ways*. But God lets them be *exalted* only for a brief time. Soon he judges them, and they *are no more*. The higher they rise, the harder they will fall. *They are laid low and shrivel up like grass* or *wither like heads of grain* beneath the scorching sun. Just as the grain is dried up before it comes to harvest, God brings them down by a miserable fate before they enjoy the fruit of their evil schemes.

25 This verse clearly belongs to Job. Certain of his position, he affirms its truth by challenging anyone to prove his argument false. If there is no rebuttal, that will stand as proof that he has established his case.

AIM

Job speaks with increasing conviction. His confidence in receiving a just resolution to his complaint from the elusive God has grown, and his lamenting his plight in self-pity has receded into the background. Having been free to lament his distress has clarified his thinking, allowing him to formulate his resolve to meet God on legal grounds. Thus he is determined to persevere, holding on to his claim of innocence, until God answers him.

While Job awaits God's answer, his mind turns to the topsy-turvy affairs in the world that allow the wicked, given to self-serving, brutal deeds of violence, to oppress the weak and powerless. His own sufferings have made him more sensitive to widespread human suffering. He longs for God to rectify matters on earth. While he grieves at social evil, he remains so confident that God does eventually execute justice that he pronounces a series of curses against the wicked. Job's concern for injustice leads him to challenge the theology of his day, but at the same time, because of his profound faith in God, his lamenting drives him to God for an answer. He is anxious that God curse the wicked, holding them accountable for their evil deeds.

20. Heb. *'abbîr* basically means strong; it is often used in reference to strong animals, like a bull. See *TDOT*, I:43; cf. Ps. 22:13 (Eng. 12); Jer. 8:16.

3. BILDAD'S THIRD SPEECH (25:1–6; 27:13–23)

Bildad's third speech, lacking both an introduction and a conclusion, is far too short. Perhaps a portion of it has become dislocated in chs. 24–28. That portion may be found in 27:13–23, for its wording is closer to the comforters' type of discussion than to Job's. By placing these verses with 25:1–6, a fuller speech is gained for Bildad. In support of this reconstruction is the fact that 27:13–23 offers a direct rebuttal to the ideas Job was struggling with in ch. 24. Because the connection between these two portions is rough, however, it may be assumed that other lines have been lost after 25:6 and both before and after 27:13–23.

The reconstructed speech contains two sections: a hymn of praise to God (25:1–6), and a discourse on the certain retribution of the wicked (27:13–23). The first section draws on Israelite hymns of praise,[1] and the second section is composed in the style of a Wisdom discourse (27:13–23). Bildad affirms God's sovereign rule and every creature's frailty and unworthiness before him. In this way he soundly repudiates Job's accusation that God rules unjustly (24:1–17) as well as his affirmation of innocence (27:4–6).

Bildad opens with lines drawn from a hymn of praise. The hymn is cast into rhetorical questions, a style typical of a Wisdom discourse. Two themes are sharply contrasted: the absolute exaltedness and purity of God (vv. 2–3) and the imperfections of all creation, especially mankind (vv. 4–6). A chiastic pattern exists among these five lines (Hakam). Verse 4, standing at the center of the chiasm, bears the emphasis. Verses 3 and 5 focus on the heavenly host; the stars and the moon (v. 5) are numbered among God's troops (v. 3). Verses 2 and 6 are antithetically parallel: the greatness of God (v. 2) stands in contrast to the insignificance of mankind (v. 6). The message conveyed by these lines is that mankind is far too limited in power to call God into question as Job is attempting to do.

a. A Hymn of Praise to God (25:1–6)

1 *Bildad the Shuhite responded:*
2 *"Dominion and dread[1] are with him*
who makes peace in his heights.

1. On these hymns see N. Snaith, *Hymns of the Temple* (London: SCM, 1951); S. Mowinckel, *The Psalms in Israel's Worship,* tr. D. Ap-Thomas (New York: Abingdon, repr. 2 vols. in 1, 1979), I:81ff.; cf. C. Westermann, *Praise and Lament in the Psalms,* tr. K. Crim (Atlanta: John Knox, repr. 1981), pp. 15–35.

1. Duhm and Gordis interpret *hamšēl wāp̄aḥaḏ* as a hendiadys for "dominion of fear, or awe-inspiring rule." Heb. *hamšēl* is an infinitive absolute used as a noun (cf. GKC, § 85c). LXX, however, reads the *h* as the interrogative *he*.

3 *Is there any number to his troops?*
On whom does his light[2] *not rise?*
4 *How can man be just before God?*
How can one born of woman be pure?
5 *Behold, even the moon is not*[3] *bright,*[4]
and the stars are not pure in his sight,
6 *how much less man, a maggot,*
and the son of man, a worm?"

2 Bildad lauds God's sovereign power. From *his heights*[5] God reigns over the entire world. He is so awesome in holiness that people stand in *dread* of him. Even in heaven there is no force that would dare challenge his rule, for his *dominion* is too great. Having complete authority, he *makes peace [šālôm] in his heights,* his place of abode. Perhaps the expression *make peace* alludes to the primordial conflict, a theme common in Near Eastern cosmogonies (cf. 9:13; 26:12–13). If it does, Bildad is asserting that all cosmic forces are now subject to God and there is no danger that the conflict might break out anew. If there are no powers in opposition to God in heaven, certainly there are none on earth. Through this line of reasoning Bildad categorically rejects Job's lament that there are numerous cases of injustice on earth (24:1–17). The truth is that God rules supreme over all creatures in heaven and on earth (cf. Jer. 33:9).

3 The heavenly hosts constitute God's *troops* or armies *(gᵉḏûḏāyw).* All of them are obedient to his command and serve to ensure his peaceful rule. The rhetorical question claims that his troops are so numerous that they are beyond counting. The opposite expression—that something can be numbered—means that it is limited and insignificant. Further, God's gracious, universal rule is affirmed through the image of light. Light shines everywhere, bringing warmth, joy, and life. God, the source of light, em-

2. For MT *ʾôrēhû,* "his light," LXX reads *ʾôrᵉḇô,* "his ambush." This variant is adopted by many (e.g., Duhm, Dhorme, Fohrer), for it offers a good parallel to "his troops" *(gᵉḏûḏāyw).* But the reading "his light" offers a fine sense, for the moon and the stars appear in v. 5, and light is associated with God's cosmic rule throughout Scripture. Thus MT is followed.

3. The predicate is introduced with *waw* after a *casus pendens* (GKC, § 143d). A few mss. do not read the *waw*.

4. MT *yaʾᵃhîl* may be a by-form of *hll,* "shine"; the ʾ may be a *mater lectionis.* Thus it may be vocalized *yāhēl* (see *BHS,* Pope).

5. Heb. *mᵉrômāyw,* "his heights," is another name for the heavens as God's dwelling place (cf. 16:19; 31:2).

powers life and sustains all his creatures, for there is none on whom *his light does not rise*.

4 This verse, standing at the center of the chiasm of vv. 2–5, is the focal point of this pericope. Bildad asserts that before the majestic God no creature can *be just (ṣāḏaq)*[6] or *pure (zāḵâ)*.[7] Thus it is impossible for a feeble, finite human to attain moral perfection. The weakness of mankind is underscored by the word for *man ('ĕnôš)* and by the phrase *born of woman (yᵉlûḏ 'iššâ)*.[8] Bildad is quoting Eliphaz's great insight presented in 15:14–15 (cf. 4:17–18). Thus he also has come to the conclusion that Job is deluded in thinking that he might be able to prove his innocence before God.

5 Bildad defends God's way of governing the world by saying that nothing except God himself is pure or flawless. The *moon,* which shines brightly enough in the Middle East for a traveler to find his way across the steppe at night, *is not bright* in God's judgment. And *the stars are not pure [zāḵaḵ] in his sight*. Even though the moon and the stars, members of God's heavenly army, appear so bright to mankind, they have no innate purity that gives them any position with God. They too must serve him out of contrition and unworthiness. If this is true of these marvelous heavenly bodies, how much more is it true of mankind.

6 The concluding hymnic line emphasizes human frailty and moral ineptitude. A human being is but *a maggot (rimmâ)* and *a worm (tôlēʿâ)*.[9] These terms symbolize a wretched, lowly existence, and they have the smell of death about them. Also, the words *man ('ĕnôš)* and *son of man (ben-'āḏām)* bear the note of human weakness and earthiness.[10] Illness and loss make a person's life so wretched that he feels like a maggot, and he can look forward only to the grave, where he will be consumed by worms (cf. Isa. 14:11).

Thus Bildad, in quoting from the hymns of the congregation, impugns Job's speculation that a human being could even attempt to enter into litigation with God. He is seeking to show Job that his hope of defending his own integrity is absurd in the light of God's absolute holiness. He is also denouncing Job's bold accusation that God does not keep times of judgment.

6. Cf. 9:15, 20; 10:15; 13:18; 33:12; 34:5; 35:7.

7. For *zāḵâ,* "be pure," cf. 13:14a; for *zaḵ,* "pure," cf. 8:6; 11:4; 16:17; 33:9.

8. Cf. 14:1; 15:14.

9. Heb. *tôlēʿâ,* "worm," also occurs for a man in Ps. 22:7 (Eng. 6) and Isa. 41:14. The noun *rimmâ,* "maggot," appears in Job 7:5; 17:14; 21:26; and 24:20; all of these are in speeches of Job. These words are parallel in Isa. 14:11.

10. Heb. *'āḏām,* "man," is related to *'ᵃdāmâ,* "ground," and *'āḏōm,* "be red": man is ruddy by reason of his origin from the reddish-brown soil; cf. 16:21; 35:8.

b. The Certain Retribution of the Wicked (27:13–23)

13 *"This is the portion of the wicked from God,*[1]
the tyrants'[2] *inheritance from Shaddai.*[3]

14 *Though he has many children, they are for the sword;*
his offspring will not have enough bread.

15 *Those who survive him*[4] *will be buried in a plague,*[5]
and his widows[6] *will not weep.*

16 *If he heaps up silver like dust*
and piles[7] *up clothing like clay,*

17 *he may accumulate, but the righteous will wear it;*
the innocent will divide the silver.

18 *He built his house like a spider's web,*[8]
like a booth that a watchman makes.

19 *He goes to bed rich,*[9] *but for the last time;*[10]
he opens his eyes and nothing is left.

1. MT *ʿim-ʾēl,* "with God," may be an error for *mēʾēl,* as in 20:29b. The *ʿayin* could have resulted from dittography. M. Dahood (*Ugaritic-Hebrew Philology,* BibOr 17 [Rome: Pontifical Biblical Institute, 1965], p. 32) has found an example in *UT,* 2065:14 of *ʿim* meaning "from." His insight enables one to follow the MT without emendation.

2. The plural ending on *ʿārîṣîm,* "tyrants," may be a result of dittography or it may be an enclitic *mem.* While the singular is preferred, the plural is possible, for in treating classes of people the numbers frequently vary.

3. Since the second line is long (12 syllables), the verb *yiqqāḥû,* "they receive," is suspect. Also 20:29, which is almost identical to this verse, does not have a verb in this position. Therefore, this verb is omitted.

4. The Qere, a plural form, *śᵉrîḏāyw,* "those who survive him," is preferred to the singular Ketib, *śᵉrîḏô,* "he who survives him," because of the plural forms in v. 14.

5. Heb. *māweṯ,* "death," is taken to mean "pestilence" with RSV and Gordis; cf. Jer. 15:2; 18:21; 43:11. This interpretation is supported by comparative uses of the word for death. As Dhorme notes, in the Amarna texts Akk. *mūtu* means "disease"; see also Syr. *mauta*ʾ, which means "cause of death, plague, pestilence," and Syr. *mautana*ʾ, which means "pestilence, mortality, slaughter" (R. P. Smith, *A Compendious Syriac Dictionary,* p. 260). Pope, however, reads MT *bmwt* as *bāmôṯ,* "a cultic term for tomb or funerary monument." But he must supply a negative to get "his posterity will not be buried in a tomb."

6. LXX and Syr. read "their widows." Some (e.g., Hölscher, Fohrer) have suggested that this reading arose to avoid a polygamous implication. Since plural and singular forms are mixed throughout this pericope, MT may be retained.

7. The Hiphil of *kûn* means "provide, furnish," with the extended meaning "store up, amass" (cf. Prov. 6:8; 30:25; Dhorme).

8. For MT *ʿāš,* "moth," there are many suggestions. Dhorme reads "nest," taking *ʿāš* as cognate to Arab. *ʿušš,* "nest," based on the argument that the object of the comparison is the building, not the builder. Gordis agrees. Pope, however, finds the comparison with the builder and takes *ʿāš* as a cognate of Arab. *ʿās,* "night watchman." LXX appears to translate *ʿāš* twice, the second time by *aráchnē,* "a spider's web"; so too Syr. This possibility is the best, for it restores balance to the first line (syllable count 8/8), which otherwise is a little short. But see Grabbe, *Comparative Philology,* pp. 89–91.

9. The noun *ʿāšîr,* "rich," an accusative of position, is placed first for emphasis.

10. For MT *lōʾ yēʾāsēp,* "he is not gathered (or removed)," it seems best to read

20 *Terrors overtake*[11] *him like waters;*[12]
in the night the tempest snatches him away.
21 *The east wind lifts him up and he is gone,*[13]
and it sweeps him from his place;
22 *it hurls itself at him without sparing*
as he tries to flee from its power.
23 *It claps its hands at him,*
and hisses him from his place."

13 In this portion of his speech, if it is correctly assigned to him, Bildad draws heavily on Zophar's words found in his last speech (ch. 20). He opens with a proverb stating that there is a set penalty for every person who transgresses God's law. This proverb stands at the head of a detailed description of the woes that befall a wicked person. The concept of reward for improper behavior is carried by the words *portion (ḥēleq)* and *inheritance (naḥᵃlâ)*. The proverb teaches that God has set the penalty for wrongdoing, and he ensures its execution. The two terms *the wicked (rāšāʿ)* and *the tyrants (ʿārîṣ)* are strong words to mark the ruthless, vicious character of those who oppose God.

14, 15 Even though the evildoer has his *many children,* whom he takes pride in and whom he expects will enjoy his wealth, God will punish them for their father's sins by appointing them *for the sword.* The thesis is that if a tyrant multiplies children in the hope of their enjoying the wealth he has amassed and spreading his fame, he brings them forth only to die a violent death (cf. 5:4; 18:19). Some of his children who *survive* the sword will starve, and others will be wiped out by *a plague.*[14] The weapons of death will strike at the evildoer's family until no survivor is left. *His widows* will be facing such hardship that they will not be able to *weep* over the loss of their own children. That is, his family will be cast into such turmoil that funeral rites with appropriate mourning will be impossible.

16, 17 Furthermore, a wicked person will lose all the wealth he has accumulated. His covetous greed has driven him to heap up *silver like dust*

(with most commentators) *lōʾ yôsîp,* "do not again," i.e., do for the last time, with LXX and Syr., since the form in MT contradicts the preceding statements.

11. An abstract feminine plural subject may take a feminine singular verb, particularly when the verb precedes it (GKC, § 145k).

12. To gain a better parallel with *laylâ,* "night," Merx reads *bayyôm,* "in the day," for MT *kammayim,* "like waters." Similarly, Dhorme reads *yômām,* "by day," which is a better suggestion grammatically. But the latter requires a greater change in MT. Since Qumran Targ. agrees with MT, MT is followed.

13. For the vocalization *yēlaḵ* see GKC, § 69p.

14. It is interesting to note with Dhorme that this threefold formula of a curse—sword, famine, pestilence—is attested in Jer. 14:12; 15:2 (with captivity a fourth); and Ezek. 5:12; 6:12.

and *clothing like clay*. Fine clothing is costly, and it bolsters its wearer's pride.[15] The vast wealth symbolized by silver and clothing he has amassed is enormous. But in just retribution *the righteous will wear* his fancy clothing and *the innocent will divide the silver*.[16] That is, the very people he has exploited will enjoy his wealth (cf. Eccl. 2:20–21, 26). The wicked person never gets to enjoy his wealth (cf. Eccl. 6:1–6). These verses are arranged chiastically: 16a/17b::16b/17a.

18 This wicked person has built a magnificent house for his own glory. But quickly built, the house is unsound. It may be compared to *a spider's web,* which, though beautifully and masterfully constructed, is the frailest of all structures. Or, it is like a flimsy, temporary *booth,* which a farmer puts up in his field as a temporary shelter for him as he guards his crops during the harvest. After the harvest, the booth, left unattended, quickly falls into ruins.

19 One fatal night this wicked person *goes to bed rich*. But it is *for the last time*. During the night tragedy strikes, sweeping away all his riches. In the morning he finds that *nothing is left* of all that he had. This description reminds Job of the sudden, total loss of his wealth. It implies pointedly that he is a wicked person.

20–22 This wicked person's loss of all his wealth is but the beginning of his end. He himself will have to pass through a tunnel of horror that leads to his own death. *Terrors [ballāhôṯ]*[17] *overtake him*. He is panic-stricken, as when a person walking in a wadi suddenly faces a rushing torrent.[18] Or *in the night the tempest snatches* [lit. "steals," *gānaḇ*] *him from his place*. His *place* is the center of his rule, his wealth, and his security.

The evildoer feels as though the hot *east wind*[19] *lifts him up* and *sweeps him* away *from his place*. On nights when the sirocco blows, the dry heat makes it difficult to sleep; a person's restless mind is troubled by nightmares. As God's instrument of punishment, this wind torments the wicked person. It pursues him relentlessly as he tries desperately to escape its force.

23 The subject of this verse is unclear. While Gordis takes it as indefinite ("men"), it could be "the east wind" of v. 21 (cf. Pope). Perhaps

15. Apparel is listed with gold and silver in Gen. 24:53, and such clothing marks great wealth in 2 K. 7:8 (cf. Josh. 7:21; Zech. 14:14). Interestingly, silver is parallel to clothing *(lbš/ksp)* in *UT,* 1115:3–5; 2101:14–17 (*RSP,* I:248, no. 329). Thus MT is supported.

16. This idea of retribution in kind is a common theme in the Wisdom literature; cf. Job 5:5; Prov. 13:22; 28:8.

17. Cf. Job 18:14.

18. See 2 Sam. 5:20; Isa. 28:17; Hos. 5:10.

19. Cf. Job 15:2; 37:17; 38:24.

the picture is that this broken, wicked person continually hears the taunts of the community in the howling of the wind. When tragedy struck him, all whom he had oppressed enthusiastically showed their hatred of him by clapping their hands and hissing at him as they drove him from his place.[20] "Clapping the hands" and "hissing" were gestures of anger and derision expressed against someone who was greatly despised (cf. Lam. 2:15).

AIM

Bildad rejects as untenable Job's desire that God grant him a trial before the heavenly court by quoting from the hymnic tradition that exalts God and teaches that the retribution of the wicked is certain. Surely a mere human being, who is prone to error, is guilty and unworthy of having the divine court hear his case. Therefore, holding firm to the doctrine of retributive justice, Bildad attempts to refute Job's lament that God permits gross injustice in the world. Bildad is certain that everyone who rejects God and heaps up his own wealth through injustice will receive a swift, harsh punishment. All his children will die and all his possessions will be given to the poor. Taunted and rejected, he will suffer an ignominious death. Bildad is convinced that Job is wrong in thinking that some wicked people go unpunished. Furthermore, if Job persists in the obstinacy of his way, his ignominy will become total.

This speech is the last from the three comforters. Their attempts to understand Job's suffering have led them to condemn their friend. In their opinion Job will die without honor, receiving the just reward for his sins, unless he repents. Having no other comfort to offer him, they turn silent, confident that God will consummate Job's suffering in just measure.

4. JOB'S EIGHTH RESPONSE (26:1–27:12)

Job has become completely exasperated at the friends' counsel. Their words have become a taunt, and their exhortations to repentance tempt him to seek God for the wrong reasons. Job, therefore, turns to meditate on God's awesome power. Then he swears to his innocence. In conclusion he pleads that his enemies be removed. Job has clearly resolved that he will hold on to his integrity to the end.

20. It was customary for those who passed by a devastated city to clap their hands, hiss, and shake their heads. With these gestures the passersby heaped contempt on those who were destroyed by such dreadful calamity; cf. Jer. 19:8; 49:17; Lam. 2:15, 16; Zeph. 2:15.

This speech is Job's last response to his friends.[1] Because of the disturbances in the third cycle, this speech has been reconstructed out of 26:1–14 and 27:1–12. It ends abruptly, for some words seem to have been lost. This speech consists of many genres: that part of a disputation speech in which one renounces his opponents (26:2–4; 27:11–12), a hymn (26:5–14), an avowal of innocence (27:2–6), and an imprecation against one's enemies (27:7–10). The four sections are: the rejection of Bildad's counsel (26:1–4), the praise of God's majestic power (26:5–14), Job's confidence and his wish (27:1–10), and Job's intent to instruct the friends (27:11–12).

a. The Rejection of Bildad's Counsel (26:1–4)

1 *Job responded,*
2 *"How have you helped the powerless!*
How have you saved the arm without strength!
3 *How have you counseled him who is without wisdom!*
And how have you declared sound wisdom abundantly!
4 *With whose help have you uttered words?*
Whose breath spoke through you?"

These verses contain Job's harshest rejection of a friend's counsel.[1] Job uses the second person masculine singular form here, whereas in his other speeches he used second person masculine plural forms in addressing the friends as a group.[2] Perhaps he is singling out Bildad for this series of harsh rhetorical questions because he has reiterated the position of each of the other comforters.

2 Job asks him how he has helped a weakling, one whose arm lacks strength, to overcome the difficulties he is facing. He has in mind a valiant effort to rescue a beleaguered victim from an oppressive situation. With biting sarcasm Job is accusing Bildad of having violated the patriarchal mores in doing nothing to rescue him from his oppressive circumstances.

3 Job next asks Bildad how he has offered counsel to one lacking wisdom. While Job has admitted that he lacks both help and sound wisdom

1. On the reconstruction of Job's last speech in the dialogue see pp. 24–26.

1. Job frequently opens his speeches with a charge against the friends for not perceiving the wisdom of his words and for taunting him instead of offering him comfort (e.g., 12:2–3; 16:2–5; 19:2–6; 21:2–3).

2. There are a few similar exceptions, once in his speech to Eliphaz (16:3) and perhaps twice in speeches to Zophar (12:7–8 and 21:3b). This fact has led some to take 26:2–4 as part of Bildad's speech (e.g., Driver-Gray, though with hesitation). But most (e.g., Fohrer, Pope, Rowley) assign these verses to Job.

(6:13),[3] he charges that Bildad has not offered him *sound wisdom (tûšîyâ)*[4] to enable him to discover a way out of his incriminating affliction. Wisdom could enable a person to rise above trying circumstances to accomplish God's purpose.[5]

4 In the light of these failings Job scathingly questions the source of Bildad's rhetoric. He asks who has inspired Bildad as to what to say. By asking the source of his inspiration Job is questioning the value of his instruction. The *breath (nᵉšāmâ)* is the principle of human life that is given by God (Gen. 2:7; Job 33:4). It may also stand for divine inspiration that stirs up special insight deep inside a person (cf. 32:8). Job, however, does not find that Bildad has any special wisdom from outside his own thinking that will help him overcome his difficulties. In fact, he has had to resort to quoting from the other friends to fill out his third speech. Therefore, by rejecting Bildad's instruction as lacking in encouragement and in wisdom at this point, Job is rejecting all the discourse of the comforters as worthless.

b. The Praise of God's Majestic Power (26:5–14)

5 *"The shades writhe*
beneath[1] *the waters, with their inhabitants.*[2]
6 *Sheol is naked before him,*
and Abaddon has no covering.
7 *He stretches out the north over chaos*
and hangs the earth over nothing.
8 *He binds the waters in thick clouds,*
and the cloud mass bursts not under their weight.

3. The close tie between 6:13 and 26:2–3 defends the authenticity of these lines as part of the oldest portion of the poem and also supports the assigning of these verses to Job.

4. Cf. 5:12; 6:13; 11:6; 12:16; 30:22.

5. Two great examples of wise men who overcame trying circumstances through their wisdom and their reliance on God were Joseph (Gen. 39–47) and Daniel. Overcoming prejudice and stern opposition, both rose to leadership in foreign governments.

1. The double prepositional phrase *mittaḥaṯ*, "from under," is difficult. Dhorme places this word in the first line and believes that a verb *yēḥattû*, "they become terrified," was lost by haplography. Blommerde (*Northwest Semitic Grammar and Job*, p. 103) believes that the *mem* is enclitic and belongs to the last word in the first line. Then he revocalizes MT to *tēḥaṯ*, a third person feminine singular Niphal form of *ḥtt*, "crush." It is followed by a plural subject understood collectively: "the waters and their inhabitants are crushed." Because the scanning of MT is balanced, 8/8, it is kept.

2. The abrupt shift between vv. 4 and 5 suggests that some lines may be missing.

9 *He encloses*[3] *the sight of his throne,*[4]
spreading over[5] *it his cloud mass.*

10 *He marks the horizon*[6] *on the surface of the waters*
at the farthest limits of light and darkness.

11 *The pillars of heaven tremble*
and are astonished at his rebuke.

12 *By his power he stilled the sea;*
by his insight[7] *he smote Rahab.*

13 *By his wind*[8] *the heavens are cleared;*[9]
his hand pierced the fleeing serpent.

3. This is the only instance of the Piel of *'ḥz,* "seize, hold," a common Hebrew verb. But KB, p. 31, lists a root *'āḥaz* II, a loan from Akk. *uḫḫuzu,* "enclosing, framing" or "overlaying with gold or silver." This root is used in Neh. 7:3 for "barring" a gate, and in 1 K. 6:10 it is an architectural term for "joining" beams to a wall.

4. MT *kissēh* appears to be a variant spelling of *kissē',* "throne." Some prefer to take MT as a faulty spelling of *kis'ōh,* "his throne" (see, e.g., Driver-Gray), but the change is not mandatory, for God's throne need not have the possessive pronoun. Dhorme follows Ibn Ezra in considering MT to be an error of vocalization for *keseh,* "full moon": "He obscures the face of the full moon." While this reading is possible, it is not followed because no other heavenly bodies are mentioned in the context. In rejecting this view Gordis points out that *keseh* means specifically "the day of the full moon."

5. MT *paršēz,* an unusual form in Biblical Hebrew, is variously explained. Dhorme thinks that it is a later error arising from a scribal conflation of *pāraś,* "spread," and *pāraz,* "extend." He believes that the original text read *pōrēś,* "unfurling." Another view takes the MT form as a quadriliteral, a *qiṭlel, pirśēś,* which became *paršēz* by dissimilation of the sibilants. Driver-Gray consider this view to be "highly artificial." Therefore, with Budde they prefer to read an infinitive absolute, *pārōś,* "spreading out." The question of the correct form remains open, but the context accepts a meaning of "spread out."

6. The expression *ḥōq-ḥāg,* "he has drawn a boundary circle," is a variation of *beḥûqô ḥûg,* "when he inscribed a circle" (Prov. 8:27). Dhorme and others, with support of LXX, Targ., and Syr., read *ḥaq-ḥug,* "he has traced a circle." Either reading is possible.

7. The Ketib *twbntw* is a scribal error; thus the Qere *tebûnātô,* "his insight," is read. See *BHS*.

8. The preposition *be* on *berûḥô,* "by his wind," may be an error of dittography (Dhorme and Gordis).

9. MT *šiprâ* is variously interpreted. In Aramaic the root means "be fair, beautiful, bright." Driver-Gray translate, "By his wind the heavens are bright." Dhorme, identifying it as a Piel perfect, takes it is a cognate of Arab. *safara,* "to shine" and "to sweep": "*His* breath has swept the heavens." Gordis vocalizes the verb as a Piel, *šipperâ,* and argues that it is a cognate of Akk. *šuparruru,* "spread out (a canopy)." He translates the line, "His breath stretched out the heavens." Thus this language refers to God's original creative act. Working with the account of Marduk's defeating the sea monster Tiamat by means of a mighty wind and a net (*ANET,* p. 67), Pope finds a relationship between *šiprâ* and Akk. *saparu,* "net"; he then divides *šmym,* "heavens," into *śm ym* to yield: "By his wind he put the Sea in a bag." While Pope gains a fine reading, the textual changes are radical. In the light of this uncertainty MT is followed, and the Aramaic meaning is assigned to the word, which in this meteorological context connotes "be clear."

14 *Lo, these are the outskirts of his ways;*
how faint a whisper we hear of him;
but the thunder of his power[10] *who can understand?"*

5, 6 God, the Creator, has complete mastery over the realm of the dead, referred to by three names, *waters (mayim), Sheol,* and *Abaddon (ʾᵃḇaddôn).*[11] Sheol was thought to lie under the ocean and to be a murky, watery abode. Its inhabitants eked out a wretched, meager existence. They are called *shades (rᵉpāʾîm),*[12] for while they have existence and identity, they are weak and helpless. Even though Sheol is far away (11:8), dark (17:13), and sealed (7:9), no one can hide from God there. *Sheol is naked before him,* i.e., God knows all that happens there. Since there is no hiding from God in Sheol, its inhabitants tremble in dread of his presence.

7 God, like a sheikh pitching a tent, created the world. *He stretches out the north over the* watery *chaos* (cf. 9:8). And he *hangs the earth* over the great void. A casual reading of this verse suggests the most abstract account of creation found in the OT. Thus Buttenwieser comments: "Our author, though naturally ignorant of the law of gravitation, had outgrown the naive view of his age about the universe, and conceived of the earth as a heavenly body floating in space, like the sun, moon, and stars." Although this description does appear to coincide rather well with a contemporary understanding of space, the worldview behind the imagery must be interpreted from the author's perspective. *north (ṣāpôn)* in this context is not a direction but a spatial term for the high heavens, the place of God's throne.[13] Standing

10. Either the Qere *gᵉḇûrōṯāyw,* "his mighty deeds," or the Ketib *gᵉḇûrāṯô,* "his power, strength," is possible. The versions support the Ketib, so it is read.

11. The noun *ʾᵃḇaddôn* may be derived from the root *ʾāḇaḏ,* "perish," thus meaning "the destruction." It is joined with "death" (*māweṯ;* 31:12) and is paralleled with "grave" (*qeḇer;* Ps. 88:11 [Eng. 12]). In Rev. 9:11 the name appears as *Apollyon.* There it is the name of the angel of the bottomless pit.

12. In the OT Heb. *rᵉpāʾîm* has two distinct uses. It sometimes refers to an ethnic group, possibly of tall stature, that occupied Canaan before the Israelites (Deut. 2:10–11, 20–21; 1 Chr. 20:4, 6, 8). Its second use is in reference to the dead. Ugaritic texts have shed new light on this meaning of the term. The Canaanites and the Phoenicians called the dead *rpʾm.* This name has recently been related to the root *rpʾ,* "heal." J. de Moor ("*Rāpiʾūma*—Rephaim," *ZAW* 88 [1976] 323–45) thinks that it was an honorific title, "healers, saviors," first used by the mighty living and later attributed to the dead men of eminence. It was carried over into Hebrew, but it eventually became embarrassing to call the dead "healers." Consequently, the root meaning was transferred from *rpʾ* to *rph,* "sink, drop, relax," i.e., "the feeble ones." The interchange of *lamed-ʾalep* and *lamed-he* verbs is not infrequent. If this view is valid, the parallel in this verse may juxtapose two classes that occupy Sheol: the noble, *rᵉpāʾîm,* and the masses, *šōḵᵉnêhem,* "their inhabitants" (cf. 3:19). Cf. R. Schnell, "Rephaim," *IDB,* IV:35; S. Parker, "Rephaim," *IDBS,* p. 739; C. L'Heureux, "The Ugaritic and Biblical Rephaim," *HTR* 67 (1974) 265–74.

13. Cf. J. Roberts, "*Ṣāpôn* in Job 26:7," *Bib* 56 (1975) 554–57. Cf. also P. Reymond, *L'eau, sa vie, et sa signification dans l'Ancien Testament,* VTSup 6 (Leiden: Brill, 1958), pp. 15, 175–76.

after the verb *stretch out (nāṭâ),* it occurs in place of the usual term "heavens" (e.g., 9:8; Isa. 40:22). This position is further supported by the fact that *earth,* which is often coupled with or parallel to "heavens" (e.g., Gen. 1:1; Isa. 44:23, 24), here stands parallel to *north.* In Ugaritic mythology the north was the place where the divine assembly gathered, and Mount Saphon (mountain of the north) was the dwelling place of Baal, the chief god. Borrowing from this imagery, some OT passages use the term *the north* to refer to the place where God reigns supreme (e.g., Ps. 48:3 [Eng. 2]). In Isa. 14:13–14 it is clear that "the north" is used symbolically, not geographically, for God's habitation. In this passage then *the north,* the highest height, is the opposite of Sheol and Abaddon (v. 6), the lowest depths.

Above the watery *chaos* (*tōhû;* cf. Gen. 1:2), God pitched his tent, the sky or the firmament (cf. Job 9:8). From the edges of the tent's roof or the sky, he hung the earth over *nothing (beli-mâ),*[14] i.e., over the vast ocean depths. In a sense the floor of God's tent, the earth, is being pictured as a disk or a plate floating on the deep. Although floating on these deep waters, the land mass is securely supported by being tied to the heavens.

8 Under the heavenly canopy God does many wonders. Amazingly he *binds (ṣōrēr)*[15] some of *the waters in thick clouds (ʿāḇîm),*[16] as one stores wine in a wineskin. But the *cloud mass (ʿānān)* does not *burst* or split open under the great weight of the water. God protects the earth from being inundated by a cloudburst.

9 God *encloses the sight of his throne* in a *cloud mass* (*ʿānān;* cf. Ps. 97:2). Since no creature can behold his glory and live, for it is too brilliant and awesome, these clouds protect his creatures from being consumed by the glory.

10 At the end of the sea's waters God drew a boundary line, the horizon, to divide the light from the darkness. The horizon is located at *the farthest limits.* This line divides the light that shines on the cosmos from the darkness that inhabits the watery chaos.

11 Whenever God appears in anger, *the pillars of heaven,* possibly the distant mountains on the horizon that support the huge canopy of the sky, shake violently.[17] The phrase *at his rebuke (geʿārâ)*[18] describes God's com-

14. Apparently *beli-mâ* is a poetic compound meaning "not anything, nothing."

15. Heb. *ṣōrēr* means "tie or bind" something or "shut in." It is used with wineskins in Josh. 9:4 and with clouds in Prov. 30:4b.

16. R. Scott ("Meteorological Phenomena and Terminology," *ZAW* 64 [1952] 23–25) defines *ʿāḇ* as "a distant cloud," a rain cloud or thunderhead, and *ʿānān* as "a dense cloud cover," such as fog or mist. The latter may also refer to dust-filled air caused by strong winds.

17. Cf. Jörg Jeremias, *Theophanie,* WMANT 10 (Neukirchen-Vluyn: Neukirchener, 1965), pp. 67–68.

18. Cf. A. Caquot, *"gāʿar," TDOT,* III:51–53.

mand to bring into subjection those cosmic forces hostile to his rule. In Ps. 18:16 (Eng. 15) par. 2 Sam. 22:16 his rebuke is expressed in "a blast of the breath of [his] nostrils." The same picture is found in the phrase "by his wind" in v. 13a. Often God expresses his rebuke by a strong blast of wind (Isa. 50:2; Nah. 1:3–4) or by a loud thunderclap (cf. Ps. 104:7). This imagery alludes to the cosmic conflict in which Yahweh, the divine warrior, comes in a storm and defeats his ancient foe, the sea *(yām),* and its chief inhabitant, the fleeing serpent (cf. Job 9:13; Isa. 27:1).[19]

12, 13 By his awesome power God *stilled* or quieted *(rāgaʿ)*[20] *the sea.* And in his insight *he smote Rahab.* Rahab is the embodiment of all evil forces. God *pierced the fleeing serpent (nāḥāš bārîaḥ),* possibly an epithet of Rahab,[21] *with his* own *hand.* Then a blast from God's nostrils clears the heavens of all dark clouds. This spectacular display of power in the heavens demonstrated to all that God reigns supreme. Evil is defeated. Peace is insured.

God overcame these foes *by his power* and *by his insight* (v. 12), even *by his wind* and *his hand* (v. 13). These words for God's instruments in defeating his foes are chiastically arranged: God's power (v. 12a) is visible in his hand (v. 13b), and his insight or wisdom (v. 12b) is manifest in his wind or breath (v. 13a). Usually in ancient Near Eastern mythologies the god of wisdom is distinguished from the god of power.[22] Because these two qualities do not exist in a single god of the pantheon, there is no god that is able to accomplish his full intentions. In contrast, the God of Scripture possesses both qualities supremely. There is no other cosmic being that is his equal in any way.

14 The mighty acts of God are merely *the outskirts* or the ex-

19. The themes found in vv. 11–13 allude to the popular motif in ancient Near Eastern myths that recount the god of order defeating in mortal combat the god(s) of chaos. In "Enuma Elish" Marduk assaults Tiamat, the deep sea. He extends her mouth with a blast of wind and then shoots an arrow into her chambers, mortally wounding her (*ANET,* pp. 66–67). In Ugaritic mythology Baal fights in mortal combat his potent enemy Yamm, the Sea (*ANET,* pp. 130–31). The OT borrows this mythical language to depict God's complete mastery over all forces, cosmic and terrestrial.

20. Interestingly Heb. *rāgaʿ* means both "stir up" (Isa. 51:15) and "be at rest, quiet" (e.g., Jer. 50:34). The idea here seems to be "to quiet" another by force.

21. The creature *nāḥāš bārîaḥ,* "the fleeing serpent," appears in Isa. 27:1: "In that day Yahweh with his hard and great and strong sword will punish Leviathan, the fleeing serpent, Leviathan, the twisting serpent, and he will slay the dragon that is in the sea." This passage appears in an Ugaritic text (*UT,* 67:I:1–4). In Isa. 27:1 the context suggests that the battle is God's final one before he restores his people Israel as a glorious nation. This imagery of the dragon is used in Rev. 12:3.

22. Cf. Y. Kaufmann, *The Religion of Israel,* tr. and abridged by M. Greenberg (New York: Schocken, repr. 1972), pp. 33–34.

tremities *of his ways.*[23] In a theophany a person hears but *a whisper* of God's ways. If the wonders of creation are far too marvelous for mankind to comprehend, it is just as impossible for a human being to comprehend *the thunder of his power*. At best a human being catches only a glimpse of God's marvelous ways.

Often in his speeches Job recites hymnic lines in praise of God. They encourage his faith in God. This time his meditation on God's majestic power as seen in creation and his defeat of the cosmic foes foreshadows Yahweh's appearing out of the whirlwind (chs. 38–41).

c. Job's Confidence and His Wish (27:1–10)

(1) An Avowal of Innocence (27:1–6)

1 *Job continued his discourse, saying,*
2 *"As God lives, who has denied my right,*
Shaddai, who has made my soul bitter,
3 *as long as*[1] *my breath is in me*
and God's spirit is in my nostrils,
4 *my lips will never speak false testimony,*
nor my tongue utter deceit.[2]
5 *Far be it from me that I should admit that you are right;*
until I die I shall not deny my integrity.[3]
6 *I hold fast my righteousness, and will not let it go;*
my conscience does not reproach me for any of my days."[4]

1 This heading seems to be secondary, for it differs from the standard introduction to the other speeches in the dialogue and it is similar to the one that introduces Job's oath of innocence (29:1). It is much more appropriate as a heading to that portion, for it indicates that Job's avowal of innocence stands outside the dialogue.[5] It was put here secondarily to indicate that Job continues to speak because Zophar remained silent.

23. Dahood ("Some Northwest Semitic Words in Job," *Bib* 38 [1957] 306–20) has argued from Ugaritic evidence that Ugar. *drkt* and Heb. *derek̲* both mean "dominion." But such a meaning is not necessary here.

1. On *kî kol-ʿôd̲,* "as long as," cf. GKC, § 128e; Gordis.

2. The double triad to describe a human being in vv. 2–4 reflects great artistic skill: "soul" (v. 2b), "breath" (v. 3a), and "spirit" (v. 3b) along with "nose" (v. 3b), "lips" (v. 4a), and "tongue" (v. 4b).

3. The second line is a little long. The omission of *mimmenî,* "from me," with LXX and Duhm would restore balance to the line (9/9 syllable count), but as Dhorme notes, *ḥāsîr* calls for *mimmenî* as a complement.

4. MT *miyyāmāy,* "my days," is variously rendered: "as long as I live" (Blommerde, *Northwest Semitic Grammar,* pp. 103–104), "(any) of my days" (Driver-Gray).

5. Cf. the discussion on pp. 24–26 above.

2–4 Job resolutely affirms his innocence with a complex oath. It opens with an oath formula (v. 2a, c), expanded by an accusation against God contained in a relative clause (v. 2b–2d), plus a parenthetical statement that God is the source of his life (v. 3), and then the oath proper asserting that he has not lied at all in his affirmations of innocence (v. 4). Typically Job swears by the confession that *God lives,* i.e., God, being alive, will confirm his oath. Should his sworn statement prove false, God will activate the curse on Job. Daringly Job adds a complaint against God after the opening formula. He accuses the very God by whom he swears of two offenses: God *has denied* or set aside *(hēsîr)*[6] his right, and Shaddai has made his soul bitter.[7] Since God has refused to answer his pleas to resolve his case, he has had to cope with resentment against God welling up within himself. These words suggest that two views of God are struggling against each other in Job's thinking: God his accuser and God the source of justice. Job is pitting God against himself in a mighty effort to compel God to answer his complaint. Both his contention and his wishful hope of resolution are with this same God. Here he abandons any hope for a third party to come to his aid (cf. 9:33–34).

3 Job acknowledges parenthetically that it is the living God who has given him the breath of life (cf. Gen. 2:7; Isa. 42:5). God both imparts life to the body and sustains that life. In this statement Job acknowledges his complete dependence on God. At the same time he believes that God, by reason of the fact that he is the giver of life, is obligated to judge each person justly, including Job. Job's double confidence—in his own integrity and in God's fidelity to justice—moves him to speak so brazenly.

4 Finally Job arrives at the oath itself. The line opens with an untranslated *ʾim.* The *ʾim* implies an imprecation: "May God curse me if I do such a thing." Job swears, *my lips will never speak false testimony* (*ʿawlâ;* cf. 6:30). Nor will he *utter (hāgâ)*[8] any guileful *deceit* (*rᵉmîyâ;* cf.. 13:7) to win his case. In the Wisdom tradition he who controlled his tongue was considered self-controlled and upright. Therefore, Job expresses his conviction about his own innocence in the strongest language. Both Job's resolve and his use of an oath pave the way for his final oath of innocence (ch. 31).

5 With an exclamatory oath Job rejects the counsel of his friends.

6. Dhorme interprets the Hiphil of *sûr* to mean "to set aside." The perfect verbs in v. 2 underscore the certainty of Job's accusation.

7. A complaint of Job throughout is that God has made his soul bitter: 7:11; 10:1; cf. 3:20; 21:25.

8. Heb. *hāgâ,* "utter," means "meditate" or "murmur," hence "devise." In ancient times thinking was usually done verbally, a person talking softly to himself. The thought being mulled over could be either distressing circumstances or hopeful dreams. Therefore, this word means both "meditate" and "moan."

This is another type of oath formula: *Far be it from me . . . until I die*. This oath is less foreboding than that in vv. 2–4, for it is grounded in Job's own fate rather than in God's being. As H. H. Rowley observes, "There is something sacrilegious or profane in the idea that is repudiated. . . . Job declares that to admit that the friends' charges were true would be a violation of his duty to God." Also, he will not deny his own *integrity (tummāṯî)*. The foundation of Job's faith in God is his personal conviction that he has been blameless in his relations with God and human beings. This verse is a direct allusion to 2:3, in which God confesses Job's integrity after his losses (cf. 2:9; 31:6). If Job would concede to the friends that he was suffering for some wrong he had committed, he would destroy the central fiber of his stalwart moral character, for he would be seeking their approval by speaking a lie.

6 Job backs up his oaths with a firm resolution. He will hold tenaciously to his *righteousness (ṣᵉḏāqâ)*. He will not relax his grip on it for a single moment. He can be so determined because his *conscience* (lit. "heart," *lēḇāḇ*) does not reproach him for a misdeed done in *any of my days*. Not a single day's memory torments his thinking with regret. His conscience is clear.

(2) An Imprecation against the Enemies (27:7–10)

7 *"Let my enemy be like the wicked,*
and my opponent like the unjust.
8 *For what hope has the godless when he is cut off,*[1]
when God despoils[2] *his life?*
9 *Will God hear his cry*
when distress comes on him?
10 *Will he take delight in Shaddai?*
Will he call on God at all times?"

The content of vv. 7–10 seems out of place in the mouth of Job. One would not expect him to curse his enemy after asserting his innocence. Also, the identity of the enemy stands in question. Is the enemy God, the friends, or those who heap reproach on him? Since praying for deliverance from an

1. Heb. *bṣʿ* means "cut off" in Piel and "gain by extortion or violence" in Qal. Since most apply the former meaning in this line, they revocalize it as a Piel, *yᵉḇaṣṣēaʿ*, or a Pual, *yᵉḇuṣṣāʿ* (Driver-Gray). Gordis interprets the Qal as intransitive, "he is cut off," which seems the best alternative.

2. There are many suggested readings for MT *yēšel*. It may be read as *yāšōl* from the root *šll*, "take as prey." This forms a good parallel to *bṣʿ* (see n.1 above). This interpretation has the strongest internal support and is accepted. Another suggestion interprets *yēšel* as defective writing for *yišʾal*, "When God asks for his life" (Duhm, Budde). Or it may be an error for *yiśśāʾ lᵉ*, "[when] he lifts (his soul) to (God)," i.e., "prays" (Dhorme, Fohrer).

enemy is an essential component of a personal psalm of lament, these words may be Job's. Either the author is using standard formulas or the identification of the enemy is left intentionally vague in order to emphasize that Job is requesting complete deliverance from all hostility. Job feels not only that he must be proved innocent, but also that all enmity against him must be removed.

7 After affirming his innocence Job prays that *my enemy* may be punished like *the wicked* (cf. 8:22). He wants them to be afflicted by the fate they deserve instead of enjoying life and heaping reproach on him. This wish is expressed with another type of oath formula: *y*ᵉ*hî k*ᵉ . . . *'ōy*ᵉ*ḇî,* "let my enemy be like. . . ." It is a curse uttered against an opponent.

8 The imprecatory wish in v. 7 is supported by general truths about the wicked in vv. 8–10. Verse 8 is the most difficult to interpret, for there are multiple options for the two verbs *cut off (yiḇṣaʿ)* and *despoil (yēšel).*[3] It seems best to understand the line as saying that a godless person has no hope, for God will despoil his very *life.*

9, 10 When *distress* comes on the evildoer as punishment, he may cry out to God for help, but God will not hear his cry. God refuses to deliver him because such a person calls on God solely to get out of a desperate condition. That person will experience the full brunt of the misfortune designed to punish him, for he has no intention of delighting in God by doing his will. Only those with a broken spirit have a genuine hope of deliverance from God (cf. Ps. 86:1–3).

d. Job's Intent to Instruct the Friends (27:11–12)

11 *"I will teach you about God's power;*
I shall not conceal that which concerns[1] *Shaddai.*
12 *Behold, all of you have seen it;*
why do you speak so vainly?"

11 Here Job adopts an instructive disposition similar to the style of his friends.[2] He will instruct them about *God's power (yāḏ),* particularly as it is

3. One could also interpret the verse: "What is the hope of the profane? For he will be cut off when he prays to God." Cf. Tur-Sinai.

1. The preposition *ʿim,* lit. "with," bears the concept, "What is in one's mind?" (Dhorme and Gordis).

2. The location of vv. 11–12 is uncertain. V. 12 is unquestionably an utterance of Job, for the second masculine plural form appears four times, the form Job uses for addressing the friends. The friends, of course, employ second person singular forms. V. 12 fits well with v. 11 by reason of content and the use of the second person plural form in v. 11a. While v. 12 may possibly stand as a heading to the Wisdom poem found in ch. 28, it emphasizes the power of God more than God's wisdom, so it is better to keep them with Job's speech. Still, some of the original text seems to be missing, for these lines end abruptly.

expressed in afflicting punishment. In his teaching he will not *conceal (kiḥēḏ)* anything that concerns Shaddai (cf. 15:18). He will speak the truth, the whole counsel of God. He will not cover up any discrepancies between reality and dogma with his rhetoric.

12 Since the friends have seen God's power and purpose, Job wonders why they speak so vainly. In his opinion their discourses have been futile and unreliable.[3] Job thus concludes with a final and full rejection of his friends' wisdom.

AIM

In his last speech of the dialogue Job sings the praises of God's glorious might and affirms once again, with even more determination, his own uprightness. His sublime view of God impels him to continue reaching out to God as the one who will restore his honor, even though God himself appears to be the cause of his bitter affliction. His genuine faith is grounded in his conviction that God is just and merciful despite the evidence to the contrary. The other pillar that keeps his faith from being swallowed up by fear is his assurance that he is blameless. In using an oath form to assert his integrity he has come close to his final course of action, swearing an avowal of innocence (ch. 31). Then out of distress, hoping to end his agony, Job prays that the causes of his affliction, personified as an enemy, will be defeated by the mighty God who defeats all his foes. Job's firm resolve thus paves the way for his avowal of innocence coming in his next speech (chs. 29–31).

3. The placing of the noun before the verb as cognate accusative intensifies the concept of futility (GKC, §§ 117p, q).

IV. HYMN TO WISDOM (28:1–28)

Here is a magnificent hymn in praise of wisdom.[1] Wisdom is extolled as the noblest divine trait.[2] God knows wisdom fully and employs it in all of his ways, but its abode is hidden from mankind.

This hymn consists of three pericopes plus a conclusion: human skill in mining technology (vv. 1–11); wisdom's value, beyond purchase (vv. 12–19); God's knowledge of wisdom (vv. 20–27); wisdom for mankind (v. 28).

This hymn comes at the end of the disturbed third cycle. Since its abstract, reflective tone does not match well any of the speakers, it is taken to be a piece that stands outside the dialogue. It functions as a bridge between the dialogue and the groups of speeches that are coming.

A. HUMAN SKILL IN MINING TECHNOLOGY (28:1–11)

1 *There[1] is a mine[2] for silver*

1. Cf. P. Zerafa, *The Wisdom of God in the Book of Job* (Rome: Herder, 1978), esp. pp. 126–84; G. von Rad, *Wisdom in Israel,* tr. J. D. Martin (Nashville: Abingdon, 1972), pp. 144–57; G. Fohrer, *TDNT,* VII:476–96; N. Habel, "Of Things beyond Me: Wisdom in the Book of Job," *Currents in Theology and Missions* 10 (1983) 142–54; J. Lévêque, *Job et son Dieu* (Paris: Gabalda, 1970), II:593–679. For more on the critical issues of this hymn see the Introduction, pp. 26–27.

2. In this hymn there exists a tension between wisdom as a self-existing entity and as a personification of one of God's attributes. Many understand that wisdom is coexistent with God. But when this hymn is interpreted in comparison with other texts in which wisdom is personified, esp. Prov. 3:19–20; 8:22–31 (cf. Sir. 1:1–10), it can be seen that vv. 23–24 teach that God brought forth wisdom and determined its essence, employing it in his creation of the world. This wisdom has no existence independent of God.

1. The opening *kî,* "because," leads many to postulate that some lines preceded this verse. Duhm thinks that a refrain like that in v. 12 and v. 20 stood before v. 1, but if that were so, it would lessen the impact of the refrain. According to Gordis, however, Heb. *kî* is functioning as an introductory particle with asseverative force ("surely"). Such a *kî* stands at the head of a poem in Isa. 15:1; cf. Josh. 22:34. Ugaritic usage also supports this use of *kî;* cf. *UT,* p. 416 no. 1184. Possibly the *kî* works in conjunction with the *waw* of v. 12. The former introduces things accessible, the latter things inaccessible.

2. MT *môṣāʾ* means lit. "a place of going out"; it is taken from the root *yṣʾ* ("go

and a place where gold is refined.[3]

2 *Iron is taken*[4] *from the dust;*
a stone[5] *is poured out*[6] *as copper.*[7]

3 *Man puts*[8] *an end to darkness;*
and he searches every recess
for a stone in the thick darkness.[9]

4 *He sinks a shaft*[10] *far away from habitation,*[11]
places forgotten by the foot of man;
hanging far from men they sway back and forth.[12]

---

out") rather than the root *mṣ*ʾ ("find"). It refers to the source of a spring (2 K. 2:21) or the place of the sunrise (Ps. 65:9 [Eng. 8]). But if this word comes from the root *mṣ*ʾ, it means "a place where something is found." But it would then more likely be written *mimṣāʾ*; see P. Joüon, *Bib* 11 (1930) 23.

3. MT *yāzōqqû* is from the root *zqq*, cognate with Akk. *zaqāqu*, "blow" (Pope). Thus it means "to refine" with fire as in Mal. 3:3; cf. Ps. 12:7 (Eng. 6).

4. MT *yuqqāḥ*, "taken," may be a Qal passive imperfect.

5. Heb. *ʾeḇen*, "stone," usually feminine, is masculine here (cf. Isa. 60:17).

6. MT *yāṣûq* may be a Qal passive participle of *yṣq*, "pour, cast," or a Qal imperfect of *ṣûq* II, "pour out, melt." Others read either a Hophal *yûṣaq* from *yāṣaq*, "is smelted" (Fohrer), or a Niphal *yiṣṣôq* from *ṣûq*, "one smelts" (Duhm). Since the picture is that the rock is turned into a metal, the verb is read as a Qal passive participle.

7. The form *nᵉḥûšâ*, "copper," is a secondary accusative of a product: "They melt a stone into copper" (GKC, §§ 117ii, 121d).

8. The subject of *śām*, "put," is indefinite. Budde supplies a word for "man," either *ʾĕnôš* or *ʾāḏām*. Although a subject is necessary for the English translation, there is no strong reason to supply a word in the Hebrew text.

9. Gordis takes v. 3c as part of v. 4 to gain two distichs and to eliminate the tristich. This is a good suggestion, but it lacks textual support, and the third line can be taken as balancing the first line of v. 3.

10. MT *mēʿim-gār*, lit. "from with the sojourner," is very difficult, as attested by the wide variety in both ancient versions and modern English translations. Dhorme modifies the line in this way: he takes the *m* with *naḥal*, "wadi, shaft," and revocalizes MT *ʿim*, "with," as *ʿam*, "people," and MT *gār*, "sojourners," as *gēr*, "foreigner": *nᵉḥālîm ʿam gēr*, "A foreign people (has pierced) shafts." Gordis suggests interpreting *gār* as "crater," on the basis of Arab. *jawra*, "deep hole," and *mēʿim* as "from within": "A channel from the crater." L. Waterman ("Notes on Job 28:4," *JBL* 71 [1952] 167–70) reads *nᵉḥālîm ʿam nēr:* "The people of the lamp break open passageways." He takes "the people of the lamp" as an epithet for miners; such an identification of personnel is needed in the passage. M. Dick ("Job xxviii 4: a new translation," *VT* 29 [1979] 216–21) revocalizes the consonantal text to gain this translation: "An excavation is carved out by the foreign work-force, Stooped over by disease/Nergal, Weakened from illness, they stagger about." The reference to suffering in this reading has the advantage of tying the hymn into the rest of the book, but it is strange that there is no other reference to suffering in the hymn. Dhorme's suggestion is accepted as the simplest.

11. The various words for riverbeds throughout this pericope are interpreted as technical terms for mining shafts; cf. vv. 4, 10, 11.

12. The third line is obscure. This picture appears to be that of men hanging and swinging dangerously either from ropes or in suspended cages as they work in a vertical shaft.

5 *The earth, from which comes stone,*[13]
below is turned as by[14] *fire,*
6 *a place*[15] *where its stones are lapis lazuli;*
its dust contains gold.
7 *The path no bird of prey*[16] *knows,*
no falcon's[17] *eye has spied;*
8 *proud beasts have not set foot on it;*
no lion has passed over it.
9 *Man assaults the flint stone;*
he overturns the mountains by their roots.[18]
10 *In the rocks he hews out channels;*
his eye has seen every precious thing.
11 *He searches*[19] *the sources of*[20] *the rivers*
and brings hidden things[21] *to light.*[22]

This hymn praises human technical skill as illustrated in the amazing process of mining.[23] This laudation of human ability is set against the key ques-

13. MT is lit. "earth, from which comes food," a strange image in this context. It may be a fine picture for mining operations in a cultivated land, but it is unlikely for desolate places like Sinai. Perhaps the first line needs to be understood differently. Thus Gordis takes *leḥem* to mean "heat," not "bread": "It is a land from which heat pours forth." From another direction Andersen suggests reading MT *lḥm* as *lûḥ,* "stone (-tablet)," plus enclitic *mem.* This last suggestion is tentatively accepted.

14. The preposition *k*^{e}*mô,* "like," is taken as equivalent to a substantive (GKC, § 118w): "As it were by fire." It is easier, however, to read *b*^{e}*mô,* "by"; the confusion of *b* and *k* is likely in the archaic Hebrew script.

15. It is best to take MT *m*^{e}*qôm,* "a place," as in construct to the clause *sappîr ʾ*^{a}*ḇāneyhâ,* with the relative conjunction *ʾ*^{a}*šer* understood: "a place—its stones are lapis lazuli" (Gordis). A similar construction appears in 18:21.

16. Heb. *ʿayiṭ,* "bird of prey," comes from a root meaning "scream, shriek."

17. Heb. *ʾayyâ* means a "hawk, falcon, kite" (BDB, p. 17). This word may be onomatopoeic for the call the bird makes (KB, p. 38).

18. Blommerde (*Northwest Semitic Grammar and Job,* p. 106) transfers the *m* on *miššōreš,* lit. "from the root," to the preceding verb as an enclitic *mem* and renders *hāpaḵ-m,* "he overturns."

19. MT *ḥibbēš* may be a dialectal variation of Heb. *ḥippēś,* "search" (Pope; Blommerde, *Northwest Semitic Grammar and Job,* pp. 106–107). Gordis, however, accepts the usual meaning of *ḥibbēš,* "bind": "He binds up the springs of the rivers."

20. MT *mibb*^{e}*ḵî,* "from weeping, trickling," is best read as *mabb*^{e}*ḵê,* "sources of." This reading is supported by Ugar. *mbk nhrm* (*UT,* 51:IV:21), "the source (or spring) of the rivers." Cf. H. L. Ginsberg, "The Ugaritic Texts and Textual Criticism," *JBL* 62 (1943) 111; G. Landes, "The Fountain at Jazer," *BASOR* 144 (Dec. 1956) 32; Pope; Blommerde, *Northwest Semitic Grammar and Job,* p. 107.

21. The *mappiq* in the final *h* of *taʿ*^{a}*lumāh,* "her hidden things," is for euphony, if correct. Many (e.g., Dhorme, Fohrer, *BHS*) do not accept it.

22. MT *ʾôr,* "light," is an adverbial accusative (Blommerde, *Northwest Semitic Grammar and Job,* p. 107).

23. This passage is the only treatment of mining found in the OT. According to

tion—"Where can wisdom be found?"—that heads the two central pericopes. The theme in this section is that man has amazing creative ability to discover the gems hidden deep in the earth. As Habel (OTL) keenly observes, "The mining process is a paradigm for probing a mystery in the natural domain which parallels probing wisdom at a deeper level in the cosmic domain."

1, 2 Men skillfully apply their extensive technical ability to mine ores and refine them, expressing the wonder of human ingenuity.[24] They sink shafts into the mountainside to find precious minerals. Out of the earth's bowels they take valued ores like *silver* and *gold,* as well as the more common ones like *iron* and *copper* that are essential for making tools and other vessels. And smelters have the know-how to extract metals from these ores.[25]

3 With torches or lamps the miner *puts an end to darkness,* the supposed abode of evil spirits, and *searches every recess for a* (precious) *stone in the thick darkness* (*ʾōpel wᵉṣalmāweṯ;* cf. 10:22). Miners do not fear to penetrate into the foreboding darkness of the earth's interior, the underworld, the abode of the dead (cf. 10:21–22) in search of treasures. Though men probe to the edge or limit *(taḵlîṯ),* wisdom lies beyond (cf. 11:6–9).

4 Since the civilized nations thirsted for these raw materials, mining expeditions were organized to go to desolate places far from habitation in quest of precious metals. For example, from ancient times the Egyptians undertook mining expeditions into the Sinai Peninsula, a sparsely inhabited wilderness with an austere climate. There the intense heat and the dry winds, combined with the scarcity of water, made survival next to impossible. Under these severe working conditions scores of men lost their lives. That is why the miners were usually slaves or conscripted gangs. In those distant places the miners sunk tunnels into the earth.[26] Sometimes they worked in

---

Deut. 8:9, Canaan was a land of iron and copper. Deposits of iron were found in the Transjordan, and copper came from Edom and the region of Ezion-geber. But overall Canaan was poor in minerals. Asia Minor was particularly rich in silver, while gold was abundant in Nubia and South Arabia. Small quantities of gold, however, were discovered in the Sinai Peninsula.

24. A close tie exists between v. 1 and v. 12, because of the similarity between *môṣāʾ* (v. 1a) and *timmāṣēʾ* (v. 12a) and the use of *māqôm* in both verses (v. 1b and v. 12b).

25. Verses 1 and 2 stand parallel to each other: v. 1a and v. 2a speak of mining and v. 1b and v. 2b consider the refining process. Assonance also ties these verses together.

26. Knowledge of ancient mining technology is not extensive. Three techniques are known: (1) open cast mining—a kind of stone quarrying technique in which the miner looked for copper-rich nodules in the alluvial surface of the wadi; (2) horizontal gallery mining extending into the white sandstone layers; and (3) deep shaft mining. Extensive mining goes back to the Chalcolithic period (6000–5000 B.C.). It has been discovered that

vertical shafts, hanging from ropes. They swayed back and forth precariously as they labored to dislodge the minerals from the side of the shaft.

5 Under the earth the hard ground had to be assaulted in order to tear away its rich minerals. In some mining processes a large fire was built on a platform to heat the wall of the tunnel. When the rock became hot, water was poured on it, causing the stone to crack. The miners would then rake up the fallen stones and carry them to the surface.[27]

6 Precious stones are also brought forth from the earth's bowels. Two of these stones are *lapis lazuli,* a deep dark blue stone, and *gold.*[28] In the ancient Near East lapis lazuli was highly prized, being used in jewelry like cylinder seals. Sometimes it even was accepted as tribute.[29]

7, 8 Mankind's technical skill evidenced in mining reveals his superiority over all earthly creatures. Amazingly none of the animals with all their prowess can discover the path to such beautiful gems. The *falcon* and the *lion,*[30] two magnificent creatures that dominate the sky and the land respectively, are representative of all animals. The falcon is known for its keen eyesight. From lofty heights it surveys the land, spots its prey, and swoops down on it. But it never detects the hidden path to these minerals. On the ground the stately lion stalks about, taking whatever prey it wants. It is called a *proud beast* because of its unusual strength and its lack of fear. Even though it is lord over a large area, it is absent from these mines and has no interest in them.

9–11 To uncover these hidden treasures miners vigorously attack the mountains. They *assault*[31] *the flint stone* as they carve out tunnels to

---

at Timna and later in the 14th–12th centuries B.C., Egyptian and Midianite miners honeycombed the area with vertical shafts reaching to a depth of over a hundred feet, at which point they intersected with a horizontal tunnel(s). Those galleries apparently could be entered only from the vertical shafts; see S. Singer, "From These Hills . . . ," *Biblical Archaeology Review* 4/2 (1978) 16–25. Cf. B. Rothenberg, *Were These King Solomon's Mines?* (New York: Stein and Day, 1972); and R. Forbes, *Studies in Ancient Technology,* VII (Leiden: Brill, 1963).

27. Cf. L. Waterman, "Notes on Job 28:4," *JBL* 71 (1952) 167–70.

28. Gordis points out that sapphire was not known until Roman times and that this word for gold could refer to iron pyrites, often found in lapis lazuli.

29. E.g., texts 17.383 and 17.422 in *PRU,* IV:221–25.

30. Instead of reading *šaḥal* as "lion," S. Mowinckel (*"šaḥal,"* in *Hebrew and Semitic Studies,* Fest. G. R. Driver, ed. D. Thomas and W. McHardy [Oxford: Clarendon, 1963], p. 97) translates it "lizard"; cf. Ps. 91:13. He points out that in Semitic thought a connection exists between the lion and the serpent; e.g., the serpent griffon on Marduk's temple at Nippur is a composite of features of the lion and the serpent. He then argues that the word here may designate the serpent dragon that is found in mythology (for a discussion see Pope). This is an intriguing suggestion, but this word for "lion," *šaḥal,* is chosen to parallel *šaḥaṣ,* "proud," in the first line.

31. Heb. *šālaḥ yāḏ bᵉ*, lit. "send a hand to," means "assault." It suggests an act

reach the ore. Their work makes it appear that they *overturn the mountains by their roots*. Earlier in a hymn of praise Job recounted that God overturns the mountains, causing them to quake and tremble before his presence (9:5). Here human beings, acting somewhat like God in their search for treasures, are not afraid to shake the mountains, which were considered eternal and often associated with the dwelling place of the gods.[32] Mining thus attests mankind's daring bravery.

Miners cut a series of *channels (yᵉʾōrîm)*[33] in the mountainside. In the singular this Hebrew word refers to the Nile, and in the plural it stands for the tributaries of the Nile in the Delta. In this context it functions as a technical term for mining shafts. The miner enters the earth through these paths, and his eye sees precious treasures. He penetrates even to *the sources of the rivers,* the springs deep within the earth, in hopes of finding precious gems. Truly, human beings have vast knowledge and great technical skills.

B. WISDOM'S VALUE, BEYOND PURCHASE (28:12–19)

12 *But[1] where can wisdom be found?*
Where is the place of understanding?
13 *Man does not know its abode,[2]*
and it is not found in the land of the living.
14 *The deep[3] says, "It is not in me,"*
and the sea says, "It is not with me."

---

of aggression; cf. Esth. 2:21. This translation is supported by the parallel word *hāpaḵ*, "overturn."

32. E.g., in Ugaritic mythology El, the patriarch deity, makes his abode at the source of the depths.

33. Possibly the words "Nile, canals" *(yᵉʾōrîm)* and "rivers" *(nᵉhārôṯ)* mean channels for water. The ancient miners are reported to have dammed up water in order to use it to help them remove rocks from their shafts. Gordis interprets v. 10a as the miners' hewing out a channel to wash away rocks that stand in the way and v. 11a as their damming up the flow of water in order to reach their goal deep in the earth.

1. The *waw* has adversative force (GKC, § 163a).

2. MT *ʿerkāh,* "its price," seems out of place, for the theme of wisdom's price is not developed until vv. 15–19. A word for "place" or "way" is more desirable by reason of the place references in vv. 12–14. Thus many (e.g., Duhm, Dhorme, Fohrer) emend MT to *darkāh,* "its way," with support of LXX. Gordis, however, argues that *ʿerkāh* means "place" on the basis that *maʿărāḵâ* means "row" (Exod. 39:37) and "battle line" (1 Sam. 4:2). Dahood and Pope interpret MT to mean "house" based on the parallel *ʿrk/bt* in Ugaritic (12:3–4 in J. Nougayrol, et al., eds., *Ugaritica,* V [Paris: Imprimerie Nationale, 1968]; cf. Dahood, "Hebrew-Ugaritic Lexicography VII," *Bib* 50 [1969] 355). The latter is followed, for no emendation is required and there is good Northwest Semitic support.

3. Heb. *tᵉhôm* is generally a feminine noun, but it functions here and in Jon. 2:6 (Eng. 5); Hab. 3:10; Ps. 42:8 (Eng. 7) as a masculine noun.

15 *It cannot be gotten with solid gold,*[4]
and its price cannot be weighed in silver.
16 *It cannot be bought*[5] *with the gold*[6] *of Ophir,*
with precious onyx[7] *or lapis lazuli.*
17 *Neither gold nor glass*[8] *can equal it,*
nor vessels of fine gold[9] *be its exchange.*
18 *Coral*[10] *and crystal*[11] *are not worth mention;*
wisdom's price[12] *is above rubies.*[13]
19 *The topaz of Ethiopia*[14] *cannot equal it;*
it cannot be bought with pure gold.

12 The refrain heads this section: *But where can wisdom be found? Where is the place of understanding?* This double question, which obsesses human beings even though it is unanswerable, is the nucleus of the chapter. *Wisdom (ḥoḵmâ)* is paralleled by *understanding* or insight *(bînâ),* as often in the Wisdom literature (e.g., Prov. 1:2; 4:5, 7; 9:10; Isa. 11:2). Given the human drive to control the world, mankind is strongly allured by the power of

4. MT *s^e^gôr* is generally taken as poetically short for *zāhāḇ sāgûr,* like Akk. *ḫurāṣu sagru,* "solid gold, gold bullion." The different words for gold relate either to the quality of the metal or to the place of origin.

5. The Hebrew root *slh* appears to be a by-form of *slʾ* (Lam. 4:2) and refers to "weighing, putting in a balance," which was how value was determined and items were bought and sold. It may be related to Heb. *sal,* "basket."

6. Heb. *keṯem* is derived from the Egyptian designation for Nubia, a land rich in gold. From the 20th Dynasty in Egypt the expression *nb-n-ktm,* "gold of Ktm," was well known (Pope).

7. Tur-Sinai relates Heb. *šōham* to Akk. *sāmtu.* LXX reads "onyx" and Syr. "beryl." But Dhorme suggests that *šōham* means "carnelian," for it is frequently mentioned with lapis lazuli. The precise identification of this jewel remains in doubt.

8. The word for "glass" *(z^e^ḵôḵîṯ)* comes from the root *zkk,* "clear," because, of course, glass is translucent.

9. Heb. *paz* means "refined, pure gold" (BDB, p. 808).

10. The word translated "coral" *(rāʾmôṯ)* appears in Ugaritic for pectoral ornaments.

11. Pope thinks that *gāḇîš* is related to Arab. *jibs,* "gypsum." It may be a shortened form of *ʾelgāḇîš,* "hail," i.e., hard, clear stone. In Akkadian *algamešu* means steatite or a soft stone easy to carve (*Chicago Assyrian Dictionary,* ed. I. J. Gelb, et al. [Chicago: Oriental Institute, 1964], I/1:337–38).

12. Heb. *mešeḵ,* from the root *mšk,* "draw, drag," is variously interpreted. Perhaps the imagery is that of drawing up oysters for pearls from the sea. Driver-Gray take it to mean "price" (cf. Prov. 31:10) with the extended meaning of "precious"; cf. Ps. 126:6, "precious seed" (AV).

13. Heb. *p^e^nînîm* is usually understood as "pearls." Pope suggests the meaning "rubies," for in Lam. 4:7 this gem has a reddish color.

14. MT *piṭdaṯ-kûš* is probably "yellow chrysolite" from Zabarqad, an island off the Egyptian coast, according to Pope. He mentions that Pliny (*Nat. Hist.* 27.9) called it Topaz Island.

wisdom. But its abode lies safely beyond the distant frontiers where human beings can make an entrance. No human being can bring wisdom into his own service.

13, 14 In spite of humanity's great technical genius and research skills, no one knows where wisdom has its abode. The way to wisdom is untraceable and inaccessible. Its dwelling place is neither *in the land of the living* nor *in the sea (yām). The deep [tᵉhôm] says, "It is not with me."* The *deep* is the lowest part of the sea where the entrance to the chambers of the dead was thought to be. In pushing back the boundary between light and darkness (v. 3), mankind is penetrating beyond the land of the living into the region of chaos. Nevertheless, not even in that remote place will he ever find wisdom, for it does not reside in these dark recesses.

15–19 Some people, of course, would presume that if wisdom could not be found by exploration it could be purchased with the great wealth gained from their mining operations.[15] But mankind does not realize that wisdom outweighs all earthly jewels and metals. These highly valued objects prove worthless in the marketplace of wisdom. No amount of precious metals or priceless jewels can purchase wisdom.[16] There is not enough *solid gold (sᵉg̱ôr)* or *silver* to be weighed against its price. Nor will the fine *gold [keṯem] of Ophir* balance the scales. Unfortunately the location of Ophir is unknown. Speculation as to its location includes Elam, Africa, and even India.

Wisdom also cannot be bought *with precious onyx or lapis lazuli* or with treasured *vessels of gold* or *glass. Onyx (šōham)* is one of the products of the land of Havilah, possibly located in southern Arabia (Gen. 2:12). It was used in the breastplate of the high priest (Exod. 28:20), and it could be engraved (Exod. 28:9). Tur-Sinai thinks that it is a stone of either purple or dark gray color. *Glass,* i.e., glass vessels, were highly valued in the ancient world. Egypt and later Phoenicia were famous for their glassware. *Vessels of fine gold (paz)* were also valuable both for their metal and for their artistic work. No amount of these riches, however, suffices to be used in exchange for wisdom.

Coral (rā'môṯ), crystal (gāḇîš), and *rubies (pᵉnînîm)* are so far beneath wisdom's value that they are not even *worth mention.* The coast surrounding the Sinai Peninsula is particularly noted for its beautiful corals. But when wisdom is mentioned, these stunning objects do not even come to mind. Neither does the price of wisdom's acquisition compare to highly

15. Budde and many others consider vv. 15–19 as an insertion. But LXX omits only vv. 14–16, so it does not support the elimination of vv. 15–19. In favor of retaining these verses is the fact that they balance vv. 1–2 and vv. 6–7 respectively.

16. In Proverbs wisdom is also prized above silver, gold, rubies, and all precious gems (Prov. 3:14–16; 8:10–11, 19; 16:16).

prized crystal or rubies. The last two precious stones in this list, *topaz of Ethiopia (piṭḏaṯ-kûš)* and *pure gold (keṯem ṭāhôr),* also fail to equal wisdom's value. No amount of precious metals or gems can ever be collected in order to purchase wisdom.

C. GOD'S KNOWLEDGE OF WISDOM (28:20–27)

20 *From where does wisdom come?*
Where is the place of understanding?
21 *It is concealed from the eyes of all living,*
even[1] hidden from the birds of the sky;
22 *Abaddon and Death say,*
"We have heard a report of it in our hearing."
23 *God understands the way to it;*
he knows its place,
24 *for he looks to the end of the earth,*
and he sees under the whole heavens.[2]
25 *When he allotted weight to the wind*
and set the measure of the waters,
26 *when he made a decree for the rain*
and a way for the thunderstorm,
27 *then he saw it and appraised[3] it;*
and he discerned[4] it and searched it.

20–22 At the head of this pericope stands the refrain: *From where does wisdom come?*[5] Since wisdom is transcendent, it does not reside anywhere on earth or in the depths of the sea. No eye of any living creature[6] has beheld it. Not even *the birds,* which soar high above the earth's surface, have caught a glimpse of it. The remote regions of *Abaddon (ʾaḇaddôn)*[7] and

1. Many omit the first *waw* with LXX, Syr., Vulg., but that may result from a translation preference, not from a different text. The syllable count of 9/9 favors keeping it.

2. Hakam understands *kol-haššāmayim,* "all the heavens," as referring to "the heaven of heavens," i.e., the highest heaven.

3. Heb. *sippēr* means "recount, rehearse," and in Ps. 22:18 (Eng. 17) it means "count exactly, accurately" (BDB, p. 708).

4. Heb. *hēḵîn* means "establish, set up, prepare," and can mean "arrange, set in order" (Gordis). There is no need to emend it to *heḇînāh,* "he understands it," with some mss. and Duhm, Pope.

5. There is one variation between v. 20 and v. 12: *tāḇôʾ*, "it will come," is used here in place of *timmāṣēʾ*, "it will be found." P. Zerafa (*The Wisdom of God in the Book of Job* [Rome: Herder, 1978], p. 146) suggests that the former reflects human inability to find wisdom while the latter refers to the human inability of acquiring it.

6. The term "all living" *(kol-ḥay)* includes both people and animals, but it refers esp. to people (12:10; 30:23; Ps. 143:2; 145:16; Rowley).

7. On Abaddon, see 26:6.

Death, which were thought to be located in the depths of the sea, can only say, "We have heard a report of it." Although no one, living or dead, has ever seen wisdom, all know intuitively that it exists.

23, 24 *God,* however, *understands the way to wisdom* and *he knows its* dwelling *place.* Since God's field of view encompasses the entire universe, including the remotest corners, he knows wisdom's abode. In knowing wisdom's place, God is its master. Wisdom, so to speak, discloses to him the deepest secrets of the universe. God, in contrast to man, *sees* everything *under the whole heavens.*

25, 26 God's employment of wisdom in structuring the world is amazingly evident in four mysterious forces: *the wind, the waters, the rain,* and *the thunderstorm.* Although the wind cannot be seen or held, God has assigned it *weight (mišqāl).*[8] At times the wind blows lightly, refreshing the earth. Then at God's command it gusts violently, inflicting great destruction. Furthermore, the vast, seemingly measureless waters of the oceans have been precisely measured by God (cf. Isa. 40:12). The sea, even in all its ferocity, is under God's complete control. Similarly, the sending of the rain reveals God's full understanding. God has *made a decree* or statute *(ḥōq)*[9] *for the rain.* He determines both the season for the rain to water the earth and the amount of water that is to fall. The rain must obey his decree; e.g., it may not inundate the earth. More amazing is that God made *a way for the* violent *thunderstorm (ḥᵃzîz qōlôṯ).*[10] Though the lightning jumps about in a zigzag course, God has charted the course for its forks to travel, and he has prepared the way for the roll of thunder. These marvels of nature demonstrate that God has structured the world order in wisdom.

27 God *saw (rāʾâ)* wisdom and *appraised [sippēr] it.* Verily he *discerned [hēḵîn] it* and *searched [ḥāqar] it* out. That is, from the beginning God determined wisdom's essence.[11] Knowing fully its value, he set up wisdom as his counselor (cf. Prov. 8:22–31). This means that wisdom played a vital role in creation. During his creative work God searched out wisdom's marvelous ability. Creation was a great adventure for God, as he

8. Heb. *mišqāl* means "the proper weight" (Gordis).

9. Heb. *ḥōq,* normally translated "statute," means here "limit." In 38:25, where the idea of this line is reiterated, *teʿālâ,* "a conduit or watercourse," stands in place of *ḥōq.* In Jer. 5:22 *ḥōq* is parallel to *gᵉḇûl,* "border." Pope suggests that with rain it could mean "groove," i.e., the rain falls in prescribed patterns.

10. Heb. *ḥāzîz* means "a cumulus cloud, a thunderhead." Heb. *qōlôṯ,* in the plural, means "thunderclaps" (Dhorme).

11. This language includes the idea that God created wisdom, according to von Rad (*Wisdom in Israel,* p. 147). Conversely, S. Harris ("Wisdom or creation: a new interpretation of Job 28:27," *VT* 33 [1983] 419–27) finds creation as the object of these verbs. But that would elevate creation to prominence, whereas the hymn is concerned with wisdom.

tested wisdom's capacity. But his use of wisdom did not stop there. He continues to employ it fully in his governance of the universe. As a result, the world is filled with wonders and is governed in justice. Wisdom is God's closest companion.

D. WISDOM FOR MANKIND (28:28)

28 *But he said to man,*[1]
"Behold, the fear of God[2] *is wisdom,*
and turning from evil is understanding."[3]

Although human beings cannot discover the way to wisdom, they can find wisdom by fearing God. God reveals wisdom to mankind *(ʾāḏām)*[4] as he wills. Wisdom for human beings has two foci: *the fear of God* and *turning from evil.* Fear is the proper human response in the presence of the Holy God. A person bows in contrition, committing himself to follow God's way. As he acknowledges his own limitations and God's greatness, he enters into communion with God. Desirous of God's favor he wills to shun all evil. This twofold attitude enables a person to grow in wisdom. That is, a human being increases in wisdom primarily by obedience to God, not by investigation into the unknown.

It is important to note the significant grammatical difference in the treatment of the word *wisdom* in this verse. Up to this point "wisdom" has

1. Although this heading is a prosaic postscript, Gordis points out that it can be considered an anacrusis, as evidence from other texts suggests (e.g., Ps. 1:1, 4; Prov. 4:4). Thus this introductory statement must not be surrendered too easily.

2. The word for "God" here is *ʾaḏōnāy,* "Lord." Since this is its only occurrence in the book of Job, it is suspect. The phrase in the OT is usually "the fear of Yahweh" (e.g., Prov. 1:7). The author of Job, however, avoids the use of the divine name Yahweh (cf. the problem in 12:9). Usually he uses the phrase "the fear of God" (*ʾĕlōhîm;* 1:1, 8; 2:3). But here he may have used *ʾaḏōnāy* to call to the reader's mind God's name Yahweh without explicitly using that name (cf. Habel, OTL).

3. Verse 28 is set off by a prosaic introduction and the lines are out of balance (9/6). Therefore, many (e.g., Duhm, Driver-Gray, Hölscher, Dhorme, Pope) consider it a later addition. Perhaps the author had included a closing similar to MT that became harmonized through the centuries to the standard expression of this theme. Nevertheless, he may have set this verse off from the rest of the hymn for emphasis. Although on the surface this verse appears to counter the theme of the inaccessibility of wisdom in the first 27 verses of this chapter, its content fits well with the book; it forms an inclusio with the opening characterization of Job in 1:1 (cf. Habel, OTL, p. 393), and it connects with the last concluding statement offered by Elihu (37:24). Gordis observes that the introduction, being an anacrusis, stands outside the meter. Surely this verse should not be dismissed too readily.

4. In another direction Tur-Sinai takes the word "man" *(ʾāḏām)* to mean the first man, Adam. Since allusion is made to creation, he sees that God gave the first man wisdom.

had the definite article, but in this verse it is without it. Since the same word is used, the wisdom available to mankind is qualitatively the same as that which God knows. The fact that this word is without the article indicates that it is the practical side of wisdom human beings may acquire.[5]

AIM

This masterful hymn in praise of wisdom marks the end of the dialogue. It judges the efforts of the comforters to teach Job wisdom as a failure. While they have faithfully adhered to the tradition of the fathers, they have misinterpreted Job's specific case and failed to offer him any insight into God's amazing ways in regard to his affliction. While Job has questioned the traditional wisdom, he remains without any significant insight into the mystery of how God is acting wisely in his sufferings.

Wisdom resides with God alone. It permeates all of his creative work. In mankind it finds expression in his amazing technical genius. But human ingenuity cannot find wisdom. Neither can all the wealth that man can wrestle from the earth purchase it. Wisdom for mankind can only be discovered in a devout relationship with God. Therefore, this hymn authenticates Job's turning away from his comforters to petition God directly. It is telling him that he will receive genuine insight into his suffering when God himself speaks to him. Thus this hymn prepares Job for Yahweh's appearing. More specifically, it indicates the approach that Yahweh will take in his discourses. He will address Job's lament by recounting the wise and marvelous way he has created the world. Thereby he will demonstrate that Job's suffering does not discount the truth that he rules the world wisely and justly. The only response Job can then make to Yahweh's discourse will be to fear Yahweh. In this manner the hymn links the opening characterization of Job as "one who feared God and shunned evil" (1:1, 8; 2:3) with his submissive response to Yahweh's word in the end (42:1–6).

Job's experience verifies the concluding principle of this hymn that a human being finds true wisdom only in fearing God. This wisdom is a spiritual wisdom that transcends human knowledge, but that does not mean that it is irrational. The converse is true. It is intelligible, for it is the portal into the vast resources of God's wisdom. That is why Yahweh can dialogue with Job and offer him insight into his own wonderful ways. Beyond the limits of his reason, though, a person can contemplate the mystery and the wonder of wisdom. In the words of von Rad, wisdom is "the divine mystery of creation."[1]

5. Cf. Gordis, "Special Note 24," p. 539; Habel, OTL, p. 401.

1. G. von Rad, *Wisdom in Israel*, p. 148.

V. JOB'S AVOWAL OF INNOCENCE (29:1–31:40)

Job has decided how he will rest his case. He takes a daring step in a final attempt to clear himself. He swears an avowal of innocence. His oath forces the issue, for the oath compels God either to clear him or to activate the curses. Even if God continues to remain silent, that would be an answer, for if the curses Job utters are not activated, the entire community would be convinced that Job is innocent. So after swearing this avowal of innocence, Job will sit in silence, awaiting God's answer.

This avowal of innocence consists of three distinct parts: Job's remembrance of his former abundant life (ch. 29), a lament (ch. 30), and an oath of innocence (ch. 31). The author has composed a wonderful piece by stretching the structure of a psalm of lament. At the beginning he has placed Job's reminiscence of his past glory (ch. 29). And at the conclusion he has elaborately expanded an oath of innocence, an element that appears in some psalms of lament (e.g., Ps. 7:4–6 [Eng. 3–5]; 17:3, 5).[1] The entire speech may be labeled an avowal of innocence. The oath of innocence is the focal point of the avowal, for by it Job demands from God a legal judgment on his character. The remembrance portrays by contrast the depth of Job's affliction as expressed in the lament. These two elements also reveal Job's motivation for uttering the oath. And the lament seeks to move God to respond compassionately to Job's oath. In Westermann's words, Job is "simultaneously a supplicant and an initiator of a legal proceeding."[2]

The author is drawing on legal customs of his day and molding them with the genre of the psalm of lament. In the ancient Near East a person who was suffering economically or personally from the accusations of another person, even though his accuser refused to file a formal complaint, could initiate a trial demanding that the plaintiff present the evidence that he had against him (cf. 1 Sam. 12:3).[3] In such a circumstance the defendant might

1. M. Dick ("Legal Metaphor in Job 31," *CBQ* 41 [1979] 48–49) argues that the oath takes the place of the plea for help, a central element in psalms of lament.

2. Westermann, *Structure of the Book of Job*, p. 39.

3. See M. Dick, op. cit., p. 42.

swear an oath in order to prove to the public that he was guiltless, an effort also designed to force the hand of his accuser. In the ancient world this was a fairly common practice.[4] In so doing, the accused placed himself in God's hand to decide his fate by either activating or staying the curse.[5] In taking this step Job is passionately seeking vindication. While the lament conveys the depth of Job's sorrow and expresses his yearning for God's favor, the oath reveals his undergirding confidence that God will acknowledge his integrity. If Job did not have that confidence, his oath would be the height of folly. But in bold faith Job appeals to God's compassion through the lament and to his justice through the oath.

In the structure of the book Job's avowal of innocence balances his first speech, the curse-lament (ch. 3). The curse-lament heads the dialogue, and the avowal heads the set of speeches from Elihu and Yahweh. Since Job addresses God in both speeches, neither of them functions as a soliloquy. Rather they set the tone for the speeches that follow them. In these two speeches Job expresses his strongest convictions. The curse-lament reveals the depth of his despair at his misfortune, while the avowal of innocence is his firmest statement of conviction that he is innocent. The curse-lament troubles the three comforters and moves them to exhort Job to repent, while the avowal is so strong that it silences the friends as it places the issue of Job's integrity squarely with God. After this speech only God could give an answer.

A. JOB'S REMEMBRANCE OF HIS FORMER ABUNDANT LIFE (29:1–25)

Job begins his avowal of innocence with a detailed description of his former stature in the community.[1] Then he had intimate fellowship with God. The community recognized God's favor in his life and showed him their highest respect. But Job did not rest in his glory; he diligently helped the poor and

4. For such a practice, cf. Exod. 22:7, 10–11 (Eng. 8, 11–12); 1 K. 8:31–32; 2 Chr. 6:22–23; Code of Hammurabi, §§ 8, 103, 106, 107, 249, 266 (*ANET*, pp. 170, 176, 177).

5. An analogous incident in the OT is David's being accused of plotting harm against King Saul (1 Sam. 24:8–22). In speaking to Saul, David asserts his innocence and requests Yahweh to decide between them: "Know and see that there is no evil or treason in my hand; I have not sinned against you though you are hunting my life to take it. May Yahweh judge between me and you. May Yahweh avenge me on you" (vv. 11b–12a). So confronted, Saul concedes his wrong: "You are more righteous than I, you have done good to me, but I have wronged you" (v. 17).

1. For an analysis of the grammar of these three chapters see A. Ceresko, *Job 29–31 in the Light of Northwest Semitic*, BibOr 36 (Rome: Pontifical Biblical Institute, 1980).

unfortunate. Confident that he pleased God, he looked for a long, prosperous life. This remembrance serves to portray the depth of his shame as he will express it in his lament (ch. 30).

The five sections of this chapter are God's rich blessing (vv. 1–6); the respect Job commanded (vv. 7–10); Job's striving for justice (vv. 11–19); Job's hope for a long, blessed life (vv. 19–20); and the most respected elder (vv. 21–25).

1. GOD'S RICH BLESSING (29:1–6)

1 *Job resumed his discourse.*
2 *"O that it were for me as in*[1] *the former months,*
as in the days when[2] *God watched over me,*
3 *when he made his lamp shine*[3] *above my head,*
when I walked in darkness by his light,
4 *when I was in the prime of my life,*
when God was an intimate in[4] *my tent,*
5 *when Shaddai was still with me,*
my children around me,
6 *when my steps were bathed in curds,*
and the rock poured out streams of oil for me."[5]

1 The introductory formula sets off these three chapters from the previous two chapters (chs. 27–28), which in their present position appear to be a part of Job's last speech in the dialogue. The introductory formula is the same as that for ch. 27. If either of these formulas is secondary, it would more likely be the one attached to ch. 27, for that chapter comes in a greatly disordered section. Here the introductory formula indicates that Job continues to speak,

1. This is a pregnant use of the preposition *kᵉ;* it means "after the manner of the months," i.e., "as in the months" (GKC, §§ 118s, u).

2. This is an example of a noun in construct before a relative clause (GKC, § 130d).

3. Possibly MT *bᵉhillô* is a Qal infinitive construct with the suffix anticipating the following subject (GKC, §§ 131k, o). It seems better to read a Hiphil form, *bahᵃhillô,* or a contraction, *bahillô,* "when he made it to shine" (so Dhorme, Gordis).

4. MT *bᵉsôḏ* is variously interpreted. Many, like Duhm, emend it to *bᵉsôḵ,* "when God protected." But Pope thinks that the root is *ysd,* "find, establish," and the correct reading is *bîsôḏ,* "when God founded." Gordis, however, postulates that the word is a verbal form of Heb. *sôḏ,* "close friend, intimacy," as found in Ps. 2:2 and 31:14 (Eng. 13): "When God was an intimate in my tent" (cf. 15:8a). Assonance connects this word with *bᵉʿôḏ,* "as yet," in v. 5a.

5. The preposition *ʿimmāḏî,* "for me," appears to overload the line. But since Job is applying this thought to his own former situation, it is best to keep this reading until there is further textual support for a change. Gordis posits that in some instances the concluding line to a pericope may be longer.

but that he is taking a different direction. It thus marks off Job's avowal of innocence from the dialogue.

2 Job begins his avowal of innocence by remembering his former glory. He characterizes those days as a time when God nourished and protected his life. The phrase *God watched [šāmar] over me* describes God's special care for and protection of his own servant (cf. Num. 6:24–26; Ps. 91:11; 121:7–8). In a grateful manner Job acknowledges that God, not his own wisdom and shrewdness, had been the source of his wealth. Job never lets his pride lead him to make the claim that he had been the genius behind his success. His conviction about God's blessing keeps his lament focused on the real cause of his pain, a ruptured relationship with God. Since he never abandons his gratitude for God's past favor, his lament flows from real hurt.

3 God had set *his lamp* to shine above Job's head. Light is a symbol of blessing and success (Ps. 36:10 [Eng. 9]; 18:29 [Eng. 28]). Healing and joy attend its shining.[6] When Job faced *darkness* or difficult circumstances God's *light* gave him direction and the courage to pursue the right course. As God showed Job the way, Job obeyed by walking in it.

4, 5 Prior to his misfortune Job believed that he had reached *the prime of life* (lit. "his own harvest," *ḥōrep*),[7] the time in his life when he would fully enjoy the abundance of his labor. *An intimate* in his tent, God was present with Job, giving him counsel and protection. God fully accepted his servant, for his presence is the highest blessing he bestows on a person.[8] Job was also filled with happiness at the sound of *his children* playing about his dwelling.[9] The children themselves were a concrete sign of God's blessing (cf. Ps. 128:3).

6 Job's household was filled with abundance. An abundance of *curds* and *oil* symbolize a rich, affluent life. Job's flocks produced such an abundance of *curds,* a staple food, that figuratively speaking he had the luxury of washing his feet in thick cream.[10] His olive trees produced such a

6. For the opposite picture, cf. Job 18:5–6; 21:17.

7. While Heb. *ḥōrep* means "autumn," the season of ripe fruit, Pope demonstrates that the root *ḥrp* means "be early, young" in Akkadian and Arabic. Then he argues that this root was used for the autumn in an era when the calendar began in that season. The emphasis then falls on the blessing of maturity, not on the state of decline just before the end.

8. Cf. Exod. 3:12; Josh. 1:5, 9.

9. Heb. *naʿar* covers a wide age range, from a small child to a grown man. Thus Job could be using this word even for his grown children. From his fatherly perspective he remembered them as still being young. It is doubtful that the term refers to his servants, for any wealthy noble had numerous servants, but children were viewed as a special blessing from God.

10. Cf. Deut. 32:13–14; 33:24; Ps. 81:17 (Eng. 16).

great yield that *the rock poured out streams of oil for* Job. This imagery refers either to the olive trees growing on the rocky hillside or to the olive presses, made out of stone and set up in the orchards, flowing with oil. Olive oil was a vital product for the ancients. They used it for cooking, for fuel in their lamps, and as an ointment for the body.

2. THE RESPECT JOB COMMANDED (29:7–10)

7 *"When I went through the gates[1] of[2] the city[3]*
and took[4] my seat in the square,
8 *youths saw me and kept out of sight,*
the old men rose[5] to their feet,
9 *princes refrained from talking*
and put their hands over their mouths;
10 *the voices of the nobles were hushed,[6]*
and their tongues stuck to the roof of their mouths."

7–10 Job was accustomed to go through the city gate to the square to fellowship with the elders. The broad place outside the main city gate was the hub of the ancient city. It was the area of business and government. On outspread blankets merchants displayed their wares. There the citizens gathered to discuss the news and exchange ideas. The elders also assembled there for conversation and to make decisions. At almost any time a group of citizens could be assembled as a jury headed by an elder, acting as judge, to

1. LXX reads *šaḥar,* "morning," for MT *šaʿar,* "gate." Interestingly the Qumran Targ. preserves both readings: "morning(s) in the gates of the city" (Pope). Thus the variant reading is quite ancient. While either reading is possible, the context gives a slight edge to *šaʿar.*

2. The preposition *ʿalê* is taken to mean "from," as in Moabite and Phoenician (Dahood, "Northwest Semitic Philology and Job," p. 68; Pope). Perhaps an easier explanation is offered by Hakam. Since from such a spot one could look over the whole city, the phrase "over the city" became idiomatically associated with the gate, emphasizing its strategic importance in relationship to the entire city.

3. The word for city, *qereṯ,* is a form of the Phoenician word *qiryâ.* It is used in Hebrew as a synonym for *ʿîr,* "city," esp. in poetry.

4. The imperfect verb after an infinitive phrase is taken as under the government of the preposition (GKC, § 114r; Driver, *Hebrew Tenses,* §§ 117–18).

5. The lack of a conjunction before MT *ʿāmāḏû,* "they stood," is forceful and idiomatic (Driver-Gray).

6. Heb. *ḥāḇāʾ*, "withdraw, hide," may have the extended meaning "be hushed" (Pope). Others believe that the text was corrupted by influence from v. 8a and suggest reading *neʾĕlam,* "be dumb" (Budde), or *niḵlāʾ*, "be restrained" (Duhm, Driver-Gray). Pope's view is accepted to avoid emendation. Also, this verb is plural because it is attracted to the plural genitive (GKC, § 146a) or perhaps because *qôl,* "voice(s)," is to be taken as a collective.

rule on a matter of dispute. From this practice grew the expression that justice took place in the gate (cf. Amos 5:15).

When Job, the noblest elder, entered the city square, he was accorded the greatest deference. Out of respect *youths* ceased playing and hid while *the old men* rose and stood silently. The *princes* or the officials *(śārîm) of the city* likewise ceased speaking as they raised a hand to their mouths to signal silence in the assembly. *Nobles (nᵉgîḏîm),* those who had positions of authority in the government or in the army, also *hushed* their speaking. Their esteem for Job is caught by the phrase *their tongues stuck to the roof of their mouths.*[7] Job was accorded the highest honor as he took his seat in the town square.

3. JOB'S STRIVING FOR JUSTICE (29:11–17)

11 *"Indeed,[1] when the ear heard, it blessed me,*
and when the eye saw, it commended me,
12 *because I rescued the poor who cried,*
and the orphan who[2] had no one to help.
13 *The blessing of the destitute came to me,*
and the widow's heart I made sing with joy.
14 *I put on righteousness and it clothed me,*
and the justice I practiced was like a robe and a turban.
15 *I was eyes to the blind,*
and feet to the lame was I.
16 *I was a father to the needy;*
the case of one I did not know I investigated.
17 *I broke[3] the fangs of the wicked man*
and snatched the prey from his teeth."

11, 12 Whoever heard about Job *blessed* him, and those who saw him *commended* him. Job is claiming that the high respect he was given was due to his zealous pursuit of righteousness. He showed mercy toward the afflicted. When he heard the poor and the orphan crying for help, he came to their aid. Patriarchal religion (and ancient Near Eastern society) taught that

7. This phrase expresses complete silence, sometimes resulting from the loss of strength under affliction (cf. Ezek. 3:26; Ps. 137:6). This idiom may also denote extreme thirst (Lam. 4:4; Ps. 22:16 [Eng. 15]).

1. The conjunction *kî* at the beginning of both v. 11 and v. 12 is troublesome. Duhm and Hölscher delete the first one. But Gordis reads the first as an asseverative, "indeed."

2. The *waw* on *wᵉlōʾ* is attested by the versions. It is most likely the explicative *waw* (GKC, § 154a n. 1).

3. The cohortative *wāʾašabbᵉrâ,* "and I broke," conveys the impression of determined resolve.

widows, orphans, and the poor—the powerless members of society—came under God's special concern.[4] When the wicked lorded it over them and the wealthy enriched themselves at their expense,[5] the only weapons these poor had were their pleas to God for help. They were too poor to take any legal recourse against these oppressors. Consequently, the mark of a righteous person was that he heard the cries of these miserable creatures and acted to rescue them.[6] Job affirms that he had been faithful to that standard like the ideal king described in Ps. 72:12: "For he delivers the needy who cry and the afflicted who have no one to help."

13 The one who was *destitute* (*ʾōḇēḏ*), i.e., one who was at the point of perishing from deplorable living conditions, blessed Job. Also, Job's help for the widow inspired her *heart* to hum a tune joyfully. That is, he reached out to meet the deepest needs of those who were forlorn and thereby restored their sense of worth. The fundamental spiritual law, that in giving one receives, was evident in Job's life. He gave joy and received blessing.

14 Job clothed himself with *righteousness,* and in turn righteous activity clothed him.[7] The justice he practiced enveloped him like a mantle and a turban. The *robe* or mantle (*meʿîl*) was a garment worn on dress occasions, and the *turban* (*ṣānîp̱*) symbolized one's status, e.g., that of a king (Isa. 62:3) or a high priest (Zech. 3:5). While Job presided as elder his clothes witnessed to his complete commitment to justice. Indeed, Job implanted these qualities deep within himself so that they controlled his words and decisions.

15, 16 Job's righteous disposition expressed itself in deeds of mercy to the handicapped and the unfortunate. He was *eyes to the blind* and *feet to the lame.*[8] That is, he did things for the handicapped that they were unable to do for themselves. Like *a father* Job reached out *to the needy.* He assisted in supplying whatever they lacked. *the case of one I did not know I investigated.* When someone he did not know was indicted, he took up his case. A stranger was particularly vulnerable to persecution in a foreign city. When

4. In the epilogue to his code of laws, Hammurabi says of his actions: "Hammurabi, the lord, who is like a real father to the people, bestirred himself for the word of Marduk, his lord" (25:20–25; *ANET,* p. 178; cf. Isa. 22:21; Ps. 68:6 [Eng. 5]). In an inscription Kilamuwa states: "I, Kilamuwa, the son of Hayya, sat upon the throne of my father. . . . I, however, to some I was a father. To some I was a mother. To some I was a brother" (*ANET,* p. 500). Afterward Kilamuwa describes his deeds to provide possessions for the desolate poor.

5. Cf. Ps. 10:2, 9–10; 37:14; Isa. 3:14–15.

6. Cf. Ps. 72:2, 4, 12.

7. Cf. Job 8:22; 40:10; Isa. 59:17; Ps. 132:9, 16, 18: cf. Isa. 11:5.

8. "The blind" (*ʿiwwēr*) and "the lame" (*pissēaḥ*) are often coupled in the OT; e.g., Lev. 21:18; Deut. 15:21; 2 Sam. 5:6, 8; Jer. 31:8.

something wrong or unusual happened, people quickly pointed accusingly at a stranger. Often the courts were organized so that the rich, powerful leaders could get a quick judgment against the poor and the alien in order to enhance their own wealth. To ensure a favorable decision the wealthy prejudiced the court by bribing the judge. But instead of listening to the prejudicial complaints against a stranger, Job carefully *investigated* the matter in order to render a just decision. When he had gathered the facts, he defended that person.

17 Job went a step further. He not only helped the oppressed; he also sought to break the power of the oppressors. He wanted both to deprive these scoundrels of their spoil and to put them out of commission. The cruel harshness with which these charlatans afflicted the unfortunate is captured by the word *fangs*. They acted like fierce animals, ravaging their weak prey. Job, however, championed the cause of the abused, *broke the fangs of the wicked,* and *snatched the prey from his teeth.*

4. JOB'S HOPE FOR A LONG, BLESSED LIFE (29:18–20)

18 *"I thought, 'I shall expire with my family,*[1]
and I shall multiply my days[2] *like sand;*
19 *my roots will spread out to the water,*
and the dew will lie all night on my branches;
20 *my liver will be fresh within me,*
my bow ever new in my hand.' "

18 Because of God's blessing and because of his energetic pursuit of the highest standard of justice, Job had believed that God would give him a long life: *I shall multiply my days* in numbers to equal *the sand.*[3] Secure in the

1. Heb. *qēn,* lit. "nest," may refer to one's household or family (cf. Deut. 32:11; Isa. 16:2).

2. Blommerde (*Bib* 55 [1974] 550–51) revocalizes *yāmîm,* "days," to *yammîm,* "seas," and argues that "the sand . . . of the seas" is an example of a broken construct chain.

3. The crux of this verse is the identification of MT *ḥôl* in the second line. The Masoretes of Nehardea read *ḥûl,* which Gordis explains either as a change in vocalization to distinguish this noun from the common Heb. *ḥôl,* "sand," or simply as a phonetic variant. LXX reads *phoínix,* which in this context means "palm tree." The combination of these factors plus the parallel with "nest" has led many, even quite early, to find an allusion to the legend of the rebirth of the phoenix, who rose from the ashes of its nest every 500, 600, or 1461 years. If this interpretation is accepted, then *ḥûl* means "phoenix." This view has been championed by M. Dahood ("Nest and Phoenix in Job 29:18," *Bib* 48 [1967] 542–44; idem, "*Ḥôl* 'Phoenix' in Job 29:18 and in Ugaritic," *CBQ* 36 [1974] 85–88), and it is accepted by Grabbe, *Comparative Philology,* pp. 98–101.

The possibility that the author alluded to this legend gains strength from his

doctrine that obedience to God's law brought long life,[4] he had anticipated that after many good years he would die quietly with his family about him.

19 Because of God's blessing Job had expected to experience abundant blessings, both material and spiritual. He pictures himself as a stalwart tree, a fitting image for the righteous.[5] He believed that his roots were spreading out to a perennial source of water. And in the dry season the nightly dew would refresh his branches.[6] He believed confidently that he could weather any adversity.

20 Job believed that he would have a vigorous life in all aspects. The paralleling of *liver* and *bow* means that he would be strong emotionally and physically. The *liver (kāḇôḏ)* is an organ associated with a person's most intimate feelings.[7] A *fresh liver* means that a sense of well-being permeated his inner being. From within himself he had the resilience to lead the community in the way of righteousness. The *bow (qešeṯ)* signifies manly vigor (Gen. 49:24); thus to have one's bow broken symbolizes that one becomes impotent.[8] Job believed that his bow would be *ever new,* always pliable so that he could continually rely on it to shoot an arrow with force and accuracy. That is, Job looked forward to a vigorous, healthy life and to the growth of his honor and authority in Uz.

5. THE MOST RESPECTED ELDER (29:21–25)

21 *"Men listened to me expectantly*
and kept silent for my counsel.[1]

---

frequent allusions to mythopoetic imagery and from the fact that references to this legend appear in ancient Jewish sources (*Midrash Genesis Rabbah* 19:5; T.B. *Sanhedrin* 108b). Some, e.g., W. F. Albright ("Baal Zephon," in *Festschrift für Alfred Bertholet,* ed. W. Baumgartner, et al. [Tübingen: Mohr, 1950], pp. 3–4), have argued in support of this interpretation by finding a reference to the phoenix in an Ugaritic text. But M. Pope shows the tenuousness of this supposed reading. Although it is quite possible that the author of Job had such a mythical figure in mind, the emphasis on a new life springing from the ashes of death makes this analogy less likely, esp. since Job had rejected any hope of a return to life after his death in chs. 13–14. Therefore, MT *ḥôl* is taken simply to mean "sand."

4. Cf. Deut. 5:30 (Eng. 33); 1 K. 3:14; Prov. 10:27.

5. The righteous are frequently compared to well-watered trees to connote their fresh vitality amidst a harsh or hostile environment (Ps. 1:1–3; Jer. 17:7–8; cf. Ezek. 31:2–9; Job 8:16–17; 14:7–9; and the opposite idea in 18:16).

6. Cf. Gen. 27:28; Hos. 14:6 (Eng. 5); Ps. 133:3 for the importance of dew to agriculture in Palestine.

7. Usually Heb. *kāḇôḏ* is taken to mean "honor," but in this context, which speaks of a continually vigorous life, "liver" is most appropriate and forms a good parallel with "hand" (A. Ceresko, *Job 29–31,* p. 27). Cf. Ps. 16:9: "Therefore my heart is glad; my liver *[keḇôḏî]* rejoices; indeed, my flesh dwells at ease."

8. Cf. Ps. 46:10 (Eng. 9); Jer. 49:35; Hos. 1:5.

1. The tradition alternates between grouping these letters into a single word,

22 *After my word[2] they did not speak;*
my speech fell gently on them.
23 *They waited for me as for rains,*
and they opened their mouths as for the spring rain.
24 *When I smiled on them, they scarcely believed it;*
they did not let the light of my face fall.[3]
25 *I directed their course[4] and sat as chief;*
I dwelt as king among his troops;
I was as one who comforts mourners."

Since the theme about the respect that Job's presence commanded in the community occurs twice, many scholars wish to transpose vv. 21–25 to follow v. 10 (e.g., Budde, Duhm, Dhorme, Fohrer). Although these verses fit that context well, their present location is superior (cf. Kissane, Gordis). They restate the theme for emphasis. The impact they make in their present position is heightened by the contrast they paint between Job's days of glory and his present debased condition that is expressed in the next chapter.

21–23 Job returns to recounting the respect that he received from the community, particularly in the city council, as in vv. 7–10. Although the connection between v. 19 and v. 20 is rough, this pericope underscores Job's former honor and provides a sharp relief to his coming lament (ch. 30).

The community *listened expectantly* to Job's *counsel.*[5] When he spoke, others *kept silent* out of deep respect. They anticipated excitedly that Job's words would point the direction that the community would take. His rhetoric was so insightful that no one dared to oppose him. The manner of his speaking *fell gently* on the people. Through wise, gentle counsel he inspired the community to carry out the right course of action. His words were

---

lᵉmôʿᵃṣāṯî, "by my plan" (so some mss.), or making two words, *lᵉmô ʿᵃṣāṯî,* "for my counsel" (so MT).

2. Most (e.g., Duhm and Driver-Gray) wish to emend *dᵉḇārî,* "my word," to *dabbᵉrî,* "my speaking," but the versions have a noun and that form goes best with the following verb *yišnû,* "they repeated."

3. Though most understand the root of *yappîlûn* to be *nāpal,* "to fall," Gordis offers the interesting interpretation that it is a defective spelling of *yaʾᵃpîlûn,* "they darken"; thus he translates: "They did not darken the light of my countenance." This form may have arisen by the elision of the *ʾalep,* as is frequent in Job, or by the assimilation of *lamed-ʾalep* verbs to the form of the *lamed-yod* verb.

4. A. Ceresko (*Job 29–31,* p. 31) takes MT *bḥr* as a dialectal form of a Northwest Semitic root *bḫr,* "gather, assemble," and *dereḵ* ("course, way") as meaning "dominion, assembly" ("the basis of authority"), and thus arrives at a smoother translation for this clause: "I convoked their assembly." The difficulty with this suggestion is that Ceresko assigns new meanings to two words whose sense is well established.

5. The emphasis in v. 21 falls on Job, for the preposition "to me" *(lî)* stands at the head of the verse.

awaited like the coming of the winter *rains* to water the dry earth. The community drank wisdom from them just as the ground gladly absorbs *the spring rain,* i.e., the latter rains which bring the maturing crops to a full harvest.[6]

24 At the appropriate moment Job *smiled* on the people. His expression of warmth and blessing so delighted them that they *scarcely believed it.* Whoever lets his countenance shine on others expresses his kindness toward them (cf. Ps. 4:7 [Eng. 6]). The people never let Job's cherished gesture pass unnoticed (so Dhorme); his smile motivated them to moral courage. Job was an inspirational leader and "a beneficent source of life" (Habel, OTL).

25 Job's judicious counsel prompted the people to appoint him as their *chief (rōʾš).* This verse encompasses every aspect of his role in the community, from leading the counsel in peaceful times to guiding the people through a crisis and to caring for the unfortunate. As though he were a king over his troops, he inspired the community to work with moral resolve and discipline for the common good. This picture suggests that Job addressed the assembly particularly on the occasion of their mourning some catastrophe, like drought, famine, or plague. Through his wise counsel he led the community to take steps to overcome the difficulty.

B. A LAMENT (30:1–31)

After recounting his past blessings and the respect he had in the assembly, Job laments the depths of his shame and the severity of his suffering.[1] He is deeply distressed that he is scorned by all, even the desert rabble. He also cries out from the piercing pains that torment him. It is very distressing to Job that he sees God's mighty hand behind his suffering. Moreover, God's silence to his pleas exasperates him. In anguish he laments like a psalmist who sings a psalm of lament to the tune of the harp and flute.

This lament is artfully structured in relationship to his remembrance (ch. 29). In the lament Job speaks of the shame caused by external forces, then of his personal distress, while in his remembrance he recounted his personal blessings and then the honor others bestowed on him. The three sections of this lament are Job's present disgrace (vv. 1–15); an accusation against God (vv. 16–23); and a self-lament (vv. 24–31).

6. Cf. Prov. 16:15, where the king's favor is compared to the spring rain.

1. The themes and phraseology of Ps. 38, an individual psalm of lament, are echoed in this lament. The author draws on that psalm or on one of similar structure for this passage.

1. JOB'S PRESENT DISGRACE (30:1–15)

Job deplores the extent of his dishonor by elaborately characterizing the dregs of society who taunt him (vv. 1–8), and then he describes the mockery he must bear (vv. 9–15).

a. The Mockers (30:1–8)

1 *"But now they deride me,*
men younger than I,
whose fathers I would have disdained
to put with the dogs of my flock.
2 *What use did I have for the strength of their hands,*
from whom vigor had perished?[1]
3 *Gaunt from want and hunger are*
those who roam[2] *the parched land*
at night in a desolate waste,[3]
4 *those who pluck saltwort among the shrubs,*[4]
broom-roots for warmth;
5 *they are driven out from the community;*[5]
they are shouted at like a thief.

1. Although Dhorme has a similar translation, he emends the text, reading *ʿuzzāmô,* "their vigor" (cf. Ps. 89:18 [Eng. 17]) for *ʿālêmô,* "on him," and *kullōh,* "wholly," for *kālaḥ,* "vigor." But it is better to take *ʿal* to mean "from" (Blommerde, *Northwest Semitic Grammar and Job,* p. 112) and *kālaḥ* to mean "vigor," as in 5:26.

2. The hapax legomenon *ʿāraq* appears in Aramaic, meaning either "gnaw" or "roam." If the former meaning is accepted, the object is missing. So Duhm supplies *y^{e}raq,* "green" or "vegetation," thinking that it has fallen out by haplography. Interestingly the Qumran Targ. reads *[k]pn rʿyn hwʾ yrq d[ ]:* "In their hunger their desire was the vegetation of [the desert]." Similarly Ball, followed by Dhorme, postulates that *ʿiqqārê,* "roots," has been lost by haplography: "They gnaw the roots of the waste land." But if *ʿāraq* is taken to mean "roam," *ṣîyâ* then means "land of drought," with the word "land" *(ʾereṣ),* which usually accompanies it, either suppressed or accidentally omitted (cf. Jer. 2:6). The last view is accepted because of the lack of an object for the meaning "gnaw."

3. This line is most puzzling. For MT *ʾemeš,* "at night," there are numerous suggestions, e.g., *ʾimmām,* "their mother" in the sense of "their nurse" (Budde), *y^{e}mašš^{e}šû,* "they grope" (Duhm), *yāmîšû* or *yāmûšû,* "they wander" (Gordis). But Pope posits that all three words of this line may be taken as adverbial accusatives. This possibility preserves a line with alliteration designed to describe the habitat of these outcasts: *ʾemeš šôʾâ ûm^{e}šōʾâ.* The last two words, appearing also in 38:27; Zeph. 1:15; Sir. 51:10, connote extreme desolation.

4. A suggestion going back to Saadia and followed by Tur-Sinai is to translate *ʿ^{a}lê śîaḥ* as "leaves of shrubs" and to treat this phrase as in apposition to "saltwort."

5. Heb. *gēw,* "the community," is understood in the sense of Syr. *gawāʾ,* "inside, inner part, belly," and metaphorically, "a body of people, community" (R. P. Smith, *A Compendious Syriac Dictionary,* p. 62; KB, p. 174). In another direction M. Dahood ("Some Northwest-Semitic Words in Job," *Bib* 38 [1957] 318–19) takes MT *min-gēw* as identical to *miqqôl,* "with a shout," based on the Ugar. *g,* "voice." This

6 *They are found to dwell[6] in the gullies[7] of wadis,*
in holes of the ground and the rocky cliffs;[8]
7 *among the bushes they bray;*
under the nettles they huddle.
8 *A foolish, nameless brood,*
they were brought lower[9] than the ground."

1 The displaced desert rabble deride Job, hurling taunts at him as they pass by. These mockers are doubly odious to him by reason of their youth and their lowly status.[10] In those days the young were to show respect to their elders. But the most deplorable youths mock Job, who had been the most respected person in the community. These youths are so low in Job's sight that he would not have deemed their fathers worthy even to put with the *dogs* of his flock. Since the Hebrews disdained dogs as scavengers,[11] those who were in charge of dogs were considered to have a very low job. Job also makes a play on the word *deride (śāḥaq)*. Whereas he had *smiled (śāḥaq)* on the assembly inspiring confidence (29:24), now the rabble *deride* or smile derisively *(śāḥaq)* at him.

2–8 To stress his outrage at such mockery Job enumerates the despicable characteristics of those who reproach him. They lack strength

---

reading offers a good sense, but the lack of evidence for such a meaning in Hebrew makes it suspect.

6. The infinitive construct conveys the result of the expulsion. The fuller phrase would be *hāyû liškōn,* "they are forced to dwell," but often the verb *hāyâ* is omitted (GKC, § 114k; Driver, *Hebrew Tenses,* § 204).

7. Heb. *baʿarûṣ,* "in the gullies," is taken to mean "the precipitous side of a dry streambed," like Arab. *ʿarḍ, ʿurḍ* (cf. Dhorme; Guillaume, *Studies in the Book of Job,* p. 113). Some mss. read *baʿarōṣ,* "in the most feared of (wadis)."

8. Heb. *kēp* is cognate with Akk. *kāpu,* "rock, cliff," and Aram. *kêpā',* "rock, stones." It appears elsewhere only in Jer. 4:29.

9. MT *nikkeʾû* is usually taken as an Aramaized form of *nāḵâ,* "smite, scourge." Working from the fact that the adjective forms *nāḵāʾ* and *nāḵēʾ* mean "stricken" in reference to suffering humiliation and a depressed spirit (Isa. 16:7; Prov. 15:13; 17:22; 18:14), Gordis argues that there is a root *nkʾ* meaning "bring low, depress."

10. Having presented the various aspects of his former nobility, Job dwells on the detestable characteristics of these desert rats to stress the depth of humiliation their taunts cause him. While he assigns great worth to his servants in the next chapter (31:13–15), his enlightened attitude toward the weak has not been extended to include those viewed as social outcasts. Conversely, Jesus went even to such lowly people and shared with them both his message of forgiving love and his healing power, as shown in the narrative of the Gadarene demoniac (Mark 5:1–17).

11. In the OT "dogs" are viewed as scavengers with an insatiable appetite (Exod. 22:30 [Eng. 31]; Jer. 15:3; Ps. 68:24 [Eng. 23]). They even licked up human blood (1 K. 21:19) and devoured corpses left lying in the streets (1 K. 14:11; 21:23–24). In an oracle of reproach Israel's watchmen are ridiculed for acting like voracious dogs and stupid shepherds (Isa. 56:10–12).

and vigor. *Gaunt*[12] *from want and hunger,* they have become outcasts, roaming the desolate, dry steppe in search of food and shelter. They *pluck saltwort,* a perennial shrub identified as *atriplex halimus,* which because of its saltiness is eaten only in dire circumstances.[13] From the broom tree, *retama roetam,* one of the larger plants in the desolate regions of Sinai and the Dead Sea, they collect roots, possibly to make into charcoals (cf. Ps. 120:4).[14]

When these scoundrels enter a city, the citizens are appalled, fearing that such riffraff might snatch anything in sight. As soon as they spot them, they drive them out, shouting "Thief!" Never extending any courtesy to them, the citizens refuse to let them dwell in the village. These vagabonds, therefore, must find shelter in the rugged terrain of the steppe, which, being cut through with deep wadis, offers hiding places under cliffs and in caves. Huddled among the shrubs for shelters, they *bray*[15] from their deep-seated hunger.

These repulsive outcasts are called *a foolish, nameless brood* (lit. "sons of a fool" and "sons without a name"). Belonging to the class of hardened fools *(n^{e}ḇālîm),* they continually manifest their incorrigible folly. Noted for their impious, surly nature (Isa. 32:5–6) and haughty speech (Prov. 17:7), they are men without a name, i.e., they have no honor. Since people in ancient times believed that a name defined its bearer's essential nature, whoever became *nameless* had sunk to the lowest level of infamy. Such depraved creatures are viewed as *lower than the ground.*

b. The Mockery (30:9–15)

9 *"Now I have become their mocking song;*
I am a byword[1] *to them.*
10 *They detest me and stand aloof from me;*[2]
they do not hesitate to spit in my face.

12. Heb. *galmûḏ,* "gaunt," is used also to describe rocky, sterile soil (cf. 3:7; 15:34).

13. The Talmud refers to saltwort as the food of the poor (T.B. *Qiddushin* 66a).

14. Some take MT *laḥmām* to mean "their food," but the roots of the broom tree are inedible, though their small berries may be eaten (Tur-Sinai). Another possibility is to take this word as a Qal infinitive of a geminate root, uncontracted, meaning "to warm" (GKC, § 67cc; cf. Isa. 47:14 for the same form). Since the context is recounting the hardship these ruffians face, their having to make "food" out of such a paltry source witnesses to their dire straits.

15. While some understand Heb. *nāhaq,* "bray," to describe a cry of lust like that of a wild donkey (cf. Fohrer), this word more likely describes their hoarse cries occasioned by hunger, as in 6:5 (Dhorme).

1. The context suggests that Heb. *millâ,* "word," here connotes "byword."

2. The preposition *mennî* is a poetic form for *mimmennî,* "from me."

11 *Because he loosed[3] my cord[4] and afflicted me,*
they cast off restraint in my presence.
12 *On my right hand the young rabble[5] rise;*
they send my feet to their ruin;
they build up their ways against me.[6]
13 *They break up[7] my path;*
they promote my calamity;
there is none to help[8] against[9] them.
14 *As through a wide breach they come;*
amid the devastation they roll on.
15 *Terrors are turned[10] on me;*
my dignity is chased away[11] by the wind,
and my well-being has vanished like a cloud."

3. Many (e.g., Driver-Gray) emend MT *pittaḥ,* "he loosed," to a plural, so that the rabble may be the subject. But Job sees God as his primary enemy, and his earthly foes as taking advantage of what God has done to him (cf. Gordis).

4. The Ketib *yiṯrô,* "his string," followed by LXX and Vulg., is less likely than the Qere *yiṯrî,* "my string," with Targ. and Syr., for first person pronouns are prominent in this context.

5. MT *pirḥaḥ* is an unusual singular word in the OT. It could be a form in which the third radical is reduplicated (*qiṭlal;* GKC, § 84ᵇm); its root *prḥ* means "to bud, sprout." The derived noun *ʾeprōaḥ* means "young (of birds), brood." Gordis observes that the similar word in Arabic, *farḥ,* means both "young bird" and "base man." Thus the meaning "young rabble," a deprecatory term for these outcasts, is accepted.

6. Verse 12 is filled with problems, and no suggestion has won wide favor. A particular problem is that the second line is too short and the third line is too long. The latter is similar to 19:12b, but *ʾêḏām,* "their ruin," which Syr. omits and which is absent in 19:12b, overloads the line (Dhorme). It or some other word which gave rise to it may have originally belonged to the second line. If *ʾêḏām* is transposed to the second line, *ʾorḥôṯ,* "ways," may be revocalized as a plural, *ʾᵒrāḥôṯ,* or perhaps emended to have a suffix, *ʾorḥôṯām,* "their ways." The phrase *raglay šillēḥû* in the second line is variously understood: "they have cast off my feet" or "they have sent my feet away," i.e., they have driven me from place to place. But Gordis understands the phrase to mean "they spread my feet, send me sprawling." The figure appears to be that of a military attack. Then *ʾêḏām* could follow *šillēḥû* as an accusative of place: "They send my feet to their ruin." That is, they seek to entrap Job in a way that will bring about his downfall. This suggestion, though rough, restores some balance to the tristich, 8/7/8, and is thus followed.

7. MT *nāṯas* is usually taken as cognate to *nāṯaṣ,* "pull down, break up." Pope suggests that the root *nts* may be attested in an Ugaritic text (*UT,* 68:4): *ṯm ḥrbm its,* "there with (two) swords I shall shatter (him)."

8. For *ʿōzēr,* "helper," many (e.g., Dhorme, Driver-Gray, Fohrer, *BHS*) read *ʿōṣēr,* "one who stops or hinders."

9. Blommerde (*Northwest Semitic Grammar and Job,* p. 113) shows that the preposition *lᵉ* may mean "against."

10. MT *hohpaḵ,* "be turned," is a masculine singular form preceding its feminine plural subject (GKC, § 145o). The Hophal is unusual (GKC, § 121b), but no emendation is necessary.

11. The verb *tirdōp,* "it pursues, chases," may have "terrors" as the subject, but "terrors" belongs in the first line. The parallelism suggests that it should be revocalized as a Niphal, *tērāḏēp* (Hölscher, Fohrer).

9, 10 While the noble Job, covered with sores, sits on the ash heap outside the city, these rascals, considering him to be beneath them, scoff at him. Gleefully they make him *their mocking song* (see Lam. 3:14). The noblest elder has become the *byword* of the scum of society. These rabble express their contempt for Job with rude, offensive gestures: when they pass by him, they contemptuously *spit* in his face. Job suffers the worst social disgrace possible.

11 Job looks beyond these dregs and names God as the cause of his disgrace. God has *loosed* his *cord [yeṯer]*[12] *and afflicted* him. In this metaphor Job compares his body to a tent. Since God has slackened the central cord, the tent sags. In response to God's action against his own servant, the wicked *cast off restraint* and freely abuse God's servant. By vividly recounting the misery that God's harsh treatment causes him, Job is desperately seeking to arouse God's sympathy for him.[13]

12–14 *The rabble* have attacked Job with such force that it appears as though they are besieging a fortified city. Exactly what forces or foes Job has in mind is difficult to tell. The context suggests that he is thinking of the abuse he receives from the desert dregs. Certainly the loathsome appearance and the repulsive manners of these dregs would stimulate his imagination and perhaps cause nightmares. In any case this passage is the closest Job comes to considering that some evil force is assaulting him.

Job describes their attack against his *right* side, the place of strength and honor. *They send my feet to their ruin,* i.e., they lay traps along every path of escape. They also make impassable the roads that lead to Job in order to prevent any help from reaching him. Having isolated Job, they build up a siege ramp to breach the wall. Under the drawn-out siege Job languishes. Job feels that their tactics *promote my calamity*. That is, their continuous bombardment of him increases his suffering daily without any relief. Eventually they make a wide breach in the wall and rush into the city like a mighty torrent of water.[14] Inside the walls they delight in turning the beautiful city into a heap of rubble. That is, the rabble relish tormenting Job.

12. Heb. *yeṯer*, "cord," is interpreted in different ways. In Ps. 11:2 it stands for a "bowstring." If it means "bowstring" here, God has unstrung Job's bow, i.e., broken his strength. Another view identifies it as "strings" used to tie a girdle. "To loosen a girdle" would mean to render one weak, unable to undertake a heavy task (Hakam). Another possibility is that it refers to a "tent-cord." When the central tent-cord is loosened, the tent collapses; so too when a man's life-cord slackens, he becomes frail, near the point of death (cf. 4:21). While each of these possible metaphors has a similar meaning, the last has the advantage of an earlier reference in this work (cf. 4:21).

13. This style is typical of a psalm of lament; e.g., Ps. 11:2–3; 22:13–14 (Eng. 12–13); 27:2–3; 64:3–5 (Eng. 2–4).

14. This interpretation takes MT *pereṣ*, "breach," as short for *pereṣ mayim*, "a torrent" (as in 2 Sam. 5:20; cf. Isa. 30:13). According to Gordis, the comparative preposition *k*ᵉ supports this interpretation.

15 Job feels like *terrors* (*ballāhôṯ;* cf. 18:11; 27:20) have turned on him. Such emotion is aroused by a gruesome sight or by an overwhelming force (cf. 24:17). In 18:14 the leader of the realm of the dead is called "the king of terrors." This wording hints that Job perceives that the hands of Death are behind his attackers. As a result of this attack, his *dignity (nᵉḏîḇâ)*[15] has been driven away and his *well-being*[16] *has vanished like a cloud.* Job laments that he has lost not only the dignity of his position as leading elder but also the serenity his vast estate provided.

2. AN ACCUSATION AGAINST GOD (30:16–23)

16 *"Now my soul is emptied from me;*
days of affliction seize me.
17 *At night God*[1] *painfully pierces my bones,*
and my veins[2] *do not sleep.*
18 *With great force he*[3] *seizes*[4] *my clothing*
and girds me about like the collar[5] *of my tunic.*
19 *He*[6] *has cast me*[7] *into the mire;*

15. Heb. *nᵉḏîḇâ* speaks of the honor and dignity that attend the office of a noble, *nāḏîḇ;* cf. Isa. 32:8.

16. Heb. *yᵉšûʿâ,* "well-being," is generally translated "salvation, victory, deliverance," but it also refers to the state of blessing that results from deliverance. Gordis, however, argues that since *primae-yod* and *mediae-waw* roots are often interchanged, MT *yᵉšûʿâ* comes from the root *šôaʿ*, "noble, independent," and means "the station of a nobleman." In support he cites Isa. 32:5, where *šôaʿ* is parallel to *nāḏîḇ,* "nobleman."

1. In this verse God, the cause of all of Job's affliction, is assumed to be the undefined subject of "pierce" *(niqqar).* Two other possibilities of treating MT *niqqar* are to take *laylâ,* "night," as its subject or to revocalize it as a Pual, *nuqqar,* with *ʿaṣāmay,* "my bones," as its subject: "At night my bones are pierced with pains."

2. Of the many suggestions for MT *ʿōrᵉqay,* two are more likely. One is "my veins," gained from the Arab. *ʿirq,* "veins and sinews" (Tur-Sinai, Gordis). This view has the advantage of having a part of the body parallel to "bones." The other is "my gnawing pains," based on a cognate root in Syriac and Arabic. A major problem with this position is that since the Syriac version translates the word here "my body," the Syriac translators did not equate *ʿōrᵉqay* with the same root in their language.

3. The subject of the verb *yiṯḥappēś,* "he seizes," is either indefinite, alluding to the disease, or God (Pope, NIV). Either way God is the final cause and thus is accepted as the subject.

4. For MT *yiṯḥappēś,* "disguise oneself," Dhorme, Fohrer, and Pope read *yiṯpōś,* "he seizes," based on LXX. But Gordis thinks that Heb. *ḥāpaś* may be a phonetic variant of *ḥāḇaš,* "bind up." He argues that the Hithpael arose as a conflation of second and third person forms by reason of the shift from third person (vv. 17, 19) to second person (vv. 20–23).

5. Some (e.g., Pope and Gordis) think that for *kᵉpî,* "like the collar of," it is better to read *bᵉpî,* "by the collar of." Since it is possible to make sense out of MT, it is better not to emend the text.

6. Since the first line is unusually short, Pope may be correct in supplying "God" as the subject.

7. Many (e.g., Duhm, Hölscher, Fohrer) believe the verb *hōrānî,* "throw me,"

I have become as dust and ashes.
20 *I cry to you, but you do not answer me;*
I stand, but you do not[8] *heed me.*
21 *You have grown cruel toward me;*
with your strong hand you act hatefully against me.
22 *You lift me up and mount me on the wind;*
you toss[9] *me about with a tempest.*[10]
23 *I know that you will bring me to death,*
to the meeting house for all the living."

Job continues his lament by directly accusing God of causing his ills. Shifting to second person forms, Job addresses God directly, complaining that no matter how much he cries out to him for help God not only remains heedless to his petitions but also punishes him more cruelly. Job fears that God is bringing him to the chambers of death. Only in vv. 20–23 of this entire speech does Job address God directly. Not surprisingly, these verses are at the virtual center of this long speech.[11]

16, 17 Job grieves over the pain that continually pierces his body. He feels that his *soul (nep̱eš),* his vitality, has been poured out like water from a jar (cf. Ps. 22:15 [Eng. 14]).[12] All that is left is a limp body, throbbing with pain. He has no strength left to fight his compounding illness. *Days of affliction seize* him without relief. Instead of being able to get some sleep at night, Job feels that *God painfully pierces my bones, and my veins do not sleep.* Possibly the pounding of his heart is so loud that it disturbs his sleep, or perhaps convulsions awaken him in the night. He cannot find even a moment's rest.

18 Since every part of his body aches, Job imagines that God has grabbed him by his *clothing* and pulled it so tightly about him that every part of his body screams out in agonizing pain. He feels as though he were

---

often used of shooting arrows, is an error of haplography for *hōriḏanî,* "he has sent me down." This view is possible, but not compelling.

8. It seems best to read *lō'*, "not," or *w^elō'*, "and not," before *tiṯbōnen,* with Vulg. (so Dhorme, Rowley).

9. Heb. *mûg* means "wave, billow, toss, dissolve" (KB, p. 526; cf. Amos 9:5; Ps. 46:7 [Eng. 6]). By extension it has the psychological meaning of "despair, become dejected" (Isa. 14:31; Josh. 2:9, 24).

10. The Qere *tušîyâ,* "success," is less preferable than the Ketib *t^ešuwwâ* as a variant spelling of *t^ešu'â,* "noise, roar" (of a storm) (cf. 36:29; 39:7). Dhorme takes it as the subject, but it is possible to interpret it as the accusative of place (Gordis).

11. Cf. A. Ceresko, *Job 29–31 in the Light of Northwest Semitic* (Rome: Pontifical Biblical Institute, 1980), pp. 80–81.

12. Hakam believes that this language describes the physical responses to suffering—flowing tears, outcries from pain, and vomiting (cf. Lam. 2:11–12).

confined in a straitjacket that is gripping him tighter and tighter. Or it seems that God is girding him with a girdle which is no wider than *the collar* of his tunic.[13] When God puts the girdle on him, it binds him so tightly that he cannot breathe. No wonder his body feels as if it is about to collapse. In the previous verse Job described his inner pains, and in this verse he depicts the agony caused by the withering of his diseased skin.

19 After emaciating Job's body, God *has cast* him *into the mire* to disgrace him. Job has been made to feel that he is merely *dust and ashes* (cf. 2:8; 27:16; 42:6). He is not thinking that God has soiled him indelibly (cf. 9:31), but rather that God has so discredited him that he has no honor left.

20 Job protests that though he has fervently petitioned God for relief, God remains silent. With determination and a sense of urgency he *stands* to make his plea for help,[14] but still God fails to acknowledge him. God's unresponsiveness to his cries causes Job much spiritual anguish.

21 Job complains boldly that God has *grown cruel* (*'akzār*)[15] toward him. Because he has assailed Job with such might, Job believes that God *acts hatefully* (*śāṭam*) against him. Most likely the author is making a play on the verb *śāṭam,* "act hatefully," and the title *Satan* (*śāṭān;* cf. 1:6; 16:9). God has acted so bitterly against him that Job feels that God is his foe, his satan. That is, Job is poignantly accusing God of cherishing animosity against him.

22, 23 Job continues his complaint by making a parody on the hymnic language that pictures God as riding on the wings of the wind when he comes to deliver his people (cf. Ps. 18:11 [Eng. 10]). Turning this metaphor upside down, Job sarcastically complains: *you [God] . . . mount me on the wind; you toss me about with a tempest.* Job says: *I know that you will bring me to death,* i.e., Job knows that God is wearing him down before he brings him to death. Here *death* is called *the meeting house for all the living*. The word *bring* (*hēšîḇ*) is used with a note of sarcasm. It often means "restore, bring back," but here it means to transport from one place to another. Also, the opening formula *I know* is used sarcastically. It contrasts with Job's great affirmation of faith in 19:25. Here his knowledge comes out of hopelessness and fear, not out of faith. In this way Job is venting his bitter frustration at the way he feels God is treating him.

13. The tunic was a garment with long skirts and long sleeves worn next to the body.

14. Cf. Jer. 15:1, where "standing" is the posture for presenting an earnest petition to God. Cf. A. Ceresko, *Job 29–31,* p. 32.

15. Heb. *'akzār,* "cruel," is often used in reference to the hostilities of war (Isa. 13:9; Jer. 6:23; 30:14). Cruel deeds are motivated by wrath (Prov. 27:4) and are executed without loyal love (*ḥeseḏ;* Prov. 11:17) or compassion (*raḥam;* Jer. 6:23).

3. A SELF-LAMENT (30:24–31)

24 *"Yet God does not stretch out his hand in destruction,*
if one cries to him for help in his disaster.[1]
25 *Did I not weep for him whose day was hard?*
Was not my soul grieved[2] *for the poor?*
26 *But*[3] *when I looked for good, evil came;*
when I hoped for light, darkness came.
27 *My bowels boil unceasingly;*
days of affliction meet me.
28 *I go about blackened, but not by the sun;*[4]
I stand in the assembly and cry for help.[5]
29 *I am a brother of jackals*
and a companion of ostriches.
30 *My skin blackens and peels;*
my body[6] *burns with fever.*

1. Verse 24 is very difficult and has received numerous reconstructions. For MT *ʿî*, "heap," Pope and Dhorme read *ʿānî,* "needy, afflicted": "One does not turn his hand against the needy, when in distress he cries for help." Hakam takes *b*^{e}*ʿî* as equivalent to a common Aramaic word for "prayer, request" (cf. Dan. 6:8, 14 [Eng. 7, 13]), with the preposition *b*^{e} omitted for assonance. This word parallels *šûaʿ* in the second line, which is elliptical for *ʿāraḵ šûaʿ*, "cry for help." As for the antecedents of *lāhen,* "to them," Hakam identifies them as "death" and Sheol ("meeting house") in v. 23 and "hand" in v. 24a, and he reasons that *lāhen* is a feminine plural, for *š*^{e}*ʾôl* and *yāḏ* are feminine: "Surely God does not bring death by petition, If in his distress one cries for them (i.e., death, its instrument and its abode)." Although this interpretation is somewhat strained, it has the advantage of reading the existing text.

Gaining a clue from T.B. *Aboda Zara* 4a, Grabbe (*Comparative Philology,* pp. 101–103), believes that *ʿî* could mean "destruction": "Indeed let him not send (his) hand with (complete) destruction/ruin if in his calamity there is accordingly a cry (for help)." This suggestion, too, has the advantage of no textual change plus some rabbinic support. This view of *ʿî* is accepted tentatively, but it seems best to find *lōh y*^{e}*šawwēaʿ*, "one cries to him," in *lāhen šûaʿ* (see *BHS*). Such a view takes the *n* as a scribal error rising from the coalescing of an *h* and a *y*.

2. The meaning of *ʿāgam,* "be grieved," is clear from its use in Mishnaic Hebrew. Perhaps this word occurs in the Ugaritic text Krt 26–27: *yʿrb bḥdrh ybky bṯn [ ]gmm wydmʿ*, "He entered his chamber to weep; while repeating his grief, he shed tears" (cf. A. Ceresko, *Job 29–31*, pp. 91–92).

3. Gordis suggests that the *kî* gives the reason for v. 27.

4. The expression *b*^{e}*lōʾ ḥammâ,* "without the sun," may be elliptical for "without the light of the sun" (Delitzsch), or it may mean that one's face is covered so that he does not see the sun (Hakam). Duhm, Budde, and Fohrer read *b*^{e}*lōʾ neḥāmâ,* "where there was no comfort." Although this change makes excellent sense, both LXX (despite its own textual problem) and Syr. read the same consonants as MT, which is thus retained.

5. The use of the imperfect *ʾ*^{a}*šawwēaʿ*, "I cry for help," after the perfect *qamtî,* "I stand," comes close to having the sense of a final clause (Driver-Gray; GKC, § 120c; Driver, *Hebrew Tenses,* § 163).

6. Dhorme shows that *ʿaṣmî* (lit. "my bone[s]") in the singular denotes one's frame; cf. Ps. 102:6 (Eng. 5): "My frame *[ʿaṣmî]* cleaves to my flesh."

31 *My lyre is tuned to wailing,*
and my flute to the voice of mourners."[7]

24 Job has assumed that whenever one who faces *disaster* cries to God for help, God will extend to him a saving hand, not a hand stretched out to inflict another blow. But instead of showing him kindness, God has increased his affliction. No wonder Job can hardly believe God's abusive behavior. His experience shakes deeply his firmest convictions about God's goodness.

25 With rhetorical questions Job accuses God of failing to act toward him as Job has acted toward others. When Job saw someone *whose day was hard,* i.e., languishing under hard conditions,[8] he wept for him. For *the poor* he was deeply *grieved,* and he took steps to relieve their suffering. He spent much time and effort in showing mercy (29:12–17). By recounting his deeds of compassion Job is indirectly affirming once again that he has lived a blameless life.

26 Job had expected that God would reciprocate his deeds of mercy with blessing. *I looked for good . . . I hoped for light.* For many years his belief was supported by the amazing increase of his estate. Suddenly all was turned upside down. Instead of good, *evil* befell him; instead of light, *darkness.*[9] His experiencing the complete reversal of his fortune was like being forced to eat something sour after eating a sweet, delightful morsel.

27 Now, Job's *bowels* are so agitated that they feel as though they *boil unceasingly.* A tragic fate arouses deep psycho-physical reaction (cf. Lam. 1:20; 2:11). Similarly, when Jeremiah heard the trumpet blast that ordered the troops to march against Jerusalem, he cried: "My bowels, my bowels! I writhe in pain. The walls of my heart! My heart pounds in me; I cannot keep silent, for I have heard the sound of the trumpet, the shout of war" (Jer. 4:19). Like Jeremiah, Job's whole body writhes in pain from his anguish.

28 Job's complexion has been *blackened*[10] by his illness and emotional turmoil, *not by the sun.* By referring to the dark color of his skin he reveals his anxiety about how the disease is distorting his appearance. Distraught, he stands in the midst of the assembly and cries for help, hopeful

7. Gordis suggests that *bōḵîm,* "those who weep," may be an abstract noun, "weeping," parallel to *'ēḇel,* "mourning."

8. The expression is *qᵉšēh yôm,* lit. "hard of day."

9. For this theme, cf. Isa. 59:9, 11; Jer. 13:16; 14:19.

10. Heb. *qōḏēr,* "being dark," is interpreted as referring either to Job's complexion or to the color of his garments; cf. Ps. 38:7 (Eng. 6), which has the identical expression *(qōḏēr hillaḵtî).* If the latter possibility is followed, the phrase "without the sun" should be emended to "without comfort" (see n.4 above). But taking the literal meaning of that phrase and considering the parallel that exists between vv. 28–29 and vv. 30–31, it seems better to take *qōḏēr* as referring to the color of Job's skin.

that someone would come to his aid. Since Job would have been barred from the public assembly because of his disease, the language of the second line is figurative to describe his resolve in lamenting publicly on the ash heap.

29 Job's continuous lamenting makes him *a brother of jackals* and *a companion of ostriches*. The jackal's howl is a doleful, mourning sound, said to sound like the wailing of a child, while the ostrich gives out a hissing moan.[11] Their moaning cries convey the stark loneliness of the steppe. Job feels so lonely that he senses that his only companions are these animals in their doleful crying.

30 Once again Job deplores the severe discomfort caused by his diseased body. His skin blackens and peels, and his body burns with fever. His physical suffering causes him to moan woefully.

31 In pain and despair Job has poured out his lament like a psalmist who sings a dirge with his *lyre* or as one who plays a *flute*[12] to accompany the lamenting of *mourners* (cf. Jer. 48:36; Matt. 9:23). Reference to these musical instruments underscores the sad tone of his lamenting.

Job suffers totally. His body is bent over by pain. His emotions are distraught. He is disgraced, being taunted by the dregs of society. The contrast between his former glory and his present disgrace is stark. Abandoned by all, Job laments the full scope of his misery. Against this background Job will offer his oath of innocence. The lament underscores the strength of Job's conviction and the desperation that have led him to swear the oath of innocence.

C. AN OATH OF INNOCENCE (31:1–40)

After having reminisced about the glory of his former days and having lamented his present disgrace, Job swears an oath of innocence in a final move to prove that he is not guilty of any wrongdoing. The oath requires God either to activate the curses of the oath or to clear the swearer. Should God remain silent, Job would be declared innocent by not being cursed. A common formula for an oath of innocence is, "May God do such to me, if I do (or do not do) so and so."[1] The swearer usually suppresses the actual curse either with evasive language or abbreviated formulas, no doubt fearful

11. In Mic. 1:8 these two animals are paralleled because of their moaning sounds.

12. Pope thinks that Heb. *ʿûgāḇ* is a single pipe or tone flute in contrast to Heb. *ḥālîl,* the double pipe.

1. See S. Blank, "The Curse, the Blasphemy, the Spell, and the Oath," *HUCA* 23 (1950–51) 87–92; idem, "An Effective Literary Device in Job XXXI," *JJS* 4 (1951) 105–107.

of the very verbalizing of a specific curse. But Job is so bold that four times he specifies the curse that should befall him if he be guilty (vv. 8, 10, 22, 40).[2] His wreckless bravery reflects his unwavering confidence in his own innocence.

This oath is similar to an Egyptian oath of innoçence, which is attested in "The Book of the Dead." On entering the realm of the dead, the deceased's heart was weighed against a feather. Before the weighing he swore to his innocence by reciting a list of ethical and religious sins he had not committed. Although the sins in Job's list are quite different from those in "The Book of the Dead," these two situations have a similar purpose, for in both the swearer desires to clear himself of any guilt from the slightest wrongdoing.[3] There exists a parallel in Israel. When worshipers were about to enter the temple precinct, they recited a ritual confession that they had adhered to the law and were pure from any evildoing, not merely from overt transgressions but also from the subtle sins of a poor attitude and lack of compassion for others (e.g., Deut. 26:12–15; Ps. 15; 24:3–6).

In this oath Job enumerates a long list of sins that he had never committed. The sins he denies, however, follow no order attested elsewhere in the OT or related documents.[4] They appear to be those sins that were foremost in his mind. The uneven flow of the oath may be symptomatic of Job's qualms about taking such a brazen step.

Instead of denying blatant acts of transgression punishable by law, Job scrupulously tests his attitudes and motives. His primary interest is to demonstrate that he has maintained right relationships on all levels. Because Job is focusing on his attitudes toward others he mentions only two sins that are found in the Decalogue, adultery (vv. 9–12) and covetousness (vv. 7–8). Moreover, he asserts that he has never abused his servants, the poor, or the weak (vv. 13–23, 31–32). He considers them persons toward whom he is obligated to show respect and compassion. He believes that it is wrong to hate his enemy or even to gloat over his enemy's troubles (vv. 29–30). In relationship to God he asserts zealously that his devotion has never wavered (vv. 24–28). Job believes that his motives have always been pure. He has not lusted (vv. 1–2) or coveted (vv. 7–8). He has avoided falsehood (vv. 5–

2. A parallel to the imprecation that his shoulder should fall from its socket and his arm be broken at the elbow if he has harmed an orphan (vv. 21–22) occurs in Ps. 137:5–6: "If I forget you, O Jerusalem, let my right hand [wither]. Let my tongue stick to my palate, if I do not remember you" (cf. Ps. 7:4–7 [Eng. 3–6]).

3. See J. Murtagh, "The Book of Job and the Book of the Dead," *Irish Theological Quarterly* 35 (1965) 166–73.

4. See G. Fohrer, "The Righteous Man in Job 31," in *Essays in Old Testament Ethics,* Fest. J. P. Hyatt, ed. J. Crenshaw and J. Willis (New York: Ktav, 1974), pp. 1–22. He argues persuasively that the author draws heavily on the ethical teaching of the Wisdom tradition in formulating the list of precepts.

6), and he has never concealed any wrong (vv. 33–34). It is clear that Job knows that one is accountable not only for overt acts of sin but also for contemplating immoral behavior and cherishing cruel, vengeful thoughts against others. His moral insight is highly refined, pointing toward the Sermon on the Mount.

Job concludes his avowal of innocence by appending his signature (vv. 35–37). He demands that God, the plaintiff, give him a written document that he may wear on his shoulder as visible evidence to all that he is innocent. The conviction that God, being true to his nature, will act justly, is the basis for this oath. Job leaves God no option but to answer him. If God fails to answer, he is no longer the personal God actively concerned with the behavior of human beings. If such is the case, a person's commitment to faithful observance of the moral code fails to hold any meaning. If God treats human beings capriciously, their hope of building their character through communion with God is an illusion. Job, therefore, has sworn this oath of innocence out of his desperate need to hear from God, not out of arrogance.

1. THE LIST OF SINS DENIED (31:1–34, 38–40B)

Job enumerates fourteen sins in his negative confession.[1]

1. Lust (vv. 1–4)
2. Falsehood (vv. 5–6)
3. Covetousness (vv. 7–8)
4. Adultery (vv. 9–12)
5. Mistreatment of one's servants (vv. 13–15)
6. Lack of concern for the poor (vv. 16–18)
7. Failure to clothe the poor (vv. 19–20)
8. Perversion of justice against the weak (vv. 21–23)
9. Trust in wealth (vv. 24–25)
10. Worship of the heavenly bodies (vv. 26–28)

1. The listing of the sins is variously enumerated (from 10 to 16) depending on how the verses are grouped. For example, Fohrer finds twelve sins. He considers the sins mentioned in vv. 16–23 as belonging to one class: hardness of heart against the poor. He postulates that the author began with a list of ten transgressions, which was expanded to twelve sins by additions at the beginning (vv. 1–4) and at the end (vv. 38–40a). These two additional transgressions are set apart in that Job does not use the oath formula but mentions a covenant designed to keep himself from sinning in the first pericope. The original listing is also apparent in the similarity between the first sin, "falsehood" (vv. 5–6), and the last, "hypocrisy" (vv. 33–34). While this analysis makes only a mild modification of the text, the first pericope is viewed as paving the way for conditional self-imprecation clauses, and the last sections may have been accidentally misplaced in transmission. However, vv. 38–40b are placed after v. 34, because they are the conclusion to the oath of innocence.

11. Satisfaction at a foe's misfortune (vv. 29–30)
12. Failure to extend hospitality to a sojourner (vv. 31–32)
13. Concealment of a sin without confession (vv. 33–34)
14. Abuse of the land (vv. 38–40b).

Herewith Job wishes to affirm his complete avoidance of any wrongdoing. Since seven is the number of perfection or completeness, the use of two sevens in the list points to his faithful adherence to the entire moral law. Also, his great concern in regard to his attitudes and thoughts reveals that Job holds himself to be free from transgression in thought as well as deed.

a. Lust (31:1–4)

1 *"I made a covenant with my eyes,*
that I would never[1] look longingly at a maiden.
2 *What would be one's lot from God above,*
his heritage from Shaddai on high?
3 *Is it not disaster for the unrighteous*
and ruin to the workers of iniquity?
4 *Does he not see my ways*
and count all my steps?"

1 Job begins his oath of innocence with an affirmation. He states that he had made a covenant with his eyes that he would never look longingly after a *maiden* or a virgin *(bᵉṯûlâ)*.[2] He has resolutely controlled his *eyes* to keep any sinful longing from entering his heart. In the OT the eyes were considered the gateway to the heart, for their gaze may arouse the deepest desires and so spur their owner to transgress God's laws (e.g., Gen. 3:6; 2 Sam. 11:2; cf. Sir. 9:8; Matt. 5:28). The people were, therefore, enjoined to remember God's commandments and not prostitute themselves by following the lusts of their hearts and eyes (Num. 15:39).

2 In a series of three questions—one each in the next three verses—Job considers how God would treat him if he had looked longingly at a maiden. He believes that God, who is exalted, living on high, fixes a *lot (ḥēleq)* or plans a *heritage (naḥᵃlâ)* for every person on earth in just measure to his deeds. Parenthetically this question counters Eliphaz's accusation that Job has acted wickedly because he believes that God, dwelling *on high,* is concealed by dense clouds that prevent him from taking notice of events on

1. This is an example of Heb. *mâ* used as a negative rather than an interrogative (Pope).

2. Job's concern with the potential hazard in a lustful gaze points toward the standard set by Jesus in his Sermon on the Mount: whoever looks lustfully on a woman sins (Matt. 5:28). But as Driver-Gray observe, Job differs from Jesus, for he does not consider the gaze a sinful act but acknowledges that it is liable to result in wrongdoing.

earth (22:12–18). Here it is clear that although Job believes that God is transcendent, he is also convinced that God knows and judges every human deed. This question indicates that prior to his trial Job held a view of retribution similar to his friends' view. There should be no surprise at Job's uttering this line, even in the light of his complaint against God, for he still believes that if he had violated the covenant he would have been judged by God. But the issue for him now is whether his suffering can be taken as proof that he has violated the standard of his day.

3 Next Job ponders the consequences of pursuing iniquity. The portion that God assigns *the unrighteous,* i.e., *the workers of iniquity,* is *disaster* (*ʾêḏ*) or *ruin* (*nēḵer;* cf. 18:12; 21:17, 30).[3] God breaks the prosperity of the wicked by causing a disaster to wipe out everything he has (cf. Prov. 6:15). A disaster fills a person with panic (cf. Prov. 1:26–27). Wishing to avoid such a frightening situation, Job has snuffed out every longing to sin.

4 With another question Job affirms that God knows exactly whether he has let his eyes wander. From his lofty abode God observes all of each person's *ways* and counts all of his *steps.*[4] In his own case Job is convinced that God is fully aware of everything he has done and is completely knowledgeable about the reasons for Job's present sufferings. He knows whether Job is deserving of them. At the very opening of this declaration of innocence, Job reveals his basic conviction that makes him willing to risk such an oath. Since God discerns all matters, he is surely not deceived in regard to his servant's obedience. Job hopes that this oath will move God to reverse matters and act justly toward his faithful servant.

b. Falsehood and Covetousness (31:5–8)

5 *"If[1] I have walked with falsehood*
and my foot hastened[2] to deceit,

3. MT *nēḵer* is unknown in Hebrew. The *qaṭl* form appears to mean the same as the *quṭl* form, *nōḵer,* meaning "disaster" (Obad. 12). According to Dhorme the root *nkr* means "to be alien" and also "to be hostile" (cf. Akk. *nakāru*) or "to be harsh, hateful" (Arab. *nakura*).

4. This theme appears frequently in Scripture, e.g., Ps. 33:13–15; 119:168; 139:1–4; Prov. 5:21; Sir. 15:17.

1. Gordis thinks that often in this type of oath structure *ʾim* is not the "if" that introduces the protasis, especially in that there is no apodosis. He takes it as an interrogative particle introducing a question expecting a negative answer. This is the case then in vv. 13, 16, 24, 25, 26, 33, and possibly vv. 19, 20. While the interrogative form affords an easier English translation, it seems better to follow through with "if," assuming that the oath dominates the chapter, including those constructions without an expressed apodosis. S. Blank observes that often in a curse the condition, i.e., the protasis introduced by *ʾim,* "if," or *ʾim lōʾ,* "if not," may itself function as the oath with no apodosis ("The Curse, the Blasphemy, the Spell, and the Oath," *HUCA* 23 [1950–51] 90).

2. MT *wattaḥaš,* "and it hastened," instead of the expected *wattāḥaš* may be a

6 *let him weigh me in a just balance,*
that God may know my integrity.
7 *If my step has turned from the way,*
or my heart has gone after my eyes,
or a spot[3] *has stuck to my hands,*
8 *let me sow and another eat,*
and let my crops be uprooted."[4]

5, 6 Job states that he has avoided *falsehood (šāw')* in every aspect of his life. He has not used falsehood to promote his own ventures; he has not kept company with those who advance themselves through perverting the truth. And he has not denied God. *Falsehood (šāw')* describes something as insubstantial, worthless.[5] It is especially applied to improper speech, e.g., wrong use of God's sacred name (Exod. 20:7), false testimony given in court (Exod. 23:1; Deut. 5:17 [Eng. 20]), lies that pour forth from a person given to violent acts (Ps. 144:8, 11), oracles delivered by uninspired prophets that mislead the people (Ezek. 12:24; 13:6–9, 23; 21:28, 34 [Eng. 23, 29]; 22:28; Zech. 10:2). It is also used for inauthentic acts of worship (Isa. 1:13) and for the idols themselves (Jer. 18:15).

Job has never let his *foot*[6] hasten to follow a path of *deceit* or treachery *(mirmâ)* by which he could advance himself at the expense of others. The Wisdom tradition taught that whoever advanced himself through deceitful practices is a fool (Prov. 14:8; cf. 26:24). But Job has acted wisely by pursuing that which is true and genuine. He has lived by the same standard as that required of those about to enter the temple precinct: "He who has clean hands and a pure heart, who does not lift up his soul to *what is false [šāw'],* and does not swear *deceitfully [mirmâ]*" (Ps. 24:4). Should anyone suspect him of using deceit, Job requests that God *weigh* him in the scales of justice as a proof of his *integrity (tummâ).* In the Wisdom tradition a scale symbolizes God's precise testing of human motives in contrast to the individual's own estimate, which is so biased that it is considered unreliable (cf. Job 6:2, 3; Prov. 16:2; 21:2; 24:12). Confident of his innocence, Job is certain this test would convince God of his integrity or blameless character (cf. 1:1).

7 Job avows that he has never *turned* aside *from the way* that God

---

so-called Aramaic form of the Hiphil (GKC, § 72ff), but Gordis thinks that the guttural prefers a double *pataḥ* (cf. *watta'aṭ* in 1 Sam. 15:19).

3. MT *mu'ûm* (cf. Dan. 1:4) is taken as identical with *mûm,* "blemish," written here with a quiescent ' (see Dhorme). LXX and Syr. apparently read *me'ûmâ,* "anything."

4. Heb. *šāraš* means both "take root" (Isa. 40:24) and "uproot" (Ps. 52:7 [Eng. 5]).

5. See *TWOT,* II:908; cf. J. Sawyer, *THAT,* II:882–84.

6. The "foot" is frequently used to express the ethical bearing of a person's life (Job 23:11; Ps. 119:59, 101; Prov. 1:15–16; 4:26; 6:18).

has set before him (cf. Ps. 119:67). He has never let his *heart* follow his *eye,* i.e., his mind has not been controlled by his lusts. Any wrongful suggestion that has entered through the eye has been squelched in his heart. Never have his hands been stained by a *spot* from a wicked act. Each sinful act was thought to place a deep stain on the doer's hands. Job is claiming that his hands are spotless, free from the stains made by any wrongdoing (cf. 16:17). In these verses the entire body is pictured as participating in a sinful act: the eye covets, the heart plots, the feet turn aside, the hand acts. Job asserts that he has kept his body under control.

8 For the first time Job boldly specifies the consequence that should befall him if what he affirms is false. *let me sow and another eat.* If Job has been lying, may another feast on his crops, the produce of his toil, while he goes hungry. *let my crops be uprooted.* The uprooting of his crops[7] just before harvest would demoralize him, for his long, hard labor done in anticipation of a good harvest would have been in vain.[8] If a farmer's crop is wiped out, he is also put in jeopardy of losing his land from indebtedness.

c. Adultery (31:9–12)

9 *"If my heart has been enticed by a woman*
or I have lurked at my friend's door,
10 *let my wife grind for another,*[1]
and let others bend over her.
11 *For that would be a heinous crime,*
that would be a punishable iniquity,[2]
12 *because it is a fire which consumes*[3] *unto Abaddon;*
it will burn[4] *all my produce."*

9 Job disavows lustful fantasies or any stealthy schemes designed to seduce a friend's wife. Earlier he had affirmed that he had never lusted after or

7. "Yield" or "crops" (*ṣeʾĕṣāʾ*) stands for both the produce of the land (Isa. 34:1; 42:5) and human offspring (Isa. 48:19; Job 5:25; 21:8; 27:14). The context emphasizes produce here, but Hakam thinks that the term could refer to both in the light of the phrase in Deut. 28:18a: "Cursed shall be the fruit of your body, and the fruit of your ground."

8. Cf. Deut. 28:38; Amos 5:11; Mic. 6:15; Zeph. 1:13.

1. The Aramaic plural ending *-n* on *ʾaḥērîn* is chosen for assonance with the *nun energicum* on the verb: *yiḵreʿûn ʾaḥērîn*.

2. Possibly the text should read the construct form, *ʿawōn,* instead of the absolute *ʿāwōn.* Also, MT *pelîlîm* (see n.9 below) could be read without the final *-m,* or, even better, the *-m* could be treated as an enclitic (Gordis).

3. The relative pronoun is understood before *tōʾḵēl,* "consumes" (GKC, § 155f).

4. MT *tešārēš,* "uproot," may be an error influenced by *yešōrāšû* in v. 8b; it does not offer a suitable parallel to the first line. Therefore, *tiśrōp,* "burn," is read with Dhorme and Fohrer. Gordis keeps MT and takes *teḇûʾāṯî* as "offspring": "That will consume all my increase to the roots."

taken advantage of a virgin (v. 1). In this instance he states that he has never let himself be *enticed by a woman.* These words picture Job's observing a neighbor's house stealthily, watching for an opportune moment when, undetected, he could make intimate contact with the lady of the house. *door* may have a double meaning: access to his neighbor's house and access to his neighbor's wife's womb.

The violation of another's wife was a treacherous act, breaking the bond of trust among neighbors. At the same time it was a sin against one's own wife, a violation of the covenant of marriage. Moreover, whenever a person sins against another, God's name is profaned (cf. Amos 2:7). No wonder both the law (Exod. 20:14) and the Wisdom literature (e.g., Prov. 6:23–35) categorically forbid adultery.

10 For the second time Job specifies the curse for such reprehensible behavior. He swears that his wife be reduced to menial slave labor. She would have to submit to enter the service of another master and *grind* his grain.[5] Both "grind" *(ṭāḥan)* and "bend" *(kāraʿ),*[6] particularly the latter, carry a sexual connotation. Being enslaved, she may be ordered about and used as her new master pleases.[7] If Job has lurked after his neighbor's wife, his wife will bear greater shame in serving her new master's wishes. Thus her punishment would be multiple—strenuous work, humiliation, and despair from the fact that the results of her labor would profit another. Though this curse is strange to a modern audience, in the ancient world it would be viewed as an acrid curse against her husband, for a wife is so closely identified with her husband that his disgrace is as great as hers for letting this grave injustice happen to her.

11, 12 These lines express the repugnant nature of adultery; it *would be a heinous crime [zimmâ].* This Hebrew word depicts violent, wanton deeds (Ps. 26:10; Judg. 20:6), particularly abhorrent sexual sins such as incest and prostitution (Lev. 18:27; 19:29; 20:14) or lewd acts (Jer. 13:27; Ezek. 16:27, 43, 58; 22:9, 11; 23:21, 27).[8] Such an *iniquity (ʿāwōn)* is a *punishable* offense *(pᵉlîlî).*[9] So if Job were guilty of seducing his neighbor's wife, the court would render a stiff judgment against him.

5. During his imprisonment in Philistia Samson was assigned to the hard labor of drawing a millstone (Judg. 16:21; cf. Exod. 11:5; Isa. 47:2; Lam. 5:13).

6. In a positive sense MT *kāraʿ* means "kneel to rest." It also means "bow under physical exhaustion" or "bow in humiliation." Most likely this word connotes the humiliation both from hard labor and from sexual abuse.

7. The idea that a sin of adultery should result in retributive punishment against one's wife is evident also in Deut. 28:30 and 2 Sam. 12:11.

8. See S. Steingrimsson, *"zmm," TDOT,* IV:89–90.

9. Heb. *pālîl* means "assessable" in this verse and in v. 28 according to E. Speiser, "The Stem *Pll,* in Hebrew," *JBL* 82 (1963) 301–306. D. Ap-Thomas (*VT* 6 [1956] 233), however, takes it to mean "an iniquity which outlawed the sinner from society," for he takes the verb *pālal* to mean "cut off" or "break off."

The power of sexual lust is likened to *a fire* burning out of control in one's breast (cf. Prov. 6:27–29; Sir. 9:9; 23:17). Its flames reach all the way to *Abaddon,* the abode of the dead (26:6; 28:22; Deut. 32:22).[10] While the guilty person is headed toward the grave, the flames consume all his produce, either burning the grain standing ripe in the fields or devouring it in storage. The teaching is that such a sinful deed consumes all one's wealth and destroys one's household.

d. Mistreatment of Servants (31:13–15)

13 *"If I have rejected the cause of my manservant*[1]
or my maidservant when they had a complaint against me,
14 *what shall I do when God rises up?*
When he makes inquiry, what shall I answer?
15 *Did not he who made me*[2] *in the belly make him?*
Did not one[3] *fashion us in the womb?"*

13, 14 More so than in other ancient Near Eastern cultures, slaves in Israel had rights as persons (e.g., Exod. 21:2–11, 20–21, 26–27; Lev. 25:39–55), but they were still limited because of their status. Israelites were to be kind toward slaves, remembering that they had been slaves in Egypt (Lev. 25:42–43, 55; Deut. 15:15; 16:12). Job contends that he has treated his slaves fairly and kindly. He insists that he has never refused to listen to a just complaint from either his male or his female slaves, including a complaint against himself. He has accepted the responsibility of treating his slaves justly as a God-given obligation, convinced that in the time of judgment God, either as a judge or a witness, will *rise (qûm)* to their defense.[4] Before rendering his decision God *makes inquiry (pāqaḏ)* into the way Job has managed his household. Possibly this means that as judge God will interrogate Job, the defendant, about his servants' complaints. Job knows that if he has mistreated any of his slaves, he could not *answer* God.

15 Besides having to give an account of his actions to God, Job

10. On Abaddon, see 26:6. The Wisdom writers also teach that whoever yields to sexual passion blindly travels the road to Sheol (cf. Prov. 7:21–27; 9:18).

1. For balance it is best to place the *'aṯnaḥ,* or caesura, under *'aḇdî,* "my manservant."

2. MT *wayᵉḵunennû* may be a Qal imperfect, but it seems best to take it as Polel (with Dhorme), a contracted form of *wayᵉḵônᵉnennû* to avoid four *n*s in succession (GKC, § 72cc).

3. Since MT *bāreḥem,* "in the womb," has the article, *'eḥāḏ,* "one," stands as the subject (so Vulg.). But the other versions take *'eḥāḏ* as an adjective modifying *reḥem,* i.e., "one womb."

4. In legal contexts *qûm* means "to stand up in court" as a plaintiff presenting a case (Mic. 6:1; Ps. 74:22), as a judge passing sentence (Ps. 76:10 [Eng. 9]; 82:8), or as a witness offering evidence (16:8; 19:25; Deut. 19:15–16; Ps. 27:12; 35:11; cf. Gordis).

bases his compassionate concern for each of his servants as a person in his conviction that God has made both himself and his servant in the same way.[5] Both were *made* (*ʿāśâ*) or *fashioned* (*kônēn*), each in his mother's womb,[6] by the same God. The word *fashion* suggests the arrangement of the parts of the body into an intricate structure. Earlier Job had marveled at the conception and birth of a child (10:10–11). The wondrous origin of a human life is true for both slave and free, although their earthly status differs markedly. From God's perspective the slave possesses value as well as the nobleman. Therefore, what God has made with such careful skill must be treated with respect. Job shows that he feels responsible to God for the management of his household just as his servants are accountable to him for the care of his fields and flocks. His faith has led him to a liberated attitude toward those who were usually considered as having little worth. In this regard he was way ahead of his time.

e. The Poor and the Weak (31:16–23)

16 *"If I refused the desire of the poor,*
or have caused the widow's eye to grow weary,
17 *and eaten my bread alone,*
and the orphan did not eat some of it—
18 *for from my youth he grew up with me as with a father,*[1]
from my mother's womb I guided her![2]
19 *If I have seen anyone perishing for lack of clothing,*
or a poor man without covering;
20 *and his loins did not bless me,*
warmed by the fleece of my sheep;
21 *if I have raised my hand against an orphan,*[3]
because I saw support for me[4] *in the gate,*

5. Cf. Prov. 22:2 and esp. Mal. 2:10.

6. This sequence of these verbs occurs also in Deut. 32:6 and Ps. 119:73.

1. Gordis suggests that MT *keʾāḇ,* "like a father," may be a contraction of two prepositions, *kiḇʾāḇ,* "like with a father."

2. As this verse stands in MT it seems to be out of context. Thus Hölscher deletes it. Others (e.g., Duhm, Driver-Gray) accept God as the subject and Job, in the first person, as the child. Then MT *ʾanḥennâ,* "I guided her," is read as *nāḥannî* or *yanḥēnî,* "he led me." Budde, Dhorme, and Pope understand Job as the subject of the verse, however, and therefore they read *ʾagaddelennû,* "I raised him," for MT *geḏēlanî* (see *BHS*). But Hakam and Gordis take the suffix on *geḏēlanî,* an intransitive verb in the Qal, as indirect, "he grew up with me." Either of the last two views preserves the parallelism between *minneʿûray,* "from my youth," and *mibbeṭen ʾimmî,* "from my mother's womb." The latter one is better, for it avoids emendation.

3. Many, e.g., Budde, Driver-Gray, Fohrer, and *BHS,* propose to emend MT *ʿal yāṯôm,* "against the orphan," to *ʿalê ṯām,* "against the innocent." But this proposal has no textual support and is unnecessary since the orphan is mentioned in v. 17b.

4. The exact sense of *ʿezrāṯî,* "my help, support," is uncertain. Perhaps it refers

22 *let my shoulder fall from its socket;*
let my arm be broken at the elbow.
23 *I have a dread of disaster from God;*[5]
I could not endure his majesty."

16, 17 Job defends his treatment of the disenfranchised members of society—*the poor, the widow,* and *the orphan.* Whenever any of these people begged for food and cried out for shelter, Job responded to their pleas. While begging for basic needs is degrading, being turned away by one who is able to help produces a feeling of utter worthlessness, as captured by the language *caused the widow's eye to grow weary.* Job did not sit down to eat bread by himself without being concerned about an orphan's hunger. He shared the abundance from his fields with the unfortunate.

18 Job inserts a parenthetical thought expressing the longevity of his compassionate treatment of the orphan and the widow. This understanding of the difficult pronouns throughout the verse takes the antecedent of *he* in the first line as the orphan of v. 17, and the antecedent of *her* in the second line as the widow of v. 16. *from my youth* is hard to explain. But it cannot be too easily dismissed, for it has an excellent parallel in the phrase *from my mother's womb.* Possibly the phrase *he grew up with me* indicates that Job learned to care for the unfortunate because his father raised orphans alongside his own children. The other possibility is to change the pronoun *my* to "his" and to understand the verse to say that Job raised orphaned infants, being to them like a father.

19, 20 Job showed compassion to whoever was languishing from exposure to the elements due to *lack of clothing.* When he came upon an ill-clad person, he gave him clothes. As a result, Job says that the loins of the poor, *warmed* with a garment made from the wool of his own flocks, *blessed* him for his kindness. *loins* is a synecdoche for the whole person. Good

---

to a friend or servant of the plaintiff who took a place in the crowd assembled in the gate to hear a case. When the plaintiff signaled, he would arouse the crowd to shout down or even beat down an opponent (cf. Pope). From evidence found in Ugaritic texts, M. Dahood (*RSP,* II:25–26) suggests that *ʿezrāṯî* may mean "liberation, acquittal" (cf. 3 Aqht, rev. 14). On this basis he translates this line: "If I raised my hand against the orphan, when I saw his acquittal at the gate." This idea is an interesting possibility, but it has two problems. It requires the *yod* suffix to be taken as a third person form, rather than the normal first person form, and *ʿzr* in 3 Aqht needs to mean "rescue," rather than "help," being parallel to *plṭ,* "save, deliver." The reason the author chose this particular word is that it is similar in sound to *ʿezrōʿî,* "my arm," in v. 22b. In this way the author enhances the tie between the offense and the punishment.

5. For the last three words of this line, *ʾēlay ʾêḏ ʾēl,* "to me (is) a disaster (from) God," Budde and Fohrer read *ʾēl yeʾĕṯâ ʾēlāy,* "because the dread of God has come over me." Since Syr. and probably LXX support this second reading, it needs consideration. But MT is followed as the more difficult reading.

works done with an attitude of superiority or contempt demean the recipient, but when they are done out of genuine concern, they have the potential of establishing a bond between the parties and enriching both lives.

21 Job next defends his conduct as a member of the court assembled at the city *gate*. He has not abused his position to pressure the judge to decide a case against an orphan to his own or to a friend's advantage. The *orphan* exemplifies one without any power or means to influence the court. Specifically Job says that he has not *raised his hand against an orphan,* i.e., he has not made a gesture designed to indict another (cf. Isa. 10:32; 19:16). Such an action undertaken by an influential party could turn the mood of the court against the defendant, regardless of his innocence. Another possible interpretation of this gesture is that Job did not signal one of his servants, i.e., his supporter standing by to help his master, to arouse the crowd in shouting down the poor defendant as he presented his defense. In ancient courts if a party was silenced, that party lost the case.

22 Job specifies the punishment if he should use the system of justice to distort the cause of the poor: *let my shoulder fall from its socket,* i.e., be separated, and *let my arm be broken at the elbow.*[6] This curse would break his strength, leaving him helpless.[7]

23 Job states the reason for his driving compassion for the unfortunate. He fears *disaster from God* should he abuse his wealth and power. God's *majesty* would overwhelm him. By this statement Job does not mean that he acted continually out of fear and was, therefore, afraid to venture anything. Rather it is to be understood in terms of the Wisdom literature, which taught that the fear of God or reverence is the basis of wisdom. A profound awareness of God's majestic holiness guides a person to pursue righteousness and to shun evil. A person who believes this acts in all matters as though he is directly accountable to God. If he had denied helping the unfortunate, Job knows that he could not *endure God's majesty.* In God's presence he would be condemned.

f. Trust in Wealth and Worship of the Heavenly Bodies (31:24–28)

24 *"If I have made gold my confidence,*
or called fine gold my security,

6. Heb. *qāneh* means "stalk, reed, beam of a scale, shaft of a lampstand," and in postbiblical Hebrew it can mean "radius." Pope argues from Ugaritic evidence that *qn ḏrʿh* means "the upper arm, including the flesh." Kissane thinks that it means "the elbow." The parallelism favors the latter view.

7. In the OT a broken arm indicates that one's power has been decisively broken. Often God is the one who does the breaking (cf. Ps. 10:15; 37:17; Jer. 48:25; Ezek. 30:21–22).

25 *if I have rejoiced because my wealth was great,*
or because my hand has gotten[1] much,
26 *if I have looked at the light shining radiantly,*
or the moon moving[2] in splendor,[3]
27 *and my heart was secretly enticed,*
and my hand threw a kiss from[4] my mouth,
28 *that also is a punishable iniquity;*
I would have denied God on high."

24, 25 Job claims that he has never *made gold* his *confidence*. Riches pull hard at the heart of their owner to trust in them, for with their possession go power, prestige, and freedom from want. Riches also create a tremendous thirst for more riches (Eccl. 5:9 [Eng. 10]). As a result, the wealthy use their skills and influence to increase their wealth, often by squeezing it out of the weak or poor. Also, the rich flaunt their gold to impress others with their affluence (cf. Jer. 9:23–24). In ancient society a wealthy person would be prone to have some of his gold cast into an idol (see Judg. 17:3–5) or used to plate a wooden idol (see Isa. 40:18–20). But Job asserts that he has never yielded to such a temptation. He has never based his joy in or gloated over his great wealth, nor has he vaunted himself as the maker of his own fortune. The phrase *my hand* means that a person proudly acquires his wealth by his own power. Resolutely Job disputes Eliphaz's insinuation that he has raised gold above God as his first love (22:24–25). To the contrary, he knows that he has always remembered that God himself is the one who gave him the strength and wisdom to earn his abundance (cf. Deut. 8:17–18).

26, 27 Job's affection has never been so drawn by the heavenly bodies, the brightness of the sun (lit. "light"; Heb. *'ôr;* cf. Hab. 3:4),[5] or the lure of the moon, moving across the sky in splendor, that he has bowed down to them. In the wide-open expanse of the Near Eastern landscape, the sun's shining in brilliant splendor day after day created the feeling that the sun ruled the earth. The glory of the moon, mysterious in its phases and marvelous in its fullness, allured human affection. No wonder these bodies were

1. Heb. *māṣā'*, "find," also has the nuance "arrive at, reach, attain," according to Ceresko, *Job 29–31*, p. 156.

2. Ceresko (ibid., p. 160) suggests that *hālak*, lit. "walk, go," here means "wane," and that *hll*, "shine," in the first line means "wax."

3. Cf. Deut. 4:19; 2 K. 23:5; Jer. 8:1–2. Heb. *yāqār*, "precious, splendid," is used esp. for gems (Rowley). This word stands immediately before the verb for emphasis and functions as an accusative of state (GKC, § 118n). Gordis believes that the language refers specifically to the full moon.

4. The preposition *le*, "to," has the sense here of "from" (Pope).

5. Hakam takes *'ôr*, lit. "light," to mean "the stars," but the parallelism with "moon" suggests that *'ôr* means "the sun" (cf. Zech. 14:6).

widely worshiped as gods throughout the Near East. But the lure of these bodies has never caused Job's confidence in God to waver. He never *threw a kiss* to them as a sign of affection and devotion, a widespread pagan practice. Apparently Job is referring to the gesture in which one kissed his hand and threw the kiss to the heavenly bodies. He has never shown other gods affection even in secret.

28 Job states that such idolatrous worship was *a punishable iniquity [ʿāwōn]*.[6] He knew that such worship would be a direct denial of the very God who stood far above the heavenly bodies. To worship the creature rather than the Creator was to him absurd, for in so doing he *would have denied God,* separating himself from God's favor. Job has guarded himself against such folly.

g. Satisfaction at a Foe's Misfortune and Failure to Extend Hospitality to a Sojourner (31:29–32)

29 *"If I have rejoiced at my foe's ruin*
and exulted[1] when evil befell him,
30 *I have never[2] given my mouth to sinning,*
asking for his life with a curse.
31 *If the men of my tent have ever said,*
'Who has not[3] been sated from his meat?'
32 *The sojourner has not had to lodge in the street;*
I have opened my doors to the traveler."[4]

29 At this point in the oath a series of three conditional clauses states the sin Job disavows (vv. 29–34), but there are no main sentences stating the curse or consequences of such action. These clauses could be made into sentences by framing them as questions. However, to preserve their relation to the oath, the *if* form is continued.[5]

6. In a law found in Deut. 17:2–5 death by stoning was the punishment for false worship.

1. Dhorme thinks that the verb *wᵉhiṯʿōrartî,* "I stirred myself," can mean "exult" in the Hithpolel. Others (e.g., Gordis; cf. *BHS*) follow the Targ. and read *wᵉhiṯrōʿaʿtî,* "I shouted for joy." It is preferable to follow MT if that root can bear the meaning "exult." This verb is an example of the perfect consecutive after an imperfect referring to repeated acts in the past (GKC, § 112c).

2. With Ceresko, *Job 29–31,* p. 165, the *waw* on *wᵉlōʾ* is taken as emphatic (so Blommerde, *Northwest Semitic Grammar and Job,* p. 115).

3. The negatives in both lines reinforce the strength of conviction undergirding Job's hospitality.

4. Heb. *ʾōraḥ,* "traveler," may be a variant spelling of the more common *ʾōrēaḥ* (cf. Gordis, *BHS*). Cf. Jer. 14:8 for the parallel of *gēr,* "stranger," and *ʾōrēaḥ* (Ceresko, *Job 29–31,* p. 170).

5. See p. 410 n.1.

Job claims not to *have rejoiced at* his *foe's ruin.* The term for *foe* is literally "the one hating me." When a person learns that his antagonist has fallen into dire straits, he naturally feels like giving forth a gleeful shout, happy that at least God is giving that person his due. But Job never became ecstatic with joy when *evil* or misfortune *befell* his enemy. He was reaching beyond the standard of loving his neighbor (Lev. 19:18, 34) to that of showing compassion to an enemy. He was mindful of the proverb: "Do not rejoice when your enemy falls, and let not your heart be glad when he stumbles; lest the Lord see it, and be displeased, and turn away his anger from him" (Prov. 24:17–18; cf. 17:5). Again Job's moral sensitivity points toward the ideal standard taught by Jesus (cf. Matt. 5:43–48; Luke 6:27–36).

30 Job has never spoken harmful words against any of his enemies with his *mouth* (*ḥikkâ,* lit. "palate"). In Hebraic thought the palate and the tongue are the instruments of speech (cf. Job 6:30). Job has not used his organs of speech *asking for his life [nepeš] with a curse,* i.e., he has not pronounced a curse that was intended to cause a foe's premature death.[6]

31, 32 In the true nomadic spirit Job entertained his guests graciously and generously. He knew that not to show hospitality was a disgraceful act (cf. Judg. 19–21). The phrase *the men of my tent* is taken to mean guests invited to dine at Job's table. This phrase may, however, mean kinsmen, for the family ties of tribal people are far-reaching. Whomever a sheikh received as a guest was greeted warmly. His feet were washed, and he was fed a sumptuous meal. No guest could ever have said that he left Job's table hungry.

Job extended his generous hospitality also to *the sojourner* or foreigner *(gēr)* and *the traveler (ʾōraḥ).* When such transients entered the city, they often sought refuge at the plaza or the broad place of the city. There they were permitted to stay the night. The usual custom, though, was for a citizen of the village to invite the sojourner to his house, care for his donkey, prepare a meal for him, and give him a place to sleep (cf. Gen. 19:1–3; Judg. 19:16–21). To such wayfarers Job's door was always open, so to speak.[7] Nightly he may have sent his servants out to the city's plaza in search of any travelers without lodging. Whomever they found, they graciously invited to Job's residence. Job provided a substantial meal for his guests, as the term *meat* indicates, for meat was usually reserved for festive occasions. Job's house guests would bear witness to his warm hospitality.

6. Cf. the power of the curse against a life in 1 K. 3:11.

7. A saying in *Pirke Abot* 1:5 captures the same flavor: "May your house be open to the broad place; and may the poor be your guests."

h. Concealment of a Sin without Confession (31:33–34)

33 *"If I have covered my transgression like a man,*[1]
concealing[2] *my iniquity in my bosom*[3]
34 *because I feared the large crowd,*
and the contempt of the clan terrified me,
so that I kept silent and did not go out the door."

33, 34 Job is sure that he has never *covered* any *transgression* that he has done. He overcame the human tendency to conceal his mistakes and wrongs in order to avoid embarrassment and to skirt the responsibility of that error. The phrase *concealing my iniquity in my bosom* means that the transgressor hides the object related to his iniquity, e.g., a stolen item was concealed next to the chest under his tunic, a garment without external pockets. An evil deed spawns secrecy. But Job had never yielded to this strong human inclination. He confessed his mistakes and publicly bore the responsibility of his faults. He shied away from the slightest taint of hypocrisy.

If Job had concealed his iniquity, he would have been acting out of fear of public opinion. Even more terrifying was *the contempt* that his own *clan* would express to him. If he had done wrong, the clan might have ostracized him, forcing him to live like a vagabond. No wonder a person in those days kept silent about his transgressions. But because he never transgressed God's law, Job had no need of concealing any deed. He never worried about the shame of exposure. It is this high commitment to personal integrity that motivates Job to swear this oath of innocence in order hopefully to win a public vindication from God.

i. Abuse of the Land (31:38–40b)

38 *"If my land has cried out against me,*
and at the same time[1] *its furrows have wept,*
39 *if I have eaten its yield without payment,*
or snuffed out the life of its tenant,[2]

1. Some, e.g., Gordis, take *ʾāḏām* to mean Adam and his reaction of hiding from the presence of God after he had sinned. But the reference to "bosom" suggests the garments of Job's contemporaries, not those from primeval times. Others, e.g., Budde and Fohrer, wish to read *mēʾāḏām,* "from man," but MT is quite satisfactory and is supported by the versions.

2. The infinitive construct *liṭmôn* is taken as a gerund (cf. GKC, § 45f), identifying how the covering up was done.

3. MT *ḥōḇ,* a cognate to the common Aram. *ḥubbāʾ*, means "bosom, hollow."

1. In this context *yaḥaḏ* is taken to mean "at the same time, simultaneously" (Fohrer); BDB, p. 403, and Gordis, however, take it to mean "altogether."

2. Heb. *baʿal* usually means "owner," but Job is the master. It appears that he is thinking of those who supervise an area of his vast holdings, i.e., "tenant." Possibly *baʿal*

40 *let briers grow instead of wheat,*
stinkweeds[3] *instead of barley."*

38, 39 The last injustice Job denies is any abuse of his land. It appears doubtful that Job would add another specific item after affixing his signature (vv. 35–37), so most modern interpreters place these verses earlier in the declaration of innocence. Perhaps a scribe discovered that they had been inadvertently omitted from the text and copied them at the end to preserve them. No consensus has been reached regarding the proper placement of these verses; they are placed before v. 35 simply because of their proximity to that location.[4]

The structure of these verses is that of a conditional oath, with the condition contained in v. 40a. As already noted this is the strongest possible type of oath. Job swears that he has not abused his land. Although in Hebraic society the land was not worshiped as a god as it was among the neighboring peoples, it was treated as having personality. If the people engaged in lewd sins, the land became defiled, i.e., infertile, and spewed out the inhabitants. When this happened, the people would have to leave that land in search of a place that would support them (cf. Lev. 18:24–28).

The OT teaches that there is a bond between a people's right to occupy a land and their moral behavior. So the Sinaitic covenant had various regulations related to the land (cf. Lev. 18:24–28); e.g., it was not to be sown with two kinds of seeds (Lev. 19:19), and it was to receive rest every seven years (Exod. 23:10–11; Lev. 25:2–7; 26:34–35). Most of all, shed blood defiled the land, which in response cried out against the violator, demanding vengeance (cf. Gen. 4:10–12; Num. 35:33–34; Ps. 106:38). So when the people are disobedient, the land withers and mourns beneath the

---

is a dialectal variant of *paʿal,* "worker" (as in Ugaritic; see Pope). In another direction this word has been taken to mean "protecting spirits"; cf. M. Dahood, *Bib* 41 (1960) 303; idem, 43 (1962) 362.

3. The word for "stinkweeds," *boʾšâ,* comes from the root *bʾš,* "have a bad smell, stink" (cf. Akk. *buʾšu,* "stinkplant"). It refers to an obnoxious, foul-smelling weed (cf. *beʾušîm,* "wild grapes" or "stinking things," in Isa. 5:2, 4; see BDB, p. 93). Dhorme identifies it with annual mercury, called dead or malodorus nettle, *Lolium temulentum* (see KB, p. 103). Or it may be equated with the darnel *(zizánion)* of the NT; cf. Matt. 13:25–27, 29–30, 36, 38, 40.

4. Many other locations for these verses have been made; e.g., Hölscher places them after v. 7, Pope after v. 8, Budde after v. 12, Kissane and Dhorme after v. 32. Terrien cautions against rearrangement of the text based on modern logic. He suggests that the present location of these verses may be another example of the author's flair for the device of the afterthought (e.g., 3:16; 9:32; 14:13). The result then is a relaxing of the extreme tension Job's oath has created. Nevertheless, the finality of the oath from Job's view favors placing the verses about his signature as the conclusion to the avowal of innocence.

weight of their sins (cf. Hos. 4:1–3; Isa. 24:1–13). Conversely, when the people obeyed God's laws, he blessed the land so that it yielded abundantly.

In Job's day there must have been regulations regarding the use of the land, for he acknowledges that a bond exists between the land and its owner's deeds. If the owner abuses his workers by withholding their wages or shortens the life span of his servants by demanding excessive production under poor working conditions, the land and all its furrows will cry out against the lord on behalf of those oppressed. The phrase *eaten its yield without payment* could mean that the tithe had not been paid or gleanings had not been left for the poor (cf. Lev. 19:9–10; 23:22). But Job knows that he has been free of any such mismanagement of his land.

40a, b Job specifies what must befall him if he has abused his land. His land should lie fallow while *briers* and *stinkweeds* grow instead of *wheat* and *barley*. This is the typical description of land left untended (cf. Prov. 24:30–31). The prophet proclaimed that God executed a curse against his wayward people by causing the land to grow briers, thorns, and thistles (cf. Isa. 5:6; 34:13; Hos. 9:6). This kind of curse wiped out a tribe's food supply, and, if severe enough, it could cause them to migrate to find food for themselves and their flocks. If Job had violated his land and its workers, he asks that a curse of this kind rob his fields of their fertility. His land then would no longer support him and he would be driven from his household to wander about in poverty. But Job affirms his innocence in regard to his management of his own land.

2. THE SEALING OF THE OATH (31:35–37, 40C)

35 *"Oh, that my judge would give me[1] a hearing!*
Behold my signature! Let Shaddai answer me!
Let my accuser write a document.
36 *I would surely carry it on my shoulder;*
I would bind it on like a crown.
37 *I would give him an account of my steps;*
like a prince I would present myself before him."
40c *Job's words are ended.*

1. There is great emphasis on "me" *(lî),* for this pronoun occurs twice. Some mss., LXX (Theod.), and Syr. omit the first *lî,* while many, e.g., Driver-Gray, wish to eliminate the second *lî.* Gordis finds the double preposition acceptable for emphasis; in fact, the first line would have too few syllables with the removal of either *lî.* E. Sutcliffe (*Bib* 30 [1949] 67) suggests that the first *lî* was originally *'ēl,* "God," having arisen from a displaced *'*; this offers a fine reading, but it would detract from the emphasis on *šadday* in the second line, according to Fohrer.

Job has sworn that he is guiltless of committing any sin, particularly the fourteen sins he has enumerated. Through this list he protests that he has lived justly and avoided the appearance of all wrong. Confident that he is innocent, he seals his oath with his own signature. God now must either verify Job's oath or activate the curses it contains.

35 Job ends his oath of innocence with an exclamation, pleading that the heavenly *judge (šōmēaʿ)* would give his case a hearing. M. Dick demonstrates that Heb. *šmʿ*, "hear," in Northwest Semitic is a technical term for "to hear (a case)"; then he argues that the participle *šōmēaʿ* means "an official who mediates legal disputes" (e.g., 2 Sam. 15:3–4).[2] Job informs the court that his *signature (tāw)* is appended to his oath of innocence. He is resolutely affirming everything he has sworn. Heb. *tāw* is the last letter of the Hebrew alphabet, and in ancient times it was written like an English *X*. An illiterate person could authenticate a document by marking it with a *tāw*. Since Job probably had a cylinder seal to certify any documents, the reference to the *tāw* suggests that he personally signed the oath rather than only impressing on it his seal. With his signature Job makes the document official. Legally he has demanded that Shaddai answer him.

Earlier Job had said to God: "Then call and I shall answer, or let me speak and you respond" (13:22). Since God has not responded, Job, as defendant, has sworn an oath in order to compel God, the plaintiff, to file his complaint and then substantiate it. If God remains silent, then all the world will know that the defendant has been falsely accused.

Job makes this desperate plea, hopeful that God will act in justice toward him. Because he has forced the issue, God, the supreme Ruler, has two apparent options, either to activate the curses contained in the oath or to write *a document*. Job, of course, asks for the latter. The text reads simply "book" *(sēp̄er)*. This term may refer to various kinds of legal documents, e.g., "a bill of divorce" (*sēp̄er kᵉrîṯûṯ;* Deut. 24:1; Isa. 50:1) or "a bill of sale" (*sēp̄er hammiqnâ;* Jer. 32:11–12, 14, 16). Here it could be a formal indictment.[3] But in the light of v. 36 Job anticipates that his opponent-at-law

2. M. Dick, "Legal Metaphor in Job 31," *CBQ* 41 (1979) 47–49.

3. Another view, offered by Fohrer, understands the document to be a written accusation; e.g., in Egyptian judicial customs a written accusation was issued before a trial proceeding began. The background to this practice is the belief that a writ of indictment is laden with curses and will cause the death of its bearer if he is guilty. Such an ordeal functioned as the test for an oath of innocence. That Job lives despite his wearing this curse-laden writ will become proof to all that he is innocent. By taking this step Job is certain of victory. This position stumbles over having to view the type of trial as a trial by ordeal; earlier Job had totally rejected an ordeal as a way of establishing his innocence (9:30–31).

will have to issue an acquittal. Thus the document is taken to be a writ of innocence.

36 Job would be so proud of this document that he says *I would surely carry it on my shoulder*[4] in full public display. It would be his *crown.*[5] Just as a person's position or authority is immediately revealed by his headgear or by the insignia on his shoulders, so Job's wearing of this writ of innocence would testify to all of his blameless, upright character. Having been humiliated publicly, Job would be vindicated publicly. This theme carries through the metaphor that his misfortune has soiled his robe of righteousness and turban of justice (29:14). Now he needs something to wear as proof of his innocence so that all, particularly his scoffers, may know that God has cleared him. It is important to observe that Job does not seek the restoration of his wealth or his family. Instead, he addresses his most fundamental need—a right relationship with God and respect from his neighbors.

37 Job declares that he would speak his complete case. *I would give him an account of my steps [ṣeʿāḏîm];* i.e., Job would disclose all his ways and thoughts. There is nothing that his contender might uncover and present as surprising, convicting evidence. *Like a prince [nāḡîḏ]*[6] Job will approach the court confidently. That is, he will bear himself in God's presence like a righteous ruler, not like a criminal. In turn he expects the court to treat him with respect. If a convincing case can not be presented against him, the court will be obligated to restore his honor. To the end Job remains tenacious. He will not succumb without a final verdict rendered by the divine Judge himself. Having sworn to his own innocence, Job will remain silent until God speaks.

40c At the conclusion of this speech is a note that Job's words are ended. He rests his case. He will not even lament any more. He will wait for God to answer his oath, hopeful of being declared innocent. The next chapter will open a new section. This line is probably an editorial comment like that found in Jer. 51:64 and Ps. 72:20.

4. Heb. *šeḵem* is "the nape of the neck" or "shoulder" on which burdens were borne (Driver-Gray). Symbolically a ruler is said to bear the authority of government on his shoulder; cf. Isa. 9:5 (Eng. 6); 22:22.

5. Heb. "crown" *(ʿaṭārôṯ)* is in the plural, for the plural may represent the tiers of a crown (Rowley). In the Wisdom literature the crown is a symbol of honor, beauty, and blessing (Prov. 4:9; 12:4; 17:6; Sir. 6:31; 15:6; 25:6).

6. The title *nāḡîḏ* (cf. 29:10) was used for the king of Israel at various times, but esp. at the rise of the kingship (1 Sam. 9:16; 10:1; 13:14; 25:30; 2 Sam. 5:2; 6:21; 7:8; 1 K. 1:35). In the earliest times it designated the close bond between Yahweh and the king. It is no accident that Job chose this title for himself. If nothing more, it conveys his high and important role in the community. Cf. C. Westermann, *THAT,* II:34–35.

AIM

Job's last speech is a masterpiece. He recounts his former honor (ch. 29), mourns his humiliation (ch. 30), and then swears an oath of innocence (ch. 31). His confidence has grown so strong that he enumerates specific sins that he has not done, under threat of a terrible curse should he be lying. He has lived by the highest moral standard, concerned not only with his acts but more importantly with his attitudes and motives. Job has had regard for the dignity of all people, be they nobles, servants, or foreigners, and his affection for God survives underneath his complaints.

The clarity of Job's conviction reveals that he has risen above his deep despair as expressed in his curse-lament (ch. 3). Even though his pain has not lessened, he has been able to give form to his thoughts. By verbally lamenting his bitterest feelings, he has not let the bitterness and anger of his sorrow drive him to utter despair. He gives focus to his frustration by addressing God as his opponent. Complaining to God about his wretched condition keeps him from falling into subjective disorientation. Although frustrated at God's apparent hostility, Job has, throughout the dialogue, kept a high view of God in his thinking by reciting hymnic lines in praise of God. Now he rests his case with God, believing that in the end God will do justice by him.

In these chapters Job is a model of how the human spirit can struggle against all aspects of suffering—physical, emotional, social, spiritual—and sustain a search for God while God remains hidden. The ability to express genuine faith under extreme duress enables the human spirit to bear the severest tragedy and prevail. Job disciplines his thoughts and his emotions as he demands an answer from God. Since God is the supreme ruler, Job has nowhere to turn but to God, with the hope that God will answer him. If God does answer him, his experience will prove that every misfortune can have a redemptive outcome. To cope with a hard, trying experience, the afflicted must keep his focus on God in order not to compromise his confidence in God. Such persistent faith will strengthen the bond between God and the afflicted. Evil will never triumph over a person who trusts in God. Job will find justification. In this speech the bifocal image of the patient Job of the prologue and the agitated Job of the dialogue comes into clear focus: the persevering Job. Assuredly Job demonstrates that God's confidence in him has been well-founded, for his most basic motivation for serving God, the very motivation that urges him to persevere, is his longing for the dynamic communion he finds in God's presence.

VI. THE ELIHU SPEECHES (32:1–37:24)

Job's avowal of innocence is so audacious and final that it leaves the comforters speechless. All are terrified, waiting for an answer from the heavens. But God remains silent. Then a young man named Elihu arises. Taking advantage of the silence, he asks for permission to address Job. Possessed by a compelling need to defend God's honor, he is convinced that he can instruct Job even though the others have failed. Who should change the mood but the youthful, bombastic Elihu. What a surprise! Elihu's verbose, overly apologetic style offers comic relief to break the tight, fearful atmosphere created by Job's oath.[1]

On the serious side Elihu claims divine inspiration as the source of his wisdom (32:18–22). Enlightened by God's Spirit, he offers special insight into the way God instructs people. Thus he functions as God's forerunner both by his position between Job's avowal of innocence and Yahweh's answer and by the content of his speeches.

After a lengthy apology for speaking, Elihu delivers four unanswered discourses. His thesis is twofold: God disciplines a person to turn him from the error of his way, and God governs justly without exception. Although Elihu's approach is close to that of the three friends, he differs from them in that he does not assume that all suffering is punishment for past sins. He teaches that misfortune may befall a person in order to awaken him to some wrongful attitude or unconscious error and thus keep him from taking a wrong course. Another major difference in his teaching is the emphasis that suffering may be an expression of God's mercy more than his wrath. With these theses Elihu makes a significant contribution to the core issue of the book, namely, how the righteous should respond to suffering.

Furthermore, the Elihu speeches stress God's sovereignty. If God had spoken immediately after Job's oath, it would appear that Job's oath had compelled him to answer. That God remains silent indicates that his coming

1. W. Whedbee ("The Comedy of Job," *Studies in the Book of Job,* Semeia 7, ed. R. Polzin and D. Robertson [Missoula: Society of Biblical Literature, 1977], pp. 18–20) finds Elihu playing the role of the *alazṓn* or buffoon, "a comic figure whom the author exposes and ridicules" (p. 20).

appearance rests in his sovereign decision. God always keeps the initiative with himself. In addition, through Elihu the author presents some major insights into God's use of suffering.[2] Also, the importance of Elihu's role among the various speakers should not be overlooked; it is attested in the fact that he delivers four speeches, one more than each of the comforters.

A. INTRODUCTION OF ELIHU (32:1–5)

1 *These three men ceased answering Job because he was righteous in his own sight.*[1]

2 *Then Elihu,*[2] *son of Barachel,*[3] *the Buzite*[4] *of the family of Ram,*[5] *became exceedingly angry with Job because he made himself more righteous than God.*

3 *And he became angry at his three friends because they did not have an answer and so put God in the wrong.*[6]

2. See the Introduction above, pp. 28–30. This idea has been well argued by R. Gordis in *The Book of God and Man: A Study of Job* (Chicago: University of Chicago Press, 1966), pp. 104–16.

1. A textual variant reads "in their eyes" (LXX, Syr.) and is followed by many (e.g., Dhorme, Hölscher, Fohrer). Driver-Gray and Gordis point out that *hāyâ,* "he was," would be the correct grammar with the variant reading rather than *hû'*, "he." After Job's last speech the singular seems more appropriate. Also, there is no clue that the friends have come to the position that Job is right. If they do not continue to speak, however, they will be conceding that Job is right. Although the variant is the harder reading, the grammar supports MT.

2. Elihu is a name borne by others in the OT, including one of Samuel's ancestors (1 Sam. 1:1), a chief of a tribe in Manasseh (1 Chr. 12:21 [Eng. 20]), a member of the Korahites, the temple gatekeepers (1 Chr. 26:7), and a brother of David (1 Chr. 27:18).

3. This reference is the single occurrence of the name Barachel in the OT. Pope posits that it is found in Akkadian documents as Barikilu/i. It is attested several times in the business documents of the Murashu house (possibly Jewish) from Babylon (5th century B.C.).

4. In Gen. 22:20–21 Buz, brother of Uz, was a nephew of Abraham; this would suggest that Elihu was an Aramean. But in Jer. 25:23 Buz is mentioned along with Dedan and Tema, locales in the Edomite area.

5. In the OT an ancestor of David is named Ram (Ruth 4:19). Another Ram is associated with Jerahmeel (1 Chr. 2:9–10, 25, 27). Perhaps this name is a hypocoristicon for "(God) is exalted." Interestingly the Targ. identifies Ram as Abraham.

6. MT reads *wayyaršîʿû ʾeṯ-ʾîyôḇ,* "they declared Job guilty." An alternative reading is *wayyaršîʿû ʾeṯ-hāʾĕlōhîm,* "they made God appear guilty." This variant is one of the eighteen *Tiqqune sopherim,* instances in which harsh or inappropriate language in reference to God appeared in the original text and the scribes altered the text to alleviate the embarrassment. Here they wished to avoid the occurrence of God as the direct object of this negative verb. It is easier to account for a textual variant moving from "God" to "Job" than vice versa.

4 *Elihu had waited while they spoke*[7] *with Job*[8] *because they were all older than he was.*

5 *When Elihu saw that these three men had no answer, he became angry.*

1 Since Elihu had not been mentioned in the prologue, the author introduces him in a prose section.[9] Compared to the brief, compact scenes of the prologue, this introduction is long and wordy, a foreshadowing of Elihu's style. The first verse makes the transition from Job's avowal of innocence to the introduction of Elihu. It states that the three men who have addressed Job and sought to convince him of the error of his way have abandoned their attempts because they could not dissuade Job from his conviction that he was a righteous man. Perhaps the chasm between the comforters and Job is reflected in the term used for the comforters, *these men (ʾᵃnāšîm),* rather than "friends" *(rēʿîm)* as in 2:11; 19:21; 42:10.

2 Elihu is introduced in the traditional style with a full patronym. His father, Barachel, is named along with his tribe, Buz, and his clan, Ram. This full genealogy reflects Elihu's youth and lack of personal accomplishment. The name *Elihu* means "he is my God." It is similar to the name Elijah *(ʾēlîyāhû),* "Yahweh is my God." His name bears witness that El is the highest God. His father's name, Barachel, means "Bless, Oh God" or "God has blessed." Although the setting of this book is to the east of Canaan, the combined weight of the names in Elihu's lineage identifies him with the kin of Abraham, a faithful worshiper of the one true God. His name and his function in the book indicate that he is Yahweh's forerunner. True to his name, Elihu will defend God's honor, teaching that God mercifully and justly disciplines his servants. His teaching prepares for Yahweh's appearance to Job.

In this introduction Elihu's youth and his anger are given prominence. In four verses (vv. 2–5) there are four references to his anger. His *anger* is righteous indignation, for he sees the whole dialogue between Job and the three friends as having been argued poorly on both sides. He is particularly angry with Job, for in holding on to his own innocence Job has

7. MT *biḏḇārîm,* "with words," is most difficult. A revocalizing offers an excellent reading: *bᵉḏabbᵉrām,* "while they were speaking."

8. MT *ʾeṯ-ʾîyôḇ* is taken by Hölscher, Tur-Sinai, and Pope as a dittography from the end of v. 3, but the full nature of this prose section favors its inclusion. "With Job" could go with "wait," as explained by Gordis, or with "speaking." The latter is preferred, for Elihu waited during the whole dialogue.

9. The entry of a new person requires some background material. That material is presented in prose as elsewhere, e.g., the headings to chs. 3, 27, 29, 38, and at the end of ch. 31.

made himself more righteous [ṣeḏeq] than God. Elihu cannot tolerate anyone casting a shadow on God's righteousness.

3 Elihu is also angry at the three friends because in their failure to *have an answer* to Job they *put God in the wrong*. Elihu assumes that since these men have ceased speaking, not having convinced Job of the error of his position, they appear to have conceded that Job has won the debate.[10] This thinking reflects an ancient legal practice in which a party could win a dispute by silencing his opponent with his arguments.

4, 5 Elihu was a bystander listening to the dialogue. During the dialogue he often had an insight that would clarify an idea being articulated by one of the friends, but he remained silent out of deference to his elders. The social custom of that time was for only the elders to speak; everybody else remained silent. Another person could offer a word only when properly recognized by them. Elihu adhered to this custom until it became evident to all that the elders had no intention of responding to Job's oath. His anger, however, had been slowly simmering. Since it has now reached the boiling point, Elihu feels that he must vent it by speaking.

B. ELIHU'S SPEECHES (32:6–37:24)

Elihu delivers four unanswered speeches. The substance of each speech is as follows. In his first speech Elihu develops the theme that God instructs a person through dreams and afflictions. God uses these means to turn a person from wrongdoing, either potential or real, that will result in a premature death. To guarantee the release of that person from death's grip, he sends a special mediating angel to offer that person's ransom should he turn and pray for God's help (32:6–33:33). In his second speech Elihu defends the tenet that God governs the world in justice without exception (34:1–37). In the third speech Elihu reasons that human beings cannot affect God either by their sins or by their righteous acts. In no way, therefore, can God be placed under obligation as Job has attempted to do by demanding that God acknowledge his innocence (35:1–16). In his last speech Elihu returns to his opening thesis that God disciplines anyone in jeopardy, even the mightiest, with suffering. Then he prepares Job for God's appearing by contemplating the divine glory that is manifest in a thunderstorm. He concludes with the conviction that the wise are those who fear God (36:1–37:24).

10. Cf. H. Richter, *Studien zu Hiob: Der Aufbau des Hiobbuches dargestellt an den Gattungen des Rechtslebens,* Theologische Arbeiten 11 (Berlin: Evangelische Verlagsanstalt, 1958), pp. 40–41, 104–10. Also, in Isa. 41:21–29 it is implied that whoever fails to answer in a legal dispute loses.

1. ELIHU'S FIRST SPEECH (32:6–33:33)

After a wordy apology in defense of his speaking, Elihu presents his thesis that God disciplines a person through dreams and pain in his effort to bring about moral growth. The speech may be divided into an apology (32:6–22) and the teaching about discipline (33:1–33).

a. An Apology (32:6–22)

6 *Then Elihu, son of Barachel, the Buzite spoke:*
"I am young in years,
and you are aged;
therefore I was timid and afraid
of offering[1] *my view to you.*
7 *I thought,*[2] *'Days should speak,*
and many years should make known[3] *wisdom.'*
8 *But it is the spirit in man,*
the breath of Shaddai, which gives him[4] *insight.*
9 *Seniors*[5] *may not be wise,*
and elders may not understand what is justice.
10 *Therefore, I say, 'Listen*[6] *to me;*
I, even I, will offer my view.'
11 *Behold, I have waited for your words;*
I have listened[7] *to your reasoning*[8]
while you searched out words.

1. MT *ḥiwwâ,* "declare," is an Aramaic word used in lieu of the more common Heb. *higgîd,* "tell, declare." It appears frequently in Elihu's speeches (32:10, 17; 36:2). But it is also found in 15:17, and the related noun *'aḥwâ,* "declaration," occurs in 13:17.

2. One way to express a former thought in Hebrew is with the verb *'āmar,* "he said or thought," in the perfect. Then the new thought is marked by *'āḵēn,* "but, indeed" (v. 8; cf. Isa. 49:4; Ps. 31:23 [Eng. 22]; 82:6–7).

3. The verb *yōḏîʿû,* "make known," is plural by its attraction to the plural *nomen regens.* LXX, however, reads it as a Qal, "know," instead of a Hiphil.

4. The plural suffix on *teḇînēm,* lit. "it gives them insight," understands *'ĕnôš,* "man," as a collective (Dhorme).

5. Heb. *rabbîm,* "seniors," means here "the aged," not "the great," for it parallels *zeqēnîm,* "elders," and is so used in the Manual of Discipline from Qumran (Pope). G. R. Driver (*Textus* 4 [1964] 91) finds in *rabbîm* a misunderstood abbreviation of *rabbê yāmîm,* "great in days," "aged men." Either way it is not necessary to emend MT to *rōḇ yāmîm,* "many of days," with Syr., as some do (e.g., Duhm and Fohrer).

6. MT *šimʿâ,* "hear," is translated in the plural by LXX, Syr., and Vulg. Whether they had a different text or preferred the plural for a smoother translation is moot. MT could be correct, for it is the harder reading and Elihu addresses the bulk of his words to Job. Nevertheless, since plural forms of "you" are used in this context and the apology is directed first to the elders in order that Elihu might receive their leave to speak to Job, the plural form *šimʿû* is read.

7. MT *'āzîn* is elliptical for *'a'azîn* (cf. GKC, § 68i).

8. For MT *teḇûnōṯêḵem,* "your reasoning," Syr. seems to have read *tklytkm,*

12 *I have paid close attention to you,*[9]
but, behold, no one has been able to refute Job;
none of you has answered his statements.
13 *Do not say, 'We have found wisdom;*
let God rebuke him,[10] *not man.'*
14 *He has not*[11] *ordered his words against me,*
I will not answer him with your sayings.
15 *Dismayed, they do not answer again;*
words have forsaken them.
16 *Shall I wait*[12] *because they do not speak,*
because they have stopped and answer no more?
17 *I, even I, shall answer*[13] *my portion;*
I, even I, shall offer my insight.
18 *For I am full of*[14] *words;*
the spirit within me constrains me.
19 *My insides are like wine, not yet opened,*
like new wineskins[15] *ready to burst.*[16]

"your completion" (Dhorme). Since this is the reading of the Qumran Targ., it has good support. If this variant is accepted, Heb. *ḥāqar,* "search" (third line), should be understood in the direction of "end or limit," as Gordis suggests.

9. Heb. *hiṯbônan,* "pay close attention," with *ʿaḏ,* "to," appears also in 38:18. The primary position of *ʿaḏ* is for emphasis.

10. MT *yiddᵉpennû* is variously understood. It has been read as an apocopated form of either *yirdᵉpennû,* "they persecute him," or *yehdᵉpennû,* "they repel him." Others, e.g., Dhorme and Hölscher, emend it to *yallᵉp̄ēnû,* "he will teach us," with the loss of the ʾ as in *mallᵉp̄ēnû* (35:11). Gordis argues that MT is a form of the verb *nāḏap,* "drive," used abstractly to mean "rebut, refute." This suggestion has the advantage of not requiring an emendation.

11. Instead of the negative *lōʾ* the precative *lûʾ* might be read (Pope; cf. Tur-Sinai). Blommerde (*Northwest Semitic Grammar and Job,* p. 117) puts these letters with the verb *ʿāraḵ,* "order," to get *ûlᵉʾaʿᵃrōḵ,* "I will indeed prepare (my own discourse)." The *l* is emphatic, and the ʾ is a first person preformative of the verb. Cf. also G. Gray, *AJSL* 36 (1919–20) 101–102.

12. The verb in the perfect with a *waw* may introduce a question (GKC, § 112cc).

13. MT *ʾaʿᵃneh,* "I shall answer," could be taken as a Hiphil, but such a form of this root is not well attested in the OT. The vocalization may have developed by analogy from the vocalization of the second and third Qal imperfects with a *pataḥ* (Gordis). Others, e.g., Tur-Sinai, *BHS,* wish to revocalize it as *ʾeʿᵉneh.* It is best not to eliminate unusual forms for which an explanation (such as Gordis's) is available.

14. MT *mālēṯî* is a defective spelling as in many cases of a quiescent ʾ (GKC, § 23f); some mss. read *mālēʾṯî.*

15. A. Guillaume ("An Archaeological and Philological Note on Job XXXII, 19," *PEQ* 93 [1961] 147–50) believes that *ʾōḇôṯ* means "wine jars," not "wineskins." He connects it with Arab. *waʾb.* In support of "wine jars" over "wineskins" is the evidence from excavations at Gibeon that ancient Israelites used wine jars.

16. Duhm and others emend the masculine form of the verb *yibbāqēaʿ,* "it will burst," to a feminine *tibbāqēaʿ,* to agree with *beṭen,* "belly, insides." The form in MT

20 *I must speak and get relief;*
I must open my lips and answer.
21 *I will not be partial*
nor flatter any man,
22 *for I do not*[17] *know how to flatter;*[18]
else my Maker would quickly[19] *carry me off."*

6 Elihu opens with a lengthy apology for rising to speak among the elders. The practice of offering an apology is well attested in ancient Near Eastern documents, particularly when one assumes a role not rightly his by position, status, or age.[20]

There is another heading to Elihu's speech, restating his lineage possibly to lend authority to his speaking because of his youth. Elihu begins with an apology for speaking. He concedes that he is too *young* to have the right to address Job, recognizing that traditionally wisdom is associated with the *aged (yᵉšîšîm).* Although he has restrained himself from speaking because he is *timid (zāḥal)*[21] and *afraid (yārēʾ),* his drive to speak now cannot be checked. So he sets aside tradition and begins to voice his views. Apprehensive that his perspective might not be given serious consideration, he earnestly defends the value of his insight in this apology.

7, 8 Elihu expresses his keen disappointment with the wisdom spoken by the aged.[22] Although he too has been taught that wisdom resides

---

may have arisen by influence of the parallel verb *yippāṭēaḥ* at the end of the first line, or a standard form of the verb may have been used because of the distance between the subject and the verb. Or *beṭen* may have been treated as a masculine noun. Gordis gives another possibility: the passive verb, the logical subject, becomes a grammatical object. Thus MT is explicable.

17. Gordis suggests a variant interpretation by taking *lōʾ*, "not," as *lûʾ (= lû),* "if," creating a conditional clause: "If I did know how to flatter."

18. The second finite verb in the first line, *ʾᵃḵanneh,* "I flatter," bearing a complementary verbal idea, is subordinate to the first verb (GKC, § 120c). Driver-Gray observe that this style of asyndeton is more common in Syriac.

19. Heb. *meʿaṭ* is taken to mean "in a little time, quickly, easily"; cf. also Ps. 2:12; 81:15 (Eng. 14); perhaps 94:17 (Tur-Sinai).

20. E.g., in "The Protests of the Eloquent Peasant" (*ANET*, pp. 407–10) a peasant defends his right to speak in his own defense before the pharaoh, and in "The Apology of Hattusilis," Hattusilis, the Hittite emperor, gives the rationale for his taking the reign, though his nephew has the right to the throne by lineage.

21. Heb. *zāḥal* appears to be a Canaanite form attested in Ugar. *dḥl,* "fear," and Aram. *dᵉḥal,* "fear, worship." In the OT it appears only here in Hebrew, but in Aramaic it occurs in Dan. 2:31; 4:2 (Eng. 5); 5:19; 6:27 (Eng. 26); 7:7, 19. It also appears as *zḥl* in the Aramaic inscription of Zakir, king of Hamath (9th century B.C.).

22. A passage that extols the virtue of old men is found in Sir. 25:4–6 (JB): "How fine a thing: sound judgment with gray hairs, and for graybeards to know how to advise! How fine a thing: wisdom in the aged, and considered advice coming from men of distinction! The crown of old men is ripe experience, their true glory, the fear of the Lord."

with the aged, he has come to the conviction that the *insight* inspired by *the spirit in man* is superior to that delivered by an elder. By *spirit* does he mean his own spirit or the Spirit of God? Since the phrase *the spirit in man* is paralleled by *the breath of Shaddai,* it seems to be referring to the insight that the human spirit receives from the Spirit of God, i.e., *the breath*[23] *of Shaddai,* which gives human beings life (cf. Gen. 2:7), also inspires the human spirit with insight.

The spirit in a human being is an essential source of insight, for it searches one's deepest thinking (cf. 1 Cor. 2:10–16). It is the seat of a person's reflective thought. The spirit enables one to evaluate ideas and actions and to discern attitudes. Moreover, the Spirit of God may endow the spirit of a particular human being with a special wisdom, e.g., skill in artisan's work (Exod. 31:2–5; 35:30–36:1) or the art of administering justly and with the fear of the Lord (cf. Isa. 11:2–4). Thus Elihu seems to be asserting that having been inspired by the Spirit of God (cf. 1 K. 3:9, 12; 5:9 [Eng. 4:29]) he has insight that may be trusted despite his youth. No wonder he will go on to argue in a few verses that he can no longer restrain his own spirit from speaking (vv. 18–20).

9 Elihu challenges the traditional belief directly by stating that the *seniors* of the community *may not be wise* and that the *elders may not understand what is justice.* Wisdom is closely associated with *justice.* An essential part of instruction of the Wisdom books was the instruction concerning equity (Prov. 1:3; 2:9–10). To be wise meant that one followed closely the path of righteousness (Prov. 2:6–8; 8:20). That is why a wise person was respected as a judge, for it was believed that he possessed the insight to render just judicial decisions. But Elihu challenges the traditional belief that the aged are always wise.

10 Believing that his insight into God's ways is inspired, Elihu exhorts Job and the friends to listen to him while he offers his own view. He is promising to speak that which is just and wise.

11 Since Elihu has waited for their words and *listened to* (lit. "give ear to," *he'ĕzîn*) their reasoning while they *searched out [ḥāqar] words,* he wants them in turn to listen while he delivers his position. Eliphaz had claimed that his position was true and trustworthy, since it had been *searched out* (*ḥāqar;* see 5:27), and Bildad had argued that the ideas of the fathers had come *by searching* (*ḥēqer;* see 8:8). Surely they in turn ought to be patient while he searches out words to articulate his ideas.

12 Having paid *close attention* to the speeches of the three friends, Elihu perceives that they have failed *to refute Job.* He concludes that not one of them, acting as an attorney for the plaintiff, has been able to counter Job's

23. Cf. Job 33:4; 34:14; 27:3; Isa. 42:5.

complaints against God, the plaintiff. They have failed to defend their client's, i.e., God's, course of action.

13 In anticipation of their answer to this accusation Elihu cautions them not to defend themselves too confidently. Quoting them hypothetically, Elihu has them say: *We have found wisdom; let God rebuke him, not man.* The phrase *have found wisdom* means that one has mindfully studied the teachings of the wise (cf. Prov. 3:13; 8:17, 35). Elihu does not, however, think that they should let a man under punishment like Job silence them, for that casts serious doubt on their claim to wisdom.[24]

14 By contrast Elihu believes that he will be able to refute Job's carefully *ordered* (*ʿārak̲;* cf. 13:18) arguments. He will, therefore, take up the debate confidently, but he will not use the same words or aphorisms that the friends have used. Since Job has not spoken against him, he is hopeful that he is in a better position to instruct Job about the nature of his suffering. Elihu's optimism is supported by the fact that he makes a contribution found nowhere else. If, however, he should give the insight that he indicates he can give, there would be no need for the Yahweh speeches.

15–17 Again Elihu reiterates his reasons for speaking. His wordiness, however, may be a sign of uncertainty, for in challenging the tradition, he appears to be quite self-conscious. While his manner may suggest self-importance, his actual attitude depends on the tone in which he offered these words. If, for instance, Elihu paused after a statement to allow the friends an opportunity to respond, his demeanor would certainly be less pompous than appears at first reading. It is possible to view him as a reflective young man who had been irritated by some of the ideas and arguments floating about and who, believing that he had some insight to offer, with rising emotions awaited an occasion to speak. Taking advantage of that opportunity, he expressed his deference to his elders in a sincere though wordy apology.

Elihu finds that the friends have been so *dismayed* (*ḥāṯaṯ*)[25] that they offer Job no response. Words have failed them. Then, in the form of a question, both for politeness and persuasive appeal, Elihu reasons that he does not have to remain silent simply because his elders have become dumb. Therefore, he boldly affirms his resolve to speak (v. 17). The personal decision and determination are captured by the emphatic expression *I, even I* (*ʾap̄ ʾanî*) repeated in both lines of v. 17 and by the use of the first person verbal forms with the first person pronominal suffix on the nouns. Elihu will speak his *portion* of wisdom and the *insight* that he possesses.

24. Another view takes this difficult verse to mean that the friends' wisdom resides in their leaving off their arguments in order to let God refute Job.

25. Heb. *ḥāṯaṯ* means "be dismayed" and also "be shattered, broken" (Isa. 7:8). It emphasizes the fear, shame, and confusion that arise from defeat. Here the friends are daunted from debate (cf. Gordis).

18–20 In vivid imagery Elihu further reiterates his compulsion to speak. In contrast to the friends from whom words have fled, he is full of words. Deep inside him (lit. in "his belly," *beṭen*), his *spirit* pushes hard and *constrains* him to speak.[26] The ancients believed that the human spirit resided in the abdomen. The word *constrain (ṣûq)* describes the tension that builds up inside one, from pressures like the pressure caused by a person who keeps importuning for something (Judg. 14:17; 16:6). There it stirred the various organs and produced definite feelings and ideas.

Elihu compares his belly to *new wineskins* filled with fermenting wine. As the wine expands, so does the wineskin, to prevent the skin from breaking. But the fermenting action going on inside Elihu is so rapid that he fears his belly is *ready to burst*. He must, therefore, give expression to his thoughts in order to vent the wineskin and *get relief (rāwaḥ)*.[27]

21, 22 Elihu affirms emphatically that he will speak the truth without being *partial* or showing favoritism to anyone.[28] On the one hand, in his apology Elihu argues that in wisdom he is on a par with his elders. On the other hand, he is saying that he will not cloud the issue with the use of titles or with flattery (*kinnâ,* vv. 21b and 22a). The use of titles is proper, unless intended to influence a person to a favorable bearing; then their use is a kind of bribery. Elihu, though, will speak his convictions plainly and boldly regardless of how his words might offend either Job or the comforters. In fact, he declares *I do not know how to flatter*. He believes that accommodating himself to others would prompt God, his *Maker,* to *carry* him away, possibly by a storm (cf. 27:21). He thus claims unwavering allegiance to God, an allegiance that will not be altered by the prestige or persuasion of anybody.

26. In the Wisdom literature "the chambers of the belly" or "the viscera" are the storehouse of knowledge. The thoughts formed there find expression on the lips (Prov. 22:18). These inner thoughts of human beings may be cleansed by disciplinary blows (Prov. 20:30). This passage in Job indicates that the spirit may agitate one's viscera, compelling a person to speak (cf. Job 20:9). Cf. *TDOT,* II:96–97; and H. Wolff, *Anthropology of the Old Testament,* tr. M. Kohl (Philadelphia: Fortress, 1974), p. 63.

27. Heb. *rāwaḥ,* "be wide, spacious," is used the same way in 1 Sam. 16:23. There Saul found relief from a troubling evil spirit when he listened to music; cf. *rewaḥ,* "respite, relief," in Esth. 4:14 and *rᵉwāḥâ,* "respite," in Exod. 8:11 (Eng. 15).

28. There is a fine play on words here. Heb. *nāśā'*, "lift, carry, take," occurs in both v. 21a and v. 22b. In v. 21a it is used with *pᵉnê* ("face of") in the idiom "to show partiality," and in v. 22b it means "to be carried away." Furthermore, two verbs in vv. 21–22 are chiastically arranged; *nāśā'* appears in v. 21a and v. 22b and *kinnâ* is used in v. 21b and v. 22a: a:b::b:a. There is also chiasm with the grammatical order in v. 21: negated verb:prepositional phrase::prepositional phrase:negated verb. And there is play on sounds in v. 22b: *yiśśā'ēnî 'ōśēnî*.

b. A Disputation about God's Efforts to Redeem (33:1–33)

At last Elihu arrives at the body of his first speech. It consists of three parts: a further apology (vv. 1–7); the central thesis: God's disciplinary use of suffering (vv. 8–30); and an invitation for Job to respond (vv. 31–33).

(1) A Further Apology (33:1–7)

1 *"But now, Job, hear my speech;*
listen to all my words.
2 *Behold, I open my mouth;*
words are on the tip of my tongue.
3 *My words come from an upright heart;*[1]
my lips utter knowledge sincerely.[2]
4 *The spirit of God has made me,*
and the breath of Shaddai gives me life.
5 *If you can, answer me;*
prepare your case; take your stand before me.
6 *Behold, in God's sight I am just like*[3] *you;*
I, too, was pinched[4] *from clay.*
7 *Behold, no fear of me need terrify you;*
my pressure[5] *will not be heavy on you."*

1 Turning from the general audience, Elihu addresses Job directly. Having promised to speak impartially and with genuine insight, Elihu exhorts Job: *listen* carefully *to all my words*. In addressing *Job* by name he does not use any titles, showing his disregard for the position or prestige of any person, as

1. Since this verse is difficult and out of balance, 6/10, various emendations have been offered. The first line may be lengthened by placing the *ʾatnaḥ* at w^{e}*ḏaʿaṯ* to form a construct chain with the revocalizing of *ʾ*^{a}*mārāy*, "my words," to yield *ʾimrê ḏaʿāṯ*, "words of knowledge" (cf. Prov. 19:27). Others seek a verb in *yōšer*, "upright," e.g., *yāšîq*, "overflows" (Duhm, Fohrer); *yāšîr*, "sing," from *šîr* or *šûr* (Gordis); *yāšur*, "repeat," from *šûr* (Dhorme). No proposal thus far is very convincing.

2. The Qal passive participle *bārûr*, "clear," is taken to have adverbial force.

3. Heb. k^{e}*peh* (lit. "like the mouth of") is used metaphorically for a comparative relationship, "like" (KB, p. 865; Dhorme; Pope).

4. Heb. *qāraṣ* means "cut, pinch, bite, nip." In later Hebrew it includes "blinking" the eye (cf. Prov. 6:13; 10:10), "nipping" a cluster from the vine, and "pinching off" a lump from the baker's dough. In the "Epic of Gilgamesh," the god Aruru created a noble person named Enkidu by pinching off some clay and casting it on the steppe (II:34; *ANET*, p. 74).

5. MT *ʾaḵpî* is taken as a noun meaning "my pressure, weight." The Hebrew root *ʾkp* appears as a verb in Prov. 16:26: "His appetite compels him." The word also occurs in Sir. 46:5 and in Aramaic and Syriac.

he has just promised he would do. This form of address, however, also reflects Elihu's brash character in that he does not fear to address a distinguished elder by name.

2 Even though Elihu has been silent for all this time, he states, *I open my mouth; words are on the tip of my tongue*. The note of his present determination is borne both by the particle *Behold (hinnēh)* and by the verbs in the perfect.[6] By this phraseology he indicates that earlier his tongue had been cleaving to the roof of his mouth (cf. Ezek. 3:26),[7] assisting him in obeying protocol.

3 Elihu offers the assurance that his words are trustworthy on the basis that they *come from an upright heart*. Also, his *lips utter knowledge sincerely*. This appeal to listen to his words by virtue of their truth and uprightness is similar to an appeal found in Prov. 8:6–9.

4 To add authority to his speaking Elihu affirms his own origin in terms that allude to the account of the creation of the first man recorded in Gen. 2:7. Just like Adam, Elihu was made by the *spirit [rûaḥ] of God* when *the breath [nᵉšāmâ] of Shaddai gave* him, a lump of clay, *life* (cf. Job 32:8). The thought is that God was personally involved in his own creation, not just in that of the first man or pair. In referring to his origin in this way Elihu claims two things: he is equal to both Job and the comforters, and his words are worthy of careful attention, for they are inspired.

5 Although Elihu will seek to overpower Job with his rhetoric, he invites Job to return an answer. The power of his argumentation, however, will force Job to use his rhetorical skills to the utmost in composing a response. He will have to *prepare (ʿārak̠)* his case as though he were a lawyer engaged in a heated dispute, and then take a firm stand before him *(hit̠yaṣṣēb̠)* during the battle of words.[8]

6 Elihu, emphasizing himself,[9] believes that he is on a par with Job, neither one being superior in the sight of God. Both of them have been made in the same way, having been *pinched [qāraṣ] from clay* by the Master Potter. The fact that all are made by God from a lump of clay implies the bond that exists among all people and their common dependence on God.

7 Since Job had frequently expressed his fear of being so overwhelmed that he would be reduced to silence if God should enter into legal

6. For a similar style designed to capture a listener's attention, cf. Deut. 32:1; Ps. 49:2–5 (Eng. 1–4).

7. Cf. 6:30 in regard to "the tongue and the palate" as instruments of speech.

8. The verbs *ʿārak̠* ("array"; at times elliptical for *ʿārak̠ milḥāmâ,* "draw up in battle array"; cf. 13:18; 23:4; 32:14) and *hit̠yaṣṣēb̠* ("station oneself, take one's stand"; cf. 1 Sam. 17:16; Ps. 2:2; Jer. 46:4, 14) are frequently military words that may also be used in a legal setting, for a legal dispute is viewed as a contest of words.

9. Great emphasis falls on "I," for the verse begins with "behold, I" *(hēn-ʾᵃnî)* and closes with "even I" *(gam-ʾānî)*.

dispute with him, Elihu encourages him by saying *no fear [ʾēmâ] of me need terrify [bāʿaṯ]*[10] *you.* He will not pressure Job as God has done (cf. 13:21). That is, Elihu wants to create an atmosphere that will allow Job to argue his case as he wishes, although not with God himself but with God's representative—a man similar to himself. While the debate may be fierce, Job is encouraged to present his position free from awe of Elihu.

(2) The Disputation Proper (33:8–30)

Elihu wishes to be Job's instructor, leading him to God. To achieve this goal he must help Job realize the purpose of his affliction. To accomplish this he addresses Job's complaints directly and shows him when he is wrong. His style is to present Job's position in a capsulized quote (vv. 8–11) and to articulate a detailed response (vv. 12–30).

(a) Presentation of Job's Claim to Be Free from Sin (33:8–11)

8 *"Surely, you have spoken in my hearing;*
I have heard the sound of your words.[1]
9 *'I am pure*[2] *without rebellion;*
I am innocent[3] *and without iniquity.*[4]
10 *But behold, he finds occasions*[5] *against me;*
he considers me his enemy.
11 *He puts my feet in stocks*
and watches all my paths.' "

10. Heb. *bāʿaṯ,* "terrify," is a favorite word in the poetry; cf. 3:5; 7:14; 9:34; 13:11, 21; 15:24; 18:11.

1. For MT *millîn,* "words," LXX (א, A), Syr., Targ., and Vulg. read *milleyḵā,* "your words." This variant is accepted and a balanced line, 7/7, is gained.

2. Zophar had similarly quoted Job: "For you say, 'My doctrine is pure *[zaḵ],* and I am clean *[bar]* in [God's] eyes" (11:4).

3. Heb. *ḥap* appears only here in the OT. But in the Talmud *ḥāpap* means "wash, rub," e.g., washing the hair (M. Jastrow, *Dictionary of the Targumim, the Talmud Babli and Yerushalmi, and the Midrashic Literature* [New York: Judaica Press, repr. 1982], p. 492), and Syr. *ḥûp* refers to a mother's washing and rubbing her children (R. P. Smith, *Compendious Syriac Dictionary* [Oxford: Clarendon, repr. 1976], p. 132).

4. Job frequently uses *pešaʿ,* "rebellion" (7:21; 13:23; 14:17; 31:33), and *ʿāwōn,* "iniquity" (7:21; 10:6, 14; 13:23, 26; 14:17; 19:29; 31:11, 28, 33), in reference to any sin he may have committed, along with *ḥaṭṭāʾṯ,* "sin" (10:6; 13:23; 14:16).

5. MT *tᵉnûʾôṯ* may be from the root *nûʾ,* "hinder, frustrate"; the noun *tᵉnûʾâ,* "opposition," appears in Num. 14:34. But most relate this word to the Hebrew root *ʾnh,* "meet"; Piel, "cause to meet"; Hithpael, "seek an occasion (for a quarrel)" (cf. 2 K. 5:7). Duhm and Driver-Gray, however, emend MT to *tōʾᵃnôṯ,* "opportunities," based on the occurrence of the noun *tôʾᵃnâ,* "opportunity," i.e., a cause for a quarrel, in Judg. 14:4. On the other hand, Gordis suggests that MT might be an example of an aural metathesis. If that is correct, a meaning may be found without emending MT (cf. Fohrer).

8–11 Elihu constructs the core of Job's complaint in six lines after an introduction (v. 8). He quotes Job as saying *I am pure [zaḵ] without rebellion [pešaʿ]; I am innocent* or clean *(ḥap) and without iniquity [ʿāwōn].* Elihu has chosen words that have Job claim moral perfection whereas Job has asserted that he is innocent or blameless (*tām;* cf. 9:20–21). Job never uses the word "clean, innocent" *(ḥap),* and he uses the word "pure" *(zaḵ)* only in reference to his prayer (16:17). For while Job is confident that he has followed God's way faithfully (23:11–12; cf. 10:7; 27:4–5), he never asserts that he has not sinned. His position is that he cannot recall having committed any transgression that would require such harsh punishment (9:20–21).

Elihu next quotes Job as saying that God has looked for and found *occasions* or opportunities *(tᵉnûʾôṯ)* to afflict him. That is, the reason for his plight lies with God, not in some wrong he has committed. Thus Job fears that God is attacking him like an *enemy* (*ʾôyēḇ,* a word similar in sound and spelling to Job's name, *ʾîyôḇ;* cf. 13:24; 16:9; 19:11; 30:11). God's attack is so fierce that Job has complained that he feels as though he is a fortified city being razed by a mighty army (16:14) or a target at which God continually shoots his arrows (6:4; 16:12–13).

In the last couplet Elihu quotes Job exactly: "[God] puts my feet in stocks and he keeps close watch on all my paths" (13:27). This line captures Job's feeling that God's dogged observance never allows him a moment of respite so that he might catch his breath.

(b) A Response (33:12–30)

(i) The Disciplines of God (33:12–22)

12 *"Behold, in this you are not right; I shall answer you,*
for God is greater than man.[1]
13 *Why do you contend*[2] *with him*
that he does not answer any of man's words?[3]

1. Since this verse seems to present a conclusion in a context of quotes from Job, Duhm and others emend it to fit Job's wording. But in ancient Hebrew direct and indirect quotes stand next to each other. Also, such a reconstruction requires a radical change of MT with no textual support.

2. MT *rîḇôṯā,* "you contend," is an example of a Qal perfect of a middle *yod* root patterned after a Hiphil.

3. The antecedent of the pronominal suffix on *dᵉḇārāyw,* "his words," is taken to be "man" of v. 12b (with Gordis). But Dahood ("The Dative Suffix in Job 33,13," *Bib* 63 [1982] 258–59) revocalizes MT as a Qal participle, *dōḇᵉrāyw,* "the one who speaks to him." Others (e.g., Duhm and Fohrer) emend MT to *dᵉḇāray,* "my words," and take this line as a quotation of Job's words.

14 *For in one way God speaks,*
even in two, though man does not perceive it.[4]
15 *In a dream, a vision of the night,*
when sound sleep falls on men,
while they slumber on their beds,
16 *then he opens men's ears*
and he frightens them with visions[5]
17 *to turn a man from his deed*[6]
and to separate[7] *pride*[8] *from man;*
18 *so he keeps back his soul from the pit,*
his life from crossing the channel.[9]
19 *Or one may be reproved with pain on his bed,*
with continual aching[10] *in his bones,*

4. The second line is taken as a clause of concession. Gordis puts forth another possibility, reading *lû*ʾ, "if," for *lō*ʾ, "not": "If only man would perceive it." Such a construction appears in Ps. 81:14 (Eng. 13).

5. MT *ûḇᵉmōsārām yaḥtōm,* "and he seals with their fetters," has been emended in various ways. MT *yaḥtōm,* "he seals," is best revocalized to *yᵉḥittēm* (so *BHS*), "he frightens them," with LXX and Syr., also followed by Duhm, Pope, and Gordis. For MT *ûḇᵉmōsārām,* "their fetters," Gordis reads *ûḇᵉmûsārām* and takes the suffix as an objective genitive: "And with a warning administered to them." Duhm and Hölscher emend it to *ûḇᵉmōrāʾîm,* "and with terrors," while Dhorme, Driver-Gray, and Pope suggest *ûḇᵉmarʾîm:* "and with visions (or apparitions)." This last suggestion has the advantage of establishing a fine parallel, and it has the support of the joining of vision and terror in two earlier passages: Eliphaz was frightened to death by his night visitation (4:14–15) and Job says: "You (God) scare *[ḥittattanî]* me with dreams and with visions terrify me" (7:14). Also, there is some support in the LXX reading "in visions of terror."

6. The preposition *min,* "from," is added to *maʿᵃśeh,* "work," yielding *mimmaʿᵃśeh,* the first *m* having been lost by haplography (cf. *BHS*). The possessive pronoun is to be understood; perhaps it too was lost by haplography.

7. MT *yᵉḵasseh,* "he covers," is generally emended to *yiḵsaḥ,* "he cuts away" (Fohrer, *BHS;* cf. Isa. 33:12; Ps. 80:17 [Eng. 16]), or *yᵉḵallēl,* "he puts an end to" (Hölscher). But if the word "cover" may have the extended meaning of "separate" by reason of covering so as to remove the effects of something, MT may be accepted (cf. Gordis).

8. MT *gēwâ* is a defective writing of *gaʾᵃwâ,* "pride" (cf. 22:29).

9. MT *baššālaḥ* has usually been rendered "by the sword" (Fohrer). Tur-Sinai believes that it may refer to the deadly sword wielded by the deity of death. Other interpreters (e.g., Dhorme, Pope, Gordis) take *šelaḥ* to refer to the subterranean channel or canal that leads from the grave to Sheol. Pope relates it to Akk. *šalḫu* or *šiliḫtu* (*sic*), "a water conduit or channel" (cf. Neh. 3:15). In Mesopotamian myth this channel is called Hubur and in Greek, Styx. In Ugaritic (Krt 20) this word is also associated with death. Cf. M. Tsevat, "The Canaanite God Šälaḥ," *VT* 4 (1954) 41–49; Grabbe, *Comparative Philology,* pp. 103–104.

10. Although the Qere *rôḇ,* "multitude," is supported by the text of 4:14, "the totality of his bones," the Ketib *rîḇ,* "strife," "aching," is preferred in the light of the parallelism with *hûḵaḥ,* "be reproved."

20 *so that his whole being loathes*[11] *bread,*
and his appetite dainty food.
21 *His flesh wastes*[12] *from sight;*
his bones, once not seen,[13] *stick out.*[14]
22 *His soul draws near to the pit,*
and his life to the messengers of death."[15]

12 Without hesitation Elihu begins with a judgment on Job's approach to resolving his plight. He boldly says, *In this you are not right [lōʾ ṣāḏaq]*. His judgment rests on the premise that *God is greater than man*. The difference between Elihu and the friends is evident in this passage: he will argue that Job is wrong for his bold complaints against God, rather than for some undisclosed past sins. Elihu will, therefore, attempt to defend God's ways so that Job will have a clearer picture of the true God.

13 Astounded that Job would even think of taking up a legal case with God, Elihu asks Job, *Why do you contend [rîḇ] with* God, for God *does not answer [ʿānâ] any of man's words,* as though he were facing legal accusation (cf. 9:3, 14–16). In Elihu's opinion contending with God is a very presumptuous sin.

14 One of Elihu's main postulates is that God goes to great efforts to communicate with a person, above all to prevent that person from going astray. Elihu believes that God speaks to a person in many different ways and on many occasions. The sequence of the numbers *one, two* draws attention not to the small number of occasions on which God speaks but to God's repetitive efforts to speak to that person.[16] This interpretation is

11. MT *zihᵃmattû* is unclear. The word *ziham* occurs only here in MT. In Aramaic *zᵉham* means "sicken, create aversion" (M. Jastrow, *Dictionary*, p. 382); in Syriac the root *zhm* means "be greasy, dirty, smell like bad fat" (R. P. Smith, *Dictionary*, p. 111); and in Arabic *zahima* is "stink, be fetid" (Driver-Gray). Thus this word is taken to mean "feel repulsion, loathe." The suffix may be viewed as anticipating the object or, with Gordis, as an indirect object, i.e., virtually an ethical dative.

12. The jussive here bears the sense of an imperfect (GKC, § 109k).

13. MT *ruʾû,* "they were seen," may be a Qal passive perfect (so Gordis), not a Polel. It was chosen by the author for assonance with the first word of this line, *šuppû* (Qere), "stick out" (see next note).

14. The Qere *wᵉšuppû* is a verb and is preferred to the Ketib *ûšᵉpî,* a noun meaning "bareness." The meaning accepted for the Qere is "laid bare, exposed" (BDB, p. 1045). Dhorme relates it to Aram. *šᵉpāʾ*, "crush, grind"; the interpretation is that the bones are crushed so that they cannot be seen. The bones of a starved person, however, protrude. Cf. H. Rouillard, "Le sens de Job 33,21," *RB* 91 (1984) 30–50.

15. For MT *lammiṯîm* many (e.g., Budde) read *lᵉmô mēṯîm,* "to the dead." Believing that MT has resulted from haplography, Dhorme restores *limqôm mēṯîm,* "to the place of the dead," but the syllable count supports MT. Fohrer and Pope observe that the seven evil demons in Akkadian literature are called *mušmītūti,* "the death bringers." See n.21 below.

16. Cf. Ps. 62:12a (Eng. 11a): "Once God has spoken; twice I have heard this." For this poetic pattern cf. 5:19.

confirmed by the sequencing of the numbers "one, two" with "twice, thrice" at the end of the major section (v. 29). Even when a person fails to recognize the manner of God's speaking, God keeps seeking to communicate with that person. The two most prominent ways God employs to warn an individual are visions during the night (vv. 15–18) and disciplines of pain (vv. 19–22).

15 A primary mode through which God speaks is *a dream (ḥᵃlôm)* or *a vision of the night (ḥezyôn laylâ)*. This type of communication comes during *the soundest sleep (tardēmâ)*. It is this type of sleep that God often causes to fall on a person before he reveals something to him as in a dream (e.g., Gen. 15:12). In fact, Eliphaz reported that his encounter with a spirit took place when this kind of heavy sleep overcame him (cf. 4:12–16). Possibly Elihu is telling Job that his troubling dreams (7:14) are God's attempts to teach him.

In ancient times dreams were often thought to contain messages from the gods, particularly if the dream was experienced by a king, a high official, or a priest. Though dreams played a far less significant role in Israel than among its neighbors, God sometimes spoke through this medium. In the OT dreams are recounted frequently in the patriarchal narratives (e.g., Gen. 20:3; 28:11–16; 31:11, 24; 37:5–10; 40:5; 41:1–7; 46:2–4). But in contrast to neighboring cultures in which dream interpreters had an important role, a servant of God ordinarily was able to interpret his own dreams with God's help (e.g., Joseph, Gen. 37:5–10).

16 God *opens men's ears*[17] in order that they might be receptive to the truth.[18] "An open ear" means that a person is willing and prepared to receive instruction (cf. Isa. 50:5), while a "heavy" or "closed ear" characterizes a person as rebellious, one who stubbornly resists God's counsel (cf. Isa. 6:9–10). Through *visions* God reveals to a person the error of his way or shows him the course of action he should take. The numinous dimension of the dream frightens the recipient, impelling him to change his ways.

17 God's purpose is *to turn a man from* committing a *deed* that is harmful or that may lead him into sin. The use of *maʿᵃśeh,* a nonpejorative Hebrew word, for *deed* indicates that the deed in itself is not a sin. The second line suggests that the potential sin for the doer resides in his becoming proud of his accomplishments. When someone, because of his success, starts to think of himself as better or more deserving than another, he looks for ways to exalt himself and to promote his own welfare at the expense of others. Pride prods even a spiritual or disciplined person to commit deeds of

17. This idiom appears also in 1 Sam. 9:15; 2 Sam. 7:27; Ruth 4:4.

18. Verses 16–17 may be taken together, as is evidenced by the use of three words for man: *ʾᵃnāšîm,* v. 16a; *ʾāḏām,* v. 17a; *geḇer,* v. 17b.

selfishness in his continual striving to improve his own standing. As one proverb teaches, "Pride goes before destruction, and a haughty attitude before a fall" (Prov. 16:18). So God seeks to stifle an improper attitude from leading to wrongful acts by warning the person in a dream.

18 God intervenes to keep a person who is moving toward sin from experiencing the punishment of sudden death in the prime of life. If that person listens to what God says, he will not lose *his soul (nepeš)* in *the pit (šaḥaṯ),* the abode of the dead.[19] *His life (ḥayyâ)*[20] will not cross *the channel (šelaḥ)* that leads to the subterranean realm of the dead.

19–22 A second method God employs to teach or to turn one from the error of his ways is the discipline of pain. The use of pain is, of course, a more severe discipline than dreams. God may suddenly bring a serious illness on an enterprising person. With his strength broken a person is no longer able to administer his estate. His suffering is continual and intense, as the phrase *continual aching in his bones* indicates. The pain robs him of the possibility of enjoying any pleasures. Food, above all *dainty food,* becomes loathsome to him, and he cannot enjoy even a piece of *bread.* His once muscular body, symbolic of his well-being and prosperity, wastes away to nothing. His flesh shrivels up until *his bones stick out.* Sapped of all strength, he is close to the brink of the grave where *messengers of death* stand ready to take his soul to Sheol.[21] But God afflicts that person to awaken him to the seriousness of his situation. If the person responds to God's message, he will avoid a premature death.

(ii) The Angel Mediator (33:23–30)

23 *"If there is an angel on his side,*
a mediator, one among a thousand,
to declare to man what is right for him,
24 *to be gracious to him and say,*

19. Heb. *šaḥaṯ,* "the pit," also occurs in vv. 22, 24, 28, 30; cf. Ps. 16:10; 30:10 (Eng. 9); 49:10 (Eng. 9); 55:24 (Eng. 23); 103:4; Ezek. 28:8.

20. The usual phrase *nep̄eš ḥayyâ,* "a living being," is split into parallel members (see also vv. 20, 22, 28):

yaḥśōḵ napšô minnî-šāḥaṯ
wᵉḥayyāṯô mēʿᵃḇōr baššālaḥ.

21. The identity of these "messengers of death" is not evident. They may be angels who have the duty of transporting a deceased person to the pit. According to Fohrer, the plural indicates that this is not a special group of angels but all angels, and the reference is not to an angelic office but to one of their duties. But Gordis thinks that this reference may be an early forerunner of the later Jewish belief that an angel of death ushers a soul into the next world.

'Release him[1] from going down to the pit;
I have found a ransom for him,'[2]
25 *his flesh becomes fresh[3] like a lad's;*
he returns to the days of his youth.
26 *He prays to God, and he accepts him;*
he sees his face with a joyful shout;
he restores[4] to man his righteousness.
27 *He sings[5] before men and says,*
'I have sinned and perverted that which was right,
and it was not profitable for me.[6]
28 *He has redeemed my soul from going down to the pit,*
and my life[7] sees the light.'

1. MT *pᵉḏāʿēhû* is a difficult *hapax legomenon*. Many wish to read *pᵉrāʿēhû*, "let loose" (see *BHS*). The confusion of a *d* and an *r* is a common error in the later script. Possibly the original was *pᵉḏēhû* with the ʿ entering later as a *mater lectionis* (so Dhorme, et al.). Yet MT is accepted as possible, since the parallel passage in Ps. 49:8–10 (Eng. 7–9) has similar vocabulary: *pāḏâ* ("to ransom"), *kōper* ("price of ransom"), *šaḥaṯ* ("pit"). Cf. Grabbe, *Comparative Philology*, pp. 105–107.

2. Since the third line is short, Dhorme may be correct that a phrase, possibly *bᵉnapšô* or *napšô*, "for him," has fallen out (cf. Exod. 30:12; Num. 35:31; Prov. 13:8).

3. For the unusual quadriliteral *ruṭᵃpaš* scholars have offered many explanations. The context suggests the meaning "be fresh or fat." One view sees this word as an expansion of the triliteral root *rṭb* ("be moist") with a *š*, a sibilant (Guillaume, *Studies in the Book of Job*, p. 119), or similarly an expansion of the root *ṭpš* ("be wide, delicate") with an *r*, a liquid. Gordis thinks that it is a metathesis of *ṭurpaš* ("grow fat"), on the basis of the talmudic *tarpᵉšāʾ*, "a ray-like, fatty membrane." Hakam offers another possibility, that this word is a blend of *rāṭēḇ* ("be moist") and *ṭāpaš* ("be fat").

4. Many have difficulty with v. 26c. Instead of MT *wayyāšeḇ*, "and he restores," some (e.g., Duhm) read *wayyᵉḇaśśēr*, "and he proclaims," with the interpretation that the messenger announces God's righteousness to the suffering man. Gordis takes MT *yāšeḇ* to mean "ascribe" and *ṣᵉḏāqâ* to mean "goodness": "He proclaims before men His goodness." Dhorme restores this line at the end of v. 23: "(the intermediary) restore(s) to man his righteousness." That verse then becomes two distichs. In the present interpretation v. 26b is the response to v. 26a and v. 26c expands on v. 26a ("and he accepts him"). Thus MT is retained.

5. MT *yāšōr* may be taken from the root *šûr*, "behold, watch," but if it is taken from the root *šîr*, "sing," the meaning fits the context better. The MT form may be a variant spelling due to the interchange of a middle *yod* verb with a middle *waw* verb (Gordis). Many (e.g., Budde, Hölscher, Pope), however, wish to emend it to *yāšîr*, "he sings." Cf. Dhorme.

6. The third line is unusual in form and appears short. Duhm, with LXX, emends the text to read *wᵉlōʾ-šiwwâ lîḵāʿᵃwōnî:* "He did not requite me according to my iniquity." But the verb *šāwâ* + *lᵉ* in the Qal may mean "be worth" (Esth. 3:8; 5:13; 7:4). The shorter MT phrase then means "it did not prove to my advantage" (Gordis).

7. The Ketib *napšî*, "my soul," and *ḥayyāṯî*, "my life," are in the first person as a quote from an actual confession. The third person forms of the Qere, *napšô* and *ḥayyāṯô*, again witness to the lack of a clear distinction in ancient Hebrew between direct and indirect quotes.

29 *Truly, all these things God does,*
twice, thrice with a man,
30 *to restore his soul from the pit,*
to light[8] him with the light of life."

23, 24 Elihu teaches that there is a heavenly intercessor who takes up the sufferer's case.[9] This helper is an angel who functions as *a mediator (mēlîṣ),* one who will help whomever God is afflicting for disciplinary reasons. He declares to that person *what is right [yāšār]*[10] *for him,* i.e., the right way for him to take, the way that will lead him out of suffering and back to God. This mediator acts graciously on behalf of the one suffering by commanding the death angel that has come to take this person's life, *Release him!* He has authority to order that person's release, for he *has found a ransom (kōper)* to make on that person's behalf. The meaning of *ransom* is not restricted to a payment of money. It may include anything accepted in compensation for an obligation, freeing the indebted party from that obligation. In this case the exact nature of the ransom this angel makes is not specified. Whatever it is it compensates the divine justice for that person's failures, so that person is freed from the punishment demanded by his errant ways. Once this angel pays the ransom, the death angel must leave the offender. Only God himself can provide the ransom that the angel offers; as the psalmist says, "Surely a person cannot redeem another; he cannot give to God his *ransom price [koprô]* because the redemption for his soul is costly and can never suffice that he should live continually and never see *the pit [haššāḥaṯ]*" (49:8–10 [Eng. 7–9]).

The identity of this mediating angel is uncertain. There have been numerous suggestions: (1) another human being, e.g., a covenant friend, a prophet, or a teacher; (2) the sufferer's own conscience; (3) one of the angelic host; (4) the heavenly witness mentioned in 16:19; (5) the special angel or messenger of Yahweh (*mal'aḵ Yhwh;* e.g., Gen. 21:17; 22:11, 15; Judg. 6:11–22; 13:2–23); (6) the concealed Christ.[11] Since the speeches of Elihu are intricately tied to the entire book of Job, Elihu is no doubt showing Job who his witness (16:19) or his redeemer (19:25) really is and what his task will be (cf. 9:33). Elihu is also countering Eliphaz's position that there

8. MT *lē'ôr,* "to light," is a Niphal infinitive construct with the elision of the *h* (the usual form is *l^ehē'ôr;* see *BHS*). But in the light of v. 28b and Syr., Fohrer wishes to read *lir'ōṯ,* "to see."

9. Elihu's thinking builds on the idea expressed in Ps. 34:7–8 (Eng. 6–7): "This afflicted man called, and Yahweh heard and rescued him from all his troubles. The angel of Yahweh encamps about those who fear him and delivers them."

10. Prov. 14:2 says, "The man who walks in uprightness *[yāšār]* fears the Lord."

11. Cf. A. de Wilde, *Das Buch Hiob,* OTS 22 (Leiden: Brill, 1981), p. 316.

is no holy one to whom Job may turn for help. Elihu says that there is a special angel who works for the redemption of the afflicted. The phrase *one among a thousand* is taken by some to mean an ordinary angel, but from the way the phrase is used in 9:3 it is better understood as having very restrictive force. Therefore, this mediating angel is a very special heavenly creature. He may be identified with "the angel of Yahweh."[12] In some OT passages (e.g., Gen. 16:7–13; Num. 22:35) there is a close identification between Yahweh and his angel. The role of this angel allows God himself to affect events on earth without compromising his exalted transcendence. In Elihu's teaching this special angel works for the restoration of those who have strayed from the right way. This means that God does not immediately abandon any of his servants who err. The converse is the truth; he labors zealously for their full restoration to faithful service.

25 The angel's redemptive message produces immediate effects. The sufferer's *flesh,* shriveled by illness, becomes so renewed that it looks as *fresh* as *a lad's*. Youthful vigor returns to his body. With his health totally restored he can enjoy life again.

26 The renewed person enthusiastically *prays to God* and God *accepts him.* Specifically he takes the first opportunity to offer a praise offering and possibly a vow offering at the local shrine. In this way he expresses his heartfelt gratitude to God for his deliverance. When he makes his offering, at the high moment, he beholds God's presence, as the phrase *he sees his face* indicates. Filled with fear and wonder at beholding God's glory, he utters *a joyful shout (t^erûʿâ).*[13] He has the inner assurance that God accepts him. In this way God may restore to him *his righteousness (ṣ^eḏāqâ).* Here *righteousness* means that God accepts him as an upright and blameless person. All suspicion of wrongdoing that has been raised against him during his affliction fades into the dusk. Once again, he has full standing before God and the community.

27, 28 Revitalized, this person makes a public confession. He acknowledges both that he has *sinned and perverted that which was right (yāšār)* and that *it was not profitable*. Positively, he testifies that God *has redeemed* him from death and restored him to health. Now his *life sees the light*. Such a confession is an essential step in sealing his reconciliation. By witnessing to God's mercy the redeemed person glorifies God before the

12. Cf. W. Eichrodt, *Theology of the Old Testament,* tr. J. Baker, OTL (Philadelphia: Westminster, 1967), II:23–29; J. Wilson, "Angel," *ISBE,* I:125.

13. Heb. *t^erûʿâ* is "a loud, joyful shout" that commemorates a victory in battle, and it is also a cultic cry given forth at a high point in the festival. It is associated with a praise offering (cf. Ps. 27:6; 107:22) and expresses spontaneous joy with accompanying song and music (cf. Ps. 33:1, 3). The use of this word does not mean that a prescribed Levitical sacrifice was a part of the joyous worship.

entire community.[14] In this way the community shares in the joy of his new commitment to serve God. The mention of singing suggests that the person makes his confession in the words of a psalm composed to be sung before the community assembled in worship.

29, 30 Elihu recapitulates his teaching about God's efforts to correct a person through dreams or suffering. God's purpose is both preventive—to keep a person from going down to the grave—and affirmative—to illumine his life with the true light so that he will live a rich, full, meaningful life. Special attention is placed on God's extensive efforts to keep a person from dying prematurely and ignominiously by the number sequence *twice, thrice*. This series builds on the sequence "one way, even two" in v. 14 to emphasize that God is gracious enough to keep disciplining a person in order to turn him from the error of his ways. God does not give up after an initial try has been frustrated. There is, however, a necessary end to God's extension of grace should a person continually spurn God's efforts to lead him.

(3) An Invitation for Job to Answer (33:31–33)

31 *"Attend, Job, listen to me;*
be silent and I shall speak.
32 *If you have a response, answer me.*
Speak, for I wish to have you acquitted.
33 *If not, listen to me;*
keep silent; and I shall teach you wisdom."

31–33 Elihu concludes his first speech with an exhortation that Job *attend* to his words. He requests that Job *be silent* so that he may proceed to develop his ideas. Apparently Elihu wishes to proceed without a reply from Job, but remembering his own pent-up feelings, he offers Job an opportunity to speak should he feel so compelled. If not, then he enjoins Job to listen in silence as he teaches him wisdom. He desires to help Job be acquitted and procure the restoration of his status and estate. Perhaps he wishes to prevent Job from responding in a manner that might silence him as it did the three friends.

The silence of the loqacious Job may seem improbable, but it is part of the plot of the entire work. Since Job has offered his final appeal to God, he will wait for God's reply, not man's. Therefore, it must not then be thought that Elihu has reduced Job to silence. Nevertheless, since Job does not answer, Elihu takes up his second discourse after a brief pause.[1]

14. Cf. Ps. 22:23 (Eng. 22); 32:8–9; 51:15–16 (Eng. 13–14).

1. This view stands in contrast to that of Rowley. He comments: "As Job makes no reply to any of Elihu's speeches we are left to infer that he was reduced to silence and that after a pause to give him an opportunity, Elihu resumed. It is hard to think that the author of Job's speeches in the rest of the book would have been at a loss for an answer

AIM

Because Elihu is so overly apologetic in a boastful manner, his stature has suffered greatly in biblical interpretation. For example, some of the early church fathers consider him to be overconfident and arrogant. It must be taken into account, however, that Elihu's relationship with Job differs from that of the other three comforters. He is not a friend who is bound by loyalty to seek his restoration (cf. 6:14–23). Rather he is a young, promising wise man who attempts to offer some new insight into the issue of Job's suffering. He hopes to instruct and encourage Job while everybody is awaiting God's answer.

In teaching Job about the disciplinary nature of suffering, Elihu hopes to open up to Job's mind new ways of looking at his affliction. Instead of focusing on the human proneness to error as the comforters have done, Elihu stresses God's persistent love and mercy toward his followers. God does not let those who serve him go astray without any warnings of the danger they are facing nor does he allow them to hasten to the grave unaware. He employs dreams and painful tragedies both to warn and to discipline them. Moreover, he provides the ransom to restore those who trust in him. At the right time his mediating angel secures their release from death's grip. Whoever accepts the angel's work finds renewal of health and restoration of his righteousness.

Elihu is telling Job that God has not been silent, but has been speaking to him in many ways through his dreams and his pains, ways that Job has not expected. He hopes that Job will listen to God's speaking through his misfortune. Then he will turn his attention away from his complaints against God's cruel enmity to focus on God's gracious ways toward him. It can be said that Elihu is delivering to Job a message of hope, for he wants to help Job find acquittal and full restoration with God.

2. ELIHU'S SECOND SPEECH (34:1–37)

Elihu now defends God's righteous rule against Job's inflammatory complaint that since God fails to keep times of judgment the wicked prosper and the righteous suffer. Believing that God never does wrong, Elihu contends that God speedily punishes all the wicked, including powerful kings. He never shows partiality in his judgment. Elihu argues this point so intensely because he seems to fear that Job, in hardening his heart to God's disciplin-

---

here" (p. 216). The author may, however, have chosen silence as the best posture for Job. Just as the pious Job of the prologue could mourn his suffering in long periods of silence, so too could the verbose Job of the dialogue. At least Job's silence underscores the fact that he rested his case with the avowal of innocence.

ary judgment, stands in danger of the final punishment, death. Therefore, he wants to convince Job to relinquish his complaint and submit himself to God.

This speech is essentially a disputation. The three major sections of this speech are a summons to listen (vv. 1–4), a disputation (vv. 5–33), and a judgment (vv. 34–37). There is a secondary structure in the speech. Elihu addresses all in attendance (vv. 1–15); then he disputes directly with Job (vv. 16–33), as is evident in the shift from second person plural forms to second person singular forms; at v. 34 he returns to address the audience at large with plural forms. This style gives dramatic movement to the Elihu speeches even though they basically constitute a monologue.

a. A Summons to Listen (34:1–4)

1 *Then Elihu spoke:*
2 *"Hear my words, you wise men;*
listen to me, you who know;
3 *for the ear tests words*
as the palate tastes food.[1]
4 *Let us choose for ourselves what is right;*
let us determine among ourselves what is good."

2–4 Elihu politely enjoins the wise to attend to his words. The *wise men (ḥ^{a}ḵāmîm),* namely, those *who know (yōḏ^{e}ʿîm),* may be identified as either the three friends or the bystanders in general. Given Elihu's attitude toward the comforters in his first speech (32:3, 11–16), it is doubtful that he is using these titles for them. More likely he is addressing the elders of the community who, like a jury, are empowered to decide disputes argued before the city gate. In this manner Elihu attempts to win broad support for the way he is instructing Job.

Elihu asks the wise to *listen* attentively *(heʾ^{ĕ}zîn),* for *the ear* discerns the truth of the spoken word just as *the palate tastes food* (cf. 12:11). He requests that they join him in deciding which line of argumentation, Job's or his, is *right (mišpāṭ)* and *good (ṭôḇ). Right* stands for that which is legally correct and *good* for that which is morally sound. If the elders side with his position, Elihu is hopeful that Job will change his mind and leave off his complaint against God.

1. Perhaps for the infinitive construct *leʾ^{ĕ}ḵōl,* "eating," a noun such as *ʾōḵel,* "food," should be read (see LXX, Syr., Vulg.; cf. Driver-Gray), or perhaps the original text was *lô ʾōḵel,* "food for it," as in 12:11 (so Budde, *BHS*). But cf. Dhorme.

b. A Disputation (34:5–33)

(1) Presentation of Job's Complaint against God (34:5–9)

5 *"Now Job has said, 'I am innocent,*
and God has taken away my right.
6 *In spite of*[1] *my right, I am considered a liar;*[2]
my arrow-wound[3] *is incurable, though I am without transgression.'*
7 *What man is like Job,*
who drinks scorn like water?
8 *He keeps company*[4] *with evildoers*
and walks[5] *with wicked men.*
9 *For he has said, 'A man does not profit*
when he pleases God.' "[6]

5, 6 Again Elihu begins his disputation by quoting Job. This time, though, he summarizes the core of Job's complaint instead of using Job's exact wording. He has put Job's position into four interrelated axioms. First, he quotes Job as saying, *I am innocent.* Indeed, Job has tenaciously affirmed his innocence or righteousness (*ṣāḏaq;* see 10:15; 13:18; cf. 9:15, 20). Second, Elihu refers to Job's complaint, *God has taken away my right (mišpāṭ),* i.e., denied him justice (27:2; cf. 19:7). Third, he states Job's accusation that God considers him *a liar,* for God has made his illness to testify against him, speaking more loudly than his own claims of innocence

1. The preposition *ʿal,* "on," is taken to mean "in spite of, although," with Budde and Driver-Gray.

2. MT *ʾaḵazzēḇ,* "I lie," is difficult. The line could be translated: "I declare the judgment against me a lie" (cf. *The Book of Job, A New Translation according to the Traditional Hebrew Text* [Philadelphia: Jewish Publication Society, 1980]). Others, like Hölscher, emend MT to the third person *yeḵazzēḇ,* "(concerning my case) he lies." But Gordis thinks that the line is an indirect quote and the verb means "they say that I lie, i.e., I am held to be a liar."

3. Heb. *ḥiṣṣî,* "my arrow," is taken to mean "the wound caused by the arrow in me." Many (e.g., Duhm, Rowley, Fohrer) wish to read *maḥaṣî,* "my severe wound" (elsewhere only in Isa. 30:26), but *ḥēṣ,* "arrow," has the advantage of being used by Job himself in reference to his affliction (6:4; cf. 16:13).

4. Driver-Gray and Gordis identify MT *leḥeḇrâ,* "be in league," as a feminine Qal infinitive construct (cf. GKC, § 45d), while most take it as a feminine noun, "company" (KB, p. 277).

5. The infinitive construct with *waw* continues the force of the previous finite verb; it may also convey the idea of intention (GKC, § 114p).

6. Budde and Hölscher consider v. 9 as a later interpolation, for it interrupts the context and anticipates the concerns of ch. 35. But this thought is a main theme that Elihu wishes to refute; thus it is repeated in order to rebut it from various angles.

(16:8; 10:17; cf. 19:19–21). Fourth, Elihu states Job's grave concern that God has inflicted him with *incurable* wounds even though he has not transgressed God's law (6:4; cf. 16:13). Job has pictured God's hostility either as a mighty warrior attacking his foe or as a general marshalling his troops against his enemy (16:9–14; 19:7–12). This time Elihu has quite accurately capsuled Job's position.

7–9 Job's assertions and complaints have convinced Elihu that Job is a hardened sinner. Therefore, he asks, *What man [geḇer]*[7] *is like Job, who drinks scorn [laʿag̱]*[8] *like water?* The picture is that of a very thirsty person gulping down large amounts of water.[9] With a similar metaphor Eliphaz had said that a vile, corrupt man drinks iniquity like water (15:16). What Eliphaz had implied about Job, Elihu says bluntly. He charges that Job has accepted the scorn heaped on him without shame. He comes to this conclusion, for he is convinced that the taunting that Job bears does not move him to adopt a humble attitude.

Elihu goes on to accuse Job of keeping company with the *evildoers (pōʿ^{a}lê ʾāwen),* even *wicked men (ʾanšê-rešaʿ).* That is, his attitude indicates that he has joined the company of sinful men. Job has taken this way because he believes that *a man does not profit* (*sāḵan;* cf. 22:2; 15:3) by living in a way that *pleases* or is acceptable *(rāṣâ)* to God. In his view upright behavior has no earthly advantage. Such a scornful attitude is indicative of folly and rebellion against God, according to the teaching of the Wisdom literature (e.g., Prov. 17:5; 30:17). Elihu again says explicitly what Eliphaz had insinuated (22:15–17), namely, that Job has taken the way of the godless. Unfortunately Elihu perceives only the negative implications of Job's sincere questioning.

(2) A Response (34:10–30)

In his response to Job's position, Elihu states his thesis that God rules justly (vv. 10–15), and then he defends it (vv. 16–30).

(a) The Thesis: God's Just Rule (34:10–15)

10 *"Therefore, hear me, you men of understanding.*
Far be it from God to do evil,[1]

7. Cf. 3:3.

8. Cf. 9:23; 11:3; 21:3; 22:19.

9. Hakam understands this phrase to mean that Job fills his mouth with "scorn" and utters it so forcefully that it flows out like a torrent of water.

1. Instead of the abstract nouns *rešaʿ* and *ʿāwel,* Hölscher and others wish to read infinitive constructs, *r^{e}šōaʿ*, "acting wickedly," and *ʿawwēl,* "doing injustice." Although this is an excellent suggestion, the phrase found in Josh. 22:29, *ḥālîlâ lānû mimmennû,* "far be it from us," shows that a verb is not mandatory after *ḥālîlâ* (cf. Gordis). Although MT is followed, the English translation is smoother if infinitives are used.

from Shaddai[2] to do wrong,[3]
11 *for he pays a man for what he has done;[4]*
he brings back on a man his way.
12 *Surely God does not do evil;*
Shaddai does not pervert justice.
13 *Who gave him charge of the earth?[5]*
Who appointed him[6] over the whole world?
14 *If he returned[7] to himself his spirit*
and gathered to himself his breath,
15 *all flesh would perish together,*
and mankind would return to dust."

10, 11 With the conjunction *Therefore* Elihu marks the transition from his presentation of Job's position to the development of his own thesis. At this point he again entreats the wise to listen to his words. The wise are called *men of understanding (ʾanšê lēḇāḇ,* lit. "men of heart"). With the solemn adjuration *far be it (ḥālîlâ),* Elihu loudly exclaims his thesis that God could never do *evil (rešaʿ)* or *wrong (ʿāwel).* He formulates the thesis negatively to enhance its impact. Then he states the reason for this thesis positively.

God rewards or *pays (šillēm)* each one according to his deeds by *bringing back on (himṣîʾ)* a person the results of his conduct *(ʾōraḥ,* lit. "way"). This belief of exact retribution is found frequently in the OT, particularly in the Wisdom literature.[8] The idea here is not merely that a deed

2. For MT *wešadday,* some, with LXX, wish to read *ûlšadday,* "and to Shaddai," to parallel *lāʾēl,* "to God." This is possible, but it is also possible to consider the preposition *le* on *lāʾēl* as serving double duty.

3. The first line is long and the third line is short. To balance the first line and form a quatrastich, Fohrer adds after the first line *ḥaḵāmîm haʾazînû lî,* "you wise men, listen to me." A tristich is preferable, for the author frequently employs it. Perhaps a word has fallen out of the third line, but no addition commends itself.

4. In the first line one may read the preposition *ke*, "like," before *pōʿal,* "he who does," the *ke* having been lost by haplography (see *BHS*); or, more likely, the preposition *ke* in the second line may do double duty and be implied in the first (Blommerde, *Northwest Semitic Grammar,* p. 121).

5. MT *ʾārṣâ,* "earth," appears to have the locative *he* ending, meaning "earthward." Blommerde (*Northwest Semitic Grammar,* p. 122) and Gordis, however, suggest that it is the old accusative ending. This may be possible; otherwise it is best to revocalize it *ʾarṣōh,* i.e., *ʾarṣô,* "his earth" (with Budde, Dhorme, Tur-Sinai, Fohrer, *BHS*).

6. The preposition *ʿālāyw,* "on him," does double duty in the second line.

7. MT *yāśîm,* "he places," seems to be a textual error even though it is read by Targ. and Vulg. But LXX and Syr. read *yāšîḇ,* "he returns." Most likely *libbô,* "his heart," was drawn into the text by *yāśîm* to form a common idiom: "to pay attention." It is better to omit *libbô* and join *rûḥô* of the second line to the first; the scan then is 7/8 rather than 7/10. (Without the *waw* at the head of the second line it is 7/7.) An excellent parallelism results; *rûaḥ,* "wind," parallels *nešāmâ,* "breath," as in 32:8 and 33:4.

8. Cf. Prov. 12:14; 19:17; 24:12; Ps. 62:13 (Eng. 12); Jer. 25:14; Ruth 2:12.

is pregnant with its own consequences, but that God judges every deed and renders to its doer a just reward. Elihu is countering Job's assumed position that God acts as he wills whether the people are innocent or wicked (cf. 9:23–24).

12 Elihu straightforwardly states his thesis in different words. He highlights it with the word *surely (ʾap-ʾomnām)*. The truth is that *God does not do evil.* God *does not pervert justice [mišpāṭ]*. The second line is a reiteration of Bildad's thesis: "Does God pervert justice *[mišpāṭ]* or Shaddai pervert the right *[ṣeḏeq]*?" (8:3). This teaching means that whatever misfortune a person experiences is justly deserved. There are no exceptions, for God makes no mistakes. Elihu resolutely renounces Job's stern accusation against God when he said: "Know then that God has put me in the wrong and closed his net about me" (19:6). Elihu is convinced that in statements like this Job has gone too far in his questioning and is guilty of rebelling against God.

13 With rhetorical questions Elihu asks who gave God the right to rule. The answer is, of course, no one! God, being supreme, does not have to report to anyone. Since his right to rule is inherent in his being, any challenge of his rule is a disparagement of his person.

14, 15 God breathes into every person the *breath* of life (Gen. 2:7); therefore, every person is continually dependent on him for life. This divine breath is mysteriously related to the human spirit in OT thought. To take away that breath is to remove a person's *spirit.* If God wills, he may gather the life-giving breath from the entire human race. *All flesh would* then *perish together* and *return to dust,* as the psalmist says: "When you hide your face, they are terrified; when you take away their spirit *[rûaḥ]*, they expire; they return to the dust" (104:29). Since all human existence is contingent on God's will, a person risks his life in contesting God's lordship.

(b) The Defense of the Thesis (34:16–30)

16 *"Indeed,[1] understand;[2] hear this;*
listen to the sound of my words.
17 *Can one who hates justice govern?*
Will you condemn[3] the Righteous Mighty One,[4]

1. The particle *ʾim* is the emphatic "indeed" (Gordis).

2. It seems best to take MT *bînâ,* the usual form of the noun "understanding," as an imperative with an emphatic sufformative *h* (with Tur-Sinai, Gordis, Hakam). Others (Budde, Hölscher, Fohrer, *BHS*) wish to read a perfect, *bînōṯā,* "you have understood," with the versions, but the versions may be offering a free translation.

3. For the second person *taršîaʿ*, "you condemn," two Heb. mss., Targ., and Syr. read the third person *yaršîaʿ*, "he condemns," and continue in the same person as the first line. MT is preferred as the more difficult reading.

4. Heb. *ṣaddîq kabbîr* are two titles juxtaposed like *ṣaddîq ʿattîq* (MT *ʿāṯāq*) in

18 *who says[5] to a king, 'Scoundrel,'*
and to a nobleman,[6] 'Wicked';
19 *who pays no respect to princes,*
nor favors[7] the rich over the poor,
because they are all the work of his hands?
20 *They die in a moment, in the middle of the night;*
gentry are shaken[8] and pass away;[9]
the mighty are removed[10] without a hand.
21 *For his eyes are on man's ways,*
and he sees their every step.
22 *There is no darkness or deep shadow*
where evildoers may hide.
23 *For it is not for man to set[11] a time[12]*
to come before God in judgment.
24 *He shatters[13] the mighty without inquiry[14]*
and sets others in their place.

Ps. 31:19 (Eng. 18), which Dahood (*Psalms,* I:191; II:XXIV) renders "the Ancient Just One." Here the two titles may be rendered "the Righteous Mighty One." These nouns are probably official titles (cf. Tur-Sinai).

5. Since MT *haʾᵃmōr* is an anomalous use of the infinitive construct with the interrogative *he,* the definite article is read with the versions: *hāʾômēr,* "who says" (see *BHS*).

6. As Gordis explains, the plural noun *nᵉḏîḇîm,* "the nobles," may be taken as a distributive (so Dhorme), or the ending may be an enclitic *mem.*

7. MT *nikkar,* "regards, favors," is taken as a Piel although it could be read as a Niphal with *šôaʿ,* "rich," being its subject: "The rich are not favored above the poor."

8. Some (e.g., Fohrer, *BHS*) wish to emend MT *yᵉgōʿᵃšû ʿām,* "gentry are shaken," to *yiḡwᵉʿû šōʿîm,* "the rich expire," but there is no textual support for this change.

9. The plural verbs in these lines are problematic; perhaps the antecedents are to be taken as collectives. Blommerde (*Northwest Semitic Grammar and Job,* pp. 121–22) suggests that the verb forms could be understood as old indicative endings.

10. Since the subject of MT *wᵉyāsîrû* is singular, one may read either *wᵉyāsûr,* "and he removes" (Duhm, Fohrer) or else treat the MT form as an impersonal use of the plural (GKC, § 144g).

11. Gordis reads the infinitive construct *śîm,* "put, set," for the imperfect *yāśîm,* "he sets." This change (along with the emendation noted below in n. 12) offers an excellent reading: "It is not for man to set the time to go to God for judgment." The combination of *y*'s and *ś*'s could have led to the MT reading. See Tur-Sinai for a defense of MT.

12. The difficult *ʿôḏ,* "yet," at the end of the line is overcome by the old (first proposed by J. J. Reiske, *Coniecturae in Iobum et Proverbia Salomonis* [1779]) and widely accepted suggestion of reading *môʿēḏ,* "an appointed time." MT arose by haplography.

13. MT *yārōaʿ* is taken from the root *rʿʿ,* the Aramaic equivalent of Heb. *rṣṣ,* "crush, shatter."

14. The phrase *lōʾ-ḥēqer,* "without inquiry," appears also in 36:26; cf. the similar phrase *ʾên ḥēqer,* "there is no inquiry," in 5:9; 9:10.

25 *Because he regards*[15] *their deeds,*[16]
he overthrows them in the night[17] *and they are crushed.*
26 *He strikes them for their wickedness*[18]
in a public place,[19]
27 *because they turned from following him*
and heeded not any of his ways,
28 *causing the cry of the poor to come before him*
that he might hear the cry of the afflicted.
29 *If he remains silent, who could condemn him?*[20]
If he hides his face, who can behold him?[21]
Yet he is over a nation or a man alike,[22]
30 *so that a godless man should not rule*
nor lay snares for the people."[23]

16, 17 Addressing Job directly, Elihu politely exhorts him to pay careful attention to his words. Then he frames Job's complaint that the all-powerful God hates justice (cf. chs. 9, 24) as a double rhetorical question in order to refute Job's position. In the OT it is assumed that justice is the foundation of

15. Gordis wishes to take MT *yakkîr,* "he regards," which is a weak word if v. 25 is building on v. 24, as defective orthography for *yaʿakōr,* "he destroys." The suggestion is fine but lacks textual support.

16. MT *maʿbādêhem,* "their deeds," is the Aramaic form of Heb. *maʿaśeh,* "deed, action" (cf. Dan. 4:34 [Eng. 37]).

17. Heb. *laylâ,* "night," is taken as an accusative of time (GKC, § 118i).

18. The phrase *taḥaṯ-rešāʿîm,* "in place of the wicked," is awkward and conveys a meaning opposite to the one the context demands. Budde wishes to read *tāḥēṯ ḥamāṯô rešāʿîm,* "His wrath shatters the wicked." Gordis offers a less radical change, requiring only revocalizing MT as *taḥaṯ risʿām,* "in return for their evil," supported in the Syr.

19. Since v. 26b is short, some wish to transpose the verbs by moving *weyiddakkāʾû,* "they are crushed," from v. 25b to v. 26a and *sepāqām,* "he slaps, smites them," from v. 26a to v. 26b. Unfortunately, v. 25b then becomes too short. For v. 26b the Qumran Targ. reads, "He throws them in the pla[ce of . . .]." So a verb may have fallen out of MT, but since the translation unit is intelligible, no emendation is made.

20. For MT *yaršiaʿ,* "he condemns," many commentators wish to find a word that means "to stir up" in order to contrast with the verb *yašqiṭ,* "he is silent." Dhorme and Hölscher wish to read *yarʿiš,* "he stirs up." Gordis interprets *yaršiaʿ* by the Arab. *rasaʿa,* "be loose (of limbs)," but this seems too speculative. Therefore, MT is followed; the direct object ("him") is implied in the Hebrew and has been supplied for a smoother English translation.

21. The succession of imperfects expresses a condition and its consequence (GKC, §§ 159b, c).

22. MT *yāḥaḏ,* "alike, both," is problematic. Gordis thinks that *yāḥaḏ* is a poetic synonym for *kol,* "all." But many commentators think it conceals a verb meaning "see" or "watch." Thus Dhorme accepts Ehrlich's solution that *yāḥaḏ* is a corruption of *yāḥaz,* "he sees"; with the preposition *ʿal* it means "he watches over." Blommerde considers MT as a dialectal variant, *ḥdy* = *ḥzy* (*Northwest Semitic Grammar and Job,* p. 123). This suggestion is best.

23. This interpretation takes Heb. *ʿām,* "people," as an objective genitive.

God's rule (cf. Ps. 96:4–13). Elihu highlights this dogma by juxtaposing two of God's honorific titles: *the Righteous One (ṣaddîq)* and *the Mighty One* (*kabbîr;* cf. Ps. 99:4). In this way of thinking, if it is true that God fails to judge justly, as Job complains, then Job's belief that God is all-powerful is invalid. But since Job still thinks that God rules supremely, then he is surely mistaken in his charge that God hates justice. It is logically impossible in Elihu's reasoning for one who hates justice to *govern (ḥāḇaš)*. This argument had much more weight in ancient times than today (cf. Prov. 16:10–15; 20:8), for the philosophy behind Western democracies requires the separation of the judicial system from the executive branch of government. But in ancient thought justice and power were believed to be united in the ideal ruler. The word translated *govern* (*ḥāḇaš,* lit. "to bind") is significant. It has this meaning only in this passage. This word has many special usages: "to saddle (an animal)"; "to heal," i.e., to bind up a wound for healing; "to wrap" on a turban.[24] In Syriac and Arabic it also means "to put in irons, imprison." With God as its subject it often carries the sense of healing (Ps. 147:2–3; cf. Hos. 6:1; Isa. 30:26; 61:1). Elihu may have chosen this word to mean "govern" in order to emphasize the redemptive nature of God's rule.

18, 19 God rules justly, for he never shows partiality to any person by reason of position, wealth, or power. He fearlessly castigates a mighty *king* with the pronouncement *Scoundrel (beliyaʿal),*[25] and *nobles* he calls *wicked (rāšāʿ).* With these declarations God strips corrupt leaders of their rule. He *pays no respect to princes,* nor does he favor the opulent *rich [šôaʿ]*[26] *over the poor [dal],* because all people, rich and poor, leader and disenfranchised, are *the work of his hands* (*maʿaśēh yāḏāyw;* cf. 14:15). They all depend on God for their existence, and he holds them accountable for their conduct.

20 Such great people *die in a moment, in the middle of the night,* at

24. Cf. G. Münderlein, *TDOT,* IV:198–200.

25. Heb. *beliyaʿal,* "worthless, scoundrel," is one of the few compound nouns in Hebrew, composed of *belî,* "not, without," and *yaʿal,* "value, worth." This noun identifies the most vile, worthless men of society, the exact opposite of a king except when he governs unjustly. In the OT those who are called scoundrels include those who lie under oath (1 K. 21:10, 13; cf. Prov. 19:28), those with political power who use it to their own selfish advantage (2 Chr. 13:7), troublemakers who reject the authority of the king (2 Sam. 20:1; cf. Prov. 16:27), those who commit gross sexual sins, such as homosexuality, by force (Judg. 19:22; 20:13), and those who invite a city to serve a strange god (Deut. 13:14 [Eng. 13]). In later writings it became a name for the devil (cf. 2 Cor. 6:15; T. Levi 3:3; 18:12; 19:1; Jub. 1:20; 15:33; Mart. Isa. 1:8–9; 2:4; 3:11; Sib. Or. 3:63–92; 1QH 2:22; 4:13; 1QM 13:10–11; CD 4:13; etc.). See also B. Otzen, *TDOT,* II:131–36, and the bibliography listed there.

26. Heb. *šôaʿ* appears elsewhere only in Isa. 32:5; there it parallels *nāḏîḇ,* "noble," and is the opposite of *kîlay,* "rogue, scoundrel." It then refers to the wealthy upper class.

the height of their power, when they least expect to die. The suddenness of their death indicates that God himself has acted (cf. 20:4; Habel, OTL). God also *shakes [gāʿaš]*[27] *the gentry* (*ʿām*, lit. "people"), i.e., the landed aristocracy, so furiously that they *pass away*. Although they are the most stable members of society, a catastrophe dislodges them from their secure positions. The fact that their removal takes place without any human agent (lit. "not by hand")[28] further stresses that God brings about their demise.

21, 22 God executes just judgment in all these deaths and disappearances, for he constantly and insightfully observes every person's behavior. There is no place dark enough for any *evildoer* to hide from his observation.[29] Even the darkest place, described as *darkness (ḥōšeḵ)* and *deep shadow (ṣalmāweṯ)*,[30] is visible to God.

23 Conversely, no human being has the prerogative *to set a time to come before God in judgment*. God, whose reign is just and sovereign, is too exalted to have to give any accounting of his rule to anyone. In his sovereign wisdom he appropriately sets the seasons of judgment.

24, 25 Since God recognizes the work of every person for its exact worth, he may *shatter the mighty* swiftly and suddenly *without inquiry*, i.e., without a formal trial. Elihu is countering Job's complaint that God, being limited in knowledge and insight like a human being, seems to use oppressive measures to discover his sin (10:2–6). By contrast Elihu believes that God knows all matters fully. Therefore, he acts swiftly and justly every time. He topples those in power from their offices and *sets others* who are upright *in their* vacated *places* of authority. During such a judgment the wicked leaders are totally *crushed (hiddakkēʾ)*[31] so that there is no possibility of their coming back into power.

26–28 Elihu stresses God's punishment of the wicked. God *strikes* the guilty *for their wickedness in a public place*. Such punishment is a just recompense for their clandestine ways of exploiting the poor and afflicted, causing those innocent victims public disgrace. The verb *strike (sāp̱aq)* means literally "to clap hands" in anger (Num. 24:8–10) or "to beat one's thighs" in mourning (Jer. 31:19; Ezek. 21:17 [Eng. 12]). God punishes

27. Heb. *gāʿaš* means "violent shaking or quaking." It appears most frequently in the Hithpael or Hithpoal to denote continuous shaking back and forth, whether it be of the mountains (Ps. 18:8 [Eng. 7]) or the waves of the sea (Jer. 5:22). This word describes the reeling to and fro of men drunken with the wrath of God and inflicted with a fatal wound (Jer. 25:16). In this passage it means that the stable citizenry are cast into social chaos.

28. For similar use of the phrase "without hand" see Lam. 4:6; 2 Sam. 23:6; Dan. 2:34.

29. Cf. Ps. 139:7–12; Amos 9:2–4; Jer. 23:24.

30. Cf. 3:5; 10:21; 12:22; 28:3.

31. Cf. 5:4 for the use of this word in the same stem.

these arrogant rulers in a manner that shames them deeply. In their corrupt ways they have deliberately *turned from following* God and have not *heeded,* or discerned the prudence *(hiśkîl)* in, any of God's ways. The oppressive manner in which they exercise their authority causes *the cry of the poor* and *the cry of the afflicted* to come before God. In their brazen disregard of God's law, in their arrogance, they forget that God always sides with the poor. It is the evildoers themselves who arouse God's anger; they cause their own punishment.

29–30 These verses are very difficult to interpret, for they are replete with textual problems.[32] Since no reconstruction has won a consensus, it is best to work with the MT and note some of the major themes.[33]

Though God remains silent, i.e., he lets affairs on earth take their ordinary course so that a tyrant rises to rule over a nation, who among mankind would ever be in a position to *condemn him* as Job has (e.g., 24:1–17)? When God *hides his face* (i.e., himself)[34] or seems to withdraw his influence from the course of events on earth, no one can behold him. Then evil appears to reign supreme. Nevertheless, God is still in control over both *a nation (gôy)* and *a man (ʾāḏām).* God does not permit a *a godless man (ḥānēp̱)* to establish a long, enduring rule. Such a tyrant is characterized as one who *lays snares,* i.e., uses deceitful schemes, to capture or coerce *the people.* Elihu holds that even if this is true, no claim that God rules unjustly could ever be substantiated. God's slowness to act does not deny his sovereignty.

(3) A Call for a Decision (34:31–33)

31 *"But say[1] to God,*
'I am guilty;[2] I will not offend again.

32. LXX omits vv. 28–33, perhaps to shorten this verbose speech of Elihu, not necessarily because it had a different text. V. 30 is connected with v. 29b, for the word *ʾāḏām,* "man," is repeated, and *ʿām,* "people," parallels *gôy,* "nation." Although v. 30 is out of balance and difficult to interpret, it does appear to belong to this context.

33. Gordis secures a good reading by joining v. 29c with v. 30: *weʿal-gôy weʿal ʾāḏām yāḥaḏ mamlîḵ ʾāḏām ḥānēp mimmōqešê ʿām,* "When over both a nation and all its people He permits a godless man to rule, it is because of the sins [lit. the snares set by] of the people." In this translation the verse means that God uses the wicked as an instrument of punishment against nations and evildoers who have ensnared the innocent.

34. Cf. Isa. 8:17; 54:8; 64:6 (Eng. 7); Mic. 3:4; Deut. 32:20.

1. MT *heʾāmar* is an unusual form. The *he* could only be the interrogative *he* (Driver-Gray), but it is in the wrong position in the sentence. Gordis redivides the first line to read *kî ʾel ʾělôah ʾěmōr,* "But say instead to God" (cf. Tur-Sinai). This suggestion is followed, since direct address is supported by the context.

2. Heb. *nāśāʾ,* "to bear (guilt)," usually has a complement, but it may be used elliptically (Gordis). Some (e.g., Dhorme, Fohrer, Pope) wish to make a small change to read *niššēʾṯî,* "I am beguiled, deceived, led astray."

32 *'What I do not[3] see,[4] teach me;*
if I have done iniquity, I shall not continue.'
33 *Will he requite[5] on your terms that you may object?*
You must choose, not I.
What do you know? Speak!"

31, 32 Elihu formulates for Job a confession for one who has arrogantly challenged God's rule. Job should say, *"I am guilty. I will not offend [ḥāḇal][6] again."* Then he needs to ask God to *teach* him what he does not see. Also, he must be resolved to cease doing whatever iniquity he has done. These are elements of true repentance.

33 It is difficult to make full sense out of v. 33 in this context. The verse seems to contain a question put to Job, seeking to convince him of the absurdity of his resolve to demand that God prove his innocence. It is foolish for Job to think that God would recompense on his own *terms*. Particularly Job is mistaken in supposing that God would subject himself to his avowal of innocence (chs. 29–31). Elihu then summons Job to make a choice, for Elihu cannot make that choice for him. Should Job still disagree, however, Elihu enjoins him to speak what he knows.

c. A Judgment (34:34–37)

34 *"Men of understanding will say to me,*
even a wise man who hears me,
35 *'Job speaks without knowledge;*
his words lack insight.'[1]

3. Dhorme argues that MT *bilʿᵃḏê,* "except, without," arose as an error of dittography from *'eḥbōl,* "I offend," at the end of v. 31b. Thus he reads *ʿᵃḏê,* "until." The Qumran Targ., however, appears to support MT, so MT is followed.

4. For *'eḥ̆zeh,* "I see," Vulg. seems to presuppose *'eḥ̆ṭā',* "I sin," which leads Fohrer to read *ḥāṭā'ṯî,* "I have sinned" (see *BHK*); he understands *bilʿᵃḏê* in a sense similar to Dhorme (see n.3 above) and moves *ʿôḏ* from this verse to v. 31b. MT is preferred as the most difficult reading.

5. The third person feminine singular suffix on *yešalmennâ,* "he will requite it," is explained as a pronoun with neuter force referring to the actions that are to be recompensed (cf. GKC, § 135p). As Andersen points out, "requite" here may mean "retribution" or "recompense." The vagueness of its meaning also makes the choice that Elihu puts before Job unclear. The meaning "recompense" appears to be favored by the broader context of the entire speech.

6. Cf. Neh. 1:7, where *ḥāḇal* means "to act corruptly or to cause ruin."

1. MT *haśkêl,* "have insight, be wise," is an example of the infinitive absolute with a *ṣere yod* (GKC, § 53k).

36 *Oh that[2] Job were tested to the utmost[3]*
for answering like an impious man.[4]
37 *For he adds to his sin,*
he increases rebellion among us,[5]
and he multiplies his words against God."

Elihu seems to pause after v. 33 to give Job a chance to speak. But Job's demeanor must have communicated to Elihu that he definitely rejected this exhortation, for Elihu responds with an incisive accusation against him.

34, 35 Elihu gives the judgment that the *men of understanding* whom he has exhorted to listen to his disputation will render. After listening to his arguments, they will decide that *Job speaks without knowledge, his words lack insight.* That is, Job has erred in his complaints against God and in swearing his avowal of innocence.

36 Caught up in his own rhetoric, Elihu pronounces an imprecation against Job. He would that *Job were tested to the utmost for answering like an impious man* (lit. "men of evil or wrongdoing," *ʾanšê ʾāwen*). In Elihu's view Job's answers to the friends are the kind of answers that the impious would give. Therefore, being guilty of impiety, he deserves the harshest fate.

37 Elihu states that Job *adds to his sin (ḥaṭṭāʾṯ),* i.e., the sin that

2. MT *ʾāḇî,* lit. "my father," is problematic. Given this meaning, unless the name of a relative could be used as an interjection (cf. Delitzsch), the one to whom the line is addressed is not specified. Other suggestions are numerous. Duhm emends it to a wish particle, *ʾaḇôy,* "alas." Following LXX and Syr., Dhorme reads *ʾaḇāl,* "but." Cf. also M. Dahood, "Ugaritic-Phoenician Forms in Job 34,36," *Bib* 62 (1981) 548–50. Gordis thinks it best to take it as a noun from the root *ʾbh,* "wish, desire," meaning "I desire that." It seems preferable to treat *ʾāḇî* as a wish particle (cf. Driver-Gray, Pope).

3. The phrase *ʿaḏ-neṣaḥ,* "until forever," is best understood as a superlative, "completely, entirely" (cf. P. Saydon, "Some unusual ways of expressing the superlative in Hebrew and Maltese," *VT* 4 [1954] 433; and D. Thomas, "The Use of *nēṣaḥ* as a Superlative in Hebrew," *JSS* 1 [1956] 108).

4. If MT *tešuḇōṯ* is taken to mean "answers," it seems best to read MT *keʾanšê,* "like [wicked] men" (with a few mss.), instead of MT *beʾanšê,* "among [wicked] men" (so Driver-Gray, Hölscher, Gordis).

5. This verse is a tristich designed to give weight to the conclusion of the speech. But the second line is too brief. This problem may be corrected by adding *kappāyw,* "his hands" (Budde), to the line ("he claps his hands among us"), but the prepositional phrase *bênênû,* "among us," is problematic. Dhorme revocalizes MT *yispôq* as a Hiphil, *yaspîq,* and assigns it the Aramaic meaning "doubt." He also joins *pešaʿ*, "transgression," in the first line to the second line and revocalizes it as *pišʿô,* "his transgression": "In our midst he *casts doubt upon his* transgression." Gordis takes MT *yispôq* as a by-form of *śāpaq,* "suffice, abound," and he too joins *pešaʿ* to the second line: "He increases impiety among us." The advantages of Gordis's reading are that it does not alter MT and it produces an excellent parallelism.

brought on his misfortune, by *increasing rebellion (peša')* among the people. Job does this when *he multiplies his words against God,* i.e., charges God with judging injustly. Thus Elihu finds that Job is guilty of infidelity. He has not only wrongly accused God, but he has also fostered unbelief among the people.

AIM

Elihu has endeavored to refute both Job's claim of innocence and his complaint that God does not always execute justice in matters on earth by elaborating the thesis that God, the sovereign Lord, governs the world justly. Nothing escapes God's attention nor does he allow any wicked person to exert his influence unchecked. From this perspective Elihu cannot fathom how any human being could demand that God grant him a judicial hearing by filing a complaint against God himself. In fact, such a demand reeks of rebellion against God's rule. Job, therefore, needs to accept God's disciplinary punishment rather than questioning God's motives. Otherwise he is deserving of the severest penalty.

This speech seems to contrast sharply in tone and emphasis with Elihu's first speech. That is, Elihu's compassion and openness seem to have hardened into a rigid concern to protect God's just rule from the challenge of a rebel like Job. In his view Job has added unbelief to his sin by complaining so bitterly against God. He believes that that is why Job never receives any response from God. Elihu thus locates Job's plight in his inflamed rhetoric rather than in any continuance of past sins. Therein Elihu departs from the judgment of the comforters that Job is suffering because of some hidden sin that he had committed.

Elihu has also misjudged Job, however, and he has overstepped his intention of instructing Job. He too fails to allow for the particulars of an individual case. Nevertheless, he forewarns Job that he will have to abandon his complaint against God and his avowal of innocence if he is ever to find reconciliation with God. In this way Elihu prepares Job for a proper response to the theophany, but unfortunately at the high price of blatantly condemning him and making him apprehensive about being smitten with worse suffering.

3. ELIHU'S THIRD SPEECH (35:1–16)

This time Elihu disallows Job's claim to innocence. Typically he summarizes Job's position with the use of quotes (vv. 2–4) and offers a response (vv. 5–16). He addresses Job's concern about his own right (vv. 1–4) with a speech on God's sovereign justice (vv. 5–16).

a. Presentation of Job's Concern about His Own Right (35:1–4)

1 *Then Elihu replied,*
2 *"Do you think that it is just*
that you have said, 'I am more righteous than God'?
3 *Because you say, 'What does it profit you?*[1]
What do I gain by not sinning?'[2]
4 *I shall answer you*
and your friends with you."

2 Without offering any apology, this time Elihu formulates Job's position that he wishes to counter. He is concerned with Job's avowals of innocence (e.g., 6:28–30; 9:20; 13:18; 16:17; 23:7, 10–12; 31:1–40). He puts Job's claim of innocence against his complaint that God has acted unjustly toward him (e.g., 9:21–22; 10:5–7; 13:23; 16:7–14; 19:7–12). Elihu hears Job saying in these avowals, *I am more righteous than God.* While Job has not uttered those exact words, he has so fervently defended his innocence and so vigorously accused God of treating him unjustly that he seems to have claimed for himself a righteousness that surpasses God's. With a rhetorical question to underscore the absurdity of this position, Elihu asks Job if such a claim of innocence is *just (mišpāṭ).* The answer is obviously no. No mortal could be more righteous *(ṣeḏeq)* than God. By casting Job's position in the form of a rhetorical question, Elihu is reprimanding Job before answering him.

3 Next Elihu quotes Job as asking, *What does it profit you* [i.e., God; cf. 7:20]? *What do I gain by not sinning?* (cf. 22:2). It is true that Job has assumed that there surely must be some reward for obedience to God's law. But his plight has made him question his belief. For example, he complains: "It is all one; therefore I say, he destroys both the blameless and the wicked" (9:22). Job would that God rewarded the blameless and punished the wicked, but he fears that such is not the case. But Elihu takes Job's questioning of the value of moral behavior and formulates his complaint to make it sound as scandalous as possible. In that way his answer will sound far more reasonable and orthodox than Job's questioning.

1. The indirect object *lāḵ,* "to you," is emended to *lî,* "to me," by some (e.g., Duhm, Budde, Hölscher). But this may not be necessary, for this line may be an indirect quotation (Driver-Gray, Gordis), and the second line is a direct quotation. Dhorme, however, demonstrates that the quotation of Job is from 7:20; then the antecedent of "you" is God.

2. Gordis exegetes the preposition *min* on *mēḥaṭṭā'ṯî* as the *min* of separation: "what good if I avoid sin?" Another possible interpretation of *mēḥaṭṭā'ṯî* is "what advantage is there in my righteousness over my sin?" Others (e.g., Ehrlich, Dhorme) emend the text.

4 Elihu affirms forthrightly: *I shall answer you* [Job] *and your friends*. He believes that from his insight he will be able to instruct them properly. Nevertheless, Job is uppermost in his mind, as seen in his repeated use of second person masculine singular forms in vv. 5–8. The verbose, overconfident style of his first speech is again visible in this verse, including the emphatic use of the personal pronoun *I* (*'ᵃnî*).

b. A Response: God's Sovereign Justice (35:5–16)

5 *"Look at the heavens and see,*
and observe the sky high above you.
6 *If you have sinned,*[1] *what do you accomplish against him?*
If your sins are many, what do you do to him?
7 *If you are righteous, what do you give him*
or what does he receive from your hand?
8 *Your wickedness affects a man like yourself,*
your righteousness only human beings.
9 *From excessive*[2] *oppression*[3] *human beings cry out;*[4]
they call for help against the power of the mighty.
10 *But none says,*[5] *'Where is God my Maker,*
who gives songs[6] *in the night,*
11 *who teaches us*[7] *by the beasts of the earth,*
who makes us wise by[8] *the birds of the sky?'*

1. The apodoses of these conditional sentences have perfects because the actions are past or completed in relation to their effects (Dhorme).

2. Before an abstract noun Heb. *rōḇ* means "the excess of."

3. Heb. *ʿᵃšûqîm* is an abstract noun meaning "oppression." Based on some LXX mss., Syr., and Vulg., Hölscher and others (cf. *BHS*) wish to read *ʿᵃšôqîm,* "oppressors." Since the abstract noun appears in Amos 3:9 and Eccl. 4:1, it is quite possible that the MT is correct (so Dhorme, Rowley). The plural may be the plural of intensification (GKC, § 124e).

4. The Hiphil *yazʿîqû,* "they cry out," appears to have the same sense as the Qal (Dhorme, Gordis).

5. MT *'āmar* is singular in form because it is used impersonally (Gordis). Therefore, emendation to the plural *'āmᵉrû,* following Syr. (accepted, e.g., by Dhorme), is unnecessary.

6. Cf. Ps. 42:9 (Eng. 8). Tur-Sinai and Pope argue that the primary sense of *zāmîr,* usually rendered "song," is "strength" as in Exod. 15:21; 2 Sam. 23:1; Isa. 12:2; Ps. 118:14. Pope connects it with the Arabic root *ḏmr,* "violent, mighty." This view is enhanced by the Qumran Targ.'s reading *lnṣbtn',* "strength, firmness." Also, Ugar. *ḏmr* refers to a class of military troops. Thus this view has some plausibility. Singing, however, is associated with the loneliness of the night, and it certainly builds emotional strength. See further Gordis; Grabbe, *Comparative Philology,* pp. 108–10.

7. MT *mallᵉpēnû* is taken as a contraction of the usual spelling *mᵉ'allᵉpēnû,* "he who teaches us" (so Dhorme, Gordis; cf. Driver-Gray, *BHS*).

8. The preposition *min* is understood as equivalent to *bᵉ,* "in, with, by" (so Dhorme, Tur-Sinai, Pope; cf. Gordis).

12 *Then they cry, but he does not answer*
because of the pride of evildoers.
13 *Surely it is false that God does not hear,*
that Shaddai does not regard it.[9]
14 *Though you say that you cannot see him,*
the case is before him; wait for him,[10]
15 *though you say that his anger does not punish anything*[11]
and that he does not regard transgression[12] *much.*
16 *Job opens his mouth with vanity;*
he multiplies words without knowledge."

5 Elihu enjoins Job to ponder the expanse of the universe by gazing at the heavens. The sheer vastness of the solid blue sky overwhelms a person with a feeling of blank wonder. It also fills one with a profound sense of one's own smallness. The psalmist sings: "When I see your heavens, the work of your fingers, the moon and the stars, which you have stationed, what is man that you remember him and mankind that you observe him?" (8:4–5 [Eng. 3–4]). This line of reasoning indicates that Elihu grounds his moral teaching in the order of creation, as is common in the Wisdom tradition. Also, it is apparent that in answering Job he will emphasize the great chasm that exists between God and human beings.

6, 7 Since God is so exalted, how could a mere human being *accomplish* anything *against him* (cf. 11:8; 22:12–13)? No person can affect God, not even by multiplying his sins. Job has already reflected on this thought in a vague hope that God would pass over any wrong he might have done and leave him alone (7:20–21). But Job knows intuitively that God will not blink at any misconduct. Conversely one's righteous character cannot be

9. The third person feminine suffix on *y*ᵉ*šûrennâ,* "he regards it," is an indefinite pronoun referring to the oppression which causes the people to cry.

10. MT *t*ᵉ*ḥôlēl* is the Polel of *ḥîl,* "writhe," "be in labor," and is assumed to mean "wait anxiously," though the Polel has this meaning only in this passage. But since the Hithpolel has this meaning in Ps. 37:7, some wish to read a Hithpolel here. Others find a scribal error of metathesis and read *tôḥēl,* from the root *yḥl,* meaning "wait." In a different direction Gordis takes the second line as an exhortation. He relates *dîn,* the first word of the second line, to the Arabic root *da'na,* "submit, yield," and considers that *t*ᵉ*ḥôlēl* may be a denominative of *tôḥeleṯ,* "hope": "Yield before Him and trust in Him."

11. The wording *'ayin pāqaḏ 'appô* is difficult, for *'ayin,* "there is not," is not used with the perfect. Driver-Gray and Fohrer read *'ên 'appô pōqēḏ,* "Because his anger punishes not." But if this were the original text, it is hard to account for MT. It seems better to understand the structure of v. 15a as similar to that of v. 14a, a quote; then *tō'mar* is implied after the *kî* (cf. Dhorme). Dhorme interprets *'ayin* as the complement of *pāqaḏ,* "visit, punish": "his anger does not punish anything."

12. Since the phrase *bappaš* is inexplicable, most scholars (e.g., Dhorme, Gordis) treat it as an orthographic error for *b*ᵉ*peša',* "in a transgression," with LXX and Vulg. But cf. Grabbe, *Comparative Philology,* pp. 110–12.

presented as a gift to God. No amount of good works benefits God or puts him under obligation to anybody (cf. 22:2–3). There is nothing that God wants or needs from human hands. Since God is not dependent on human beings for anything, a person has no leverage with God.

8 But human deeds for good or ill work out their consequences in society. That is, moral behavior has far-reaching consequences on earth. Good deeds build society, while evil deeds cause social discord. Elihu's argument is not that moral deeds have no spiritual significance, but rather that they cannot be used to persuade or compel God (see Weiser). Elihu is seeking to allow that there is value in upright behavior without conceding that human conduct affects the heavenly realm.

9–11 Elihu next addresses the issue of innocent victims *crying out from excessive oppression,* for Job has charged that God lets violent crimes go unrequited (see esp. 24:1–17). Even though in Job's sight the victims *cry out for help against the power of the mighty,* "God does not impute error" (24:12). He fails to punish criminals. Therefore, Job holds that God's silence encourages the wicked to act more wantonly (cf. 24:1–12).

Elihu, however, does not believe that God is negligent in not responding to the cries of the oppressed. He argues that the crying heard is solely a natural response to injury and harsh treatment. The oppressed are so full of self-pity that they do not focus their cries into intercessory prayers. They never ask, *Where is God my Maker?* (cf. Jer. 2:8; Ps. 95:6–7). This question is an earnest petition for God's help.

Nor do these suffering victims petition God, *who gives songs [zāmîr] in the night.* Troubles, of course, were closely associated with the night. So during a long night of anxiety the faithful would sustain themselves by singing psalms (cf. Ps. 30:6 [Eng. 5]; 143:7–10). In song they lamented their plight and praised the glory of God, recounting God's past victories. Through their laments they vented their anger and disappointment. Also, as they sang God's praises their hope grew that God would deliver them just as he had delivered his people in the past. Terrien observes, "That man should sing praises in the deepest darkness does not explain suffering, but it negates its poison, and the ability to sing them is for God alone to give. Natural man cannot overcome suffering, but grace blunts the thorn (2 Cor. 12:9)." But these sufferers forget to sing. They fail to let God *teach* them *by the beasts of the earth* and *by the birds of the sky* (cf. 12:7–8). They do not realize how much God cares for them and how desirous he is that they become wise.

12, 13 Elihu posits that God does not answer the importuning cries of the oppressed *because of the pride of evildoers.* It is *false* to claim that *God does not hear* or *regard* these cries. The truth is that God cannot be coerced or pressured by such pleas into acting in any set way. God's apparent silence indicates that there is some fault in those making the petition, not in God.

14, 15 Difficulties in the Hebrew text make the interpretation of these two verses uncertain. Elihu believes that the principles he has articulated are surely true in Job's case. Although Job agonizes over the fact that he *cannot see* God, Elihu wants him to realize that, nonetheless, his *case is before* God. God has known about it from the beginning. But Job cannot compel God to take any specific course by his laments and complaints. Furthermore, Job must not be driven to take a presumptuous stance toward God because he is convinced that God's *anger does not punish . . . transgression.* Job should not let such an error in judgment lead him astray. Elihu exhorts that the proper attitude that he should have is to *wait for* God.

16 Elihu concludes with a judgment against Job. In his opinion *Job opens his mouth with vanity* or empty talk *(heḇel).* Heb. *heḇel* (lit. "a breath") represents that which is lacking substance and is worthless. And he believes that Job *multiplies words without knowledge.* Job, the wise elder, has acted like a fool by reason of his much lamenting. This is indeed a harsh judgment against Job.

AIM

In his concern to defend the truth that God is just, Elihu appears to be as critical and condemnatory of Job as the three comforters have been. Most of his ideas have been presented in their speeches. In contrast to them, especially to Eliphaz (22:5–9), however, he does not compose a theoretical list of sins Job has committed. Elihu is less concerned to prove that Job has committed some hidden sin that has led to his plight than to show that Job's asseverations of innocence and his charges against God are presumptuous folly. While he has made Job appear to be more arrogant than he really has been, he helps Job reflect on the presumptuous nature of his bold claims. In this manner he prepares Job for the possibility that he might have to surrender his avowal of innocence when God addresses him.

4. ELIHU'S FOURTH SPEECH (36:1–37:24)

In a more compassionate tone Elihu returns to the theme of God's disciplinary use of suffering. He teaches that God protectively watches the righteous. If they commit a transgression, he lets them know what they have done wrong, often using the cords of affliction to instruct them. If they respond to his rod of discipline, they will be restored and behold the divine splendor in awe. But if they persist in their transgression, they will die. After warning Job, Elihu focuses on God's glory that is revealed in a thunderstorm.

For this disputation speech Elihu draws heavily on hymnic lines in praise of God and on theophanic descriptions. He turns these lines into rhetorical questions in his attempt to persuade Job to seek God. The speech has four sections: an introduction (36:1–4), God's disciplinary ways (36:5–25), God's greatness (36:26–37:20), and the divine splendor (37:21–24).

a. Introduction (36:1–4)

1 *Elihu continued to speak:*
2 *"Be patient*[1] *with me a little longer that I may show you*
that there are more words on God's behalf.[2]
3 *I receive my knowledge from afar,*[3]
and I shall demonstrate my Maker to be right.
4 *For truly my words are not false;*
one complete in knowledge is among you."

1, 2 Elihu again entreats his audience, particularly Job, to *be patient* with him while he defends God. He is confident that he can offer Job more insight into God's ways.

3 Elihu insists that *his knowledge* may be trusted, for it has come *from afar,* the distant place where God dwells. The source of one's wisdom was assumed to ensure its validity. So here, as in ch. 32, Elihu claims that his words are inspired. He also states that it is his intent to *demonstrate* that God, his *Maker (pōʿēl),* acts rightly. He feels compelled to defend God's integrity before Job's complaint.

4 Elihu assures his audience that his *words are not false.*[4] He speaks confidently, for he possesses comprehensive *knowledge (dēʿôṯ).* The plural form of *dēʿâ,* "knowledge," means "full knowledge," knowledge characterized as perfect, pure, or *complete (tāmîm).* Such knowledge is beyond contradiction or rebuttal. Elihu "claims to be an expert" in argumentation (Habel, OTL).

1. The verb *kittar* means "surround" in Hebrew and "wait" in Aramaic. But Pope argues that it is possible to assign to the Hebrew the meaning "wait."

2. The preposition *lᵉ* is taken to mean "for, on behalf of." LXX eased the brashness of Elihu by reading *en emoí,* "in me": "For there are still words in me."

3. The double preposition on *lᵉmērāḥôq* is a grammatical style similar to Phoenician usage (Blommerde, *Northwest Semitic Grammar and Job,* p. 125). An alternative interpretation takes this phrase to mean "to a far distance" (cf. Ezra 3:13; Hakam). Dhorme believes it means that Elihu makes his speech "resound to the ends of the earth." Or it may be another way of saying "from the heavens of God" (Ps. 138:6; 139:2; Jer. 23:23; cf. A. Anderson, *The Book of Psalms* [*NCBC,* repr. 1981], II:903).

4. Perhaps Elihu is anticipating a reaction by Job similar to his charge against his comforters that they are "whitewashers of lies" (13:4).

b. God's Disciplinary Ways (36:5–25)

(1) The Core Teaching (36:5–15)

5 *"Behold, God, mighty in strength,*
does not despise the pure of heart.[1]
6 *He does not keep the wicked alive*[2]
but gives justice to the afflicted.
7 *He does not withdraw his eyes*[3] *from the righteous,*
but[4] *he sets them on the throne with*[5] *kings,*
and they are exalted forever.
8 *But, if they are bound with chains*
and caught with cords of affliction,
9 *he tells them what they have done*
and their transgressions, that they have acted arrogantly.
10 *He opens their ear to discipline,*
and he orders, 'Turn from iniquity!'[6]
11 *If they obey and serve him,*
they will complete their days in prosperity,
their years in pleasantness.
12 *But if they do not obey,*
they will cross the river of death
and expire from[7] *lack of knowledge.*[8]

1. The second line is quite short, and many emendations have been offered to fill out the line. Gordis eases the reading by emending *kōaḥ,* "strength," to *bar,* "pure," but the lines remain out of balance. Dhorme suggests that *kōaḥ* was transposed from the first line, belonging after the first *kabbîr,* "mighty," and that the second *kabbîr* arose by error from an original *bar.* Dhorme's emendation is followed to achieve a translation, but it is far from satisfactory.

2. Dhorme, however, understands the phrase "he does not keep alive" as a litotes meaning "he slays."

3. For MT *ʿênāyw,* "his eyes," Budde, Dhorme, and others read *dînô,* "his right," with LXX; *dîn* also occurs in v. 17b. The LXX variant makes good sense, but so does the idiom in MT (cf. Ps. 33:18; 34:16 [Eng. 15]).

4. Fohrer wishes to remove the *waw* on *wayyōšîḇēm,* but according to Blommerde (*Northwest Semitic Grammar and Job,* p. 126), it is an emphatic *waw* which throws the verb to the end of the line. The *ʾatnaḥ* is placed on this word.

5. MT *weʾeṯ,* "with," is taken as a preposition by Targ. and Theodotion. Some (e.g., Dhorme, Hölscher) wish to read for it *wešāṯ,* "and he has placed." In the context the word "righteous," not "kings," appears to be the focus, so this emendation is rejected (cf. Rowley).

6. Verses 10–12 and vv. 13–15 are arranged chiastically:
a. God's corrective discipline (vv. 10–11)
b. Death to those who disobey (v. 12)
b′. Death to the godless (vv. 13–14)
a′. God's deliverance through disciplinary suffering (v. 15).

7. The preposition *be* is used to express cause, like the preposition *min* (cf. Dhorme, Gordis).

8. This verse is divided into a tristich that parallels v. 11 (cf. Hakam).

13 *The godless in heart incur his anger;*[9]
they do not cry when he binds them.
14 *They die*[10] *in their youth;*
they lose their life in youthful shame.[11]
15 *He saves the afflicted through their affliction;*
he opens their ear with tribulation."[12]

5, 6 Elihu states his premise forthrightly: *God,* who is *mighty in strength,* punishes the wicked and defends the just. Since no person can threaten him, he never governs capriciously or out of fear. Assuredly he would never *despise* or treat lightly *the pure of heart.* On the other hand, God does not continue to support the life of the wicked so that they may prosper indefinitely in spite of their evil ways. In the proper time he judges them and terminates their success. This a direct refutation of Job's rhetorical question, "Why do the wicked live?" (21:7). Moreover, God *gives justice to the afflicted* by delivering them from their affliction. There can be no question that God is a God of compassionate justice.

7 Elihu accentuates the compassionate way God treats the righteous. God never *withdraws his eyes from* them; i.e., he continually observes them to protect and bless them. In due time he exalts them—*he sets them on the throne with kings* forever. Because God trusts them, he gives them authority. Perhaps Elihu is alluding to the theme, beloved in Wisdom literature, of the poor, afflicted, righteous person who rises to a prominent place of leadership (see, e.g., the story of Joseph, Gen. 37; 39–50; and Eccl. 4:14).

8, 9 But should the righteous ever stray from the right way, God would bind them *with chains* as though they were prisoners of war (cf. Ps. 107:10–16). Heb. *ziqqîm,* "fetters," is used for chains of captives in Nah. 3:10; Isa. 45:14; and Ps. 147:8. God curtails their movement *with cords of*

9. The phrase *yāśîmû ʾāp* is taken to mean "they incur God's anger," for the second line gives their lack of response to God's binding them. Gordis, however, understands the idiom to mean "remain obdurate."

10. The jussive is used poetically for the imperfect (Dhorme).

11. The phrase *baqqᵉḏēšîm* is taken to mean "in youthful shame." This word in the masculine plural sometimes means "sacred male prostitutes" (cf. Targ. and Vulg.; Deut. 23:18 [Eng. 17]; 1 K. 14:24; 15:12; 22:47 [Eng. 46]; 2 K. 23:7). Since it parallels *bannōʿar,* "their youth," it most likely refers to licentious practices associated with the young (cf. Gordis). In some neighboring cults youths were dedicated to the deity to perform base deeds. Perhaps as a consequence of their corrupt ways, they died a cruel, hard death while they were still young. Another view understands MT *qᵉḏēšîm* as "angels"; in that case they act as messengers of death (cf. LXX and Qumran Targ.).

12. There is a play on the sound of *yᵉḥallēṣ,* "he saves," in the first line and *ballaḥaṣ,* "with tribulation," in the second line.

affliction (ʿōnî).[13] The chains not only keep them from traveling further down a wrong road, but they also inflict pain to make the errant conscious of the impending doom that lies at the end of the wayward path they have taken. After binding them, God *tells them what they have done.* He makes them aware *that they have acted arrogantly.* Whereas pride blinds their conscience, God seeks to bring them to their senses so that they might turn from their evil course. Moved by mercy he reveals to them *their transgressions.*

10 God communicates to them: *He opens their ear to discipline* or instruction *(mûsār).* An "open ear" means that a person accepts obediently what he is being taught (cf. Isa. 50:4–5). He orders, *Turn from iniquity (ʾāwen).* "Turn away" *(šûḇ)* is equivalent to "repent." The phraseology indicates that a person who genuinely repents puts an end to his evildoing. It is through discipline then that God seeks to move any of the righteous who have sinned to forsake their wrongful ways and to serve him faithfully again.

11, 12 The errant righteous respond to God's speaking in one of two ways: either they willingly obey his words or they stubbornly refuse to obey them.[14] Some who are afflicted hear God speaking through their affliction. Welcoming the divine instructions, they humbly submit themselves to God. As they begin to *serve (ʿāḇaḏ)* God, a gracious change takes place in their lives. Their despair is turned to hope, since they know that *they will complete their days in prosperity (ṭôḇ).* That means God will richly bless *their years* with pleasant experiences *(neʿîmîm).* Conversely, if these sufferers *do not obey* God's instruction, they will experience a premature death. A subtle play on words in v. 11a and v. 12a underscores the consequences of these different responses to God's word. In v. 11a *obey (šāmaʿ)* and *serve (ʿāḇaḏ)* are used affirmatively, while in v. 12a refusal to obey *(lōʾ šāmaʿ)* will be punished by crossing *(ʿāḇar) the river of death (šelaḥ).*[15] To put it another way, they *expire from lack of knowledge.*[16] The phrase *lack of knowledge* means that they do not faithfully obey God. Since they reject him, God withdraws his sustaining presence, and they expire.

13, 14 *The godless in heart,*[17] i.e., those who are obstinate toward

13. Cf. Ps. 105:18, "His feet were hurt *[ʿinnû]* with fetters."

14. These alternatives of promise and threat are similar to those in Isa. 1:17–20 (Weiser).

15. Heb. *šelaḥ* is taken to mean "the river of death" as in 33:18b.

16. Cf. Hos. 4:6a: "My people are destroyed for lack of knowledge. Because you have rejected knowledge, I have rejected you from being my priests" (cf. 4:1b). In some contexts Heb. *yāḏaʿ*, "know," means to be in covenant with another person. Conversely, the phrase "lack of knowledge" means one party no longer abides by, i.e., obeys, the terms of the covenant. One covenant party is unfaithful to the other. Cf. H. Huffmon, "The Treaty Background of Hebrew *yāḏaʿ*," *BASOR* 181 (Feb. 1966) 31–37; G. Botterweck, *TDOT,* V:468–70, 476–79.

17. The phrase "godless or impious of heart" *(ḥanpê-lēḇ)* appears in Ugaritic as descriptive of the goddess Anat in her selfish design to steal the lad Aqhat's bow (Pope).

God, arouse God's *anger*. When *he binds* or imprisons them (cf. v. 8) in an effort to alert them to the error of their ways, *they do not cry* for help. Unresponsive to God's discipline, they will *die in their youth . . . in youthful shame*.

15 In summary Elihu reaffirms that God's purpose in using the discipline of pain is to turn *the afflicted through their affliction*. He increases their *tribulation* in order to *open their ears* to his speaking. His purpose is to lead them into the blessings he has prepared for them. God then is mankind's most patient, compassionate, and persistent teacher.

(2) A Warning to Job (36:16–25)

16 *"He lures[1] you from the mouth of distress*
to a broad place free from constraint;
your table will be filled with rich food.[2]
17 *But you are laden with judgment due to the wicked;*
just judgment will be upheld.[3]
18 *Lest one lure you by riches,[4]*
let not a large bribe turn you aside.
19 *Can one arrange your deliverance without distress*
or without all kinds of mighty efforts?[5]

1. Heb. *hēsîṯ*, the Hiphil of *sûṯ*, usually has a negative meaning, "incite, allure, instigate." Nevertheless, it may be used with a positive meaning (e.g., 2 Chr. 18:31, "Remove or turn [the enemy] away from him").

2. MT *naḥaṯ*, "rest of," is difficult to translate, for its meanings of "rest, quietness, and tranquility" do not fit the context. Gordis takes this word from the root *nḥt*, "descend," and assigns to it the meaning "that which is set on your table, i.e., food." Others (e.g., Budde, Hölscher, Dhorme, Fohrer) wish to eliminate it as a dittography of the preceding *taḥteyhā*, "under it." While both suggestions yield the same translation, Gordis's view is favored, for it requires no emendation and finds some support in the versions.

3. Verse 17 is very difficult to explain in this context. Many alterations have been suggested. Following Tur-Sinai's idea, Pope redivides the verse to read: "But the case of the wicked you did not judge, the orphan's justice you belied." At the end of the line Pope adds *kizzaḇtā*, "you belied." Gordis also reapportions the consonantal text in order to read: "But you did not plead the cause of the poor or the suit of the orphan." Although these suggestions deserve careful consideration, MT provides some sense. Perhaps "judgment and justice" *(dîn ûmišpāṭ)* are a hendiadys for "just judgment."

4. It seems best to remove the words *kî ḥēmâ*, "because wrath," at the beginning of the verse. Not only do they overload the first line, but in this context "wrath" *(ḥēmâ)* does not fit as the subject of the verb "lure." Many emendations have been suggested; e.g., Dhorme, Pope, and Gordis revocalize the noun as an imperative, *ḥᵃmēh*, "beware," from the verb *ḥāmâ*, "see," common in Aramaic: "Now beware, lest you be seduced by your wealth."

5. The meaning of v. 19 is virtually impossible to establish. Any suggestion is tentative. MT *šûᶜᵃḵā* is variously understood; e.g., "your wealth" (related to *šôaᶜ*, "nobleman, rich person"; cf. Arab. *saᶜat*, "wealth"), "your salvation" (from the root *yšᶜ*, "save,

20 *Do not pant after the night*
when peoples vanish from their place.[6]
21 *Beware lest you turn to evil,*
which[7] *you seem to prefer to affliction.*
22 *Behold, God is exalted in power;*
who is a teacher[8] *like him?*[9]
23 *Who has held him accountable for his way,*
and who has said to him, 'You have done wrong'?
24 *Remember that you must extol*[10] *his works,*
of which men have sung praises.
25 *All mankind has beheld it;*
people gaze on it from afar."

16 Elihu exhorts Job to accept God's disciplining of him so that he can have his health restored. He says to Job that God *lures (hāsîṯ)* him *from the mouth* or the jaws *of distress (mippî-ṣar)*. This imagery stresses that God is endeavoring to pull Job away from experiencing greater sorrow. God wants to lead him to *a broad place free from constraint* or anguish *(mûṣāq)*. In Hebraic thought a broad, open space symbolized deliverance or prosperity.[11] Conversely, a cramped, narrow location connoted distress, oppres-

deliver"), "your cry" (from *šāwaʿ*, "cry for help"), while MT *beṣār* may mean "in distress" or it may be revocalized *beṣer*, "gold." If these words mean "your salvation" and "in distress," the question asked is whether Job expects to be granted deliverance without any distress. Working from the structure of v. 18, Gordis looks for the initial verb to have a second person pronominal suffix. He gains such a form by revocalizing the MT *hayaʿarōḵ* to *hayʿîreḵā*, a Hiphil of *ʿûr*, "guard, watch," hence: "Will your possessions guard you from trouble, or all your exertions to achieve riches?"

6. Fohrer thinks that v. 20 is hopelessly corrupt. The second line is extremely difficult. Dhorme believes that the second line, lit. "that peoples go up to their place," alludes to some event in which one people displaces another, as in a revolution. For him this idea belongs to the context of 34:17–20, rather than here. He argues that because both v. 19 and v. 20 have been added, they fail to offer a coherent sense. Pope suggests that MT *ʿālâ*, "go up," here has the sense of "vanish" (cf. also Gordis). This suggestion is accepted to achieve a translation.

7. The use of the preposition *ʿal*, "on," with *bāḥar*, "choose," is unusual, but Dhorme and Gordis think that it is possible. Driver-Gray and Fohrer, however, feel that it is necessary to read *ʿalwâ*, "injustice," for *ʿal-zeh*, "for this": "You have chosen unrighteousness rather than affliction."

8. Instead of MT *môreh*, "teacher," LXX has "ruler," perhaps having read *mārēʾ*, which in Aramaic means "lord." Although the OT does not usually talk about God in the role of teacher, Elihu prefers that term, as in 33:14–26; 34:32; 35:11; cf. Isa. 28:26; 30:20–21.

9. The phrase *mî kāmōhû*, "who is like him," is a formula of admiration that appears in prophetic and cultic speech, in the latter mostly as a hymnic question, according to Fohrer (cf. Exod. 15:11; Deut. 33:29; Isa. 44:7; Ps. 35:10; 71:19; 89:9 [Eng. 8]).

10. Hiphil *taśgîʾ* is to be exegeted as a declarative, "you must extol" (cf. Gordis).

11. Cf. J. Sawyer, "Spaciousness," *ASTI* 6 (1967–68) 20–34.

sion, and failure. Elihu believes that God wants to restore Job as head of a large household. With his *table filled with rich food,* he will be able to celebrate again a festive meal with his family.

17 Elihu states that God has found it necessary to devastate Job's former tranquil life for his own good. In an effort to discipline him, God has brought on him the kind of *judgment due to the wicked,* a *just judgment.* From Elihu's viewpoint that which has befallen Job is God's merciful way of leading him out of some hidden error. Elihu has no doubt that God has acted justly in Job's case. This means that in his thinking Job would gain nothing should he win the privilege of arguing his case before the divine court. The court would uphold God's just judgment.

18 The meaning of this verse is far from clear. Elihu seems to admonish Job not to be enticed (Hiphil of *sûṯ*) by *riches (sep̄eq).* Heb. *sep̄eq* is taken to mean "a generous gift," as the parallel "a large bribe" suggests (cf. Gordis). Riches blind a person from seeking justice.[12] Perhaps Elihu suspects that Job begrudges the high cost *(kōp̄er)* of his redemption (cf. 33:24). The thought of it is turning his mind away from God. Therefore, Elihu urges him to respond to the lure of God (v. 16a), not the lure of a generous gift (v. 18a). The play on the word *lure* (Hiphil of *sûṯ*) indicates that Elihu is anxious that Job seek God from pure motives.

19, 20 The text of these two verses is so obscure that it is next to impossible to establish any meaning for them. Perhaps Elihu wishes to convince Job that he will never find deliverance without experiencing distress and without expending great effort. Certainly Job should not *pant after the night* in order that he might expire, like those who *vanish from their place.* Job expresses his desperate longing for night's deep darkness in ch. 3, and he often ends a speech on this note.[13] Possibly then Elihu is countering Job's longing to escape his suffering through a premature death by encouraging him to learn from his suffering.

21 Elihu warns Job not to *turn to evil (ʾāwen)* as a way of alleviating his *affliction (ʿōnî).* Job must realize that the purpose of his test is to learn whether he will be true to God or whether he will seek relief through improper means. Fearful that Job has taken a wrongful course of action, Elihu warns him about the dangers inherent in shunning the pain of God's discipline.

22 To encourage Job to accept God's discipline in his life, Elihu praises God's greatness and his skill as a teacher. God, being highly *exalted in power,*[14] is sovereign. No one could make him change his course of action by a threat, such as Job's threat of taking him to court. God is the supreme

12. Cf. Exod. 23:8; Deut. 10:17; 16:19.
13. Cf. 7:21; 10:18–22; 17:13–16.
14. Cf. Isa. 2:11, 17; Ps. 148:13.

teacher.[15] As a caring teacher he uses discipline to prod his students along the right path, not as a capricious tyrant who enjoys seeing his servants suffer.

23 Since God is subject to no one, no one has ever *held him accountable [pāqaḏ] for his way.* He and the way he takes cannot be called into question by some power or person that inspects his work. Consequently, no one, not even Job, could ever be in a position to accuse him of having *done wrong (ʿawlâ),* i.e., of perverting justice,[16] as Job has thought of doing.

24, 25 Elihu exhorts Job to remember that he is to *extol* God's works. A mere man, he is to adopt an attitude of praise toward God, not a posture of challenge. He needs to sing the songs that people have sung, praising God's wondrous deeds. God has revealed his works in order that all humanity might behold the vistas of nature with a sense of wonder and joy. People are overwhelmed before the splendor of God's creative deeds, even though they view them from a far distance. When Job remembers to praise God, he will leave off his complaint. Then he will reap all the benefits of his suffering.

c. God's Greatness (36:26–37:20)

Elihu praises God for his greatness as seen in the storm (36:26–37:13) and then challenges Job to reconsider his challenge of God with a view to abandoning his demand for a trial (37:14–20).

(1) God's Glory Visible in the Thunderstorm (36:26–37:13)

26 *"Behold, God is great beyond[1] our understanding;*
the number of his years is unsearchable.
27 *He draws the waterdrops*
that distill[2] as rain from[3] the heavenly stream;
28 *when the clouds pour down,*
they shower on numerous people.[4]

15. The role of God as teacher occurs also in Ps. 25:8–14 and 94:12.

16. In Ps. 92:16 (Eng. 15) the people confess: "Yahweh is upright, My Rock, and there is no wickedness *[ʿa(w)lāṯâ]* in him."

1. The *waw* on *wᵉlōʾ*, lit. "and not," introduces a predicate clause.

2. The verb *yāzōqqû,* "distill," occurs only here in the Qal. Elsewhere it occurs in the Piel or Pual with the meaning "refine, purify." In regard to rain it is thought to mean "reduce to vapor" (Dhorme) or "distill." The third person plural form may be understood as impersonal (with Gordis).

3. The preposition *lᵉ* here bears the meaning "from" as in Ugaritic (Pope).

4. In the phrase *ʾāḏām rāḇ,* scholars posit that it is unlikely that *raḇ* means "many," for *ʾāḏām,* "man," is a collective. Pope takes *raḇ* to mean "showers," a form of *rᵉḇîbîm.* This idea gains support from Ugaritic, in which both *rb* and *rbb* mean "show-

29 *Indeed,[5] he soars[6] amidst the spreading clouds,[7]*
with thunderings from his pavilion.
30 *Behold, he spreads his light over it;*
he uncovers[8] the roots of the sea.
31 *For with them he nourishes[9] the people;*
he gives food in abundance.[10]
32 *He lifts up[11] lightning[12] in his hands[13]*
and orders it to the mark.[14]

ers." But the fact that it does not come after the verb is problematic. As for the term *'ādām*, "man," Pope follows Dahood ("Zacharia 9,1, *'ên 'Ādām*," *CBQ* 25 [1963] 123–24), who thinks that *'ādām*, "man," has the same meaning as *'adāmâ*, "ground," in a few contexts. He thus translates the line: "Pour on the ground in showers." But the Qumran Targ. translates these words "numerous people." Therefore, the joining of these two words must not be so hastily viewed as incorrect, and MT is followed.

5. For MT *'im*, "if," many (e.g., Duhm, Budde, Fohrer) wish to read *mî*, "who." A question, though, does not fit this context. Tur-Sinai and Gordis take *'im* as emphatic, "indeed."

6. Gordis takes MT *yāḇîn* as a denominative of *bên*, "between," to mean "go between, soar" (when the metaphorical background is that of a bird of prey). Although speculative, this suggestion is tentatively followed, for the context prefers an action verb.

7. The phrase *mipreśê-'āḇ* is taken to mean "spreading out of the clouds." Perhaps it is a phonetic variant of *mipleśê-'aḇ* in 37:16. Dhorme points out that MT is supported by the reading in Ps. 105:39a: *pāraś 'ānān lemāsāḵ*, "He spreads out a cloud as a covering."

8. Heb. *kissâ* usually means "cover," but Gordis suggests that this word may also have the opposite meaning, "reveal." If that meaning is valid, Gordis's view has the advantage of avoiding textual emendation. A few, e.g., Pope, wish to read *kissôh* = *kis'ô*, "his throne." The parallelism suggests that a verb is preferable, so Gordis is followed.

9. MT *yāḏîn*, "he judges," appears to be out of context. The parallelism favors reading *yāzûn*, "he feeds" (cf. Jer. 5:8). Pope and Blommerde (*Northwest Semitic Grammar and Job*, pp. 128–29) keep MT by treating it as a dialectal variant of *yāzûn*.

10. MT *maḵbîr*, "abundance," is taken as a noun from the root *kbr*, which is similar in form to *mašḥîṯ*, "destruction" (Gordis).

11. This *kissâ* is also variously understood (cf. n. 8 above). Dhorme and Fohrer postulate that it is an error for *niśśā'*, "he lifts" = "he brandishes" (cf. Ps. 91:12). Pope offers another possibility. Connecting it with Akk. *nasāsu*, "move to and fro, vibrate" (cf. Ps. 60:6 [Eng. 5]; Zech. 9:16), he reads *nassâ* to describe the flickering action of lightning. The first suggestion is followed tentatively.

12. Heb. *'ôr*, "light," here means "lightning flashes"; such is also an extended meaning of Akk. *urru* (Dhorme). The feminine suffix on the preposition *'al*, "on," in the second line suggests that it is treated as a feminine noun here.

13. Gordis treats *kappayim*, "two palms," in a unique manner by relating it to Mishnaic Heb. *kippâ*, "arch." The dual form stands for the heavens as a double arch. Nevertheless, the ancients thought lightning was hurled from the deity's hand; thus the usual understanding of MT may be retained.

14. MT *mapgîa'* is usually emended to *mipgā'*, "target," as in 7:20 (see *BHS*). Following Delitzsch, Pope keeps MT and assigns to it the meaning "sure aim." The text is obscure, and the present translation accepts the picture of God as a warrior hurling forth his arrows of lightning.

33 *His thunder*[15] *announces his presence,*
the storm,[16] *his indignant wrath.*[17]
37:1 *Indeed,*[18] *at this my heart trembles*
and leaps from its place.
2 *Listen, listen to the roar of his voice*
and the rumble that comes from his mouth.
3 *Under*[19] *the whole heaven he flashes*[20]
his lightning to the corners of the earth.
4 *After it his voice*[21] *growls;*
he thunders with his majestic voice;
one cannot stay[22] *them*
when his voice is heard.[23]
5 *God thunders marvelously with his voice;*
he does great things beyond our understanding.

15. Heb. *rēaʿ* means "shouting, roar" (BDB, p. 929), and by extension, "thunder." The emendation to *raʿmô,* "his thunder" (Budde), is unnecessary.

16. MT *ʿôleh,* "one coming up," is revocalized *ʿawlâ,* "injustice," by Pope and *BHS*. Others, e.g., Dhorme and Gordis, wish to read MT *ʿal-ʿôleh* as *ʿilʿôlâ,* "storm, whirlwind," an Aramaic word found also in Rabbinic Hebrew. This suggestion is tentatively accepted.

17. MT *miqneh,* "cattle," is a difficult word in this context. Delitzsch and Dhorme reason that cattle are alert to an approaching storm and announce its coming. The Targ., however, takes *miqneh* from the root *qnʾ*, "be jealous, excite to jealous anger," and Gordis suggests vocalizing the text *miqnēh ʾap̱,* "the wrath of indignation." This suggestion keeps the picture of the storm and thus is followed.

18. Heb. *ʾap* is used as an emphatic to mean "indeed" (Gordis).

19. In Ugaritic the preposition *tḥt,* "under," parallels *ʿl,* "in," as here; cf. ʿnt II:9–10 (*RSP,* I:373, no. 589).

20. MT *yišrēhû* is variously understood. Many (e.g., Dhorme, Rowley) relate it to Aram. *šᵉrāʾ*, "untie, loosen, release." Gordis, however, believes that the parallelism demands a noun, so he takes it as a noun, *yōšer,* meaning "strength, power." The same noun stands in the title *sēp̱er hayyāšār,* "The Book of the Upright," which he more accurately renders "The Book of Heroes" (Josh. 10:13; 2 Sam. 1:18). Thus he translates this line: "His power is heard everywhere beneath the sky." Another interpretation finds insight from an Ugaritic text, 51:V:68–71, in which the word *šrh* appears: "Now Baal will begin the rainy season, the season of wadis in flood; and he will sound his voice in the clouds, flash his lightning to the earth *[šrh larṣ brqm]*" (M. Coogan, *Stories from Ancient Canaan* [Philadelphia: Westminster, 1978], p. 101). A. Schoors (*RSP,* I:24–25, nos. 18e, g) thinks that it is best to take MT *yšrhw* as an old Hebrew *yaqṭulu* form with an archaic ending rather than as a third person singular pronominal suffix: "Under all the heavens he flashes." The Ugaritic evidence is accepted, for it accounts for the unusual verb form.

21. Possibly *qôlô,* "his voice," for *qôl,* "a voice," should be read with a couple of mss. The *waw* could have been lost either by haplography or by influence from the next *qôl,* which lacks the pronominal suffix.

22. Most assign to Heb. *ʿiqqēḇ* the meaning "hold back, restrain." Gordis gains this meaning by treating it as a metaplastic form of *ʿikkēḇ,* "hold back, restrain, delay."

23. The line makes an excellent quatrastich, 6/7/6/6.

6 *To the snow he says, 'Fall[24] to the ground';*
to the downpour of rain,[25] 'Be mighty.'[26]
7 *He seals up[27] every man*
so that all men[28] may know his work.
8 *Animals[29] enter into[30] their lair;*
they lie down in their dens.[31]
9 *The tempest comes from its chambers,*
cold, from the scattering winds.[32]
10 *By the breath of God ice comes;*
the expanse of water is turned into a frozen solid.[33]
11 *He loads[34] the thick clouds with moisture;[35]*
he scatters his lightning from the clouds.[36]

24. Dhorme and Guillaume (*Studies in the Book of Job,* p. 127) understand MT *hĕwēʾ* as cognate to Arab. *haway,* "fall from above."

25. There is obviously a dittography in the redundant *wegešem māṭār wegešem miṭrôṯ*. Three mss. omit the first phrase, and Syr. does not read the second phrase. The plural verb and the unusual form suggest that the latter may be the original text, with the last word vocalized *meṭārôṯ*. Duhm and Fohrer, though, prefer to read *gešem māṭār*.

26. Heb. *ʿuzzô,* "his strength," is a noun. The context requires a verb, so Fohrer reads *ʿuzzû,* "be strong." Gordis, however, reads *ʿûzû,* "flee, run," from the root *ʿûz.*

27. The phrase *beyaḏ,* "by the hand of," is better read as the preposition *baʿaḏ,* "behind, about," which is used with a verb meaning "seal," as in 9:7 (Duhm, Pope).

28. The plural construct *ʾanšê,* "men of," is incorrect if *maʿaśēhû* is the object of the infinitive construct. It seems best to read *ʾanāšîm,* "men" (Hölscher, Pope, *BHS*), the *m* having been lost by haplography. Duhm and Fohrer, however, prefer the singular *ʾĕnôš*.

29. Heb. *ḥayyâ,* "beast," is most likely a collective.

30. The preposition *bemô,* "in," is a poetic form as in 9:30; 16:4, 5; 19:16.

31. The habitation of animals is often in the plural, so MT *meʿônōṯeyhā,* translated "her dens," is correct.

32. Heb. *mezārîm* is a meteorological term, but its precise meaning is unknown. The favored identification is "the scattering winds." For this meaning the form is taken as a Piel participle from the root *zārâ,* "scatter." Since in Mesopotamia the four points of the compass were identified by names for the winds (Dhorme) and since in the Koran (50:1) there is a word meaning "scatterers" for the cold winds out of the north (Pope), it is likely that this word means "winds (from the north)."

33. One understanding of MT *mûṣāq* is a noun from the root *yāṣaq,* "pour, cast out," meaning "a casting, a hard mass" in 38:38 (Gordis). Here it is taken to mean "frozen solid." The usual identification, though, is with *ṣûq,* "constrain, press on," with the noun *mûṣāq* meaning "narrowness, constraint, distress" (BDB, p. 848; KB, p. 530).

34. Heb. *ṭāraḥ* means "load, burden," as in Aramaic and later Hebrew.

35. MT *berî* is variously interpreted, e.g., as "corn, wheat" (from *bar;* so Jerome) or "chosen one" (from the Hebrew root *brr,* "pure"); or it is emended to *bārāḏ,* "hail" (Duhm), or *bārāq,* "lightning" (Dhorme, Pope; cf. Driver-Gray). Hölscher and Gordis, however, take *rî* as a noun, "moisture," from the root *rwh,* "saturate," with the preposition *be*. In Sir. 31:28 it is written *reʾî*. See also Grabbe, *Comparative Philology,* pp. 114–16.

36. Perhaps the absolute *ʿānān,* "clouds," should be read for the construct *ʿanan* and treated as an adverbial accusative (Pope).

12 *They turn round about by his guidance,*
wherever he commands them over the world.[37]
13 *Whether for discipline—if they are not obedient*[38]*—*
or for mercy, he causes it to be realized."

26 Certainly God is *great [śaggî'] beyond our understanding* (cf. Eccl. 8:17). And he is eternal beyond limitation of years: *the number of his years is unsearchable* (cf. Ps. 102:28 [Eng. 27]). Job must be mindful that such a God is worthy of praise rather than seeking a legal challenge with him.

27, 28 Elihu meditates on the wondrous phenomenon of a raging thunderstorm. In a land marked by months without rain, the fall rains bring great joy as they relieve the fear of drought. On the steppe, where the horizon is visible for miles, the gathering and the movement of the clouds as a storm approaches is a spectacular sight. Just as amazing is the way that God empties the clouds by pouring down drops of water on the earth. These raindrops are distilled *from the heavenly stream* or ocean *('ēḏ),* the great body of water believed by ancient people to encircle the earth.[39]

29, 30 God, the Rider of the clouds (cf. Isa. 19:1), *soars amidst the spreading clouds* and sends forth *thunderings from his pavilion.* God is master of every kind of rain, from the gentle dew to the violent thunderstorm. To the sound of thunder *(tᵉšu'ôṯ)*[40] he sends forth lightning. These forks of lightning *spread over* the landscape and *uncover the roots,* i.e., the depths, *of the sea.* When their brightness lights up the sky, all is revealed for a moment.

37. Verse 12 seems unusually bulky, which suggests that it probably has suffered greatly in transmission. Perhaps three words were originally explanatory glosses: *mᵉsibbôṯ,* "in circles," for *miṯhappēḵ,* "it turns about"; *lᵉpoʿolām,* "their working," for *bᵉtaḥbûlōṯāw,* "his directions"; and *'ārṣâ,* "earthward," for *tēḇēl,* "world." This possibility is supported by the singular translations of these dual words in the Qumran Targ. Interestingly, at the head of the verse the Qumran Targ. reads, "He speaks and they hear him."

38. The phrase *'im lᵉ'arṣô,* "if for his land," is difficult to fit into the context. Many suggestions for improvement have been offered. Duhm and Driver-Gray wish to read *lim'ērâ,* "for a curse," as in Deut. 28:20 and Prov. 3:33. Pope posits that there may be a noun *'rṣw,* with a prefix ', meaning "favor, grace." Tur-Sinai and Gordis redivide *lᵉ'arṣô* into *lō' rāṣû,* "they are unwilling." This suggestion has the advantage of working with the consonantal text without creating a new word.

39. Heb. *'ēḏ* appears only here and in Gen. 2:6 and has traditionally been translated "mist." W. F. Albright (*JBL* 58 [1939] 102n.25) identified it as a loanword from Akk. *edū,* Sum. ID, which means the subterranean waters. These are the waters above and below the earth. Working from E. A. Speiser's ideas presented in *BASOR* 140 (1955) 9-11, Pope suggests that the *-ô* of *'ēḏô* may be a modification of the Akk. *edū* and not the pronominal suffix "his."

40. Heb. *tᵉšu'ôṯ* means "a loud noise" as from a crowd (Isa. 22:2) or a storm.

31 The giving of the rain testifies to God's gracious care for mankind. In order that there may be *food in abundance* to nourish *the people,* he turns the dry, thirsty soil into fertile land.

32, 33 Like a warrior God *lifts up lightning in his hands* and *orders* it toward its *mark* like an arrow shot from his bow. These arrows are released with such sure aim that they always strike their target; this phenomenon is utterly amazing since they are hurled forth in a zigzag pattern. In their trajectory they obediently follow God's command. The *thunder announces* God's *presence,* and the fury of *the storm* reveals that *his indignant wrath* is burning hotly. God makes his passion visible in the storm.

37:1, 2 Before this amazing display of God's majestic power, Elihu's *heart trembles and leaps* in excited apprehension. Awestruck at this display of God's lordship, he exhorts his listeners to hearken well to God's voice in the thunder. Before God, people should be fearful and submissive rather than bellicose and demanding. When God speaks in the heavens, it is with *roaring (rōgez)* and *rumbling (hegeh).* The first word, *rōgez,* captures both the clash of the thunder and the fear it arouses in the human breast (Dhorme; cf. 3:26). While Job has stated that his sufferings have disturbed him deeply (30:17, 26), Elihu asks him why he should not expect to be unsettled by God's presence.

3, 4 The thunderstorm dominates the whole landscape. God *flashes his lightning to the corners of the earth* and lights up *the whole heaven.* Right behind the flashes of light God's *majestic voice thunders,* puncturing the stillness with a roar like the growling (*šāʾag;* cf. 4:10) of a lion. No human being can *stay* the lightning or keep back the thunder.[41] Before a storm a human being is powerless.

5 The spectacle of the thunderstorm is one of the *great things* or miracles (*g^e^dōlôṯ;* cf. 9:10) God performs. Marvelous deeds like this are *beyond* human *understanding.*

6 Sometimes in the hills of Palestine the winter rains turn into falling snow. The *downpour* is a marvel, and the seldom seen *snow* is even more wondrous. God commands the snow to *fall to the ground* just as his word orders the rain to descend in torrents. Since all these elements are obedient to his command, God can turn a steady downpour, which soaks the earth and makes it fertile (Isa. 55:10; Amos 4:7), into a destructive torrent (cf. Ezek. 13:11).

7, 8 God uses the weather to restrict human and animal activity on earth. The cold, driving rains of winter shut people indoors. *Animals,* too,

41. The third line may be viewed as a further description of the lightning. Pope's suggestion that it depicts a human response to the storm as in the Ugaritic passage alluded to above (n.20) has much to commend it.

are forced to seek cover. Even the mightiest of beasts are confined to their lairs. Since these natural forces keep human beings from doing as they would like to do, they are made aware of a higher ruler who governs their destiny. That is, God reveals himself to human beings through his works such as the torrential rains.

9, 10 As people and animals seek cover, *the tempest comes from its chambers* to vent its full fury across the landscape. According to ancient belief, the various winds were stored in *chambers* in the heavens. Whenever God willed, he opened the doors to the appropriate chambers and let out those winds to blow on the earth.[42] In the appropriate season he sent *the scattering winds,* which blow out of the north, to chill the earth and its inhabitants. These winds bring the cold, driving rain. The temperature turns so cold that there is frost on the ground, and an *expanse of water* freezes over. Figuratively it can be said that God breathes out ice (cf. Ps. 147:17).

11, 12 God *loads the thick clouds with moisture* and has them carry rain to a certain location. From these clouds God *scatters his lightning.* These dark, heavy clouds move across the sky at God's *guidance* or direction *(taḥbûlôṯ).*[43] God is the captain who wisely and masterfully charts their course, and they obediently go *wherever he commands.*

13 The storm serves God's purpose, for good or for ill. Skillfully God uses it as his rod of *discipline,* particularly if his people have been *disobedient.* Conversely, the rain is a great blessing as it drenches the thirsty ground so that the soil may yield its fruit. In that mode the storm is an expression of God's faithful kindness or *mercy (ḥeseḏ)* to his obedient people. The storm evidences that God governs the world wisely, i.e., both caringly and judiciously.

(2) An Admonition to Job (37:14–20)

14 *"Give ear to this, Job;*
be still and consider God's wondrous works.
15 *Do you know how God controls them*
and makes lightning appear[1] *in his clouds?*
16 *Do you know the spreading out of*[2] *the clouds,*
the wondrous works of one perfect in knowledge?

42. Cf. Ps. 135:7; Jer. 10:13; 51:16.

43. The noun *taḥbûlôṯ* comes from the root *ḥbl,* "bind." The noun *ḥeḇel* from the same root means "cord, rope." It is associated with the skill of navigation, and in the Wisdom tradition it emphasizes great skill in tactical areas, as in solving a problem or in leadership (cf. Prov. 1:5; 11:14; 20:18; 24:6). See W. McKane, *Proverbs,* OTL (Philadelphia: Westminster, 1970), p. 266.

1. The perfect consecutive carries on the construction of the infinitive with a preposition (GKC, § 114r).

2. MT *mipl^{e}śê* is often taken from the root *plś* = *pls,* "equalize, balance," to

17 *You whose[3] garments are hot*
when the earth lies still[4] under the south wind,
18 *can you with him spread out the sky,*
hard as a molten mirror?
19 *Tell us what we should say to him;*
we cannot prepare our case[5] because of darkness.
20 *Should it be told him that I wish to speak?*
Can a man speak when he is confused?"

14 Not wanting his teaching to escape Job's attention, Elihu exhorts him to *give ear,* i.e., to pay close attention, to what he has said. He believes that if Job would *be still and consider God's wondrous works* (*nipl*ᵉʾ*ôṯ;* cf. 9:10), he would gain significant insight into his own situation and would come to realize both God's superior wisdom and man's limited knowledge and ability.

15, 16 To stimulate Job's thoughts Elihu puts to him some rhetorical questions. Does Job know how *God controls* the clouds and *makes lightning* flash forth through them? The answer, of course, is no. Surely the one who designed these *wondrous works (mipl*ᵉʾ*ôṯ)* is *one perfect in knowledge*.

17, 18 When the sirocco or *south wind*[6] blows off the desert, village life comes to a standstill. The land becomes still as every creature seeks shelter under some shade. The silence can be felt. People become listless and irritable. Clothing becomes unbearably hot.[7] Everyone feels as though he is suffocating. On such days the sky is such a bold blue that it looks as *hard as a molten mirror.*[8] Elihu asks Job if he could assist God in *spreading out* (lit. hammering out, *hirq̧îa*ʿ) the solid sky—especially on such a hot day when he is so robbed of strength that he does not want to do

---

indicate the free suspension of the clouds in the sky. It seems better to interpret *mipl*ᵉ*śê* as a phonetic variant of *mipr*ᵉ*śê,* "spreading out of" (36:29). The alternate form is used here for alliteration with *mipl*ᵉʾ*ôṯ,* "wondrous works" (cf. Gordis).

3. The antecedent of "who," ʾ*ᵃšer,* is the "you" in v. 16; for clarity "you" is added in the translation.

4. The Hiphil of *šāqaṭ,* "it lies still," bears the nuance of being in a quiet condition (GKC, § 53e).

5. As in 33:5, Heb. ʿ*āraḵ,* "arrange," stands here elliptically without *millîn,* "words," or *mišpāṭ,* "justice, legal case," to mean "prepare a case"; cf. 13:18; 23:4; 32:14.

6. Only here is the sirocco called the south wind; usually it is referred to as the east wind (*qāḏîm;* 15:2; 27:21; 38:24), but cf. Luke 12:55.

7. Cf. W. Thomson, *The Land and the Book* (London: Nelson, 1913), p. 536.

8. Ancient mirrors were cast out of bronze, so they were hard and unbreakable. Cf. Deut. 28:23, where the sky is said to be bronze when it gives no rain.

anything. Of course not. This picture makes it clear that God is the Mighty One.

19 If Job does not know how God performs wonders in nature, how can he, out of his darkened understanding, *prepare* his *case* so well that he could convince God (cf. 13:18)? Any person would become speechless before this marvelous Creator.

20 Is it necessary to tell the Creator that a mortal wishes to speak in his presence? Can a mortal speak persuasively when he is confused? These rhetorical questions demand a strong negative reply. Surely no mortal, *confused* or bewildered *(billaʿ)*[9] in his reasoning, would wish to defend himself before God. No doubt, the double thrust of *billaʿ*—to be confused in argument and to be destroyed—is present in the question (cf. 10:8). God would easily overpower the arguments of such a defendant and secure a stiff verdict against that person. Wisdom, therefore, surely advises one against pursuing a course of action that has no possibility of achieving any of one's goals.

d. The Divine Splendor (37:21–24)

21 *"Now after they had not seen the light,*
it is bright in the sky,
for the wind has blown, sweeping the sky clean.
22 *From the north comes golden*[1] *splendor;*
God is clothed in awesome majesty.
23 *Shaddai, far beyond our reach,*
great in power and justice,
great in righteousness,[2] *he does not oppress.*
24 *Therefore, men fear him;*
indeed, all the wise of heart see him."[3]

9. Gordis argues that Heb. *billaʿ*, "swallow," may also mean "be confused, confounded." In Isa. 28:7 it describes the confused mental state of those under the influence of too much wine (cf. Isa. 3:12), and in Isa. 19:3 it describes the dissolution of carefully formed plans (cf. Ps. 55:10 [Eng. 9]). While the meaning "confused" is present, its primary meaning of "swallow up, destroy" captures the results of such a brazen course of action. Cf. *TDOT*, II:136–39.

1. Many (e.g., Duhm, Driver-Gray) wish to read *zōhar*, "brightness," for *zāhāḇ*, "gold." This change, though, diminishes the poetic picture.

2. The construct chain *rōḇ-ṣᵉḏāqâ*, "great of righteousness," is variously understood. Dhorme vocalizes it *raḇ-ṣᵉḏāqâ*, "a master of righteousness," as a title for God. Gordis considers it as referring to man and grammatically as the object of the verb: "The man abounding in righteousness, He does not torment." The MT, however, is kept, for *rōḇ* is parallel to *saggîʾ*, "great."

3. The second line is difficult. The phrase "wise of heart" is an affirmative phrase throughout the OT, and there is no contextual reason to consider it to be pejorative

21, 22 A wind comes up *sweeping* the skies of the rain clouds. The sun shines brightly in the clear *sky*. As the rays of the setting sun play on the clouds gathering in the north, the sky lights up with a brilliant display of colors. The new storm gathering in the north forebodes God's majestic appearance.[4] Intertwining the terms *the north*[5] and *the storm,* both symbolic of a theophany, Elihu sees that God is about to appear from the glorious sunset. *God,* the sovereign Lord, *is clothed in awesome majesty*. The word *awesome (nôrā')* emphasizes the terror that a display of the divine power arouses in earthly creatures, and the word *majesty (hôḏ)* represents the splendor that attends the holiness of God.[6]

23 In his appearing God remains *far beyond* human *reach*. Nevertheless, those who behold his coming sense his exalted *power* and his *justice*. These two qualities, power and justice, so often divided on earth, are inexorably bound together in God. *Great in righteousness,* Shaddai will never violate justice—he will not *oppress* the people capriciously. That is, when God reveals himself to Job, Job will be reduced to silence as God will convince him that he has been treated justly.

24 Men *fear* (*yārē'*; cf. 1:1) this terrible and righteous God. Those who are *wise in heart* are able to *see* or perceive God when he displays his glory in the north. This line is a direct reference to Job's concern in his second speech (ch. 9). Job was afraid that when God revealed himself under the canopy of the heavens, he would not be able to behold him (9:2–13, esp. v. 11). No one could be wise enough (9:4) to challenge this God in a legal dispute. Elihu's response is that the wise in heart fear God and have no need to dispute with him.

The conclusion to the Elihu speeches parallels the conclusion to the hymn of wisdom (ch. 28): "Behold, the fear of the Lord is wisdom."

(cf. 9:4; Prov. 10:8; 11:29; 16:21). Therefore, it is best to interpret *lō'*, "not," as asseverative *lû'*, "surely, indeed." Gordis also suggests revocalizing *yir'eh,* "he will see," as *yîrā'uhu,* "they will fear him," for the author sometimes likes to repeat a verb in both lines. But it seems better to revocalize MT as *yir'ēhû,* "they see him," for it is supported by LXX and accords with the plural subject.

4. Cf. Deut. 4:11; Ps. 18:8–16 (Eng. 7–15); Hab. 3:2–15.

5. In Ugaritic mythology the gods held their solemn assembly on the high mountain in "the north," Mt. Casius. Israel used this language metaphorically for the place of God's ruling (cf. Ps. 48:3 [Eng. 2]). See R. Clifford, *The Cosmic Mountain in Canaan and the Old Testament* (Cambridge, MA: Harvard University Press, 1972), pp. 55–79.

6. Cf. G. Warmuth, *"hôdh," TDOT,* III:353–55.

AIM

In his final speech Elihu seeks to persuade Job to focus on God, the Supreme Teacher. The mighty power of God is emphasized in order to make it crystal clear to Job that no human being is ever in a position to dispute with God. Nevertheless, God is compassionate, insistently luring a person from the error of his ways through discipline. Whoever listens to God's instruction will receive blessing.

This time Elihu focuses more on the Teacher than on the Teacher's instructional methods. The incredible wisdom of this Teacher is clearly visible in nature, the particularly marvelous thunderstorm. God's marvelous ways of directing a storm testify to his great wisdom. God masters all forces, and his ways cannot be surpassed. In fact, he uses the weather to affect the course of human and animal activity. In doing this he wishes that all people may know his work. His direction of the clouds and the winds leads people to ponder his perfect knowledge. Such a wise and a good Creator instructs human beings in order that they might revere him.

Elihu's description of a theophany prepares Job to hear Yahweh's words out of the tempest, for in revering God a human being finds true wisdom. In his conclusion Elihu agrees with the final line of the hymn to wisdom (28:28). His teaching thus prepares Job to abandon his avowal of innocence in an act of full submission to God as his Lord. He enjoins Job to realize that the proper human response to a display of God's splendor is the fear of God (37:21–24). Elihu's exhortation thus foreshadows the response Job will have to Yahweh's theophany (42:1–6).

ELIHU'S CONTRIBUTION

Elihu's major contribution to ancient Israel's Wisdom tradition is a significant reshaping of the doctrine of retribution. Though he is more verbose and less skilled in the use of poetic metaphor than the three comforters, his understanding of the dynamic of the interaction between God and human beings is far more complex and realistic. He accepts the possibility that the righteous may suffer. Whereas the comforters hold the position that a person suffers either because of an inherent human weakness or as the direct consequence of some sinful deed, he develops the thesis that God freely uses suffering as well as dreams to instruct a person (33:12–22). Through these means God mercifully reaches out to correct a person likely to commit some wrong. Elihu is saying to Job that his terrifying nightmares and his seizures of pain are God's merciful, disciplinary blows designed to rescue him from a worse fate. Job needs to believe that God can and is prepared to rescue him from the power of death and restore his health and fortune. With this teaching Elihu focuses more on Job's present plight than on his past life. He thereby avoids a futile search like that of the comforters for some sin that Job may have committed as the cause of his pain. He is more interested in Job's present response to God's discipline than in any past transgressions. Although Job may not have done anything gravely wrong to be so afflicted by God, he must obediently accept God's discipline instead of resisting it so stubbornly.

Elihu fears, however, that Job has defied God himself by complaining that God has unjustly afflicted him and that God fails to govern the world justly (34:5–9, 34–37). He judges Job's avowal of innocence to be an act of treason (34:32). Therefore, he forewarns Job that if he does not abandon his complaint and confess his pride, he will be punished more, a punishment that will lead to the grave. He wants to awaken Job to the necessity of learning from his misfortune. Job must willingly accept Yahweh's instruction.

In order to counter Job's complaint against God, Elihu teaches that God governs the world justly (34:10–30). God constantly observes the entire earth and judges all justly without inquiry (34:21–30). No one gets away with wrongdoing, not even the mightiest kings (34:18). Furthermore, God is not accountable to anyone, let alone a human being, for any action. It is absurd to think that a human being could enter into litigation with God Almighty. Job must, therefore, abandon his presumptuous demand for an acquittal and respond humbly to God's wooing (36:16).

Elihu exhorts Job to hear God's instruction. Although God does not listen to empty pleas (35:13), in the morning he comes to deliver one who earnestly sings his praises during the night of affliction (35:10; 36:22–26). Through the distress God is opening the ears of the afflicted in order that such a one might listen attentively to his instruction, i.e., that he might willingly follow the right way. God will abundantly prosper that person (36:11). How may an afflicted person find God during his troubles? The answer is by meditating on God's power and extolling his work in song (36:24–37:20). God, whose glory is attested throughout creation, specially manifests his presence in the fury of the thunderstorm. In such an encounter with God, the sufferer, forgetting his plight, fearfully bows in submission to God.

VII. THE YAHWEH SPEECHES (38:1–42:6)

Out of a tempest Yahweh addresses Job.[1] In breaking his silence Yahweh fulfills Job's deepest yearning. Although the plot requires a word from God, his coming surprises everyone.[2] The air is full of excitement. The greatest wonder of all is that God himself speaks to a mere man. Job has had to wait for the moment of Yahweh's choosing. It is important also to note that Yahweh comes out of concern for his servant, not because he has been coerced by Job's oath of innocence (ch. 31). In answering Job he expresses his merciful goodness to his suffering servant.

Amazingly, Yahweh ignores Job's complaints and avoids making a direct response to his avowal of innocence, and, contrary to the friends' expectations, he does not reprove Job for some wrongdoing. Rather he addresses Job like a teacher instructing a student who fails to understand an important matter, for he wishes to open up for him new ways of understanding the created order and his wise care of that order. Yahweh seeks to temper the bitter strains of Job's lament by having Job contemplate his gracious

1. On Job 38–42 see R. MacKenzie, "The Purpose of the Yahweh Speeches in the Book of Job," *Bib* 40 (1959) 435–45; G. Fohrer, "Gottes Antwort aus dem Sturmwind Hi, 38–41," in *Studien zum Buche Hiob* (Gütersloh: Gerd Mohn, 1963), pp. 108–29; P. Skehan, "Job's Final Plea (Job 29–31) and the Lord's Reply (Job 38–41)," *Bib* 45 (1964) 51–62 (repr. in *Studies in Israelite Poetry and Wisdom,* CBQMS 1 [Washington, D.C.: Catholic Biblical Association, 1971], pp. 114–23); M. Tsevat, "The Meaning of the Book of Job," *HUCA* 37 (1966) 73–106 (repr. in *Studies in Ancient Israelite Wisdom,* ed. J. Crenshaw [New York: Ktav, 1976], pp. 341–74); S. Terrien, "The Yahweh Speeches and Job's Response," *RevExp* 68 (1971) 497–509; H. Preuss, "Jahwes Antwort an Hiob und die sogenannte Hiobliteratur des alten Vorderen Orients," *Beiträge zur alttestamentlichen Theologie,* Fest. W. Zimmerli, ed. H. Donner, et al. (Göttingen: Vandenhoeck & Ruprecht, 1977), pp. 323–42; O. Keel, *Jahwes Entgegnung an Ijob* (Göttingen: Vandenhoeck & Ruprecht, 1978); J. Williams, "Deciphering the Unspoken: The Theophany of Job," *HUCA* 49 (1978) 69–72; V. Kubina, *Die Gottesreden im Buche Hiob* (Freiburg: Herder, 1979); A. Brenner, "God's Answer to Job," *VT* 31 (1981) 129–37; B. Malchow, "Nature from God's Perspective: Job 38–39," *Dialog* 21 (1982) 130–33.

2. The height of the dramatic action is expressed in numerous ways: Yahweh himself speaks, a tempest attends his appearing, the special name Yahweh is used.

ways in governing the world. He also hopes to persuade Job to perceive the false inferences that have led to his complaint that God fails to keep the times of judgment.

The Yahweh speeches consist of two discourses: Yahweh's first speech (38:1–40:2), and Yahweh's second speech (40:6–41:26 [Eng. 34]). Both speeches are followed by a short response from Job (40:3–5; 42:1–6).

The Yahweh speeches, being a blend of multiple genres—theophany, hymn of praise, dispute, interrogation of a defendant, myths of the divine battle with primordial monsters—create a unique form. The essential nature of these speeches is a hymn of praise,[3] but the list of natural phenomena and the series of rhetorical questions dominate their structure. Von Rad has observed a correspondence between the list of meteorological phenomena in Job 38:12–37 and that enumerated in an Egyptian scientific work named "The Onomasticon of Amenope."[4] He argues that such encyclopedic lists were known in Israel and that there were sages who composed instructional poems from such lists. But the use of rhetorical questions is not attested in any other OT hymn of praise. It is a style more common to a controversy.[5] Comparisons with other Near Eastern texts indicate that the Yahweh speeches are closer to a disputation than to a plaintiff's interrogation of a defendant. The disputation genre offers Yahweh the opportunity to challenge Job's perspective without filing a formal indictment against him. Yahweh rebukes Job for the audacity of thinking that he could dispute with God as an equal, but he does not charge Job with committing any specific transgression.

3. Fohrer posits that elements of these speeches are borrowed from the hymnic genre in which a deity praises his own exalted lordship. This genre is attested in Isaiah (e.g., 43:11–13; 44:6–8, 24–28). Westermann (*Structure of the Book of Job*, pp. 105–23) finds two elements present in Yahweh's speech, praise of the Creator and praise of the Lord of history. Reordering the text, he assigns these two themes to 38:2–39:30 (minus 39:9–12, 13–30) and 40:6–14 + 40:25–41:3 (Eng. 41:1–11) respectively.

4. Similar lists have been preserved in Hebrew poetry, e.g., Ps. 148. This example establishes a tie between encyclopedic lists and a hymn of praise. Von Rad postulates that the author of Job drew from such lists in composing the Yahweh speeches (G. von Rad, "Job xxxviii and Ancient Egyptian Wisdom," in *The Problem of the Hexateuch and Other Essays*, tr. E. W. Trueman Dicken [New York: McGraw-Hill, 1966], pp. 281–91; repr. in *Studies in Ancient Israelite Wisdom*, ed. J. Crenshaw [New York: Ktav, 1976], pp. 267–77).

5. An Egyptian text that has some similarities to the Yahweh speeches is Papyrus Anastasi I, for it employs a rhetorical use of questions composed from an encyclopedic list. A scribe named Hori sought to persuade Amenemope, a colleague, of his errors by means of a barrage of rhetorical questions about the geography of Palestine. No doubt he drew on a geographic list that he had memorized in school. This text indicates how an encyclopedic list could be employed in a dispute. Furthermore, Hori's style, like Yahweh's, is satirical as he endeavors to refute the position of his rival.

By casting the hymn of praise into rhetorical questions that draw an agreeing nod from Job, Yahweh establishes a bond between himself and his servant. Such a rhetorical style leads "the auditor [to] accept the speaker's claims out of his own consciousness rather than having the information imposed on him from the outside."[6] Yahweh also employs irony throughout the speeches in order to break through Job's defense and to defuse the bitterness of his complaint. He wishes to persuade Job to surrender his complaint and his avowal of innocence. Then Job may trust his honor and his destiny to Yahweh, confident that Yahweh is sovereign and that he rules in justice and in kindness.

The Yahweh speeches thus relate to the two dominant elements in Job's speeches, lament and lawsuit. By addressing Job directly, Yahweh fulfills his demand for a hearing, and by employing a barrage of rhetorical questions, Yahweh puts Job in his place, showing him that he is no match for God in a dispute. As a result Yahweh wins the lawsuit by reducing Job to silence.[7] As for the lament, Yahweh delivers to Job a word of hope, similar to an oracle of salvation.

A. YAHWEH'S FIRST SPEECH (38:1–40:2)

After an introduction and opening challenge to Job (38:1–3), Yahweh interrogates Job about the created order (38:4–39:30), and concludes by extending an invitation for Job to respond (40:1–2). In the first speech Yahweh considers the structure of the world (38:4–24) and the maintenance of the world (38:25–39:30).[1] He presents himself first as Creator and then as Lord. As Creator, Yahweh established the earth securely on its foundation (38:4–7), bounded the sea (38:8–11), and created the light (38:12–15). As Creator, he knows and rules the farthest recesses: the deep (38:16–18); the distant horizons, the residence of light and darkness (38:19–21); the height, the storehouse of snow and hail (38:22–24). As Lord, Yahweh judiciously manages all the elements in heaven (38:25–38) and all creatures on earth (38:39–39:30). Although there is no mention of mankind in this speech, no doubt intentionally, Job can easily discern Yahweh's implication that he

6. M. Fox, "Job 38 and God's Rhetoric," *The Book of Job and Ricoeur's Hermeneutics*, Semeia 19, ed. J. D. Crossan (Chico: Scholars Press, 1981), p. 58.

7. Cf. Westermann, *Structure of the Book of Job*, p. 106.

1. A major break exists between 38:24 and 38:25, although it is not immediately obvious since the theme of rain seems to unite vv. 22–24 with vv. 25–30. But vv. 22–24 join with vv. 16–24 in focusing on the heavenly storehouse as one of the recesses of the world order, while vv. 25–27 belong with vv. 25–38 in presenting the rainstorm as one of the heavenly phenomena tied with the seasons (cf. Westermann, *Structure of the Book of Job*, pp. 110–13).

cares for human beings even more wisely and compassionately than for the other creatures.

1. INTRODUCTION AND OPENING CHALLENGE TO JOB (38:1–3)

1 *Then Yahweh answered Job out of*[1] *the tempest saying,*
2 *"Who is this that darkens counsel*
with words lacking knowledge?
3 *Gird your loins like a man;*[2]
I will ask you, and you shall tell me."

1 *Out of the tempest (s^{e}ʿārâ),* like the one Elihu has just described or possibly the very one Elihu has seen gathering in the north (37:21–24), *Yahweh answered Job.* A storm often attended Yahweh's coming.[3] The clouds and mist both conceal and reveal the divine glory. A theophany is so portentous that nature presents an awesome display of power—thunder (Ps. 77:18–19 [Eng. 17–18]), dark clouds (Ps. 18:10–13 [Eng. 9–12]; 97:2), earthquake (Judg. 5:4; Ps. 18:8 [Eng. 7]), and fire (Isa. 30:27; Ps. 50:3). This panorama of natural phenomena witnesses that Yahweh, the holy God, is actually present.[4] The clouds protect the audience from being consumed by the divine holiness. Those who behold such a display are filled with dread and wonder. The awe strikes the beholder dumb. Each worshiper, drawn out of his self-centered existence as by a powerful magnet, bows reverently before his God.

1. The writing of a *nun* in medial style suggests that at one time the two Hebrew words, "from the storm," were written together. Fohrer, however, suggests that it could be an error for the poetic form *minni,* "from."

2. In the light of 3:3 it is not necessary to read *k^{e}gibbôr,* "like a mighty man," with some mss., for MT *k^{e}geḇer,* "like a man."

3. Heb. *s^{e}ʿārâ* may be either "a whirlwind" (2 K. 2:11) or "a tempest" (Ezek. 13:11, 13). At various times Yahweh appeared through this medium. In a mighty storm of lightning and thunder Yahweh appeared to all Israel assembled at Mt. Sinai (Exod. 19:16–20). He also appeared to Ezekiel by the brook Chebar in a whirlwind coming out of the north (Ezek. 1:2–4). The prophets speak of God's coming in "the tempest" to judge the nations and the wicked in general (Isa. 29:5–6; Jer. 23:19; 25:32 *[saʿar];* 30:23; Nah. 1:3 *[ś^{e}ʿārâ]*). Zech. 9:14–17 describes Yahweh's appearing in a tempest to protect his people while totally destroying their enemies (cf. Ps. 18:8–16 [Eng. 7–15] = 2 Sam. 22:8–16; Ps. 77:17–20 [Eng. 16–19]).

In his definitive study of the OT theophanic tradition, Jörg Jeremias argues that this account of a theophany is a major departure from the oldest theophanic form like that found in Judg. 5:4–5. No longer is there any description of the wonders in nature that attend God's appearance, and the statement of his coming is so abbreviated that only the single word "tempest" remains (*Theophanie: Die Geschichte einer alttestamentlichen Gattung,* WMANT 10 [Neukirchen-Vluyn: Neukirchener, 1965], pp. 69, 162).

4. Cf. R. Otto, *The Idea of the Holy,* tr. J. Harvey (London: Oxford University Press, repr. 1967), pp. 5–40.

38:1–3 Introduction and Opening Challenge to Job

For the first time since the prologue the author uses God's special name, *Yahweh.*[5] He chooses this name for God because it is inextricably tied to the OT theophanic tradition, especially to the redemptive events of the Exodus (cf. Exod. 6:2–9). For clarity it is specifically stated that Yahweh addresses *Job.* After the Elihu speeches the person addressed needs to be identified. This fact means that Yahweh's words are primarily spoken to Job, not to the comforters or to the audience at large.

2 Yahweh, the Wise Teacher, takes the offensive and interrogates Job, his complaining servant. Job has pondered his dilemma from many sides, and his questioning has led him to challenge the traditional belief that God governs the world in justice (e.g., chs. 21 and 24). Without presenting a self-defense against these accusations, Yahweh opens by putting Job in his place with a question that casts doubt on Job's insight (v. 2). Without discounting Job's moral integrity, Yahweh challenges Job's perception of his governance of the world. By opening with the words *Who is this?* Yahweh asserts his superiority. Moreover, he shows respect for Job by addressing him as a virile *man (geḇer).* This choice of words means that neither his affliction nor his inflamed rhetoric has diminished his intrinsic worth as a human being.

Before beginning a series of questions designed to lead Job to abandon his position, Yahweh accuses Job of *darkening counsel (ʿēṣâ)*[6] and of speaking *with words lacking knowledge.* Certainly Job lacks insight into the counsel of God, i.e., the wisdom that permeates his creative acts and guides his governance of the universe (cf. Jer. 32:19). At times Job approached the truth of his situation with penetrating insight, but he fell quickly into despondent outbursts. His anxious fears about his humiliating circumstance have clouded his thinking about Yahweh's purpose. Job has darkened this counsel because he lacks a broad, comprehensive perspective of God's ways. His perception has been darkest when he has accused God of acting arbitrarily without regard for justice and when he has assumed that he himself could dispute with God as an equal.

This divine rebuke, nevertheless, stands in tension with the coming statement in which Yahweh will affirm that Job has spoken rightly about God (42:7). Putting these two statements together, it could be said that Job has complained and agonized out of a sincere heart with an increasing faith, but he has not discerned the judicious counsel of God that permeates all of his deeds throughout the world. Although Job has lacked insight, Yahweh

5. This fact attests that the divine revelation belonged to the oldest layers of the epic of Job. The only other occurrence of the name Yahweh in the poetry is in 12:9, which is usually evaluated as an error.

6. For a discussion of Heb. *ʿēṣâ* see J. Lévêque, *Job et son Dieu,* Études bibliques (Paris: Gabalda, 1970), II:510–13.

does not say that Job has sinned. He never rebukes Job for swearing his avowal of innocence. But he contends that Job's limited understanding hinders him from disputing wisely with his Creator about his own fate. As Fohrer observes, Job has not sought for the solution of his plight in God himself alone, but in the pursuit of his rights. In that search he has erred, but he has not sinned. It needs to be restated that it has been Job's conviction that he is innocent that has enabled him to press the issue until God's appearing. Nevertheless, a danger inherent in basing his self-defense on his own personal integrity is that pride may arise and pervert his thinking. It is to thwart any undue pride in Job that Yahweh opens with a rebuke, for such pride will prevent Job from yielding his avowal of innocence in order to be reconciled with Yahweh.

3 Accepting Job's challenge to settle their differences, Yahweh summons him to *gird* up his *loins*. Job is enjoined to prepare himself as though they were to have a wrestling match.[7] "Girding the loins" means literally tucking in the skirt of the robe in one's belt; this is done so that one can work unhindered. It symbolizes pulling together all one's strength in order to wrestle energetically with a difficult task. In this match God will address questions to Job and expect an answer. Earlier Job had said to God: "Call and I will answer, or I shall speak and answer me" (13:22; cf. 10:2). God accepts the former alternative and puts Job on the defensive. Job will need every ounce of his wit and wisdom to answer God.

2. INTERROGATION ABOUT THE CREATED ORDER (38:4–39:30)

Yahweh questions Job on two points: the structure of the world (38:4–24) and the maintenance of the world (38:25–39:30).

a. The Structure of the World (38:4–24)

(1) The Fundamental Structure of the World (38:4–15)

4 *"Where were you when I laid the earth's foundation?*
Tell me if you know fully.

7. C. Gordon considers this passage an allusion to the ordeal of belt wrestling in which two contestants girded with a belt wrestled to resolve a dispute ("Belt Wrestling in the Bible World," *HUCA* 23 [1950–51] 131–36; cf. 9:3). Some (e.g., Fohrer) accept this custom as background for the language of v. 3, but others (e.g., H. Ginsberg, "Interpreting Ugaritic Texts," *JAOS* 70 [1950] 158; Gordis) vigorously reject it.

5 *Who traced[1] its dimension, if[2] you know?*
Who stretched a line across it?
6 *On what were its sockets set,*
or who laid its cornerstone—
7 *while the morning stars sang together*
and all the sons of God shouted[3] for joy?
8 *Who[4] knit the sea together[5] behind doors;*
who brought it forth[6] gushing from the womb
9 *when I made clouds its garment*
and dark mist its swaddling band,
10 *when I fixed[7] limits[8] for it*
and set its bolted doors,
11 *and I said, 'Unto here you may come and no farther,[9]*
and here[10] your proud waves will break'?[11]

1. M. Dahood ("Hebrew-Ugaritic Lexicography X," *Bib* 53 [1972] 399) takes Heb. *śām,* "put, place," to mean also "write down, trace, draft" (cf. 22:22 [M. Dahood, "The Metaphor in Job 22,22," *Bib* 47 (1966) 108–109]; Ps. 56:9 [Eng. 8]): "Who drafted its dimensions?" This definition is accepted, for it affords an excellent parallel to "stretch across" *(nāṭâ ʿal).*

2. Heb. *kî* is a variation on the *ʾim* of v. 4 and serves the same function (Fohrer).

3. The finite verb continues the nuance of the infinitive construct governed by a preposition (GKC, § 114r; Driver, *Hebrew Tenses,* §§ 117–18).

4. Following the Vulg., Dhorme gains the interrogative pronoun by reading *mî sāḵ* for MT *wayyāseḵ,* "and he shut up." Otherwise the interrogative "who" is implied by the immediate context.

5. For MT *wayyāseḵ,* "and he shut up," Blommerde (*Northwest Semitic Grammar and Job,* pp. 132–33) suggests reading *wayyussaḵ,* either as a Hophal or as a Qal passive imperfect from *nsk,* "when sea poured out. . . ." Possibly the root is *skk,* "to weave, knit," a metaphor for the growth of a fetus in a womb, as in Ps. 139:13b: "You knit me together in my mother's womb." This interpretation affords an excellent parallel with "bring forth" *(yāṣāʾ).* Also, the double doors are picturesque for the labia of the womb.

6. A Hiphil *yôṣîʾ*, "it is brought forth," is read instead of MT's Qal *yēṣēʾ*, "it goes out," since God is the logical subject (Andersen).

7. In this context Heb. *šāḇar,* "break," is difficult. Either it has a special legal meaning, "decree, decide" (Targ.; Gordis), or there is a textual error. Guillaume ("Arabic Background," p. 123) connects it with Arab. *šabara* ("span"): "And I measured it by span." Driver-Gray read *wāʾāšîṯ,* "and I prescribed." The first suggestion is best, for it avoids emendation.

8. Many (e.g., Duhm, Hölscher) wish to read *ḥuqqô,* "his limit," for MT *ḥuqqî,* "my limit," but the suffix may be subjective, "limit set by me," as Gordis states.

9. To restore symmetry Duhm deletes *ṯāḇôʾ*, "you may come," while Budde and Hölscher delete *wᵉlōʾ tōsîp,* "and no farther." But Gordis argues that *wāʾōmar,* "and I said," is an anacrusis, an introductory word that lies outside the meter.

10. This is a singular writing of *pōʾ*, "here," with an ʾ instead of the usual *pōh,* as in the first line.

11. MT *yāšîṯ,* "it will put," is difficult, so most commentators emend. Many

12 *Have you ever commanded the morning*
or shown[12] the dawn[13] its place,
13 *to seize the edges of the earth*
and shake the wicked[14] out of it?
14 *The earth takes shape like clay under a seal;*
its features stand out[15] like those of a garment.
15 *The wicked are denied their light;*
their upraised arm is broken."

In this first series of questions Yahweh considers the initial stage of creation under various images. Like a master builder he laid the earth's foundation (vv. 4–7), like a midwife he brought forth the sea (vv. 8–11), and like a general he commanded the light to shine (vv. 12–15). With these questions Yahweh raises Job's sight from his own troubles to the marvelous order that undergirds the world. Since the thrust of Yahweh's speech focuses on the manner in which he sustains the world more than on the creation process itself, only the first creative acts which gave definitive structure to the world are considered.

4 Since Job has doubted that God consistently rules the world in righteousness, Yahweh queries him as to whether he has the understanding necessary to *know fully (yāḏaʿ bînâ)* the inner structure of the created order. Heb. *bînâ* refers to both the faculty of understanding and the object of knowledge.[16] As the object of the verb *yāḏaʿ*, "know," it means "endued with understanding."[17] Job is asked to make known his knowledge of the

(e.g., Fohrer, Gordis, *BHS*) read *yišbōṯ g^{e}ʾôn,* "Here your high waves must stop," resulting from an error of metathesis and subsequent redivision of words. But Pope finds the same radicals as MT in an Ugaritic text (*UT*, 68:27): *yqṯ bʿl wyšt ym,* "Baal cut down and *št* Sea." In this context Heb. *šîṯ* certainly means "destruction," but its precise nuance has not yet been discovered. Again, one must not emend MT too quickly.

12. This is the only occurrence of *yāḏaʿ*, "know," in the Piel, although some (e.g., Gordis) have suggested that *ydʿ* in Ps. 104:19b should be a Piel form.

13. The Ketib *yiddaʿtâ šaḥar* may be preferred to the Qere *yiddaʿtā haššaḥar,* for the anarthrous noun is preferred in poetry (so Driver-Gray, Gordis). But since there are many exceptions to this rule in the book of Job, the Qere is accepted (so Dhorme).

14. The suspended ʿ here and in v. 15a suggests a correction as the result of an early scribal error (cf. Gordis, Tur-Sinai).

15. For MT *w^{e}yiṯyaṣṣ^{e}ḇû,* "they stand out," Dhorme reads *w^{e}ṯiṣṣāḇaʿ*, "it is dyed." Fohrer emends it to *w^{e}ṯiṣṭabbaʿ*, "it becomes colored." (See also *BHS*.) Gordis finds excellent sense for the verse by making three changes—*baḥōmer* for *k^{e}ḥōmer, ḥayyāṯām* for *ḥôṯām,* and *kullām yēḇōšû* for *k^{e}mô l^{e}ḇûš:* "and they be plunged into the mire, and be arraigned, all put to shame." This makes a fine transition from v. 13 to v. 15 and coordinates with 30:19. The suggestion is worthy of careful consideration, but the number of changes cautions against adopting it.

16. See *TWOT*, I:104.

17. H. Ringgren, *"bîn," TDOT*, II:105–106; cf. Prov. 4:1; 1 Chr. 12:33 (Eng. 32); 2 Chr. 2:11–12 (Eng. 12–13).

initial stages of the creation of the world as though he were the primordial man who had witnessed the laying of the earth's foundation (cf. 15:7). From an OT perspective, however, wisdom was God's sole companion present at creation (ch. 28; Prov. 8:22–31). Therefore, since Job lacks this essential knowledge, how could he expect to dispute successfully with God?

5–7 Yahweh questions Job about the formation of the earth under the imagery of the construction of a major building.[18] The site for the building was carefully *traced,* i.e., surveyed. A measuring *line (qaw)* was stretched out to ensure that the earth was constructed exactly according to Yahweh's blueprints. By implication it is being said that everything created corresponds precisely to God's plan. But who made sure that the building was framed according to those plans? Who stretched out the measuring line? Was it Job? Of course not!

The *sockets* for the pillars, just like the pillars that support the roof of a palace, *were* securely *set.*[19] Then *the earth's cornerstone was* precisely *laid.*[20] In an ancient community the laying of a foundation stone for a public building such as a temple was a high occasion and was commemorated by a festive ceremony. On the occasion of laying the earth's cornerstone, *the morning stars*[21] were assembled as an angelic chorus to sing praises to God for the glory of his world. At the moment the stone was set in place *the sons of God,* i.e., the angels, broke out in joyous singing, praising God, the Creator. Since no human being was present at this occasion, the inner structure of the universe remains a secret hidden from mankind.

8–11 The next set of questions concerns the origin of the sea. The ancient Semites thought that the sea or the waters of the deep were the original element of the world (cf. Gen. 1:2). Several ancient Near Eastern myths, e.g., "Enuma Elish" from Babylon and the Baal Cycle from Ugarit, recount the fierce battle in which the supreme deity won his right to rule by defeating the sea god(dess). Furthermore, the sea, no doubt because of its

18. For the picture of the earth constructed as a building compare Ps. 24:2; 89:12 (Eng. 11); 102:26 (Eng. 25); 104:5; Prov. 3:19; Isa. 48:13; 51:13, 16; Zech. 12:1.

19. Cf. Cant. 5:15. In Ps. 104:5 this metaphor emphasizes the earth's stability.

20. Cf. Ps. 19:2–3 (Eng. 1–2); 148:1–6. The language alludes to a joyous ceremony held at the laying of the cornerstone of a great building, e.g., the second temple (Ezra 3:10–11).

21. In various Near Eastern religions the morning stars were venerated as gods and goddesses. Many of them had an important role in the pantheon, esp. Venus. In this reference they are identified among the sons of God, or angels, who were created by God for special service. In Gen. 1 the stars were created on the fourth day, but here they existed at the initial stages of creation. This apparent discrepancy indicates that "the morning stars" in this context is primarily a term that forms a synonymous parallelism with "the sons of God," who, it is assumed, existed prior to the creation of the earth. It is, therefore, used metaphorically to refer to these heavenly creatures independent of the existence of the physical stars.

raging fury in a storm, symbolized the forces of chaos hostile to life. Many OT texts affirm that Yahweh is the master of the sea (e.g., Job 26:10; Ps. 77:16 [Eng. 15]). Having brought forth the sea and having harnessed it, he commands it and it does his bidding (cf. Ps. 104:6–9). This is a way of affirming that there are no belligerent cosmic forces beyond Yahweh's authority.

In contrast to mythical thought, the sea here is an infant in complete submission to Yahweh. Deep in the recesses of the universe's womb, enclosed by double *doors,* suggestive of the womb's labia, Yahweh skillfully *knit the sea together* like a fetus. At the end of its gestation Yahweh *brought it forth gushing from the womb.* It needs to be underscored that there is no hint here of sexual congress between Yahweh and (mother) nature. The picture is that Yahweh, the sea's Creator, determined the sea's every characteristic. Since he brought it into existence, he never had to subdue it in mortal combat as the ruling gods Marduk or Baal in ancient Near Eastern mythology had to do. It has always been subservient to him. In fact, Yahweh took care of the sea as gently as one cares for a newborn infant. He clothed the sea with *clouds* (*ʿānān;* cf. 26:8–9; 37:11, 15) and swaddled it with *dark mist* (*ʿărāpel;* cf. 22:13). This is a graphic description of the heavy, dark clouds that often hover over the sea.

With another metaphor Yahweh states that he *fixed limits* or statutes *(ḥōq),* i.e., natural boundaries, that the sea cannot cross (cf. Gen. 1:6–9; Prov. 8:29). Or, using another figure, he shut the sea behind *bolted doors,* as though it were confined in a fortress (e.g., Deut. 3:5).[22] Since he fully controls or restricts the sea, never can it at will inundate the inhabited land. This wording means that the sea may encroach on the land, but only so far. Its mighty, proud waves break at the seashore, the line drawn by God. Even when the sea is aroused in a violent storm and its waves reach far inland, there is a boundary it may not cross.

12–15 The next set of questions ponders the marvels of the dawn. Whereas darkness is associated with primordial powers of evil, light, the source of life, represents God (cf. Ps. 27:1; Isa. 60:19–20; John 1:9; 1 John 1:5). On the first day of creation God commanded the light into existence (Gen. 1:3–5). And each dawn thereafter is a reenactment of that first day. That is, ancient people, not viewing nature as a system of impersonal, mechanical laws, did not consider the succession of days guaranteed, but believed that God spoke each new day into existence. Yahweh asks Job if he

22. By comparison, when Marduk, the chief Babylonian god, set about to create the world: "He split [Tiamat (the salt waters)] like a shellfish into two parts; Half of her he set up and ceiled it as sky, Pulled down the bar and posted guards" ("Enuma Elish," V:137–39; *ANET,* p. 67).

ever commanded the morning light even once to shine on any given day or if he ever assigned the colorful rays of dawn to their place. The answer is obviously negative, for the light obeys only Yahweh's voice. He alone can bring forth a new day.

The rays of dawn overcome the blackness of night and ensure the continuance of life on earth. Every morning, just as a maid vigorously shakes the crumbs from a huge tablecloth, the rays of dawn reach out and grasp the mountains, the corners of the earth's tablecloth, and shake the wicked off the earth's surface.

As the morning light etches multiple designs on the horizon in an array of colors, the darkened earth begins to take shape before the human eye. The dawn lights up the hills, valleys, trees, and shrubs. Just as a lump of *clay* is turned into a beautiful design beneath a *seal,* so too the earth glistens in beauty beneath the sun's first rays. In another picture the early light of day makes the earth appear as a beautiful *garment,* exquisite in design and glorious in color.

At dawn the *wicked,* who love darkness, flee into hiding (cf. 24:13–17). The sun eclipses the *light* of the wicked, i.e., it deprives them of the good fortune and protection night offers them. The sun's rays prevent them from pursuing their evil designs. *Their upraised arm*—a sign of their arrogant determination to enforce violently their evil will—*is broken.* This wording may allude to the fact that during the day the court sits and delivers a stiff sentence of physical impairment against the wicked for their doing evil during the night. Such harsh sentences were designed to break the power of the wicked.

These verses speak directly to Job's concern that the wicked prosper unchecked (chs. 21, 24). Yahweh counters Job's complaint with the position that his own command of the light confines the work of the wicked. He has contained the wicked within limits just as he has stayed the encroachment of the sea against the land. Like the sea the wicked may cause terror and turmoil, but the light is the boundary that holds them in. Although God grants a measure of freedom to mankind, the wicked never move outside his control.

(2) The Recesses of the World (38:16–24)

16 *"Have you journeyed to the springs of the sea*
or walked in the recesses of the deep?
17 *Have the gates of death been disclosed to you?*
Have you seen the gates[1] of deep darkness?

1. Blommerde (*Northwest Semitic Grammar and Job,* p. 134) assigns emphatic force to the *waw* before a word repeated in the same verse.

18 *Have you contemplated the underworld's[2] vast expanse?[3]*
Tell me if you know all of this.
19 *Where is the way to where light dwells,*
and darkness, where is its place,
20 *that you may take it to its border,*
that you may understand[4] the paths to its house?
21 *You surely know, for you were already born;*
the number of your days is so many![5]
22 *Have you entered the storehouses of snow,*
yes,[6] seen the storehouses of hail,
23 *which I reserve for troublous times,*
for a day of war and battle?
24 *Where is the way to the place where the west wind[7] is dispersed,*
where the east wind is scattered over the earth?"

Yahweh inquires of Job about his acquaintance with the extremities of the created world. He asks if Job has ever traversed the recesses or the outer limits of the world, whether they be the depths of the sea (vv. 16–18), the distant east (vv. 19–21), or the heights of the heavens (vv. 22–24). The axiom is that whoever knows or controls the extremities of the world has control over the universe. If Job could answer Yahweh's questions in the affirmative, it would mean that he had comprehensive knowledge about the universe and understood the way it was governed. But he has never visited these remotest places. The world remains an intriguing enigma to him, as to all human beings.

16–18 Yahweh asks Job if he has ever *journeyed to the springs of the sea*. It was thought that the sea was fed by springs in its depths (cf. Gen. 7:11; 49:25). Has Job ever *walked in the recesses of the deep (tᵉhôm)?*

2. Andersen shows that Heb. *ʾereṣ,* "earth," here means the "underworld"; cf. Ps. 9:14 (Eng. 13); 107:18; Isa. 38:10.

3. The plural *raḥᵃḇê* is the plural of intensity, "the vast expanse" (Tur-Sinai).

4. For MT *tāḇîn* many (e.g., Duhm; cf. Driver-Gray, *BHS*) read *tᵉḇîʾennû,* "you will bring it," but the versions support MT.

5. The adjective *rabbîm* agrees with the genitive, for which it is the primary idea (GKC, § 146a).

6. This is the use of the emphatic *waw* before repetition; see n. 1 above.

7. MT *ʾôr,* "light," appears out of place. Many readings have been suggested: e.g., *ʾēḏ,* "mist" or "cosmic water reservoir" (Duhm, Dhorme, Pope, Rowley), and *rûaḥ,* "wind" (Hölscher, Driver-Gray). Tur-Sinai argues that it is a word for "wind," cognate with Akk. *amurru,* "land of the west wind." Gordis suggests that it may be related to Gk. *aḗr,* "air, air currents," which had a Semitic origin. The parallelism certainly calls for a word for "wind," and Tur-Sinai's suggestion gives the line the best balance.

Beyond the recesses of the deep is Sheol, the dark, dreary abode of the dead. At the springs of the sea lie the gates to Sheol. These gates are guarded by *deep darkness* (*ṣalmāweṯ;* cf. Job 3:5). If Job had walked there, he would have seen the gates through which the shades must pass on their way to Sheol and which prevent their returning to earth. Yahweh asks Job if he has contemplated the *vast expanse* of the underworld. This probing question is especially germane since Job has often expressed his longing for the comforts of death offered by Sheol. At this point Yahweh orders Job to speak, but he remains silent.

19–20 Moving from the depths of the sea to the far-off horizons, Yahweh asks Job if he knows *the way [dereḵ] to where light dwells* or *the place [māqôm] of darkness [ḥōšeḵ]?* Beyond the horizon are two chambers, one in the east for light and one in the west for darkness. Every morning the sun rises and rules the world as it journeys across the sky (cf. Ps. 19:5b-7 [Eng. 4b-6]). At night while the sun rests in the tent God has pitched for it, darkness comes from its chamber and reigns. If Job knew the paths to these abodes, he would have control over the light and the darkness. He could command them to fulfill their task.

21 Affirmative answers to these questions would mean that Job is very old, for he would have been present when these places and paths were set up (cf. 15:7–9). *The number of your days is so many!* His ignorance of this information indicates, however, that his understanding is limited. Since he is not so ancient, his position before God must be that of a contrite servant.

22–24 Yahweh moves on to question Job about the remote, heavenly *storehouses (ʾōṣᵉrôṯ),* where *snow* and *hail* are housed. *Hail* is a potent weapon which God can use to create havoc among troops fighting in an open field, vulnerably exposed to the heavens (e.g., Josh. 10:11). A hailstorm causes so much damage that it was considered to be a plague (Exod. 9:18–26; Ps. 78:47–48; 105:32; Isa. 28:17; 30:30). *Snow* too can severely cripple or even wipe out an army, especially if a blizzard catches an army making their way through a mountain pass (cf. Ps. 68:15 [Eng. 14]). No wonder Yahweh stores up these elements in the heavenly arsenal, keeping them in *reserve for troublous times.* When his people are attacked by a powerful enemy, he may open his arsenal and hurl down hail to route the enemy's army.

In the distant heights Yahweh apportions the winds according to his purpose. He disperses the gentle *west wind* to bring rain on the marshes and to dry out the land. Or he calls for the *east wind (qāḏîm),* the mighty sirocco, to parch the earth and make it so hot that the population finds it intolerable. Does Job know what causes these winds to spread over the earth? Of course not.

b. The Maintenance of the World (38:25–39:30)

Yahweh now turns to address the issue of the way in which he governs the world. Continuing to question Job, he asks him about his ability to direct the inanimate world (38:25–38) and to care for the animate world (38:39–39:30). With this line of questioning Yahweh underscores his wisdom and compassion in governing the created order justly.

(1) The Inanimate World (38:25–38)

25 *"Who cut a channel for the downpour*
and a path for the thunderbolt,
26 *to rain on the earth where no one lives,*
a desert with no one in it,
27 *to saturate a desolate wasteland,*
and to make the steppe[1] *sprout with grass?*
28 *Does the rain have a father?*
Who sired the dew drops?
29 *From whose womb comes the ice?*
Who gives birth to the frost of heaven,
30 *when water hardens*[2] *like stone,*
and the surface of the deep is frozen?
31 *Can you bind the fetters*[3] *of Pleiades*
or loose Orion's bonds?[4]
32 *Can you bring forth the planets in their times*
or lead the Bear with[5] *her cubs?*[6]

1. Heb. *mōṣāʾ*, "source," does not lend itself as a good parallel to "a desolate wasteland" *(šōʾâ ûmešōʾâ)*. Possibly a metathesis has occurred from an original *ṣāmēʾ*, "thirsty (land)" (Duhm, Driver-Gray, Pope). However, another suggestion is preferred: *miṣṣîyâ*, "from the steppe" (cf. 30:3; Dhorme, Fohrer).

2. The verb *yiṯḥabbāʾû*, lit. "it is concealed," could have an extended meaning of "harden" or "freeze" when used with water. Some (e.g., Dhorme, Pope) view it as a dialectal variant of *yiṯudḥammāʾû*, "harden." But Grabbe (*Comparative Philology*, pp. 118–20) shows the lack of any support in finding a verb *ḥmʾ* in Semitic.

3. As most scholars point out, MT *maʿadannôṯ* is an error of metathesis, oral or written, for *maʿanaddôṯ*, "bonds" (cf. 1 Sam. 15:32). So Dhorme, Tur-Sinai, Driver-Gray, Gordis, etc.

4. This may be an allusion to the myth in which Orion, a giant of great strength, was transferred to heaven at his death and bound to the sky. See W. Brueggemann, "Orion," *IDB*, III:609.

5. The preposition *ʿal* here means "in addition, together with" (Dhorme).

6. The phrase *ʿayiš ʿal-bāneyhā* is generally taken either as the Great Bear and the Little Bear (Dhorme) or as Leo and its encroachment on Cancer. The latter position gains support from its Arabic cognate *ʿay(y)ūṯ*, meaning "lion" (Pope).

33 *Do you know the statutes of heaven*
or establish their[7] *rule*[8] *over the earth?*
34 *Can you raise your voice to the clouds*
and cause a stream of water to cover you?
35 *Do you send the lightning bolts on their way,*
saying to you, 'Here we are'?
36 *Who imparted wisdom to the ibis?*
Who gave understanding to the cock?[9]
37 *Who can count the clouds in wisdom?*
Who can tip the heavenly water jars
38 *when the dust fuses to lumps*
and the clods stick together?"

25–27 Yahweh begins to account for his wise, judicious maintenance of the world by looking at the way he manages the weather for the benefit of every region of the world. Between the heavenly storehouses and the earth he *cuts a channel* for the rain, and he makes *a path for the thunderbolt* to travel. God sends rain to the *wasteland,* for he does not forget the uninhabited wilderness. The utter barrenness of this land is expressed in the alliterative phrase *šōʾâ ûmešōʾâ,* "a desolate wasteland" (30:3; Zeph. 1:15). Though no one lives there, the rain God sends nourishes the multitude of

7. The singular suffix refers to the dual *šāmayim* ("heaven") taken as a unit (cf. GKC, § 145m).

8. The hapax legomenon *mišṭār,* "order, rule, inscription," is taken as a cognate of Akk. *mašṭāru,* "writing" (Dhorme, Pope). In Akk. *šiṭir šamē* or *šiṭirtu šamāmi,* "the heavenly writing," stands for the starry sky (cf. KB, p. 609).

9. The meaning of v. 36 is difficult. Both *baṭṭuḥôṯ* and *laśśekwî,* translated here "the ibis" and "the cock," are obscure. In the context they have something to do with the sky or clouds unless the line is a refrain about wisdom. These words may be taken as two different types of clouds (cf. BDB, pp. 376, 967): *ṭuḥôṯ,* from *ṭûaḥ,* "plaster, cover," and *śekwî,* from *śkh* = *śkk* or *skk,* "cover, screen." It is difficult, though, to understand how clouds are given wisdom even though the clouds seem to have a will of their own as they move across the sky (cf. Duhm). Another view relates these words to the inner organs of the body where wisdom resides (cf. Vulg.); *ṭuḥôṯ* then is "the kidneys, inner organs" (cf. Ps. 51:8 [Eng. 6]), and *śekwî* is "the heart," from *śkh,* "look, see." The latter view seems somewhat overextended. Another view finds in these two words birds noted for wisdom and associated with announcing changes in the weather. In rabbinic tradition, *śekwî* is "the cock," which is considered the proclaimer of the fall rains; cf. O. Keel, "Zwei kleine Beiträge zum Verständnis der Gottesreden im Buch Ijob (xxxviii 36f., xl 25)," *VT* 31 (1981) 220–23. In fact, a cylinder seal found in the eighth-century level at Nimrod has a cock and water pots in the sky (cf. v. 37). Then *ṭḥwt* is identified with the ibis, the bird of thought and wisdom. In Egyptian lore the moon god Thoth *(ḏḥwty)* was represented with an ibis head. To this god the Egyptians attributed the invention of the alphabet and identified him as the god of wisdom (cf. W. F. Albright, *Yahweh and the Gods of Canaan* [Garden City: Doubleday, 1968], pp. 245–47).

desert life. This set of questions implies that human beings, motivated by greed and utilitarian attitudes, would never disperse the precious rain to water this desolate land. In their imagined wise (though selfish) planning they would manage the weather for their own profit and pleasure. As a result the balance of nature would be upset and the cultivated land would become a desert. Only God has the wisdom to make it rain in the desert, giving evidence of his wise care for the entire world.

28–30 Yahweh next asks Job how the *rain, dew, ice,* and *frost* originate, since they have no *father* or mother. The variety of forms that moisture takes is fascinating, from the rain to the gentle dew, from the picturesque images etched by the frost to the solid form of ice. In fact, water can *harden like stone (yiṯḥabbāʾ),* and even *the surface of the deep (tᵉhôm)* can be *frozen (yiṯlakkēḏ).* The phenomenon of how water changes into so many different forms bears witness to God's creative genius (cf. Ps. 147:16–18). This picture discounts the pagan belief in the natural generation of these elements. Yahweh alone brings them forth.

31–33 Yahweh then inquires into Job's knowledge about the movement of the constellations *Pleiades, Orion,* and *the Bear,* as well as *the planets.* The three constellations are the same ones mentioned in 9:9, but the precise meaning of the fourth word translated *planets (mazzārôṯ)* is not known.[10] The stars indicate the time, announce the seasons, and chart directions. Many of the ancients thought that their movements forecast the weather and influenced earthly affairs. This belief, of course, was much stronger in societies for whom the myths of the gods were a living reality.[11] In Israel, however, these heavenly bodies were not thought of as gods but as powerful forces completely subordinate to God's command. God created the stars and put them in the heavens to rule the night (Gen. 1:14–19). He could also employ them in his service; e.g., he marshalled them to help his earthly servant Barak defeat the Canaanites (cf. Judg. 5:20).

In the ancient way of thinking, the stars were believed to be controlled by chains. Each day God loosened their cords so that they could make their journey across the sky. Perhaps Hakam's suggestion for the terms *bind* and *loose* in relation to the stars is preferable; he takes these terms to mean

10. The precise identification of *mazzārôṯ* is debated. The Vulg. reads *Lucifer,* a name for Venus equivalent to *mazhᵃrôṯ,* "the shining one." Some relate it to *manzārôṯ,* "crown," i.e., the Corona Borealis (cf. Dhorme). Others see it as a dialectal variant of *mazzālôṯ,* meaning either "the planets" or "the Zodiac circle" (2 K. 23:5; G. R. Driver, *JTS* 7 [1956] 3). Gordis finds support for its meaning "the Zodiac circle" by relating the word to *maʾᵃzārôṯ,* "girdle," with the elision of ʾ. Since no one specific suggestion is compelling, it is translated generally, "the planets."

11. As is well known, the Babylonians were most interested in astrology and constantly observed the patterns in the sky (cf. Isa. 47:13). Cf. J. Hirschberg, "Job XXXVIII 31," *REJ* 99 (1935) 130–32.

that when a constellation rises, it is harnessed to its course, and when it sets, the harness is loosed.

Yahweh questions Job as to his authority over these constellations. Can he affect their rising, their setting, or their movements? Does Job *know,* i.e., determine or decree, *the statutes* that these heavenly bodies obey? Is he in a position to *establish their dominion over the earth?* If so, he might be able to alter the course of earthly affairs, including his own distress. If he cannot answer these questions, it means that his inexplicable suffering falls within God's wise governance of the world.

34–38 Yahweh now asks Job about the giving of the rain in a storm. *Can you raise your voice* and command *the clouds* to open up and pour out *a stream of water to cover you?* The cry for rain in a season of drought is legendary. But no human being has the authority to summon the clouds and to order them to release their rain. Neither can Job command the lightning to flash across the sky. *Lightning bolts* do not present themselves before him saying, *Here we are.* This language indicates that a party reports eagerly to do the master's bidding.

Yahweh asks *who imparted wisdom* to certain birds to announce the morning or approaching rainstorms? The *cock (śeḵwî)* heralds the morning and possibly also the approach of the storm, and the *ibis (ṭuḥôṯ)* was believed to announce a change in the weather. Did Job give these birds this wisdom? Surely not!

Yahweh also asks *who can count the clouds in wisdom,* directing them to the right places? When they arrive at the chosen location, *who can tip the heavenly water jars,* pouring their contents on the thirsty land? The clouds are pictured as water skins or jars of heaven *(niḇlê šāmayim)* which are tilted or *tipped (yaškîḇ)*[12] to empty their contents. The rain is desperately needed when the earth is parched with thirst. Beneath the scorching sun the ground becomes hard as stone. When *the dust fuses to lumps,* then *the clods stick together* so tightly that the land is unworkable.[13] The rains, however, soften the hardened ground so that it can be prepared for planting. Only Yahweh has the wisdom to bring the rain and turn the hard, dry ground into fertile soil.

(2) The Animate World (38:39–39:30)

After lauding his mastery over the heavenly forces, Yahweh deliberates on the unusual qualities and peculiar habits of several wild animals. He is

12. See H. Orlinsky, "The Hebrew Root *škb,*" *JBL* 63 (1944) 19–44.

13. Others (e.g., Dhorme and Rowley) find here the results of a rainstorm; the dry earth becomes muddy after a downpour. But it is more usual to think that the ground becomes as hard as bronze during the long, hot summer (cf. Deut. 28:23).

affirming that he is the designer of all these creatures, endowing them with stately beauty and amazing abilities as well as assigning to them strange features or humorous ways. People love to be amused by watching animals at play. Their beauty inspires admiration. Through observing their habits one gains insight into life (cf. 1 K. 4:32–33). Wild beasts, however, fill one with terror and are a threat to one's existence. Living in the wilderness, they refuse to submit to mankind and will not turn to him for their food. Their only lord is Yahweh.

The animal portraits include the lion, the raven, the mountain goat, the hind, the wild ass, the wild ox, the ostrich, the horse, and birds of prey. In the OT these animals are particularly associated with the desert or the desolate steppe, the habitation of adverse, demonic spirits. They are also the sole inhabitants of postwar desolate ruins (e.g., Isa. 34:6–7; Ezek. 34:8). For example, the wild ass is the enemy of cultivated land and the lion the enemy of a shepherd's flocks. With these portraits Yahweh asserts his lordship over the entire earth—the cultivated land and the wilderness, the domesticated animals and the wild beasts. No part of the world lies outside his rule. No hostile forces exist beyond his authority. That which seems unruly and demonic to mankind is assuredly subject to God's rule. This picture of God's sovereign rule parallels numerous glyphs from the ancient world that depict the might of the monarch's dominion with the motif that he is lord of the animals (see also various biblical texts that mention God's care for animals, e.g., Ps. 104:14a, 21; 145:15–16; 147:9; Matt. 6:26; 10:29; Luke 12:24). As Lord of the universe he governs the whole world for the well-being of every creature, including those mankind despises.

(a) The Lioness and the Raven (38:39–41)

39 *"Do you hunt prey for the lioness*
and satisfy the hunger[1] of her whelps
40 *when they crouch in their dens*
or lie in ambush in their lair?
41 *Who provides food for the raven*
when its young cry out to God
and wander about without food?"

39–41 The first set of questions about animals is concerned with the care that God gives them. Whether it be the mighty *lioness (lāḇîʾ)* or the little *raven (ʿōrēḇ),* God makes provision for their food.

The lioness terrifies mankind.[2] Her loud growling sends chills

1. Here Heb. *ḥayyâ,* "life," means "appetite" or "hunger" (BDB, p. 312).

2. The lion serves as a metaphor for the wicked throughout the OT (e.g., Ps. 7:3 [Eng. 2]; 10:9–10; 17:12).

throughout a town. In ancient thought the people drew a close parallel between wild animals and their enemies; e.g., Ashurbanipal (668–627 B.C.) describes his hunting expedition for wild game, especially the lion, both as a fight against a powerful enemy and as a fight against the powers of chaos.[3] But Yahweh provides *prey* for this stout beast and sees that she has an adequate supply to feed *her whelps.* The lioness usually makes her den among thickets, like the thick brush growing along the banks of the Jordan, for they offer her good protection and afford an excellent *ambush* (*'āreḇ*)[4] where she may lie in wait for some unsuspecting prey.

Yahweh also *provides food for the raven,* a bird classified as ritually unclean. Although the raven has a diet similar to the lion's, it does not capture its own prey. Instead, from a lofty height it spots a carcass, perhaps one left by the lioness, and swoops down to feed upon it. In times of scarcity its young *cry out* in supplication *to God* for food, hopping about frantically, ever hopeful that God will satisfy their hunger. Compassionately God upholds these small, winged creatures.

This short pericope, functioning as an introduction to the long discourse on animals, teaches that Yahweh sustains both the strong and the delicate among the wild animals. He shows his care and protection for all of his creation, and he does so in a way that far surpasses what any human being could or would do.

(b) The Mountain Goat and the Hind (39:1–4)

1 *"Do you know the time when the mountain goats[1] give birth?[2]*
Do you observe the calving of the hind?
2 *Do you count the months they fulfill,*
and do you know the time when they give birth?
3 *They crouch and bring forth[3] their young;*
they are delivered of their fetus.[4]

3. See O. Keel, *The Symbolism of the Biblical World: Ancient Near Eastern Iconography and the Book of Psalms,* tr. T. J. Hallett (New York: Seabury, 1978), pp. 79–80.

4. There is a play on *'āreḇ,* "ambush," in v. 40b and *'ōrēḇ,* "raven," in v. 41a.

1. Although the form for mountain goats (*ya'ᵃlê*) is masculine, the female is implied by reason of the activities described (Driver-Gray).

2. The length of the first line has led some to suspect that either *'ēṯ,* "time," or *leḏeṯ,* "giving birth," is unnecessary. Budde and Hölscher delete *leḏeṯ* as an inaccurate gloss of *'ēṯ.* Dhorme suggests that *'ēṯ* is an error of dittography, repeating the last two letters of the first word, *hyd't* (see also *BHS*). But since these suggestions lack textual support, MT is retained.

3. Heb. *pālaḥ* means "to split or cleave." Some, like Dhorme, have emended it to *tᵉpallēṭnâ,* "they cast forth, drop," but the root *plḥ* may be related metaphorically to the birth process. Gordis suggests that it originally referred to the hatching of eggs.

4. For MT *ḥeḇlêhem,* "their fetuses," the feminine suffix would be expected, not

4 *Their young are healthy and grow up in the open;*[5]
they leave and do not return."[6]

1–4 *Mountain goats (yaʿalê-selaʿ),* the Nubian ibex, inhabit the steep cliffs of the wilderness. In Israel today they are present in the regions of Qumran, En-gedi, and Sinai. These animals go about in small herds of eight to ten. Their light tan bodies with lighter brown stomachs blend in well with the rocky hillside. The male has two magnificent horns that curl backward. These graceful creatures are very shy and are endowed with a keen sense of smell. The *hind,* or the fallow deer *(ʾayyālâ),* has similar characteristics.[7]

The question put to Job is, *Do you know the time when the mountain goats give birth?* Does anyone assist the females while they are giving birth as a shepherd helps the members of his flock that are calving? The answer is that these animals complete their months of pregnancy without help from any human being. Nobody watches over them or protects them. The phrase *count the months* means that one compassionately cares for a mother during the days of her pregnancy. For the ibex, however, parturition *(pālaḥ)* takes place quickly and easily.[8] She needs no helper. Soon her healthy fawns go their own way, never to return to their mother. It is implied that God himself mercifully looks after the welfare of the departed young.

(c) The Wild Ass (39:5–8)

5 *"Who let the wild ass go free*
and loosed the reins of the onager,[1]

---

the masculine. Either there is an error or else the distinction between the feminine and masculine plural pronominal suffixes was not carefully maintained at the time this piece was written (cf. GKC, § 135o). While this word often connotes the pain of labor, Rowley and Guillaume (*Studies in the Book of Job,* p. 132) take it to mean "the fetus," the cause of the pain; for there is no stress here on pain. Dahood points to the Ugaritic parallel *yld//ḥbl,* with *ḥbl* meaning "flock" (*RSP,* I:201, nos. 227a, d, e).

5. MT *bar,* "field," is an Aramaic word; cf. Dan. 2:38, *ḥêwaṯ bārāʾ* for "open field, the outdoors."

6. The preposition *lāmô,* "to him," has "the mothers" as its antecedent, for the poetic form is the same for both genders (Hakam).

7. The parallel of ibex *(yaʿāl)* and hind *(ʾayyāl)* is attested in Ugaritic literature (*RSP,* II:6, no. 2) and in Prov. 5:19.

8. In v. 1b the word *ḥōlēl,* "calving," emphasizes the birth process, not the severe pain which usually attends a human birth and which is suggested by the root's literal meaning "writhe in pain" *(ḥûl).*

1. "Onager," *ʿārôḏ,* is an Aramaic word. Most likely it is the Aramaic equivalent of *pereʾ,* the parallel word. Cf. L. Köhler, "Archäologisches. Nr. 21. *pereʾ* = Equus Grevyi oustalet," *ZAW* 44 (1926) 59–62; P. Humbert, "En marge du dictionnaire hébraïque," *ZAW* 62 (1949-50) 202–206.

6 *to whom I gave the desert as its home,*
the salt flats for its dwelling?
7 *It laughs at the noise in the city;*
and the driver's shout it does not hear.
8 *It ranges[2] the mountains for its pasture*
and searches for anything green."

5–8 Yahweh next interrogates Job about *the wild ass (pereʾ)* or *the onager (ʿārôḏ).*[3] In contrast to the domesticated donkey, a docile though stubborn animal that serves mankind well as a beast of burden, the wild species roams the wilderness, avoiding human beings. Its speed and its lust for freedom are legendary (cf. Jer. 2:24). At its own pleasure it wanders about the vast open spaces of the desert, for God has *loosed the reins* that a master would put on it (cf. Jer. 14:6).[4] The *desert (ʿᵃrāḇâ)* may specifically refer to the Jordan Valley and the region of the Dead Sea south to the Gulf of Aqaba, which, being well below sea level, is a hot, dry, desolate land. It is labeled *the salt flats (mᵉlēḥâ),* an uninhabited (Jer. 17:6) and uncultivated land (Ps. 107:34). The wild ass frolics about these wastelands, *laughing* at the tumult in the marketplace where its domesticated counterpart toils long and hard beneath heavy loads. It is delighted that it does not have to obey a *driver's* loud *shout,* forcing it to move against its will. Nevertheless, its freedom comes at the price of having to range the barren hills far and wide in search of *anything green.* God watches over the wild ass, making sure that it enjoys its freedom amid scarcity.

(d) The Wild Ox (39:9–12)

9 *"Will the wild ox[1] be willing to serve you*
or stay the night by your manger?
10 *Can you bind the wild ox to the furrow with a rope,[2]*
or will it till the valley behind you?

2. MT *yᵉṯûr* could be a seldom used noun form, but the sentence and the parallelism suggest that a finite verb *yāṯûr,* "he ranges," is preferable. Cf. M. Dahood, *Bib* 55 (1974) 185.

3. See Cansdale, *Animals of Bible Lands,* pp. 94–95.

4. The Hebrew phrase *šillaḥ ḥop̄šî* means "release, set free (a slave)"; cf. Deut. 15:13, 18.

1. The wild ox, the aurochs or bison, is variously spelled in the OT: *rēmîm* (Ps. 22:22 [Eng. 21]), *reʾêm* (Ps. 92:11 [Eng. 10]), *rᵉʾēm* (Num. 23:22). LXX translates it "unicorn" (so AV), and Vulg. has "rhinoceros," but recent scholarship has more accurately identified the animal as the *Bos primigenius.* Cf. A. Godbey, "The Unicorn in the Old Testament," *AJSL* 56 (1939) 256–96; J. Klotz, "Notes on the Unicorn," *Concordia Theological Monthly* 32 (1961) 286–87.

2. The MT phraseology *bᵉṯelem ʿᵃḇōṯô,* "in a furrow of his rope," yields little sense. Many emendations have been offered: *baʿᵃḇōṯ talmô,* "by the cord of his furrow"

11 *Can you rely on it since its strength is great*
or leave to it your work?
12 *Can you trust him to return*[3]
and gather in your grain to the threshing floor?"[4]

9–12 *The wild ox,* or the aurochs *(rêm),* is another example of a powerful creature not subject to mankind.[5] The bull is huge, surpassing six feet in breadth at the shoulders with long horns pointed forward and a dark brown or black coat.[6] Its horns combined with its brute strength make this animal very dangerous (cf. Num. 23:22; 24:8; Ps. 22:22 [Eng. 21]). This animal loves to graze in wooded areas. Thus it was prime game for a royal hunt; e.g., the great Egyptian Pharaoh Thutmose III published on a scarab that he killed seventy-five aurochs on a hunt. An Ugaritic epic recounts the story of the deity Baal hunting for a wild ox in the marshes of Lake Huleh, located in the fertile valley north of the Sea of Galilee (*UT*, 76:II:9, 12). This last reference offers evidence that these animals roamed that area of Palestine in the 2nd millennium B.C.

Whereas the ox serves mankind willingly, the aurochs defies any attempt to tame it. No human being can harness its massive strength. It is ridiculous to think that this freedom-loving creature would ever *stay the night by a manger*. Unwilling to put its neck to the yoke, it will never drag a plow *to till* the earth. No one can rely on this splendid animal to bring the harvested grain from the field. This stalwart animal, which is endowed with more strength than wisdom, is, nevertheless, shrewd enough to stay out of bondage. From a human perspective, its strength, being available only for its own needs, goes to waste. God, however, is its master and its sustainer.

(Duhm); *baʿᵃḇōṯ ʿonqô,* "with the rope of his neck" (Hölscher); *bᵉṯelem baʿᵃḇōṯô,* "to the furrow by his rope" (de Wilde). Gordis suggests that *ʿᵃḇōṯô* is an abbreviated plural for *ʿᵃḇōṯôṯ,* "ropes," and that the accusative case functions as the *bᵉ* of means, "by ropes." The suggestion offered by de Wilde is the simplest. The preposition *bᵉ* may have been lost by haplography, for there are three *b*'s in the phrase.

3. The Qere is *yāšîḇ zarʿeḵā,* "he may bring back your seed"; the Ketib is *yāšûḇ,* "he returns"—the *ʾatnah* is placed on it and "your seed," vocalized *zarʿᵃḵā,* is read with the second line. The Ketib is preferred, for it offers a more balanced line.

4. The two nouns *zarʿeḵā,* "your seed, grain," and *wᵉgornᵉḵā,* "and your threshing floor," are taken as a hendiadys for "the grain to your threshing floor" (cf. Gordis).

5. Often in the OT the ox is mentioned with the donkey (cf. Exod. 21:33; 23:4–5, 12; Deut. 22:10; Isa. 1:3; 32:20), so this may account for the fact that discussion about the wild ox follows that about the wild donkey. The wild ox represents formidable strength, either positively (e.g., Deut. 33:17) or negatively (e.g., Ps. 22:22 [Eng. 21]).

6. See G. Cansdale, *Animals of Bible Lands,* p. 83.

(e) The Ostrich (39:13–18)

13 *"Do the wings of the ostrich beat joyously?[1]*
Do[2] her pinions lack feathers?[3]
14 *She lays[4] her eggs on the ground*
and lets them be warmed[5] in the sand,
15 *unmindful that a foot may crush them,[6]*
that a wild beast may trample them.
16 *She treats[7] her young[8] harshly, as though they were not hers,*
not fearful that her toil may be in vain,
17 *because God deprived her of wisdom[9]*
or did not apportion to her understanding.[10]
18 *Yet when she flaps[11] her wings,*
she laughs at the horse and its rider."

1. The word "rejoice," *ʿālas,* is a metaplastic form of *ʿālaz* and *ʿālaṣ* (Gordis).

2. The particle *ʾim* is best taken as introducing the second half of a double question with the initial *ha* suppressed (GKC, § 150f).

3. Verse 13b is very difficult to interpret. A literal reading, "are they the pinions and plumage of love" (RSV), makes little sense, so many changes have been suggested. Some (e.g., Hölscher) see in *ḥᵃsîḏâ* the name of a bird, "the stork." Hölscher then emends *nōṣâ,* "plumage," to *niṣṣâ,* "falcon": "Is it the wing of the stork and the falcon?" Pope finds in this line a further description of the ostrich's wings rather than a comparison between two kinds of birds. This view is attractive, for there is no further allusion to the other birds in this portrait. Thus the reading *ʾim ʾeḇrâ ḥᵃsērâ nōṣâ,* "though her pinions lack feathers," is adopted. MT arose from the confusion of *r* and *d* common in a later Hebrew script. The change to *ḥᵃsēḏâ* led to the inclusion of the *waw* conjunction on *nōṣâ.*

4. The verb *taʿᵃzōḇ,* "she lays," agrees with its logical subject, ostrich, not with its grammatical subject, *rᵉnānîm,* a masculine plural form. This is another occurrence of *ʿzb* II, "put, place, lay," instead of *ʿzb* I, "leave, forsake" (see M. Dahood, "The Root *ʿzb* II in Job," *JBL* 78 [1959] 307–308).

5. The verb *tᵉḥammēm,* "she lets them be warmed," seems to have the masculine plural suffix omitted for euphony (Dhorme), but Gordis wishes to restore it: *tᵉḥammᵉmēm.*

6. The third person feminine singular suffix refers to the plural of things, *eggs* in v. 14a (GKC, § 135b).

7. For MT *hiqšîaḥ,* "he treats harshly," it seems best to read the feminine imperfect *taqšîaḥ* (Kennicott mss., Hölscher, Fohrer) or possibly the infinitive absolute *haqšîaḥ* (Ewald). The latter is preferred, for it requires only a change in the vowel under the preformative.

8. Gordis suggests taking *bāneyhâ,* "her young," as subject, with the preceding verb being in the singular: "Her young ones grew tough without her." The flow of the context, however, does not favor Gordis's view.

9. Verse 17 is a possible addition, for God, the speaker, refers to himself in the third person and there is no parenthetical line of this nature in any other strophe.

10. The preposition *bᵉ* on *babbînâ* is used partitively, "no part of understanding" (see Blommerde, *Northwest Semitic Grammar and Job,* p. 135).

11. The verb *tamrîʾ,* "she flaps," appears only here. Gordis assumes a metathesis and reads *taʾᵃmîr,* "she goes aloft," a denominative of *ʾāmîr,* "summit." Guillaume (*Studies in the Book of Job,* p. 134) takes it from Arab. *marā,* "whipping or spurring a

13–18 The *ostrich (rᵉnānîm)* is a huge, peculiar-looking bird.[12] Its small head, attached to a large body by a long, skinny neck, makes one chuckle. In addition, although it joyously beats its wings, it fails to fly. The hen also has the seemingly careless custom of *laying her eggs on the ground* instead of building a nest for them. During the day she leaves the eggs partly buried in the sand while she searches for food. She seems *unmindful* of the danger that *a foot may crush* the eggs or that *a wild beast may trample them.* And it appears that *she treats her young harshly, as though they are not hers.* In these ways she seems unconcerned about her offspring, not worrying *that her toil may be in vain.* This poetic description, however, draws on popular opinion rather than on detailed observation. The ostrich is more protective of her eggs than a casual reading of the passage might suggest. Often when hunters attack, the parents run away leaving the young behind to lie flat on the ground. But the parents are not unheedful of the young, for they are attempting to draw away the hunters.[13] Nevertheless, the peculiar habits of the hen have resulted in proverbs about the ostrich's stupidity.

Even though the ostrich is a bird that cannot fly, astonishingly it can run faster than the stately horse. In a chase this strange creature *laughs at the* majestic *horse and its rider.* Even though it appears that God has deprived the ostrich of wisdom, in this one aspect he has made it superior, raising it above ridicule to a place of respect. God's wisdom has marvelously created even the strangest of animals.

(f) The Horse (39:19–25)

19 *"Do you give the horse strength?*
Do you clothe its neck with a flowing mane?[1]

horse." The flapping of the wings may appear the same as spurring a horse for speed. The comparison with the horse in this verse fits the analogy.

12. The Hebrew word for the ostrich means lit. "the one of piercing cries, the screamer" (BDB, p. 943). No doubt the name arises from the shrill cries made by this bird. The ostrich is known to have inhabited the semidesert region of southern Palestine, Arabia, and northern Africa. Possibly it was numbered among the unclean animals (Lev. 11:16; Deut. 14:15), if the phrase *baṯ hayyaʿᵃnâ* is equivalent to it (RSV); but Cansdale, *Animals of Bible Lands,* pp. 190–92, does not think so, for he takes the latter term to mean "owl" (p. 145). See also G. R. Driver, "Birds in the Old Testament: II. Birds in Life," *PEQ* 87 (1950) 137–38; idem, "Birds in the Old Testament: I. Birds in Law," *PEQ* 87 (1955) 5–20; cf. J. Boehmer, "Was ist der Sinn von Hiob 39 13–18 an seiner gegenwärtigen Stelle," *ZAW* 53 (1935) 289–91.

13. Cansdale, *Animals of Bible Lands,* p. 193.

1. Heb. *raʿmâ* (lit. "quivering or thunder") is taken to mean "mane" by reason of the context. This interpretation is supported by LXX. Perhaps it connotes the mane as that which quivers in the wind. In Arabic the hyena is called "the mother of the mane" (*umm riʿm;* see Pope). Thus there may be a play on the homonyms "quiver" and "mane." Cf. J. Slotki, "A Study of *rʿm,*" *AJSL* 37 (1920–21) 149.

20 *Do you make it leap like a locust,*
striking terror with its proud snorting?
21 *It paws[2] in the valley[3] joyously;*
mightily it charges into the fray.[4]
22 *It laughs at fear, undaunted;*
it does not recoil from the sword.
23 *The quiver rattles[5] at its side,*
the glittering spear and sword.[6]
24 *In a frenzy it devours the ground;*
it does not stand still when the trumpet sounds.
25 *At the blare of[7] the trumpet it snorts, 'Aha!'*
It catches the scent[8] of battle from afar,
the shout[9] of officers and the battle cry."

19–25 Next Yahweh questions Job about *the horse (sûs),* a creature of beauty, power, and courage. The Creator has masterfully designed the

2. The singular form *yaḥpōr,* "it paws," is read with LXX, Syr., and Vulg. for the plural *yaḥpᵉrû*.

3. The phrase *bāʿēmeq* means lit. "in the valley," where an army sets itself in battle array. Ugaritic, however, seems to have a root *ʿmq* II, "strong"; if related, MT *bʿmq* may mean "strongly, violently." Also, Akk. *emūqu* means "force, strength." The parallelism with *bᵉḵōaḥ* is taken as support for finding this second root here. But Grabbe, *Comparative Philology,* pp. 124–26, severely doubts this position, for the Akkadian evidence is indecisive and the possibility of a second root in Ugaritic rests primarily on one passage.

4. Since Heb. *nešeq,* "weapon," is a metonym for the battle, the fierce hand-to-hand combat, it is translated "fray."

5. MT *terneh,* "rattles," is a geminate vocalized as a *lamed-he* root. Gordis may be right in his position that there is no need to change MT. Some (e.g., Dahood, "Northwest Semitic Philology and Job," p. 24; and Blommerde, *Northwest Semitic Grammar and Job,* p. 135) revocalize it *tārōnnâ;* the ending is then a *nun energicum*. The root meaning is "a loud ringing cry." If MT is kept, the Qal is best taken as a verb, probably an archaic Qal participle (Gordis).

6. Heb. *kîḏôn* is best understood as "a sword" or "a scimitar," a curved sword about 27 inches in length and 3 inches wide. This term appears in the Qumran War Scroll (1QM vii.2). See K. Kuhn, "Beiträge zum Verständnis der Kriegsroll von Qumran," *TLZ* 8 (1956) 29–30; G. Molin, "What Is *Kidon?*" *JSS* 1 (1956) 334–37.

7. Pope and Blommerde (*Northwest Semitic Grammar and Job,* p. 136) relate *bᵉḏê* to Ugar. *bd,* "song," hence "at the call of the trumpet." Another possibility considered by Pope is to relate *dê* to *day,* "sufficiency," and understand the preposition *bᵉ* to mean "from." The phrase would mean "as often as."

8. P. de Boer ("*wmrḥwq yryḥ mlḥmh*—Job 39:25," in *Words and Meanings: Essays Presented to David Winton Thomas,* ed. P. Ackroyd and B. Lindars [Cambridge: Cambridge University Press, 1968], pp. 29–38) argues for an intransitive meaning for *hērîaḥ,* "one gives out an odor," for when facing the heat of battle the horse emits a penetrating smell. Thus he translates the lines: "And even from afar he recalls war, thunder of captains, and battle-cry."

9. Instead of interpreting *raʿam* as "thunder" or "burst of shouting," Gordis finds an enclitic *mem* and takes the noun as *rēaʿ,* "shouting" (cf. 36:33).

horse. Majestic in appearance and free from any strange characteristics, it is universally honored.

The horse comes from the steppes of central Asia. From ca. 2000 B.C. on, it was imported to Mesopotamia and Egypt. By the 1st millennium B.C. they were incorporated into the military, greatly strengthening the army. The Israelites, however, did not readily accept horses. Saul and David tended to reject them, but Solomon added them into his army (cf. 1 K. 5:6, 8 [Eng. 4:26, 28]; 10:26). As one of many commercial adventures, he imported and exported these fine animals (10:28–29). Nevertheless, throughout the OT the kings of Israel were advised not to trust in them (Prov. 21:31; Ps. 33:17; cf. Isa. 30:15–16; 31:1, 3).

The horse is lauded for its fierceness in battle. While galloping headlong toward the fray *with a flowing mane,* it communicates fearless courage (Nah. 3:2). Its majestic bearing is manifest in its leaping ability and in its proud snorting. The horse, though a large animal, is so agile and strong that it can *leap [hirʿîš] like a locust,* which has amazing similarities of appearance (cf. Joel 2:4). Delitzsch thinks that this is a reference to "a curved motion forwards in leaps, now to the right, now to the left, which is called the caracol." Or this word could depict the horse's prancing about eagerly as the descending of a swarm of locusts on crops makes the earth appear to shake (Gordis).

Having a keen sense of smell, it catches the scent of battle. *It paws* the ground *fiercely, anxiously awaiting the order to charge.* Its excited, *proud snorting* strikes *terror* in the warriors. The snorting is described as *proud (hôḏ)*—a word used for "the splendor" of the Lord or of the king.[10] This word communicates that the horse is the king of the fracas. Its loud snorting heard above the noise of battle proclaims its dominion. Unafraid of sword or foe, it rushes headlong *into the fray, it laughs* at the danger. Neither the rattling of the quiver nor *the glittering spear and sword* daunts the horse. Galloping swiftly and determinedly, it appears to *devour the ground* like the locust. *The shout of officers* and *the blare of the trumpet* spur it on. Truly the Creator has masterfully designed the horse.

(g) Birds of Prey (39:26–30)

26 *"Does the hawk take flight by your understanding*
and spread its wings to the south?[1]
27 *Does the eagle soar at your command*
or[2] *make its nest on high?*

10. Cf. G. Warmuth, *"hôdh," TDOT,* IV:352–56.

1. Heb. *têmān* may refer to seasonal migration to the south or to the south wind, as in Ps. 78:26 and Cant. 4:16.

2. Evidence from the Qumran Targ., which reads "falcon," and LXX, which

28 *It dwells on a cliff and spends the night there;*
a rocky crag is its stronghold.[3]
29 *From there it spies its food;*
its eyes behold it from afar.
30 *Its young*[4] *extract*[5] *blood,*
and where the slain are, there it is."

26–30 Lastly Yahweh inquires of Job about his control over birds of prey.[6] The two terms—*nēṣ* (v. 26), the sparrow hawk, falcon, or kestrel, and *nešer* (v. 27), the golden eagle or the griffon vulture—appear to be generic terms.[7] Yahweh asks Job if he gave the hawk the remarkable *understanding (bînâ)* that directs it to migrate to the south in autumn and then, spreading out its wings, to return to Syria in the spring. "The reference to 'discernment' *(bīnā)* in the final vignette of this speech forms an *inclusio* with the pivotal use of the word in 38:4. Thus both the opening and closing units focus on the key question of Job's capacity to 'discern' mysteries of the universe and, by his wisdom, to control their movements" (Habel, OTL). No, it is their Creator who has equipped them with such understanding.

The *eagle* dominates the sky. Its authority in the sky is comparable to

reads "vulture," indicates that MT *kî* may be another species of "vulture" or that it is the textual remnant of such a word. J. Reider ("Etymological studies in Biblical Hebrew," *VT* 4 [1954] 294) relates *ky* to Arab. *ky*, "pelican," and G. R. Driver ("Job 39:27–28: The KY-Bird," *PEQ* 104 [1972] 64–66) takes *ky* as the name of the ibis. Grabbe (*Comparative Philology*, pp. 126–28) also favors the possibility of a word for an unrecognized bird. But if v. 27 is similar to v. 26, it is most likely that a bird's name appears only in the first line. Furthermore, in the other pericopes no more than two different names for the animals appear. Thus there is no great reason to alter the text and find another new word.

3. Blommerde (*Northwest Semitic Grammar and Job*, p. 136) takes the *waw* on *ûm*^{e}*ṣûḏâ* as an emphatic *waw*.

4. The Hebrew root *prḥ* means "to shoot forth, sprout," so *ʾeprōaḥ* is taken to mean "young, brood" (cf. Deut. 22:6; Ps. 84:4 [Eng. 3]).

5. MT *y*^{e}*ʿalʿû* is anomalous. It seems best to take it as a Pilpel of *lôaʿ* (Syr. "lick, lap up") or possibly *l*^{ʿʿ} II (an Arabic root with a similar meaning; see KB, p. 506). The text should then read *y*^{e}*laʿl*^{e}*ʿû*. Another possibility is to vocalize it *yālōʿû*, an Aramaic Peal form (Dhorme). In a creative venture Pope considers the MT as an Aramaized form of Arab. *ʿlḍ*, "shake a thing (in order) to pull it out." Grabbe (*Comparative Philology*, pp. 128–30) suggests taking it from an original root *ǧll*, "enter, plunge into," with the connotation of "the young falcons wading or plunging into blood" (cf. Ugar. *ǵll;* Heb. *ʿll* II [Job 16:15]; Aram. *ʿll*). There would thus need to be a development: *ʿll > ʿlʿl > ʿlʿ*. Although the best solution remains in doubt, the context suggests a reference to some act of eating, and as Pope points out, "extract" seems more appropriate for a bird than "lick."

6. The eagle follows the horse in this passage possibly because the horse is compared to the eagle for its speed and fierceness.

7. Heb. *nešer* appears frequently in the OT, while *nēṣ* occurs only two other times, and each of those is in a list of unclean birds (Lev. 11:16; Deut. 14:15). On the identification, see Cansdale, *Animals in Bible Lands*, pp. 142–47; G. R. Driver, "Birds in the Old Testament," *PEQ* 87 (1955) 5–20.

the lion's on land (2 Sam. 1:23). It *soars* high and builds *its nest* far from the reaches of danger (Obad. 4; Jer. 49:16). Its nest, constructed on *a rocky crag,* is impregnable, like a *stronghold.* Endowed with keen sight, the eagle is able to spot prey from its lofty perch. It swoops down on its victim with amazing speed and accuracy. The prey taken by the eagle is brought back to the young so that they may feast on fresh meat (cf. Deut. 32:11). While the young remain in the nest from eight to twelve weeks before they can fly, the parents care for them.[8]

After a battle the eagle has a feast. The *slain (ḥalālîm),* left without burial, become its prey. It brings back food for the newly hatched *young (ʾeprōaḥ)* to have a feast picking at this food. Proverbially it is said that *where the slain are, there it is.*[9]

The eagle's power and beauty have led to its widespread veneration. It has served as the symbol of many great empires. A dreadful army is also likened to an eagle (Deut. 28:49; Lam. 4:19; Jer. 48:40; 49:22), and because of its speed, even horses are complimented by being compared to the eagle (Hab. 1:8; Jer. 4:13). Yahweh queries Job: *Does the eagle soar at your command* (*pîkā,* lit. your mouth)? Of course not. Only its wise Creator is its commander.

Interestingly, Yahweh ends this speech with a description of his providing carrion for the young of the eagles. In the light of Job's frequent references to death and the grave, it is quite appropriate that an allusion to death be found at the close of Yahweh's first speech. Job would quickly catch this allusion because of his deep concern for his own fate. Although the meaning of a human being's existence seemingly evaporates before the tragic death of warriors slain in battle, God reigns above the battle. Amid the gloom and destruction he gently feeds the young eagles. Even human hostility and aggression can be used by God to satisfy the needs of one of his creatures.

3. AN INVITATION FOR JOB TO RESPOND (40:1–2)

1 *Yahweh answered Job,*
2 *"Will one who contends[1] with Shaddai correct[2] him?*
Let him who instructs God give an answer."

8. Cansdale, *Animals in Bible Lands,* pp. 142–43.

9. This line appears to be a proverbial saying (Pope) and has the same meaning as the aphorism in Matt. 24:28: "Wherever the body is, there the eagles will be gathered together."

1. For MT *rōḇ* there are various interpretations. Fohrer views it as an infinitive absolute, standing in place of an imperfect in an indignant question (cf. GKC, § 113ee). Another possibility is to vocalize it as a participle, *rāḇ,* "he who argues" (cf. Isa. 45:9; Dhorme), but Gordis argues that the MT form is an older spelling of the participle of an *ʿayin-waw* verb. The parallelism favors exegeting it as a participle.

2. MT *yissôr,* "he will discipline, correct," is usually emended to *yāsûr,* "he

1 To conclude his first discourse Yahweh directly questions Job about his complaint. Since this question has a different tenor than the preceding questions and since it specifically applies the discourse to the legal demands made by Job, this short interrogation by Yahweh receives its own introduction.[3]

2 The tables have been turned. Job, the questioner, is being questioned. Building on the evidence just given, Yahweh asks Job a penetrating question that pinpoints the implication of his complaint. That is, in advocating the rightness of his own position so tenaciously, Job has implied that God needs to be corrected. Having presented his position, Yahweh now offers Job the opportunity to articulate such a correction. Moreover, since Yahweh has spoken in response to Job's challenge, Job may not remain silent without voiding his oath of innocence. His silence would imply his concession. But if he continues to argue, he will leave himself open to divine rebuke.

AIM

Yahweh seeks to convince Job that he created the world in wisdom and that he governs it wisely, in justice and with compassion. He laid the world's foundation precisely according to the blueprints. Then he brought forth the sea and established its limits. Afterward he called forth the sun to enlighten the earth and to send the wicked into hiding. All of this is proof that he has placed justice at the center of the world's structure. In the pericope about the sun Yahweh says that although he does not always punish the wicked immediately for their wicked deeds, these evildoers are subject to his authority. As with the sea, he restricts their activity.

Yahweh asserts that he rules supreme over the world he has created. He knows and controls all the recesses of the universe. No area or region is beyond his governance. Furthermore, he manages the various forces in the world for the benefit of all creation. For example, he commands the rain clouds to travel over the desert where no human being lives, and there he orders them to pour out their water. The implication of this point is that if human beings could direct the weather patterns, they would guide them for their own selfish benefit. They would preserve the precious rain solely for

---

will cease, yield" (Dhorme, Kissane, Pope). Another view takes it as a noun meaning "faultfinder" (RSV; BDB, p. 416). A third view treats it as a Qal imperfect of *yāsar*, "instruct, discipline" (Andersen). Although the Qal in this root is rare, it is a possible form, especially since the Niphal stem does occur (Gordis).

3. Whether this heading was originally present is hard to tell. Hölscher and Fohrer, among many, wish to delete it as a gloss. In the present text it stands to indicate a shift in theme and emphasis.

the cultivated land and neglect the barren steppe. But such an egocentric policy would upset the balance of nature and cause havoc to the cultivated lands. By contrast Yahweh manages these natural forces in a way that bears witness to his wise sustenance of the entire creation.

Yahweh next portrays himself as Lord of the wild animals. He makes sure that all of them, from the mighty lion to the little raven, find food, both for their young and for themselves. Under his supervision the hinds bear their young without any help. Also, Yahweh has skillfully assigned special traits to each species. For example, he gives the wild ass and the wild ox a love for freedom, such a love that they refuse to surrender their freedom for the abundance of food they could have at a master's trough. Thus a highly valued trait or quality is often achieved or preserved at the expense of another trait or quality.

Other creatures Yahweh has majestically fashioned. He gave the horse a magnificent form and endowed it with strength, speed, and courage. By contrast, he designed the ostrich as a peculiar-looking bird, and he bestowed strange habits on it. It is very strange that no matter how fast it flaps its wings, it cannot fly. The uniqueness of this creature surely testifies to the divine humor. Yet Yahweh has not left the ostrich without its glory. Amazingly, this peculiar bird can outrun the stately horse. Yahweh has equipped the birds of prey with keen eyesight and with the ability to soar high above the landscape. From great heights they can spot their prey and swoop down on it swiftly. Yahweh has also endowed these birds with the wisdom to build their nests high on a rocky cliff, making them very secure. All of these wild animals, free from human control, honor Yahweh as their Lord. Each one contributes to the variety and the beauty of the world order. In these portraits Yahweh demonstrates to Job that he graciously rules the remotest spheres of the world, those that lie far beyond human control. The way that he cares for these creatures testifies to his wise goodness.

If Yahweh is Lord of the wild animals that inhabit the desolate steppe, he assuredly is in full control of the inhabited world, particularly the affairs of human beings. Yahweh's message to Job is that he cares for him even more than for these wild animals. He cares for Job both in the abundance that Job formerly experienced and in his present suffering. His suffering has taken place within the world structure without upsetting that structure. His misfortune does not call into question Yahweh's lordship, as Job has argued. Nor does it demonstrate that Yahweh acts unjustly or that he permits unjust situations to occur capriciously. All happenings occur within his wise counsel. That means Job's suffering has taken place within, not outside, God's wise governance. Just like the wild ass which has to go hungry in exchange for its freedom, so Job has had to endure suffering in exchange for the integrity of his relationship with Yahweh. A human being's integrity carries far greater value than his physical and emotional health. And Job has proven that a person can preserve his integrity despite grave misfortune and the severest suffering. Adverse circumstances do not have to tarnish one's faith in God, for the basis of a a person's relationship with God is his fear of God and his shunning of evil, not his health and his wealth.

If Job had repented of some contrived sin to find relief, he would have compromised his own integrity and violated the purity of his faith in God by seeking to use God for personal gain. Now the issue Yahweh puts before him is whether he will continue to place his trust in Yahweh as a good and faithful God or reject God, thinking him to be a capricious, hostile force. According to Yahweh's argument, it is improper for Job to judge his governance of the world based on the appearance of matters on earth. Since Job is not knowledgeable enough to discover why things take place on earth as they do, he is left with a decision—either to trust Yahweh, believing that he wisely rules his created world, or to pursue his complaint that exalts himself above Yahweh. Yahweh leaves the initiative with Job either to believe him or to continue to accuse him.

B. JOB'S ANSWER (40:3–5)

3 *Then Job answered Yahweh,*
4 *"Behold, I am small, how can I answer you?*
I put my hand over my mouth.
5 *I have spoken once, but I cannot answer,*
twice, but I can add nothing."

3–5 As usual, a heading introduces a new speech. Amazingly, the loquacious Job has been reduced to a few words. The brevity of his reply indicates that he has nothing to add to his avowal of innocence, not even in the light of what Yahweh has said. Overwhelmed by Yahweh's majesty, he is aware of his own insignificance. He confesses, *I am small (qallōṯî)*. This word for "being small or light" is the opposite of "honor" (*kāḇôḏ*, lit. "heavy").[1] Although Job has been vexed that his misfortune has discredited his prestige (cf. 19:9; 29:20), he defers his personal honor to Yahweh's greater honor. He concedes that he is in no position to answer Yahweh. It has happened just as he feared. In his second speech of the dialogue (ch. 9) he stated his apprehension that if granted a meeting with God he would not be able to find words to dispute with him (9:14). The reasons for his silence, however, are different from those he had imagined. Whereas he thought that God would beat him down with his power, it is the power of Yahweh's

1. See M. Tsevat, *HUCA* 37 (1966) 91.

rhetoric that causes him to put his hand over his mouth in dumbfounded astonishment (cf. 21:5; 29:9; Fohrer).

By this gesture he also restrains himself from speaking. While he does not wish to take up a new line of argument or to introduce other matters, he does not yet renounce the position he has taken *once*, yea even *twice* (cf. 33:14). He is saying that he continues to stand behind his avowal of innocence. However, the fact that he does not want to *add* to his case shows that he feels the impact of Yahweh's speech. His confidence of winning a debate with Yahweh has greatly diminished before the power of God's presence. But given this response from Job it will be necessary for Yahweh to continue his discourse to persuade Job to submit completely to his lordship.

C. YAHWEH'S SECOND SPEECH (40:6–41:26 [ENG. 34])

Yahweh continues to challenge Job about his intention of disputing his case before the heavenly court. If Job is correct in supposing that God has acted unjustly in his regard, he should be able to adorn himself in regal apparel and humble all the proud. So Yahweh challenges Job to demonstrate his prowess by defeating in mortal combat the ominous creatures Behemoth and Leviathan. If he cannot master these symbols of cosmic powers, he will have to abandon his complaint. Furthermore, Yahweh is arguing that he masters every force in the world.

By continuing to question Job Yahweh is expressing his care for his servant. He is seeking to overcome Job's resistance by gently and persuasively leading him to submission. The unusual length of the portrait of Leviathan gives the impression that Yahweh drags out his description of Leviathan waiting for Job's stubborn resolve to weaken. That is, Yahweh continues to speak until Job gives signs that his stubborn attitude has completely melted and he is willing to relinquish his avowal of innocence. In his mercy Yahweh does not leave off speaking to Job until he humbles himself.

This speech consists of two parts: questions to Job about his power (40:6–14), and portraits of two foreboding beasts: Behemoth (40:15–24) and Leviathan (40:25–41:26 [Eng. 41:1–34]). In the opening section the author draws on the hymnic tradition and formulates it into a direct examination of the defendant. The rhetorical use of question and exhortation is designed to motivate Job to surrender his complaint against Yahweh.

1. QUESTIONS CONCERNING JOB'S POWER (40:6–14)

6 *Yahweh answered Job out of the tempest:*
7 *"Gird your loins like a man;*
I shall ask you, and you inform me.
8 *Would you impugn[1] my justice?*
Would you condemn me that you might be innocent?
9 *Have you an arm like God's?*
Can you thunder with a voice like his?
10 *Adorn yourself with majesty and grandeur;*
robe yourself in glory and splendor.
11 *Unleash your furious anger;*
glance at every proud one and humble him.
12 *Glance at every proud one and abase him;*
trample down[2] the wicked where they stand.
13 *Hide them all in the dust;*
shroud their faces in the grave.
14 *Then I myself will laud you,*
for your own right hand can deliver you."

6, 7 Yahweh's second discourse begins with the same introduction as his first speech. Since Job has not withdrawn his case, Yahweh will continue to question him.

8 Yahweh confronts Job with the major flaw in his accusations. In defending his own innocence so emphatically and lashing out so vehemently at God because of his suffering, Job has essentially charged God with acting unjustly. For a mortal to presume himself guiltless and to *impugn* God's just governance of the world approaches the sin of presumptuous pride.

It is important to observe that Yahweh does not accuse Job of any specific sin, thereby agreeing that Job has lived a righteous life. Nevertheless, if the relationship between himself and his servant is to be restored, Job's self-righteous attitude must be altered and his complaint against God's just governance of the world must be corrected. In his avowal of innocence Job places himself in danger of trusting proudly in his own righteous deeds, and in his complaints he seems to make himself appear more righteous than God. Pride is a treacherous attitude, especially when it arises from adherence to a correct position. One who glories in his good deeds is easily

1. In this context Heb. *pārar*, "break," bears the nuance "impugn, discredit." The Hiphil form is taken as having declarative force (GKC, § 53c).

2. Heb. *hāḏaḵ* is understood as cognate to Arab. *hadaka*, "wreck a building," hence of people "tread down," i.e., "trample" (KB, p. 229).

tempted to think of himself more highly than he ought. Pride distorts his perspective. While Job has the right to complain to God about his misfortune, he is now facing the peril of not assenting to God's purpose for him.

9 Furthermore, Job's avowal of innocence and his complaint against God imply that he claims to know more than God. If Job knows so much, he should be able to rule according to the ideal he espouses. If Job can prove his superiority, Yahweh will acknowledge his complaint. If not, Job must acknowledge Yahweh's sovereignty.

Yahweh specifically challenges Job to exercise authority over the mighty and the proud among men by punishing those who violate justice. When God appears, he displays his power and authority, represented here by the symbols *arm* and *voice*. In the OT "God's outstretched arm" means that God intervenes mightily in earthly affairs to accomplish his purpose.[3] And when he speaks, his voice thunders forth, inspiring fear in his subjects. Can Job prove his demands by manifesting such authority?

10 To demonstrate his rulership, Job must *adorn himself with majesty and grandeur* and *robe himself in glory and splendor*. The heaping up of words for incomparable majesty captures the grandeur that attends God's manifestation of his kingship (cf. Ps. 93:1; 96:6). Even an earthly king displays his authority in regal dress and in the terribleness of his bearing (cf. Ps. 21:6 [Eng. 5]; 45:4 [Eng. 3]).[4]

11, 12 Yahweh exhorts Job to exercise his supreme authority by wiping out the proud,[5] who abuse justice and oppress the weak to establish their own dominion. This injunction for Job to act is stressed by a chiasm of four lines (11a:11b::12a:12b), with the center expressed in virtually the same words. Yahweh is powerfully addressing Job's complaint that the wicked increase their wealth unpunished and exercise dominion unchecked (cf. 21:30–33; 24:1–17). If Job should rule the world by his own standard, he must let his anger burn furiously against the wicked. With his angry *glance* he could *abase* the *proud*. Like a mighty warrior leading a campaign he could *trample down the wicked where they stand,* i.e., devastate them in their place of authority.[6] As the victor he could inaugurate a world order based on the standards he has advocated.

13 When unleashing his fury against the arrogant wicked, Job would put them to death for their evil deeds. With their proud *faces shrouded*

3. Cf. Exod. 6:6; 15:16; Deut. 4:34; 5:15; 7:19; 9:29; 26:8; Ps. 44:4 (Eng. 3); 89:11, 14 (Eng. 10, 13); Isa. 40:10; 51:5, 9; 52:10; 59:16; 63:5.

4. For a discussion of the way one's garments express one's character see above on 29:14.

5. In judgment God poured his hot wrath on the proud, e.g., Isa. 2:12–17; 13:11.

6. Isaiah, in particular, describes the day of Yahweh as the day of his vengeance against the proud (e.g., 2:11–22; 10:33; 13:11).

they would be given a common burial *in the grave,* an infernal crypt *(baṭ-ṭāmûn).*[7] Such treatment would be the final, humiliating blow to a proud person for whom the height of glory was to receive a stately funeral followed by interment in his own majestic monument (cf. 3:14, 15; 21:32, 33). But under Job's rule the wicked would receive their just reward.

14 Should Job clothe himself in kingly majesty and defeat the proud, God would *laud* him as the victor in the present contest. He would have proved his complaint that God rules without regard for justice. There is a strongly ironic tone in Yahweh's argument: if Job could do all of this, he would not need God. Job would have no need of pleading for a vindicator, for his *own right hand*[8] could *deliver* him.

2. PORTRAITS OF TWO FOREBODING BEASTS (40:15–41:26 [ENG. 34])

To persuade Job that he must abandon his complaint in order to keep from committing the fundamental sin of usurping God's place (Gen. 3:4–7), Yahweh quizzes Job about two ominous beasts, Behemoth and Leviathan. Yahweh's purpose in these long animal portraits, patterned after animal sketches found in nature wisdom (cf. 38:39–39:30), is to convince Job to submit to his lordship. In these two portraits he uses irony and absurd arguments as bold tactics intended to awaken Job to the dire implications of his stance. Rightly used, irony penetrates a person's self-defense and awakens him to the danger of his present stance. Yahweh is laying bare the pride that underlies Job's defense of his innocence. If Job realizes his own creatureliness, he may humble himself and admit anew God's authenticating presence into his life. God's hard questioning of Job is a witness to his grace (Weiser).

The identification of the Behemoth and Leviathan is disputed, ranging from earthly creatures to mythical monsters.[1] As earthly beasts they are identified as the hippopotamus and the crocodile respectively.[2] Realistic, detailed descriptions keep the portrait from becoming purely mythical. Nevertheless, into the factual description the author skillfully blends fanciful

7. The phrase *baṭṭāmûn,* lit. "in the hidden place," is variously interpreted: "dungeon" (Dhorme); "the dark recesses of Sheol" (Rowley); "the infernal crypt" (Pope). Pope's suggestion fits the context best.

8. The right hand symbolizes authority and power over one's enemies (in reference to mankind, see Judg. 7:2; 1 Sam. 25:26, 35; in reference to God, see Exod. 15:6; Ps. 20:7 [Eng. 6]; 44:4 [Eng. 3]).

1. Scholars are found on each side of this issue. Pope and Fohrer, e.g., interpret them as mythical creatures, while Andersen finds here portraits of real animals.

2. Dhorme notes that a painting on the ceiling of the Ramesseum depicts a hippopotamus bearing a crocodile on its back. Interestingly, Herodotus (2.68–71) describes the crocodile and the hippopotamus in succession.

metaphors drawn from mythic accounts of monsters in order that these beasts may represent both mighty terrestrial creatures and cosmic forces.[3] In this way Yahweh addresses the cosmic dimensions of Job's affliction. In other passages the author has alluded to God's defeat of and control over cosmic forces under various names: Leviathan (3:8), Tannin (7:12), and Rahab (9:13; 26:12). The author employs this imagery to address in the speeches the transcendent dimension of Job's conflict, the dimension that the role of the Satan provides in the prologue. Like the Satan these creatures are totally subservient to Yahweh. This is the ancient way of affirming that Yahweh is the Master of whatever force might lie behind Job's ordeal.

If Job could rule the world in justice, he would have to capture Behemoth and defeat Leviathan. The argument is that if Job cannot subdue these mighty earthly creatures, symbols of cosmic powers, it is inconceivable that he could prove that God is treating him unjustly. This is Yahweh's response to Job's frequent request to be permitted to enter into litigation with him (e.g., 9:16; 13:3, 13–28). Yahweh is demonstrating to Job that a direct confrontation with himself is a course fraught with danger and certain defeat.

If this interpretation is granted, Yahweh's second speech is more than a continuation of the first. Whereas the first speech addresses the issue of God's gracious and just maintenance of the world, the second looks at the cosmic dimensions of Job's plight. In the first speech Yahweh emphasized that he put justice in the fabric of the created order. In the second speech Yahweh demonstrates that he has the power to execute his justice. In God power and justice are not at odds as they are in human beings. In him they are complementary qualities that accomplish the greatest good for the entire world. If Job accepts Yahweh's arguments, he may rest his case with God and trust him to do justice in his case. God's mercy assures him that God will act justly on his behalf, and God's power guarantees him that God is able to achieve what he purposes for Job.

3. In the OT God creates these amazing creatures, and they playfully enjoy God's world (cf. 9:13; 26:12; Gen. 1:21; Ps. 104:25–27). They are never viewed as rival forces on a par with God. Yahweh, however, must defeat foes that threaten his purpose in the course of the redemptive history. To convey the cosmic dimensions of these battles Israel's enemies are labeled *Leviathan* and *Rahab* (cf. Isa. 27:1; 51:9; Ps. 74:13–14; 89:11 [Eng. 10]). Apocalyptic literature, concerned with the cosmic dimensions of conflict between good and evil, also employs the terms *Behemoth* and *Leviathan* to represent primordial cosmic forces in conflict with God (1 Enoch 60:7–9; 4 Ezra 6:49–52; 2 Bar. 29:4).

a. Behemoth (40:15–24)

15 *"Behold Behemoth,*[1]
which I made along with you;[2]
it eats grass like an ox.
16 *What strength it has in its loins,*
what power in the muscles of its belly.
17 *It stiffens its tail like a cedar;*
the sinews of its thighs are tightly knit.
18 *Its bones are tubes of bronze,*
its limbs[3] *like iron bars.*[4]
19 *It is the first of God's ways;*
its Maker[5] *can approach it with his sword.*
20 *The hills bring it food,*[6]
and all the wild animals play nearby.
21 *Under the lotus it lies,*
in a covert of reeds and swamp.
22 *The lotuses conceal it in their shadow;*
the poplars by the stream surround it.

1. In Hebrew *b*^{e}*hēmôṯ* is plural and usually means "cattle"; cf. 35:11; Joel 1:20; 2:22; Ps. 8:8 (Eng. 7); 49:13 (Eng. 12); 73:22. Here the plural has intensive force, meaning "a super beast," i.e., the noblest and strongest beast. The suggested derivation of the Hebrew word from the Egyptian *p*ʾ*-iḥ-mw,* "the ox of the water," has never been substantiated (cf. Delitzsch). Cf. E. Ruprecht, "Das Nilpferd im Hiobbuch," *VT* 21 (1971) 209–31. There have been other identifications for these creatures. Thomas Aquinas, e.g., identified Behemoth as the elephant and Leviathan as the whale. Under the scholarly influence of G. R. Driver (*Book List, Society for OT Study* [London: Society for OT Study, 1972], p. 18) the NEB translates the terms "crocodile" and "whale."

2. Due to the absence of the phrase "which I made like you" in LXX and because of its prosaic nature, many (e.g., Duhm, Dhorme, Fohrer) omit it. Gordis retains it, however, interpreting it as a break in the metrical pattern designed to capture the reader's attention.

3. The term *gerem,* "bone, limb," more common in Aramaic, appears in poetic passages in Hebrew: Gen. 49:14; Prov. 17:22; 25:15.

4. B. Lang ("Job xl 18 and the 'bones of Seth'," *VT* 30 [1980] 360–61) observes that in Egypt there was "the mythical appellation of iron as 'bones of Seth'," the hippopotamus god.

5. Instead of MT *hāʿōśô* the text should read *ʿōśô,* "its maker," for the article is redundant before a noun with a pronominal suffix. LXX reads *heʿāśû,* "the one who is made," an archaic form of the Qal passive participle of a *lamed-he* verb. Many (e.g., Duhm, Dhorme, Fohrer) accept this variant, but then they find it necessary to emend the rest of the second line, *yaggēš ḥarbô,* to *nōgēś ḥ*^{a}*ḇērā[y]w:* "(He who was created) a tyrant to his companions."

6. MT *bûl* is taken as a shorter form of *y*^{e}*ḇûl,* "produce, tribute" (Gordis). Dhorme supports this view by showing that *bûl . . . nāśā*ʾ corresponds to Akk. *našū bilta,* "bring tribute."

23 *When the river gushes forth,*[7] *it is not alarmed;*
it is secure, though the Jordan surges to its mouth.
24 *With a trap*[8] *can one capture it*[9]
or with a snare pierce its nose?"

The first creature portrayed is Behemoth, which is usually identified as the hippopotamus. The hippopotamus is known to inhabit Egypt and Africa. Today it comes no farther north than between the second and third cataracts of the Nile, but in ancient times it lived in lower Egypt.[10] Possibly Behemoth is a buffalo, for in the Palestine of the 2nd millennium B.C. buffaloes roamed about the Lake Huleh region, and there is some evidence that they might have grazed in the Jordan Valley.[11] In Egypt only the divine pharaohs or the ruling god Horus could hunt this powerful animal.[12] A royal hunt was a religious ritual, considered to be a battle against evil. In taking such a mighty beast the pharaoh confirmed his right to rule.

7. Heb. *ʿāšaq* means "oppress, extort" (BDB, pp. 798–99), but its meaning in this context is uncertain. Possibly its meaning could be extended to "rush violently," but this seems doubtful. Various alternative readings have been suggested: *yišqaʿ*, "sinks" (Budde); *yišpaʿ*, "overflows" (Fohrer); *yāšōq*, "gushes forth" (Duhm). The last is followed, for it has the advantage of forming a parallel with *yāgîaḥ*, "surges forth."

8. The phrase *beʿēnāyw*, lit. "by his eyes," is difficult. Dhorme refers to Herodotus 2.70, which mentions a process of plastering a crocodile's eyes in order to control it. Gordis suggests insightfully that since in archaic script ʿ (which is both a letter of the alphabet and the word for "eye") was written in the form of a circle, it might have the technical meaning "trap." Thus it stands parallel to "snare," not "nose." The preposition favors the latter interpretation.

9. The brevity of the first line has led several to supply *mî hû'l*, "who has," at its beginning (e.g., Dhorme, Fohrer, Gordis), but since the syllabic scanning is balanced, 7/7, no addition is necessary.

10. Egyptian pharaohs took pride in slaying a hippopotamus. There are numerous pictures in which the pharaoh, hunting a hippopotamus from a papyrus boat, is poised to hurl his harpoon into the animal's opened mouth, thereby inflicting a fatal blow. This feat lauded the extraordinary strength of Pharaoh as an incarnate god. In Egyptian myths this creature also symbolized the powers hostile to the throne. For example, in "The Contest of Horus and Seth for the Rule" (*ANET*, pp. 14–17), Seth, the god of Upper Egypt, turned himself into a hippopotamus to sink Horus's ship. But when Horus, the god of Lower Egypt, was about to hurl his harpoon at Seth, the Ennead stayed him and proclaimed him victor. There was also a festival known as "Harpooning the Hippopotamus"; central to the festival was the ritual slaying of a hippopotamus, symbolic of the king's enemies. Cf. E. Ruprecht, "Das Nilpferd im Hiobbuch. Beobachtungen zu der sogennanten zweiten Gottesrede," *VT* 21 (1971) 211–18; T. Säve-Söderbergh, *On Egyptian Representations of Hippopotamus Hunting as a Religious Motive* (Upsala: Gleerup, 1953).

11. Cf. G. Haas, "On the Occurrence of Hippopotamus in the Iron Age of the Coastal Area of Israel (Tell Qasîleh)," *BASOR* 132 (Dec. 1953) 30–34.

12. See O. Keel, *Jahwes Entgegnung an Ijob* (Göttingen: Vandenhoeck & Ruprecht, 1978), p. 132.

40:15–24 BEHEMOTH

The account of Behemoth is an animal portrait about double the length of the portraits found in 38:39–39:30. It treats Behemoth's strength and bodily form (vv. 15–18), its prominence (vv. 19–20), and its habits (vv. 21–23). Only the last couplet is cast in the form of a rhetorical question (v. 24). It asks if anyone, save Yahweh himself, could capture this magnificent beast.

15 Behemoth, like Job, is God's creation, and both are servants of God. Endowed with a hearty appetite, this huge beast cuts great swaths through a grassy plain.[13] It can devour an entire field of grain, impoverishing a village.

16 Although some (e.g., Pope) find here a reference to its virility, the dominant theme is the animal's *strength,* which is legendary. Its mighty *loins* (considered the seat of strength, e.g., Deut. 33:11; Ps. 69:24 [Eng. 23]; Nah. 2:2 [Eng. 1]) and the massive *muscles of its belly* witness to its unusual might.

17 Curious features of this animal are noted. Its *tail,* which is short, hairless, and thick at the base, is likened to a *cedar* tree, a symbol of majestic power (cf. Ezek. 17:22–24; 31:1–18).[14] Fohrer thinks it refers to the thickness of the base of the tail. But the smallness of its tail in relationship to its huge body makes the comparison of its tail to a cedar seem absurd. Perhaps this couplet speaks of Behemoth's virility, with *tail* referring to the male genitals and *thighs* to the testicles.[15] If so, this verse alludes to the mating of the beast.

18, 19 This solidly constructed beast is *the first of God's ways* (cf. Prov. 8:22), i.e., the crown of the animal creation. Because Yahweh is *its Maker,* its power and greatness do not exist in opposition to him. In contrast to mythical thought Yahweh did not have to defeat Behemoth to gain control over the forces of chaos. Rather Behemoth obeyed him from the first moment of its origin. In addition, its imposing form bears witness to the majesty of its Creator. Unafraid, Yahweh *can approach* Behemoth *with his sword.* Such an act symbolizes his complete mastery of this beast.

20 The Creator has, so to speak, placed the hills at Behemoth's service. It leaves the waters of the Nile and grazes peacefully on its steep banks, where grass grows in abundance especially for Behemoth. The double meaning of *bûl* ("produce" and "tribute") indicates that the hills are pictured as paying tribute to their lord. The hills are the home of many animals, who, secure under the protection of the lordship of Behemoth, *play*

13. Cansdale, *Animals of Bible Lands,* p. 101.

14. Ruprecht, *VT* 21 (1971) 218n.2.

15. In later Heb. *zānāḇ,* "tail," colloquially has this meaning, and the Targ. renders MT *paḥaḏ,* "thigh," by *paḥdîn,* "testicles."

(*śāḥaq;* cf. 41:17–21 [Eng. 25–29]) joyfully nearby. This picture portrays Behemoth as king of the wild animals.

21, 22 A favorite habit of this splendid beast is to *lie* on the river bank, shading itself *under the lotus (Zizyphus lotus),* a thorny tree which grows in the hot, damp areas of Israel and Africa. Satisfied with food, it finds safety in a swampy area thick with *reeds* or on the bank, concealed by *lotuses* and *poplars* (*Populus Euphratica;* cf. Ps. 137:2; Isa. 15:7; 44:4).

23 When *the river* floods, Behemoth *is not alarmed,* for it can outswim the swirling waters. Since the term *Jordan* may be used symbolically for any river with a strong current, here it represents the Nile at flood stage.[16]

24 The hippopotamus was hunted, but with caution and trepidation. The hunter who captured one of these terrifying creatures was a champion. In popular lore, however, it was considered impossible to capture this great creature. In hunting a hippopotamus a favorite tactic was to *pierce its nose* so that it must breathe through the mouth; then a fatal blow could be inflicted through its opened mouth.[17] The implication of Yahweh's questions is that Job dare not hunt, at least alone, such a powerful beast.

b. Leviathan (40:25–41:26 [Eng. 41:1–34])

25 (41:1) *"Can you draw out Leviathan by a hook*
or tie down[1] its tongue with a line?
26 (2) *Can you put a cord[2] through its nose*
or pierce its jaw with a barb?
27 (3) *Will it keep begging for mercy?*
Will it speak to you gently?
28 (4) *Will it make a covenant with you*
that you may take it as a perpetual slave?
29 (5) *Can you play with it as with a bird[3]*
or can you put it on a leash for your girls?
30 (6) *Will traders barter for it?*
Will they divide it among the merchants?

16. So Rowley, Kissane, Tur-Sinai, Dhorme. Cf. Pope.

17. See Ruprecht, *VT* 21 (1971) 209–31.

1. Heb. *hišqîaʿ* usually means "sink." The context suggests a meaning of "bind" or "tie down," but such a meaning has no linguistic support. Cf. A. Guillaume, *BSO(A)S* 16 (1954) 10.

2. The primary meaning of *ʾagmôn* is "reed, rush," but it may also refer to "a cord" of rushes or rush-fibers, as it does here.

3. The phrase *kaṣṣippôr,* "like the (a) bird," is short for *kᵉḇaṣṣippôr,* "like with the (a) bird" (Gordis).

31 (7) *Can you fill its hide with harpoons*[4]
or its head with a fishing spear?
32 (8) *Place your hand on it;*
consider the battle; do not do it again.
41:1 (9) *Hope of subduing it is false;*
one is laid low at the mere sight[5] *of it.*
2 (10) *No one is brave enough to stir it up.*
Who can stand before me?[6]
3 (11) *Who could confront me that I must pay?*[7]
Everything under heaven is mine.[8]
4 (12) *I shall not be silent about its limbs,*
its strength[9] *and the grace*[10] *of its form.*
5 (13) *Who can penetrate its outer garment*
and enter[11] *its double coat of mail?*[12]
6 (14) *Who may pry open the doors of its face?*[13]
Surrounding its teeth is terror.
7 (15) *Its back*[14] *is as rows of shields,*

4. Heb. *śukkôṯ* may be related to *śikkîm,* "thorns," by reason of their sharp, piercing point. Thus it means either harpoons (Gordis) or darts (Dhorme).

5. The original *y* of the root is preserved in this writing of *mar'āyw,* "sight of it" (GKC, § 93ss).

6. Many (e.g., Dhorme, Pope, Gordis; cf. *BHS*) wish to read *lᵉp̄ānāyw,* "before him," for MT *lᵉp̄ānay,* "before me," but MT has good support and is the more difficult reading.

7. Many (e.g., Dhorme, Hölscher, Driver-Gray; cf. Pope) emend the first line to read the third person: *mî hiqdîmô wayyišlām:* "Who has confronted him and come out safe?" While this makes the wording fit the context better, MT is followed as the harder reading.

8. MT *lî hû'*, "he is mine," is sometimes changed to *mî hû'*, "who is it?" (Pope) or *lō' hû'*, "there is no one" (Dhorme, Gordis), but since MT offers a good reading, there is no compelling reason to change it.

9. For MT *gᵉḇûrôṯ,* "strengths," it is best to read *gᵉḇûrāṯô,* "its strength," as an error of metathesis (see Dhorme, Driver-Gray).

10. MT *ḥîn,* which occurs only here, is problematic. Some (e.g., Dhorme; cf. Rowley) emend it to *'ên,* "not"; others (e.g., Driver-Gray) read *ḥêl,* "strength"; while Pope takes it as a proper name or epithet of an Ugaritic deity. But perhaps the easiest solution and the one most commonly offered is to take *ḥîn* as a variant of *ḥēn,* "grace," i.e., a plene writing of the *sere;* see Gordis.

11. Interestingly *gyl* and *bw'* are parallel also in Ugaritic (*UT,* 49:I:6–7; 51:IV:23). The meaning here may be "penetrate, enter" (*RSP,* I:160–61, no. 142).

12. MT *risnô,* "its halter," appears to be an error of metathesis from *siryōnô,* "its coat of mail," as read by LXX (see *BHS*).

13. On the basis of Syr., MT *pānāyw,* "its face," is often emended to *pîw,* "its mouth" (so Dhorme, Budde), but this emendation is not necessary.

14. With support from LXX and Vulg., nearly all commentators revocalize MT *ga'ᵃwâ,* "pride," as *gēwōh,* "his back"; the ' is pleonastic.

shut by a tight seal,[15]
8 (16) *each one joining the other,*
so that no air can come between them.
9 (17) *They cleave fast to one another;*
they are interlocked and cannot be parted.
10 (18) *Its sneezing flashes*[16] *forth light;*
its eyes are like the rays of dawn.
11 (19) *Firebrands stream*[17] *from its mouth;*
sparks[18] *of fire leap forth.*
12 (20) *From its nostrils comes smoke,*
as from a steaming, boiling[19] *pot.*
13 (21) *Its breath ignites coals,*
and a flame comes out of its mouth.
14 (22) *Strength resides in its neck;*
vigor[20] *leaps*[21] *before it.*
15 (23) *The folds of its flesh stick together,*
firm on it and immovable.
16 (24) *Its breast is firm like a rock,*
firm like a lower millstone.

15. Instead of *ṣar,* "narrow," some (e.g., Dhorme, Fohrer) read *ṣōr,* "rock, flint," based on LXX. The picture would be hardness similar to that of a rock-like seal (so Rowley; cf. Pope). But MT, meaning "a tight seal" (so Gordis), makes sense, and thus no change is necessary.

16. The feminine singular verb *tāhel,* "it flashes," is used with a plural subject for names of things (GKC, § 145k).

17. MT *yahᵃlōḵû* is a seldom-used form for the usual *yēlᵉḵû,* "it walks, goes." Driver-Gray believe that this form suggests greater rapidity of movement.

18. The context suggests that the unique *kîḏôḏîm* means "sparks." M. Dahood (*Bib* 46 [1965] 327), relating it to Ugar. *kdd,* "child, son," assigns it the meaning "sons of fire"; cf. *bᵉnê rešep,* "sons of Resheph," in 5:7. But *kîḏôḏ* appears to be analogous to *nîḥôaḥ,* "pleasant," from the root *nûaḥ,* so a root *k(y)d,* "make a spark," is more likely (Dhorme).

19. Heb. *ʾagmōn* is puzzling in this context. If it means "reeds," it may refer to fuel for fire. Gordis wishes to read *waʾᵃgam,* "and (like) a marsh." The simile then is of a swamp from which a mist continually rises. The usual emendation (see, e.g., Budde, Dhorme, Pope) is *ʾōgēm,* "boiling," based on Arab. *ʾajama,* "be burning hot." Pope finds some support for this position in Qumran Targ., which reads "live coals." This emendation is followed to gain some sense for the line, but only tentatively, for it creates another new Hebrew word.

20. For MT *dᵉʾāḇâ,* "despair, dismay, languish," *dbʾh,* "strength," is read. MT resulted from an error of metathesis (F. Cross, *VT* 2 [1952] 163–64). This change is supported by Qumran Targ.'s translation *ʿlmw,* "vigor," and by the parallel *ʿz,* "strength," in this passage.

21. For MT *tāḏûṣ,* "leap, dance," LXX and Qumran Targ. read *tārûṣ,* "run." MT is preferred as the harder reading.

17 (25) *Before its majesty*[22] *the mighty*[23] *fear;*
shuddering[24] *they withdraw.*[25]

18 (26) *If one reaches*[26] *to it with a sword, it would have no effect,*
nor does spear or dart[27] *or javelin.*[28]

19 (27) *It considers iron as straw*
and bronze as rotten wood.

20 (28) *Arrows*[29] *do not make it flee;*
slingstones are turned by it to chaff.

21 (29) *A club is considered*[30] *as straw,*
and it laughs at the whirring of a javelin.[31]

22 (30) *Its undersides are sharp potsherds;*
it leaves marks in the mud like a threshing sledge.

23 (31) *It brings the depths to a boil like a caldron,*
and makes the sea like a pot of ointment.

24 (32) *Behind it, it leaves a glistening wake;*
it makes the deep appear like white hair.

22. MT *miśśēṯô* is defective for *miśśeʾṯô*. It means either "from its majesty" or "when it rises up." The former is preferred because Leviathan's movements, not his characteristics, are being described in this context.

23. Heb. *ʾēlîm* may mean "chiefs" (Ezek. 31:11; 32:21), with support from Vulg., Targ., Syr. Others, e.g., Gordis, wish to render it "gods."

24. Building on the reading "gods" for *ʾēlîm* (see n. 23 above), Gordis vocalizes MT *mšbrm* as *mišbārîm,* "waves, breakers," and renders the passage: "When he raises himself up, the gods are frightened and the mighty breakers make supplication to him." An excellent sense is gained, but it is hard to see how this reading fits the immediate context. MT *miššeḇārîm,* "breaking," may refer to shuddering in fear (Pope). With this meaning it usually stands in the idiom *šiḇrôn moṯnayim,* "breaking of the loins," a metaphor for loss of strength and courage as legs tremble in fear; but perhaps "loins" has been omitted elliptically here.

25. Heb. *yiṯḥaṭṭāʾû,* usually "they purify themselves," here has the sense of "withdraw," which has support from Ethiopic *ḥṭʾ*, "withdraw," and Arab. *ḥṭʾ*, "cast down" (Pope).

26. The participle, standing at the beginning of the sentence, introduces a condition (cf. R. Gordis, "Note on General Conditional Sentences in Hebrew," *JBL* 49 [1930] 200–203; GKC, § 116w).

27. MT *massāʿ* is difficult. If it is taken from Arab. *nasağa,* "throw," then it could mean "dart, missile, arrow" (Gordis, Dhorme). The other possibility is that it refers to "a stone," perhaps one shot from a sling, for in 1 K. 6:7 it refers to an unworked stone.

28. MT *širyâ* appears only here. In Arab. *sirwat* means "a short arrow" and *siryat* means "an arrowhead" (Gordis). Gordis takes this evidence to render *širyâ* as "javelin."

29. Heb. *ben qešeṯ,* "arrow," is lit. "son of a bow" (cf. GKC, § 128v).

30. The plural verb *neḥšeḇû* is difficult. Possibly one should read *neḥšaḇ lô,* "is considered by him," with Budde, Hölscher, and Fohrer (cf. Dhorme).

31. The meaning "javelin" or "mace" is assigned to MT *tôṯāḥ* on the basis of Akk. *tartaḫu,* "shaft, club" (Dhorme), or Arab. *mitaḫat,* "club" (Rowley). Cf. G. R. Driver, *ETL* 26 (1950) 339–40.

25 (33) *Nothing on earth is its equal,*
one made[32] *without fear.*
26 (34) *All who are high fear it;*[33]
it is king over all that are proud."

Continuing the theme of human inability to capture and control the most imposing creatures, Yahweh draws Job's attention to Leviathan, often identified as the crocodile. Crocodiles were numerous in Egypt, and there is evidence of crocodiles in Israel, e.g., along the coastal streams such as the Yarkon and the Kishon.[34] According to Strabo (6.27), a town north of Caesarea bore the name Crocodilopolis.

Another view interprets Leviathan as a serpentine sea monster, the embodiment of the chaotic forces of evil.[35] In the OT Yahweh defeated the sea monster in the deliverance of his people from Egypt (cf. Ps. 74:14), and he will defeat Leviathan again in the final apocalyptic battle (Isa. 27:1). In Ugaritic literature this same creature, known as Lotan, is a sea monster hostile to Baal. In fierce combat Baal, the ruling deity, defeated this creature, described as a twisting serpent or a seven-headed dragon.[36] The poetic description reveals that the author skillfully weaves into the portrait of an earthly serpentine animal the features of a mythical dragon. The implication of Yahweh's questioning is that Job could not master this earthly creature, let alone its cosmic counterpart.

25, 26 (41:1, 2) Yahweh questions Job's ability to capture this creature and make it his perpetual servant.[37] A baited hook was often used for hunting a crocodile. When the bait was swallowed and the hook lodged inside the mouth, the tongue was pressed down by the rope tied to the hook.

32. MT *heʿāśû,* "is made," is an archaic form of the Qal passive participle (cf. GKC, § 75v).

33. Since MT *yirʾeh,* "he sees," does not mean "look down on," it seems best to read *ʾōṯô . . . yîrāʾ*, "(all who are high) fear it," with Budde, Driver-Gray, Gordis, *BHK*, etc. But cf. Dhorme.

34. G. Gray, "Crocodiles in Palestine," *PEQ* (1920) 167–76.

35. For example, in Egypt the crocodile served as the symbol of kingly power and greatness. An interesting line in this regard is found in "The Hymn of Victory of Thutmose III": "I cause them to see thy [Thutmose III's] majesty as a crocodile, the lord of fear in the water, who cannot be approached" (*ANET*, p. 374).

36. See *UT*, 67:I:1–3.

37. A vignette in the Papyrus of Cha (1430 B.C.) pictures a man who controls a crocodile by a rope which comes from the animal's mouth. He threatens to kill the crocodile with a knife in his hand which is raised over its head (O. Keel, "Zwei kleine Beiträge zum Verständnis der Gottesreden im Buch Ijob (xxxviii 36f., xl 25)," *VT* 31 [1981] 223–25; cf. idem, *Jahwes Entgegnung an Ijob* [Göttingen: Vandenhoeck & Ruprecht, 1978], pp. 144–56).

After the animal was dragged alongside the shore, the hunter smeared its eyes with mud in order to subdue it for the fatal blow.[38]

27 (3) Will a subdued Leviathan petition Job to ease these cords? Instead of frightening people with its awesome appearance, will it utter its petitions with gentle, appeasing words (lit. "soft, tender things," *rakkôṯ*)?

28 (4) This question alludes to an ancient suzerainty covenant in which a weaker party sues for peace with a superior. In exchange for limited freedom and some self-determination, a local king would swear his allegiance to the monarch of an empire. If Job were so superior, Leviathan would seek a treaty with him and become his *perpetual slave,* subject to his orders forever.[39]

29 (5) In the ancient Near East children loved to play with doves and sparrows, which were considered safe pets even for little children. Can Job turn Leviathan into such a docile pet? The picture of Job's daughters playing with Leviathan as a small pet is absurd. In contrast to human fear, Yahweh has put Leviathan in the sea to *play (śāḥaq)* about (cf. Ps. 104:26) as evidence of his mastery over his creation.

30 (6) The next question paints another absurd picture: the excited merchants arguing over the price of a captured Leviathan. Such a prize would bring them huge profits at an auction. The second question implies that Leviathan is too large for a single merchant to be able to sell.

40:31–41:1 (7–9) Does Job think that he can capture this large creature with *harpoons (śukkôṯ)* and *a fishing spear?* Before he attempts to capture Leviathan, he needs to take account of the mighty *battle* that would ensue. Should he fight this creature once, he would not do so again. Any *hope of subduing* Leviathan that he has is *false*. Its very appearance strikes such terror in the human heart that a person is *laid low (ṭûl)*[40] before the beast. The picture is that of one cringing before a brute force without any ability to resist.

2, 3 (10, 11) Yahweh addresses the central issue in his interrogation of Job. If Job is not brave *(ʾaḵzār)*[41] enough to incite (*ʿûr,* the same verb used with Leviathan in 3:8) Leviathan to do battle, how can he *stand before (hiṯyaṣṣēḇ lipnê,* i.e., enter a superior's presence to present a report or to

38. There is a description of the way the Egyptians captured a crocodile in Herodotus (2.70), cited by Pope.

39. Compare esp. 1 Sam. 27:12, where Achish thinks that David has become his perpetual servant, a relationship probably sealed with a covenant (cf. Exod. 21:6; Deut. 15:17).

40. The Hophal of the verb *ṭûl* means "to be hurled down, headlong" (BDB, p. 376; cf. Ps. 37:24).

41. Heb. *ʾaḵzār* suggests insolent boldness, rash and reckless approach, not fearing to take on anything.

defend one's own action) God? Indeed, who could ever confront *(hiqdîm)* God, i.e., advance himself before God, and expect God to concede to a complaint against himself? It is impossible for anyone to win a judgment against God, for everything under heaven is subject to him. Unequivocally Yahweh confronts Job with the audacity of his plan to argue his case with God himself.

4 (12) Yahweh will *not be silent,* for he who stops speaking concedes his opponent's point and the one reduced to silence is the loser (cf. 9:3). He will continue to laud his creation as he waits for Job to respond. Proud of his creature, Yahweh speaks about the union of *strength and grace* in this marvelous beast.

5, 6 (13, 14) Leviathan is impregnable. Since nothing can pierce its *double coat of mail,* hunters used hooks and ropes against its mouth (cf. 40:25 [Eng. 41:1]), but no one can *pry open* Leviathan's large mouth. If one daringly succeeded in getting its mouth open, its numerous sharp teeth would fill him with *terror ('êmâ).* In contemplating taking up his case with God, Job has been concerned with being overcome by terror (cf. 9:32–35; 13:20–21). Now Yahweh is showing Job that his apprehensions were on target. If he would have to retreat in terror before Leviathan, surely he could not stand before God at court.

7–9 (15–17) Beneath the glistening sun Leviathan's *back* looks like *rows of shields.* Nothing can penetrate its tightly sealed hide.

10–13 (18–21) In these verses the poetic imagery moves beyond a real animal to a mythical dragon with ominous characteristics. When this creature sneezes, the water spray sparkles in the sunlight like flashes of light. The reflection of the light in its reddish eyes makes them appear *like the rays of dawn.*[42] When this creature emerges from the water, it spews out its pent-up breath in a steaming spray that appears like *sparks of fire* or like *smoke from a boiling pot.*

14 (22) Leviathan is exceptionally strong. This is expressed by a common idiom for referring to the center of an animal's strength, even though this would not be literally true if this creature is a crocodile. As this creature crawls along, *vigor leaps before it.* That is, its very movement communicates its awesome strength to onlookers, making them flee for cover.

15, 16 (23, 24) Leviathan's hard body makes it invincible. The quality of hardness is stressed by the use of the term "hard" or *firm (yāṣûq)*

42. In ancient Egyptian hieroglyphs the eyes of the crocodile stood for morning red.

three times in these two verses and by the comparison of its *breast (libbô)*[43] to *a lower millstone,* which is harder than the upper millstone because it must bear both the weight of the upper millstone and the brunt of the grinding.

17–21 (25–29) Even the mightiest heroes on facing Leviathan are terrified by its majestic appearance. Instead of attacking it they *withdraw, shuddering* in fear, for they have no weapon that could pierce its hard armor or make it flee in terror. It taunts its foes by laughing at their inability to harm it. As Habel (OTL) notes, "laughing" (Heb. *śāḥaq*) is a thread that runs through the animal portraits: the wild ass laughs at the noise in the city (39:7), the ostrich laughs at the horse and its rider (39:18), the horse laughs at fear (39:22), the wild animals play (laughingly) near Behemoth (40:20), and no one can play (laughingly) with Leviathan (40:29 [Eng. 41:5]). The one in control laughs at what others admire or fear. This motif further indicates that God in wisdom has created a world of creatures that enjoy play (cf. Prov. 8:30–31).

22 (30) When Leviathan moves along the bank of the river, *it leaves marks in the mud like a threshing sledge.* This implement, constructed out of two boards with pieces of basalt or flint attached to its underside, was used to crush grain (cf. Rowley). These marks left by Leviathan give the impression that *its undersides* are composed of *sharp,* rough *potsherds.*

23, 24 (31, 32) When Leviathan plunges into the water, *the depths* seem to *boil* like water in *a caldron.* The bubbling water is comparable to the foam of ingredients boiling to make perfume. As it moves through the water, it leaves *a glistening wake* of white water as beautiful as the prized, silvery *white hair* of an elder.

25, 26 (33, 34) No creature *on earth* (lit. "on dust," i.e., earth in contrast to heaven) is equal to Leviathan. This fearless creature cannot be intimidated. Since Yahweh made all earthly creatures to fear before mankind (Gen. 9:2), the fact that Leviathan is *without fear* indicates that it is a primordial creature. Even *all who are high* i.e., the great rulers, *fear it.* Leviathan is the *king over all that are proud.* Yahweh's argument is that since no human being can subject Leviathan, surely then no person can ever be so mighty or exalted as to challenge successfully Yahweh's rule.

43. An alternative interpretation of MT *libbô* is a literal rendering, "his heart," the seat of courage (Driver-Gray). It would mean then that Leviathan's courage is strong, unwavering.

AIM

Yahweh raises the key question for Job. Does he have to argue that Yahweh is guilty of governing the world unjustly in order to prove his own innocence? If Job thinks Yahweh fails to rule the universe justly, then he is setting himself up as wiser than God, even as one who could rule better than God. Yahweh thus exhorts Job to prove his claims by adorning himself in regal apparel and punishing the wicked. And Yahweh challenges him to show his mastery over the great primordial monsters, Behemoth and Leviathan, which are symbolic of cosmic forces that at times are hostile to Yahweh's rule. But if Job cannot subdue them, he is in no position to discredit God, his Creator and Master, for treating him unjustly. Furthermore, the only conclusion he can come to is that Yahweh is the supreme Lord of the universe. This means that all creatures must fear him. This echoes the conclusion to the hymn to wisdom (28:28) and Elihu's conclusion (37:24).

By questioning Job about the primordial monsters Behemoth and Leviathan, Yahweh is trying to persuade Job that he is Master of all powers in the world, both earthly and cosmic. Certainly then he is Lord of all forces, earthly and cosmic, that brought on Job's affliction. Therefore, if Job is to find Yahweh's favor again, he must submit to Yahweh as his Lord by relinquishing his avowal of innocence and by conceding his complaints against Yahweh's just governance of the world. Yahweh is thus calling Job to decide whether to argue his case and lose or submit to Yahweh, accepting in trust the blessing and the curse, the riches and the ash heap.

D. JOB'S ANSWER (42:1–6)

1 *Job answered Yahweh:*
2 *"I know*[1] *that you can do all things.*
No purpose of yours can be foiled.
3 *Who is this that obscures counsel without knowledge?*
Surely[2] *I have told things that I did not understand,*
matters too wonderful for me to know.
4 *Hear now and I shall speak;*
I shall ask and you tell me.

1. Some first person perfect verbal forms appear without the *y* (cf. GKC, § 44i).

2. Instead of MT *lāḵēn,* "therefore," which does not fit this context, Blommerde (*Northwest Semitic Grammar and Job,* p. 140) analyzes it as an emphatic *lamed* plus *kēn,* "thus."

5 *I had heard of you with my ears,*
but now my eyes have seen you.[3]
6 *Therefore I abase myself*[4]
and recant[5] *in dust and ashes."*

Contritely confessing that he has spoken beyond his knowledge (vv. 2–3), Job submits himself to the God who has appeared to him (vv. 4–6). This short passage blends together many genres: a confession of God's power and wisdom (v. 2), an admission of limited knowledge (v. 3), an invitation to dispute a case (v. 4), an acknowledgment of Yahweh's appearing (v. 5), and a recantation (v. 6).[6]

2 The formula *I know (yāḏaʿtî)* typically heads a supplicant's answer to an oracle given in response to his prayer or lament (e.g., Ps. 20:7 [Eng. 6]; 41:12 [Eng. 11]; 56:10 [Eng. 9]). Confessing that God *can do all things,* Job accepts Yahweh's argument as the answer to his complaint and his avowal of innocence.

Throughout his speeches Job has held firmly to his conviction that God is all-powerful. In his lamenting, however, he has questioned God's consistent execution of justice in the face of numerous examples that seem to contradict the standard of justice. Nevertheless, Yahweh's words have reaffirmed Job's conviction of his wise and judicious governance of the world. With an enhanced awareness of Yahweh's lordship, Job concedes that *no purpose* (*m*ᵉ*zimmâ,* i.e., "detailed plans")[7] of Yahweh's *can be foiled* or thwarted *(bāṣar).* Job's concession means that he believes that everything occurring on earth takes place within the framework of the divine wisdom.

3. Cf. B. Lang, "Ein Kranker sieht seinen Gott," in *Der Mensch unter dem Kreuz,* ed. R. Bärenz (Regensburg: Pustet, 1980), pp. 35–48.

4. MT *'em'as* comes either from the Hebrew root *m's,* "despise, loathe" (the object either having fallen out or supplied from the context), or from *mss,* "melt away, sink down." There are many objections to the first option. Pope believes that it is his miserable condition that Job rejects. L. Kuyper ("The repentance of Job," *VT* 9 [1959] 91–94) finds the understood object in v. 3, namely, his arguments and demands. Since the tone of vv. 5–6 is quite personal and Job confesses contritely before the Holy God, the translation "I abase myself" (cf. LXX), based on a reflexive meaning of the verb *m's,* fits the context well.

5. Heb. *nāḥam,* often translated "repent," does not necessarily bear the idea of sorrow for some wrong, but means "to retract a declared action" (cf. H. Parunak, "A Semantic Survey of *NḤM,*" *Bib* 56 [1975] 512–32). Frequently this word depicts Yahweh relenting, out of compassion, to inflict the misfortune he has intended against Israel (e.g., Exod. 32:14; Jer. 18:8, 10; Amos 7:3, 6; Joel 2:13, 14).

6. Cf. J. Curtis, "On Job's Response to Yahweh," *JBL* 98 (1979) 497–511.

7. Heb. *m*ᵉ*zimmâ* can refer to the "plans" of God (Jer. 23:20) and of human beings (Job 21:27). Often when it is used for human thinking it stands for schemes and evil devices (Prov. 12:2; Ps. 139:20). S. Steingrimsson notes that the negative connotation comes from the context, not from the word itself (*TDOT,* IV:88–89).

No hostile force, be it earthly or heavenly, prevents God from carrying out his purpose.

3 Having been confronted by the amazing way God has created the world, Job admits that *matters* are *too wonderful* for him to understand. He comes to realize that the divine wisdom is beyond the ability of any human being to grasp. In faith based on Yahweh's words, Job acknowledges that Yahweh is true to justice in his governance of the cosmos. He expresses his submission to God's sovereignty by recasting Yahweh's opening accusation (38:2) into a self-judgment. This fact confirms that Job is responding to Yahweh's speeches. In his complaints that God rules unjustly he admits that he has spoken beyond his knowledge and insight. He has approached the sin of hubris by claiming to have better insight than God into matters on earth.

At this point it is important to restate that Job committed no sin that led to his affliction and that he has not sinned in his lamenting. That is why Job does not confess any sin here. But Yahweh has made him aware of the danger of his self-confidence turning into pride. His self-confidence has compelled him to defend his innocence vigorously. In his strong complaints against God, he has moved dangerously close to pride, i.e., being certain that he is able to judge God. Should Job persist in holding on to his avowal of innocence, he would sin by yielding to pride. But on becoming aware of the danger inherent in continuing to charge God with injustice, he humbles himself before God, conceding that he has misstated his case by speaking about things beyond his ability to know. In taking this path Job confirms that humility is essential for a vital relationship with God. With this concession Job demonstrates that he serves God for himself alone and not for any personal gain or benefit, not even his own justification. Yahweh's confidence in his servant in the face of the Satan's challenge has been completely vindicated.

The wording in v. 2a means that Job agrees with Yahweh's second speech, and the wording in v. 3 that he accepts the argument of the first speech.

4 This verse, which is a reiteration of Yahweh's words in 40:7, is hard to interpret in this context. Earlier Job had offered God the opportunity to speak or to answer his servant's complaint (13:22). Now he enjoins Yahweh to listen to the response he will offer. Perhaps the second line is a part of the formulaic request for a legal hearing. Habel (OTL) simply takes them as a quote of Yahweh's words similar to v. 3a. In any case, these lines serve to highlight Job's coming recantation of his avowal of innocence.

5 Previously Job had heard about God through the tradition perpetuated in songs sung at the festivals and in the teaching of the elders. Rejoicing in what his *ear* heard about God, Job zealously lived by the precepts. Now he has a far superior basis for his faith—*now my eyes have* *seen* Yahweh![8] Job had a direct encounter with the living God and heard him speak clearly. Yahweh veiled himself in a tempest, which resembles in many respects his appearance at Sinai (Exod. 19), so that Job was not consumed by his holiness. His presence, however, was so unmistakably real that Job could say *now my eyes have seen you*. His deepest longing—to behold his Redeemer with his own eyes—has been fulfilled (19:25–27). The vision of Yahweh overwhelms him, filling him with a sense of wonder and awe and reducing all his complaints to insignificance. In appearing to his servant, Yahweh vindicates Job's integrity (Habel, OTL).

6 Job abases himself and recants, confessing himself to be no better than the *dust and ashes* on which he has been sitting. Job has come to a true assessment of himself before the holy God, as indicated by the similarity of his words to those of Abraham when he interceded for the sparing of Sodom and Gomorrah for the sake of the righteous left in those cities: "Behold, I have been bold to speak, though I am but dust and ashes" (Gen. 18:27). Job both renounces all false pride and concedes that God has been true to justice in allowing him, the noblest sheikh, to be brought so low that he has had to sit outside the city on the ash heap. The term *recant (niḥam)* means to turn from a planned course of action and take up a new course. It implies the strongest resolve to change direction, but not an attitude of remorse. It is affirmative action based on conviction. In recanting Job surrenders to God the last vestige of his self-righteousness, i.e., he withdraws his avowal of innocence. From now on he will locate his self-worth in his relationship with Yahweh, not in his own moral behavior or innocence. Thus Job commits his fate into God's hands knowing that he can bear any fate, for he has seen Yahweh.

AIM

Filled with wonder and awe at Yahweh's appearing, Job confesses his own unworthiness. His attention shifts from his concern for vindication to his need to prepare his heart before God. The integrity of Job's faith shines brightly. He humbles himself before God because communion with God is more important to him than release from his affliction. It has not been wrong for him to complain, even against God himself. Nor has it been wrong for him to swear an oath of innocence. But the zealous pursuit of a right eventually erects a barrier between God and the offended person. Therefore, when God makes himself known, the supplicant must surrender everything to God, including his just grievances, if he is to avoid sinning and to find God's favor again. Thus Job renounces all personal claims that could be construed to put himself above God. In humility he glorifies God.

8. Cf. Ps. 25:14–15; 123:1–2; 141:8.

VIII. EPILOGUE (42:7–17)

The author has retained a portion of the old epic account of Job's fate and reworked it as an epilogue to the speeches. In the oldest epic account this portion, which recounts the resolution of the conflict between the parties, was an integral part of the narrative. Here, however, the author has placed the reconciliation between Job and God within the structure of the poem. Nevertheless, the epilogue is more than an appendix, for it recounts Job's full reconcilation with Yahweh.

The epilogue has two divisions: the condemnation and the restoration of the three friends (vv. 7–9), and God's blessing and restoration of Job (vv. 10–17).

A. THE CONDEMNATION AND RESTORATION OF THE THREE FRIENDS (42:7–9)

7 *After Yahweh had spoken these words to Job, he said to Eliphaz the Temanite, "My anger burns against you and your two friends, because you have not spoken of me what is right, as my servant Job has.*
8 *So now take seven bulls and seven rams and go to my servant Job and offer up a whole burnt offering for yourselves; and my servant Job will pray for you, because I accept him so that I will not treat you according to your folly. You have not spoken of me what is right, as my servant Job has."*
9 *So Eliphaz the Temanite, Bildad the Shuhite, and Zophar the Naamathite went and did just as Yahweh had spoken to them; and Yahweh accepted Job's prayer.*

7 In his address to Eliphaz, the leader of the three friends who had come to comfort Job, Yahweh holds all of them responsible for the implications of their teachings and exhortations to Job. The absence of any mention of Elihu is puzzling. It may be that Yahweh did not find any serious error in his speeches or that his speeches are viewed as standing outside the main dialogue.

42:7–9 The Condemnation and Restoration of the Three Friends

Yahweh is angry with the friends because they *have not spoken of* him *what is right [nᵉḵônâ]*[1] *as Job had.*[2] Whereas Yahweh has accused Job of darkening knowledge (38:2), his charge against the friends is much stronger. Job has been genuinely groping for the truth, but the friends have spoken falsely in their attempt to defend God. More than failing to comfort Job, they have tempted him to take the wrong course out of his affliction. Since their counsel would lead Job away from the true worship of Yahweh, they are accused of *folly (nᵉḇālâ),* the denial of God's goodness and redemptive activity in the affairs of mankind. In the prologue Job used this same root in accusing his wife of speaking as one of the foolish woman for counseling him to curse God and die (2:10). Thus the friends' discourses, coming after his wife's foolish counsel, became Job's second temptation to curse God. Had he followed their exhortations, he would have denied God's faith in him by seeking God for his own personal gain.

Yahweh calls Job *my servant (ʿeḇeḏ)* four times in vv. 7 and 8. This title suggests a close, bonded relationship and in the OT is a title of honor for one who serves God. In his conversations with the Satan Yahweh referred to Job as his servant (1:8; 2:3). His use of this title again signifies that he has accepted Job's recantation and acknowledges that he has the same high status that he had prior to his trial.

8 The sacrifice demanded of the comforters consists of *seven bulls* and *seven rams,* a very costly offering.[3] The kind of animals and the significance of the number seven reflect an early setting like that of the prologue. Only nobility could afford such a rich offering. Job, acting as a patriarch and not as an ordained priest, intercedes for his friends. His prayer will be efficacious, for God *accepts him* (*nāśāʾ pānîm,* lit. "lift up the face"; cf. 13:8). That is, God has such high regard for Job that he receives favorably any requests from Job.

9 Without any resistance the friends obeyed Yahweh's instructions. True to his word, Yahweh accepted Job's prayer and forgave the three friends. This scene shows that Job's restored favor with God possesses vicarious benefits for others. It also reveals that Job's attitude had been purged, i.e., he did not bear a grudge against those who had condemned him so harshly. Acting as intercessor, he assisted them in finding favor with

1. Cf. Ps. 5:10 (Eng. 9).

2. Fohrer believes that only Job's words in 40:4–5; 42:2–6 may be judged *correct (nᵉḵônâ).* It can be argued that the whole of Job's words, when placed against his final confession, are "correct" in that they are honest and lead him to an encounter with God. If the author has adapted the epilogue to his purpose as the present interpretation suggests, this statement about Job must encompass more than his final words.

3. For example, Balaam offered seven bulls and seven rams on three different occasions in his efforts to entreat God to curse Israel (Num. 23:1, 14, 29).

God. Also, the comforters showed their strong commitment to God by obeying him in humbly letting Job, against whom they had spoken so harshly, offer up sacrifices for them.

This sequence of events is essential to the theology of the book. If the friends had not been reprimanded, they would have come out victorious and Job alone would have been humbled. Furthermore, from Job's intercession for his so-called comforters, it is learned that Job was fully restored to God's favor and that he had gained spiritual authority by faithfully enduring his trial. Also, Yahweh shows that he permits far more latitude in genuine human searching than that tolerated by those who hold rigidly to a narrow theology.

B. GOD'S BLESSING AND RESTORATION OF JOB (42:10–17)

1. RESTORATION (42:10)

10 *Yahweh restored*[1] *Job's fortune after he prayed for his friends. Then Yahweh doubled all that Job had.*

10 After Job had submitted to Yahweh and faithfully carried out his directives, demonstrating a gracious, forgiving spirit in praying for his "comforters," Yahweh restored Job's fortunes. The fundamental spiritual principle that in giving one receives and in forgiving one is forgiven is demonstrated here (cf. Luke 6:38). The doubling of Job's estate does not mean that he received a bountiful reward for the endurance of undeserved affliction, but rather that Yahweh freely and abundantly blessed him. The blessing proves that Yahweh is a life-giving God, not a capricious deity who takes pleasure in the suffering of those who fear him. In his sovereign design he may permit a faithful servant to suffer ill-fortune for a season, but in due time he will bring total healing. Moreover, the doubling symbolizes Yahweh's full acceptance of Job.

1. The phrase *šûḇ šeḇûṯ* has received much discussion, for this is its only occurrence with an individual as its subject. In prophetic literature it describes the restoration of a captive nation to its homeland (e.g., Jer. 30:3, 18; 31:23). Possibly this term also had a more general usage, as is attested in this passage. Since Job has not experienced captivity, the phrase seems to mean "take a new direction." Cf. E. Preuschen, "Die Bedeutung von *šûḇ šeḇûṯ* im Alten Testament," *ZAW* 15 (1895) 1–74; E. Dietrich, *Schub Sch'but. Die endzeitliche Wiederherstellung bei den Propheten,* BZAW 40 (Giessen: Töpelmann, 1925); E. Baumann, "*šûḇ šeḇûṯ*, eine exegetische Untersuchung," *ZAW* 47 (1929) 17–44; N. Schlögl, *"šwb šbwt," WZKM* 38 (1931) 68–75; R. Borger, "Zu *šwb šbw/yt,*" *ZAW* 66 (1954) 315–16; W. Holladay, *The Root "Šubh" in the Old Testament* (Leiden: Brill, 1958), pp. 111–14.

2. THE VISIT OF JOB'S KINSMEN AND FRIENDS (42:11)

11 *And all his brothers and sisters and his former close friends came and ate bread with him at his house. They sympathized with him and consoled him concerning all the misfortune which Yahweh had brought on him, and each one gave him a coin and a gold ring.*

11 The close members of Job's family, *his brothers* and *sisters* (which may include cousins) as well as *his close friends (yōḏeʿîm)*, perhaps members of the town council (cf. 19:19), came to *sympathize* with Job and to *console* him. Eating together reestablished their fellowship and affirmed their willingness at last to share his sorrow. Like the dialogue, this scene attributes the cause of Job's misfortune to Yahweh. There is no discussion of intermediate causes, for it was believed that Yahweh was the cause of all that takes place.

To help Job overcome his losses each visitor *gave him a coin [qeśîṭâ]*[1] *and a gold ring*. The *gold ring* may have been a nose ring or possibly an earring such as the wealthy wore.[2] This detail bears witness to the way God allows people to participate in another's restoration. The money provided Job a basis for rebuilding his estate. That is, Job's estate must have grown to double its former size over a period of time as a result of God's special blessing of what the friends had given him and his own endeavors.

This verse presents a nagging question: why did the relatives come to console at the end of his struggle? Perhaps their action typifies human nature, which comes to the aid of one who has suffered great loss after the brunt of the trouble is over and the outcome assured. Another view finds here a seam in the old epic account, taking this verse as originally part of the prologue because the verse assumes the mourning situation as pictured in the prologue.[3] This verse then may have stood originally after 2:10. When the author adapted the epic account to the dialogue, he substituted the three comforters for the relatives and friends, as is attested by the close similarity in language between this verse and 2:11.[4] He preserved this part of the original narrative as an account of Job's being reunited with his relatives and friends and of their assistance in his becoming reestablished.

1. Heb. *qeśîṭâ* is an unspecified weight of money; it might have been of gold or silver. Since the ring is specified as gold, the other object was something of silver, for these two metals are usually mentioned together. This unit of money belonged to the patriarchal age; it appears elsewhere only in Gen. 33:19 and Josh. 24:32. Since Jacob paid a hundred *qeśiṭas* for a large plot of land, this unit probably possessed moderate value.

2. Cf. Gen. 24:22, 30, 47; 35:4; Isa. 3:21; Hos. 2:15 (Eng. 13).

3. G. Fohrer, "Zur Vorgeschichte und Komposition des Buches Hiob," in *Studien zum Buche Hiob,* pp. 30–31, 40–41.

4. Cf. the Introduction, pp. 21–24.

3. THE ENUMERATION OF JOB'S BLESSINGS (42:12–15)

12 *Yahweh blessed Job's later life more than his earlier life. He had fourteen thousand sheep, six thousand camels, a thousand yoke of oxen, and a thousand donkeys.*
13 *And he also had seven*[1] *sons and three daughters.*
14 *He named his daughters: the first Jemimah, the second Keziah, and the third Keren-Happuch.*
15 *No women in all the earth were*[2] *more beautiful than Job's daughters, and their father gave them an inheritance with their brothers.*

12, 13 *Yahweh blessed Job's later life more than his earlier life* as a demonstration of his grace and love for his obedient, faithful servant. The emphasis is not so much on rewards as on the visible evidence of Yahweh's favor bestowed anew on Job. The description of Yahweh's rich blessings corresponds to the description of Job's estate given in the prologue. All that Job had was doubled.

In addition, Yahweh gave Job *seven sons* and *three daughters*.[3] In his restored life, why were not Job's children doubled as his possessions were? Perhaps because the value of human life is so much greater than the value of property. From another perspective, one could say that the belief that his first set of children continued to live in Sheol means that with his new family the number of his children did double. Since no mention is made of their mother, presumably she was Job's same wife.

14, 15 In fine epic style, which delights in beautiful or successful women,[4] the hero's daughters receive special prominence. They are named and their beauty is noted, a further witness to Yahweh's gracious blessing. In addition, they received an inheritance, usually reserved solely for the sons as long as there was a male heir.[5] Job continues to demonstrate a very progres-

1. The number "seven" is written in an unusual way, *šiḇʿānâ*. Dhorme explains the *-â* ending as a feminine ending of a cardinal number while Gordis opts for an otiose suffix for euphony after the diphthong spelled defectively: *šiḇʿayin*. The Targ. and many others have taken the ending as a dual ending such as exists in Akkadian and Aramaic. A major difficulty with taking "seven" as dual is that the number "three" for the daughters does not appear in the similar form. This writing of the number is then better viewed as an archaism rather than as a dual; cf. Ugar. *šbʿny* (N. Sarna, *JBL* 76 [1957] 18).

2. The masculine singular verb with a feminine plural subject is an example of a passive used impersonally (GKC, §§ 145o n. 1; 121a).

3. In Ugaritic myths Baal has seven/eight sons and three daughters, but only the daughters are named.

4. See, e.g., C. H. Gordon, *The Common Background of Greek and Hebrew Civilizations* (New York: W. W. Norton & Company, 1965), p. 145.

5. In Israelite law daughters could inherit if there were no sons (e.g., Num. 27:1–11; 36:1–13). This custom provides some evidence that the epic account predates the

sive attitude toward the equity of people for his day (cf. ch. 31). The daughters' names are *Jemimah,* "turtle-dove," a name used for graceful birds,[6] plants, or precious stones; *Keziah,*[7] the name of the aromatic plant *cassia,* a prized variety of cinnamon; and *Keren-Happuch,* a horn of eye paint, i.e., black rouge used to highlight the eyes.

4. JOB'S EPITAPH (42:16–17)

16 *After this Job lived one hundred and forty years; he saw his children and their children, four generations.*[1]

17 *Job died, old and full of years.*[2]

16, 17 Job *lived one hundred and forty years,*[3] double the ideal age (cf. Ps. 90:10), and saw his children's children up to *four generations,* the crown of a blessed life (cf. Ps. 128:6; Prov. 17:6). The one hundred and forty years may be his life span, or more likely the years added to his life after his trial.[4] Either way, he lived a long life, even by patriarchal standards. Since long life was a key promise for obedient service to God (e.g., Exod. 23:25, 26), old age was accepted as proof of a person's righteousness. Job experienced

---

priestly law. A few Ugaritic texts take daughters into consideration regarding inheritance; thus daughters possessed some rights to the family property in that culture (cf. Fohrer, who refers to Ugaritic texts 16.252; 15.138; 16.393B in *PRU,* III:66, 101–102).

6. In Cant. 2:14 the dove stands as an affectionate name for the bride, having a fine form and a lovely voice.

7. Another view relates this name to Ugar. *qṣʿt,* "bow," emphasizing the lady's figure (C. Gordon, *UT,* p. 479, no. 2258), but "bow" does not commend itself as a feminine name.

1. Since only three generations are mentioned, some (e.g., Rowley, de Wilde) suppose that something such as *bᵉnêhem,* "their sons," has fallen out. This conjecture is unnecessary, however, for the sequence of sons may be stated elliptically or the four generations may include Job himself.

2. The LXX adds: "It stands written that he will rise again with those whom the Lord raises. This is translated from a Syrian book, for Job was living in Ausitis at the boundaries of Idumea and Arabia. He was formerly named Jobab. He took an Arabian wife and had a son named Ennon. He, however, was a son of his father Zare, one of Esau's sons, and of his mother Bosorra so that he was the fifth from Abraham. . . . The friends who came to him were Eliphaz of the sons of Esau, king of the Temanites, Bildad, ruler of the Sauchaeans; Sophar, king of the Minaeans."

3. D. Christensen ("Job and the Age of the Patriarchs in Old Testament Narrative," a privately circulated paper) points out that the number 140 played a significant role in the number schemes of Genesis; e.g., Abraham was 140 years old when his son Isaac married, and Jacob was 140 years old when he returned to Canaan. Christensen also observes that 140 is the sum of the squares of the numbers 1–7 (cf. N. Sarna, *Understanding Genesis* [New York: Schocken, 1966], p. 84).

4. The LXX reads that Job lived 170 years after his trial to the age of 240, with a variant of 248. According to this tradition then Job was 70 when he was sorely afflicted.

Yahweh's favor as described in Ps. 91:16: "I shall satisfy him [i.e., the one who seeks refuge in God] with a long life, and I shall show him my salvation."

Job died, old and full of years. This epitaph is the same as that used for the noblest among God's servants, i.e, Abraham (Gen. 25:8), Isaac (Gen. 35:29), David (1 Chr. 29:28), and Jehoiada the priest (2 Chr. 24:15).

AIM

Although Job has experienced excruciating suffering, he has persevered until he has found full reconciliation with Yahweh. Throughout the entire ordeal Job has shown that he serves Yahweh from a pure heart. He trusts Yahweh for no ulterior motive, but solely for Yahweh's presence in his life. So when he is given the opportunity, he mercifully prays for his three friends, whose tirades have increased his suffering. The fact that Yahweh has Job intercede for the comforters indicates that Job has gained spiritual authority for having endured undeserved suffering and then yielding his complaint to God.

Job's reconciliation with Yahweh also changes all of his relationships. His relatives and neighbors come and dine with him in a renewal of their friendship, and they participate in his restoration by giving him a present of money and a gold ring. Also, as an expression of his love and goodness Yahweh restores Job's wealth and his family.

The recounting of Job's restoration and his greater prosperity after the trial is integral to the book's message. Many modern interpreters focus on Job's humbling himself before God in dust and ashes as the conclusion and thus dislike the epilogue as anticlimactic and unrealistic. The epilogue, however, preserves an essential statement of Yahwistic faith: fear of Yahweh leads to an abundant life. If fear of Yahweh led inevitably to hardship and suffering, such a faith would be sadistic. Pain would be the highest expression of devotion and the heroes of that faith would be those who endured the greatest suffering. Such is not the case, as the epilogue teaches. In his own time, Yahweh reaches out to help his servant who perseveres amid agonizing adversity. While the book of Job does not categorically reject the doctrine of retribution, it endeavors ardently to correct erroneous applications of that doctrine, especially the views that suffering is conclusive proof that the sufferer has sinned, that the righteous always prosper, and that the wicked are swiftly punished for their evil deeds. While the dialogue establishes the position that suffering does not necessarily imply sin, the epilogue recounts Job's great prosperity as Yahweh's free gift, not as a reward earned for his faithful bearing of suffering. In the framework of the whole book, Yahweh is the giver of life and blessing, not a capricious tyrant who takes pleasure in the suffering of those who serve him merely to test their loyalty. Yahweh may withdraw his favor for a season, but his love is for a lifetime.

INDEXES

SUBJECTS

Abaddon, 365, 366, 381, 414
Abraham, 3, 71, 537, 544
Accusation, 38, 39, 45, 56, 135–39, 193–95, 268, 323–27, 357, 369, 401–403
Adultery, 349, 350, 407, 408, 412–14
Aldebaren, 171–72
Alienation, 47, 286–89, 298–99
Angel, 114, 117, 247, 264, 293, 317, 430, 444, 495; mediator, 45, 49, 117, 430, 446–48, 449
Anger, human, 117, 247, 260, 274, 429–30; divine, 170, 173, 190, 192, 215, 236, 260, 285–86, 296, 307, 308, 316–17, 342, 366–67, 467, 471–72, 480, 538–39
Anguish. *See* Despair.
Animals, 16, 126–27, 209, 260, 262, 273, 274, 291, 392, 466, 481; portraits of, 16, 32, 42, 503–14, 516–17, 533
Apology, 42, 258, 427, 431–36, 437–43
Arbiter, 181–82, 185, 192, 246–65, 293
Arcturus, 171
Arrow, 132, 307, 451
Ass (wild), 132–33, 199, 347, 398, 504, 506–507, 516, 533
Avenger, 264

Baal, 68, 149, 366, 367, 477, 496, 508, 530, 542
Bear (constellation), 502
Behemoth, 32, 42, 46, 49, 518, 521–26, 533, 534
Bildad, 24–26, 38–40, 85, 86, 103, 154–65, 177, 193, 203, 208, 231, 234, 242, 257, 272–81, 282, 284, 286, 321, 322–23, 352, 355, 362–63, 434
Birds, 32, 209, 381, 466, 504, 512–14, 516
Bitterness, 176, 183, 228, 318–19, 338, 339, 426, 487, 489
Blessing, 43, 47, 68, 70, 124–25, 184, 201–203, 322, 387–89, 390, 392–93, 416, 471, 542–43
Blood, 263, 349, 422
Bow, 307, 393, 543
Bribe, 333
Burial, 97–98, 321, 520–21

Camel, 68–69, 77
Caravans, 18, 137, 138
Chaldeans, 21, 77
Children, 19, 47, 68–70, 118, 127–28, 156, 240, 254, 268–69, 289, 305, 314, 317, 346, 359, 361, 388, 531, 542–43
Clay. *See* Dust.
Clothing, 77, 164, 181, 261–62, 347, 360, 391, 402–403, 416, 421, 425, 497, 520
Cloud, 147, 304, 329, 339, 366, 367, 382, 401, 420, 479, 481, 482, 484, 490, 496, 503
Cock, 503
Complaint, 40, 50, 99, 147–50, 153, 183–85, 205–206, 217–21, 241, 256, 260–61, 272–74, 281–89, 311, 325, 336, 338, 342–50, 369, 385, 414, 426, 435, 442, 450, 463, 467, 487, 491, 514, 519, 520–21, 534, 541
Confidence, 81, 106–107, 127, 161, 201, 241, 336, 337–41, 354, 369, 386, 406–409
Consolation, 38, 39, 44, 86, 104–107, 246, 257, 310–11, 541
Cosmic conflict, 13, 41, 94, 149, 167, 168–73, 234–35, 356, 366–67, 488, 496, 518, 522, 525, 530
Council (heavenly), 20, 71–72, 79, 246, 339–40
Covenant, 85, 127, 228
Covetousness, 407, 408, 412, 546
Creation, 13, 32, 42, 46, 49–50, 168–72,

AUTHORS

SCRIPTURES

OLD TESTAMENT

Genesis

NONBIBLICAL TEXTS

HEBREW WORDS

EXTRABIBLICAL WORDS

Akkadian

Ugaritic